☞ W9-DBO-119

Universal Instantiation (UI), in two forms

$$(x)\mathcal{P}x$$
$$\therefore \mathcal{P}c$$

Where the bold **x** stands for any individual variable and the bold **c** stands for any individual constant, and $\mathcal{P}c$ comes from $\mathcal{P}x$ by substituting **c** for each free occurrence of **x** in $\mathcal{P}x$.

$$(x)\mathcal{P}x$$
$$\therefore \mathcal{P}y$$

Where the bold **x** and **y** stand for individual variables, and $\mathcal{P}y$ comes from $\mathcal{P}x$ by replacing each free occurrence of **x** in $\mathcal{P}x$ with a free occurrence of **y** in $\mathcal{P}y$.

Existential Instantiation (EI)

$$(\exists x)\mathcal{P}x$$
$$\therefore \mathcal{P}y$$

Where the bold **x** and **y** stand for variables, and $\mathcal{P}y$ comes from $\mathcal{P}x$ by replacing all the free occurrences of **x** in $\mathcal{P}x$ with free occurrences of **y** in $\mathcal{P}y$. *Restriction:* The variable we instantiate to (**y** in the above formulation) may not occur *free* previously in the proof.

Universal Generalization (UG)

$$\mathcal{P}y$$
$$\therefore (x)\mathcal{P}x$$

Where the bold **x** and **y** stand for individual variables, and $\mathcal{P}x$ comes from $\mathcal{P}y$ by replacing all free occurrences of **y** in $\mathcal{P}y$ with free occurrences of **x** in $\mathcal{P}x$. *Restriction:* **y** must not be free in a line arrived at by EI. *Restriction:* UG cannot be used within the scope of an assumption for RAA or CP if **y** occurs free in the assumption.

Existential Generalization (EG), in two forms

$$\mathcal{P}c$$
$$\therefore (\exists x)\mathcal{P}x$$

Where the bold letter **c** stands for any individual constant and **x** is an individual variable and $\mathcal{P}x$ comes from $\mathcal{P}c$ by replacing one or more occurrences of **c** in $\mathcal{P}c$ with occurrences of **x** free in $\mathcal{P}x$.

$$\mathcal{P}y$$
$$\therefore (\exists x)\mathcal{P}x$$

Where the bold **x** and **y** stand for individual variables, and $\mathcal{P}x$ comes from $\mathcal{P}y$ by replacing one or more free occurrences of **y** in $\mathcal{P}y$ with occurrences of **x** free in $\mathcal{P}x$.

Quantifier Negation (QN), in two forms

$$\sim(\exists x)\mathcal{P} :: (x)\sim\mathcal{P}$$
$$\sim(x)\mathcal{P} :: (\exists x)\sim\mathcal{P}$$

The Power of Logic

Alternate Printing

C. Stephen Layman

Seattle Pacific University

The second printing of the *Power of Logic* provides an opportunity to introduce some improvements based on feedback from teachers. Chief among these improvements is a more accessible metalanguage used to state the inference rules—Roman letters replace the Greek letters of the first printing.

Mayfield Publishing Company
Mountain View, California
London • Toronto

For Velma Layman

Copyright © 2000 by Mayfield Publishing Company

All rights reserved. No portion of this book may be reproduced in any form or by any means without written permission of the publisher.

Library of Congress Cataloging-in-Publication Data

Layman, Charles S.
    The power of logic / C. Stephen Layman.
        p.   cm.
    Includes index.
    ISBN 0-7674-1773-9
    1. Logic.   I. Title.
BC61.L28   1998
160—dc21   98-13617
                                                          CIP

Manufactured in the United States of America
10   9   8   7   6   5   4   3   2   1

Mayfield Publishing Company
1280 Villa Street
Mountain View, CA 94041

Sponsoring editor, Ken King; *production editor,* Carla White Kirschenbaum; *manuscript editor,* Tom Briggs; *text designer,* John Edeen; *design manager,* Jean Mailander; *art editor,* Amy Folden; *illustrator,* Anne Eldredge; *manufacturing manager,* Randy Hurst. The text was set in 10.5/12 Goudy by TBH Typecast, Inc., and printed on 45# Highland Plus by R. R. Donnelley & Sons, Inc.

Chapter Opening Photos: Ch. 1 Copyright © 1996 PhotoDisc, Inc.; Ch. 2 Copyright © 1996 PhotoDisc, Inc.; Ch. 3 Copyright © 1993 PhotoDisc, Inc.; Ch. 4 Copyright © 1997 PhotoDisc, Inc.; Ch. 5 Copyright © 1996 PhotoDisc, Inc.; Ch. 6 Copyright © 1992 PhotoDisc, Inc.; Ch. 7 Copyright © 1993 PhotoDisc, Inc.; Ch. 8 Copyright © 1992 PhotoDisc, Inc.; Ch. 9 Copyright © 1992 PhotoDisc, Inc.; Ch. 10 Copyright © 1995 PhotoDisc, Inc.; Ch. 11 Copyright © 1994 PhotoDisc, Inc.; Ch. 12 Copyright © 1996 PhotoDisc, Inc.

Cover image: Victor Vasarely. *Tekers-MC, 1981.* Erich Lessing/Art Resource, New York. © 1998 Artists Rights Society (ARS), New York/ADAGP, Paris.

Contents

Preface

We live in a time when many cultural forces and academic trends are unfavorable to the study of logic. Accordingly, my goal in writing this book has been to provide a text that removes as many obstacles to the learning of logic as possible. These obstacles include a dull or wordy style of writing, a shortage of interesting exercises, and an imbalance of content.

It is difficult to overemphasize the importance of writing style in a logic textbook. While logic is undeniably technical at many points, *The Power of Logic* is written with the conviction that a cut-to-the-chase style is a great asset. I can only hope that I have remained loyal to that conviction.

The Power of Logic is written with the conviction that the tools of logic are indeed powerful, and that the study of logic is one of the best ways to increase students' skills in critical thinking. Rather than requiring the student to acquire powerful logical tools *only to apply them to relatively uninteresting arguments*, I hope that this book illustrates, chapter by chapter, that the tools of logic can be put to work in analyzing and evaluating significant arguments on important subjects.

The Power of Logic is written with the belief that the best introductory courses in logic include a combination of traditional logic and modern symbolic logic. Too much emphasis on the former leaves students unacquainted with the most powerful tools logic has to offer. Too much emphasis on the latter tends to produce students who can manipulate symbols but cannot apply logic to English arguments.

Finally, *The Power of Logic* is written with the conviction that students need more logic, not less. Accordingly, I have included enough material for a two-course sequence. This may be optimistic, but it is also realistic in this sense: It takes a lot of practice to become proficient in logic. Also, the further one goes in the study of logic, the more interesting the applications become. Thus, I have included chapters and sections in some of the relatively advanced areas of logic. I believe, and hope I've shown, that these areas can be made more accessible and interesting than is commonly supposed.

The study of logic increases one's ability to understand, analyze, evaluate, and construct arguments. For this reason, logic makes a vital contribution to the curriculum of the modern university. Accordingly, if this book does something to make logic a bit easier both to learn and to teach, it will have achieved its purpose.

Because it isn't always easy to keep students interested in logic, better ways to teach logic are, I assume, welcome. Consider the following pedagogical features of *The Power of Logic:*

- Each chapter includes numerous exercises designed to show the power of logic as a tool for (a) formulating issues in a revealing way and (b) evaluating significant arguments on interesting topics. Skim the exercises and I believe you will find a high percentage of *interesting* arguments to analyze and evaluate in every chapter, including the chapters on relatively technical topics.

- The writing is concise and lively throughout the text. You'll be the judge of this, of course! But if *The Power of Logic* is more readable than most texts that cover similar topics, then it has at least one very significant pedagogical advantage.

- A relatively simple set of definitions is provided for basic terms such as: *valid, invalid, strong, weak, deductively sound* and *inductively sound.* (For details, see Chapter 1.)

- The material on recognizing arguments is delayed until Chapter 3, after students have already seen a large number of examples of very simple arguments, examined the concept of argument form, and learned some basic forms of statement logic. This provides the students with helpful background information as they attempt to identify arguments, premises, and conclusions.

- Prior to the study of argument diagrams, students learn these argument forms: *modus ponens, modus tollens,* hypothetical syllogism, disjunctive syllogism, and constructive dilemma. This helps the student understand argument diagramming because it provides a better understanding of how premises combine as logical units.

- Exercises on argument diagramming are included in three chapters. This provides an opportunity to integrate the material on argument diagramming with the material on definitions and informal fallacies.

- Categorical syllogisms are treated prior to informal fallacies. This gives the students a better grasp of what a well-constructed argument looks like *before* they begin to learn how to identify the fallacies.

- Venn diagrams are introduced prior to the discussion of the Aristotelian approach to categorical syllogisms. The modern understanding of categorical statements is also introduced before the Aristotelian. Although the coverage of Aristotelian logic is detailed, the text is designed so that the Aristotelian material is optional—later chapters do not depend on it.

- The informal fallacies are organized into four groups that are relatively easy to explain: Fallacies Involving Irrelevant Premises; Fallacies Involving Insufficient Evidence; Fallacies Involving Ambiguity; and Fallacies Involving Unwarranted Premises.

■ Frequent summaries of key definitions and main points are placed in boxes throughout the text. These boxes help students stay on track.

■ The chapter on truth tables includes a discussion of the material conditional and its relation to the English if-then, emphasizes abbreviated truth tables, and provides numerous English-argument exercises.

■ The system of natural deduction for statement logic is entirely standard: eighteen Inference Rules (introduced in three distinct sections), Conditional Proof, and *Reductio ad Absurdum*.

■ In the chapter on predicate logic, the finite universe method of demonstrating invalidity is introduced *before* the inference rules. This provides students early on with a means of understanding the subtle differences in meaning that result from shifts in the placement of parentheses and quantifiers.

■ The chapter on induction includes standard material on statistical syllogisms, induction by enumeration, arguments from authority, Mill's methods, scientific reasoning, and arguments from analogy.

■ The exercises on arguments from analogy require the student to evaluate a *stated criticism* of each argument, which makes the exercises relatively easy to grade. The treatment of arguments from analogy includes a novel section on the use of *metaphors* in arguments from analogy.

■ The chapter on probability keeps the focus on argument evaluation. The exercises on Bayes' Theorem involve a wide variety of applications, including applications to philosophical issues.

■ The chapter on modal logic provides a system of natural deduction for modal propositional logic. The inference rules are introduced in three distinct sections to make the system easy to learn.

Various paths through this book are possible, depending on the time available, the needs of the students, and the interests of the instructor. In an ideal two-course sequence, most of the book can be covered. In the case of a quarter-long course, three main paths through the book are possible, though variations on each will readily come to mind:

I. A course emphasizing traditional logic, covering Chapters 1 through 6 and 10: Basic Concepts, Argument Forms, Identifying Arguments, Logic and Language, Categorical Syllogisms, Informal Fallacies, and Induction.

II. A course giving equal emphasis to traditional and symbolic logic, covering, say, Chapters 1, 2, 3, 5, 7, and 8: Basic Concepts, Argument Forms, Identifying Arguments, Categorical Syllogisms, Statement Logic (Truth Tables), and Statement Logic (Proofs).

III. A course emphasizing modern symbolic logic, covering Chapters 1, 2, and 7 through 9: Basic Concepts, Argument Forms, Statement Logic (Truth Tables), Statement Logic (Proofs), and Predicate Logic.

If you are on semesters, you can add a chapter or two to each scenario.

This text is not designed for self-mastery. It is for courses taught by instructors. Thus, I have not tried to answer every question that might come to a student's mind as he or she works on assignments. The dangers of a highly detailed approach are that students will miss the forest for the trees and/or that students feel that coming to class is unnecessary. I have tried to write a text that explains the crucial points but avoids excessive detail. I shall have achieved my purpose if instructors find that the text makes it a little easier to keep students interested and willing to take on the "next topic."

A comprehensive ancillary package has been developed to accompany *The Power of Logic:*

- An **Interactive Tutorial** can be accessed free of charge at *www. mayfieldpub.com/logic.* This Internet-based study guide provides students with numerous ways to test their understanding of logic. Features of the study guide include randomized quizzes on the text's chapters; a proof-checker that allows students to independently check their work and receive feedback; and exercises in constructing truth tables, abbreviated truth tables, Venn diagrams, and argument diagrams.

- A **Printed Study Guide** gives students the opportunity to review the text material and to work through exercises in addition to those in the text. The study guide provides chapter summaries, discussions of key concepts, supplementary exercises with answers, and additional discussion of selected answers for exercises in the text.

- The **Instructor's Manual** includes includes an answer key for every exercise in the text, chapter tests, and a final exam.

- The **Computerized Test Bank** contains the chapter and final exams from the Instructor's Manual (available in Windows and Macintosh formats). The questions can be edited and new questions can be added.

For more information on any of these ancillary materials, please contact your local Mayfield sales representative or the Marketing and Sales Department at (800) 433-1279. You can also e-mail us at *calpoppy@mayfield pub.com.*

Acknowledgments

Many individuals have helped me with this book. I should start with the logic teachers who got me hooked on the subject (in temporal order): Carl Ginet, Alvin Plantinga, Donald Kalish, and David Kaplan. I have also been helped by colleagues and former colleagues, who read and commented on parts of the book, and sometimes used drafts of the early chapters in the classroom: Terence Cuneo, Philip Goggans, Daniel Howard-Snyder, and Richard McClelland. My students have also provided many constructive criticisms over the past four years, as I tried out drafts of the manuscript in class. One student, Nathan King, deserves special mention, as he provided initial drafts of the answer keys for two chapters.

I am also indebted to a number of textbooks that I have used in the classroom over the years. These include: Irving M. Copi and Carl Cohen, *Introduction to Logic*; Wilfred Hodges, *Logic*; Howard Kahane, *Logic and Philosophy: A Modern Introduction*; Donald Kalish, Richard Montague, and Gary Mar, *Logic: Techniques of Formal Reasoning*; Richard L. Purtill, *A Logical Introduction to Philosophy*; and Wesley C. Salmon, *Logic*. Other logic texts that I have drawn inspiration and insight from include: Kenneth Konyndyk, *Introductory Modal Logic*; Patrick Hurley, *A Concise Introduction to Logic*; and Brian Skyrms, *Choice and Chance*.

Thanks are due to the editors at Mayfield Publishing Company for their support and advice throughout the project. Special thanks goes to Kenneth King, Senior Editor at Mayfield, who has guided the manuscript through extensive revisions. Whatever the value of the book, it is far better for having undergone these revisions. I also wish to thank Jim Bull, who was Senior Editor when Mayfield first took on this project. And I am grateful to the staff at Mayfield who have patiently guided me throughout the process of publication: Joshua Tepfer, Editorial Assistant; Carla White Kirschenbaum, Production Editor; Marty Granahan, Permissions Editor; and Shari Countryman, Marketing Product Manager.

I am greatly indebted to the reviewers, who provided me with a tremendous amount of constructive criticism. They are Edwin Martin, Rutgers University; Steve Naragon, Manchester College; Robert Berman, Xavier University of Louisiana; Frank E. Wilson, Bucknell University; Gregory Mellema, Calvin College; Richard N. Lee, University of Arkansas; Andrew G. Black, Southern Illinois University-Carbondale; Professor Paul C. L. Tang, California State University, Long Beach; Keith Coleman, Johnson County Community College; Dick Gaffney, Siena College; Paul Newberry, California State University, Bakersfield; Victor F. Fontaine, Moorpark College; Daniel E. Flage, James Madison University; Michael Neville, Washington State University; Dan Barnett, California State University, Chico; Dr. William H. Hyde, Golden West College; Harmon R. Holcomb III, University of Kentucky; Scott MacDonald, Cornell University; V. L. Harper, St. Olaf College; Thomas R. Foster, Ball State University; David Christensen, University of Vermont; and Gary Iseminger, Carleton College.

Two people provided special help in the late stages of the project. Greg Mellema of Calvin College took on the exacting job of checking the penultimate draft for errors. And Tom Briggs, my copyeditor, also read the entire manuscript, correcting errors and removing infelicities. I greatly appreciate the efforts of Greg and Tom, though, of course, I must take responsibility for any errors or infelicities that remain.

I owe a special debt to my family. I thank my wife Marla and son J. D. for putting up with my frequent absences as I worked on this project. And I dedicate this book to my mother, Velma P. Layman, whose love for books has shaped my life in more ways than I can tell.

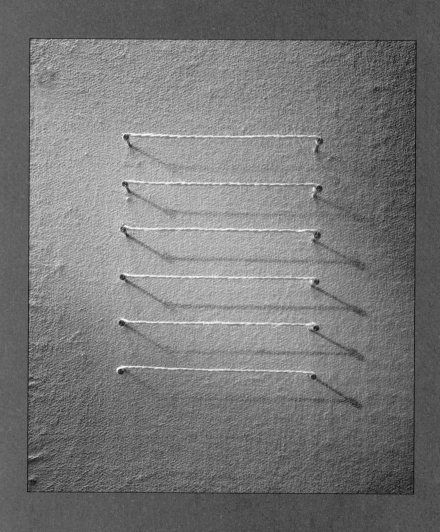

Chapter 1

Basic Concepts

Everyone thinks. Everyone reasons. Everyone argues. And everyone is subjected to the reasoning and arguing of others. We are daily bombarded with reasoning from many sources: books, speeches, radio, TV, newspapers, employers, friends, and family.

Some people think well, reason well, and argue well. Some do not. The ability to think, reason, and argue well is partly a matter of natural gifts. But whatever our natural gifts, they can be refined and sharpened. And the study of logic is one of the best ways to refine one's natural ability to reason and argue. Through the study of logic, one learns strategies for thinking well, common errors in reasoning to avoid, and effective techniques for evaluating arguments.

But what is logic? Roughly speaking, **logic** is the study of methods for evaluating arguments. More precisely, logic is the study of methods for evaluating whether the premises of an argument adequately support (or provide good evidence for) its conclusion. To get a better grasp of what logic is, then, we need to understand the key concepts involved in this definition: *argument, premise, conclusion*, and *support*. This chapter will give you an initial understanding of these basic concepts.

An **argument** is a set of statements, one of which, called the *conclusion*, is affirmed *on the basis* of the others, which are called the *premises*. The premises of an argument are offered as support (or evidence) for the conclusion, and that support (or evidence) may be adequate or inadequate in a given case. But the set of statements counts as an argument as long as one statement is affirmed on the basis of others. Here is an example of an argument:

1. All Quakers are pacifists. Jane is a Quaker. So, Jane is a pacifist.

The word "so" indicates that the conclusion of this argument is "Jane is a pacifist." And the argument has two premises—"All Quakers are pacifists" and "Jane is a Quaker."

An **argument** is a set of statements, one of which, called the *conclusion*, is affirmed *on the basis* of the others, which are called the *premises*.

What is a statement? A **statement** is a sentence that is either true or false. For example:

2. Some dogs are collies.

3. No dogs are collies.

4. Some dogs weigh exactly 124.379 pounds.

Statement (2) is true—that is, it describes things as they are. And (3) is false, because it describes things as other than they are. Truth and falsehood are the two possible **truth values**. So, we can say that a statement is a sentence that has truth value. The truth value of (2) is *true* while the truth value of (3) is *false*, but (2) and (3) are both statements. Is (4) a statement? Yes. You may not know its truth value, and perhaps no one does, but (4) is either true or false, and hence it is a statement.

Are any of the following items statements?

5. Get your dog off my lawn!

6. How many dogs do you own?

7. Let's get a dog.

Item (5) is a *command*, and one may obey or disobey a command, but it makes no sense to pronounce it true or false. So, although (5) is a sentence, it is not a statement. Item (6) is a *question*, and as such it is neither true nor false; hence, it is not a statement. Finally, item (7) is a *proposal*, and proposals are neither true nor false, so (7) is not a statement.[1]

The **premises** of an argument are the statements on the basis of which the conclusion is affirmed. To put it the other way around, the **conclusion** is the statement that is affirmed on the basis of the premises. In a well-constructed argument, the premises *give good reasons for believing that the conclusion is true*. But a poorly constructed argument is still an argument. For example, compare the following arguments:

8. All uncles are male. Chris is an uncle. So, Chris is male.

9. Some uncles are skinny. Chris is an uncle. So, Chris is skinny.

The premises of argument (8) support (or provide a basis for) the conclusion in this sense: If they are true, then the conclusion must be true. But the premises of

(9) fail to support the conclusion adequately: Even if true, they do not provide good reason to believe that the conclusion is true. So, (9) is a bad argument, but it is still an argument.

Arguments are used frequently in our verbal and written interactions with others. And we may use arguments either to *persuade* others or to *discover truth*. For example, we often use arguments to persuade others to believe our political or ethical views. But we also use arguments as tools for *discovering truth*. Suppose a detective is investigating a crime: Who shot Alvin Smith? There are only two suspects, Griggs and Brooks. The detective establishes that Brooks was out of town at the time of the shooting and argues as follows:

10. Either Brooks or Griggs shot Smith. Brooks did not shoot Smith. So, Griggs shot Smith.

In this case, the argument is used to discover truth. Of course, a given argument can be used *both* to discover truth *and* to persuade others to believe the conclusion. Persuasion and truth seeking are often compatible goals. Sometimes, however, one of these goals interferes with the other. For example, in a political campaign, one candidate might try to persuade the voters that his opponent is dishonest even though he knows his opponent is honest.

We now have a preliminary understanding of what logic is. We can gain a deeper understanding by taking a closer look at what it means for the conclusion of an argument to be adequately *based on* or *supported by* the premises. To do this, we must explore the important concepts of validity and strength.

Logic is the study of methods for evaluating whether the premises of an argument adequately support (or provide good evidence for) its conclusion.

1.1 Validity and Deductive Soundness

A valid argument is one in which the premises support the conclusion *completely*. More formally, a **valid argument** is one such that *it is impossible for its conclusion to be false while its premises are true*. In other words, a valid argument has the following essential feature: Assuming its premises are true, its conclusion *must* be true. Each of the following arguments is valid:

11. All biologists are scientists. John is not a scientist. So, John is not a biologist.

12. If Alice stole the diamonds, then she is a thief. And Alice did steal the diamonds. So, Alice is a thief.

13. Either Bill has a poor memory or he is lying. Bill does not have a poor memory. So, Bill is lying.

In each case, it is impossible for the conclusion to be false *while* (i.e., given that) the premises are true. Notice that one doesn't have to know whether the premises of an argument actually *are* true in order to determine its validity. One simply has to ascertain that the conclusion must be true *assuming* the premises are true.

In everyday English, the word *valid* is often used simply to indicate one's overall approval of an argument. But logicians focus their attention on the linkage between the premises and the conclusion, rather than on the actual truth or falsity of the statements comprising the argument. Thus, in ordinary English, *valid* has a less precise meaning than it does for logicians.

The following observations about validity may help to prevent some common misunderstandings. First, notice that an argument can have one or more *false* premises and still be valid. For instance:

14. All birds have beaks. Some cats are birds. So, some cats have beaks.

Here, the second premise is plainly false, and yet the argument is valid. It is impossible for the conclusion of argument (14) to be false *assuming that* its premises are true. And in the following argument, both premises are false, but the argument is still valid:

15. All sharks are birds. All birds are politicians. So, all sharks are politicians.

Although the premises of argument (15) are in fact false, if they *were* true, the conclusion would *have* to be true as well. It is *impossible* for the conclusion to be false *assuming that* the premises are true. So, the argument is valid.

Second, we cannot rightly conclude that an argument is valid simply on the grounds that its premises are all true. For example:

16. Some Americans are women. Clint Eastwood is an American. So, Clint Eastwood is a woman.

The premises here are true, but the conclusion is in fact false. So, obviously, it is *possible* that the conclusion of argument (16) is false while its premises are true; hence, (16) is not valid. Is the following argument valid?

17. Some Americans are Republicans. George Bush is an American. So, George Bush is a Republican.

Here, we have true premises and a true conclusion. Nevertheless, it is *possible* that the conclusion is false *while* the premises are true. (Bush could switch political parties while remaining an American.) So, even if an argument has true premises and a true conclusion, it isn't necessarily valid, for the premises may not support the conclusion in the right way. (Of course, in many cases, we simply do not know whether the premises of an argument are true or false, and yet we may know that the argument is valid.) Thus, the question "Are the premises actually true?" is distinct from the question "Is the argument valid?"

Third, suppose an argument is valid and has a false conclusion. Does it necessarily have at least one false premise? Yes. If it had true premises, then it would have to have a true conclusion, since it is valid. *Validity preserves truth;* that is, if we start with truth and reason in a valid fashion, we will always wind up with truth.

Fourth, does validity also preserve falsehood? In other words, if we start with false premises and reason validly, are we bound to wind up with a false conclusion? It is tempting to answer yes, because "error in its own right breeds error—if the first step in an argument is wrong, everything that follows will be wrong."[2] But the correct answer is no. Consider the following argument:

18. All dogs are ants. All ants are mammals. So, all dogs are mammals.

Is argument (18) valid? Yes. It is impossible for the conclusion of (18) to be false *assuming that* its premises are true. However, the premises here are false while the conclusion is true. So, *validity does not preserve falsehood.* In fact, false premises plus valid reasoning may lead to either truth or falsity, depending on the case. Here is a valid argument with false premises and a false conclusion:

19. All birds are cats. Some dogs are birds. So, some dogs are cats.

The lesson here is that although valid reasoning guarantees that we will end up with truth if we start with it, we may wind up with either truth or falsehood if we reason validly from false premises.

A **valid argument** has this essential feature: It is impossible for its conclusion to be false while its premises are true.

An **invalid argument** is one such that *it is possible for its conclusion to be false while its premises are true.* Each of the following arguments is invalid:

20. All dogs are animals. All cats are animals. Hence, all dogs are cats.

21. If Pat is a wife, then Pat is a woman. But Pat is not a wife. So, Pat is not a woman.

22. Bill likes Sue. Therefore, Sue likes Bill.

The premises of argument (20) are in fact true, but its conclusion is false; so, (20) is obviously invalid. Argument (21) is invalid because its premises leave open the possibility that Pat is an unmarried woman. And (22) is invalid, because even if Bill does like Sue, that is no guarantee that she likes him. In each of these cases, then, the conclusion could be false while (i.e., assuming that) the premises are true.

> An **invalid argument** has this essential feature: It is possible for its conclusion to be false while its premises are true.

Validity matters because true premises by themselves do not make good arguments. But we obviously want our arguments to have true premises. A **deductively sound argument** has two essential features: *It is valid, and all its premises are true*. Notice that a deductively sound argument cannot have a false conclusion. Because a sound argument is valid and has only true premises, it must have a true conclusion. Here are two deductively sound arguments:

23. All collies are dogs. All dogs are animals. So, all collies are animals.

24. If Akron is in Ohio, then Akron is in the United States. Akron is in Ohio. So, Akron is in the United States.

> Valid + All Premises True = Deductively Sound

A **deductively unsound argument** falls into one of the following three categories:

It is valid but has at least one false premise.

It is invalid but all its premises are true.

It is invalid *and* has at least one false premise.

In other words, a deductively unsound argument is one that either is invalid or has at least one false premise. For example, both of the following arguments are deductively unsound:

25. All birds are animals. Some grizzly bears are not animals. So, some grizzly bears are not birds.

26. All birds are animals. All grizzly bears are animals. So, all grizzly bears are birds.

Argument (25) is unsound, because although it is valid, it has a false (second) premise. And (26) is unsound, because although it has true premises, it is invalid. We can easily construct an unsound argument of the third type—that is, one that both is invalid *and* has at least one false premise—by replacing "birds" in (26) with "trees":

27. All trees are animals. All bears are animals. So, all bears are trees.

A **deductively unsound argument** is one that either is invalid or has at least one false premise.

Deductive logic is the part of logic that is concerned with tests for validity and invalidity.[3] And much of this book is devoted to an exploration of deductive logic. In fact, chapter 2 will provide us with our first set of methods for establishing the validity and invalidity of arguments.

A note on terminology is in order at the close of this section. Given our definitions, *arguments* are neither true nor false, but each *statement* is either true or false. On the other hand, *arguments* can be valid, invalid, deductively sound, or deductively unsound; but *statements* cannot be valid, invalid, deductively sound, or deductively unsound. Therefore, a given premise (or conclusion) is either true or false, but it cannot be valid, invalid, deductively sound, or deductively unsound.

The following exercises provide you with an opportunity to explore the concepts introduced in this section.

◆ Exercise 1.1

Note: For each exercise item preceded by an asterisk, the answer appears in the Answer Key at the end of the book.

Part A: Recognizing Statements   Which of the following are sentences? Which are statements?

* 1. The sky is blue.
  2. Let's paint the table red.
  3. Please close the window!
* 4. Murder is wrong.
  5. Abraham Lincoln was born in 1983.
  6. If San Francisco is in California, then San Francisco is in the U.S.A.

* 7. Davy Crockett died at the Alamo.
  8. How are you?
  9. If seven is greater than six, then six is greater than seven.
* 10. Let's have lunch.

Part B: True or False?   Which of the following statements are true? Which are false?

* 1. All valid arguments have at least one false premise.
  2. An argument is a set of statements, one of which, called the *conclusion,* is affirmed *on the basis* of the others, which are called the *premises.*
  3. Every valid argument has true premises and *only* true premises.

* **4.** Logic is the study of methods for evaluating whether the premises of an argument adequately support its conclusion.

  5. Some statements are invalid.

  6. Every valid argument has true premises *and* a true conclusion.

* **7.** A deductively sound argument can have a false conclusion.

  8. Deductive logic is the part of logic that is concerned with tests for validity and invalidity.

  9. If a valid argument has only true premises, then it must have a true conclusion.

* **10.** Some arguments are true.

  11. If a valid argument has only false premises, then it must have a false conclusion.

  12. Some invalid arguments have false conclusions but (all) true premises.

* **13.** Every deductively sound argument is valid.

  14. Every valid argument with a true conclusion is deductively sound.

  15. Every valid argument with a false conclusion has at least one false premise.

* **16.** Every deductively unsound argument is invalid.

  17. Some premises are valid.

  18. If all of the premises of an argument are true, then it is deductively sound.

* **19.** If an argument has (all) true premises and a false conclusion, then it is invalid.

  20. If an argument has one false premise, then it is deductively unsound.

  21. Every deductively unsound argument has at least one false premise.

* **22.** Some statements are deductively sound.

  23. Every valid argument has a true conclusion.

  24. Every invalid argument is deductively unsound.

* **25.** Some arguments are false.

Part C: Valid or Invalid?   Much of this text concerns methods of testing arguments for validity. While we have not yet discussed any particular methods of testing arguments for validity, we do have definitions of "valid argument" and "invalid argument." Based on your current understanding, which of the following arguments are valid? Which are invalid?

* **1.** If Lincoln was killed in an automobile accident, then Lincoln is dead. Lincoln was killed in an automobile accident. Hence, Lincoln is dead.

  2. If Lincoln was killed in an automobile accident, then Lincoln is dead. Lincoln was not killed in an automobile accident. Therefore, Lincoln is not dead.

  3. If Lincoln was killed in an automobile accident, then Lincoln is dead. Lincoln is dead. So, Lincoln was killed in an automobile accident.

* **4.** If Lincoln was killed in an automobile accident, then Lincoln is dead. Lincoln is not dead. Hence, Lincoln was not killed in an automobile accident.

  5. Either 2 plus 2 equals 22 or Santa Claus is real. But 2 plus 2 does not equal 22. Therefore, Santa Claus is real.

6. Either we use nuclear power or we reduce our consumption of energy. If we use nuclear power, then we place our lives at great risk. If we reduce our consumption of energy, then we place ourselves under extensive governmental control. So, either we place our lives at great risk or we place ourselves under extensive governmental control.

* 7. All birds are animals. No tree is a bird. Therefore, no tree is an animal.

8. Some humans are comatose. But no comatose being is rational. So, not every human is rational.

9. All animals are living things. At least one cabbage is a living thing. So, at least one cabbage is an animal.

* 10. Alvin likes Jane. Jane likes Chris. So, Alvin likes Chris.

Part D: Deductive Soundness   Which of the following arguments are deductively sound? Which are deductively unsound? If an argument is deductively unsound, explain why.

* 1. All cats are mammals. All mammals are animals. So, all cats are animals.

2. All collies are dogs. Some animals are not dogs. So, some animals are not collies.

3. All citizens of Nebraska are Americans. All citizens of Montana are Americans. So, all citizens of Nebraska are citizens of Montana.

* 4. "Let's party!" is either a sentence or a statement (or both). "Let's party!" is a sentence. So, "Let's party!" is not a statement.

5. No diamonds are emeralds. The Hope Diamond is a diamond. So, the Hope Diamond is not an emerald.

6. All planets are round. The earth is round. So, the earth is a planet.

* 7. If the Taj Mahal is in Kentucky, then the Taj Mahal is in the U.S.A. But the Taj Mahal is not in the U.S.A. So, the Taj Mahal is not in Kentucky.

8. All women are married. Some executives are not married. So, some executives are not women.

9. All mammals are animals. No reptiles are mammals. So, no reptiles are animals.

* 10. All mammals are cats. All cats are animals. So, all mammals are animals.

1.2 Strength and Inductive Soundness

Even if an argument is not valid, its premises may still provide significant support for its conclusion. A strong argument is one in which the premises provide *partial* support for the conclusion. More precisely, a **strong argument** is one such that *it is unlikely (though possible) that its conclusion is false while its premises are true.* In other words, a strong argument has this essential feature: It is probable (but not necessary) that if its premises are true, then its conclusion is true. For example:

28. Ninety percent of American males over 50 years of age cannot run a mile in less than 6 minutes. Thomas is an American male over 50 years of age. So, Thomas cannot run a mile in less than 6 minutes.

The premises of argument (28) do not absolutely guarantee the truth of the conclusion. Possibly Thomas belongs to that small percentage of American men over 50 who can run a mile in less than 6 minutes. Nevertheless, it is unlikely that the conclusion of (28) is false assuming its premises are true.

Now, let's alter argument (28) systematically to clarify the concept of strength. Suppose we replace "ninety" with "ninety-nine." Does the argument remain strong? Yes, of course. In fact, it is even stronger. This indicates that *strength*, unlike validity, is very much a matter of degree. Suppose we replace "ninety" with "fifty-one." Is the argument then strong? Strictly speaking, yes, because the conclusion remains *slightly* more probable than not. Of course, once we replace "ninety" with "fifty-one," the argument is of little value: The amount of support given to the conclusion is scarcely worth mentioning. But the important point to keep in mind is that because strength comes in degrees, we can legitimately speak of arguments that are *slightly* strong, *moderately* strong, or *very* strong. By contrast, it would make no sense to speak of "slightly valid" or "moderately valid" arguments. Validity is an all-or-nothing affair.

What if we replace "ninety" with "fifty" in argument (28)? Then the argument is not strong, but weak. A **weak argument** has this essential feature: *It is not likely that if its premises are true, then its conclusion is true.* If we replace "ninety" with "fifty," then it is just as likely, given the premises, that Thomas *can* run the mile in less than 6 minutes as that he *cannot*. So, the argument is weak. And, of course, the argument becomes progressively weaker as we replace "ninety" with "forty," "thirty," and so on.

At the other end of the scale, what if we replace "Ninety percent of" with "all" in argument (28)? Does the argument remain strong? No. At that point, the argument becomes *valid*—it is impossible for the conclusion to be false while the premises are true. But, by definition, in a strong argument, it is *possible* that the conclusion is false while the premises are true. Thus, no valid argument is strong and no strong argument is valid.

A **strong argument** has this essential feature: It is unlikely (though possible) that its conclusion is false while its premises are true.

A **weak argument** has this essential feature: It is not likely that if its premises are true, then its conclusion is true.

We will explore the concept of strength more fully in subsequent chapters, but it will be helpful at this point to consider some additional examples of strong arguments, in order to underscore the fact that they come in very different types.

For instance, **arguments from authority** can be strong. They have the following structure:

> 29. 1. R is a reliable authority regarding S.
>   2. R sincerely asserts that S.
>   So, S.

(Here, "R" stands for a person or reference work while "S" stands for any statement.) For example:

> 30. According to historian Howard Zinn, by 1933, the worst year of America's Great Depression, one fourth to one third of America's labor force was out of work. So, a fourth or more of American workers were unemployed in 1933.[4]

This appeal to authority is legitimate, but authorities can make mistakes, so it is possible that the conclusion of (30) is false while its premises are true—possible, but unlikely. Hence, the argument is strong. Yet it would be impossible to state the degree of strength with numerical precision.

Like arguments from authority, **arguments from analogy** are very common, and they, too, can be strong. The structure of an argument from analogy is as follows:

> 31. 1. Object (event or situation) A is similar to object (event or situation) B in certain relevant respects.
>   2. B has property P.
>   So, A has property P also.

Here is an example. Suppose Jack and Jill are riding horseback. Jill's horse jumps a fence, but Jack is unsure whether his horse can jump the fence. Jill points out that his horse is very similar to hers in size, speed, strength, and training. She adds that because Jack is an experienced rider and weighs no more than she does, Jack's horse is not operating with a handicap. She concludes that Jack's horse can jump the fence, too. We could outline Jill's reasoning as follows:

> 32. Jack's horse is similar in relevant respects to Jill's horse (and is similarly situated). Jill's horse is able to jump the fence. So, Jack's horse is able to jump the fence also.

This argument is not valid, because its conclusion can be false while its premises are true. For example, unknown to Jill, Jack's horse may have been given a drug that renders it unable to jump well today. Still, it is more probable than not that if the premises of (32) are true, then the conclusion is true, and hence the argument is at least slightly strong.

As we noted previously, deductive logic is that part of logic that concerns tests for validity and invalidity. **Inductive logic** is the part of logic that concerns tests for the strength and weakness of arguments. An **inductively sound argument** is one that has two essential features: It is strong, and all its premises are true. Here is an example:

> 33. All or nearly all lemons that have been tasted were sour. So, all or nearly all lemons are sour.

This argument is not valid because the conclusion concerns not merely the lemons that have been tasted but lemons in general, *including those that have not been tasted.* And the premise does not rule out the *possibility* that a large percentage of untasted lemons are not sour. Nevertheless, it is unlikely that the conclusion is false given that the premise is true. And the premise is true. So, the argument is inductively sound.

An inductively sound argument can have a false conclusion, for its premises do not absolutely guarantee the truth of its conclusion. In this respect, *inductively* sound arguments differ markedly from *deductively* sound arguments. A deductively sound argument cannot have a false conclusion, because it is valid and all its premises are true. (And if a valid argument has only true premises, its conclusion must be true also.)

Strong + All Premises True = Inductively Sound

An **inductively unsound argument** is one that is either (a) weak or (b) strong with at least one false premise. (Note that by this definition, a weak argument with a false premise counts as inductively unsound.) Here is an example of an argument that is inductively unsound because it is weak:

> 34. Slightly less than 50 percent of Americans are men. Julia Roberts is an American. So, Julia Roberts is a man.

Although argument (34) has true premises, the premises do not provide even partial support (in our technical sense) for the conclusion: It is *not* likely that if the premises are true, then the conclusion is true. (*Note:* This is not because Julia Roberts is a woman. If we replace "Julia Roberts" with "Woody Allen," the argument is still weak, even though its conclusion is true.)

Here is an example of an argument that is inductively unsound because it is strong but has a false premise:

> 35. There is intelligent life on all of the following planets: Mercury, Venus, Earth, Jupiter, Uranus, Neptune, and Pluto. So, there is intelligent life on Mars.[5]

As far as we know, the premise of argument (35) is false, and so is the conclusion. But it is unlikely that the conclusion is false *given that* the premise is true. So, the argument is strong but inductively unsound.

An **inductively sound argument** has two essential features: It is strong, and all its premises are true.

An **inductively unsound argument** is one that is either (a) weak or (b) strong, with at least one false premise.

Note that according to our definitions, no deductively sound argument is inductively sound, for no valid argument is strong. Similarly, no inductively sound argument is deductively sound, since no strong argument is valid. Note also that a valid argument with a false premise is deductively unsound, but it is not inductively unsound, because a valid argument is neither strong nor weak.

We now have many of the basic concepts of logic before us. However, because it is easy to become confused about the relationships between these basic concepts, let us pull back and sketch a map of the ground we have covered. We defined *logic* as the study of methods for evaluating whether the premises of an argument adequately *support* its conclusion. And we have seen that arguments can be evaluated in terms of two different standards: validity and strength. Deductive logic is the branch of logic concerned with methods of evaluating arguments for validity and invalidity. Inductive logic is the branch of logic concerned with methods of evaluating arguments for strength and weakness.

Some logic texts state that there are two different kinds of *arguments*, deductive and inductive, and that deductive logic is about deductive arguments while inductive logic is about inductive arguments. These texts provide the following classification of arguments:

	Deductive arguments	Inductive arguments
Logically correct	Valid	Strong
Logically incorrect	Invalid	Weak

However, from the standpoint of this text, this classification is misleading.[6] For example, given our definitions, every inductively sound argument is invalid, and hence deductively unsound. And every inductively unsound argument is also deductively unsound, because every inductively unsound argument is invalid.

Therefore, *deductive and inductive logic do not differ according to the kinds of arguments they treat, but according to the different standards by which they evaluate arguments—namely, validity and strength.* From our point of view, arguments may be classified as shown in the accompanying diagram.

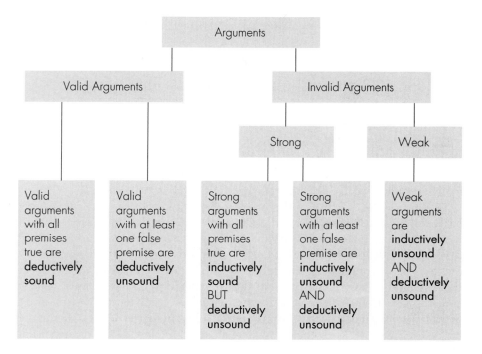

Note that in this scheme, any argument that is not deductively sound is deductively unsound. For example, all *inductively sound* arguments are *deductively unsound* because they are invalid. Strong arguments with false premises are inductively unsound, but they are also deductively unsound for two reasons: (a) They are invalid and (b) they have false premises. All weak arguments are inductively unsound (whether or not they have a false premise). And all weak arguments are also deductively unsound, because all weak arguments are invalid.

Some general remarks on terminology are in order at the close of this section. Notice that given our definitions, *arguments* can be strong, weak, inductively sound, or inductively unsound. But *arguments* are never true, and they are never false. Both *premises* and *conclusions* are either true or false. But neither *premises* nor *conclusions* are ever strong, weak, inductively sound, or inductively unsound.

The following exercises give you an opportunity to apply the concepts introduced in this section.

Summary of Definitions

An **argument** is a set of statements, one of which, called the *conclusion,* is affirmed *on the basis* of the others, which are called the *premises.*

Logic is the study of methods for evaluating whether the premises of an argument adequately support (or provide good evidence for) its conclusion.

A **valid argument** has this essential feature: It is impossible for its conclusion to be false while its premises are true.

An **invalid argument** has this essential feature: It is possible for its conclusion to be false while its premises are true.

A **deductively sound argument** has two essential features: It is valid, and all its premises are true.

A **deductively unsound argument** is one that either is invalid or has at least one false premise.

Deductive logic is the part of logic that concerns tests for validity and invalidity.

A **strong argument** has this essential feature: It is unlikely (though possible) that its conclusion is false while its premises are true.

A **weak argument** has this essential feature: It is not likely that if its premises are true, then its conclusion is true.

Inductive logic is the part of logic that concerns tests for strength and weakness.

An **inductively sound argument** has two essential features: It is strong, and all its premises are true.

An **inductively unsound argument** is one that is either (a) weak or (b) strong with at least one false premise.

◆ Exercise 1.2

Part A: Matching   In the space provided, write the letter of the item on the right that best characterizes the item on the left.

____ **1.** Valid	**A.** A sentence that is either true or false.
____ **2.** Invalid	**B.** An argument that is either invalid or has a false premise.
____ **3.** Strong	**C.** A strong argument with (all) true premises.
____ **4.** Weak	**D.** The part of logic concerned with tests for validity and invalidity.
____ **5.** Deductively sound	**E.** It is not likely that if the premises are true, then the conclusion is true.
____ **6.** Inductively sound	**F.** A valid argument with (all) true premises.
____ **7.** Statement	**G.** The part of logic concerned with tests for strength and weakness.

_____ **8.** Deductively unsound

_____ **9.** Inductively unsound

_____ **10.** Deductive logic

_____ **11.** Inductive logic

_____ **12.** Logic

_____ **13.** Argument

_____ **14.** Arguments by analogy

_____ **15.** Arguments from authority

H. The study of methods for testing whether the premises of an argument adequately support its conclusion.

I. It is impossible for the conclusion to be false while the premises are true.

J. A set of statements, one of which, called the _conclusion,_ is affirmed _on the basis_ of the others, which are called the _premises._

K. R is a reliable authority regarding S. R sincerely asserts that S. So, S.

L. An argument with the following essential feature: It is possible that the conclusion is false while the premises are true.

M. Object A is similar to object B in certain relevant respects. B has property P. So, A has property P also.

N. It is unlikely (though possible) that the conclusion is false while the premises are true.

O. An argument that is either (a) weak or (b) strong but has a false premise.

Part B: True or False?

* **1.** All arguments having only true premises are inductively sound.

  2. All strong arguments are inductively sound.

  3. All weak arguments are inductively unsound.

* **4.** All arguments with a false premise are inductively unsound.

  5. Some inductively sound arguments have a false conclusion.

  6. Some deductively sound arguments have a false conclusion.

* **7.** The following argument is true: "Over 90 percent of Americans speak English. Hank Williams is an American. So, Hank Williams speaks English."

  8. The following argument is an argument from analogy: "According to Flew's _Dictionary of Philosophy,_ the British philosopher Bertrand Russell died in 1970. So, Bertrand Russell died in 1970."

  9. A strong argument has this essential feature: It is impossible for its conclusion to be false while its premises are true.

* **10.** Every inductively unsound argument has at least one false premise.

  11. Every inductively unsound argument is weak.

  12. Some arguments have valid premises, and some do not.

* **13.** The following argument is an argument from authority: "Scholars are like the Roman emperor Nero. Nero, you'll recall, played his violin while Rome burned. Similarly, scholars play with ideas while civilization is threatened by the 'flames' of greed, poverty, racism, and violence. Now, plainly, Nero was morally irresponsible. Hence, scholars are morally irresponsible also."

14. A strong argument has these two features: (a) It is possible that if its premises are true, its conclusion is false, and (b) it is probable that if its premises are true, then its conclusion is true.

15. A weak argument has this essential feature: It is not likely that if its premises are true, then its conclusion is true.

Part C: Valid or Invalid? Strong or Weak?   As best you can determine, which of the following arguments are valid? Which invalid? Which are strong? Which weak?

* **1.** Fifty percent of serial killers were abused as children. Ted Bundy was a serial killer. Therefore, Bundy was abused as a child.

2. This lovely china plate is similar in size, weight, and composition to the one I just dropped. The one I just dropped broke. So, if I drop this lovely china plate, it will break.

3. According to Lillian Roxon's *Rock Encyclopedia,* Buddy Holly, who wrote "Peggy Sue," "That'll Be the Day," and other early rock hits, died in an airplane crash on February 3, 1959. So, Buddy Holly died in an airplane crash in 1959.

* **4.** One hundred percent of the frogs that have been dissected had hearts. Therefore, 100 percent of the entire frog population have hearts.

5. It is always wrong to kill an innocent human intentionally. A fetus is an innocent human. So, it is always wrong to kill a fetus intentionally.

6. Research based on Gallup polls indicates that a random sample of 4000 is sufficient to support highly accurate conclusions about large populations—conclusions having a margin of error of only two percentage points. And according to a recent poll, 83 percent of a random sample of 4000 American voters favors Jones for President. Thus, approximately 83 percent of American voters favor Jones for President.

* **7.** A porpoise is similar to a human being. It has lungs rather than gills. It is warm-blooded rather than cold-blooded. And porpoises nurse their young with milk. Therefore, porpoises, like humans, are capable of speaking languages.

8. Every serial killer is a psychopath. Some criminals are not psychopaths. So, some criminals are not serial killers.

9. Ninety percent of the cars in the parking lot were vandalized, and your car was in the parking lot. Therefore, your car was vandalized.

* **10.** No spiders are humans. Dawn is a human. So, Dawn is not a spider.

11. All observed emeralds have been green. So, the next emerald to be observed will be green.

12. Linda is younger than Maria. So, Maria is older than Linda.

* **13.** According to H. W. Janson, professor of fine arts at New York University, the Norwegian artist Edvard Munch painted *The Scream* in 1893. So, Munch painted *The Scream* prior to 1900. (See Janson's *History of Art* [New York: Abrams, 1971], p. 513.)

   14. Sixty-five percent of the students at St. Ambrose College are Democrats. Joan is a student at St. Ambrose College. So, Joan is a Democrat.

   15. Mark Twain is identical with Samuel Clemens. Mark Twain wrote *Huckleberry Finn*. So, Samuel Clemens wrote *Huckleberry Finn*.

* **16.** No circles are squares. All circles are figures. So, no figures are squares.

   17. According to Lewis Hopfe, a noted authority on world religions, the religion called Jainism originated in India in the sixth century B.C.E. It is the goal of Jainism to liberate the soul from matter. All life, but especially animal life, is sacred to the Jains. And the Jains hold that the gods cannot help humans attain salvation. Therefore, at least one religion does not teach humans to rely on the gods for salvation. (See Hopfe's *Religions of the World*, 4th ed. [New York: Macmillan, 1987], pp. 134–138.)

   18. In a certain factory, there is a machine that produces tin cans. Quality-control inspectors examine (in a random fashion) one tenth of the tin cans produced by the machine. Of the tin cans examined by the inspectors, 5 percent are malformed. So, approximately 5 percent of all the tin cans produced by the machine are malformed.

* **19.** Computers are similar to humans in that both are capable of complex calculations. Humans generally feel ashamed if they make a mistake. Hence, computers generally feel ashamed if they make a mistake.

   20. According to the *Encyclopedia Britannica*, the first use of poison gas as a weapon in modern warfare occurred on April 22, 1915, when the Germans launched a highly successful chlorine gas attack against the Allied positions at Ypres, Belgium. So, the first use of poison gas as a weapon in modern warfare occurred on April 22, 1915.

Part D: Inductive Soundness   Which of the following are inductively sound? Which are inductively unsound? (If the argument is inductively unsound, explain why.) Which of the arguments are neither inductively sound nor inductively unsound?

* **1.** Most humans fear death. Woody Allen (the famous comedian and filmmaker) is a human. So, Woody Allen fears death.

   2. Fifty percent of the students at Seattle Pacific University are Republicans. Kathy is a student at Seattle Pacific University. So, Kathy is a Republican.

   3. All humans are mortal. Socrates is a human. So, Socrates is mortal.

* **4.** All of the birds that have been observed (in the entire history of the world) can fly. So, all birds can fly.

   5. War is similar to playing a game of chess. For instance, in both war and chess, strategy is important. And in both war and chess, there is a struggle for victory.

Now, when one is losing a game of chess, one should not attack one's opponent with lethal weapons. So, when a nation is losing a war, it should not attack its opponent with lethal weapons.

6. Ninety percent of Americans speak Chinese. Harrison Ford (the famous actor) is an American. So, Harrison Ford speaks Chinese.

* 7. Sue is taller than Tom. Tom is taller than Fred. So, Sue is taller than Fred.

8. The vast majority of Americans are fluent speakers of English. The Queen of England is an American. So, the Queen of England is a fluent speaker of English.

9. Most Americans live in Nevada. Aretha Franklin (the famous singer) is an American. So, Aretha Franklin lives in Nevada.

* 10. Forty percent of students at Reed College are from the Northwest. Sally is a student at Reed College. So, Sally is from the Northwest.

Notes

1. I have said that arguments are composed of statements. Some logicians would prefer to say that arguments are composed of *propositions*. For more about this issue, see section 4.1.
2. C. S. Lewis, *The Problem of Pain* (New York: Macmillan, 1962), p. 116.
3. My characterizations of deductive and inductive logic are borrowed from Brian Skyrms, *Choice and Chance*, 3rd ed. (Belmont, CA: Wadsworth, 1986), p. 12.
4. Howard Zinn, *A People's History of the United States* (New York: HarperCollins, 1995), p. 378.
5. This example is borrowed from Skyrms, *Choice and Chance*, p. 9.
6. The simplicity of this picture of logic is also more apparent than real. For instance, suppose we ask, "Why aren't strong arguments invalid?" The standard answer is that we cannot speak simply of strong arguments and invalid arguments; rather, we must speak of "strong inductive arguments" and "invalid deductive arguments." Deductive arguments are then defined as ones in which the premises are *claimed* or *intended* to support the conclusion in such a way that the conclusion cannot be false while the premises are true. Inductive arguments are defined as ones in which the premises are *claimed* or *intended* to support the conclusion in such a way that it is possible but unlikely that the conclusion is false while the premises are true. In this view, to know whether an argument is strong, weak, valid, or invalid, one must first know what sort of support is *claimed* or *intended*. And this raises complicated questions because arguments themselves do not claim or intend anything. And an arguer's claims or intentions may be muddled or inconsistent. For example, suppose an argument meets the standard of validity provided in this text, but the arguer merely *claims* that it is strong. Are we to categorize the argument as inductive? Thus, an apparently simple picture of logic turns out to rest on a problematic distinction. The approach taken in this chapter avoids these problems entirely. For more about this issue, see "Myths About Inductive Logic" in section 10.1.

Chapter 2

Argument Forms

We have seen that deductive logic is the part of logic that concerns tests for validity and invalidity. This chapter introduces the concept of an argument form and explains how an understanding of argument forms can be used to establish that an argument is valid or invalid.

2.1 Forms and Counterexamples

Consider the following two arguments:

1. 1. All oaks are trees.
   2. All trees are plants.
   So, all oaks are plants.

2. 1. All monauli are flageolets.
   2. All flageolets are fipple-flutes.
   So, all monauli are fipple-flutes.[1]

These two arguments have the same *form*—that is, they exemplify the same pattern of reasoning. We can represent the form as follows:

Form 1

1. All *A* are *B*.
2. All *B* are *C*.
So, all *A* are *C*.

Here, the letters *A*, *B*, and *C* stand for *terms*. For the purposes of this chapter, let us say that a **term** is a word or phrase that stands for a class (i.e., collection or set) of things, such as the class of oaks or the class of trees. Thus, the words "oaks," "trees," and "plants" are terms in argument (1) above. (Certain descriptive phrases such as "oak trees less than 2 years old" also count as terms in the sense defined.) Form 1 provides a representation of the pattern of reasoning common to arguments (1) and (2). With regard to (1), A stands for the term "oaks," B for the term "trees," and C for the term "plants." With regard to (2), A stands for term "monauli," B stands for the term "flageolets," and C stands for the term "fipple-flutes."

Argument (1) is clearly valid: If all members of class A (oaks) are members of class B (trees), and all members of class B (trees) are members of class C (plants), then all members of A (oaks) are members of C (plants). We can diagram the logic as follows:

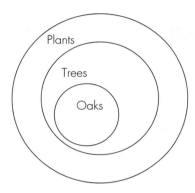

And as regards argument (2), while you may not have any idea whether the premises are true, you can see that (2) is valid because it has the same form as (1). Any argument having Form 1 has the following feature: Its conclusion cannot be false while its premises are true. So, *the validity of the argument is guaranteed by its form and does not depend on its content* (i.e., its specific subject matter).

Using Form 1, we can generate valid arguments at will by substituting terms for the letters A, B, and C. An argument that results from uniformly replacing letters with terms (or statements) in an argument form is called a **substitution instance** of that form. Note that the replacement must be uniform. For example, if "oaks" replaces A in one instance, "oaks" must replace A in all instances.

Here is another valid form of argument, along with two substitution instances:

Form 2

1. All *A* are *B*.
2. Some *C* are not *B*.
So, some *C* are not *A*.

Substitution Instances

3. 1. All emeralds are gems.
   2. Some rocks are not gems.
   So, some rocks are not emeralds.

4. 1. All collies are dogs.
   2. Some animals are not dogs.
   So, some animals are not collies.

In argument (3), "emeralds" replaces A, "gems" replaces B, and "rocks" replaces C. In (4), "collies" replaces A, "dogs" replaces B, and "animals" replaces C. Every argument having this form is valid. We can diagram the logic as follows:

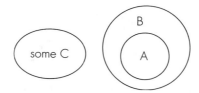

Clearly, if all members of class A are members of class B, and some members of class C are not members of B, then some members of C are not members of A. Thus, it is impossible for an argument having this form to have a false conclusion given that its premises are true.

An **argument form** is a pattern of reasoning.

An argument that results from uniformly replacing letters in an argument form with terms (or statements) is called a **substitution instance** of that form.

Let us now consider the relationship between form and invalidity. The following argument has true premises and a false conclusion, so it is plainly invalid.

5. 1. All birds are animals.
   2. All dogs are animals.
   So, all birds are dogs.

If we let A stand for "birds," B for "animals," and C for "dogs," we can represent the form of the argument as follows:

Form 3

1. All A are B.
2. All C are B.
So, all A are C.

This argument form is invalid, because it allows us to move from true premises to a false conclusion. Argument (5) proves this, for it is a substitution instance of Form 3.

The relationship between argument (5) and Form 3 suggests a procedure for showing that an argument is invalid. First, identify the form of the argument. Second, if the validity of the argument is suspect, produce a substitution instance of the argument form in which the premises are true and the conclusion is false. This will show that the argument form is invalid. Third, given that the validity of the argument depends on the form identified, we may conclude that the argument itself is invalid. Let us now make this procedure a bit more explicit and note some complications that may arise.

Consider the following argument:

6. 1. All determinists are fatalists.

2. Some fatalists are not Calvinists.

So, some Calvinists are not determinists.

Argument (6) has this form:

Form 4

1. All *A* are *B*.
2. Some *B* are not *C*.

So, some *C* are not *A*.

We can prove that this form is invalid by producing a substitution instance that has premises known to be true and a conclusion known to be false. For example:

7. 1. All dogs are animals. [true]

2. Some animals are not collies. [true]

So, some collies are not dogs. [false]

A substitution instance with premises known to be true and a conclusion known to be false is a **counterexample** to the form in question. A counterexample demonstrates the invalidity of an argument form by showing that the form does not preserve truth—that is, that the form can lead from true premises to a false conclusion. A good counterexample must have the following features:

It must have the correct form.

Its premises must be *well-known* truths.

Its conclusion must be a *well-known* falsehood.

A **counterexample** to an argument form is a substitution instance whose premises are *well-known* truths and whose conclusion is a *well-known* falsehood.

Counterexample (7) shows that Form 4 is invalid: "All A are B; some B are not C; so, some C are not A." And argument (6)—"All determinists are fatalists;

some fatalists are not Calvinists; so, some Calvinists are not determinists"—has Form 4. Therefore, we may provisionally conclude that (6) is invalid. (The *provisional* nature of the conclusion will be explained momentarily.)

Now, let's break the process of finding a counterexample down into steps. We begin with an argument:

8. 1. No capitalists are philanthropists.

    2. All philanthropists are altruists.

    So, no capitalists are altruists.

If we let A stand for "capitalists," B for "philanthropists," and C for "altruists," we can represent the form as follows:

Form 5

1. No A are B.

2. All B are C.

So, no A are C.

Next, we construct a substitution instance whose premises are well-known truths and whose conclusion is a well-known falsehood. It is best to employ terms whose interrelations are well understood—for example, simple biological terms such as "dog," "collie," "mammal," "cat," and "animal," or simple geometrical terms such as "square," "figure," "rectangle," and "circle." It often helps to begin by writing a blatantly false conclusion and then work backwards. For instance:

9. 1. No dogs are B.

    2. All B are animals.

    So, no dogs are animals.

Notice that since "dogs" replaces A in the conclusion, it must also replace A in the first premise; and because "animals" replaces C in the conclusion, it must replace C in the second premise. Now we merely need to find a term to replace B with—a term that will make the premises well-known truths. "Cats" is an obvious choice. So, our completed counterexample looks like this:

10. 1. No dogs are cats.

    2. All cats are animals.

    So, no dogs are animals.

Because the premises are well-known truths but the conclusion is a well-known falsehood, Form 5 is invalid ("No A are B; all B are C; so, no A are C"). And we may provisionally conclude that argument (8) is invalid.

The counterexample method has some limitations and complications that should be noted at this time. First, although the counterexample method can be used to prove that an invalid argument form is invalid, it cannot show that a valid form is valid. For example, suppose we show that a given argument form has a substitution instance that has true premises and a true conclusion. Does that show that the argument form is valid? No. Invalid forms often have such substitution instances. Here is one for Form 5 ("No A are B; all B are C; so, no A are C):

11. 1. No cats are collies. [true]
     2. All collies are dogs. [true]
     So, no cats are dogs. [true]

Nevertheless, the argument form remains invalid because it *can* lead from true premises to a false conclusion, as counterexample (10) illustrates. Again, the point is that the counterexample method cannot establish validity, but only invalidity.

Of course, it is impossible to construct a counterexample to a valid form. If an argument form is valid, then any substitution instance with true premises is bound to have a true conclusion. This indicates a second limitation of the counterexample method. What if we suspect that an argument form is invalid but have difficulty constructing a counterexample? Perhaps the form is valid after all, or perhaps we simply need to be more creative in thinking of substitution instances. How do we tell which? The counterexample method does not answer this question.

A third limitation of the counterexample method should be mentioned at this point. It cannot be used to show that an argument is either strong or weak, for the strength and weakness of an argument depends only partly on its form. (We will explore this issue in chapter 10 on induction.)

A minor complication that arises when constructing counterexamples concerns the word "some." In logic, the word "some" means "at least one." Hence, the statement "Some dogs are animals" is true: *At least one dog* is an animal. And "Some dogs are animals" does *not* imply that some dogs are not animals. Both of the following are true statements: "Some dogs are animals" and "All dogs are animals."

A more interesting complication regarding counterexamples stems from the fact that an argument can have more than one form. This complication explains why the counterexample method allows us to draw only *provisional* conclusions regarding the invalidity of *arguments* (as opposed to argument *forms*). Let's consider an argument having Form 1:

12. All cats are mammals. All mammals are animals. So, all cats are animals.

Like all arguments having Form 1, argument (12) is valid. But suppose we let the letters A, B, and C stand for *statements* (instead of terms, as we have been doing). Such a use of letters is entirely legitimate. And if we let A stand for the first premise, B for the second premise, and C for the conclusion, we can rightly say that argument (12) has the following form: "A; B; so, C." This form, however, is invalid—here is a counterexample:

13. Trees exist. Frogs exist. So, unicorns exist.

(To obtain the counterexample, simply substitute "Trees exists" for A, "Frogs exist" for B, and "Unicorns exist" for C.) Have we shown that argument (12) is invalid? No. We have merely shown that it has *one* form that is invalid. As a matter of fact, we might add that every argument has at least one invalid form, because we can represent *any* argument as a series of statements, followed by a conclusion, along these lines: "A; B; C; D; so, E" (where the letters stand for *statements*). And it is easy to construct a counterexample, similar to (13), to prove that any such form is invalid.

Very well then. A single argument can have both valid and invalid forms. But here is a key point to remember: *An argument is valid if any of its forms is valid.* In other words, if an argument has a valid form, then it is impossible for its conclusion to be false while its premises are true. To illustrate, argument (12) is valid because it has a valid form, namely, Form 1.

We can now see why the counterexample method yields only provisional results. Suppose we have correctly identified one of the argument's forms and shown *that* form to be invalid by means of a counterexample. It remains possible—at least in theory—that the argument has an additional form that is valid. And, as we have just seen, it is not the possession of an invalid form that makes an argument invalid; rather, it is the lack of a valid form that makes an argument invalid.[2]

What good is it, then, to show that an argument has a form that is invalid? Generally speaking, if we identify the form of an argument *with due sensitivity to its key logical words and phrases,* and if the form thus identified is invalid, then the argument has no further valid form, and so it is invalid. And this is why the counterexample method is a powerful tool for evaluating arguments even though it cannot rigorously prove that a given *argument* is invalid. In addition, bear in mind that the counterexample method *can* be used to prove *rigorously* that invalid *forms* are invalid, and it is of great value for this reason also.

The following exercise gives you an opportunity to apply your knowledge of argument forms.

◆ Exercise 2.1

Counterexamples   Use counterexamples to show that the following arguments are invalid. Remember, it is usually best to employ terms whose interrelations are well known, such as "dog," "cat," "collie," "animal," and "mammal."

* 1. No genuine Americans are communist spies. Some Oregonians are not communist spies. Therefore, some Oregonians are genuine Americans.

2. All dogmatists are hypocrites. All dogmatists are bigots. So, all bigots are hypocrites.

3. All who seek public office are noble. Some who seek public office are not wise persons. So, some wise persons are not noble.

* 4. No rock is sentient. Some mammals are sentient. Hence, no mammal is a rock.

5. All fatalists are determinists. Some predestinarians are not fatalists. So, some predestinarians are not determinists.

6. All vegetarians who refuse to eat animal products are vegans. No vegetarians who refuse to eat animal products are cattle ranchers. Hence, no vegans are cattle ranchers.

* 7. Some intelligent people are highly immoral. All highly immoral people are unhappy. Therefore, some unhappy people are not intelligent.

8. No perfect geometrical figures are physical entities. No physical entities are circles. Therefore, no circles are perfect geometrical figures.

9. All Fabians are socialists. Some socialists are not communists. So, some Fabians are not communists.

* 10. All trespassers are persons who will be prosecuted. Some trespassers are not criminals. So, some criminals are not persons who will be prosecuted.

11. All observable entities are physical entities. Some quarks are not observable entities. Therefore, some quarks are not physical entities.

12. No wines are distilled liquors. Some beers are not distilled liquors. So, some beers are not wines.

* 13. All statements that can be falsified are scientific. All empirical data are scientific. Hence, all statements that can be falsified are empirical data.

14. All diligent persons are individuals who deserve praise. Some students are individuals who deserve praise. So, some students are diligent persons.

15. All black holes are stars that have collapsed in on themselves. All black holes are entities that produce a tremendous amount of gravity. So, every entity that produces a tremendous amount of gravity is a star that has collapsed in on itself.

* 16. Every rock musician is cool. No nerd is a rock musician. Hence, no nerd is cool.

17. All miracles are highly improbable events. Some highly improbable events are cases of winning a lottery. So, some cases of winning a lottery are miracles.

18. No positrons are particles with a negative charge. No neutrons are particles with a negative charge. Therefore, some positrons are neutrons.

* 19. All people who despise animals are neurotic. No veterinarian is a person who despises animals. Hence, no veterinarian is a neurotic.

20. All destructive acts are evil. Some wars are evil. So, some wars are destructive acts.

2.2 Some Forms with Names

We have seen how the concept of an argument form can be used to establish that an argument is invalid. And we have seen that if an argument has a valid form, then it is valid. In this section, we will identify some basic valid forms that occur so often that they have been given names by logicians. We will also identify the names of two frequently occurring invalid forms. Prior to identifying these forms, however, we need to understand conditional ("if-then") statements, because some of the most important argument forms centrally involve conditional statements.

Understanding Conditional Statements

Each of the following are conditional statements (often called simply "conditionals" by logicians):

14. If it is snowing, then the mail will be late.

15. If Abraham Lincoln was born in 1709, then he was born before the American Civil War.

16. If Abraham Lincoln was born in 1809, then he was born after the American Civil War.

Conditionals have several important characteristics. First, note the components of conditionals. The if-clause of a conditional is called its **antecedent**; the then-clause is called the **consequent**. But the antecedent does not include the word "if." Hence, the antecedent of statement (14) is "it is snowing," not "*If* it is snowing." Similarly, the consequent is the statement following the word "then," but it does not include that word. So, the consequent of (14) is "the mail will be late," not "*then* the mail will be late."

Second, conditionals are hypothetical in nature. Thus, in asserting a conditional, one does not assert that its antecedent is true. Nor does one assert that its consequent is true. Rather, one asserts that *if* the antecedent is true, *then* the consequent is true. Thus, statement (15) is a true conditional even though its antecedent is false (Lincoln was born in 1809, not 1709). If Lincoln was born in 1709, then, of course, his birth preceded the American Civil War, which began in 1860. And (16) is a false conditional even though its antecedent is true. If Lincoln was born in 1809, then he certainly was not born *after* the American Civil War.

Third, there are many ways to express a conditional in ordinary English. Consider the following conditional statement:

17. If it is raining, then the ground is wet.

Statements (a) through (f) following are all stylistic variants of (17), that is, alternate ways of saying the same thing:[3]

    a. *Given that* it is raining, the ground is wet.

    b. *Assuming that* it is raining, the ground is wet.

    c. The ground is wet *if* it is raining.

    d. The ground is wet *given that* it is raining.

    e. The ground is wet *assuming that* it is raining.

    f. It is raining *only if* the ground is wet.

A knowledge of such stylistic variants is an aid to identifying argument forms. So, a close look at these variants is warranted. Consider (c). Note that "if" comes not at the beginning, but in the middle of the statement. Yet, (c) has the same underlying logical meaning as (17). And the phrase "given that" in (d) plays a role exactly analogous to the "if" in (c). We might generalize from these examples by saying that "if" and its stylistic variants (e.g., "given that" and "assuming that") *introduce an antecedent.* But we must hasten to add that this generalization applies only when "if" or its stylistic variants appear by themselves. When combined with "only," as in (f), the situation alters dramatically. Statement (f) has the same logical force as (17), but the phrase "only if" is confusing to many people and bears close examination.

    To clarify the logical force of "only if," it is helpful to consider very simple conditionals, such as the following:

    18. Rex is a dog *only if* Rex is an animal.

    19. Rex is an animal *only if* Rex is a dog.

Obviously, (18) and (19) say different things. Statement (19) is false. Rex may well be an animal even if Rex isn't a dog. Thus, (19) says, in effect, that "If Rex is an animal, Rex is a dog." But (18) says something entirely different, and something true—namely, that if Rex is a dog, then Rex is an animal. In general, statements of the form "A only if B" are logically equivalent to statements of the form "If A, then B." They are *not* logically equivalent to statements of the form "If B, then A." Another way to generalize the point is to say that "only if" (unlike "if") *introduces a consequent*, that is, a then-clause.

Basic Argument Forms

We are now ready to examine some basic argument forms.

Modus Ponens

Let us begin with **modus ponens**. Consider the following argument:

    20. 1. If it is raining, then the ground is wet.

        2. It is raining.

        So, the ground is wet.

This argument is obviously valid: Its conclusion cannot be false while its premises are true. Using letters to stand for statements, the form of the argument is as follows:

Modus Ponens

1. If *A*, then *B*.
2. *A*.
So, *B*.

(*A* stands for "it is raining"; *B* stands for "the ground is wet.") This form of argument is always valid. It is called *modus ponens* (which means "the mode of positing") because the second premise posits (i.e., sets down as fact) the antecedent of the conditional (first) premise.

Two points about *modus ponens* are worth noting. First, the order of the premises does not matter. For example, both of the following count as *modus ponens*:

21. If Einstein was a physicist, then he was a scientist. Einstein was a physicist. So, Einstein was a scientist.

22. Einstein was a physicist. If Einstein was a physicist, then he was a scientist. So, Einstein was a scientist.

In other words, arguments of the form "*A*; if *A*, then *B*; so, *B*" count as examples of *modus ponens*.

Second, the conditionals involved in *modus ponens* can be rather long and complex. For example:

23. If every right can be waived and each person has a right to life, then euthanasia is permitted in those cases in which the person to be "euthanized" waives his or her right to life. Moreover, every right can be waived and each person has a right to life. So, euthanasia is permitted in those cases in which the person to be "euthanized" waives his or her right to life.

The conditional premise in argument (23) is relatively long and complex, but the form is still *modus ponens*. ("Every right can be waived and each person has a right to life" replaces *A*; "euthanasia is permitted in those cases in which the person to be euthanized waives his or her right to life" replaces *B*.)

Modus Tollens

A second basic argument form is called **modus tollens.** Like *modus ponens*, one of its key premises is a conditional:

24. 1. If it is raining, then the ground is wet.
    2. The ground is not wet.
    So, it is not raining.

Modus tollens means "the mode or way of removing." The argument form gets its name from the second premise, which denies (removes the truth of) the consequent of the first premise. The form is as follows:

Modus Tollens

1. If A, then B.
2. Not B.
So, not A.

"Not A" and "not B" stand for negations. A **negation** of a statement is its denial. For example, in argument (24), "the ground is not wet" plays the role of "not B." The negation of a statement can be formed in various ways. Take the statement, "the ground is wet." Each of the following are negations of it:

a. *It is not the case that* the ground is wet.

b. *It's false that* the ground is wet.

c. *It is not true that* the ground is wet.

d. The ground is *not* wet.

As with *modus ponens*, the order of the premises does not matter. In other words, arguments of the form, "Not B; if A, then B; so, not A," count as *modus tollens*.

Consider a more complicated example of *modus tollens*. According to some physicists who endorse the Big Bang theory, the universe cannot be infinitely old. The second law of thermodynamics tells us that in a closed physical system, entropy always tends to increase; that is, energy gets diffused over time. (For instance, the radiant energy of a star will gradually become spread out evenly into the space surrounding it.) According to these physicists, if the physical universe has existed for an infinite period, there are now no concentrations of energy (e.g., no stars or planets). But obviously, there are stars and planets, so the physical universe has not existed for an infinite period. We can put this reasoning explicitly into the *modus tollens* form as follows:

25. 1. If the physical universe has existed for an infinite period, then all the energy in the universe is spread out evenly (as opposed to being concentrated in such bodies as planets and stars).

    2. It is not true that all the energy in the universe is spread out evenly (as opposed to being concentrated in such bodies as planets and stars).

    So, it is not true that the physical universe has existed for an infinite period.

Notice how putting the argument into explicit form helps to focus attention on the key issues. There is no debate whatsoever about the second premise of this argument. Stars and planets exist, so energy is not in fact spread out evenly throughout the physical universe. Nor is there any debate about the validity of the argument. Every argument having the form *modus tollens* is valid. The focus of the debate must therefore be on the first premise, and that is just where physicists have placed it. For example, some physicists think that the universe oscillates, that is, goes through a cycle of "Big Bangs" and "Big Crunches." And if the universe can oscillate, then its diffuse energy can be reconcentrated into usable forms, in which case the first premise is doubtful.[4]

Denying the Antecedent

Having examined two valid forms of argument, let us now take note of two invalid forms with which they are often confused. These invalid forms are called *fallacies*. (A fallacy is an error in reasoning.) Let us begin with the **fallacy of denying the antecedent**, which is often confused with *modus tollens*. Consider:

26. 1. If it is raining, then the ground is wet.
    2. It is not raining.
    So, the ground is not wet.

The first premise here is a conditional, as in the case of *modus tollens*. However, whereas the second premise of *modus tollens* denies the consequent of the conditional, the second premise of this argument denies the antecedent. This difference in form is crucial, because even if the premises of this argument were true, the conclusion could still be false. For example, let us suppose that the ground is soaking wet due to the sprinkler's being left on all night. Then, even if it is not raining, the ground is wet. (And remember, the first premise, being hypothetical, does not assert or imply that it is raining.) Denying the antecedent is an invalid form of argument. We can represent its form as follows:

Fallacy of Denying the Antecedent
1. If *A*, then *B*.
2. Not *A*.
So, not *B*.

(The order of the premises does not matter; hence, arguments of the form "Not A; if A, then B; so, not B" count as examples of denying the antecedent.) Here is a counterexample which shows that denying the antecedent is invalid:

27. 1. If lemons are red, then lemons have a color. [true]
    2. Lemons are not red. [true]
    So, lemons do not have a color. [false]

In thinking about this counterexample, it is important to recall that conditionals are hypothetical statements. Thus, premise (1) does not say that lemons *are* red; it merely says that *if* lemons are red, *then* they have a color.

Affirming the Consequent

A second fallacy, often confused with *modus ponens*, is the **fallacy of affirming the consequent**. Here is an example:

> 28. 1. If it is raining, then the ground is wet.
>   2. The ground is wet.
>   So, it is raining.

The form is as follows:

> Fallacy of Affirming the Consequent
> 1. If *A*, then *B*.
> 2. *B*.
> So, *A*.

(The order of the premises does not matter; hence, arguments of the form "B; if A, then B; so, A" are examples of affirming the consequent.) Again, the example of a sprinkler left on overnight reveals the invalidity of the argument. One cannot assume that rain is the only thing that will make the ground wet. The fallacy of affirming the consequent gets its name from its second premise, which affirms the consequent of the conditional premise. Here is a counterexample which shows that the form is invalid:

> 29. 1. If lemons are red, then lemons have a color. [true]
>   2. Lemons have a color. [true]
>   So, lemons are red. [false]

Again, in thinking about this counterexample, bear in mind that the conditional premise is hypothetical in nature.

Two issues should be considered here before going on. First, it is sometimes alleged that we can imagine circumstances in which *modus ponens* or *modus tollens* fail—that is, in which the premises are true and the conclusion is false. For example, let's go back to *modus ponens*: "If it's raining, then the ground is wet. It's raining. So, the ground is wet." What if the ground is covered, you might ask? What if the whole earth were enclosed in a plastic bag? Then, even if it was raining, the ground wouldn't be wet. Wouldn't *modus ponens* fail in such (admittedly farfetched) circumstances? No. These are not circumstances in which the premises are true and the conclusion is false. Rather, they are circumstances in which the conditional premise ("If it's raining, the ground is wet") is false. And remember: When we are testing for validity, we must assume that the premises are true and consider whether this assumption forces us to assume that the conclusion is true as well.

Second, while the invalidity of denying the antecedent and affirming the consequent is readily apparent in the examples used thus far, the error isn't always quite so obvious. Consider the following example of affirming the consequent:

> 30. If lying causes ill feelings, then it is wrong. And lying is wrong. So, it causes ill feelings.

Argument (30) is invalid because it overlooks the possibility that an act might be wrong for some reason other than its causing ill feelings. For instance, some say lying is wrong simply because society disapproves of it or because the liar violates a moral rule. The following example of the fallacy of denying the antecedent involves a similar error:

> 31. If using placebos causes harm, then doing so is wrong. But using placebos does not cause harm. Hence, using placebos is not wrong.

Argument (31) overlooks the possibility that an act might be wrong even if it doesn't harm anyone. For example, some say that acts are wrong simply because God disapproves of them (and regardless of the effects the actions have on other people).

Hypothetical Syllogism

Let us now return to valid forms. Consider the following argument:

> 32. 1. If tuition continues to increase, then only the wealthy will be able to afford a college education.
> 2. If only the wealthy will be able to afford a college education, then class divisions will be strengthened.
> So, if tuition continues to increase, then class divisions will be strengthened.

We can represent the form as follows; it is called **hypothetical syllogism**:

Hypothetical Syllogism
1. If A, then B.
2. If B, then C.
So, if A, then C.

(The order of the premises does not matter; hence, arguments of the form "If B, then C; if A, then B; so, if A, then C" are examples of hypothetical syllogism.) The argument is called "hypothetical syllogism" because it involves only hypothetical (i.e., conditional) statements. *Syllogism* comes from Greek roots meaning "to reason together," or to put statements together into a pattern of reasoning. Every argument that exemplifies the form hypothetical syllogism is valid. Here is another example of this form:

33. If I am morally responsible, then I can choose between good and evil. If I can choose between good and evil, then some of my actions are free. Therefore, if I am morally responsible, then some of my actions are free.

Note that the conclusion of a hypothetical syllogism is a conditional statement.

Disjunctive Syllogism

Thus far, we have focused on argument forms that centrally involve conditional statements. Not all argument forms are like this. Some make central use of **disjunctions**, that is, statements of the form "Either A or B." For example:

34. 1. Either Michelangelo painted *Guernica* or Picasso painted it.
    2. Michelangelo did not paint *Guernica*.
    So, Picasso painted *Guernica*.

The argument has the following form, which is called **disjunctive syllogism**, because of its "either-or" premise:

Disjunctive Syllogism
1. Either A or B.
2. Not A.
So, B.

Arguments having this form are *always* valid. (The order of the premises does not matter; hence, arguments of the form "Not A; either A or B; so, B" are examples of disjunctive syllogism.)

Some brief remarks about disjunctions are in order here. First, some terminology: The statements comprising a disjunction are called its **disjuncts**. For instance, the disjuncts of premise (1) in argument (34) are "Michelangelo painted *Guernica*" and "Picasso painted *Guernica*."

Second, we will take "Either A or B" to mean "Either A or B (or both)." This is called the **inclusive** sense of "or." For instance, suppose a job announcement reads: "Applicants must have either work experience or a bachelor's degree in the field." Obviously, an applicant with *both* work experience *and* a bachelor's degree is not excluded from applying.

Third, some authors speak of an **exclusive** sense of "or," claiming that "Either A or B" sometimes means "Either A or B (but not both)." For example, in commenting on a presidential election, one might say, "Either Smith or Jones will win the election," the assumption being that both will not (indeed cannot) win. However, it is a matter of controversy whether there really are two different meanings of the word "or" *as opposed to* there simply being cases in which the context indicates that A and B are not (or cannot) both be true. Rather than let this controversy sidetrack us, let us simply assume that the locution "Either A or B" means "Either A or B (or both)."

Having made this assumption, however, we must immediately add that arguers are free to use the locution "Either A or B (but not both)." This locution is equivalent to two statements: "Either A or B. Not both A and B." Consider the following argument:

> 35. Either Millard Fillmore was the 13th president of the United States or Zachary Taylor was the 13th president of the United States (but not both). Millard Fillmore was the 13th president. So, Zachary Taylor was not the 13th president.

We can represent the form of argument (35) as "Either A or B; not both A and B; A; so, not B." This form is valid, but notice that it differs from disjunctive syllogism.

Also note that disjunctive syllogism differs from the following form of argument:

> 36. Either Hitler was a Nazi or Himmler was a Nazi (or both were). Hitler was a Nazi. Therefore, it is not the case that Himmler was a Nazi.

The form of argument (36) can best be represented as "Either A or B (or both); A; therefore, not B." As a matter of historical fact, the premises of (36) are true, but its conclusion is false, so this argument form is definitely invalid.

Now, what is the form of the following argument?

> 37. Either Bloggs is guilty or Brennan is guilty. It is false that Bloggs is guilty. So, Brennan is guilty.

Yes, the form is disjunctive syllogism, and the argument is valid.

Constructive Dilemma

Let's look at one more form to complete our initial list of basic argument forms. This form is called the **constructive dilemma,** and it combines both conditional and disjunctive statements. Here is an example:

> 38. 1. Either Donna knew the information on her tax returns was inaccurate or she did not know it.
> 2. If Donna knew the information was inaccurate, she was lying.
> 3. If Donna did not know the information was inaccurate, then she was negligent.
> So, either Donna was lying or she was negligent.

The form of this argument is as follows:

Constructive Dilemma

1. Either *A* or *B*.
2. If *A*, then *C*.
3. If *B*, then *D*.
So, either *C* or *D*.

Arguments of this form are always valid. (The order of the premises in a constructive dilemma does not matter. For example, sometimes the conditional premises are given first, followed by the disjunctive premise.) The age-old problem of evil can be put in the form of a constructive dilemma:

> 39. If God cannot prevent suffering, then God is not omnipotent. If God does not want to prevent suffering, then God is not perfectly good. But either God cannot prevent suffering or God does not want to prevent suffering. So, either God is not omnipotent or God is not perfectly good.

This dilemma nicely illustrates how logic can be used to formulate a problem in a revealing way. Because argument (39) is valid, the conclusion must be true if the premises are true. And the first premise seems undeniable. Moreover, theists, against whom the argument is directed, can hardly deny the third (disjunctive) premise. (If God *can* prevent suffering, then God must not want to prevent it for some reason.) Historically, the second premise has been the focus of debate, with theologians suggesting that God does not want to eliminate all suffering because suffering is the necessary means to certain good ends (e.g., the spiritual maturation of free creatures).

Summary of Forms

Valid Forms

Modus ponens: If *A*, then *B*. *A*. So, *B*.
Modus tollens: If *A*, then *B*. Not *B*. So, not *A*.
Hypothetical syllogism: If *A*, then *B*. If *B*, then *C*. So, if *A*, then *C*.
Disjunctive syllogism: Either *A* or *B*. Not *A*. So, *B*.
Constructive dilemma: Either *A* or *B*. If *A*, then *C*. If *B*, then *D*. So, either *C* or *D*.

Invalid Forms

Denying the antecedent: If *A*, then *B*. Not *A*. So, not *B*.
Affirming the consequent: If *A*, then *B*. *B*. So, *A*.

At this point you have in your possession a set of useful argument forms. To test your understanding, complete the following exercises.

◆ Exercise 2.2

Part A: Stylistic Variants   Rewrite each of the following conditional statements in the form "If A, then B."

* **1.** The room is hot *given that* the sun is shining.
  2. The car won't start *if* the battery is dead.
  3. *Assuming that* you work hard, you will do well.
* **4.** Maria is a physicist *only if* Maria is a scientist.
  5. Tolstoy is justly famous *assuming that* he wrote *War and Peace*.
  6. Fred is an animal *only if* Fred is an eagle.
* **7.** *Given that* Joe is late, Wendy is angry.
  8. Inflation will cease *if* the Fed increases the prime interest rate.
  9. The car will start *only if* there is gas in the tank.
* **10.** Valerie isn't from Oregon *if* she's from Seattle.
  11. *Given that* you like football, you will like rugby.
  12. Jack is a bat *only if* Jack is a mammal.
* **13.** *Assuming that* Ted is guilty, he should go to prison.
  14. Madonna is married *only if* she has a husband.
  15. Murphy is funny *given that* he makes people laugh.
* **16.** Simone is a mathematician *only if* she is smart.
  17. *Given that* Bob wins, I'll eat my hat.
  18. Jody is not wicked *if* she is not destructive.
* **19.** Van Gogh's *Starry Night* is beautiful *only if* it is worth big bucks.
  20. Bruce is not a murderer *given that* he hasn't killed anyone.

Part B: Matching   Write the relevant letter(s) or number under the appropriate heading. You may need to use your knowledge of stylistic variants to identify the argument forms.

Evaluation	Name of Form	Form
V: Valid	MP: *modus ponens*	1. If A, then B. A. So, B.
I: Invalid	MT: *modus tollens*	2. If A, then B. Not B. So, not A.
	HS: hypothetical syllogism	3. If A, then B. If B, then C. So if A, then C.
		4. Either A or B. Not A. So, B.

DS: disjunctive syllogism

CD: constructive dilemma

DA: denying the antecedent

AC: affirming the consequent

5. Either A or B. If A, then C. If B, then D. So, either C or D.

6. If A, then B. Not A. So, not B.

7. If A, then B. B. So, A.

Evaluation	Name of Form	Form	
———	———	———	* **1.** The sky is cobalt blue only if it is blue. The sky is blue. Hence, the sky is cobalt blue.
———	———	———	**2.** If it is always wrong to kill an innocent human, then abortion in the case of ectopic pregnancy is wrong. But abortion in the case of ectopic pregnancy is not wrong. So, it is not always wrong to kill an innocent human.
———	———	———	**3.** Kidnapping is wrong if society disapproves of it. Kidnapping is wrong. So, society disapproves of kidnapping.
———	———	———	* **4.** Eating meat is unhealthy if meat contains a lot of cholesterol. Meat does contain a lot of cholesterol. Therefore, eating meat is unhealthy.
———	———	———	**5.** Either the "eye for an eye" principle is interpreted literally or it is interpreted figuratively. If it is interpreted literally, then the state should torture torturers, maim maimers, and rape rapists. If the "eye for an eye" principle is interpreted figuratively, then it does not necessarily demand death for murderers. So, either the state should torture torturers, maim maimers, and rape rapists, or the "eye for an eye" principle does not necessarily demand death for murderers.
———	———	———	**6.** Affirmative action is preferential treatment of disadvantaged groups, and preferential treatment of disadvantaged groups is reverse discrimination. If affirmative action is preferential treatment of disadvantaged groups and preferential treatment of disadvantaged groups is reverse discrimination, then affir-

mative action is wrong. Hence, affirmative action is wrong.

_____ _____ _____ * **7.** If the zygote lacks a brain, then the zygote lacks a soul. If the zygote lacks a soul, then killing the zygote is permissible. So, if the zygote lacks a brain, then killing the zygote is permissible.

_____ _____ _____ **8.** Either men are superior to women or women are superior to men. Men are not superior to women. Therefore, women are superior to men.

_____ _____ _____ **9.** If you want to ruin your life, you should take hard drugs. But you don't want to ruin your life. So, you should not take hard drugs.

_____ _____ _____ * **10.** Either acts are right because God approves of them or God approves of acts because they are right. It is not true that acts are right because God approves of them. Therefore, God approves of acts because they are right.

_____ _____ _____ **11.** Lying is wrong only if it causes social discord. But lying does not cause social discord. Hence, lying is not wrong.

_____ _____ _____ **12.** It is wrong to eat animals if souls transmigrate. Souls do transmigrate. So, it is wrong to eat animals.

_____ _____ _____ * **13.** Either the animals used in research are a lot like humans or they are not a lot like humans. If the animals are a lot like humans, then experimenting on them is morally questionable. If the animals are not a lot like humans, then experimenting on them is pointless. So, either experimenting on animals is morally questionable or it is pointless.

_____ _____ _____ **14.** The state cannot uphold the value of life by taking it. And if the state cannot uphold the value of life by taking it, then the death penalty should be abolished. Therefore, the death penalty should be abolished.

_____ _____ _____ **15.** If my society approves of genetic engineering, then genetic engineering is right. But my society does not approve of genetic engineering. Hence, genetic engineering is not right.

Part C: Identifying Forms   If an argument exemplifies a form named in this section, identify the form and indicate whether the form is valid or invalid. If the argument does not exemplify any of the forms named in this section, indicate that it does not by writing, "unnamed form."

* 1. Overeating is foolish only if it causes disease. Overeating does not cause disease. So, overeating is not foolish.

  2. Either films depicting graphic violence have caused the increase in violent crime or bad parenting has caused it. Movies depicting graphic violence have produced the increase in violent crime. Therefore, bad parenting has not caused the rise in violent crime.

  3. Corporations contribute huge sums of money to political campaigns. If that is so, then corporations exert undue influence on elections. So, corporations exert undue influence on elections.

* 4. You will win the chess tournament if you are very good at chess. Unfortunately, you are not very good at chess. Hence, you will not win the chess tournament.

  5. Either virtue is good for its own sake or it is good as a means to an end. It is not the case that virtue is good for its own sake. So, virtue is good as a means to an end.

  6. Contraception is immoral given that sex is strictly for procreation. But sex is not strictly for procreation. Hence, contraception is not immoral.

* 7. You should be an optimist if pessimists are less likely to succeed than optimists. And it is a fact that pessimists are less likely to succeed than optimists. Therefore, you should be an optimist.

  8. Either God can arbitrarily decide what is morally right or God cannot arbitrarily decide what is morally right. If God can arbitrarily decide what is morally right, then God can make cruelty right. And if God cannot arbitrarily decide what is morally right, then morality is not entirely in God's control. Therefore, either God can make cruelty right or morality is not entirely in God's control.

  9. Either Clinton won the election or Bush won the election. It is false that Clinton won the election. So, Bush won the election.

*10. The dinosaurs vanished due to a sudden, extreme drop in temperature. The earth must have suffered some sort of cataclysm millions of years ago assuming that the dinosaurs vanished due to a sudden, extreme drop in temperature. So, the earth must have suffered some sort of cataclysm millions of years ago.

 11. Bill Gates is rich given that he has exactly $2 million. But Bill Gates does not have exactly $2 million. Hence, Bill Gates is not rich.

 12. The death penalty is inequitably applied to the poor and to minorities. And given that the death penalty is inequitably applied to the poor and to minorities, it is unjust. Therefore, the death penalty is unjust.

*13. Michael Jordan is over 6 feet tall if he is over 10 feet tall. Jordan is over 6 feet tall. So, he is over 10 feet tall.

14. If Tom is taller than Mike and Mike is taller than Jim, then Tom is taller than Jim. If Tom is taller than Jim, then Jim is shorter than Tom. Therefore, if Tom is taller than Mike and Mike is taller than Jim, then Jim is shorter than Tom.

15. If you join the military, you give up a lot of freedom. If you go to college, you incur enormous debts. However, you either join the military or you go to college. Therefore, you either give up a lot of freedom or you incur enormous debts.

*16. Either Blaise Pascal or David Hume was Scottish. Blaise Pascal was not Scottish. So, David Hume was Scottish.

17. You must either love or hate. If you love, then you suffer when your loved ones suffer. If you hate, then you suffer when your enemies flourish. Hence, either you suffer when your loved ones suffer or you suffer when your enemies flourish.

18. Mercy killing is morally permissible only if it promotes a greater amount of happiness for everyone affected than the alternatives. And mercy killing does promote a greater amount of happiness for everyone affected than the alternatives. Therefore, mercy killing is morally permissible.

*19. Either the Mariners will win or they will lose. The Mariners will win. So, the Mariners will not lose.

20. A severe depression will occur given that the economy collapses. The economy collapses if inflation soars. So, inflation soars only if a severe depression will occur.

Part D: Constructing Arguments   Construct your own substitution instances for each of the following argument forms: *modus ponens, modus tollens,* hypothetical syllogism, disjunctive syllogism, constructive dilemma, denying the antecedent, and affirming the consequent. Make your substitution instances for the two fallacies counterexamples.

Part E: Quiz on Argument Forms   In the space provided, write the names of the forms of the following arguments. If the argument form is valid, circle *valid*. If the argument form is not valid, circle *invalid*.

valid   invalid   _____   1. If the solution turns blue litmus paper red, then the solution contains acid. The solution turns blue litmus paper red. So, the solution contains acid.

valid   invalid   _____   2. If the solution turns blue litmus paper red, then the solution contains acid. The solution does not contain acid. So, the solution does not turn blue litmus paper red.

valid   invalid   _____   3. If Lewis is a famous author, then he knows how to write. But Lewis is not a famous author. Hence, Lewis does not know how to write.

valid   invalid   _____   4. If Susan is a famous author, then she knows how to write. Moreover, Susan knows how to write. So, she is a famous author.

valid   invalid   _____   5. Either Jones is an innocent bystander or Jones fired a shot at the mayor. Jones is not an innocent bystander. Therefore, Jones fired a shot at the mayor.

valid   invalid   _____   6. Either you marry young or you wait. If you marry young, you incur a high risk of divorce. If you wait, the field of available partners grows ever smaller. So, either you incur a high risk of divorce or the field of available partners grows ever smaller.

valid   invalid   _____   7. If you study hard, you refine your communication skills. If you refine your communication skills, then your job opportunities increase. Hence, if you study hard, your job opportunities increase.

valid   invalid   _____   8. Ben is a rat. Ben is a rat only if Ben is a mammal. So, Ben is a mammal.

valid   invalid   _____   9. Sam is wealthy if he has over a billion dollars. But Sam does not have over a billion dollars. Therefore, Sam is not wealthy.

valid   invalid   _____   10. There is life on Mars given that there is life on Earth. There is life on Earth. So, there is life on Mars.

Notes

1. The example is borrowed from Wesley C. Salmon, *Logic*, 3rd ed. (Englewood Cliffs, NJ: Prentice-Hall, 1984), p. 21.
2. Some logicians would qualify this statement. These logicians are not convinced that validity is always due to form. Their views are based on such examples as the following: "Some things are green. So, some things have a color." This argument is clearly valid, but it is difficult to specify any valid form for which it is a substitution instance. Of course, one might reply that the argument has an unstated premise: "All green things have a color." But some logicians would counter that the argument already

seems to be valid without *adding* a premise, so why insist that validity is always determined by form? From this perspective, validity is sometimes due to specific content, even if it is typically determined by form.

3. A more complete list of stylistic variants for "if-then" is provided in chapter 7. The intent here is to provide a short list of the more common stylistic variants.
4. For a useful discussion of these issues, see P. C. W. Davies, *The Physics of Time Asymmetry* (Berkeley and Los Angeles: University of California Press, 1977), chap. 7, pp. 185–200.

Chapter 3

Identifying Arguments

The arguments we examined in the previous chapters were short and simple. Moreover, it was obvious which statements were premises and which conclusions. But, as you probably already realize, authors don't commonly put their arguments in such a simple "textbook" form. The conclusion may be given first or sandwiched between various premises. And a long argument may actually be a chain of shorter arguments, in which case it becomes vital to distinguish between the final (or overall) conclusion of the argument and the various sub-conclusions that lead up to it.

This chapter tells you how to identify arguments as they appear in ordinary language, how to distinguish extraneous verbiage from premises and conclusions, and how to identify the structure of the argument (i.e., which statements support which).

3.1 Arguments and Nonarguments

We must first learn to distinguish arguments from nonarguments. Recall that an argument is a set of statements, one of which, called the *conclusion*, is affirmed on the basis of the others, which are called *premises*. Obviously, one can do many things with language besides argue: extend greetings, tell a story, make a request, express one's feelings, provide information, tell a joke, pray, and so on. In this section, we will examine some nonargumentative uses of statements that are sometimes confused with arguments.

In general, it is important to distinguish between arguments and **unsupported assertions**. For example:

1. From 1964 to 1972, the wealthiest and most powerful nation in the history of the world made a maximum military effort, with everything short of atomic bombs, to defeat a nationalist revolutionary movement in a tiny, peasant country [Vietnam]—and failed. [1]

As it stands, this passage is not an argument, but simply a statement about the war in Vietnam. No supporting statements (i.e., premises) are provided here, and no inferences are drawn. Of course, supporting statements could be supplied, but because they do not appear in the quoted passage, it is not an argument in and of itself.

Unsupported assertions come in a variety of types, some of which may be confused with arguments. For example, a **report** is a set of statements intended to provide information about a situation, topic, or event. A report may contain many informational statements without containing any arguments. For instance:

> 2. Total global advertising expenditures multiplied nearly sevenfold from 1950 to 1990. They grew one third faster than the world economy and three times faster than world population. In real terms, spending rose from $39 billion in 1950 to $256 billion in 1990—more than the gross national product of India or than all Third World governments spent on health and education.[2]

Again, these statements could be backed up with further statements, but the passage, as it stands, is a report and not an argument. No inferences are drawn—the passage merely contains a series of informational statements.

An **illustration** is a statement together with an explanatory or clarifying example:

> 3. Mammals are vertebrate animals that nourish their young with milk. For example, cats, horses, goats, monkeys, and humans are mammals.

Because the word "thus" is often used to indicate the conclusion of an argument, illustrations are easily confused with arguments when the word "thus" is used to introduce the examples:

> 4. Whole numbers can be represented as fractions. Thus, 2 can be represented as 8/4 and 5 can be represented as 15/3.

In statement (4), the examples seem merely illustrative. Sometimes, however, examples are given not merely to explain or clarify but to support (provide evidence for) a thesis, in which case the passage in question is an argument rather than an illustration:

> 5. You just said that no mammal can fly, but that is inaccurate. At least one mammal has wings and can fly. For example, bats are mammals.

And sometimes a passage can reasonably be interpreted either as an illustration or as an argument. It all depends on the answer to this question: Do the examples merely clarify (or explain) a statement, or are they used to *provide evidence* for it? If the examples are used to provide evidence, then the passage is an argument.

Sometimes statements are used not to *provide evidence* for another state-ment, but to provide **explanations** or reasons for the occurrence of some phe-nomenon. For example:

6. Judy got sick because she ate too much.

7. The dinosaurs are extinct because a "large comet or asteroid struck the earth some 65 million years ago, lofting a cloud of dust into the sky and blocking sunlight, thereby suppressing photosynthesis and . . . drastically lowering world temperatures. . . ."[3]

Such passages are easily confused with arguments since the word "because" is often used to indicate a premise. (More on this in the next section.) But con-sider each case carefully. Is (6) best construed as an argument for the conclusion that Judy got sick? More likely, it is already accepted that Judy got sick and the question is, "Why did she get sick? What caused her sickness?" So, (6) appears to be simply an assertion about what caused Judy's sickness, and not an argument. Similarly, (7) doesn't seem to be an argument for the conclusion that dinosaurs are extinct. *That* is a widely accepted fact. The question is, "What explains it?" And (7) states one possible explanation.

A complication should be mentioned at this point. Some arguments are arguments to the effect that a certain statement or hypothesis is the *best explana-tion* of some phenomenon (or that some statement is probably true *because* it is the best explanation of some phenomenon). These are arguments rather than mere assertions because premises are provided. For instance:

8. Three explanations have been offered for the extinction of the dinosaurs. First, a global rise in temperature caused the testes of male dinosaurs to stop func-tioning. Second, certain flowering plants (namely, angiosperms) evolved *after* the dinosaurs evolved; these plants were toxic for the dinosaurs, which ate them and died. Third, a large comet struck the earth, causing a cloud of dust that blocked out the sunlight, which in turn created a frigid climate for which the dinosaurs were ill-suited. Now, there is no way to get any evidence either for or against the first hypothesis. And the second hypothesis is unlikely because it is probable that angiosperms were in existence 10 million years before the dinosaurs became extinct. There is, however, some evidence in favor of the third hypothesis. If the earth was struck by a large comet at the time the dinosaurs became extinct (some 65 million years ago), then there should be unusually large amounts of iridium (a rare metal) in the sediments of that period, for most of the iridium on earth comes from comets and other objects from outer space. And, as a matter of fact, unusually large amounts of iridium have been found in the sediments of that period. So, the third explanation seems best.[4]

Passage (8) is an argument because evidence is given to support the claim that one of the three explanations is best.

Conditional statements, taken by themselves, are typically not arguments. For instance,

> 9. If Lucy works hard, then she will get a promotion.

There is some temptation to think that the antecedent (if-clause) of a conditional is a premise and that the consequent (then-clause) is a conclusion. But this is typically not the case. Remember that a conditional statement is hypothetical in nature. Thus, statement (9) merely asserts that if Lucy works hard, then she will get a promotion. It does not assert that Lucy works hard. Nor does it assert that she will get a promotion. By contrast, consider the following argument:

> 10. Lucy works hard. Therefore, Lucy will get a promotion.

Here, we clearly have a premise–conclusion structure. And the conclusion is asserted on the basis of the premise (which is also asserted).

Although conditionals, taken by themselves, are not arguments, in context they may serve to express an argument. For example, during a tournament, a tennis coach might give this advice to one of the players: "If you want to win, you should hit to your opponent's backhand." In this context, "you want to win" need not be explicitly stated; it can be assumed. So, by expressing a conditional, the coach may in effect be offering a *modus ponens*–type argument: "If you want to win, then you should hit to your opponent's backhand. You want to win. So, you should hit to your opponent's backhand." Note, however, that adding unstated premises (and conclusions) to arguments can get tricky; we will return to this issue in a later section. The main point here is that outside of special contexts, conditionals by themselves are not arguments.

The following exercise will test your understanding of the difference between arguments and nonarguments.

Unsupported assertions are not arguments. But some types of unsupported assertions may be confused with arguments—for example, reports, illustrations, explanations, and conditionals.

◆ *Exercise 3.1*

Arguments and Nonarguments   Which of the following passages are arguments? Which are not arguments? If a passage is an argument, identify its conclusion. If a passage is not an argument, classify it as a report, illustration, explanation, or conditional statement.

* **1.** Americans are materialistic because they are exposed to more advertising than any other people on earth.

2. A person is dead if his or her brain has stopped functioning.

3. The world fish catch dropped from its 1989 high of 100 million tons to 97 million tons in 1990 and has remained at about that figure ever since. Harvests have increased in some oceans but have fallen in others. And rising catches of some species are offset by falling catches of others. Breaking with a historical trend of constantly growing catches, stagnation in the global catch now appears likely to continue . . . —Hal Kane, "Fish Catch No Longer Growing," in Lester Brown, Hal Kane, and Ed Ayres, eds., *Vital Signs 1993: The Trends That Are Shaping Our Future* (New York: Norton, 1993), p. 32.

* 4. Waging war is always wrong because it involves killing human beings. And killing humans is wrong.

5. When we calculate what the surface temperature of the planet should be, based on the heat it radiates to space, we find the whole globe should be a frozen wasteland, colder than today by about 33 degrees Celsius (60 degrees Fahrenheit) on average. The force saving us from this frigid fate is the atmosphere. The layer of air surrounding our globe contains important gases such as water vapor and carbon dioxide, which absorb the heat radiated by Earth's surface and reemit their own heat at much lower temperatures. We say they "trap" Earth's radiation and call this planetary warming mechanism the "greenhouse effect." —National Oceanic and Atmospheric Administration, *The Climate System* (Winter 1991), p. 7

6. Never has the nation been safer from foreign menaces, and never before has the nation been graduating students less well educated than those of the immediately preceding generation. These facts warrant this conclusion: Today the principal threat to America is America's public-education establishment. —George F. Will, *The Leveling Wind* (New York: Viking Press, 1994), p. 199

* 7. Since particle-like behavior and wave-like behavior are the only properties that we ascribe to light, and since these properties now are recognized to belong not to light itself, but to our interaction with light, . . . it appears that light has no properties independent of us! To say that something has no properties is the same as saying that it does not exist. The next step in this logic is inescapable. Without us, light does not exist. —Gary Zukav, *The Dancing Wu Li Masters* (New York: Bantam Books, 1979), p. 95

8. If humans are created beings, then the Creator wills the ultimate fulfillment of each human.

9. U.S. food producers feed livestock 20 million tons of plant protein per year that could be consumed by humans, and the livestock yields only 2 million tons of protein.

* 10. Wars occur because humans desire to control other humans.

11. The earth is getting warmer. Why? There are many reasons, but here are two important ones. First, the burning of coal, oil, and natural gas has greatly increased the carbon dioxide in the atmosphere. And carbon dioxide retains heat. Second, chlorofluorocarbons, which are used in air conditioners and refrigerators, have

attacked the ozone layer, thus leaving the earth exposed to ultraviolet rays from the sun.

12. In 1950, the population of the world was about 2.5 billion. In 1967, the population of the world was almost 3.5 billion. In 1980, the population of the world was almost 4.5 billion. And in 1992, the population of the world was almost 5.5 billion. So, the population of the world has grown both steadily and rapidly since 1950.

* 13. Global oil demand still lies well below the peak level of 1979. Improved energy efficiency and the expanding role of natural gas in many countries is cutting into petroleum's market. But oil is still the world's leading source of energy, supplying 40 percent of the total . . . —Christopher Flavin and Hal Kane, "Oil Production Steady," in Lester Brown, Hal Kane, and Ed Ayres, eds., *Vital Signs 1993: The Trends That Are Shaping Our Future* (New York: Norton, 1993), p. 46.

14. If it is permissible for humans to eat animals, then it is permissible for super-intelligent extraterrestrials to eat humans.

15. America is a powerful nation primarily because it has one of the strongest economies in the world.

* 16. Prime numbers are divisible only by themselves and one. For example, 3, 5, 7, and 11 are prime numbers.

17. If Oswald did not kill Kennedy, then someone else did.

18. Roman numerals as well as Arabic numerals can be used to stand for numbers. Thus, the Roman numeral IX stands for the number nine.

* 19. If one sets one's heart on humaneness, one will be without evil. —Confucius, *The Analects* (New York: Oxford University Press, 1993), p. 13

20. During the Cold War, the United States pursued a policy of nuclear deterrence. Missiles with nuclear warheads were aimed at many locations in the former Soviet Union. The threat of destruction was real. Had the missiles been launched, millions of innocent people would have been killed. But in my opinion, the U.S. policy of nuclear deterrence was immoral. Let me give you an analogy. Suppose two angry men face each other with machine guns. Behind each one stands many innocent bystanders. Each man holds the other in check by threatening to pull the trigger, thus killing many innocent people. I submit that it is obvious that such men would be acting immorally. Hence, the U.S. policy of nuclear deterrence was immoral also.

3.2 Putting an Argument into Textbook Form

Putting an argument into **textbook form** involves identifying an argument's premises and conclusion, eliminating nonessential verbiage, and putting the steps of the argument (i.e., the premises and conclusion) in proper order. This section describes and illustrates the basic principles involved in putting arguments into textbook form. Being able to put arguments into textbook form is a powerful tool for evaluating arguments.

Principle 1: Identify the premises and the conclusion.

Recall that the **premises** of an argument are the statements on the basis of which the conclusion is affirmed, and the **statements** are sentences that are either true or false. Each step of an argument, whether premise or conclusion, must be a statement. Consider the following simple example:

11. We should abolish the death penalty because it does not deter crime.

This is an argument. The word "because" often indicates a premise, and it does so in this case. Thus, we can put argument (11) into textbook form as follows:

12. 1. The death penalty does not deter crime.
So, 2. We should abolish the death penalty.

From now on, whenever we put arguments into textbook form, let us adopt the convention of making the conclusion of the argument the final step. Let us also write "so" to mark a conclusion, as I have done here. Further, let us place a number before each step of the argument (whether premise or conclusion). A step of an argument without the word "so" in front of it will be understood to be a premise. In this case, statement (1) is the only premise. We can drop the word "because" since our convention tells us that (1) is a premise.

Short as it is, argument (11) illustrates at least two things worth noting. First, the conclusion of an argument often comes first in English prose. For example, the thesis sentence in a paragraph is often a conclusion that is supported by the statements appearing later in the paragraph. Thus, one cannot assume that an author first will state his or her premises and then draw a conclusion later on. In ordinary prose, the order is often reversed.

Second, argument (11) illustrates a typical use of premise indicators—in this case, the word "because." **Premise indicators** are frequently followed by a premise, that is, a supporting reason. Common premise-indicator words or phrases include these:

because	after all
since	the reason is that
for	in light of the fact that
as	based on the fact that

Now, one cannot assume that these words and phrases indicate premises on every occasion of their use. As we have already seen, the word "because" is often used in explanations. But the point here is that these words are frequently used as premise indicators, and knowing this is a great aid when putting arguments into textbook form.

Just as premise indicators typically signal premises, **conclusion indicators** typically signal conclusions. Common conclusion indicators include:

so	thus
therefore	accordingly
hence	consequently
implies that	we may infer that
it follows that	which proves that

Consider the following argument:

13. I was bitten by several dogs when I was a child. Therefore, dogs are dangerous.

In textbook form, argument (13) looks like this:

14. 1. I was bitten by several dogs when I was a child.
So, 2. Dogs are dangerous.

Of course, this argument is weak, but a weak argument is still an argument.

At this point, you know what premise and conclusion indicators are. The good news is that authors frequently use such words and phrases to clarify their intentions. The bad news is that authors often rely on more subtle methods (e.g., context, order, emphasis) to identify the structure of their reasoning. There is no substitute in such cases for logical and linguistic insight. But *a good rule of thumb is to identify the conclusion first*. Once you figure out what the author is trying to prove, the rest of the argument often falls into place.

Let's now consider a slightly more complicated argument:

15. Since the average American consumes 30 times the amount of the earth's resources as does the average Asian, Americans (taken as a group) are selfish. After all, excessive consumption is a form of greed. And greed is selfish desire.

What is the conclusion of the argument? That Americans (taken as a group) are selfish. "Since" is a premise indicator, and so is "after all." Thus, in textbook form, the argument looks like this:

16. 1. The average American consumes 30 times the amount of the earth's resources as does the average Asian.
2. Excessive consumption is a form of greed.
3. Greed is selfish desire.
So, 4. Americans (taken as a group) are selfish.

You may be wondering whether the order of the premises matters. From the standpoint of logic, the order makes no difference, so we simply list the premises in the order in which they appear in the original. Note, however, that in the textbook form of an argument, the premises must precede the conclusion, because our conventions tell us that the last statement in the textbook form is the conclusion of the argument.

As we saw in chapter 2, conditional statements have a number of stylistic variants. When putting an argument into textbook form, you should put any conditional premises or conclusions into **standard form**—that is, "If A, then B"—for two reasons. First, most people find it easier to grasp the logical meaning of conditionals when they are in standard form. Second, putting conditionals into standard form facilitates the recognition of argument forms. Consider the following example:

> 17. It is not permissible to eat cows and pigs, for it is permissible to eat cows and pigs only if it is permissible to eat dogs and cats. But it is not permissible to eat dogs and cats.

The textbook form is as follows:

> 18. 1. If it is permissible to eat cows and pigs, then it is permissible to eat dogs and cats.
>   2. It is not permissible to eat dogs and cats.
> So, 3. It is not permissible to eat cows and pigs.

The argument form is *modus tollens*. Recall that common stylistic variants of "If A, then B" include "B if A," "B assuming that A," "B given that A," "A only if B," "Given that A, B," and "Assuming that A, B."

Before leaving the topic of identifying premises and conclusions, we need to address two slight complications involving rhetorical questions and commands. As noted in chapter 1, not all sentences are statements. For example, questions are sentences, but questions are not statements. There is, however, one kind of question that serves as a disguised statement, namely, the so-called rhetorical question. A *rhetorical question* is used to emphasize a point. No answer is expected because the answer is considered apparent in the context. For example:

> 19. The common assumption that welfare recipients like being on welfare is false. Does anyone like to be poor and unemployed? Does anyone like to be regarded as a parasite?

In this context, the arguer clearly expects a "no" answer to both questions. So, these questions are in effect statements. And, in putting the argument into textbook form, we change them into statements, like this:

> 20. 1. No one likes to be poor and unemployed.
>   2. No one likes to be regarded as a parasite.
> So, 3. The common assumption that welfare recipients like being on welfare is false.

Commands (or imperatives) are also sentences but not statements. If someone issues the command "Shut the door!" it makes no sense to reply, "That's true" (or "That's false"), because no truth claim has been made. However, imperatives sometimes turn up as premises or conclusions in arguments. Such imperatives are disguised "ought" statements. For example, consider the following argument:

21. Be a doctor! You've got the talent. You would enjoy the work. You could help many people. And you could make a lot of money!

In this case, the imperative "Be a doctor!" is naturally interpreted as "You ought to be a doctor," and this latter sentence expresses something either true or false.[5] When an imperative is a disguised "ought" statement, you should make this explicit when putting the argument into textbook form:

22. 1. You've got the talent.
    2. You would enjoy the work.
    3. You could help many people.
    4. You could make a lot of money.
    So, 5. You ought to be a doctor.

It would be equally correct to write the conclusion this way: "You should be a doctor."

Principle 2: Eliminate excess verbiage.

Four types of excess verbiage are extremely common in arguments. One is discounts. A **discount** is an acknowledgment of a fact or possibility that might be thought to render the argument invalid, weak, or otherwise unsound. For example:

23. Although certain events in the subatomic realm occur at random, I still say that the universe as a whole displays a marvelous order. Perhaps the best evidence for this is the fact that scientists continue to discover regularities that can be formulated as laws.

The conclusion of this argument is "the universe as a whole displays a marvelous order." The premise is "scientists continue to discover regularities that can be formulated as laws." But what are we to do with "Although certain events in the subatomic realm occur at random"? It does not seem to be a premise, for events that occur at random are not evidence of order. In fact, the statement "Certain events in the subatomic realm occur at random" seems to be evidence *against* the conclusion of the argument. And that is why it is best regarded not as a premise, but as a discount.

Discounts are very important rhetorically. Roughly speaking, **rhetorical elements** in an argument are ones that increase its psychological persuasiveness without affecting its validity, strength, or soundness. And discounts often increase the psychological persuasiveness of an argument by anticipating potential objections. An audience is often to some degree disarmed by the realization that the arguer has already considered a potential objection and rejected it. But discounts aren't premises, since they don't support the conclusion. Therefore, we shall omit them from our textbook forms. To illustrate, the textbook form of argument (23) is as follows:

> 24. 1. Scientists continue to discover regularities that can be formulated as laws.
> So, 2. The universe as a whole displays a marvelous order.

Words or phrases often used as **discount indicators** include these:

although	while it may be true that
even though	while I admit that
in spite of the fact that	I realize that . . . , but
despite the fact that	I know that . . . , but

A second type of excess verbiage is repetition. Authors and speakers who use **repetition** restate a premise or conclusion, perhaps altering the wording slightly. When this occurs, select the formulation that seems to put the argument in its best light, and drop the others. Here's an example:

> 25. The study of logic will increase both your attention span and your patience with difficult concepts. In other words, if you apply yourself to the subject of logic, you'll find yourself able to concentrate for longer periods of time. You will also find yourself increasingly able to approach complex material without feeling restless or frustrated. Therefore, a course in logic is well worth the effort.

A textbook version of argument (25) might look like this:

> 26. 1. The study of logic will increase both your attention span and your patience with difficult concepts.
> So, 2. A course in logic is well worth the effort.

Now, you may feel that something is lost in dropping the repetition in a case like this, and indeed, something of rhetorical importance *is* lost. Repetition itself aids memorization. And a slight alteration of terminology can correct possible misunderstandings and/or make an idea more vivid. But our streamlined textbook version has advantages of its own; in particular, it enables us to focus on the argument's essential logical features.

A third type of excess verbiage is the assurance. An **assurance** is a statement, word, or phrase which indicates that the author is confident of a premise or inference. For example:

> 27. Ben will do well in the marathon for he is obviously in excellent condition.

Here is the textbook form:

> 28. 1. Ben is in excellent condition.
>
> So, 2. Ben will do well in the marathon.

The word "obviously" indicates the author's confidence in the premise, but it does not contribute to the validity, strength, or soundness of the argument. Common assurances include these:

obviously	everyone knows that
no doubt	it is well known that
certainly	no one will deny that
plainly	this is undeniable
clearly	this is a fact

Assurances are rhetorically important, since confidence often helps to win over an audience. But they seldom affect the validity, strength, or soundness of an argument, so we are usually free to omit them from our textbook forms.

A fourth type of excess verbiage is the hedge, which is the opposite of an assurance. That is, a **hedge** is a statement, word, or phrase that indicates that the arguer is tentative about a premise or inference. For instance:

> 29. In my opinion, we have lost the war on drugs. Accordingly, drugs should be legalized.

"In my opinion" is a hedge, so the textbook form would be as follows:

> 30. 1. We have lost the war on drugs.
>
> So, 2. Drugs should be legalized.

Common hedges include these:

I think that	I believe that
it seems that	I guess that
perhaps	it is reasonable to suppose that
maybe	this seems reasonable
in my opinion	this is plausible

Hedges are rhetorically important, because without them one sounds dogmatic and close-minded. But hedges usually do not contribute to the validity, strength, or soundness of an argument. So, we normally omit them from our textbook forms.

Assurances and hedges usually can be dropped when putting an argument into textbook form. But they cannot always be dropped, for they sometimes contribute to the validity, strength, or soundness of the argument. For example:

> 31. I am in pain if it seems to me that I am in pain. And it seems to me that I am in pain. Therefore, I am in pain.

The textbook form is as follows:

> 32. 1. If it seems to me that I am in pain, then I am in pain.
>   2. It seems to me that I am in pain.
> So, 3. I am in pain.

The main point of this argument is that in the case of pain, there is a special connection between what *seems* to be so and what *is* so. Hence, while we can usually drop "it seems to me that" as a hedge, in this case we cannot. This example underscores the fact that we must remain vigilant when putting arguments into textbook form. The role of every word or phrase must be carefully evaluated in context.

> Principle 3: Employ uniform language.

Compare the following two arguments:

> 33. If God is omniscient, then God knows whether or not you will steal a car tomorrow. And, in fact, God is all-knowing. So, God is cognizant of whether or not you will commit car theft tomorrow.

> 34. If God is omniscient, then God knows whether you will steal a car tomorrow. And, in fact, God is omniscient. So, God knows whether you will steal a car tomorrow.

The logical links between premises and conclusions in these arguments are strongly dependent on the terms involved: "omniscient," "steal," "all-knowing," and so on. Argument (33) appears to have been written by someone using a thesaurus, substituting "omniscient" for "all-knowing," "commit car theft" for "steal a car," "is cognizant of" for "knows," and so on. In short, the language in (33) is not uniform, but varied. The result is that the linkage between premises and conclusion is obscured. By contrast, the premise–conclusion linkage is crystal clear in (34). And yet the underlying form of argument is the same in both cases, namely, *modus ponens*.

One good textbook version of (33) would be this:

35. 1. If God is all-knowing, then God knows whether you will steal a car
        tomorrow.

     2. God is all-knowing.

So, 3. God knows whether you will steal a car tomorrow.

Of course, you might just as well have used "omniscient" in place of "all-knowing." The important thing is to stick with one term throughout the argument, so as to highlight the logical form or pattern of reasoning.

Before leaving the topic of uniform language, let's consider one more example:

36. If you study other cultures, then you realize what a variety of human customs
     there is. If you understand the diversity of social practices, then you question
     your own customs. If you acquire doubts about the way you do things, then
     you become more tolerant. Therefore, if you expand your knowledge of
     anthropology, then you become more likely to accept other people and
     practices without criticism.[6]

Once again, the lack of uniform language makes it difficult to see whether (and how) the premises logically connect with the conclusion. Here is a good textbook version of the argument:

37. 1. If you study other cultures, then you realize what a variety of human customs
        there is.

     2. If you realize what a variety of human customs there is, then you question
        your own customs.

     3. If you question your own customs, then you become more tolerant.

So, 4. If you study other cultures, then you become more tolerant.

Now, we can see that the argument actually is a tightly linked chain of reasoning. The use of uniform language is enormously beneficial in exhibiting the logical structure of an argument. By clarifying the linkages between premises and conclusions, uniform language helps us to avoid fuzzy thinking, which frequently stems from the careless use of words with *similar but slightly different* meanings.

Principle 4: Be fair and charitable in interpreting an argument.

Fairness involves being loyal to the original, not distorting the clear meaning. *Charity* is needed when the original is ambiguous in some respect; it involves selecting an interpretation that puts the argument in its best possible light. Both of these concepts need to be explained in some detail.

With regard to fairness, many people tend to read more into an argument than they should. Instead of letting the author speak for him- or herself, they re-create the argument in their own image. Key statements may be loosely reworded or couched in emotionally loaded phrasing. Important premises may be omitted. New premises, not provided in the original, may be added. And so on. Now, there is indeed a place for identifying assumed but unstated premises in evaluating an argument. (We'll get to this in section 3.4.) But before one can usefully identify unstated assumptions, one must first accurately represent the *stated* or *explicit* version of the argument, without distorting the meaning.

Fairness demands that we not let our biases interfere with the process of providing a textbook form that is true to an author's original intent. For example, if an author argues in favor of euthanasia for permanently comatose patients, it almost certainly distorts his intent to describe him as in favor of our "playing God." Similarly, a person who argues against promiscuity does not necessarily believe that all sex is evil, and she should not be so represented in the absence of solid evidence to the contrary. Or, again, someone who supports affirmative action isn't necessarily advocating the use of strict quotas to achieve greater equality. It is unfair to interpret this person as advocating strict quotas unless he or she has *clearly* stated or implied this.

At the same time, we must not conceive of fairness in too narrow or wooden a fashion. To interpret well, we must take into account various rhetorical devices, such as irony and deliberate exaggeration. Suppose an American newspaper reporter argues as follows:

38. Oh, yes, we are all deeply appreciative of the full and accurate information we received from our government during the Vietnam War. So, how can anyone doubt that we received full and accurate information during the war in the Persian Gulf?

Since it is well known that Americans were sometimes not told the truth by their own government during the Vietnam War, the reporter's real meaning is probably the exact opposite of the surface meaning of her words. A good textbook version of the argument would therefore have to make some changes, perhaps along these lines:

39. 1. Americans did not receive full and accurate information from their government during the Vietnam War.

So, 2. Americans possibly (or probably) did not receive full and accurate information from their government during the war in the Persian Gulf.

Incidentally, notice that in the textbook version, the rhetorical question is phrased as a statement.

Charity enters the picture when an argument has been presented unclearly. Perhaps a premise can be understood in either of two ways. Or perhaps the structure of the argument is unclear—which statement is supposed to support which? Where such ambiguities occur, charity demands that we put the argument in its best possible light. In other words, when we are confronted with an interpretive choice, we should try to select an interpretation that makes the argument valid, strong, or sound (as the case may be), rather than invalid, weak, or unsound. For instance:

40. Flag burning should be outlawed. I realize that there are worse things than flag burning, such as murder or kidnapping, but it ought to be illegal. Many people are disturbed by it. And it is unpatriotic. How important is freedom of expression, anyway?

Consider the following attempt to put the argument into textbook form:

41. 1. Many people are disturbed by flag burning.
    2. Flag burning is unpatriotic.
    3. Freedom of expression is not important.
    So, 4. Flag burning should be outlawed.

Premise (3) is stated in an uncharitable fashion. Admittedly, the meaning of the question "How important is freedom of expression, anyway?" is unclear. But as stated, premise (3) is an easy target. Charity demands that we rephrase premise (3), perhaps along these lines: "Freedom of expression is not the most important thing" or "Freedom of expression is not the highest value."

Principle 5: Do not confuse subconclusions with (final) conclusions.

Some arguments proceed by establishing subconclusions, which, in turn, become premises supporting the (final) conclusion of the argument. A **subconclusion**, then, has a dual role: It is supported by a premise (or premises), but it also supports at least one further statement (which may be either the conclusion or another subconclusion). Consider this example:

42. It is not always moral to save five lives at the cost of one life. For if it is always moral to save five lives at the cost of one life, then it is moral to remove the organs of a healthy person *against his wishes* and transplant them in five people who need organ transplants. But it is not moral to perform such transplants because doing so violates the rights of the healthy person. Therefore, it is not always morally right to save five lives at the cost of one life.

The textbook form runs as follows:

43. 1. If it is always moral to save five lives at the cost of one life, then it is moral to remove the organs of a healthy person against his wishes and transplant them in five people who need organ transplants.
    2. Removing the organs of a healthy person *against his wishes* and transplanting them in five people who need organ transplants violates the rights of the healthy person.

So, 3. It is not moral to remove the organs of a healthy person *against his wishes* and transplant them in five people who need organ transplants.

So, 4. It is not always moral to save five lives at the cost of one life.

Note that premise (2) supports subconclusion (3). This structure is required by the premise indicator "because" in argument (42). And final conclusion (4) follows from (3) and (1), which work together as a logical unit (the form is *modus tollens*). To make the structure of the argument clear, shorthand expressions in the original such as "doing so" are here expanded and made explicit. (The extent to which this is helpful in a given case is a matter of judgment.)

Let us adopt the convention of always listing the (final) conclusion of the argument as the last step in the textbook form, marked by the word "So." Subconclusions are also marked by the word "So" and are distinguished from (final) conclusions because they have a dual role—that is, they are supposed to follow from earlier steps in the argument and to support later steps. Of course, a subconclusion may, in fact, not be adequately supported by earlier steps, and it may not adequately support any later steps. But the textbook version is supposed to represent the arguer's intentions, even if those intentions are logically flawed.

Let us consider another argument that contains subconclusions:

44. Murder victims X, Y, and Z were apparently killed by the same person, whom police call "the Golden Gunner," for victims X, Y, and Z were all shot with a gold-plated bullet from the same .38 caliber pistol. Now, we know that most serial killers select members of their own ethnic group as victims. And X, Y, and Z are white. Finally, nearly all serial killers are men. We may infer that the Golden Gunner is a white male.

The textbook form is as follows:

45. 1. Murder victims X, Y, and Z were all shot with a gold-plated bullet from the same .38 caliber pistol.

So, 2. Victims X, Y, and Z were killed by the same person, whom police call "the Golden Gunner."

3. Most serial killers select members of their own ethnic group as victims.

4. Victims X, Y, and Z are white.

5. Nearly all serial killers are men.

So, 6. The Golden Gunner is a white male.

Here, subconclusion (2) is supported by statement (1). And steps (2), (3), (4), and (5) combine to support final conclusion (6).

When evaluating an argument with subconclusions, one must evaluate the support for each subconclusion, as well as the support for the final conclusion of the argument. For example, if the argument for a given subconclusion is weak or invalid, then the overall argument is logically flawed. However, even if a given subconclusion is poorly supported by a premise that is supposed to support it, the overall argument may still retain merit under two conditions: (a) The subconclusion is adequately supported by other premises in the argument, and/or (b) the subconclusion is plausible taken all by itself.

You now have five principles in hand for identifying arguments and putting them into textbook form. The following exercises give you an opportunity to apply these principles to arguments.

Summary of Principles for Putting Arguments Into Textbook Form

1. Identify the premises and the conclusion.
2. Eliminate excess verbiage (e.g., discounts, repetition, assurances, hedges).
3. Employ uniform language.
4. Be fair and charitable in interpreting an argument.
5. Do not confuse subconclusions with (final) conclusions.

◆ Exercise 3.2

Part A: Identifying Arguments   If a given passage is an argument, put it into textbook form. (Be sure to apply the five principles developed in this section. Pay especially close attention to premise and conclusion indicators.) If a passage is not an argument, simply write "not an argument."

* **1.** The defendant is not guilty of murder since she is insane.

2. One does not worry about the fact that other people do not appreciate one. One worries about not appreciating other people. —Confucius, *The Analects*, trans. Raymond Dawson (New York: Oxford University Press, 1993), p. 5

3. Folly is a more dangerous enemy to the good than malice. You can protest against malice, you can unmask it or prevent it by force. Malice always contains the seeds of its own destruction, for it always makes men uncomfortable, if nothing worse. There is no defense against folly. Neither protests nor force are of any avail against it, and it is never amenable to reason. —Dietrich Bonhoeffer, *Prisoner for God: Letters and Papers from Prison*, ed. Eberhard Bethge (New York: Macmillan, 1959), p. 18

* **4.** Will power, the kind that, if need be, makes us set our teeth and endure suffering, is the principal weapon of the apprentice engaged in manual work. But, contrary to the usual belief, it has practically no place in study. The intelligence can only be led by desire. [And] for there to be desire, there must be pleasure and joy in the work. —Simone Weil, *Waiting for God* (New York: Harper & Row, 1951), p. 110

5. It can hardly be denied that people fear death more than they fear life imprisonment. Are we not then forced to conclude that the death penalty is a greater deterrent than life imprisonment?

6. Science does not deal with the whole of life. For there are many kinds of human experiences, and science can deal with only a portion of them. Specifically, the task of science is to describe the behavior of the material (or physical) world. —A. R. Patton, *Science for the Non-Scientist* (Minneapolis: Burgess, 1962). p. 3 (*Note:* This passage has been slightly altered for use as an exercise.)

* 7. Since affirmative action involves giving a less qualified person the job, affirmative action is unjust. After all, the most qualified person deserves the job.

8. Abraham Lincoln died because John Wilkes Booth shot him with a pistol.

9. If alcoholism is a disease, then it is treated medically. But alcoholism is not treated medically for the primary mode of treatment is the 12-step program of Alcoholics Anonymous. And AA's 12-step program is religious in nature. Therefore, alcoholism is not a disease.

* 10. Since the Vietnam War, America has been reluctant to get militarily involved except in situations where success was virtually certain.

11. A galaxy is a complex system of many stars. The galaxy in which we live is called the Milky Way. It is shaped like a hamburger bun 10,000 light years thick and 100,000 light years in diameter. It contains most of the stars we are able to see at night. But there is one of these stars which we can never see at night; we call this star the Sun. It is about 93 million miles away. Orbiting the Sun at 66,600 miles per hour is our own personal space vehicle, the planet Earth. . . . The Milky Way is also spinning around. We are in orbit around the center of the Milky Way at the fantastic speed of 600,000 miles an hour. —A. R. Patton, *Science for the Non-Scientist* (Minneapolis: Burgess, 1962), p. 27

12. While it is true that people in general fear death more than they fear life in prison, most murders are crimes of passion. That is to say, most murderers, at the time when they commit the act, are so full of hate or anger that they are completely unconcerned with the long-term consequences of their actions. How, then, can anyone assert with confidence that the death penalty deters murder?

* 13. The familiar statement that God cannot be proved is fundamentally ambiguous. On one hand it may mean that the existence of the One whom Christ called Father cannot be proved beyond a shadow of a doubt, but on the other hand it may mean, and often does mean, that there is no valid evidence for the being of God. One does not need to be a professional philosopher to see that these two meanings differ. . . . —Elton Trueblood, *A Place to Stand* (New York: Harper & Row, 1969), p. 21

14. Pacifists are either deeply insightful or greatly mistaken. But if pacifists are deeply insightful, then it is immoral for a police officer to kill a sniper who is firing at schoolchildren. Frankly, I don't think it takes a moral genius to see that it isn't wrong for a police officer to kill a sniper who is firing at schoolchildren. So, in my

opinion, pacifists are not deeply insightful. And hence, in my estimation, they are greatly mistaken.

15. All wrong translations, all absurdities in geometry problems, all clumsiness of style, and all faulty connection of ideas in compositions and essays, all such things are due to the fact that thought has seized upon some idea too hastily, and being thus prematurely blocked, is not open to the truth. The cause is always that we have wanted to be too active; we have wanted to carry out a search. —Simone Weil, *Waiting for God* (New York: Harper & Row, 1951), p. 112

* 16. Obviously, empirical data are scientific. But only what can be falsified (i.e., what can in principle be shown false) is scientific. Therefore, although many people regard empirical data as fixed and unchangeable, empirical data can be falsified.

17. Joan and Carl had been living together for a year and had maintained their separate friendships with both sexes. They were in agreement that they were committed to monogamy, but did not want to sacrifice the opportunity to have close friends. This informal contract proved to be workable, until Carl began spending time with his young research assistant who was in the process of going through a divorce. In response, Joan found herself feeling jealous, threatened, and angry. —Harriet Goldhor Lerner, *The Dance of Anger* (New York: Harper & Row, 1985), p. 104

18. In spite of the fact that the vast majority of contemporary scientists and intellectuals accept the theory of evolution, it is highly questionable for at least two reasons. First, the probability of life evolving from nonlife is so low as to be in the category of the miraculous. Second, if evolution is true, then there are "missing links" (e.g., animals midway between reptiles and birds). But apparently there are no "missing links" since the fossil record contains none. Therefore, the theory of evolution is very much open to question.

* 19. In Stanley Milgram's obedience experiments, first performed at Yale in 1963, subjects were ostensibly recruited to take part in a study of memory. They were then duped into believing they were to be "teachers" in an experiment in which they would administer painful electric shocks of increasing strength to "learners" whenever the latter made mistakes. The so-called learners were actually actors who grunted, screamed, begged to be released from the experiment. As the subject-teachers administered what they thought was ever stronger punishment, they were observed to see whether they continued or protested, and what their reactions were. A large fraction of them were induced to give the highest range of electric shock, even when the pseudo-learners cried out that they feared a heart attack. —Sissela Bok, *Lying: Moral Choice in Public and Private Life* (New York: Random House, 1978), p. 193

20. While many endorse the principle of *equal pay for equal work*, it is in fact untrue. For if this principle is true, then college professors with the same work load *should* receive equal pay. But in almost every college, faculty salaries differ quite significantly *by discipline*. For example, among private colleges in 1993, assistant profes-

sors in business management averaged about $45,000 while assistant professors in the social sciences averaged about $32,000. And full professors in engineering averaged about $70,000 while full professors in English literature averaged about $50,000. Thus, if we were to apply the principle of equal pay for equal work, one of two things would happen: Either the colleges would go broke trying to pay all faculty a relatively high salary or the more highly paid disciplines (such as engineering and business management) would be demoralized by huge salary cuts. Hence, it is false that college professors with the same work load should receive equal pay. Therefore, the principle of equal pay for equal work is untrue.

Part B: More Identifying Arguments   If a given passage is an argument, put it into textbook form. If it is not an argument, simply write "not an argument."

* **1.** The ozone layer has a hole in it primarily because of the large amounts of chlorofluorocarbons that have been released into the atmosphere. These chemicals are manufactured by human beings for use in refrigerators and air conditioners.

2. The most essential and fundamental aspect of culture is the study of literature, since this is an education in how to picture and understand human situations. —Iris Murdoch, *The Sovereignty of the Good* (London: Ark, 1970), p. 34

3. Language is the incarnation of the mentality of the race which fashioned it. Every phrase and word embodies some habitual idea of men and women as they ploughed their fields, tended their homes, and built their cities. For this reason there are no true synonyms as between words and phrases in different languages. —Alfred North Whitehead, *The Aims of Education and Other Essays* (New York: Macmillan, 1929), p. 66

* **4.** That our minds contain elements which are normally inaccessible to us is made clear by the phenomenon of hypnotism. For by plunging a man into a state of profound hypnosis, he can be made to remember events that have long vanished from his normal mind, and that he is quite unable to recover by ordinary voluntary effort—events belonging, for example, to his very early childhood. —J. W. N. Sullivan, *The Limitations of Science* (New York: Viking Press, 1957), pp. 116–117 (*Note:* This passage is slightly altered for use as an exercise.)

5. Assuming that global warming continues, the polar ice caps will melt.

6. We live in the best of all possible worlds. For there is a God. And if God exists, a perfect being exists. Moreover, if God exists, God created the world. So, a perfect being created the world. But if a perfect being created the world, then we live in the best of all possible worlds.

* **7.** I emphatically deny that each culture should be judged only by its own moral standards, for if each culture should be judged only by its own moral code, then no culture's moral standards should be criticized. But the ethical standards of some cultures ought to be criticized because some cultures permit slavery, cannibalism, and/or the oppression of women. Hence, it is not the case that each culture should be judged only by its own ethical standards.

8. Failure to study literature in a technical way is generally blamed, I believe, on the immaturity of the student, rather than on the unpreparedness of the teacher. I couldn't pronounce on that, of course, but as a writer with certain grim memories of days and months of just "hanging out" in school, I can at least venture the opinion that the blame may be shared. At any rate, I don't think the nation's teachers of English have any right to be complacent about their service to literature as long as the appearance of a really fine work of fiction is so rare on the best-seller lists, for good fiction is written more often than it is read. —Flannery O'Connor, *Mystery and Manners* (New York: Noonday Press, 1957), p. 127

9. Americans of this generation read less than those of the previous generation. What explains this fact? In a word, television.

* 10. We [Americans] had roughly 10,000 handgun deaths last year. The British had 40. In 1978, there were 18,714 Americans murdered. Sixty four percent were killed with handguns. In that same year, *we had more killings with handguns by children 10 years old and younger than the British had by killers of all ages.* The Canadians had 579 homicides last year; we had more than 20,000. —Adam Smith, "Fifty Million Handguns," *Esquire*, April 1981, p. 24

11. Either murderers are rational enough to be deterred by the death penalty or they are not. If they are not rational enough to be deterred by the death penalty, then the death penalty is not necessary. On the other hand, if murderers are rational enough to be deterred by the death penalty, then they are rational enough to be deterred by life imprisonment. And if murderers are rational enough to be deterred by life imprisonment, then capital punishment isn't necessary. So, the death penalty is not necessary. Now, if the death penalty isn't necessary, it should be abolished. Therefore, we should get rid of capital punishment.

12. It may fairly be said that a just man becomes just by doing what is just, and a temperate man becomes temperate by doing what is temperate, and if a man did not so act, he would not have much chance of becoming good. But most people, instead of acting, take refuge in theorizing; they imagine that they are philosophers and that philosophy will make them virtuous; in fact, they behave like people who listen attentively to their doctors but never do anything that their doctors tell them. But a healthy state of the soul will no more be produced by this kind of philosophizing than a healthy state of the body by this kind of medical treatment. —*Aristotle's Nicomachean Ethics*, trans. James Weldon (New York: Macmillan, 1897), Bk. II, chap. 3

* 13. It is now widely recognized that absolute proof is something which the human being does not and cannot have. This follows necessarily from the twin fact that deductive reasoning cannot have certainty about its premises and that inductive reasoning cannot have certainty about its conclusions. —Elton Trueblood, *A Place to Stand* (New York: Harper & Row, 1969), p. 22

14. Although advocates of the "prochoice" view sometimes claim that a woman has an unlimited right over what happens in and to her own body, this claim is plainly false. For if a woman has an unlimited right over what happens in and to

her own body, then she has the right to drink heavily during pregnancy. But if drinking lots of alcohol during pregnancy causes birth defects, then a woman does not have the right to drink heavily during pregnancy. And it is a well-known fact that heavy drinking during pregnancy does cause birth defects. So, a woman does not have the right to drink heavily during pregnancy. And therefore, a woman does not have an unlimited right over what happens in and to her own body.

15. Although rewards and punishments do indeed play a role in its formation, they do not by themselves *yield* the moral life. The tendency to avoid acting in a racist manner may first be developed in children by rewards and punishments, but they are not yet moral agents until they act in nonracist fashion even when discipline is not in view, and do so by acting *on the principle* of love and respect. —Nicholas P. Wolterstorff, *Educating for Responsible Action* (Grand Rapids, MI: Eerdmans, 1980), pp. 48–49

* 16. The conscientious law breaking of Socrates, Gandhi, and Thoreau is to be distinguished from the conscientious law testing of Martin Luther King, Jr., who was not a civil disobedient. The civil disobedient withholds taxes or violates state laws knowing he is legally wrong, but believing he is morally right. While he wrapped himself in the mantle of Gandhi and Thoreau, Dr. King led his followers in violation of state laws he believed were contrary to the Federal Constitution. But since Supreme Court decisions in the end generally upheld his many actions, he should not be considered a true civil disobedient. —Lewis H. Van Dusen, Jr., "Civil Disobedience: Destroyer of Democracy," in Lynn Z. Bloom, ed., *The Essay Connection*, 4th ed. (Lexington, MA: Heath, 1995), pp. 564–565

17. Youth is imaginative, and if the imagination be strengthened by discipline this energy of imagination can in great measure be preserved through life. The tragedy of the world is that those who are imaginative have but slight experience, and those who are experienced have feeble imaginations. Fools act on imagination without knowledge; pedants act on knowledge without imagination. Therefore, the task of a university is to weld together imagination and experience. —Alfred North Whitehead, *The Aims of Education* (New York: Macmillan, 1929), p. 93 (*Note:* This passage is slightly altered for use as an exercise.)

18. Madame Curie is perhaps the most inspirational scientist of modern times. Simply consider the facts. She was raised in genteel poverty. She endured great hardships during her years of advanced study in Paris as she was often without heat in the winter months, seldom had enough food, and once collapsed from hunger. Yet, in the face of such hardships, she devoted herself completely to the study of physics and mathematics. Finally, as everyone knows, she made spectacular discoveries regarding radioactivity. To cite only two: She discovered polonium (naming the element after her native country, Poland) and radium.

* 19. I find every [religious] sect, as far as reason will help them, make use of it gladly: And where it fails them, they cry out. It is a matter of faith, and above reason. —John Locke, *An Essay Concerning Human Understanding*, Bk. IV, chap. XVIII, p. 2

20. All segregation statutes are unjust because segregation distorts the soul and damages the personality. It gives the segregator a false sense of superiority, and the segregated a false sense of inferiority. To use the words of Martin Buber, the great Jewish philosopher, segregation substitutes an "I-it" relationship for the "I-thou" relationship, and ends up relegating persons to the status of things. So segregation is not only politically, economically and sociologically unsound, but it is morally wrong and sinful. Paul Tillich has said that sin is separation. Isn't segregation an existential expression of man's tragic separation, an expression of his awful estrangement, his terrible sinfulness? So I can urge men to disobey segregation ordinances because they are morally wrong. —Martin Luther King, Jr., "Letter from the Birmingham City Jail," in James Rachels, ed., *The Right Thing to Do* (New York: Random House, 1989), pp. 242–243

Part C: Argument Forms and Textbook Forms   Put the following arguments into textbook form. Indicate which steps support each subconclusion. Also, identify the following forms wherever they appear: *modus ponens, modus tollens*, hypothetical syllogism, disjunctive syllogism, and constructive dilemma. To save laborious writing, you may use capital letters (as indicated) to stand for the statements comprising the arguments. (See the Answer Key for an illustration.)

* **1.** Large corporations have done much to weaken family ties given that the corporations require a high degree of mobility on the part of their employees, for a high degree of mobility ensures that families will be separated geographically. And the corporations do require a high degree of mobility on the part of their employees. Hence, large corporations have done much to weaken family ties. (L: Large corporations have done much to weaken family ties; M: The corporations require a high degree of mobility on the part of their employees; H: A high degree of mobility ensures that families will be separated geographically)

2. It is wrong to risk one's life unnecessarily. But given that it is wrong to risk one's life unnecessarily, it is wrong to race autos. Hence, it is wrong to race autos. And if it is wrong to race autos, then the Indy 500 should be banned, even though most Americans enjoy watching it. Therefore, the Indy 500 should be banned. (W: It is wrong to risk one's life unnecessarily; A: It is wrong to race autos; I: The Indy 500 should be banned)

3. If the plane landed safely, then radio contact has been maintained. But radio contact has not been maintained. So, the plane did not land safely. Now, either the plan landed safely or it crashed. Therefore, the plane crashed. (P: The plane landed safely; R: Radio contact has been maintained; C: The plane crashed)

* **4.** God predestines human acts only if God fully causes human acts. God fully causes humans acts only if humans lack free will. So, God predestines human acts only if humans lack free will. But humans do not lack free will. Hence, God does not predestine human acts. (P: God predestines human acts; C: God fully causes human acts; F: Humans lack free will)

5. We have an obligation to use that form of punishment which is most likely to deter crime if we have a strict obligation to protect innocent victims. And we have an obligation to torture criminals if we have an obligation to use that form of punishment which is most likely to deter crime, for extreme torture is feared even more than death. Accordingly, if we have a strict obligation to protect innocent victims, then we have an obligation to torture criminals. But in spite of the law-and-order rhetoric we hear these days, it is not true that we have an obligation to torture crimnals. Hence, we do not have a strict obligation to protect future victims. (D: We have an obligation to use that form of punishment which is most likely to deter crime; S: We have a strict obligation to protect innocent victims; T: We have an obligation to torture criminals; E: Extreme torture is feared even more than death)

6. Either the order in the world is due merely to chance or the order in the world is due to intelligent design. The order in the world is not due merely to chance. So, the order in the world is due to intelligent design. Now, there is a God, assuming that the order in the world is brought about by intelligent design. Hence, God exists. (O: The order in the world is due merely to chance; D: The order in the world is due to intelligent design; G: God exists)

* 7. You do not love art, for you love art only if you love Cezanne's paintings. And you do not love Cezanne's paintings. But either you love art or you are uncultured. It follows that you are uncultured. (L: You love art; C: You love Cezanne's paintings; U: You are uncultured)

8. Either the defendant should be put to death or he should be permanently hospitalized. For either the defendant is guilty or he is insane. And assuming that he is guilty, he should be put to death. But assuming that he is insane, he should be permanently hospitalized. Obviously, the defendant should not be put to death if the evidence is less than compelling. And the evidence is less than compelling. So, the defendant should not be put to death. And hence, the defendant should be permanently hospitalized. (D: The defendant should be put to death; H: The defendant should be permanently hospitalized; G: The defendant is guilty; I: The defendant is insane; E: The evidence is less than compelling)

9. Humans have souls. For assuming that humans are identical with their bodies, human acts are determined by prior states of the physical universe. And if human acts are determined by prior states of the physical universe, then humans lack free will. So, humans lack free will if humans are identical with their bodies. But obviously, humans do not lack free will. Therefore, humans are not identical with their bodies. And if humans are not identical with their bodies, then they must have souls. (S: Humans have souls; B: Humans are identical with their bodies; D: Human acts are determined by prior states of the physical universe; F: Humans lack free will)

* 10. If Syria attacks Israel, Israel will counterattack. If Israel counterattacks, then the other Arab states will join in. So, if Syria attacks Israel, then the other Arab states will join in. If the other Arab states join in, then the United States will

defend Israel. So, if Syria attacks Israel, the United States will defend Israel. And if the United States defends Israel, there will be a world war. Therefore, if Syria attacks Israel, there will be a world war. (S: Syria attacks Israel; C: Israel will counterattack; A: The other Arab states will join in; U: The United States will defend Israel; W: There will be a world war)

3.3 Argument Diagrams

Although putting arguments into textbook form is useful, it does require a lot of writing. Argument diagrams involve less writing while yielding many of the benefits of textbook forms. Also, the process of diagramming provides many insights into the structure of an argument.

To diagram an argument, one first places brackets around each statement in the argument, taking note of any premise or conclusion indicators and numbering each statement. To illustrate:

46. ¹[Campaign reform is needed] because ²[many contributions to political campaigns are morally equivalent to bribes.]

We will use an arrow to indicate the relationship of support between premise and conclusion. The arrow is drawn downward from the number that stands for the premise to the number that stands for the conclusion. Thus, the diagram for argument (46) looks like this:

The arrow means that (1), the conclusion, is affirmed on the basis of (2), the premise. In other words, (2) is given as a support for (1).

Subconclusions can readily be accommodated using this procedure. Here is an example:

47. ¹[Charles is unpleasant to work with] since ²[he interrupts people constantly.] Therefore, ³ [I do not want to serve on a committee with Charles.]

This diagram says that premise (2) is given as a support for (1), the subconclusion, and that (1) is given as a support for (3), the conclusion.

Sometimes, two or more premises provide *independent* support for a single conclusion. In such a case, if one of the premises were removed, the support provided by the other(s) would not decrease. For instance:

48. Although ¹[Americans like to think they have interfered with other countries only to defend the downtrodden and helpless], ²[there are undeniably aggressive episodes in American history.] For example, ³[the United States took Texas from Mexico by force.] ⁴[The United States seized Hawaii, Puerto Rico, and Guam.] And ⁵[in the first third of the 20th century, the United States intervened militarily in all of the following countries without being invited to do so: Cuba, Nicaragua, Guatemala, the Dominican Republic, Haiti, and Honduras.]

The diagram is as follows:

Note that statement (1) is omitted from the diagram since it is a discount. The diagram says that the three premises support the conclusion *independently*.

Sometimes, two or more premises are *interdependent*. In such a case, the premises work together as a logical unit, so that if one is removed, the support of the others is decreased. Here's an example:

49. ¹[No physical object can travel faster than light.] ²[A hydrogen atom is a physical object.] Hence, ³[no hydrogen atom can travel faster than light.]

If two or more premises provide *interdependent* support for a single conclusion (or subconclusion), write their numbers in a horizontal row, joined by plus signs, and underline the row. The plus signs serve as an abbreviation for "in conjunction with." To illustrate, the diagram for argument (49) looks like this:

This diagram tells us that premises (1) and (2) provide *interdependent* support for conclusion (3).

Because English grammar is subtle and flexible, there are no hard-and-fast rules for bracket placement. But the main goal is to bracket the argument in a way that fully reveals the patterns of reasoning within it. The following rules of thumb will help you to do this.

First, always take note of any premise and conclusion indicators. For instance, two statements joined by the premise indicator "because" need to be bracketed separately, since one is a premise and one is a conclusion (or sub-conclusion).

Second, recognize that statements joined by the words "and" or "but" often need to be separated into distinct units for the purpose of diagramming. For example, whenever the word "and" joins two premises, the diagram must indicate whether the premises operate independently or interdependently. Again, the overriding principle is to bracket the statements in such a way as to make an accurate picture of the logical structure of the argument. For instance:

> 50. ¹[The defendant is guilty.] After all, ²[he confessed to stealing the jewels] and ³[he was undoubtedly present at the scene of the crime] since ⁴[his fingerprints are on the safe.]

The argument can be diagrammed as follows:

The diagram indicates that premises (2) and (3) support conclusion (1) *independently*. In addition, (4) supports (3) but not (2).

Third, note that conditionals (if-then statements) and disjunctions (either-or statements) should *never* be broken down into parts and joined with the plus sign. As noted previously, the plus sign is a special form of "and" linking statements that operate in a logically *interdependent* fashion. Of course, "and" is very different from "if-then" or "either-or." For example, take the statement "If I will fall, then I will hurt myself." This conditional statement obviously does *not* have the same meaning as, "I will fall *and* I will hurt myself." So, we must treat conditional statements as units for the purposes of diagramming. The same goes for disjunctions. The following words form compounds that should be treated as a single unit in diagramming arguments:

if . . . then	assuming that
only if	either . . . or
given that	neither . . . nor

Consider the following example:

> 51. ¹[If China attacks Taiwan, Taiwan will fight,] for ²[the Taiwanese are ready to defend themselves.] ³[Their air force is formidable.] ⁴[And their navy is well trained and well equipped.]

Argument (51) can be diagrammed as follows:

Note that conclusion (1) stands for an entire conditional statement.

When bracketing and numbering an argument, simply take the statements in the order in which they appear in the original, marking the first statement (1), the second (2), and so on. This will help to ensure that your numbering system is similar to that of your classmates. All statements should be numbered even though some statements, such as discounts and repeated statements, may not appear in your diagram. This convention helps in two ways: It makes the process of bracketing and numbering relatively mechanical, and it ensures that your numbering system is like that of your classmates. (This, in turn, is a great aid to communication.) Finally, where rhetorical questions and commands serve as premises or conclusions, they, too, should be bracketed and numbered.

The complexity of an argument diagram mirrors the complexity of the original. Accordingly, argument diagrams can become rather complex. Here's an example:

> 52. Although ¹[some have argued that nuclear weapons introduce nothing genuinely new into the disputes about the morality of war,] I believe that ²[nuclear weapons raise novel moral issues.] First, ³[nuclear weapons have new and undreamed-of long-term effects] since ⁴[the radioactive fallout pollutes the environment and alters human genes.] Second, ⁵[a nuclear war could destroy human civilization in its entirety.] Third, ⁶[in case of nuclear war, the dust caused by the explosions would prevent the sun's rays from reaching the earth's surface.] So, ⁷[a nuclear war would result in a drastic lowering of the earth's temperature.] In other words, ⁸[a nuclear war would result in a "nuclear winter."] And ⁹[no human or human group has a right to gamble with the very climate upon which life itself is based.]

The argument can be diagrammed as follows:

A number of things are worthy of note in this diagram. First, statement (1) is omitted from the diagram because it is a discount. Second, statement (8) is omitted because it is a repetition of (7). One could put (8) in the diagram, but in that case one would omit (7). Third, the conclusion is supported by three *independent* lines of reasoning:

- (4) supports (3), which, in turn, supports (2).
- (5) supports (2).
- (6) supports (7), and (7) operates in conjunction with (9) to support (2).

Each of these lines of reasoning is independent of the others because if we eliminate any one of them, the support of the others remains unaltered. Finally, statements (7) and (9) operate as an *interdependent* logical unit.

The following exercises will test your understanding of the principles of argument diagramming.

◆ Exercise 3.3

Part A: Argument Diagrams   Make a photocopy of the arguments below. Then, on your photocopy, bracket and number the statements in the arguments, using the techniques outlined in the previous section. Finally, construct a diagram for each argument, placing it beside the argument on the photocopy.

* **1.** Photography makes representational art obsolete because no one, not even the best artist, can be more accurate than a camera.

 2. In spite of the fact that electrons are physical entities, they cannot be seen. For electrons are too small to deflect photons (i.e., light particles). Hence, electrons are invisible.

 3. There is a healthy kind of individualism—the kind that is resistant to group tyranny. . . . But capitalist individualism is not concerned about promoting the growth of the person into emotional, intellectual, ethical and cultural fullness; rather, it fosters the development of individual traits only so far as these are useful for maximizing profits. Thus, ironically, capitalist individualism turns into a group despotism under which personal becoming is sacrificed to the external tyrannies of material gain. —Eugene C. Bianchi, "Capitalism and Christianity Are Contradictory," in David L. Bender, ed., *American Values: Opposing Viewpoints* (San Diego: Greenhaven Press, 1989), p. 147

* **4.** While there is much wickedness in the world, there is also much good. For if there is evil, then there must be good, since good and evil are relative, like big and small. And no one will deny that evil exists.

 5. Since major historical events cannot be repeated, historians aren't scientists. After all, the scientific method necessarily involves events (called "experiments") that can be repeated.

 6. The scientific method doesn't necessarily involve experimentation. For if anything is a science, astronomy is. But the great cosmic events observed by astronomers cannot be repeated. And, of course, an experiment is by definition a repeatable event.

* **7.** There is no better way to arouse the American citizen than to order him around or to tell him what to think. Although there are many people in this country who would like to organize us more thoroughly and tidy up the freedom we have by a little more control, we still reserve the personal right to plunge our own way into our own mistakes and discoveries, in art, philosophy, education, or politics. . . . —Harold Taylor, *Art and the Intellect* (New York: The Museum of Modern Art, 1960), p. 43

8. Although people often say that beauty is in the eye of the beholder, there are various reasons for thinking that beauty is objective. First, there is wide agreement about natural beauty. After all, virtually everyone finds the Grand Canyon, Niagara Falls, and the Rocky Mountains beautiful. Second, even though art critics frequently disagree with one another, they do defend their views with principled reasoning. Third, art critics tend to agree among themselves about which historical works of art are truly great. And this agreement is no mere coincidence since the critics are not, in general, reluctant to disagree with one another.

9. In the new order, when voters are concerned about what benefits the elected officer will provide them, promises, hypocrisy, deceit, log-rolling and clout are fast becoming the characteristics of electability. As Harold Blake Walker noted, of 21 Congressmen linked in one way or another with political wrongdoing or personal scandal prior to the 1976 election, 19 were re-elected. —John A. Howard, "Democratic Values Are Being Lost to Self-Interest," in David L. Bender, ed., *American Values: Opposing Viewpoints* (San Diego: Greenhaven Press, 1989), p. 57

* 10. Despite the fact that contraception is regarded as a blessing by most Americans, using contraceptives is immoral. For whatever is unnatural is immoral since God created and controls nature. And contraception is unnatural because it interferes with nature.

11. Of course, of all the various kinds of artists, the fiction writer is most deviled by the public. Painters and musicians are protected somewhat since they don't deal with what everyone knows about, but the fiction writer writes about life, and so anyone living considers himself an authority on it. —Flannery O'Connor, *Mystery and Manners* (New York: Noonday Press, 1957), pp. 121–122

12. While some people seem to be under the impression that humans are making moral progress, I submit that the 20th century is a movement backwards into violence and cruelty. For in spite of the fact that science and technology have developed rapidly, the greatest mass murders in history have all occurred in this century. Millions died on the battlefields of World Wars I and II. Six million Jews died in Nazi prison camps. And from 1917 until the end of Stalin's reign, 20 million people died in Soviet work camps. More recently, we have Pol Pot's slaughter of the Cambodians as well as the atrocities in the former Yugoslavia.

* 13. There is no life after death. For what's real is what you can see, hear, or touch. And you cannot see, hear, or touch life after death. Furthermore, life after death is possible only if humans have souls. But the notion of a soul belongs to a prescientific and outmoded view of the world. And hence, the belief in souls belongs to the realm of superstition.

14. Politicians are forever attributing crime rates to *policies*—if the crime rates are decreasing, to their own "wise" policies; if the crime rates are increasing, to the

"failed" policies of their opponents. But the fact is that crime rates are best explained in terms of demographics. For crime is primarily a young man's game. Whenever there is a relatively large number of young men between the ages of 15 and 30, the crime rates are high. And whenever this part of the population is relatively small, the crime rates are relatively low.

15. A liberal arts education is vital to any great nation. Why? For one thing, a liberal arts education provides the best possible skills in communication. And without good communication at all levels, a nation cannot move forward. For another, work is not the whole of life. And it is well known that a liberal arts education increases one's capacity to enjoy life by substantially broadening the range of one's interests.

* 16. For beginners, portrait painting is perhaps the most difficult branch of art to understand and enjoy *as painting*. If we happen to know, either from personal acquaintance or from photographs, what the subject of a portrait is actually like in physical appearance, we are inclined to think more about whether it is a good likeness than whether it is a good painting. And if it is a portrait of someone who lived long ago but is not in the history books, we may think that because the subject is of no interest to us the painting must also be without interest. —A. C. Ward, *Enjoying Paintings* (New York: Penguin Books, 1949), p. 90

17. Psychotherapy is a religion for many Americans. After all, fewer and fewer Americans regularly attend church, synagogue, or temple, but more and more see their psychotherapists regularly. And what do they talk about with their psychotherapists? They talk about their inner lives, or, in other words, about the state of their souls. For they speak of strange impulses, confess dark thoughts, and put their deepest fears into words. And because only 50 years ago these same outpourings would have occurred only in the presence of a priest or pastor, it seems fair to say that psychotherapy is indeed a religion for many Americans.

18. The human sciences have . . . made a major contribution to cynicism about human greatness, especially as they treat the subjects of motivation and freedom. We are told that human choice is not what it appears to be. If we accept the sophistications of some views of psychology, we know that what appears to be heroic—for example, a man or woman's act of courage in saving another's life—is, in fact, a desperate attempt to win the approval of a long-dead parent who had withheld love in the childhood years. What, then, has become of the hero? He or she is transformed in our minds into a neurotic, and with a slight turn of the mind, admiration is changed to pity and condescension. —Dick Keyes, "America Must Rediscover Heroism," in David L. Bender, ed., *American Values: Opposing Viewpoints* (San Diego: Greenhaven Press, 1989), p. 84

* 19. Violence as a way of achieving racial justice is both impractical and immoral. It is impractical because it is a descending spiral ending in destruction for all. The old law of an eye for an eye leaves everybody blind. It is immoral because it seeks to humiliate the opponent rather than win his understanding; it seeks to annihilate rather than to convert. Violence is immoral because it thrives on hatred

rather than love. It destroys community and makes brotherhood impossible.
—Martin Luther King, Jr., *The Words of Martin Luther King, Jr.*, selected and introduced by Coretta Scott King (New York: Newmarket Press, 1983), p. 73

20. Although God created all *dependent* beings, God did not create everything. For numbers have existed from all eternity since God has existed from all eternity, and there has always been exactly *one* God. Moreover, nothing that has existed from all eternity is created because each cause must precede its effect.

Part B: More Argument Diagrams   Make a photocopy of the paragraphs below. Then determine which of the paragraphs are arguments and which are not. If a paragraph is not an argument, write "not an argument" beside the paragraph. If a paragraph is an argument, bracket and number the statements involved on your photocopy; then, beside the argument, construct a diagram.

* **1.** John and Robert Kennedy and Martin Luther King were, like them or not, this country's last true national leaders. None of John Kennedy's successors in the White House has enjoyed the consensus he built, and every one of them ran into trouble, of his own making, while in office. In the same way, none of this country's national spokespeople since Robert Kennedy and Dr. King has had the attention and respect they enjoyed. —Warren Bennis, *Why Leaders Can't Lead* (San Francisco: Jossey-Bass, 1989), p. 61

2. If . . . our government is to function it must have dissent. Only totalitarian governments insist upon conformity and they—as we know—do so at their peril. Without criticism abuses will go unrebuked; without dissent our dynamic system will become static. —Henry Steele Commager, "True Patriotism Demands Dissent," in David L. Bender, ed., *American Values: Opposing Viewpoints* (San Diego: Greenhaven Press, 1989), p. 248

3. It is because of the ideal of freedom that we have organized our particular form of democracy, since the political structure of any society is . . . formed to support the demands which the people make for the attainment of certain values. Because of . . . the variety and richness of the social and natural resources with which the country has abounded, in order to realize the full potential which has always existed here, we have needed the idea of freedom as a social instrument to be used for our full development. —Harold Taylor, *Art and the Intellect* (New York: The Museum of Modern Art, 1960), p. 53

* **4.** For a variety of reasons, private colleges are in trouble. First, private colleges have repeatedly increased tuition well beyond the rate of inflation. And any business that increases prices in such a fashion is likely to run into trouble. Second, many people are beginning to question the value of higher education since a college degree no longer guarantees an attractive salary. Third, rightly or wrongly, the American public believes that colleges have not practiced good financial management, and hence the public thinks that tuition dollars often subsidize inefficiency.

5. From 1979 through 1994, attacks by dogs resulted in 279 deaths of humans in the United States. Such attacks have prompted widespread review of existing local and state dangerous-dog laws, including proposals for adoption of breed-specific restrictions to prevent such episodes. —*The Journal of the American Medical Association*, 278(4) (1997): 278

6. The legalization of drugs is neither unwise nor immoral. It is not unwise because, by legalizing drugs, we would eliminate the illegal drug trade. Hence, by legalizing drugs, we would rid our nation of all the violence that goes along with the illegal drug trade. Furthermore, the legalization of drugs is not immoral since it can be combined with a massive program of moral education.

* 7. The Peloponnesian War deeply altered the future course of Greek history. By changing the movement of men, the geographical distribution of genes, values, and ideas, it affected later events in Rome, and through Rome, all Europe. . . . In turn, in the tightly wired world of today, . . . Europeans influence Mexicans and Japanese alike. Whatever trace of impact the Peloponnesian War left on the genetic structure, the ideas, and the values of today's Europeans is now exported by them to all parts of the world. Thus today's Mexicans and Japanese feel the distant, twice-removed impact of that war even though their ancestors, alive during its occurrence, did not. In this way, the events of the past, skipping as it were over generations and centuries, rise up to haunt and change us today. —Alvin Toffler, *Future Shock* (New York: Bantam Books, 1970), p. 16

8. During the 1930s, there were 1667 executions in the United States. During the 1940s, there were 1284. During the 1950s, there were 717. And during the rehabilitation-mad 1960s, the numbers plummeted to 191. Then came the *Furman v. Georgia* decision in 1972, which resulted in a grand total of 3 executions during the 1970s. While the numbers began to creep back up in the 1980s, with a total of 117 executions in that decade, we are forced to conclude that America has not had a serious practice of capital punishment since about 1960. Therefore, it is not true that America's currently high murder rate proves the ineffectiveness of the death penalty.

9. It is difficult, and you may be sure that we know it, for us to oppose your power and fortune, unless the terms be equal. Nevertheless we trust that the gods will give us fortune as good as yours, because we are standing for what is right against what is wrong; and as for what we lack in power, we trust that it will be made up for by our alliance with the Spartans. . . . Our confidence, therefore, is not so entirely irrational as you think. —The Melians to the Athenians, in Thucydides, *The Peloponnesian War*, trans. Rex Warner (New York: Penguin Books, 1954), p. 404 (The Athenians had demanded that the Melians surrender, but the Melians refused.)

* 10. All Gaul is divided into three parts, one of which is inhabited by the Belgae, another by the Aquitani, a third by . . . [the] Celtae. . . . Of all these peoples the bravest are the Belgae, because they are farthest removed from the civilization and refinement of the Roman Province and are very rarely visited by traders who bring in those wares which tend to make people effeminate; and also because they are nearest to the Germans, who live across the Rhine, with whom they are constantly

at war. —Julius Caesar, *Caesar's Gallic War,* trans. Joseph Pearl (New York: Barron's Educational Series, 1962), p. 1

11. Two distinct lines of reasoning support the thesis that the physical universe is temporally finite. First, the galaxies are speeding away from each other *and* from a central point. Moreover, there isn't enough matter in the universe to reverse this process. And if we trace this process back, it appears that the universe began with a "bang" some 15 to 20 billion years ago. Second, if the universe is temporally infinite, it must have gone through an infinite number of cycles (each Big Bang followed by a Big Crunch). But according to physicists, each Big Bang/Big Crunch cycle would cause a decrease in the overall amount of available energy. Thus, if the universe were temporally infinite, there would now be no energy available at all. But obviously, lots of energy is still available.

12. Besides the natural and the human law it was necessary for the directing of human conduct to have a divine law. And this for four reasons. First, because it is by law that man is directed how to perform his proper acts in view of his last end. . . . [And] since man is ordained to an end of eternal happiness which exceeds man's natural ability, . . . therefore it was necessary that, in addition to the natural and the human law, man should be directed to his end by a law given by God. Secondly, because, by reason of the uncertainty of human judgment . . . different people form different judgments on human acts. . . . Thirdly, because man . . . is not competent to judge of interior movements, that are hidden, but only of exterior acts which are observable; and yet for the perfection of virtue it is necessary for man to conduct himself rightly in both kinds of acts. . . . Fourthly, because, . . . human law cannot punish or forbid all evil deeds, since, while aiming at doing away with all evils, it would do away with many good things. . . . —Anton C. Pegis, ed., *Introduction to St. Thomas Aquinas* (New York: Random House, 1948), pp. 621–622.

* 13. While colleges and universities have come under heavy criticism in the last decade, they will undoubtedly remain a vital force in American social life for generations to come. For one thing, although both the public and the media seem to have a thirst for stories about people who've gotten rich or famous with only a high school degree, the fact remains that a college or university degree is the surest way to increase one's social and occupational status. For another, college grads as a group indicate higher levels of satisfaction with their lives than do those with lesser educational attainments. Finally, you show me a nation with a weak system of higher education and I'll show you a nation with little power. And Americans will never willingly accept a position of relative powerlessness among the nations of the world.

14. As I crisscross the United States lecturing on college campuses, I am dismayed to find that professors and administrators, when pressed for a candid opinion, estimate that no more than 25 percent of their students are turned on by classwork. For the rest, college is at best a social center or aging vat, and at worst a young folks' home or a prison that keeps them out of the mainstream of economic life for a few more years. —Caroline Bird, "College Is a Waste of Time and Money," in

Stephen R. C. Hicks and David Kelley, eds., *The Art of Reasoning* (New York: Norton, 1994), p. 200

15. The war in Vietnam was immoral, for a variety of reasons. First, although America's leaders insisted that the war was needed to stop the expansion of communism, there was no good reason to suppose that communism would have spread from Vietnam to any place else significant. Second, the war in Vietnam was a civil war. Hence, North Vietnam was no more wrong to fight for union with South Vietnam than the northern states were wrong to fight for union with the southern states during the American Civil War. Third, in Vietnam, the Americans did a lot of indiscriminate killing through bombing and massive artillery strikes. Finally, during the war, the Americans (and their allies) killed some 600,000 Vietnamese. Only the achievement of a great good could justify so many deaths, but no great good was achieved.

* 16. There are no easy answers, no quick fixes, no formulas. It's time to face facts, lest we all follow Boesky, North, Hart, and the Bakkers into the abyss. We are not supermen. We cannot remake the world to suit us. It's not some mere trick of fate that the high and the mighty are tumbling off their pedestals in record numbers. It is rather the inevitable result of ambition outstripping competence and conscience. Whatever the question, competence and conscience are part of the answer. . . . . —Warren Bennis, *Why Leaders Can't Lead* (San Francisco: Jossey-Bass, 1989), p. 154

17. Since God is love, he must always have had an object for his love. Since the world did not exist from everlasting, but was created at a certain moment in time, God must have had another object for his love in the countless aeons before this world was made. If there is an eternal Lover, there must be an eternal Beloved, since love without an object is an abstraction. The Son, therefore, must have existed eternally as the object of the Father's love. —Alan Richardson, *Creeds in the Making: A Short Introduction to the History of Christian Doctrine* (London: SCM Press, 1935), pp. 58–59

18. Although the great majority of homicides in the United States involve assailants of the same race or ethnic group, current evidence suggests that socioeconomic status plays a much greater role in explaining racial and ethnic differences in the rate of homicide than any intrinsic tendency toward violence. For example, Centerwall has shown that when household crowding is taken into account, the rate of domestic homicide among blacks in Atlanta, Georgia is no higher than that of whites living in similar conditions. Likewise, a recent study of childhood homicide in Ohio found that once cases were stratified by socioeconomic status, there was little difference in race-specific rates of homicide involving children 5 to 14 years of age. —John Henry Sloan et al., "Handgun Regulations, Crime, Assaults, and Homicide: A Tale of Two Cities," in Stephen R. C. Hicks and David Kelley, eds., *The Art of Reasoning* (New York: Norton, 1994), p. 305

* 19. The only proof capable of being given that an object is visible, is that people actually see it. The only proof that a sound is audible, is that people hear it; and so of the other sources of our experience. In like manner, I apprehend, the sole evidence

it is possible to produce that anything is desirable, is that people do actually desire it. [Thus,] no reason can be given why the general happiness is desirable, except that each person . . . desires his own happiness. —J. S. Mill, *Utilitarianism* (New York: Bobbs-Merrill, 1957), pp. 44–45

20. There is an undoubted psychological easing of standards of truthfulness toward those believed to be liars. It is simply a fact, for instance, that one behaves differently toward a trusted associate and toward a devious, aggressive salesman. But this easing of standards merely explains the difference in behavior; it does not by itself justify lies to those one takes to be less than honest. Some of the harm the liar may have done by lying may be repaid by the harm a lie can do to him in return. But the risks to others, to general trust, and to those who lie to liars in retaliation merely accumulate and spread thereby. Only if there are separate, and more compelling, excuses, can lying to liars be justified. —Sissela Bok, *Lying: Moral Choice in Public and Private Life* (New York: Random House, 1978), p. 134

Part C: Diagrams and Argument Forms Make a photocopy of the following arguments. On your photocopy, bracket and number the statements in each argument, and then construct a diagram, placing it beside the argument. *If* an inference exemplifies any of the following forms, write the name of the form next to the numbers of the statements involved: *modus ponens* (MP), *modus tollens* (MT), hypothetical syllogism (HS), disjunctive syllogism (DS), constructive dilemma (CD), the fallacy of denying the antecedent (DA), and the fallacy of affirming the consequent (AC). You may wish to use abbreviations for the names of the forms, as indicated. (See the Answer Key for an illustration.)

* 1. America must reform its sagging educational system, assuming that Americans are unwilling to become a second-rate force in the world economy. But I hope and trust that Americans are unwilling to accept second-rate status in the international economic scene. Accordingly, America must reform its sagging educational system.

2. Affirmative action is morally permissible only if it promotes efficiency in the workplace. But affirmative action does not promote efficiency in the workplace since it sometimes involves hiring the less qualified of two applicants. Hence, affirmative action is not morally permissible.

3. Two distinct lines of evidence converge on the idea that Smith is the murderer. First, either Thomson or Smith pulled the trigger. And since Thomson's fingerprints are not on the murder weapon, Thomson did not pull the trigger. So, Smith pulled the trigger. Furthermore, if Smith pulled the trigger, then Smith is the murderer. Second, Smith hated the victim. And Smith had a motive given that Smith hated the victim. So, Smith had a motive.

* 4. Either humans evolved from matter or humans have souls. Humans evolved from matter. Hence, humans do not have souls. But there is life after death only if humans have souls. Therefore, there is no life after death.

5. Morality is relative to cultures only if the aggression of warlike societies is moral. But the aggression of warlike societies is not moral. Furthermore, morality is not relative to cultures if at least one moral principle is absolute. And at least one moral principle is absolute. For example, here is one moral absolute: "It is always wrong to torture people for fun." Hence, morality is not relative to cultures, despite the fact that customs do differ to some extent from culture to culture.

6. Some abortions are permissible. First, in rare instances, the growth of the fetus threatens the mother's life. And if this is so, then obviously *some* abortions are permissible. Second, in some cases, pregnancy is due to rape. But if in some cases pregnancy is due to rape, then in some cases it is wrong to force a woman to carry a fetus to term. And if in some cases it is wrong to force a woman to carry a fetus to term, then some abortions are permissible. So, if in some cases pregnancy is due to rape, then some abortions are permissible. Third, in the case of severe birth defects, abortion is allowable because the emotional and financial costs of having a severely disabled child are very high indeed.

* 7. Either Boris drowned in the lake or he drowned in the ocean. But Boris has salt-water in his lungs. And if Boris has saltwater in his lungs, then he did not drown in the lake. So, Boris did not drown in the lake. It follows that Boris drowned in the ocean.

8. Obviously, there is an objective moral law (i.e., a truth about right and wrong independent of human opinion), for every sane person will agree that it is immoral to kill people at will. However, there is an objective moral law only if there is a moral Lawgiver who exists independently of human thinking. Hence, there is a moral Lawgiver who exists independently of human thinking. But God exists if there is a moral Lawgiver who exists independently of human thinking. Accordingly, God exists.

9. Moral principles cannot be known. For if moral principles can be known, then either they are known via the senses or they are true by definition. And obviously, moral principles are not true by definition. Furthermore, if moral principles are known via the senses, then moral rightness must be visible. But if moral rightness is visible, then it has a certain shape or color. So, if moral principles are known via the senses, then moral rightness has a certain shape or color. Plainly, however, moral rightness does not have a certain shape or color. Hence, moral principles are not known via the senses. And therefore, they cannot be known at all.

* 10. If affirmative action (AA) has better overall consequences than the alternatives, then AA is right. And if AA promotes social equality by countering unconscious bias among those who interview job candidates, then AA has better overall con-sequences than the alternatives. It follows that if AA promotes social equality by countering unconscious bias among those who interview job candidates, then AA is right. Furthermore, AA does promote social equality by countering unconscious bias among interviewers. Therefore, AA is right. Moreover, either we should endorse untrammeled networking or we should endorse AA. But we should not endorse untrammeled networking if it has the effect (whether intended or not) of excluding minorities. And untrammeled networking does have this effect. So, we should not endorse untrammeled networking. Hence, we should endorse AA. Once again, then, we arrive at the conclusion that AA is right.

3.4 Enthymemes

An **enthymeme** is an argument with an unstated premise, an unstated subconclusion, and/or an unstated conclusion. If we use the more general term *step* to refer to premises, subconclusions, and/or conclusions, we can say that an enthymeme is an argument with one or more unstated steps. Unstated steps are also referred to as *missing* or *implicit* steps. Enthymemes complicate the attempt to identify arguments, because the missing steps must be supplied. This section explains how to supply the unstated steps in enthymemes.

Arguers often provide the premises of an argument and leave it up to their audience to draw the obvious conclusion or subconclusions. For instance:

53. If you want to win this election, you should respond publicly to your critics. And I know you want to win this election.

Here, the unstated conclusion is, "You should respond publicly to your critics." Note that if we add this step to the original, the form of the argument is *modus ponens*.

Arguers also often leave a premise unstated. For instance:

54. The rich will get richer if the Republicans win. And taxes will increase if the Democrats win. Hence, either the rich will get richer or taxes will increase.

The unstated premise here is, "Either the Republicans win or the Democrats win." Note that if this premise is added to the original, the argument has the form of a constructive dilemma.

In dealing with enthymemes, it will be helpful to keep in mind a distinction between the textbook form, which does not fill in the missing steps, and an **elaborated textbook form**, which does fill in the missing steps. In evaluating an enthymeme, one begins by constructing the textbook form—listing only those premises, subconclusions, and conclusions that are actually stated. Then, to arrive at the *elaborated* textbook form, one adds such steps as are needed to render the argument valid (or strong). To illustrate, the textbook form for argument (54) is as follows:

55. 1. If the Republicans win, then the rich will get richer.
    2. If the Democrats win, then taxes will increase.
So, 3. Either the rich will get richer or taxes will increase.

By contrast, the elaborated textbook form for argument (54) looks like this:

> 56. [1. Either the Republicans win or the Democrats win.]
>   2. If the Republicans win, then the rich will get richer.
>   3. If the Democrats win, then taxes will increase.
> So, 4. Either the rich will get richer or taxes will increase.

Note the use of brackets to indicate the unstated (or implicit) step that has been added.

When constructing an elaborated textbook form for an enthymeme, it is important not to get carried away listing possible background assumptions the original author *may* have been making. We risk misrepresenting an author when we attempt to fill in unstated steps in an argument. Here are some principles of charity to bear in mind when constructing elaborated textbook forms:

> **Principle A:** An elaborated textbook form should be a *valid* argument unless one of the following conditions holds: (a) The argument is clearly presented as invalid or strong or (b) one cannot make the original argument valid without adding a false (or doubtful) premise but one *can* make the original argument strong without adding a false (or doubtful) premise. (*Note:* In this section, we are focusing on valid arguments. We will discuss strong arguments in chapter 10.)

> **Principle B:** If you intend for an elaborated textbook form to be valid, add only those steps to the original argument that are needed to give it a form known to be valid, such as *modus ponens*. (*Note:* A good working knowledge of argument forms is indispensable for the construction of elaborated textbook forms, and we will add to our list of valid forms in later chapters.)

> **Principle C:** If you intend for the elaborated textbook form to be strong, add only those steps needed to make the original argument strong.[7]

Now, let's apply these principles to some examples. Consider:

> 57. One often hears left-leaning critics say that the United States pursued a genocidal policy during the Vietnam War. But if the United States pursued a genocidal policy in Vietnam, the major cities in North Vietnam were utterly annihilated by bombing. Thus, the only reasonable conclusion is that the United States did not aim at genocide in Vietnam.

The elaborated textbook form of argument (57) is as follows:

> 58. 1. If the United States pursued a genocidal policy in Vietnam, then the major cities in North Vietnam were utterly annihilated by bombing.

[2. It is not true that the major cities in North Vietnam were utterly annihilated by bombing.]

So, 3. The United States did not pursue a genocidal policy in Vietnam.

Following Principle A, we have constructed a valid argument. And following Principle B, we have added just one step needed to give the argument a form known to be valid, namely, *modus tollens*. Again, we use brackets to indicate the missing step.

Note that it is quite common for the conditional premise of the *modus ponens* or *modus tollens* forms to be left unstated. Consider the following examples:

59. Since Henry can run a mile in under 5 minutes, he is in excellent physical condition.

60. Since this stone will not scratch glass, this stone is not a diamond.

Here is the elaborated textbook form for argument (59):

61. [1. If Henry can run a mile in under 5 minutes, then he is in excellent physical condition.]

2. Henry can run a mile in under 5 minutes.

So, 3. Henry is in excellent physical condition.

Here, the form is *modus ponens*. Note the brackets around the conditional premise to indicate that it is not explicit in the original. The elaborated textbook form for argument (60) is as follows:

62. [1. If this stone is a diamond, this stone will scratch glass.]

2. This stone will not scratch glass.

So, 3. This stone is not a diamond.

Here, the form is *modus tollens*.

Occasionally, an enthymeme is clearly presented as invalid. For instance:

63. If people respect the boss, then the boss is talented. My fellow employees, we are forced to conclude that the boss is not talented.

Plainly, the unstated premise is, "People do not respect the boss." So, Principle A tells us that the elaborated textbook form will exemplify the fallacy of denying the antecedent:

64. 1. If people respect the boss, then the boss is talented.

[2. People do not respect the boss.]

So, 3. The boss is not talented.

It is rather rare, however, for an enthymeme to be clearly presented as a fallacy. And an elaborated textbook form should not contain fallacies unless the original argument is clearly presented as such.

Arguments may be presented as strong rather than valid. For example:

65. Judy Smith is an American. So, it is likely that Judy disapproves of communism.

The important phrase "it is likely that" indicates that the argument is claimed to be strong. So, the elaborated textbook form looks like this:

66. [1. Most Americans disapprove of communism.]
    2. Judy Smith is an American.
So, 3. Judy Smith disapproves of communism.

Notice that if we try to turn (65) into a *valid* argument, we run into certain difficulties. Consider the following two attempts:

67. [1. All Americans disapprove of communism.]
    2. Judy Smith is an American.
So, 3. Judy Smith disapproves of communism.

68. [1. If Judy Smith is an American, then she disapproves of communism.]
    2. Judy Smith is an American.
So, 3. Judy disapproves of communism.

Although arguments (67) and (68) are both valid, in each case the first premise is false or doubtful. These examples are included here simply to illustrate clause (a) of Principle A. We will develop tools for handling strong arguments in chapter 10.

Subconclusions are also frequently left unstated. For example, consider the following argument:

69. Pollution will increase dramatically if the population will continue to grow at the current rate. And the environment will be destroyed if pollution will increase dramatically. Unfortunately, the population will continue to grow at the current rate. Accordingly, the environment will be destroyed.

To cut down on writing, let's use capital letters to stand for the statements in argument (69) as follows:

P: Pollution will increase dramatically
G: The population will continue to grow at the current rate
E: The environment will be destroyed

Using this scheme of abbreviation, the textbook form looks like this:

70. 1. If G, then P.
    2. If P, then E.
    3. G.
So, 4. E.

A subconclusion has been left unstated, but we make it explicit when constructing an *elaborated* textbook form:

71. 1. If G, then P.
    2. If P, then E.
 [So, 3. If G, then E.]   1, 2, hypothetical syllogism
    4. G.
So, 5. E.   3, 4, *modus ponens*

Now the argument is a tightly linked chain exemplifying two valid argument forms. In the case of arguments with subconclusions, it is helpful to indicate which steps support which and to indicate which argument forms are exemplified, as above. For example, "1, 2, hypothetical syllogism" written to the right of step (3) means that subconclusion (3) is supported by premises (1) and (2) and that the argument form involved is hypothetical syllogism. And "3, 4, *modus ponens*" written to the right of step (5) means that (5) is supported by (3) and (4) and that the argument form involved is *modus ponens*.

A brief word about the background assumptions of an argument may be helpful at this point. These background assumptions are often called presuppositions. A **presupposition** of an argument is a statement that is *implied* by one or more premises of the argument but that is not itself a step in the argument (i.e., not a premise, not a subconclusion, and not the conclusion). In identifying arguments, it is important not to confuse premises and presuppositions. For instance, consider the following argument:

72. Pruning trees is wrong because it involves torturing trees.

Here is a correct, elaborated textbook form of argument (72):

73. 1. Pruning trees involves torturing them.
    [2. If pruning trees involves torturing them, then it is wrong.]
So, 3. Pruning trees is wrong.

Since torture necessarily involves inflicting pain, the first premise of this argument implies that trees can feel pain. Thus, the argument *presupposes* that trees can feel pain. But notice that this presupposition does not appear in our elaborated textbook form. We have added only a single step needed to give the argument a form known to be valid, namely, *modus ponens*.

Identifying an argument's presuppositions is useful in evaluating the truth of its premises, for any statement that implies something false is itself false. Thus, if it is false that trees can feel pain, then premise (1) of argument (73) is false, because it implies that trees *can* feel pain. But while identifying an argument's presuppositions is often helpful when evaluating for soundness, two common errors regarding presuppositions must be avoided.

First, presuppositions must not be confused with unstated premises. Typically, one adds unstated premises in order to render an argument valid (or strong). (The only exception is when the argument is clearly presented as invalid or weak.) But adding presuppositions will not render an argument valid (or strong). Again, a presupposition of an argument is a statement that is not a step in the argument (not even an unstated step), but that is implied by one or more premises of the argument.

Second, it is notoriously easy to think that an argument presupposes something when it really doesn't. Indeed, one of the most common errors of reasoning among well-educated people could be generalized as follows: "Your argument presupposes statement S (when the argument doesn't *necessarily* presuppose S), and since S is false or dubious, your argument is unsound." For example, consider the following argument:

> **74.** The choices a human being makes are influenced by his past because a person's upbringing limits the options that occur to him.

Through carelessness or inattention, one might suppose that the premise of this argument, "a person's upbringing limits the options that occur to him," implies *determinism* with respect to human acts—that is, the view that the past causally necessitates a *unique* future. (According to determinists, I may *think* I can choose either option A or option B, but factors in the past *cause* me to select A rather than B, or vice versa.) Note, however, that the premise of argument (74) doesn't really imply determinism. The premise says only that our choices are limited by our upbringing. For instance, a person deprived of an education might be unaware that *certain* alternatives are open to him (e.g., that he could enroll in a particular government program) and yet still have *other* alternatives to choose

---

Summary of Key Terms

An **enthymeme** is an argument with one or more unstated steps. A **step** is either a premise, a subconclusion, or the conclusion.

An **elaborated textbook form** includes the unstated steps in an argument whereas a **textbook form** does *not* include the unstated steps.

A **presupposition** of an argument is a statement that is *implied* by one or more premises of the argument but that is not itself a step in the argument.

from (e.g., get a job, live on the streets, or enter a life of crime). The lesson here is to take care when claiming that an argument presupposes something; be sure that a premise or premises really imply the statement in question.

The following exercise provides you with an opportunity to construct elaborated textbook forms for enthymemes.

◆ Exercise 3.4

Elaborated Textbook Forms Put the following arguments into *elaborated* textbook form, supplying the missing premises, subconclusions, or conclusion. Place brackets around each missing step to indicate that it does not appear in the original argument. Also indicate which steps support each subconclusion, and identify all the argument forms. To save laborious writing, use capital letters (as indicated) to stand for the statements comprising the arguments. (For the purposes of this exercise, your elaborated textbook forms should be *valid* as opposed to *strong*. Strong arguments will be discused in chapter 10.) (See the Answer Key for an illustration.)

* **1.** According to the contractual theory of fair pay, you are paid a fair wage if you are paid the wage you agreed to work for. But if the contractual theory of fair pay is true, then any woman who agrees to less pay than a man would receive for the same work is paid fairly (even if she agrees only because she desperately needs a job). So, the contractual theory of fair pay is not true. (C: The contractual theory of fair pay is true; W: Any woman who agrees to less pay than a man would receive for the same work is paid fairly)

  2. Since the Democrats are in office, we can expect another round of tax-and-spend politics. (D: The Democrats are in office; W: We can expect another round of tax-and-spend politics)

  3. If we employ economic sanctions, the poor will suffer. If we send in the troops, a lot of innocent people will be killed outright. Therefore, either the poor will suffer or a lot of innocent people will be killed outright. (E: We employ economic sanctions; P: The poor will suffer; T: We send in the troops; K: A lot of innocent people will be killed outright)

* **4.** Pacifism is not true. For if pacifism is true, then it is always wrong to kill. But if it is always wrong to kill, then it is wrong to kill even in self-defense. (P: Pacifism is true; K: It is always wrong to kill; S: It is wrong to kill even in self-defense)

  5. Either the American way of life is envied by no other country or capitalism is basically a good thing. Therefore, capitalism is basically a good thing. (A: The American way of life is envied by no other country; C: Capitalism is basically a good thing)

  6. One should believe in ESP only if it is supported by the total evidence. But ESP is not supported by the total evidence since the evidence for ESP is equally balanced by the evidence against it. It follows that one should not believe in ESP. (O: One should believe in ESP; E: ESP is supported by the total evidence; B: The evidence for ESP is equally balanced by the evidence against ESP)

* 7. Many people misrepresent their income when filling out their tax forms. But this is wrong. For if lying is wrong, then misrepresenting one's income on a tax form is wrong. (M: Misrepresenting one's income on a tax form is wrong; L: Lying is wrong)

8. If religion can be proved true, then religion is a form of science. If religion is a matter of faith, then religion is a form of superstition. Therefore, either religion is a form of science or religion is a form of superstition. (P: Religion can be proved true; S: Religion is a form of science; F: Religion is a matter of faith; R: Religion is a form of superstition)

9. Since the economy is in recession, the Federal Reserve Bank will lower the interest rate. (E: The economy is in recession; F: The Fed will lower the interest rate)

* 10. The so-called just-war theory is not credible. For it is credible only if war is an effective way to settle problems. But violence never solves problems; it simply creates worse ones. (J: The just-war theory is credible; W: War is an effective way to solve problems; V: Violence never solves problems; it simply creates worse ones)

11. If we keep our chemical weapons, we will set a bad example for other nations. If we give up our chemical weapons, we will make ourselves vulnerable. We will not set a bad example for other nations. Hence, we will make ourselves vulnerable. (K: We keep our chemical weapons; B: We will set a bad example for other nations; G: We give up our chemical weapons; V: We make ourselves vulnerable)

12. If the religion commonly referred to as Christian Science is true, then suffering is an illusion. But unfortunately, suffering is real. Accordingly, Christian Science is false. (T: Christian Science is true; S: Suffering is an illusion; R: Suffering is real)

* 13. Either it is perfectly moral to destroy the entire human race or nuclear war is wrong. I must conclude that nuclear war is wrong. (P: It is perfectly moral to destroy the entire human race; N: Nuclear war is wrong)

14. Either truth is relative to persons or it is objective (i.e., it is what it is regardless of anyone's opinion). Now, if truth is relative to persons, then the earth can be flat and round at the same time. Therefore, truth is objective. (R: Truth is relative to persons; O: Truth is objective; E: The earth can be flat and round at the same time)

15. Assuming that the Bible is infallible, children who curse their parents deserve the death penalty (Exodus 21:17). I can only conclude that the Bible is not infallible. (B: The Bible is infallible; D: Children who curse their parents deserve the death penalty)

* 16. Plainly, you are out of touch with public opinion. For if you intend to vote for Smith, then you want higher taxes. And if you want higher taxes, then you are out of touch with public opinion. (P: You are out of touch with public opinion; S: You intend to vote for Smith; T: You want higher taxes)

17. You should not drink coffee all day long. For you should drink coffee all day long only if you want to be dehydrated. (S: You should drink coffee all day long; D: You want to be dehydrated)

18. Either you are extroverted or you'll hate being a sales representative. But, obviously, you are introverted. Thus, although I would like to offer you the job, I am forced to conclude that you'll hate being a sales representative. (E: You are extroverted; H: You will hate being a sale representative; I: You are introverted)

* 19. Given that killing innocent people is murder, euthanasia is murder. And if euthanasia is murder, then it is wrong. Therefore, euthanasia is wrong. (K: Killing innocent people is murder; E: Euthanasia is murder; W: Euthanasia is wrong)

20. If I have a job, then I have money to spend but little time to enjoy myself. If I am unemployed, then I have time to enjoy myself but lack the requisite funds. Hence, either I have money to spend but little time to enjoy myself or I have time to enjoy myself but lack the requisite funds. (J: I have a job; M: I have money to spend but little time to enjoy myself; U: I am unemployed; T: I have time to enjoy myself but lack the requisite funds)

Notes

1. Howard Zinn, *A People's History of the United States: 1492–Present* (New York: HarperCollins, 1995), p. 460.
2. Alan Thein Durning, "World Spending on Ads Skyrockets," in Lester Brown, Hal Kane, and Ed Ayres, eds., *Vital Signs 1993: The Trends That Are Shaping Our Future* (New York: Norton, 1993), p. 80.
3. Stephen Jay Gould, "Sex, Drugs, Disasters, and the Dinosaurs," in Stephen R. C. Hicks and David Kelley, eds., *The Art of Reasoning: Readings for Logical Analysis* (New York: Norton, 1994), p. 145.
4. This argument is a summary of some of the main ideas in Gould, "Sex, Drugs, Disasters, and the Dinosaurs," pp. 144–152.
5. Some philosophers, such as the emotivists, have denied that "ought" judgments are either true or false. But I am here speaking from the standpoint of common sense. For a classic statement of the emotivist position, see Alfred Jules Ayer, *Language, Truth and Logic* (New York: Dover, 1952), pp. 102–120. This work was first published in 1935.
6. This example is borrowed from Anthony Weston, *A Rulebook for Arguments* (Indianapolis, IN: Hackett, 1987), p. 8. My textbook version of this argument also is borrowed from Weston.
7. There is a complication regarding strong arguments that will be discussed in chapter 10—namely, correct form does not ensure the strength of an argument.

Chapter 4

Logic and Language

In order to construct, analyze, and evaluate arguments *well*, one must pay close attention to language. Many errors of logic stem from a careless or imprecise use of language, and many misunderstandings about logic stem from misunderstandings about the nature of language. This chapter provides a series of clarifications about the relationships between logic and language.

4.1 Logic, Meaning, and Emotive Force

Let us begin by noting that the meaning of words can change over time. For example, in the King James Version of the Bible, first published in 1611, we read, "Let no man despise thy youth, but be thou an example of the believers, in word, in conversation, in charity, in spirit, in faith, in purity" (1 Tim. 4:12). But the word "conversation" did not then mean, as it now does, "talking together." Rather, it meant what we should call "conduct," and this shift in meaning has been taken into account in more recent translations.

The fact that the meaning of words can change over time raises some important questions about the nature of logic. For example, do logical relationships change as linguistic meaning changes? Let us examine this question briefly.

In chapter 1, we said that a statement is a sentence that has truth value (i.e., a sentence that is either true or false). And we said that arguments are composed of statements. Some logicians would prefer to say that arguments are composed of *propositions*—an interesting point that needs to be considered at this time. In order to grasp the concept of a proposition, consider the following sentences:

1. Grass is green.

2. *Das Gras ist grün.*

Sentence (2) translates sentence (1) into German. So, it is natural to suppose that (1) and (2) can be used to express the same truth (or falsehood). In other words, (1) and (2) can be used to express the same **proposition**—a proposition being a truth or a falsehood that may or may not be expressed in a sentence. Whereas a sentence (and hence a statement) belongs to a particular language, such as English or German, a proposition does not.

We can get at the distinction between statements and propositions in another way. Consider the following:

> 3. All squares are rectangles.

What if the meaning of the word "rectangle" were to change over time, so that in, say, the year 2096, "rectangle" were to mean what we now mean by the word "circle"? Such reversals of meaning do sometimes occur in the history of a language. Would (3) become false? Not if by (3) we mean the *proposition* (i.e., truth) currently expressed by the *sentence* "All squares are rectangles" (assuming the words are used in the standard way). Given the current, conventional meaning of the terms, no square can fail to be a rectangle. But it could indeed happen that the meaning of the word "rectangle" would change, in which case we would have to use a different sentence to express the proposition that we now express via the sentence "All squares are rectangles." So, once again, there seems to be a distinction between a sentence and the truth (or falsehood) it expresses, and hence a distinction between statements and propositions.

As noted previously, some logicians regard arguments as *sets of propositions* rather than as sets of statements. We will not here enter into the highly theoretical debate about whether arguments are best regarded as sets of statements or sets of propositions. We do not need to do this in order to grasp an important point about the nature of logic that arises from that debate. Logic is sometimes characterized as a "word game," as if logical reasoning were simply a matter of manipulating words, with *any* conclusion being possible provided that the players are sufficiently clever. However, once we see that logic is fundamentally about the connections between truths and falsehoods, it becomes apparent that logic is not merely a word game. Of course, we must use words to communicate truths and falsehoods (and hence arguments). But logical connections are fundamentally connections between those truths and falsehoods, and this is so whether we regard arguments as composed of statements or propositions.

Thus far, we have considered the fact that the meanings of words can change over time. But we also need to take note of the fact that statements often have *emotive force* as well as *cognitive meaning*. Failure to distinguish these two factors can easily lead to errors in logic. Consider the following statements:

> 4. There are approximately 20,000 homicides in the United States each year, with handguns being the most frequent instrument of death.

5. The number of murders per year in America is now so high that you've got to have a death wish to walk the streets, day or night. Every lunatic and every thug carries a "heater," just waiting to blow you away.

Statement (4) is designed primarily to provide information, whereas statement (5) is designed, at least in part, to express feelings or elicit an emotional response. To the extent that a sentence conveys information, it is said to have **cognitive meaning**. Words such as "approximately," "20,000," and "homicides" help to give (4) its cognitive meaning. To the extent that a sentence expresses or elicits emotions, it is said to have **emotive force**. Words and phrases such as "death wish," "lunatic," "thug," and "blow away" contribute heavily to the emotive force of (5). Of course, a single sentence can have both cognitive meaning and emotive force. Take (4), for instance. It conveys information, and so it has cognitive meaning, but the information conveyed is itself apt to provoke emotions such as fear or outrage; hence, (4) also has emotive force.

Logic mainly has to do with cognitive meaning—that is, with the logical connections between the informational content of statements. But one often needs to distinguish between the cognitive meaning and the emotive force of a sentence in order to understand its logical relationships, for emotionally loaded language is apt to interfere with logical insight. This can happen in at least two ways. First, loaded language can interfere with our attempt to understand the cognitive meaning of a sentence. We may be so carried away with or blinded by the feelings a sentence evokes that we fail to grasp its informational content precisely. Second, emotionally loaded language can blind us to the need for evidence. When our positive emotions are aroused, we may be inclined to accept a statement without argument even though an argument is definitely called for.

Let's consider some examples:

6. Should capital punishment be abolished? No way! The inmates on death row are nothing but human vermin.

7. You should ignore the company's arguments against the strike. Those arguments are nothing but capitalist propaganda aimed at workers.

The phrase "human vermin" in argument (6) is apt to have considerable emotive force. Vermin are small, troublesome animals (such as mice or rats), and we routinely kill vermin without qualms. So, if we accept the label "vermin" for the inmates on death row, we may readily accept the claim that they should be killed. But what exactly is the *cognitive meaning* of the premise "The inmates on death row are nothing but human vermin"? Perhaps this: "The inmates on death row are very bad people, morally speaking." Putting the premise into emotionally neutral terms helps us not to be swayed too easily by the emotive force of the original verbiage. It also helps us to think of relevant critical questions to ask about the argument. For example, do we really believe that *all* "very bad people" should be put to death? Can't a person be very bad, morally speaking, without committing murder? If so, does argument (6) in effect extend the death penalty to many persons who have never killed anyone? It would seem so.

Argument (7) illustrates the way in which the emotive force of language may blind us to the need for evidence. Once we've labeled someone's reasoning as propaganda, we are apt to dismiss it out of hand. After all, propaganda is a systematic form of indoctrination, often involving deliberate deception or distortion of the facts. But if arguments have been offered, then we need to explain *why* they are rightly labeled as propaganda. For example, wherein lies the deception or distortion of facts? Perhaps some of the company's arguments against the strike are sound, even if it *is* in the company's interest to avoid a strike.

To underscore the distinction between cognitive meaning and emotive force, let's consider two further arguments:

8. If we harvest the organs (hearts, liver, kidneys, etc.) of certain animals, such as baboons, and transplant the organs into humans who need them, many human lives will be saved. Therefore, we ought to harvest the organs of baboons and use the organs to save human lives.

9. Most of the people at the party were bureaucrats. Therefore, not surprisingly, the party was quite boring.

Argument (8) illustrates how a word with positive emotive force can be used to downplay certain negative facts or aspects of an issue. Literally speaking, "to harvest" means "to gather in a crop," an agricultural activity that has everyone's approval. But, of course, "harvesting" the vital organs of animals involves killing the animals, and this unsavory or questionable aspect of obtaining the organs is to some degree obscured by the emotive force of the word "harvest." Again, there is less likelihood of downplaying negative aspects of the case if we express the argument in more neutral language—for instance: "If we remove the vital organs of certain kinds of animals, such as baboons, and transplant their organs into humans who need them, the animals will die but many human lives will be saved. So, we ought to remove the vital organs of baboons and use the organs to save human lives."

As for argument (9), the word "bureaucrat" has a strong negative connotation. And the emotive force of the word may lead us to suppose that the premise of (9) supports its conclusion. But in less emotionally loaded language, the argument would look like this: "Most of the people at the party were government officials. So, the party was quite boring." Again, the more neutral language immediately suggests relevant critical questions: Are government officials on average less interesting than other people? If so, how is this known? What is the evidence? If not, then the premise seems to provide little support for the conclusion.

Thus far, we have emphasized that emotionally loaded language can interfere with logical insight. But this does not mean that arguments should always be expressed in emotionally neutral language. In fact, it is neither possible nor desirable to rid argumentative speech and writing of emotive force. For example, the information conveyed in the premises of almost any argument about a controversial moral issue is apt to have emotive force. Furthermore, it is often appropriate to engage the emotions of one's audience when defending an important belief or course of action. For example, it is entirely proper for a person to be stirred by a profound insight or by the revelation of serious injustice. "If you have a logical argument to back up a conclusion, there is nothing wrong with stating it in such a way that your audience will endorse it with their feelings as well as with their intellects."[1] The key point to remember, however, is that emotional verbiage should not be used as a substitute for sound arguments. If, upon "translating" an argument into emotionally neutral language, it becomes clear that the premises do not support the conclusion, then emotional language has replaced logic.

Let us here consider an argument that involves a skillful use of emotive language, taken from the famous "I Have a Dream" speech of Dr. Martin Luther King, Jr.:

> 10. I have a dream that one day this nation will rise up and live out the true meaning of its creed: "We hold these truths to be self-evident—that all men are created equal." I have a dream that one day, on the red hills of Georgia, the sons of former slaves and the sons of former slaveowners will be able to sit down together at the table of brotherhood. I have a dream that one day even the state of Mississippi, a state sweltering with the heat of injustice and oppression, will be transformed into an oasis of freedom and justice. I have a dream that my four little children will one day live in a nation where they will not be judged by the color of their skin but by the content of their character.[2]

While this passage has considerable emotive force, it does not substitute an appeal to the emotions for substantive argument. This can readily be seen if we restate its central argument in more neutral language: "All persons are created equal. So, people should not be judged by the color of their skin but by the content of their character."

The following exercise gives you some practice in distinguishing between cognitive meaning and emotive force.

◆ *Exercise 4.1*

Cognitive Meaning and Emotive Force　Each of the following arguments involves the use of emotionally loaded language. Put the arguments into textbook form, replacing the emotionally loaded verbiage with more neutral language. You may find it helpful to use a dictionary. (Do *not* fill in any missing steps.)

*　**1.** Sir, terrorism in the Middle East is one of the greatest threats to world peace today. Therefore, I strongly recommend that we neutralize the leaders of each of the main terrorist groups.

　　2. Since the Chinese have a lousy record on human rights, to give China "Most Favored Nation" status is simply to give in to injustice.

3. It's pretty ridiculous to tell people to drive their cars less often in order to reduce air pollution. After all, we can't go back to the caves.

* 4. What's wrong with playing the lottery? Nothing. Playing the lottery simply involves making a modest investment with the possibility of a substantial return.

5. As Senator Smith is a demagogue, she should be removed from office. No free country should indulge a demagogue.

6. Ever since Franklin D. Roosevelt introduced welfare programs into American life, this country has become increasingly socialistic. But Americans reject socialism. So, the sooner we eliminate welfare, the better.

* 7. Your reluctance to take this job is beyond comprehension. The pay is good and the hours are reasonable. Furthermore, the work of a sanitary removal engineer is of great importance.

8. I admit that American foreign policy suffered a temporary setback in Vietnam during the late 1960s and early 1970s. But it's the essence of a great country to turn temporary setbacks into stunning success stories. Hence, all the moaning and groaning about the American "defeat" in Vietnam is just blather.

9. The CIA has engaged in electoral sabotage in some countries. For example, the CIA dropped a bomb on the elections in Brazil one year by giving a total of $20 million to conservative candidates.

* 10. If you're against genetic engineering, you're against progress. So, why don't you just accept the fact that genetic engineering is here to stay?

11. Plato lured us into a mystical realm of ideas separated from physical reality. Aristotle taught us how to be logic choppers. Descartes tried to frighten us with the possibility that we might be dreaming all the time. Kant did nothing but take ordinary moral rules and put them into his own pompous and obscure technical language. Haven't philosophers done a lot for the world?

12. I utterly repudiate the notion that God will punish the immoral, for it is nothing but a deception used to frighten children and weak-minded adults.

* 13. Gun control is utterly misguided! Do not be deceived: There is a war on. And politicians who promote gun control are collaborating with the enemy. But the enemy will remain fully armed—you can bet on that!

14. The lyrics of many rock music hits are obscene. We must cleanse our society of this moral filth. That's why I think rock music should be banned.

15. While the right wing of the Republican party masquerades as the bastion of moral values, it has in fact done little but provide rationalizations for the selfishness of the yuppies. As for the Democrats, they are a loose-knit coalition of left-wing ideologues and social outcasts. So, cast your lot with the moderate Republicans.

* 16. The world is full of horror, shocking cruelty, grinding poverty, starvation, and debilitating illness. In short, we humans inhabit one gigantic disaster area. And yet, some people believe that a loving God controls the universe. It just goes to show: People believe what they want to believe regardless of the facts.

17. If a gang of criminals were systematically executing 1.6 million citizens in our society per year, decent folks would take a stand, using force of arms if necessary. But this is precisely the situation America is in given the current rate of abortion. Hence, I think that those who have bombed abortion clinics are fully justified.

18. The insanity plea is a joke. Here's how the process works: (a) Vicious murderers go out and kill innocent people in cold blood; (b) the police haul the sadistic killers into court, where they claim to have been temporarily insane at the time they performed their cruel deeds; and (c) the psychotic killers spend a few months being treated in a mental hospital, are miraculously "cured," and then are released so they can go out and massacre more law-abiding citizens.

*19. Son, you must not marry her! She's nothing but a selfish little Barbie Doll.

20. Would it be wrong to fight a nuclear war? Yes, of course. Just imagine it: millions of people vaporized in a few moments. Millions more, including children and the aged, literally melting from the intense heat. Of those who aren't killed immediately, many freeze to death as great clouds of dust block out the sun's rays. The rest perish in agony from the nasty effects of radioactive fallout.

4.2 Definitions

Ambiguous or vague language often interferes with clear thinking. A word is **ambiguous** if it has more than one meaning. For example, in the statement "I walked to the bank," the word "bank" might mean either a kind of financial institution or the edge of a river. A word is **vague** to the extent that it is imprecise, and a word is imprecise if there are "borderline cases" in which there is no way to determine whether the word applies. For example, how much does a person have to have in the way of material possessions in order to count as *rich*? We would all agree that millionaires are rich. But as we mention lesser sums, there would come a point at which we would not be sure whether a person who has such-and-such a net worth is rich.

Definitions play an important role in argument because definitions can be used to clear up ambiguity and to make vague terminology more precise. In this section, we will examine various types of definitions, focusing on those types that are most helpful in clarifying and sharpening arguments.

Types of Definitions

As we discuss the various types of definitions, we will focus mostly on *terms* rather than on words in general. For present purposes, a **term** *is a word or phrase that can serve as the subject of a statement.* For example, proper names, such as "Teddy Roosevelt," "New York City," and "Mount Rainier," are terms.

Common nouns, such as "tree," "mammal," "human," "event," and "chair," are also terms. Finally, certain descriptive phrases, such as "the 16th president of the United States" and "the furniture in my office," serve as terms. Words or phrases that are not terms include verbs, adverbs, prepositions, and conjunctions—for example, "to waltz," "slowly," "of," and "but." (Note that this definition of *term* is broader than the one used in chapter 2, in which *term* was defined as a word that stands for a class or collection of things.)

Intensional and Extensional Definitions

We can attain greater clarity about linguistic meaning if we distinguish between the extension and the intension of a term. The **extension** of a term consists of the set of things to which the term applies. Thus, the extension of the term "collie" consists of Lassie, Rex, Shep, and so on. The **intension** of a term consists of the properties a thing must have in order to be included in the term's extension. In the case of "collie," the intension includes such properties as being a Scottish sheep dog, being long-haired, and having a narrow head and pointed nose.

The **extension** of a term consists of the set of things to which the term applies.

The **intension** of a term consists of the properties a thing must have in order to be included in the term's extension.

As Wesley Salmon observes, we "may specify the meaning of a word through its extension, or we may specify its meaning through its intension. There is thus a basic distinction between extensional definitions and intensional definitions."[3] Extensional definitions themselves come in two basic types: nonverbal (or ostensive) and verbal. To give an **ostensive definition**, one specifies the meaning of a term by pointing to objects in its extension. Usually, we can't point to them all, but only to a representative sample. Thus, if you are trying to teach a child the meaning of the word "rock," you might point to a rock, utter the word "rock," then point to another rock, utter the word "rock" again, and so on. Of course, this type of definition is not without its problems. For instance, if the rocks you point to are all small, the child may fail to realize that large rocks are rocks as well.

Many times, however, we use *verbal* extensional definitions to specify the meaning of a term. We can do this by naming the members of the extension *individually* or *in groups*. An **enumerative definition** names the members of the extension *individually*. For example:

11. "Philosopher" means someone such as Socrates, Plato, Aristotle, Descartes, Kant, or Hegel.

Such a definition may be either partial or complete. Definition (11) is partial since we have not listed every philosopher. An enumerative definition is complete if all members of the extension are listed. For instance:

12. "Scandinavia" means Denmark, Norway, Sweden, Finland, Iceland, and the Faroe Islands.

Generally speaking, however, it is either impossible or impractical to list all the members of a term's extension. For example, it is impossible to list all the whole numbers because there are infinitely many of them. And it would be impractical for most purposes to define "Ohioan" by listing all the inhabitants of that state.

Another kind of verbal extensional definition names the members of the extension *in groups* (rather than individually). This is called a **definition by subclass**. For instance:

13. "Feline" means tigers, panthers, lions, leopards, cougars, cheetahs, bobcats, house cats, and the like.

Definitions by subclass can also be partial or complete. Definition (13) is partial since some classes (kinds or types) of felines have been omitted, such as jaguars and lynxes. Here is an example of a complete definition by subclass:

14. "North American marsupial" means an opossum.[4]

While extensional definitions are sometimes very useful, they also have their drawbacks. One drawback is this: Some terms cannot be defined extensionally because their extensions are empty. To illustrate:

15. "Unicorn" means a horselike creature having one long, straight horn growing from the center of its forehead.

Because unicorns are mythical creatures, the extension of the term "unicorn" is empty. Nevertheless, "unicorn" has a meaning that can be specified via an intensional definition, as above. A second drawback of extensional definitions is that they are often inadequate for the purposes of argument and rational dialogue. For example, suppose Smith and Jones are debating whether affirmative action is just. Jones requests a definition of "justice." Smith mentions a few examples of just social practices—for example, punishment only for the guilty, the progressive income tax, and the prohibition against poll taxes for voters. Even if Jones agrees that these practices are just, such an extensional definition is unlikely to facilitate an enlightening discussion of the justice of affirmative action. Careful and insightful thinking about controversial issues demands more precise terminology—hence the need for intensional definitions, which specify the meaning of a term by indicating the properties a thing must have in order to be included in the term's extension.

Lexical Definitions

A **lexical definition** *reports the conventional or established intension of a term.* Dictionary definitions are standard examples of lexical definitions. For example:

16. "Immanent" means existing or remaining within, that is, inherent.

17. "Imminent" means about to occur.[5]

Note that lexical definitions have truth value—that is, they are either true or false. They are true if they correctly report the established intension of the term and false if they fail to do this.

For the purposes of critical thinking, it is important to know when conventional meanings are at issue. To illustrate, in the middle of a philosophical conversation, someone may assert that no one knows what "truth" means. Well, thinking about the nature of truth may give rise to some puzzling questions, but since "truth" is a word in the English language, it has a conventional meaning. Surely no one would suggest that witnesses in court have *no idea* what a judge means when she admonishes them to "tell the truth, the whole truth, and nothing but the truth"!

Stipulative Definitions

A **stipulative definition** *specifies the intension of a term independently of convention or established use.* For various reasons, a writer or speaker may wish to introduce a new word into the language or give an old word a new meaning. For example, the word "double-dodge" currently has no generally accepted meaning. But we could make a proposal:

18. "Double-dodge" means the anticipatory movements people commonly make when they nearly collide (as when walking toward each other in a confined space) and are trying to avoid such collision.[6]

To illustrate: "Marsha and Fred nearly ran into each other in the hallway; but at the last moment they double-dodged and then came to a full stop, whereupon Fred burst into laughter." Thus, by introducing a stipulative definition, we can gain a shorthand means of expressing a complex idea.

Stipulative definitions are often useful in science. For example, in 1967, the physicist John Wheeler introduced the term "black hole" as shorthand for a star that has completely collapsed in on itself due to gravitational forces.[7] When first introduced, this definition was stipulative, for there was then no conventional use of "black hole" to refer to astronomical entities. (Of course, since 1967, "black hole" has come into common use, so that it now has a conventional meaning that can be reported in a *lexical* definition.)

Note that a stipulative definition is a *recommendation* or *proposal* to use a term in a certain manner. In other words, a stipulative definition has the form "Let's use term X to mean . . ." And since a recommendation or proposal is neither true nor false, a stipulative definition is neither true nor false. However, if the recommendation to use a term in a certain manner takes hold and becomes part of established use, then the stipulative definition turns into a lexical one, as is the case with "black hole." And as we have seen, lexical definitions are true (or false) because they report conventional meanings.

Precising Definitions

A **precising definition** *reduces the vagueness of a term by imposing limits on the conventional meaning.* It differs from a stipulative definition because it is not independent of the conventional meaning, but rather simply sharpens the conventional meaning, making it more exact. The definition of "valid argument" provided in chapter 1 is a good example of a precising definition. In ordinary English, the phrase "valid argument" is rather vague, so logicians sharpen it up to make it more useful in understanding and evaluating arguments. However, the logician's definition of "valid" is not stipulative, because the conventional meaning of "valid" is not ignored, but simply rendered more exact.

Precising definitions are common in both science and law. For example, the term "velocity" simply means "speed" in ordinary English, but physicists have given it a more precise meaning for their own purposes, namely:

19. "Velocity" means rate of motion in a particular direction.

Precising definitions are also essential in constructing workable laws. For instance, suppose Congress wishes to write legislation that provides a tax break for the poor. Since the word "poor" is quite vague, a precising definition will be needed if the law is to be applicable—for example, a family of four will count as poor if it has an annual income of $15,000 or less. Or again, suppose a law is being written to determine when care-givers may remove a patient from life-support systems (such as a respirator). A precising definition of "dead" will be helpful for this purpose, because presumably there are no objections to removing life-support systems if the patient is dead. But is a person "dead" when her heart has ceased to function? When she stops breathing? When she is permanently unconcious? When her brain has stopped functioning? For legal purposes, we obviously want to be rather precise about this. In most states, a person is now considered legally dead if he or she is "brain-dead." That is, a precising definition along these lines is used:

20. A "dead" person is one whose brain functions have permanently ceased.

And an electroencephalograph can be used to determine whether this definition applies in a given case.

Theoretical Definitions

A theoretical definition is an intensional definition that attempts to provide an adequate understanding of the thing(s) to which the term applies. For example, when philosophers or scientists disagree about the definition of important terms, such as "knowledge," "virtue," "mass," "temperature," "space," or "time," they are not disagreeing about the lexical definitions. Nor are they simply trying to stipulate meanings or make conventional meanings more precise. They are trying to reach a deeper and more accurate understanding of the nature of things. For example, in one of Plato's dialogues (entitled "Euthyphro"), the following definition is discussed:

>   21. "Right" means approved of by the gods.[8]

This definition is not lexical, not stipulative, and not precising. Rather, it attempts to provide deeper insight into the nature of moral rightness. Interestingly, however, within the dialogue, Plato has his hero, Socrates, object to this definition, pointing out that the same act may be approved by one god but disapproved by another god. Would such an act be both right and not right, according to definition (21)? Apparently so. Thus, within the dialogue, the definition is rejected as inadequate. (Because the ancient Greek religious context was polytheistic, the possibility of conflict between the gods was acknowledged as relevant by all parties in the dispute.)

The scientific definition of "temperature" as "the motion of molecules" also provides an example of a theoretical definition (the more rapid the motion of the molecules, the higher the temperature). Obviously, this definition of "temperature" could not be given prior to the development of molecular theory. Note that in offering this definition of "temperature," scientists are not reporting the conventional meaning. Nor are they offering a stipulative definition or making a conventional definition more precise. They are offering a theoretical definition intended to provide a deeper and more adequate understanding of the nature of temperature.

Definition by Genus and Difference

One technique for constructing definitions is worth special attention, because it can be applied in a wide variety of cases and because it is one of the best ways to eliminate ambiguity and vagueness. This is the method of definition by *genus* and *difference*. This method is often useful in constructing stipulative, precising, and theoretical definitions, but we will here focus primarily on lexical definitions.

To explain this method, we need some technical terms. First, as is customary among logicians, let us call *the word being defined* the **definiendum**, and let us call *the word or words that do the defining* the **definiens**. To illustrate:

22. "Puppy" means young dog.

Here, "puppy" is the *definiendum* while "young dog" is the *definiens*.

The **definiendum** is the word being defined.
The **definiens** is the word or words that do the defining.

Second, we need to define *proper subclass*. A class X is a **subclass** of another class Y given that every member of X is a member of Y. For example, the class of collies is a subclass of the class of dogs. Note, however, that the class of collies is also a subclass of itself. By contrast, class X is a **proper subclass** of class Y given that X is a subclass of Y but Y has members X lacks. Thus, the class of collies is a *proper* subclass of the class of dogs, but the class of collies is not a *proper* subclass of the class of collies.

Now we can say that the **species** is simply a *proper subclass* of the **genus**. This use of the terms differs from the use they are given in biology. For example, in logic (unlike biology), we may speak of the genus dog and the species puppy, of the genus animal and the species dog, or of the genus animal and the species mammal. The **difference** (or specific difference) is the attribute that distinguishes the members of a given species from the members of other species in the same genus. For example, suppose sibling is the genus and sister is the species. Then the difference is the attribute of being female, which distinguishes sisters from the species brother, which also belongs to the genus sibling. Or suppose dog is the genus and puppy is the species. Then the difference is the attribute of being young, which distinguishes puppies from other species in the same genus—for example, adult dogs.

The relationship between genus, species, and difference is shown in the accompanying diagram, with the rectangles standing for classes. Again, a species is a proper subclass of the genus. The difference is the attribute that distinguishes the members of a given species from the members of other species belonging to the same genus.

GENUS (Example: horse)

SPECIES: Filly

DIFFERENCE: Young female

SPECIES: Colt

DIFFERENCE: Young male

One constructs a definition by genus and difference as follows. First, choose a term that is more general than the term to be defined. This term names the genus. Second, find a word or phrase that identifies the attribute that distinguishes the species in question from other species in the same genus. Here are some examples:

Species		Difference	Genus
"Stallion"	means	male	horse
"Kitten"	means	young	cat
"Banquet"	means	elaborate	meal
"Lake"	means	large	inland body of standing water

In many cases, of course, the difference is a rather complicated attribute that takes many words to describe. For example:

23. "Dinosaur" means any of a group of extinct reptiles of the Mesozoic Era, with four limbs and a long, tapering tail.[9]

The genus here is reptile, and the rest of the definition specifies the difference.

A definition by genus and difference is inadequate if it fails to meet certain criteria. Let us now examine the six standard criteria for evaluating definitions by genus and difference.

Criterion 1: A definition should not be obscure, ambiguous, or figurative.

To illustrate:

24. "Desire" is the actual essence of man, insofar as it is conceived, as determined to a particular activity by some given modification of itself.[10]

This definition employs obscure technical jargon. And since the point of defining a term is to clarify its meaning, one should use the simplest words possible in the definiens.

Sometimes, a definiens contains a word that, in the context, has two possible meanings. Then the definition is ambiguous:

25. "Faith" means true belief.

Does "true belief" here mean "sincere or genuine belief," or does it mean "belief that is true as opposed to false"? Either meaning seems possible in the context of a definition of "faith," so the definition is ambiguous. Note, however, that many words have multiple meanings listed in the dictionary, and this mere fact does not render the words ambiguous in a given case. For instance, the word "store" may mean "a place where merchandise is sold," as in, "I bought a shirt at the store"; or it may mean "to provide for a future need," as in, "Squirrels store nuts for the winter." But the context usually indicates which of the meanings is relevant. It is only when the context does not make clear which meaning is relevant that ambiguity occurs.

Figurative (or metaphorical) definitions are generally either obscure or ambiguous. For example:

> 26. "Art" is the stored honey of the human soul, gathered on wings of misery and travail.[11]

Definition (26) may be suggestive and interesting, but as is common with figurative language, it invites multiple interpretations and so is ambiguous.

> Criterion 2: A definition should not be circular.

A definition is circular if the definiendum (or some grammatical form thereof) appears in the definiens. To illustrate:

> 27. "Metaphysics" means the systematic study of metaphysical issues.

Of course, if one doesn't know the meaning of the term "metaphysics," one isn't likely to find a definition employing the word "metaphysical" informative. Note, however, that depending on the context, some kinds of circularity in definitions are not problematic. For instance, suppose my audience knows what a triangle is but does not know what an acute triangle is. In such a context, I might define "acute triangle" as follows:

> 28. "Acute triangle" means any triangle in which each of the three angles is less than 90 degrees.

This type of circularity is harmless because (in the context) the part of the definiendum that appears in the definiens (namely, "triangle") is not what needs to be defined.

> Criterion 3: A definition should not be negative if it can be affirmative.

For example:

> 29. A "mineral" is a substance that is not an animal and not a vegetable.
> 30. "Mammal" means an animal that is not a reptile, not an amphibian, and not a bird.

A relatively affirmative definition is more informative than a relatively negative one and is therefore to be preferred. However, it is impossible to give affirmative definitions in every case. For instance, a typical dictionary definition of "geometrical point" is "something that has position in space but no size or shape."

And the word "spinster" is defined as "an elderly woman who has never married." These definitions would be hard to improve on, though they are largely negative.

Criterion 4: Definitions should not be too wide (or too broad).

A definition is too wide (or too broad) if the definiens applies to objects outside the extension of the definiendum. For instance:

31. "Bird" means animal having wings.

Taken as a lexical definition, (31) is too wide, since bats and some types of insects have wings, and yet neither bats nor insects are birds.

In order to determine whether a definition is too wide, we need to know the context and/or type of definition. For example, in the context of the formal study of logic, the following definition is too wide:

32. A "valid" argument is one such that the premises support the conclusion.

In the context of the study of logic, definition (32) is too wide because the definiens also applies to strong arguments. But (32) may not be too wide if it is taken as a lexical definition, designed to report the conventional meaning of "valid."

Criterion 5: Definitions should not be too narrow.

A definition is too narrow if the definiens fails to apply to some objects in the extension of the definiendum. To illustrate:

33. "Bird" means feathered animal that can fly.

Taken as a lexical definition, (33) is too narrow because some birds cannot fly—for example, penguins, kiwis, ostriches, and cassowaries.

To determine whether a definition is too narrow, we need to know the context and/or type of definition. For example, in the context of the formal study of logic, the following definition is too narrow:

34. A "valid" argument is one that (a) has only true premises and (b) is such that its conclusion cannot be false while its premises are true.

This definition is too narrow because the definiens does not apply to valid arguments with false premises. Taken as a lexical definition, (34) is incorrect because it is far more precise than the established meaning of "valid." But (34) would probably be too narrow from this perspective as well, because in ordinary English, "valid" is applied to both strong inductive arguments and valid deductive arguments.

As you may have realized, the same definition can be both too wide and too narrow. For example:

35. "Bird" means animal that can fly.

On the one hand, this definition is too wide, because bats and certain insects are not birds, but they are animals that can fly. On the other hand, this definition is too narrow since the definiens does not apply to penguins, kiwis, ostriches, and so on, and yet these animals are birds.

Criterion 6: A definition is flawed if the definiens picks out the right extension via attributes that are unsuitable relative to the context or purpose.

For example, suppose we are trying to construct a lexical definition of the word "triangle." The following definition would violate Criterion 6:

36. "Triangle" means my favorite geometrical figure.

Since triangles are my favorite geometrical figure, the definiens applies to the correct extension, namely, the members of the class of triangles. But the attribute of "being my favorite geometrical figure" is unsuitable to the context of forming a lexical definition. What would be suitable is the attribute English speakers implicitly agree to mean by the term "triangle," namely, "being a closed-plane figure with three angles (or three sides)."

Because Criterion 6 is not always easy to apply, let us consider some further examples. For instance:

37. "Seven" means the number of days in a week.

Since there are indeed seven days in a week, the definiens picks out the right extension. But taken as a lexical definition, this definition is flawed, because it does not make reference to the attribute associated with established usage, namely, "being one more than six." (In principle, one could know the ordinary meaning of "seven" without knowing how many days there are in a week.) Furthermore, taken as a theoretical definition, (37) is flawed, because it fails to pick out attributes relevant for mathematical purposes—for example, that of "being a whole number between six and eight."

If we translate the proposal of certain ancient Greek philosophers into English, we get the following definition of "human":

38. "Human" means featherless biped.

Now, let's assume that this definition is neither too narrow nor too wide—that is, that all and only humans lack feathers *and* normally walk upright on two legs. Still, if (38) is taken as a lexical definition, it violates Criterion 6. As evidence, we can cite the fact that the attribute of "being a featherless biped" is not alluded to in dictionary definitions of the term "human." We might add that the attribute seems unsuitable if the definition is taken to be theoretical in nature, for (38) surely fails to provide any noteworthy insight into the nature of human beings.

To sum up, definitions can be used to eliminate ambiguity and vagueness. Both extensional and intensional definitions can be used for these purposes, but certain kinds of intensional definitions (e.g., stipulative, lexical, precising, and theoretical definitions) are especially useful in argumentation. The method of definition by genus and difference can often be used to construct stipulative, lexical, precising, and theoretical definitions; hence, this method is very useful for the purposes of constructing and evaluating arguments. Finally, definitions by genus and difference must conform to the six criteria set down in this section.

The following exercises give you an opportunity to apply the concepts introduced in this section.

◆ Exercise 4.2

Part A: Types of Definitions   Match the letter of the item on the right that best characterizes the type of definition on the left.

_____ * **1.** Let us use the word "grellow" to mean the color of things that are either green or yellow.

_____ **2.** "Vixen" means female fox.

_____ **3.** "Southern state" means Alabama, Arkansas, Georgia, Louisiana, Mississippi, North Carolina, South Carolina, Tennessee, Texas, and Virginia.

_____ * **4.** "Tall man" means male human over 6 feet in height.

_____ **5.** "Living things" means plants and animals.

_____ **6.** "Motorized vehicle" means cars, motorcycles, trucks, and the like.

_____ * **7.** "Tome" means large book.

_____ **8.** A "wrong act" is one that fails to promote the general happiness.

_____ **9.** "Aunt" means sister of one's father or mother.

_____ *__10.__ A "deductively sound argument" is one that (a) has only true premises and (b) is valid (i.e., its conclusion cannot be false while its premises are true).

_____ **11.** "Religion" means Hinduism, Christianity, Judaism, Buddhism, Islam, Sikhism, and the like.

A. Enumerative definition

B. Definition by subclass

C. Lexical definition

D. Stipulative definition

E. Precising definition

F. Theoretical definition

_____ 12. Let us use the term "zangster" to mean a person who steals zirconium.

_____ *13. "Human" means rational animal.

_____ 14. "Subatomic particles" means electrons, protons, neutrons, quarks, and the like.

_____ 15. "Miracle" means an event that (a) is an exception to a law of nature and (b) is brought about by the decision of a divine being.

Part B: Lexical Definitions   Identify one defect in each of the following definitions, using the six criteria for definition by genus and difference:

1. Obscure, ambiguous, or figurative
2. Circular
3. Unnecessarily negative
4. Too wide
5. Too narrow
6. Unsuitable attribute

Explain your answer briefly. For example, if you say a definition is too narrow, give an example that illustrates your point. Assume that the definitions are meant to be lexical definitions. You may find it helpful to use a dictionary.

* 1. "Penguin" means bird that can't fly, but not an ostrich, cassowary, or emu.

2. "Quadrilateral" means a closed-plane figure having four sides of equal length and four right (i.e., 90-degree) angles.

3. "Marsupial" means an Australian mammal.

* 4. An "octagon" is a figure shaped like a stop sign.

5. "Square" means a closed-plane figure having four right (i.e., 90-degree) angles.

6. "Right" means not wrong.

* 7. A "triangle" is a closed-plane figure having three sides of equal length.

8. "Jellyfish" means an animal without a spine.

9. "Wine" means a beverage made from grapes.

* 10. An "ellipse" is a cross between a circle and a rectangle.

11. "Coward" means a spineless person.

12. "Wolf" is defined as a flesh-eating mammal having four legs.

* 13. "Homosexual" means a man who is erotically attracted exclusively (or at least primarily) to other men.

14. "Dog" means a flesh-eating domestic mammal similar to a wolf but having specifically doglike characteristics.

15. A "murderer" is a human who has killed another human.

* 16. A "wealthy person" is one who has as much money as Bill Gates or Donald Trump.

17. "Camel" means ship of the desert.

18. "Snake" means a widely feared animal that symbolizes evil or deception in many cultures.

* 19. "Evil" is defined as the darkness that lies within the human soul.

20. "Wife" means spouse who is not a husband.

Part C: More Lexical Definitions   Evaluate the following definitions, using the six criteria for definition by genus and difference:

1. Obscure, ambiguous, or figurative   4. Too wide

2. Circular   5. Too narrow

3. Unnecessarily negative   6. Unsuitable attribute

Explain your answer briefly. For example, if you say a definition is too narrow, give an example that illustrates your point. Assume that the definitions are meant to be lexical definitions. If a definition meets all six criteria, simply write "OK" in the blank space.

* 1. "Blue" means having a bluish color.

2. "Fifty" means the number of states in the U.S.A.

3. "Rectangle" means a plane figure having four equal sides and four right (i.e., 90-degree) angles.

* 4. Time is the great container into which we pour our lives.

5. "Wise person" means one who displays wisdom.

6. A "trapezoid" is a closed-plane figure that is neither a triangle nor a rectangle nor a circle nor an ellipse.

* 7. "Oligarchy" means a form of government in which the ruling power belongs to a few persons.

8. A "circle" is a closed-plane figure bound by a single curved line, every point of which is equally distant from the point at the center of the figure.

9. "Atheist" means person who believes that there is no God.

* 10. "Spherical" means shaped like the earth.

11. A "trumpet" is a brass wind instrument with three valves.

12. A "painting" is a picture made with water colors.

* 13. "Reptile" means snake.

14. A "scrupulous person" is one who has scruples.

15. "God" means a being Billy Graham often speaks about.

Part D: Precising Definitions   Evaluate the following as precising definitions *in the context of the formal study of logic,* using the six criteria for definition by genus and differ-ence. These definitions presuppose that you know the definition of "argument," so they should not be evaluated as circular simply on the grounds that the definiens contains the word "argument" (or a pronoun that refers to "argument").

* **1.** An *inductively sound* argument is an argument that is strong, has only true premises, and has a true conclusion.

 2. A *deductively unsound* argument is an argument that has at least one false premise.

 3. A *valid* argument is one in which the conclusion is validly deduced from the premises.

* **4.** A *strong* argument is one in which the premises support the conclusion.

 5. A *valid* argument is one in which there is an airtight connection between the premises and the conclusion.

 6. *Logic* is the study of tests for the validity and invalidity of arguments.

* **7.** A *valid* argument is one in which the premises lead to the conclusion.

 8. An *invalid* argument is one having true premises and a false conclusion.

 9. An *inductively unsound* argument is one that either (a) is weak or (b) has at least one false premise.

* **10.** A *weak* argument is one such that if its premises were true, then the negation of its conclusion would *more likely be true* than its conclusion.

Part E: Theoretical Definitions Match the definiendum on the left with the *best* definiens available on the right. These definitions are theoretical in type.

_____ **1.** Courage

_____ **2.** Justice

_____ **3.** Faith

_____ **4.** Evidence

_____ **5.** Wisdom

_____ **6.** Virtues

_____ **7.** Belief

_____ **8.** Suspending judgment

_____ **9.** Vices

_____ **10.** Disbelief

A. Confidence that a proposition is true

B. A tendency to perform acts the agent considers dangerous but worth the risk

C. Knowledge of which ends are worth achieving and of how to achieve them

D. Traits that hinder one from living well

E. Considerations relevant to the truth of the proposition in question

F. Confidence that a proposition is false

G. Believing in spite of factors that may tend to cause doubt

H. Giving each individual his or her due

I. Traits enabling one to live well

J. A lack of confidence in the truth of a proposition combined with a lack of confidence in its falsehood

4.3 *Using Definitions to Evaluate Arguments*

In the absence of good intensional definitions, two negative results are likely to occur: equivocation and merely verbal disputes. **Equivocation** occurs when a word (or phrase) is used with more than one meaning in an argument but the validity of the argument depends on the word's being used with the same meaning throughout. For example:

> 39. Only man is rational. But no woman is a man. Hence, no woman is rational.

Here, of course, the word "man" is used with two different meanings. In the first premise, it means "humans," while in the second, it means "male humans." When we rewrite the argument making the two meanings explicit, the invalidity is apparent:

> 40. Only humans are rational. No woman is a male human. So, no woman is rational.

The use of the single word "man" in argument (39) gives it a superficial appearance of validity. But our rewrite, argument (40), indicates that in reality, the two meanings of the word "man" destroy the logical linkage between premises and conclusion. Etymologically, "equivocate" comes from two Latin words, one meaning "equal" and one meaning "voice" or "word." When one equivocates, one makes it sound as if the same word (or phrase) is being used *with the same meaning* throughout the argument, when, it fact, more than one meaning is present.

Let's consider another example of equivocation:

> 41. John has a lot of pride in his work. He is already a superb craftsman and he is constantly improving. But, unfortunately, pride is one of the seven deadly sins. So, John is guilty of one of the seven deadly sins.

Here, the equivocation is on the word "pride." In its first occurrence, "pride" means "justifiable self-respect." But in its second occurrence, "pride" means "arrogance" or "an exaggerated opinion of oneself." Clearly, these two meanings differ. And it is plainly invalid to argue that John has grave moral faults simply on the grounds that he has a justifiable self-respect with regard to his work.

A **merely verbal dispute** occurs when two (or more) disputants appear to disagree (i.e., appear to make logically conflicting assertions) but an ambiguous word (or phrase) hides the fact that the disagreement is unreal. Here is an example:

> 42. Mr. X: Bob is a good man. I can always count on him to do his job. And he doesn't make excuses. I wish I had more employees like him.
>
> Ms. Y: I disagree. Bob is not a good man. He has been divorced four times, he drinks too much, and he is addicted to gambling.

For Mr. X, "good man" means "good man on the job"—that is, a person who does quality work efficiently. But for Ms. Y, "good man" means "a morally virtuous person." Accordingly, there is no real disagreement here between Mr. X and Ms. Y, for there is no logical conflict between the statement that *Bob does quality work efficiently* and the statement that *Bob is not morally virtuous*. Even if Bob does have some moral vices, it may still be true that he is a good employee.

A merely verbal dispute is similar to equivocation in that a double meaning is involved. But a merely verbal dispute necessarily involves *two or more people* who misunderstand each other due to the ambiguity of a key word or phrase, whereas equivocation occurs when an ambiguity destroys the validity of an argument (and no dialogue partner need be involved). The American philosopher and psychologist William James provides a striking and humorous example of a merely verbal dispute:

> Some years ago, being with a camping party in the mountains, I returned from a solitary ramble to find every one engaged in a ferocious . . . dispute. The *corpus* of the dispute was a squirrel—a live squirrel supposed to be clinging to one side of a tree-trunk; while over against the tree's opposite side a human being was imagined to stand. This human witness tries to get sight of the squirrel by moving rapidly round the tree, but no matter how fast he goes, the squirrel moves as fast in the opposite direction, and always keeps the tree between himself and the man, so that never a glimpse of him is caught. The resultant . . . problem now is this: *Does the man go round the squirrel or not?* He goes round the tree, sure enough, and the squirrel is on the tree; but does he go round the squirrel? In the unlimited leisure of the wilderness, discussion had been worn threadbare. Everyone had taken sides, and was obstinate. . . .[12]

At this point, the dispute can be summed up as follows:

43. Side 1: The man goes around the squirrel.
　　　Side 2: No. The man does not go around the squirrel.

James goes on to explain how he resolved the dispute:

> Mindful of the scholastic adage that whenever you meet a contradiction you must make a distinction, I immediately sought and found one, as follows: "Which party is right," I said, "depends on what you practically mean by 'going round' the squirrel. If you mean passing from the north of him to the east, then to the south, then to the west, and then to the north of him again, obviously the man does go round him, for he occupies these successive positions. But if on the contrary you mean being first in front of him, then on the right of him, then behind him, then on his left, and finally in front again, it is quite as obvious that the man fails to go round him, for by the compensating movements the squirrel makes, he keeps his belly turned toward the man all the time, and his back turned away.[13]

Here, the dispute is merely verbal, due to the ambiguity in the phrase "going round." The disputants fail to communicate because they do not realize that their assertions are logically compatible. There is an appearance of contradiction, but no real logical conflict is present.

Consider one last example of a merely verbal dispute:

> 44. Mr. X: Modern physics has shown that medium-sized physical objects, such as bricks, walls, and desks, are not solid.
>
> Ms. Y: How absurd! If you think this wall isn't solid, just try putting your fist through it, buster.[14]

Mr. X presumably has in mind the fact that according to modern physics, medium-sized physical objects are composed of tiny particles—atoms, protons, electrons, quarks, and the like. And, according to modern physics, these particles are not packed tightly together. Rather, the spaces between the particles are vast relative to the size of the particles (just as the spaces between the sun and the planets in the solar system are vast relative to the size of these bodies). In a nutshell, the two parties talk past each other because Mr. X uses "solid" to mean "dense or tightly packed" while Ms. Y uses "solid" to mean "hard to penetrate."

At this point, we need to consider another error in reasoning that is sometimes confused with the merely verbal dispute. This is the improper use of persuasive definitions. A **persuasive definition** is one *slanted (or biased) in favor of a particular conclusion or point of view*. In practice, persuasive definitions often amount to an attempt to settle an argument by verbal fiat. Here's an example:

> 45. "Affirmative action" means reverse discrimination. But discrimination is always wrong. So, affirmative action is wrong.

Obviously, by defining "affirmative action" as "reverse discrimination," one puts a particular slant on matters. But this definition hardly characterizes a useful concept for the purposes of rational discussion. Notice that a person who did not know the conventional meaning of "affirmative action" would not get a clear grasp of the concept from this definition. A better definition of "affirmative action" would be "preferential treatment of disadvantaged groups." This definition enables us to focus on the heart of the issue: Should disadvantaged groups receive special treatment?

Persuasive definitions sometimes have considerable rhetorical power, and this power is often exploited in politics. Here's a typical example:

> 46. I will speak frankly and without the verbal fuzziness so typical of my opponent. "National health care" means socialized medicine. That's why I oppose it and why you should, too.

This argument may well succeed in associating national health care with something an audience fears or disapproves of, namely, socialism. But it is hardly a fair and neutral definition that will enable both sides to confront the issues squarely.

Persuasive definitions generally violate one or more of the six criteria for definition by genus and difference. Thus, they may be obscure, too wide, or too narrow, or they may involve attributes that are unsuitable relative to the context or purpose. The most common failing is this: When the context calls for a neutral (unbiased) definition of a key term for the purposes of rational discussion, then a persuasive definition makes reference to an attribute that is not suited to the purpose. A definition that slants things in favor of one side in the dispute is obviously not a definition acceptable to all parties in the dispute.

The use of persuasive definitions is sometimes confused with the phenomenon of the merely verbal dispute. This is the case especially when disputants trade persuasive definitions slanted in favor of opposing points of view. For example, a political conservative may define "conservative" as "a liberal who has wised up." In retaliation, the liberal may define "conservative" as "a person bent on protecting his own privileges." But the use of persuasive definitions differs from the merely verbal dispute precisely because definitions are provided. By contrast, in a merely verbal dispute, different meanings are employed but no definitions are provided.

It should be noted that it is not necessarily an error in reasoning to employ persuasive definitions. The error comes only when persuasive definitions are substituted for substantive argument. This error can be exposed by restating the argument without using any persuasive definitions. If such a restatement is an argument whose premises do not support its conclusion, then an error in reasoning has occurred. But such a summary may reveal a valid or strong argument, with plausible premises, that does not depend on persuasive definitions. In that case, persuasive definitions may well have been used appropriately as a rhetorical device. Persuasive definitions can be both humorous and insightful, and thus legitimate rhetorical tools, provided they are not substituted for arguments where arguments are needed.

The following exercises provide you with some practice in identifying equivocation, merely verbal disputes, and the misuse of persuasive definitions.

◆ Exercise 4.3

Part A: Equivocation   Each of the following arguments is invalid due to a word or phrase that has a double meaning. Identify the ambiguous word or phrase in each argument, and succinctly describe the double meaning involved. (It is a common tendency to ramble on in an attempt to identify such double meanings. Avoid this. Instead, provide two brief definitions of the relevant word or phrase.) You may find it helpful to use a dictionary. (See the Answer Key for an illustration.)

* 1. A boring job at the minimum wage is better than nothing. But nothing is better than going to heaven. So, a boring job at the minimum wage is better than going to heaven.

  2. If a tree falls in the forest and no one is there to hear it fall, does it make a sound? Modern science says, "Yes, for there are vibrations in the air even if no humans are nearby." But this is easily refuted. Sound is something heard. That's really quite obvious when you think about it. So, if no one was there to hear the sound, there was no sound.

3. We are in the dark because the light bulb burnt out. But if we are in the dark, then we are ignorant. Therefore, we are ignorant.

* 4. The Bible says you need faith, but lots of people disagree with the Bible on this point. Unfortunately, these folks just aren't thinking straight. The fact that you go out to your car in the morning shows you have faith it's going to start. And the fact that you pull out of the driveway shows you have faith the car won't fall apart on the way to work. Everybody needs faith.

5. A basketball player is a person. A male basketball player is a male person. Consequently, a short male basketball player is a short male person.

6. When the recession hit us, I lowered your salary by 20 percent. You moved from $30,000 to $24,000. I know that was tough, and I'm sorry about it. But I have some good news. Things are looking up again. We're showing a profit. So, I'm going to raise your salary by 20 percent. I hope you appreciate this. I lowered your salary by 20 percent; now I'm raising it by 20 percent. So, you see, this policy will bring you back up to where you were before the recession hit.

* 7. People nowadays say they can't believe in the Christian religion. They say they can't believe in miracles. Is it that they can't or that they won't? They believe in the miracles of modern science, don't they? You bet they do. They believe in vaccines, space-walks, and heart transplants. They believe in fiber optics, laser surgery, and genetic engineering. They can believe in miracles, all right. They just don't want to believe in the Christian miracles.

8. An ant is an animal. And an Australian ant is an Australian animal. There-fore, a large Australian ant is a large Australian animal.

9. You are a free creature. So, you are free to do good or evil. But if you are free to do evil, then you should not be punished for doing evil. Hence, you should not be punished for doing evil.

* 10. See how foolish and inconsistent it is to say, "I would prefer not to be, than to be unhappy." The man who says, "I prefer this to that," chooses something; but "not to be" is not something, but nothing. Therefore, you cannot in any way choose rightly when you choose something that does not exist. You say that you wish to exist although you are unhappy, but that you ought not to wish this. What, then, ought you to have willed? You answer, "Not to exist." But if you ought to have willed not to exist, then "not to exist" is better. However, what does not exist cannot be better; therefore, you should not have willed this.
—St. Augustine, *On Free Choice of the Will*, trans. Anna S. Benjamin and L. H. Hackstaff (Indianapolis, IN: Bobbs-Merrill, 1964), p. 104

11. I have a duty to do what is right. And I have a right to run for office. Hence, I have a duty to run for office.

12. We can all agree that sick people should not be punished for displaying the symptoms of their sickness. For instance, you shouldn't punish a flu victim for having a high fever. But, you know, a person has to be sick to commit murder. Murder is a symptom of a sick mind. Thus, contrary to popular belief, murder-ers should not be punished.

13. Alice is crazy. She'll do anything to get a laugh! Of course, if she is crazy, then she should be put in a mental hospital. So, Alice should be put in a mental hospital.

14. A boxer is a human being. A 6-foot-tall boxer is a 6-foot-tall human being. Accordingly, an old 6-foot-tall boxer is an old 6-foot-tall human being.

15. It is good to act natural. And it is natural for boys to fight. Therefore, it is good for boys to fight.

Part B: Merely Verbal Disputes and Persuasive Definitions   The following brief dialogues provide examples of either merely verbal disputes or the improper use of persuasive definitions. If a persuasive definition is employed, explain its weakness in terms of the six criteria for definitions. Remember, a persuasive definition occurs *only when* an explicit definition of the relevant word or phrase appears. (And, of course, not every explicit definition is persuasive.) In the case of a merely verbal dispute, identify the word or phrase that has a double meaning, and provide a definition for both meanings. (*Note:* A merely verbal dispute is similar to equivocation in that a double meaning is involved, but a merely verbal dispute necessarily involves *two or more people* who misunderstand each other due to the ambiguity of a key word or phrase. Equivocation occurs when an ambiguity destroys the validity of an argument, and no dialogue partner need be involved.)

* 1. **Ms. Y:** Homework is sheer agony!

   Mr. X: Oh, come on. You love to do your logic homework.

   Ms. Y: Well, yes, but logic is fun. I can't really count logic assignments as homework.

2. **Ms. Y:** Pacifists are the only hope for the future of the human species.

   Mr. X: I disagree. "Pacifist" means a wimp who's afraid to stand up for his own rights. I see nothing hopeful about that.

3. **Ms. Y:** Secular humanism is a religion, for it is just as much a worldview or way of life as Judaism or Christianity. And yet, secular humanists claim to be free of religious bias.

   Mr. X: No. Secular humanism is not a religion. After all, secular humanists deny the supernatural altogether.

* 4. **Mr. X:** The Republican party will be the salvation of this country.

   Ms. Y: Give me a break! The "Republican party" is best defined as the party whose primary concern is to protect the wealth of its own members. The only "country" Republicans will ever save is the country club.

5. **Mr. X:** I don't care for Reverend Boggs myself. Judging from his sermons, I don't even think he is a Christian. He denies the doctrine of the Trinity and the deity of Christ. Once he even preached a sermon claiming that heaven and hell are entirely mythical.

   Ms. Y: How can you say that! Reverend Boggs is a fine Christian man. He is genuinely loving, tolerant of others, and helps people in every way he can.

6. **Ms. Y:** This canyon is really beautiful. Look at these sweeping lines of natural geometry! And the background is the brightest blue sky imaginable.

Mr. X: On the contrary, this canyon is nothing but a big, ugly hole in the ground.

Ms. Y: You are mistaken. The word "beautiful" simply means enjoyable for the speaker to see or hear, and therefore the canyon is beautiful since I *do* enjoy looking at it.

* **7. Ms. Y:** Most atheists are inconsistent. On the one hand, they say there is no God, but then they turn around and say that certain things are right and certain things are wrong.

Mr. X: Well, I'm an atheist and I don't get your point. Stealing and murder can be wrong whether or not there is a God.

Ms. Y: No way. "Wrong" simply means disapproved of by God. So, the minute you say something is wrong, you imply that God exists. I rest my case.

8. Mr. X: Our society is losing its reverence for life. For example, euthanasia is widely practiced in American hospitals.

Ms. Y: You are misinformed. Euthanasia is illegal, and in our litigious society, doctors have a tremendous motivation to avoid illegal procedures.

Mr. X: But many patients are taken off respirators when their hearts are still pumping. Then they stop breathing and die. *That* is euthanasia.

Ms. Y: No, it's not euthanasia, because the electroencephalograms of the patients indicate that they were dead before the respirators were removed.

9. Ms. Y: We are not free, because our behavior is determined by our genes in conjunction with environmental influences.

Mr. X: I disagree. This is a free country. Americans are a free people!

* **10. Ms. Y:** Moral codes vary from society to society. For example, polygamy is "right" in some societies but "wrong" in others.

Mr. X: No. Polygamy is never right. It is degrading to women.

11. Mr. X: I know that I am reincarnated.

Ms. Y: Nobody can know that.

Mr. X: I disagree. "To know" means to believe with all your heart. And I believe with all my heart that I am reincarnated. Therefore, I know that I am reincarnated.

12. Ms. Y: Although many people claim to be atheists, there really are no atheists.

Mr. X: I beg to differ.

Ms. Y: Beg all you want, but "God" means the greatest being. And everyone thinks that something or other is the greatest being. For example, if you don't believe in supernatural entities, you will probably think that the entire physical universe is the greatest being. So, while not everyone accepts the traditional view of God, everyone does believe that God exists, and hence there are no atheists.

* 13. **Mr. X:** Did you have a nice weekend?

  Ms. Y: Yes, we went to the Jackson Pollock exhibit at the art museum. He is truly one of the greatest artists of the century.

  Mr. X: On the contrary, Pollock's abstract paintings aren't even art. You can't even tell what the paintings are supposed to be *of*.

14. **Ms. Y:** I'll never be a political conservative. Never!

  Mr. X: Oh, but you are mistaken. After all, the word "conservative" means a liberal who has been mugged. So, given the rate of violent crime, I think you will likely one day find yourself a conservative.

15. **Mr. X:** Nietzsche was one of the most intelligent people in the history of the world. His books caused a revolution in philosophy.

  Ms. Y: Intelligent? I don't think so. If Nietzsche was so smart, then why was his personal life such a total disaster? He couldn't keep a job, he alienated all his friends, and the older he got, the weirder he got. Personally, I think Nietzsche was stupid.

Part C: Argument Diagrams, Equivocation, and Persuasive Definitions   Make a photocopy of the following passages. Then diagram the arguments, bracketing and numbering the steps in the manner indicated in chapter 3. Beside each diagram, identify any equivocations or persuasive definitions. (See the Answer Key for an illustration.)

* 1. Every free action is prompted by a motive that belongs to the agent (i.e., the person who performs the action). So, every free act is pursued in an attempt to satisfy one of the agent's own motives. But, by definition, a "self-serving act" is one pursued in an attempt to satisfy one's own motives. Hence, every free act is self-serving.

2. Many people say there is poverty in America today. They cite the number of homeless men and women living on the streets. But there is no real poverty in America today. The people living on the streets of Calcutta are poor. They are literally starving. Now that's poverty. Therefore, poverty doesn't really exist in America today.

3. Whenever 2 gallons of water are poured into a barrel and 2 gallons of alcohol are added, the barrel will contain slightly less than 4 gallons of liquid (due to the way water and alcohol combine chemically). Thus, when you add 2 and 2, you do not always get 4. Of course, this is entirely contrary to what any mathematician will tell you—namely, when 2 and 2 are added, you always get 4. Therefore, mathematics is sometimes contrary to empirical fact.

* 4. There ought to be a law against psychiatry, for "psychiatrist" means person who makes a living by charging money for talking with deeply troubled people. And it is wrong to exploit deeply troubled people.

5. Many atheists complain about the harshness of nature "red in tooth and claw." They say that a loving Creator would not set up a system in which some animals must kill and eat other animals in order to live. Hogwash! "The law of the survival

of the fittest" is best defined as God's way of achieving population control among the animals. Thus, although the struggle for survival *appears* harsh to us, the law of the survival of the fittest is in fact a very good thing. For without it the environment would be destroyed by an overabundance of animals.

6. Wherever there is a law, there is a person or group who established it. So, since the law of gravity is a law, there is a person or group who established the law of gravity. Now, no human or group of humans could establish the law of gravity. Therefore, some superhuman person or group of superhumans established the law of gravity.

* 7. Any fetus of human parents is itself human. And if any fetus of human parents is itself human, then abortion is wrong if human life is sacred. Furthermore, since being human consists in having faculties higher than those of other animals (such as the capacity to choose between good and evil), human life is sacred. It follows that abortion is wrong.

8. Frankly, it amazes me that there are people who oppose capitalism. "Capitalism" means an economic system characterized by a free market, fair competition for the goods available, minimal interference from the state, and the sacred right to keep what you've earned. Accordingly, capitalism is a good thing, indeed, a marvelous thing. I can only conclude that those who oppose capitalism are either seriously confused or perverse.

9. If you become a socialist, you will be making a very big mistake. For "socialist" means someone who thinks the government should own everything and that the individual person has no moral value and no rights. So, the very foundations of socialism are evil.

10. It is reasonable to appeal to legitimate authority to settle disputes. If it is reasonable to appeal to legitimate authority to settle disputes and legitimate authority in a democracy resides in the people, then in America, it is reasonable to appeal to the people to determine whether nuclear weapons are needed. And you will undoubtedly agree that legitimate authority in a democracy resides in the people. So, in America, it is reasonable to appeal to the people to determine whether nuclear weapons are needed. Now, if in America it is reasonable to appeal to the people to determine whether nuclear weapons are needed, then if the majority of Americans regard them as needed, they are needed. The majority of Americans regard nuclear weapons as needed. Hence, nuclear weapons are needed.

Notes

1. David Kelley, *The Art of Reasoning*, exp. ed. (New York: Norton, 1990), p. 114.
2. *The Words of Martin Luther King, Jr.*, selected and introduced by Coretta Scott King (New York: Newmarket Press, 1983), p. 95.
3. Wesley Salmon, *Logic*, 3rd ed. (Englewood Cliffs, NJ: Prentice-Hall, 1984), p. 145.
4. This example is borrowed from Frank R. Harrison, III, *Logic and Rational Thought* (New York: West, 1992), p. 463.
5. Definitions (16) and (17) are taken from *The American Heritage Concise dic-tion-ar-y*, 3rd ed. (New York: Houghton Mifflin, 1994), p. 417.
6. I owe the interesting observation that the English language has no conventional term for this phenomenon to my friend Dr. Gary Gleb, in conversation.

7. This example is borrowed from Irving M. Copi and Carl Cohen, *Introduction to Logic*, 9th ed. (Englewood Cliffs, NJ: Prentice-Hall, 1994), p. 170.

8. See Plato, *Five Dialogues,* trans. G. M. A. Grube (Indianapolis, IN: Hackett, 1981), p. 12. My example is admittedly a loose paraphrase of the original for the sake of illustration.

9. *Webster's New World Dictionary of the American Language* (New York: World, 1966), p. 412.

10. Benedict de Spinoza, *The Ethics*, trans. R. H. M. Elwes (New York: Dover, 1955), p. 173. Quote marks added.

11. Definition (26) is borrowed from H. L. Mencken, ed., *A New Dictionary of Quotations on Historical Principles from Ancient and Modern Sources* (New York: Knopf, 1978), p. 62. Quote marks added. Mencken attributes (26) to Theodore Dreiser.

12. William James, *Pragmatism and Four Essays from* The Meaning of Truth (New York: New American Library, 1974), p. 41. This quotation is from chap. 2 of *Pragmatism,* "What Pragmatism Means." *Pragmatism* was originally published in 1907 by Longman, Green.

13. James, *Pragmatism,* p. 41–42.

14. The gist of this example is borrowed from Salmon, *Logic,* p. 162.

Chapter 5

Categorical Syllogisms

In chapter 2, we noted that the validity of many arguments depends on the relationships between classes or sets of things. We might have put the same point this way: In a wide range of cases, validity depends on the relationships among *categories* of things. In this chapter, we will take a deeper look at arguments whose validity depends centrally on the relationships among classes, sets, or categories.

5.1 Categorical Statements

To understand categorical arguments, we must first understand categorical statements. A **categorical statement** is a statement that relates two classes, sets, or categories. Here are some examples of categorical statements:

1. All ducks are animals.
2. No humans are horses.
3. Some soldiers are cowards.
4. Some subatomic particles are not electrons.

Statement (1) says that every member of the class of ducks is a member of the class of animals. Statement (2) says that the class of humans and the class of horses have no members in common. Statement (3) says that some (i.e., at least one) member of the class of soldiers is a member of the class of cowards. And statement (4) says that some (i.e., at least one) member of the class of subatomic particles is not a member of the class of electrons.

There are four different **standard forms** of categorical statements. We can summarize the four standard forms as follows:

Categorical Statement	Example	Form
Universal affirmative	All trees are plants.	All S are P.
Universal negative	No plants are animals.	No S are P.
Particular affirmative	Some trees are oaks.	Some S are P.
Particular negative	Some trees are not oaks.	Some S are not P.

The letter S stands for the subject term, and the letter P stands for the predicate term. The terms in a categorical statement denote classes. When a categorical statement is in standard form, the subject term appears first and is followed by the predicate term. For example, the word "trees" is the subject term in "All trees are plants" while the word "plants" is the predicate term. And in the statement "Some trees are not oaks," the word "trees" is the subject term while the word "oaks" is the predicate term.

Every categorical statement has a **quality**, affirmative or negative. If a statement affirms that one class is wholly or partially included in another class, then the statement's quality is *affirmative*. If a statement denies that one class is wholly or partially included in another, its quality is *negative*. Every categorical statement also has a **quantity**, universal or particular. *Universal* statements refer to all members of the class denoted by the subject term. *Particular* statements refer to only some members of the class denoted by the subject term.

A **universal affirmative** statement has the form "All S are P"—for example, "All wives are women." A universal affirmative statement says that all members of class S are members of class P. Thus, "All wives are women" says that all members of the class of wives are also members of the class of women.

A **universal negative** statement has the form "No S are P"—for example, "No men are women." A universal negative statement says that no members of class S are members of class P. In other words, a universal negative says that classes S and P have no members in common. Thus, "No men are women" says that no members of the class of men are members of the class of women.

A **particular affirmative** statement has the form "Some S are P"—for example, "Some animals are carnivores." A particular affirmative statement says that some members of class S are members of class P. Thus, "Some animals are carnivores" says that some members of the class of animals are also members of the class of carnivores. Here, it is important to note that for present purposes, the word "some" means "at least one." In ordinary English, "some" occasionally has the force of "some but not all." But this is not the meaning assigned to "some" in logic. It is especially important to bear in mind that "Some S is P" does not imply that "Some S is not P." (For example, "Some animals are carnivores" does *not* imply that "Some animals are not carnivores.")

A **particular negative** statement has the form, "Some S are not P"—for example, "Some mammals are not land animals." A particular negative statement says that some members of class S are not members of class P. Thus, "Some mammals are not land animals" says that at least one member of the class of mammals is not a member of the class of land animals.

A number of complications regarding categorical statements should be noted at this time. First, terms can be rather complicated phrases. For example:

> **5.** All soldiers with lots of experience in combat are seasoned veterans.

Here, the subject term is "soldiers with lots of experience in combat" and the predicate term is "seasoned veterans."

Second, the terms of a categorical statement must include a noun or pronoun that denotes a class. But sometimes an adjective appears without a noun or pronoun, in which case the term is incompletely expressed. In such a case, a noun or pronoun must be added. Here are some examples:

> **6.** All humans are rational. (With noun added: All humans are rational animals *or* All humans are rational beings.)
>
> **7.** All emeralds are green. (With noun added: All emeralds are green stones *or* All emeralds are green things.)
>
> **8.** All bachelors are happy. (With noun added: All bachelors are happy persons *or* All bachelors are happy men.)

In these cases, we need to add a noun in order to have a genuine predicate *term* that denotes a class.

Third, categorical statements sometimes have to be rewritten slightly in order for the *copula* (linking verb) "are" to appear. Here are some examples:

> **9.** All fish swim. (Rewrite: All fish are swimmers.)
>
> **10.** All criminals should be punished. (Rewrite: All criminals are people who should be punished.)
>
> **11.** Everyone is happy. (Rewrite: All persons are happy persons.)

Fourth, each type of categorical statement has both a standard form and multiple *stylistic variants*. Take universal affirmative statements. The standard form is "All S are P." But universal affirmatives can be expressed in various ways in ordinary English. For example, there are many ways of saying "All cats are mammals" in ordinary English:

> Every cat is a mammal.
> Each cat is a mammal.
> Cats are mammals.
> Any cat is a mammal.
> If anything is a cat, then it is a mammal.
> Things are cats only if they are mammals.
> Only mammals are cats.

To put any of these statements into standard form, we simply write, "All cats are mammals." In the next section, we will see that a knowledge of standard forms and their stylistic variants is very useful when evaluating arguments for validity.

Take special note of the word "only" in the preceding list. Be aware that "Only P are S" means "All S are P," but it does *not* mean "All P are S." For example, "Only mammals are cats" means "All cats are mammals" (which is true), but it does not mean "All mammals are cats" (which is false). By contrast, "Only cats are mammals" (which is false) means "All mammals are cats," but it does *not* mean "All cats are mammals" (which is true).

The standard form for universal negatives is "No S are P." Again, there are common stylistic variants. For example, "No whales are humans" can be expressed in each of the following ways:

> Nothing that is a whale is a human.
>
> All whales are nonhumans.
>
> If anything is a whale, then it is not a human.
>
> Nothing is a whale unless it is not a human.

To put any of these into standard form, write, "No whales are humans." Note that "All whales are nonhumans" can be regarded as a variant of "No whales are humans," and we shall so regard it. (We can also properly regard "All whales are nonhumans" as a universal affirmative, but in this section and the next, it will be useful to regard it as a variant of "No whales are humans."[1])

The standard form for particular affirmatives is "Some S are P." This type of statement also has a number of stylistic variants. For example, "Some fish are sharks" can be expressed in each of the following ways:

> There are fish that are sharks.
>
> At least one fish is a shark.
>
> There exists a fish that is a shark.
>
> Something is both a fish and a shark.

To put any of these into standard form, we simply write, "Some fish are sharks."

The standard form for particular negatives is "Some S are not P." Again, there are common stylistic variants. For example, "Some fish are not sharks" can be expressed as follows:

> At least one fish is not a shark.
>
> Not all fish are sharks.
>
> Not every fish is a shark.
>
> Something is a fish but not a shark.
>
> There is a fish that is not a shark.

To put any of these into standard form, we simply write, "Some fish are not sharks."

Summary of Stylistic Variants	
Universal Affirmative: **All S are P.**	**Universal Negative:** **No S are P.**
Every S is a P. Each S is a P. S are P. Any S is a P. If anything is an S, then it is a P. Things are S only if they are P. Only P are S.	Nothing that is an S is a P. All S are non-P. If anything is an S, then it is not a P. Nothing is an S unless it is not a P.
Particular Affirmative: **Some S are P.**	**Particular Negative:** **Some S are not P.**
There are S that are P. At least one S is a P. There exists an S that is a P. Something is both an S and a P.	At least one S is not a P. Not all S are P. Not every S is a P. Something is an S but not a P. There is an S that is not a P.

Prior to the late 19th century, many logicians thought that all valid arguments could be analyzed in terms of classes or categories. From this perspective, the four standard forms of categorical statements are the basic elements of deductive logic. While logicians no longer hold that all valid arguments can be expressed in terms of categorical statements, many important logical insights still can be derived from the study of the logic of categorical statements.

The following exercise gives you some practice in working with categorical statements.

◆ Exercise 5.1

Categorical Statements   Categorize the statements below as universal affirmative, universal negative, particular affirmative, or particular negative. If a statement is not in standard form, rewrite it so that it is. (There are only four standard forms: All S are P, No S are P, Some S are P, and Some S are not P.) Identify the subject and predicate terms in each case (each term must include a noun or pronoun that denotes a class). For purposes of this exercise, treat statements of the form "All S are nonP" as stylistic variants of "No S are P."

* **1.** No diamonds are emeralds.
   2. Every kangaroo is a marsupial.
   3. At least one car is not a Ford.
* **4.** At least one person is a nerd.

  5. Nothing that is a spider is an insect.
  6. All highly motivated students are interesting.
* 7. All criminals are nonsaints.
  8. There are saints who are reformed criminals.
  9. Not all politicians are liars.
* 10. Some morally virtuous human beings are atheists.
  11. Each patriotic American loves justice.
  12. No liars are honest.
* 13. Not every animal that can fly is a bird.
  14. All people who have committed murder deserve death.
  15. Some good-looking people are snobs.
* 16. Each adult male human who is married is a husband.
  17. No fools are sages.
  18. All humans over the age of 70 are elderly.
* 19. No people who are unlucky are happy.
  20. Some people who choose not to attend college are highly successful.
  21. Nothing is a snake unless it is not a mammal.
* 22. Only reptiles are lizards.
  23. If anything is chimpanzee, then it is not a fish.
  24. Not every bright green stone is an emerald.
* 25. Things are birds only if they have feathers.
  26. Only diamonds are gems.
  27. There exists an animal that is a dog.
* 28. Something is a painting but not a masterpiece.
  29. Only mammals are whales.
  30. Physicists are scientists.
* 31. There exists a mountain that is beautiful.
  32. If anything is a slug, then it is not intelligent.
  33. All ghosts are nonhuman.
* 34. At least one tree is ugly.
  35. Nothing that is an odd number is divisible by two.
  36. Things are beautiful only if they are pleasant to behold.
* 37. At least one animal is vicious.
  38. If anything is a bad-tempered person, then it is a curmudgeon.
  39. Only red things are scarlet.
* 40. If anything is a sibling that is female, then it is a sister.

5.2 Venn Diagrams

Categorical syllogisms are arguments comprised entirely of categorical statements. Every categorical syllogism has two premises and one conclusion, and every categorical syllogism contains three terms. For example:

  12. All trees are plants. All oaks are trees. Therefore, all oaks are plants.

"Trees," "plants," and "oaks" are the terms in this syllogism. Some additional terminology will be useful momentarily. Note that one of the terms, namely, "trees," occurs once in each premise. The **middle term** of a categorical syllogism is the term that occurs once in each premise. The **major term** of a categorical syllogism is the predicate term of the conclusion. In argument (12), the major term is "plants." Finally, the **minor term** of a syllogism is the subject term of the conclusion. In argument (12), the minor term is "oaks."

What is the middle term of the following categorical syllogism?

13. All astronomers are scientists. Some astrologers are not scientists. So, some astrologers are not astronomers.

The middle term is "scientists," the major term is "astronomers," and the minor term is "astrologers."

In this section, we will examine a method for establishing the validity and invalidity of categorical syllogisms. This method was discovered around 1880 by the English logician John Venn. Venn's method involves the use of a special type of picture or diagram.

In order to use Venn's method, we must first learn how to diagram the four basic forms of categorical statements. Let's begin with universal negatives, such as "No dogs are cats." We use one circle to stand for the category or class of dogs and another circle to stand for the class of cats. The area of overlap of the two circles stands for those things that belong to both classes—that is, those things that are both dogs and cats. (Of course, this class is in fact empty, since in reality there are no dogs that are also cats.) The area to the left of the overlapping portion stands for the class of dogs-that-are-not-cats. The area to right of the overlapping portion stands for cats-that-are-not-dogs. Here's how we would depict this:

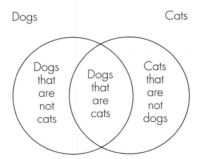

Now, to construct Venn diagrams, we indicate that the various areas of the diagram either contain objects or are empty. To show that an area contains at least one object, we use an "x." To show that an area is empty, we shade it in. If an area does not contain an "x" and is not shaded in, we simply have no information about it. Thus, to diagram a universal negative statement, such as

"No dogs are cats," we indicate that the area of overlap between the two circles is empty by shading it in, as follows:

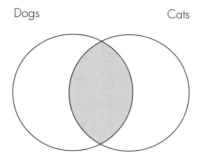

This is the sort of diagram you will always use for a universal negative statement. However, as previously noted, the English language provides various ways of saying that "No S are P," such as "All S are non-P" and "Nothing that is an S is a P." When you encounter such stylistic variants in a syllogism, simply rewrite the statement in "No S are P" form, and use a diagram similar to the one just shown. One last thing: Notice that the preceding diagram does not say that there are any dogs, nor does it say that there are any cats. It simply says that nothing belongs to the class (or set) of things that are both dogs and cats.

Universal affirmatives have the form "All S are P," and they say that the members of set S are also members of set P, or, in other words, that S has no members that are not members of P. Thus, the diagram for "All dogs are animals" looks like this:

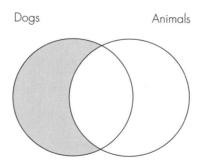

Notice that this diagram does not say that there are any dogs, nor does it say that there are any animals. It simply says, "If there are any dogs, then they are animals." This is the sort of diagram you will always use for an universal affirmative statement. However, as previously noted, the English language contains numerous stylistic variants for "All S are P," such as "Every S is a P," "If anything is an S, then it is a P," and "Only P are S." When you encounter these stylistic variants, rewrite the statement into "All S are P" form, and use a diagram similar to the one just shown.

Particular affirmatives have the form "Some S are P," and these say that sets S and P have at least one member in common. The diagram for "Some dogs are collies" looks like this:

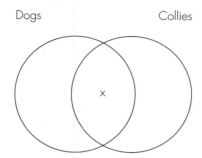

This diagram asserts that there exists at least one dog that is a collie. This is the type of diagram you will always use for particular affirmative statements. However, as previously noted, the English language contains a number of stylistic variants for "Some S and P," including "At least one S is a P" and "There are S that are P." When you encounter these variants, simply rewrite the statement into "Some S are P" form, and use a diagram similar to the one just shown.

Particular negatives have the form "Some S are not P." These statements say that set S has at least one member that does not belong to set P. The diagram for "Some dogs are not collies" looks like this:

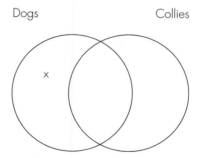

The diagram asserts that there exists at least one dog that is not a collie. This is the type of diagram you will always use for particular negative statements. But as previously noted, the English language contains a number of stylistic variants for "Some S are not P," such as "Not all S are P" and "At least one S is not a P." When you encounter these variants, simply rewrite the statement in "Some S are not P" form, and use a diagram similar to the one just shown.

Now that we know how to diagram the four relevant types of categorical statements, we can use Venn diagrams to evaluate syllogisms for validity. Since there are three terms in every syllogism, we need three overlapping circles for our diagram, as shown here:

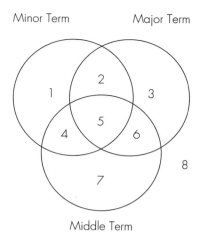

To ensure uniformity in our diagrams, we always let the circle in the middle stand for the class of things denoted by the *middle term* of the syllogism (the term that appears in both premises). The circle in the upper left stands for the class of things denoted by the *minor term* (the subject term of the conclusion). And the circle in the upper right stands for the set of things denoted by the *major term* (the predicate term of the conclusion). The numerals (1 through 8) are not normally part of a Venn diagram, but they are added here temporarily to enable us to refer to the separate areas of the diagram. Notice that there are eight areas (counting the region outside the circles). Each area represents a possible relationship among the three sets or classes. For example, if we placed an "x" in area 5, we would be saying that at least one thing belongs to all three of the sets or classes. If we shaded in area 5, we would be saying that no object belongs to all three sets. If we placed an "x" in area 8, we would be saying that at least one thing is not a member of any of the three classes in question. If we shaded in areas 4 and 5, we would be saying that nothing that belongs to the set denoted by the middle term also belongs to the set denoted by the minor term.

To determine whether a syllogism is valid, we proceed as follows. First, we diagram the premises. Second, we look to see whether our diagram of the premises tells us that the conclusion is true. This works because if an argument is valid, the content of the conclusion is contained, at least implicitly, in the premises. Consider the following example:

14. No rocks are sentient things. All animals are sentient things. Hence, no animals are rocks.

We set up our diagram and label the circles as just prescribed: The *middle term* ("sentient things") labels the circle in the middle of the diagram, the *minor term* ("animals") labels the circle in the upper left, and the *major term* ("rocks") labels the circle in the upper right. Next, we diagram the first premise:

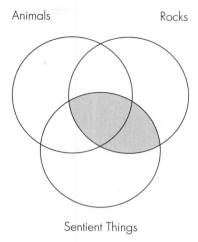

In diagramming the first premise, we focus on the two circles representing rocks and sentient things, since only those classes are mentioned in the first premise. Next, we diagram the second premise:

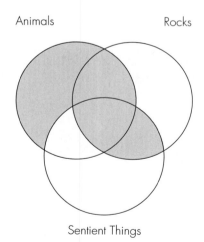

In diagramming the second premise, we need pay attention only to the circles representing animals and sentient things.

Having diagrammed the premises, we must now check to see whether the content of the conclusion has also been diagrammed in the process. In other words, does our diagram tell us that no animal is a rock? Yes, it does, for the areas of overlap between the circles representing these two classes are shaded in. Therefore, the argument is valid.

Our first example involved only universal statements. Let us now consider a syllogism involving a particular negative statement:

> 15. All humans are rational things. Some animals are not rational things. Therefore, some animals are not humans.

First, we set up our diagram, label the three circles (as prescribed previously), and diagram the first premise:

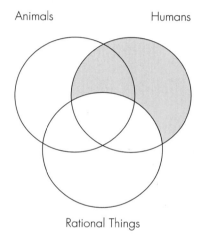

Animals   Humans

Rational Things

Once again, notice that we focus on only two circles at a time as we diagram the premises. Next, we diagram the second premise:

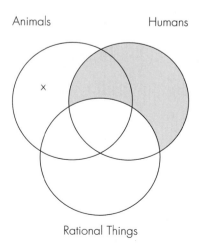

Animals   Humans

Rational Things

Why did we put our "x" in area 1 and not in area 2 of the diagram? We couldn't put it in area 2 because area 2 is shaded in. That is, the information in the first premise tells us that area 2 is empty. Thus, if we put an "x" in area 2, we would in effect be saying that the premises of the argument are logically inconsistent—that is, that the first premise says area 2 is empty while the second premise says area 2 is not empty. Clearly, this would misrepresent the content of the two premises, because they are consistent.

Now, we examine the diagram to see whether, in the process of diagramming the premises, we have diagrammed the content of the conclusion. Does the diagram tell us that some animals are not human? Yes. The "x" lies within the "animal" circle but outside the "human" circle.

In diagramming argument (15), we diagrammed the universal premise before we diagrammed the particular premise. *When a syllogism contains both universal and particular premises, always diagram the universal premise first.* Otherwise, you may run into obstacles in constructing your diagram. To illustrate, try to diagram the particular premise of argument (15) prior to diagramming the universal premise. (You won't know whether to put the "x" in area 1 or area 2.)

How does the Venn diagram method apply to invalid arguments? Consider the following syllogism:

16. All immoral persons are psychologically disturbed persons. No saints are immoral persons. Hence, no saints are psychologically disturbed persons.

We draw and label the circles and then diagram the first premise:

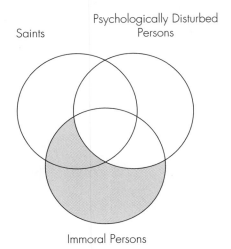

Next, we diagram the second premise:

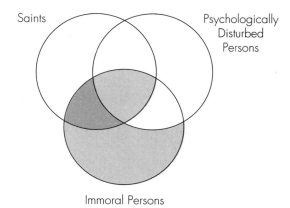

Immoral Persons

Notice that area 4 has been shaded in twice, since the diagram for each premise declares area 4 empty. This is not a problem; it merely means that our diagram is redundant as regards the emptiness of area 4.

Now that the premises are diagrammed, the crucial question is this: Does our diagram tell us that the conclusion of the argument is true? In other words, does it tell us that no saints are psychologically disturbed? The answer, of course, is that it does not. Area 2 has not been declared empty. Thus, the diagram leaves open the possibility that some saints are psychologically disturbed persons. This means that the premises do not guarantee the truth of the conclusion, and so the argument is invalid.

Let us diagram one last argument that brings out a slight complication in the Venn technique.

> 17. Some highly successful people are people of average intelligence. All famous actors are highly successful people. So, some people of average intelligence are famous actors.

We diagram the universal premise first:

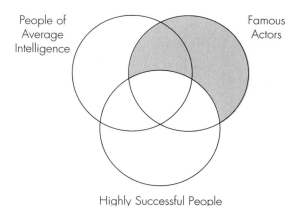

Highly Successful People

Now, when we try to diagram the first (or particular affirmative) premise, we see that the "x" could go in either area 4 or area 5. The premises do not contain more specific information than that. We indicate this by putting an "x" *precisely* on the line separating the two areas, like this:

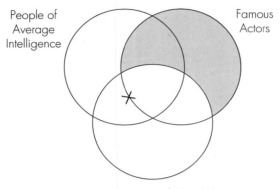

People of
Average
Intelligence

Famous
Actors

Highly Successful People

Now, for the argument to be valid, the premises must tell us that either area 2 or area 5 contains an object. But our diagram for the second premise declares that area 2 is empty. And our diagram for the first premise does not *assure* us that area 5 contains an object—it may and it may not. The "x" straddles areas 4 and 5, so the premises do not definitely say that the "x" belongs in area 4, nor do they say that the "x" belongs in area 5. Hence, the argument is invalid.

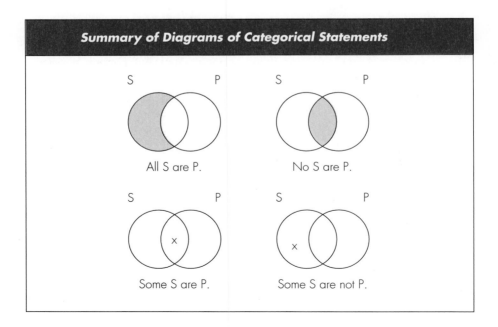

Summary of Diagrams of Categorical Statements

All S are P.

No S are P.

Some S are P.

Some S are not P.

The following exercise tests your understanding of the Venn diagram method.[2]

◆ *Exercise 5.2*

Venn Diagrams   Use Venn diagrams to determine the validity of the following syllogisms. In labeling the circles of your diagrams, remember that the middle term labels the circle in the middle, the subject term of the conclusion labels the circle in the upper left, and the predicate term of the conclusion labels the circle in the upper right. Use your knowledge of stylistic variants to rewrite any statements that are not in standard form. (Standard forms are: All S are P; No S are P; Some S are P; Some S are not P.)

*   **1.** Only Greeks are Athenians. At least one human is not an Athenian. Therefore, not all humans are Greeks.

    2. Every animal is sentient. And each sentient thing is a rights-holder. Hence, if anything is an animal, then it is a rights-holder.

    3. No evil thing is good. Every serial killer is evil. It follows that no serial killer is good.

*   **4.** Every liar is self-deceived. All liars are wicked persons. Accordingly, every wicked person is self-deceived.

    5. Every person who loves children is blessed. Some criminals are persons who love children. Hence, at least one criminal is blessed.

    6. All those who have faith are virtuous. But there are highly moral people who do not have faith. Therefore, not all highly moral people are virtuous.

*   **7.** No human is omniscient. Something is both divine and human. So, at least one divine being is not omniscient.

    8. Only wars are great evils. Some wars are ordained by God. Hence, at least one great evil is ordained by God.

    9. Anything that is worth doing is worth doing well. Not every hobby is worth doing well. Therefore, some hobbies are not worth doing, period.

* **10.** If anything is a mental event, then it is not a brain event. For only physical events are brain events; and all mental events are nonphysical.

  11. Some philosophical views are not worth considering. Every philosophical view has been held by a genius. Thus, some views that have been held by geniuses are not worth considering.

  12. No wicked person is utterly without a conscience. But all wicked persons are deeply confused individuals. Hence, no deeply confused individual is utterly without a conscience.

* **13.** Only metaphorical statements are similarity statements. And every statement is a similarity statement. Accordingly, a thing is a statement only if it is metaphorical.

  14. Contrary to what traditional Western morality says, some acts of suicide are morally permissible. For all morally permissible acts are ones that conform to the categorical imperative, and some acts of suicide conform to the categorical imperative.

  15. Only acts that maximize utility are obligatory. Not all acts that maximize utility are prescribed by the Ten Commandments. Therefore, at least one act prescribed by the Ten Commandments is not obligatory.

* **16.** Not every act is free, since every act foreknown by God is nonfree and some acts are foreknown by God.

   17. Only acts approved of by God are moral. Some acts of killing are approved of by God. Hence, some acts of killing are moral.

   18. No human is omnipotent. All divine beings are omnipotent. Therefore, no human is divine.

* **19.** Only persons who have inner conflicts are unhappy. At least one successful comedian is unhappy. We may conclude that some successful comedians are persons who have inner conflicts.

   20. At least one tycoon is a person who has walked over others to get to the top. Every person who has walked over others to get to the top is evil. It follows that at least one tycoon is evil.

   21. Some trees are maples. Some trees are oaks. So, some oaks are maples.

   22. No balalaika is a banjo. Some balalaikas are beautiful. Hence, some beautiful things are not banjos.

   23. Each tyrant is mendacious. If anything is a tyrant, then it is a liar. Consequently, all liars are mendacious.

   24. Every aphorism is an apothegm. Each epigram is an aphorism. Accordingly, only apothegms are epigrams.

   25. Every Saint Bernard is a large dog. Not all large dogs are brown. So, not all brown dogs are Saint Bernards.

5.3 Aristotelian Logic: Immediate Inferences

Long before the Venn diagram method was invented, Aristotle (384–322 B.C.E.) worked out a system of logic for categorical statements. Historically, Aristotelian logic (the tradition of logic stemming from Aristotle's work) has been of tremendous importance in Western culture. In fact, until the latter half of the 19th century, the study of logic was in large measure the study of Aristotelian logic. In this section and the next, we will explore categorical logic from an Aristotelian perspective.

When a conclusion is drawn from only one premise, the inference is labeled "immediate." In this section, we will examine immediate inferences, comparing the Aristotelian and modern traditions.

Categorical Statements and the Square of Opposition

In the Aristotelian tradition, it is customary to refer to the four types of categorical statements with the first four vowels of the alphabet, as follows:

   A Universal affirmative (All S are P.)
   E Universal negative (No S are P.)

I   Particular affirmative (Some S are P.)
O   Particular negative (Some S are not P.)

We will freely employ these abbreviations in this section and the next.

What are the logical relationships between standard-form categorical statements *having the same subject and predicate terms?* For example:

A   All dogs are collies.
E   No dogs are collies.
I   Some dogs are collies.
O   Some dogs are not collies.

Let us refer to categorical statements having the same subject and predicate terms as **corresponding statements**. Logicians in the Aristotelian tradition offer the following theses regarding the logical relationships between corresponding statements.

First, corresponding **A** and **O** statements are contradictories. Two statements are **contradictories** if they cannot both be true and they cannot both be false. (In other words, if one is true, the other must be false; and if one is false, the other must be true.) For example, "All dogs are collies" contradicts "Some dogs are not collies." Therefore, given that all dogs are collies, we can immediately conclude that it is false that some dogs are not collies. And given that some dogs are not collies, we can immediately conclude that not all dogs are collies.

Similarly, corresponding **E** and **I** statements are contradictories. For example, "No dogs are collies" contradicts "Some dogs are collies." Therefore, given that no dogs are collies, we can immediately conclude that it is false that some dogs are collies. And given that some dogs are collies, we can immediately conclude that it is false that no dogs are collies.

Second, according to the Aristotelians, corresponding **A** and **E** statements are contraries. Two statements are **contraries** if they cannot both be true but they can both be false. (For instance, the following two statements are contraries: "The Taj Mahal is pink all over" and "The Taj Mahal is blue all over." Although the Taj Mahal is, in fact, pink, it could be painted, say, green, in which case both of these statements would be false.) For example, corresponding **A** and **E** statements such as "All dogs are collies" and "No dogs are collies" are contraries. These statements can both be false if some (but not all) dogs are collies. But if one of these statements is true, the other must be false, according to the Aristotelians.

Third, according to the Aristotelians, corresponding **I** and **O** statements are subcontraries. Two statements are **subcontraries** if they cannot both be false but they can both be true. For example, according to Aristotelians, "Some dogs are collies" and "Some dogs are not collies" are subcontraries.

Fourth, according to the Aristotelians, **A** statements logically imply their corresponding **I** statements. For example, the following argument is valid according to Aristotelians: "All dogs are collies; therefore, some dogs are collies." Similarly, **E** statements logically imply their corresponding **O** statements. For example, the following argument is valid according to Aristotelians: "No dogs are collies; hence, some dogs are not collies."

All of these relationships can be pictured in a single diagram called the *Square of Opposition*, as shown here. The Aristotelian Square of Opposition, however, involves a crucial presupposition—namely, that the terms in categorical statements refer to nonempty classes. This is a presupposition that modern logicians, following the lead of the British mathematician and logician George Boole (1815–1864), are generally not willing to make. We will now consider why modern logicians reject certain aspects of the Square of Opposition.[3]

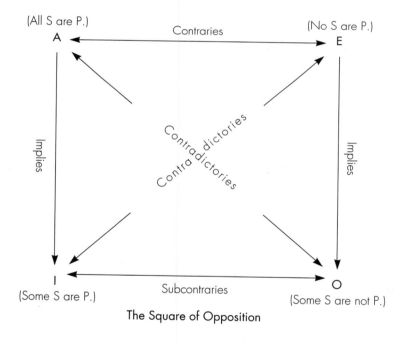

The Square of Opposition

Let us begin by noting that **I** and **O** statements have existential import; that is, they assert that their subject terms refer to classes that are not empty. For example, the statement "Some dogs are collies" says that there *exists* at least one dog who is a collie. So, "Some dogs are collies" implies "There exists at least one dog." Similarly, the statement "Some dogs are not collies" says that there *exists* at least one dog who is not a collie, which, in turn, implies that there exists at least one dog.

Now, according to the Aristotelians, **A** statements imply their corresponding **I** statements. It follows that **A** statements must have existential import, because a statement with existential import cannot be derived logically from one lacking existential import. To illustrate, according to Aristotelians, "All dogs are collies" implies "Some dogs are collies"; and as we have just seen, "Some dogs are collies" implies "There exists at least one dog." Therefore, "All dogs are collies" implies "There exists at least one dog." Similarly, according to Aristotelians, **E** statements imply their corresponding **O** statements. Therefore, **E** statements must have existential import. For example, "No dogs are collies" implies "Some dogs are not collies," which, in turn, implies "There exists at least one dog."

Unfortunately, we have now arrived at a serious problem with the Aristotelian view. According to the Aristotelians, corresponding **A** and **O** statements are contradictories, and so they cannot both be false. But consider the following **A** and **O** statements:

18. All unicorns are friendly animals.

19. Some unicorns are not friendly animals.

Now, unicorns do not exist. But if statements (18) and (19) both have existential import, then both imply that at least one unicorn exists, and hence both are false. Therefore, (18) and (19) are not contradictories after all, in spite of the fact that Aristotelians affirm that corresponding **A** and **O** statements are contradictories. (Remember, if two statements are contradictories, then if one is false, the other must be true; and if one is true, then the other must be false.)

Note that sometimes we might want to use terms that denote empty classes (or at any rate, classes that are empty as far as we know). To illustrate, consider the following statements:

20. All terrorists who have killed millions of innocent citizens by detonating a nuclear weapon in a highly populated area are people who deserve to die.

21. No perfect vacuum is a space through which sound can be transmitted.

22. Every ideal society is just.

23. No perfect sphere is a perfect cube.

In each case, the subject term refers to a class that is empty (or at least empty as far as we know). And yet, one might think that these statements are true, and even argue for them, while fully recognizing that their subject terms denote empty classes. But, again, the main point is that the Aristotelian claim that **A** and **E** statements have existential import conflicts with the thesis that corresponding **A** and **O** statements (as well as **E** and **I** statements) must be contradictory.

Modern logicians endorse the Aristotelian theses regarding contradictories—namely, that corresponding **A** and **O** statements are contradictories and that corresponding **E** and **I** statements are contradictories. In other words, modern logicians endorse the *diagonal* relationships pictured in the Square of Opposition. But this forces modern logicians to reject all of the relationships along the *sides* of the Square of Opposition. As we have just seen, to preserve the Aristotelian theses regarding contradictories, one must deny that **A** and **E** statements have existential import. This basic move carries with it a series of implications.

Implication 1: **A** statements do not logically imply their corresponding **I** statements.

Hence, the following arguments are invalid:

24. All unicorns are animals. So, some unicorns are animals.
25. All terrorists who have killed millions of innocent citizens by detonating a nuclear weapon in a highly populated area are people who deserve to die. So, some terrorists who have killed millions of innocent citizens by detonating a nuclear weapon in a highly populated area are people who deserve to die.
26. All dogs are collies. So, some dogs are collies.

In thinking about this, bear in mind that **I** statements have existential import. "Some unicorns are animals" implies "There exists a unicorn that is an animal," which, in turn, implies that at least one unicorn exists. It may also be helpful to note that the preceding arguments are invalid according to the Venn diagram method. Here is a diagram of argument (24):

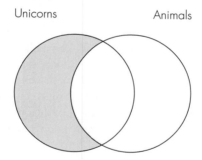

Unicorns   Animals

For the argument to be valid, an "x" must appear in the area of overlap between the two circles, but no such "x" appears. This illustrates the fact that the Venn method endorses the modern (as opposed to the Aristotelian) view of the logical relationships between categorical statements.

Implication 2: Similarly, **E** statements do not imply their corresponding **O** statements.

Thus, the following argument is invalid:

27. No perfect vacuum is a space through which sound can be transmitted. So, some perfect vacuum is not a space through which sound can be transmitted.

Note that scientists affirm the premise of argument (27) but deny the conclusion since a perfect vacuum has never been achieved. A Venn diagram indicates that (27) is invalid:

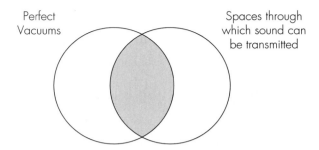

For the argument to be valid, an "x" must appear inside the "Perfect Vacuums" circle *and* outside of the other circle, but no such "x" appears.

> Implication 3: Corresponding I and O statements are not subcontraries. (Recall that subcontraries can both be true but cannot both be false.)

For example, "Some dogs are collies" and "Some dogs are not collies" can both be false. To illustrate, suppose all dogs were to die of a catastrophic disease and cease to exist. Then both of these statements would be false, because both imply that at least one dog exists.

> Implication 4: Corresponding A and E statements are not contraries. (Recall that contraries cannot both be true but they can both be false.)

The explanation of this thesis must await our discussion of predicate logic in chapter 9. Here, we can only note that according to modern logicians, **A** and **E** statements should be analyzed as involving conditionals (if-then statements). For instance, "All unicorns are animals" may be rewritten as follows:

> 28. If anything is a unicorn, then it is an animal.

And "No unicorns are animals" may be rewritten as follows:

> 29. If anything is a unicorn, then it is not an animal.

For reasons we will discuss in chapter 9, both of these conditionals are true assuming that there are no unicorns. Admittedly, this result is not intuitive, and it depends on logical theories we will examine in later chapters.

Categorical Statements: Conversion, Obversion, and Contraposition

As we have seen, modern logicians are critical of significant aspects of the Aristotelian Square of Opposition. But they endorse many Aristotelian claims

Summary of Immediate Inferences Related to the Square of Opposition

I. Valid Inferences According to Both Aristotelian and Modern Logicians

1. All S are P. So, it is false that some S are not P.
2. Some S are not P. So, it is false that all S are P.
3. No S are P. So, it is false that some S are P.
4. Some S are P. So, it is false that no S are P.

5. It is false that all S are P. So, some S are not P.
6. It is false that no S are P. So, some S are P.
7. It is false that some S are P. So, no S are P.
8. It is false that some S are not P. So, all S are P.

(*Note:* The above inferences are all based on the fact that if two statements are contradictories, then if one is true, the other must be false; and if one is false, the other must be true.)

II. Valid Inferences According to Aristotelians but Not Modern Logicians

1. All S are P. So, some S are P.
2. No S are P. So, some S are not P.

(*Note:* At issue here is whether **A** and **E** statements have existential import.)

3. It is false that some S are P. So, some S are not P.
4. It is false that some S are not P. So, some S are P.

(*Note:* At issue here is whether corresponding **I** and **O** statements are subcontraries.)

5. All S are P. So, it is false that no S are P.
6. No S are P. So, it is false that all S are P.

(*Note:* At issue here is whether corresponding **A** and **E** statements are contraries.)

regarding immediate inferences. Let us now consider these under three categories: conversion, obversion, and contraposition.

Conversion

The **converse** of a standard-form categorical statement is formed simply by interchanging its subject and predicate terms. Here are four examples of statements together with their converses:

Statement	Converse
A All dogs are animals.	All animals are dogs.
E No plants are animals.	No animals are plants.
I Some plants are trees.	Some trees are plants.
O Some plants are not trees.	Some trees are not plants.

Conversion is the inference from a categorical statement to its converse. Conversion is valid for **E** and **I** statements. For example, both of the following arguments are valid:

> 30. No plants are animals. So, no animals are plants.
>
> 31. Some plants are trees. So, some trees are plants.

(You can construct Venn diagrams to confirm this result.) But conversion is not valid in general with regard to **A** and **O** statements. The following examples should suffice to indicate why:

> 32. All dogs are animals. So, all animals are dogs.
>
> 33. Some plants are not trees. So, some trees are not plants.

Both arguments move from a true premise to a false conclusion, and hence are invalid. To sum up, then: Conversion is always valid for **E** and **I** statements, but it is not in general valid for **A** and **O** statements.

Obversion

The concept of an obverse requires a bit of explanation. First, each class has a complement. The **complement** of a class X is the class containing all things that are not a member of X. For instance, the complement of the class of trees is the class containing all nontrees, that is, everything that is not a tree (horses, hawks, humans, hamburgers, and so on).

Second, each term has a term-complement. The **term-complement** is the word or phrase that denotes the class complement. For instance, the term-complement of "dogs" is "nondogs," which denotes the class containing everything that is not a dog. And the term-complement of "nondogs" is simply "dogs," which denotes the class containing everything that is not a nondog. (*Note:* Do not confuse term-complements with contrary terms. For instance, the term-complement of "winner" is not "loser," but "nonwinner," and the class of nonwinners includes players who tie, nonplayers, *and* losers.)

The **obverse** of a statement is formed by (a) changing its quality (from affirmative to negative, or vice versa) and (b) replacing the predicate term with its term-complement. Here are four examples:

Statement	Obverse
A All trees are plants.	No trees are nonplants.
E No cats are trees.	All cats are nontrees.
I Some trees are oaks.	Some trees are not nonoaks.
O Some trees are not oaks.	Some trees are nonoaks.

Obversion is the inference from a categorical statement to its obverse. Obversion is always valid.

Contraposition

The **contrapositive** of a statement is formed by (a) replacing its subject term with the term-complement of its predicate term and (b) replacing the predicate term with the term-complement of its subject term. Here are four examples:

Statement	Contrapositive
A All cats are mammals.	All nonmammals are noncats.
E No bats are elephants.	No nonelephants are nonbats.
I Some plants are weeds.	Some nonweeds are nonplants.
O Some plants are not weeds.	Some nonweeds are not nonplants.

Contraposition is the inference from a statement to its contrapositive. Contraposition is valid for **A** and **O** statements. Thus, the following arguments are valid:

34. All rubies are stones. So, all nonstones are nonrubies.

35. Some trees are not elms. So, some nonelms are not nontrees.

It is interesting to note that these same results can be achieved by a sequence of obversions and conversions. For instance, consider the inference from an **A** statement to its contrapositive:

Step 1: All S are P.
Step 2: No S are non-P. [obverse of Step 1]
Step 3: No non-P are S. [converse of Step 2]
Step 4: All non-P are non-S. [obverse of Step 3]

Contraposition is not valid in general for **E** and **I** statements. For example, the following argument is invalid:

36. No dogs are trees. So, no nontrees are nondogs.

Argument (36) is plainly invalid. Its premise is true, but its conclusion is false. (Examples of nontrees include stones, steers, and stereoscopes; therefore, some nontrees are nondogs.) The following argument involves an inference from an **I** statement to its contrapositive and is also invalid:

37. Some animals are nondogs. So, some dogs are nonanimals.

Here, the premise is true. (The mere fact that there are cats is proof of that.) But the conclusion is false, so the argument is invalid.

The following exercises will test your understanding of immediate inferences.

Summary of Immediate Inferences Related to Conversion, Obversion, and Contraposition

Conversion

A   All S are P. So, all P are S. [not in general valid]
E   No S are P. So, no P are S. [valid]
I   Some S are P. So, some P are S. [valid]
O   Some S are not P. So, some P are not S. [not in general valid]

Obversion

A   All S are P. So, no S are non-P. [valid]
E   No S are P. So, all S are non-P. [valid]
I   Some S are P. So, some S are not non-P. [valid]
O   Some S are not P. So, some S are non-P. [valid]

Contraposition

A   All S are P. So, all non-P are non-S. [valid]
E   No S are P. So, no non-P are non-S. [not in general valid]
I   Some S are P. So, some non-P are non-S. [not in general valid]
O   Some S are not P. So, some non-P are not non-S. [valid]

◆ Exercise 5.3

Part A: Matching   In the space provided, write the letter of the item on the right that best characterizes the item on the left.

_____   1. Contradictories

_____   2. Contraries

_____   3. Subcontraries

_____   4. Converse

_____   5. Obverse

_____   6. Contrapositive

_____   7. Complement

_____   8. Conversion

_____   9. Obversion

_____   10. Contraposition

A. The inference from a statement to its obverse
B. The inference from a statement to its contrapositive
C. The inference from a statement to its converse
D. Formed simply by interchanging the subject and predicate terms
E. Can both be false but cannot both be true
F. The class containing all things not a member of the original class
G. Can both be true but cannot both be false
H. Cannot both be true and cannot both be false (If one is true, the other must be false; and if one is false, the other must be true.)
I. Formed by (a) replacing the subject term with the term-complement of the predicate term and (b) replacing the predicate term with the term-complement of the subject term

J. Formed by (a) changing the quality (from affirmative to negative, or vice versa) and (b) replacing the predicate term with its term-complement

Part B: Contradictories, Contraries, and Subcontraries   Which of the following are contradictories, contraries, and subcontraries according to Aristotelian logicians?

* **1.** All lovers are happy people./Some lovers are not happy people.
  2. Some artists are painters./Some artists are not painters.
  3. No scholars are rock stars./Some scholars are rock stars.
* **4.** All bureaucrats are mystics./No bureaucrats are mystics.
  5 Some women are not physicians./All women are physicians.
  6. All students are lovers of logic./No students are lovers of logic.
* **7.** Some politicians are honest./Some politicians are not honest.
  8. No lawyers are liars./Some lawyers are liars.
  9. All serial killers are psychopaths./Some serial killers are not psychopaths.
* **10.** No soldiers are saints./All soldiers are saints.

Part C: Valid or Invalid?   Which of the following are valid arguments according to Aristotelian logicians? Which are not valid according to Aristotelian logicians? Which are not valid according to modern logicians?

* **1.** All vampires are dangerous creatures. So, some vampires are dangerous creatures.
  2. No poltergeists are perfect creatures. So, some poltergeists are not perfect creatures.
  3. All customers are people with correct opinions. Therefore, it is false that no customers are people with correct opinions.
* **4.** No angels are mortal beings. Hence, some angels are not mortal beings.
  5. Some dinosaurs are carnivores. So, some carnivores are dinosaurs.
  6. All kangaroos are marsupials. Therefore, all marsupials are kangaroos.
* **7.** No karate experts are wimps. Hence, it is false that all karate experts are wimps.
  8. No human beings are gods. Accordingly, some human beings are not gods.
  9. It is false that some people are entrepreneurs. So, some people are not entrepreneurs.
* **10.** No nerds are snobs. Therefore, no snobs are nerds.
  11. No despicable persons are moral paragons. Thus, some despicable persons are not moral paragons.
  12. All rabbits are animals. Accordingly, all nonanimals are nonrabbits.
* **13.** No doctors are astrologers. So, no nonastrologers are nondoctors.
  14. Some plants are nontrees. So, some trees are nonplants.
  15. All citizens are residents. Therefore, no citizens are nonresidents.

* **16.** No scholars are conformists. Hence, all scholars are nonconformists.

   17. Some vegans are not pacifists. Accordingly, some vegans are nonpacifists.

   18. All extraterrestrials are highly evolved creatures. It follows that some extraterrestrials are highly evolved creatures.

* **19.** No people with flawless characters are geniuses. Thus, some people with flawless characters are not geniuses.

   20. Some athletes are professionals. So, some athletes are not nonprofessionals.

Part D: Converse, Obverse, and Contrapositive   Form the converse, obverse, and contrapositive of each of the following. Then state whether conversion, obversion, and contraposition are valid in general for statements of the type in question. (For example, is conversion valid in general for **A** statements?)

* **1.** No saints are reprobates.
   2. All executives are leaders.
   3. Some rectangles are nonsquares.
* **4.** Some bombs are not grenades.
   5. All demons are angels.
   6. No lovers are fighters.
* **7.** All forgeries are copies.
   8. No cowards are heroes.
   9. Some scientists are not chemists.
* **10.** Some theologians are nonbelievers.
   11. Some liars are statisticians.
   12. No witches are wizards.
* **13.** All scientists are nonmagicians.
   14. Some mammals are nonwhales.
   15. All portraits are pictures.

5.4 Aristotelian Logic: Categorical Syllogisms

Let us now examine categorical syllogisms from an Aristotelian perspective. Consider the following syllogism:

> 38. All therapists are altruists. Some psychologists are not altruists. So, some psychologists are not therapists.

This syllogism is in *standard form*. When a syllogism is in **standard form**, its first premise contains the major term (the predicate term of the conclusion), its second premise contains the minor term (the subject term of the conclusion), and the conclusion is stated last. In argument (38), the major term is "therapists" and the minor term is "psychologists." The **major premise** of a categorical syllogism is the premise containing the major term, and the **minor premise** is the premise containing the minor term. So, when a categorical syllogism is in standard form, the first premise is the major premise and the second premise is the minor premise.

Syllogisms differ according to their mood and figure. The **mood** of a syllogism (in standard form) is determined by the kinds of categorical statements comprising it. The mood of (38) is **AOO**. That is, the first premise is a universal affirmative statement, the second is a particular negative statement, and the conclusion is a particular negative statement. What is the mood of the following syllogism?

39. No birds are mammals. All bats are mammals. So, no bats are birds.

The mood is **EAE**. That is, the first premise is a universal negative statement, the second premise is a universal affirmative statement, and the conclusion is a universal negative statement. Two syllogisms can have the same mood and yet differ in logical form. The following syllogism has the same mood as (39), but it differs in logical form:

40. No mammals are birds. All mammals are bats. So, no bats are birds.

We can bring out the difference in form by using letters to stand for terms. Let "S" stand for the minor term (the subject term of the conclusion), "P" for the major term (the predicate term of the conclusion), and "M" for the middle term. (Recall that the middle term occurs once in each premise but does not occur in the conclusion.) Then arguments (39) and (40) have the following forms, respectively:

No P are M.	No M are P.
All S are M.	All M are S.
So, no S are P.	So, no S are P.

In the Aristotelian scheme, (39) and (40) are said to differ in **figure**. Figure is specified by the position of the middle term. There are four possible figures, which can be diagrammed as follows:

First Figure	Second Figure	Third Figure	Fourth Figure
M–P	P–M	M–P	P–M
S–M	S–M	M–S	M–S
So, S–P	So, S–P	So, S–P	So, S–P

In the first figure, the middle term is the subject term of the major premise and the predicate term of the minor premise. In the second figure, the middle term is the predicate term of both premises. In the third figure, the middle term is the subject term of both premises. In the fourth figure, the middle term is the predicate term of the major premise and the subject term of the minor premise.

The form of a syllogism is completely specified by its mood and figure. The Aristotelian approach works out which combinations of mood and figure result in valid forms, and which result in invalid forms. For example, argument (39) is a syllogism in the *second figure* having the mood **EAE**; this form is valid. On the other hand, argument (40) is a syllogism in the *third figure* having the mood

EAE; this form is invalid. Thus, according to Aristotelian logic, validity is determined by mood and figure.

How many different forms of categorical syllogisms are there? Two hundred and fifty-six. As we have seen, there are four kinds of categorical statements, and three categorical statements per categorical syllogism. Thus, there are $4^3 = 4 \times 4 \times 4 = 64$ possible moods (**AAA, AAE, AAI, AAO, AEA,** etc.). Moreover, there are four different figures, and $64 \times 4 = 256$. Out of all these possibilities, ancient and modern logicians agree that the following 15 forms are valid:

> First figure: **AAA, EAE, AII, EIO**
> Second figure: **EAE, AEE, EIO, AOO**
> Third figure: **IAI, AII, OAO, EIO**
> Fourth figure: **AEE, IAI, EIO**

According to the Aristotelians, an additional nine forms are valid:

> First figure: **AAI, EAO**
> Second figure: **AEO, EAO**
> Third figure: **AAI, EAO**
> Fourth figure: **AEO, EAO, AAI**

However, for reasons discussed in the previous section, most modern logicians do not accept the additional nine forms as valid. Note that all the forms in the additional set of nine involve an inference from two universal premises to a particular conclusion. Accordingly, such forms are valid only if *universal affirmatives and universal negatives have existential import*. And, as we saw in the previous section, modern logicians deny this because it leads to the conclusion that corresponding **A** and **O** statements are not contradictories (and to the conclusion that **E** and **I** statements are not contradictories).

How can valid syllogistic forms be identified? In the Aristotelian system, they are identified through a set of rules. Let us now formulate those rules.

> Rule 1: A valid standard-form categorical syllogism must contain exactly three terms, and each term must be used with the same meaning throughout the argument.

A *fallacy of equivocation* occurs if a term is used with more than one meaning in a categorical syllogism. A syllogism we encountered in chapter 4 illustrates this fallacy:

> 41. Only man is rational. But no woman is a man. Hence, no woman is rational.

Argument (41) violates Rule 1 because in the first premise, "man" means "human beings," while in the second premise, "man" means "male human."

The next two rules depend crucially on the concept of a term's being *distributed*. So, the rather technical concept of distribution must be explained in some detail before we proceed any further. A term is **distributed** in a statement if the statement says something about every member of the class that the term denotes. A term is **undistributed** in a statement if the statement does not say something about every member of the class the term denotes. For example:

42. All ants are insects.

Statement (42) says something about all members of the class of ants—namely, that every member of the class of ants belongs to the class of insects. Hence, the term "ants" is distributed in (42). But the term "insects" is undistributed, for the statement does not say anything about every member of the class of insects. In general, the subject term of a universal affirmative (or **A**) statement is distributed while the predicate term is not.

Both terms are distributed in a universal negative (or **E**) statement. For instance:

43. No trumpets are flutes.

This says that every trumpet is excluded from the class of flutes and that every flute is excluded from the class of trumpets. Hence, both the subject term "trumpets" and the predicate term "flutes" are distributed.

Neither term is distributed in a particular affirmative (or **I**) statement. For example:

44. Some precious stones are diamonds.

This statement makes no assertion about all precious stones. Furthermore, it makes no assertion about all diamonds. Both the subject term and the predicate term of a particular affirmative statement are undistributed.

The predicate term of a particular negative (or **O**) statement is distributed, but its subject term is undistributed. For example:

45. Some precious stones are not diamonds.

Statement (45) does not say anything about *all* precious stones. But it does refer to all members of the class of diamonds, and it says that *all* diamonds are excluded from a portion of the class of precious stones.

To recap: Universal (**A** and **E**) statements distribute their subject terms while negative (**E** and **O**) statements distribute their predicate terms. The following list summarizes our discussion of distribution:

Letter Name	Form	Terms Distributed
A	All S are P.	S
E	No S are P.	S and P
I	Some S are P.	None
O	Some S are not P.	P

We are now in position to state Rule 2.

> **Rule 2:** In a valid standard-form categorical syllogism, the middle term must be distributed in at least one premise.

Here is an example of a syllogism that violates Rule 2:

> 46. All eagles are birds. All penguins are birds. So, all penguins are eagles.

The middle term, "birds," is not distributed in either premise, since the predicate terms of **A** statements are not distributed. Within the Aristotelian scheme, a violation of Rule 2 is called a *fallacy of the undistributed middle*.

Why does the distribution of the middle term matter? Because the middle term has to serve as a link between the other terms. And if the middle term is undistributed, then neither premise makes an assertion about *all* the members of the class denoted by the middle term. Hence, it is possible that the subject term relates to one part of the class denoted by the middle term while the predicate term relates to a different part of that class, with the result that there is no guaranteed link between the subject and predicate term.

Rule 3 also involves the concept of distribution.

> **Rule 3:** In a valid standard-form categorical syllogism, a term must be distributed in the premises if it is distributed in the conclusion.

This rule can be broken in two basic ways, depending on whether the major or minor term is distributed in the conclusion but not in the premises. Consider the following examples:

> 47. All birds are animals. No bats are birds. So, no bats are animals.
> 48. All squares are rectangles. All squares are figures. So, all figures are rectangles.

In argument (47) the major term, "animals," is distributed in the conclusion but not in the premises. This sort of violation of Rule 3 is called a *fallacy of the illicit major*. In argument (48), the minor term, "figures," is distributed in the conclusion but not in the second premise. This type of violation of Rule 3 is called a *fallacy of the illicit minor*.

Why is it important for a term to be distributed in the premises if it is distributed in the conclusion? Well, suppose a term is distributed in the conclusion but not in the premises. Then the conclusion contains more information than the premises warrant, because the conclusion says something about *all* members of the class denoted by the term while the premises do *not* say something about all the members of that class. Therefore, if a term is distributed in the conclusion but not in the premises, the conclusion "goes beyond" the information contained in the premises, and hence the argument is invalid.

The next rule concerns the *quality* of the statements composing a categorical syllogism.

> Rule 4: In a valid standard-form categorical syllogism, the number of negative premises must be equal to the number of negative conclusions.[4]

Since a syllogism has only one conclusion, this rule tells us that any categorical syllogism with two negative premises is invalid. For instance:

> 49. No dogs are cats. Some cats are not cocker spaniels. So, some cocker spaniels are not dogs.

The premises of argument (49) are true while the conclusion is false, so (49) is clearly invalid.

Rule 4 also tells us that the conclusion of a categorical syllogism must be negative if one of the premises is negative. Thus, the following syllogism also violates Rule 4:

> 50. No tigers are wolves. Some felines are tigers. So, some felines are wolves.

Here again, the premises are true while the conclusion is false, so the argument is invalid.

Finally, Rule 4 tells us that a categorical syllogism is invalid if it has a negative conclusion but no negative premises:

> 51. All collies are dogs. Some animals are collies. So, some dogs are not animals.

Argument (51) has obviously true premises and an obviously false conclusion; therefore, it is plainly invalid. In fact, violations of Rule 4 are not common because the invalidity tends to be quite obvious.

At this point, our list of rules is complete from the traditional Aristotelian perspective. If we add the following rule, however, we can bring the Aristotelian system into agreement with modern systems of logic.

> Rule 5: No valid standard-form categorical syllogism with a particular conclusion can have two universal premises.[5]

Here is an example of a syllogism that violates Rule 5 but counts as valid in the traditional Aristotelian scheme:

> 52. All Americans are humans. All morally perfect Americans are Americans. So, some morally perfect Americans are humans.

The conclusion asserts the existence of at least one morally perfect American. But from the standpoint of modern logic, we can assert that "all morally perfect Americans are Americans" without asserting that there actually *are* any morally

> ### Summary of Rules for Determining the Validity of Categorical Syllogisms
>
> **Rule 1:** A valid standard-form categorical syllogism must contain exactly three terms, and each term must be used with the same meaning throughout the argument.
>
> **Rule 2:** In a valid standard-form categorical syllogism, the middle term must be distributed in at least one premise.
>
> **Rule 3:** In a valid standard-form categorical syllogism, a term must be distributed in the premises if it is distributed in the conclusion.
>
> **Rule 4:** In a valid standard-form categorical syllogism, the number of negative premises must be equal to the number of negative conclusions.
>
> **Rule 5:** No valid standard-form categorical syllogism with a particular conclusion can have two universal premises.

perfect Americans. We can analyze the statement "All morally perfect Americans are Americans" as involving a conditional, along the following lines: "If anything is a morally perfect American, then it is an American." And such a statement can be true even if the term employed in the if-clause denotes an empty class.

Check your understanding of the Aristotelian theory of the syllogism by completing the following exercises.

◆ Exercise 5.4

Part A: Constructing Valid Syllogisms   Both Aristotelian and modern logicians agree that the following syllogistic forms are valid.

> First figure: **AAA, EAE, AII, EIO**
> Second figure: **EAE, AEE, EIO, AOO**
> Third figure: **IAI, AII, OAO, EIO**
> Fourth figure: **AEE, IAI, EIO**

Write an English example of each of these 15 valid forms. Be sure your examples are in *standard form* (i.e., the major term should appear in the first premise, the minor term should appear in the second premise, and the conclusion should be stated last).

Part B: Forms   Specify the mood and figure of the following forms. Then apply the five rules set forth in this section to determine whether the forms are valid.

* **1.** No P are M. No M are S. So, no S are P.

   2. All M are P. No S are M. So, no S are P.

   3. All M are P. All M are S. So, all S are P.

* **4.** All P are M. All S are M. So, all S are P.

   5. No M are P. Some S are M. So, some S are not P.

   6. No M are P. All M are S. So, some S are not P.

* **7.** All P are M. Some S are not M. So, some S are not P.

   8. Some M are P. All S are M. So, some S are not P.

   9. All M are P. Some S are not M. So, some S are not P.

* **10.** Some P are not M. Some S are not M. So, some S are not P.

 11. All P are M. Some S are M. So, some S are P.

 12. No P are M. All M are S. So, no S are P.

* **13.** Some M are not P. All S are M. So, some S are not P.

 14. No M are P. Some M are not S. So, some S are not P.

 15. All P are M. No M are S. So, some S are not P.

* **16.** All M are P. All S are M. So, some S are P.

 17. All P are M. All M are S. So, all S are P.

 18. No P are M. All S are M. So, some S are not P.

* **19.** Some M are P. Some M are S. So, some S are P.

 20. Some P are M. All S are M. So, some S are P.

Part C: Valid or Invalid? For each of the following categorical syllogisms, specify the form using "S" to stand for the subject term, "P" for the predicate term, and "M" for the middle term. (If the English argument itself is not in standard form, be sure your form puts the major premise first, the minor premise second, and the conclusion last.) Next, identify the mood and figure. Finally, apply the five rules set forth in this section to determine whether the syllogism has a valid form.

* **1.** Some great scientists are famous. No TV stars are great scientists. So, some TV stars are not famous.

  2. No deathly ill people are hypochondriacs. All hypochondriacs are dysfunctional people. Accordingly, some deathly ill people are dysfunctional people.

  3. Some books written by Kant are not great books. For no great books are books that put their readers to sleep. But some books written by Kant are books that put their readers to sleep.

* **4.** No humans are animals. All members of *homo sapiens* are animals. Therefore, no humans are members of *homo sapiens*.

  5. All values that can be quantified are important values. No human emotions are values that can be quantified. Consequently, no human emotions are important values.

  6. No great altruists are great thinkers. Some great thinkers are people who make life better for humanity in general. It follows that some people who make life better for humanity in general are not great altruists.

* **7.** All cars are vehicles. All Ford automobiles are cars. Hence, some Ford automobiles are vehicles.

   8. All banks are edges of rivers. Some banks are financial institutions. Thus, some financial institutions are edges of rivers.

   9. All acts that promote the general welfare are commanded by God. For all acts commanded by God are obligatory acts. And all acts that promote the general welfare are obligatory acts.

* **10.** All of the greatest human achievements are accomplishments that have come at a great price. Some accomplishments that have come at a great price are not brilliant discoveries. We may conclude that some of the greatest human achievements are not brilliant discoveries.

   11. All kleptomaniacs are troubled persons. No Bodhisattvas are troubled persons. So, some kleptomaniacs are not Bodhisattvas.

   12. All biologists are vivisectionists. Some vivisectionists are well-intentioned people. Therefore, some biologists are well-intentioned people.

   13. Every schipperke is a small dog. Some small dogs are not black. Hence, not all black dogs are schipperkes.

   14. No bagatelle is important. Some important things are pleasurable. It follows that at least one bagatelle is not pleasurable.

   15. All Mennonites are Protestants. No Mennonites are Roman Catholics. Accordingly, no Protestants are Roman Catholics.

Notes

1. Negative terms such as "nonhuman" and "nondog" will be discussed more fully in section 5.3. Such terms can present problems when employing Venn diagrams (which will be introduced in section 5.2). See the next note for details.

2. Negative terms can complicate the use of the Venn method and so it is generally a good policy to avoid them. To illustrate, consider the following syllogism: "All cats are nondogs. Some mammals are dogs. So, some mammals are not cats." If we rewrite "All cats are nondogs" as "No cats are dogs," our diagram will be routine. But if instead we regard "All cats are nondogs" as a universal affirmative statement, then we have four terms in the argument: "cats," "nondogs," "mammals," and "dogs." Assuming we have just three circles in our diagram, one is labeled "mammals," one is labeled "cats," what about the third? We can label it "dogs," but if we do, our diagram for the first premise cannot be the standard diagram for a universal affirmative statement. (Try it!) On the other hand, if we label the third circle "nondogs," our diagram for the second premise cannot be the standard diagram for a particular affirmative statement.

3. The relevant work by George Boole is *The Mathematical Analysis of Logic* (London and Cambridge: Macmillan, Barclay, and Macmillan, 1847). My discussion of the Square of Opposition is indebted to that of Irving Copi and Carl Cohen, *Introduction to Logic*, 9th ed. (Englewood Cliffs, NJ: Prentice-Hall, 1994), pp. 229–234.

4. My formulation of Rule 4 is borrowed from Wesley C. Salmon, *Logic*, 3rd ed. (Englewood Cliffs, NJ: Prentice-Hall, 1984), p. 57.

5. My formulation of Rule 5 is borrowed from Copi and Cohen, *Introduction to Logic*, p. 266.

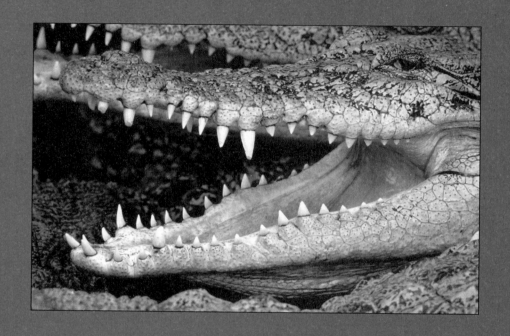

Chapter 6

Informal Fallacies

Some errors in reasoning are so obvious that no one is apt to be taken in by them. For example, probably no one would find the following argument persuasive:

1. Two plus two equals four. Therefore, Santa Claus exists.

But other errors in reasoning tend to be psychologically persuasive; these are called **fallacies**. In this chapter, we will describe some of the more common informal fallacies and classify them by type. Our first question, then, is, What is an *informal* fallacy?

Let's begin with the contrasting concept of a formal fallacy. A **formal fallacy** involves the *explicit* use of an invalid form. We encountered a number of formal fallacies in chapter 2. For example, the fallacy of affirming the consequent is a formal fallacy:

2. If nepotism is wrong, then it is destructive. And it is destructive. Hence, nepotism is wrong.

The form here is invalid: "If A, then B; B; so, A." The fallacy of denying the antecedent is another formal fallacy:

3. If good intentions make good sermons, then Reverend McGuire is a good preacher. Unfortunately, they don't; so he's not.

The form here is invalid as well: "If A, then B; not A; so, not B."

We have also seen formal fallacies in our examination of categorical syllogisms. For instance:

4. All cantaloupes are melons. All watermelons are melons. So, all watermelons are cantaloupes.

The form here is "All P are M; all S are M; so, all S are P" (using "S" to stand for the minor term, "P" for the major term, and "M" for the middle term). This form is invalid and (along with some other forms involving a similar error) is called the **fallacy of the undistributed middle** by Aristotelian logicians.

Not all fallacies are formal fallacies. **Informal fallacies** are errors in reasoning that do not involve the *explicit* use of an invalid form. Furthermore, exposing an informal fallacy requires an examination of the argument's *content*. We took note of one kind of informal fallacy in chapter 4, namely, equivocation. Here is a blatant example:

> 5. My wife's brother is a real pig. You should see him eat! And if he is a pig, then he is not human. So, he is not human.

If we ignore the content, argument (5) appears to be an example of *modus ponens*. But if we examine the content, we notice that the word "pig" is used with two different meanings. In the first premise, "pig" means "person who habitually overeats." In the second premise, "pig" means "hog" (i.e., a domesticated animal with a long snout and fat body). Once we spot the double meaning, we see that it destroys the logical linkage between the two premises. While the form initially appears to be *modus ponens*, an analysis of the content indicates that the form would be more accurately identified as follows: "A; if B, then C; so, C." This form is obviously invalid, but it is not *explicitly* employed in argument (5)— it remains hidden due to the double meaning of the word "pig." Thus, equivocation is an *informal* fallacy.

There are many types of informal fallacies, and logicians do not agree on the best way to classify them. However, the attempt to classify them has benefits, for it enables us to see some commonalities among them. In this text, informal fallacies are divided into four groups: (a) fallacies involving irrelevant premises, (b) fallacies involving insufficient evidence, (c) fallacies involving ambiguity, and (d) fallacies involving unwarranted premises. The reason for studying informal fallacies is simply this: By describing and labeling the more tempting ones, we increase our ability to resist their allure. (*Note:* Throughout this chapter, we will provide a contemporary name for each fallacy as well as the traditional Latin name when it is still used with some frequency.)

6.1 Fallacies Involving Irrelevant Premises

Some fallacies involve the use of premises that are logically irrelevant to their conclusions, but for psychological reasons, the premises may *seem* relevant. These fallacies are classified as *fallacies involving irrelevant premises.* Five varieties of this general class of fallacy are discussed in this section.

1. *Argument Against the Person* (Ad Hominem *Fallacy*)

The *argument against the person* (or *ad hominem* fallacy) involves attacking the person who advances an argument (or asserts a statement) as opposed to providing a rational critique of the argument (or statement) itself. (*Ad hominem* is a Latin phrase meaning "against the man.") Here is an example:

> 6. Jones argues for vegetarianism. He says it is wrong to kill animals unless you really need to for food, and that, as a matter of fact, nearly everyone can get enough food without eating meat. But Jones is just a nerdy intellectual. So, we can safely conclude that vegetarianism remains what it has always been—nonsense.

Here, Jones's argument is not given a rational critique; rather, Jones himself is criticized. And even if Jones is a "nerdy intellectual," this does not show that Jones's argument is flawed, nor does it show that vegetarianism is nonsense. The personal attack on Jones is simply irrelevant to the soundness of Jones's argument and irrelevant to the issue of vegetarianism.

Ad hominem arguments need not employ outright verbal abuse. In more subtle forms, they involve the attempt to discredit an opponent by suggesting that his or her judgment is distorted by some factor *even though the soundness of the opponent's argument (or truth of the opponent's view) is independent of the factor cited*. For example:

> 7. Ms. Fitch argues in favor of equal pay for equal work. She says it doesn't make sense to pay a person more for doing the same job just because he is male or Caucasian. But since Ms. Fitch is a woman, it's to her personal advantage to favor equal pay for equal work. After all, she would get an immediate raise if her boss accepted her argument! Therefore, her argument is worthless.

Here, an attempt is made to discredit the argument by showing that the arguer has something to gain if her conclusion is accepted. Of course, the activity of arguing can be, in a given case, simply a way of getting something the arguer wants. But this fact, by itself, does not prove that the arguer's reasoning is flawed. What is needed is a rational critique of the premises or inferences in question.

Another form of the argument against the person involves an attempt to suggest that the opponent is hypocritical—that is, that his views or arguments conflict with his own practice or with what he has said previously. This form of *ad hominem* argument is sometimes called the *tu quoque* (pronounced "too kwo-kway"), meaning "you too." For instance, suppose a 12-year-old argues as follows:

> 8. Dad tells me I shouldn't lie. He says lying is wrong because it makes people stop trusting one another. But I've heard my Dad lie. Sometimes he calls in "sick" to work when he isn't really sick. So, lying isn't actually wrong—Dad just doesn't like it when I lie.

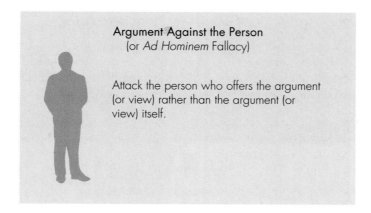

Argument Against the Person
(or *Ad Hominem* Fallacy)

Attack the person who offers the argument
(or view) rather than the argument (or
view) itself.

The *tu quoque* fallacy may succeed in embarrassing or discrediting the opponent, but the logical error should be clear upon reflection. For example, with regard to argument (8), that some people (including one's parents) lie, in no way shows that lying is morally permissible. In general, the fact that some people violate a given moral rule does not show that the rule is incorrect. So, the premise of (8), that "Dad lies," is irrelevant to the conclusion.

Let us consider one last example of the argument against the person before moving on:

9. During the 1980s, many American journalists passed harsh judgments on South African apartheid. They wrote that it was unjust, cruel, and immoral. But given the disgraceful history of race relations in America, these American journalists were in no position to pass judgment on South Africa. So, their judgments were without value.

Here again, the premises are irrelevant to the conclusion. The journalists themselves are under attack due to their American citizenship, but what is needed is evidence contrary to the moral judgments of the journalists, and that has not been offered.*

2. Straw Man Fallacy

A *straw man* fallacy occurs when the arguer attacks a misrepresentation of the opponent's view. The idea is to describe something that *sounds like* the opponent's view but is easier to knock down and then to refute it. This fallacy can be

---

*How persuasive are *ad hominem* arguments? One sociological study measures the extent to which such arguments influence third parties (not the arguers themselves, but those listening), and reaches these conclusions: (a) The persuasiveness of *ad hominem* arguments depends on the relative social status of the disputants (as perceived by third parties); (b) *ad hominem* arguments employed by either a high-status person (e.g., a boss) or a low-status person (e.g., a subordinate) are apt to be ineffective; and (c) *ad hominem* arguments are most likely to persuade third parties when the disputants are perceived as having the same social status. See David Diekema, "Social Status and the Effectiveness of Abusive Arguments," paper presented at the Annual Meeting of the Pacific Sociological Association, San Diego, 1994.

very effective from a rhetorical point of view if one's audience is not aware that the misrepresentation has taken place. However, when put bluntly, it is obvious that the premise is irrelevant to the conclusion:

> Premise: A misrepresentation of the view is false.
> Conclusion: The view is false.

Notice that the straw man fallacy results from a failure to honor Principle 4 of chapter 3: *Be fair and charitable in interpreting an argument.* Fairness demands that we represent the original accurately; charity demands that we put an argument in its best light when we are confronted with interpretive choices.

In order to demonstrate that a straw man fallacy has occurred, one obviously must provide a more accurate statement of the view that has been misrepresented. Equally obviously, one does not always have in hand the information needed to do this. But one can often "smoke out" a straw man fallacy by asking such appropriate questions as these: What were the exact words used in the original? Have any key words or phrases been changed or omitted? Does the context suggest that the author was deliberately exaggerating or leaving obvious exception clauses unstated?

Straw man fallacies often appear in political contexts. Some years ago, when the Equal Rights Amendment was being hotly debated, arguments of the following sort were sometimes offered against it:

> 10. Backers of the ERA believe in the total equality of the sexes. "Equal pay for equal work" is just the tip of the iceberg. Few realize that to ratify the ERA is to insist that 50 percent of the players in the National Football League should be women. Few realize that to ratify the ERA is to insist that there should no longer be separate public bathrooms for men and women. Believe me, it would be a great mistake to ratify the ERA.

The entire text of the proposed Equal Rights Amendment runs as follows: "Equality of rights under the law shall not be denied or abridged by the United States or by any state on account of sex."[1] Now, like many statements in the U.S. Constitution itself, this proposed amendment leaves room for interpretation. But it certainly seems unfair to describe it as requiring that half the players on professional football teams be women or as requiring that men and women use the same public bathrooms. Argument (10) attacks a straw man rather than the ERA itself.

The straw man fallacy is also committed when a view or argument is alleged to involve assumptions that it does not (or need not) involve. For example:

> 11. Susan advocates the legalization of cocaine. But I cannot agree with any position based on the assumption that cocaine is good for you and that a society of drug addicts can flourish. So, I disagree with Susan.

Of course, one can consistently advocate the legalization of cocaine and yet believe that cocaine is not good for people. For example, one may think that although drugs are harmful, legalizing them is the best way to eliminate the illegal drug traffic (and hence, the violence associated with it). Moreover, one can advocate the legalization of drugs without assuming or presupposing that a society of drug addicts can flourish. One might believe that legalization will not lead to a significant increase in the number of drug-addicted persons, especially if legalization is accompanied by a strong educational campaign on the dangers of using hard drugs.

Sometimes a persuasive (i.e., biased) definition is used to set up a straw man:

> 12. Empiricism is the view that nothing should be believed in unless it can be directly observed. Now, no one can see, hear, taste, smell, or touch protons, electrons, or quarks. So, while empiricists pretend to be advocates of science, their views in fact rule out the most advanced physical science of our times.

Professor Anthony Flew, author of A *Dictionary of Philosophy*, defines "empiricism" as "the thesis that all knowledge or at least all knowledge of matters of fact (as distinct from that of purely logical relations between concepts) is based on experience."[2] Now, since the phrase "is based on" is somewhat vague, the concept of empiricism has rather fuzzy borderlines. But Flew's definition does not have the empiricists insisting that we know only those things we have *directly* observed. We might know about the existence of some entities by extrapolation or because the best theories presuppose their existence. This knowledge would still be "based on" experience because it would be inferred using observation statements. Thus, Flew's definition is fair to the empiricist tradition in philosophy, while the definition contained in argument (12) is biased. By including the phrase "direct observation," the arguer makes empiricism a straw man. Incidentally, argument (12) illustrates how the straw man fallacy can become quite subtle when complex issues are involved. If a seemingly minor but actually important aspect of a view is distorted or omitted, the view itself may appear much easier to refute than it really is.

3. Appeal to Force (Ad Baculum *Fallacy*)

The *appeal to force* (or *ad baculum* fallacy) occurs whenever a conclusion is defended by a threat to the well-being of those who do not accept it. (*Baculum* is Latin for "staff," the staff being a symbol of power.) The threat may be either explicit or implicit. Let's start with a case involving the threat of physical harm, reminiscent of scenes from films about organized crime:

> 13. Mr. Jones, you helped us import the drugs. For this, the Boss is grateful. But now you say you're entitled to 50 percent of the profits. The Boss says you're entitled to 10 percent. Unless you see things the Boss's way, you're going to have a very nasty accident. So, you're entitled to 10 percent. Got it?

Of course, the threatened "nasty accident" has no logical bearing on the conclusion ("Jones is entitled to 10 percent"). But a credible threat might induce Jones to accept the conclusion.

An autocratic employer might argue as follows:

> 14. Lately there has been a lot of negative criticism of our policy on dental benefits. Let me tell you something, people. If you want to keep working here, you need to understand that our policy is fair and reasonable. I won't have anybody working here who thinks our policy is unfair or unreasonable.

Here, the threat of job loss is obviously irrelevant to the conclusion that the dental benefits are fair and reasonable. But again, the threat may very well influence the thinking of the employees.

The *ad baculum* fallacy may involve any sort of threat to one's well-being, including one's psychological well-being. For instance:

> 15. Listen, Valerie, I know you disagree with my view about the building project. You've made your disagreement clear to everyone. Well, it's time for you to see that you are mistaken. Let me get right to the point. I know you've been lying to your husband about where you go on Wednesday afternoons. Unless you want him to know where you really go, it's time for you to realize that I've been right about the building project all along. You follow me?

Of course, the threat to expose the lie in no way constitutes evidence for anyone's view on a building project. But fear is a strong motivator, and it can influence a person's thinking.

4. Appeal to the People (Ad Populum *Fallacy*)

The *appeal to the people* (or *ad populum* fallacy) is an attempt to persuade a person (or group) by appealing to the desire to be accepted or valued by others. (*Populum* is Latin for "people" or "nation.") For instance, a speaker at a political rally may elicit strong emotions from the crowd, making each individual want to believe his conclusion so as to feel a part of the group:

> 16. I look out at you all, and I tell you, I am proud to be here. Proud to belong to a party that stands for what is good for America. Proud to cast my lot with the kind of people who make this nation great. Proud to stand with men and women who can get our nation back on its feet. Yes, there are those who criticize us, who label our view of trade agreements as "protectionist." But when I look at you hard-working people, I know we're right, and the critics are wrong.

Of course, the strong feelings of the crowd do not lend logical support to anyone's view about trade agreements. Premises to the effect that "I am proud to be associated with you" and "you are hard-working people" are irrelevant to the conclusion (that "our view of trade agreements is right").

One doesn't have to be addressing a large group to commit the *ad populum* fallacy. Any attempt to convince by appealing to the need for acceptance (or approval) from others counts as an *ad populum* fallacy. For instance:

> 17. Ms. Riley, are you saying that President Bush made a moral error when he decided to go to war with Iraq? I can't believe my ears. That's not how Americans feel. Not true Americans, anyway. You *are* an American, aren't you, Ms. Riley?

The mere fact that Ms. Riley is an American provides her with no logical support for the conclusion that America's war with Iraq was just or moral. But like most Americans, Ms. Riley may wish to avoid being regarded as unpatriotic, and so an appeal to the people may influence her thinking.

The appeal to the people is common in advertising:

> 18. The new Electrojet 3000 cabriolet isn't for everyone. But then, you've always stood apart from the crowd, haven't you? So, the Electrojet 3000 is the car for you.

Here, the *ad populum* fallacy takes the form of "snob appeal," that is, an appeal to the desire to be regarded as superior to others.

5. The Appeal to Pity (Ad Misericordiam *Fallacy*)

The *appeal to pity* (or *ad misericordiam* fallacy) is the attempt to support a conclusion merely by evoking pity in one's audience *when the statements that evoke the pity are logically unrelated to the conclusion.* (*Misericordiam* is Latin for "pity" or "mercy.") For example, the chair of a faculty committee made the following speech to her dean:

> 19. We realize that our proposal concerning the library is flawed. But the merits of the proposal outweigh its flaws. After all, we worked awfully hard on it, and for so many hours! I hate to think we wasted all that time. Also, if you reject it, I might be denied my next promotion.

The premises here are simply irrelevant to the conclusion (that "the merits of the proposal outweigh its flaws"). Even if much time was spent developing the proposal, this in no way guarantees that its merits outweigh its flaws. And even if the dean's rejection of the proposal would lessen the likelihood of the arguer's receiving a promotion, this fact in no way supports the conclusion.

The appeal to pity is not, generally speaking, very subtle. But if the arguer succeeds in evoking sufficiently strong feelings of pity, he may distract his audience from the logic of the situation and create a desire to accept the conclusion. For this reason, lawyers often use the appeal to pity in an effort to convince judges and juries that their clients are not guilty or not deserving of a harsh sentence.

Summary of Fallacies Involving Irrelevant Premises

For psychological reasons, the premises in these arguments may *seem* relevant to the conclusion, but in fact they are not.

1. The **argument against the person** (or *ad hominem* fallacy): Instead of providing a rational critique of an argument (or statement), one attacks the person who advances the argument (or asserts the statement).
2. The **straw man fallacy**: The claim that a statement or viewpoint is false on the grounds that a misrepresentation of it is false.
3. The **appeal to force** (or *ad baculum* fallacy): The attempt to defend a conclusion by threatening the well-being of those who do not accept it.
4. The **appeal to the people** (or *ad populum* fallacy): The attempt to persuade a person (or group) by appealing to the desire to be accepted or valued by others.
5. The **appeal to pity** (or *ad misericordiam* fallacy): The attempt to support a conclusion merely by evoking pity in one's audience. *when the statements that evoke the pity are logically unrelated to the conclusion.*

The *ad misericordiam* fallacy must be distinguished from arguments that support the need for a compassionate response to persons whose plight calls for compassion. For example, the following sort of argument is *not* an example of the *ad misericordiam* fallacy:

> 20. As a result of war and famine, thousands of children in country X are malnourished. You can help by sending money to Relief Agency Y. So, please send whatever you can spare to Relief Agency Y.

While the information in the premises of this sort of argument is apt to evoke pity, the information is also logically relevant to the conclusion. Hence, there is no *ad misericordiam* fallacy here.

The following exercise gives you an opportunity to identify examples of the fallacies discussed in this section. More examples of these types of fallacies can be found in exercise 6.3, part B ("Argument Diagrams and Multiple Fallacies").

◆ Exercise 6.1

Fallacies Involving Irrelevant Premises   Most of the following passages exemplify a fallacy discussed in this section. If a fallacy is committed, name the type of fallacy and explain why the passage is an example of that type. If no fallacy is committed, simply write "not a fallacy."

* **1.** Social Darwinists, such as Herbert Spencer, hold that the development and structure of human societies can be explained in terms of evolutionary principles, such as the survival of the fittest. But I reject Social Darwinism because Spencer was a real bonehead.

2. Your Honor, it's true that I killed my parents. I fully admit that I murdered them in cold blood. But I should get a light sentence. After all, I *am* an orphan.

3. As I travel around and talk to people I find that many do not even know what genetic engineering is. Well, genetic engineering is best defined as the most recent in a long line of attempts, on the part of human beings, to play God. Of course, the proponents of genetic engineering overlook just one little fact: We humans are not God. And that's why genetic engineering is profoundly immoral.

* 4. All the really hot new thinkers are using principles from sociobiology. It's the new wave in ethics. So, you should accept the principles of sociobiology.

5. Robert, I've heard you're a communist. So, let me tell you something. Around here, we know communism is evil. And we have ways of making communists see the error of their ways. The last communist who passed through this town suddenly saw the light after some of the boys had a little "talk" with him one night. I hope these facts will clarify things for you. You do understand that communism is evil, don't you?

6. Yes, Jill argues for deconstruction. But her mind is so open her brains are falling out. You can safely ignore whatever she has to say.

* 7. It is quite clear what the proponents of legalized euthanasia are seeking. Put simply, they are seeking the power to kill anyone who has a serious illness. And that is why I stand opposed to legalized euthanasia.

8. Consuming alcohol in large quantities is bad for your health. So, if you care about your health, you should consume alcohol in moderation or abstain from it entirely.

9. So many people these days are against prayer in the public schools! Of course, the assumptions underlying this view include (a) there is no God, (b) only matter exists, and (c) life is essentially meaningless. That is why we must fight against these people who seek to remove prayer from our public schools.

* 10. Professor Jackson, this paper merits at least a "B." I stayed up all night working on it. And if I don't get a "B," I'll be put on academic probation.

11. I find it mildly amusing that Mr. and Mrs. Billings are advocating school reforms. But I certainly do not see any reason to take their proposal seriously. Both of them were poor students in high school.

12. Intelligent, refined people insist on the best wines. And our Old World Merlot is the best red wine available. Obviously, Old World Merlot is for you.

* 13. Since you became a member of this club, you've raised quite a ruckus about women's rights. And I know you sincerely believe in feminism. But if you go on holding these extreme views, I will see to it that you are never voted in as an officer of this club. And you know I can make good on that threat. I hope you follow me: Your feminist views are too radical and need to be toned down.

14. The future free actions of humans can be known in advance only if time travel is possible. But you're a fool if you think time travel is possible. So, it is not true that the future free actions of humans can be known in advance.

15. The school needs a football team. I hope you agree. One thing I can tell you for sure: If you want to fit in around here, you'll see this issue the way the rest of us do. And we all think the school needs a football team.

* 16. Dr. Herzheimer has written essays criticizing self-help books from the standpoint of logic and science. I realize Dr. Herzheimer is a famous philosopher, but I think it's immature and cold-hearted to criticize people who are trying to help others get their lives together. Thus, I myself give no credence to Dr. Herzheimer's work whatsoever.

17. Republicans are people who believe that the rich should get richer and the poor poorer. They are against welfare and against taxes for people who can well afford to pay taxes. Republicans also hold that the only good immigrants are either wealthy or well educated. Thus, I strongly urge you not to be a Republican.

18. Excuse me, Mr. Smith, did I hear you correctly? Did you say that boxing should be banned? Sure, boxing is a little dangerous, but real men love boxing. Therefore, boxing should not be banned.

* 19. Mr. Johnson argues that we should stop eating meat. But did you know that Mr. Johnson owns the Vegetables Forever Produce Company? Oh yes, he stands to gain a lot, financially speaking, if the rest of us become vegetarians. I think we can safely ignore his line of argument.

20. Nowadays, everybody that's anybody believes in reincarnation. So, you should too.

21. What is the prochoice view? This: It is permissible to kill innocent human beings at will as long as they are small and helpless. By implication, then, the prochoice view would permit the slaughter of children on a wide scale. And that is why we should all oppose the prochoice view.

* 22. Your Honor, my client does not deserve a year in prison. He has small children that need a father, and a wife that needs a husband.

23. You really think that drugs should be legalized? Think again. Dad will cut you out of the inheritance if you go on thinking like that. That should make it clear to you just how far off base your views really are.

24. Clairvoyance is the alleged ability to "see" with the mind's eye what cannot literally be seen. For example, some clairvoyants have claimed to "see" the death of a loved one from whom they were separated by many miles. Of course, you can imagine the kind of attention clairvoyants receive from the media, not to mention the money they can squeeze out of weak-minded people who are curious about the paranormal. Thus, I think the alleged reports of clairvoyance are just hype.

* 25. Joe, I know you think that the new electronics plant should be located in Seattle. Well, you're wrong. It should be located in Spokane. How do I know? Joe, I'm your boss, right? And you're up for a promotion next month, right? You want the promotion, right? Well, then, the conclusion is obvious: The new electronics plant should be located in Spokane.

26. Smoking cigarettes can harm one's health. So, it's best to avoid smoking assuming one wants to be healthy.

27. You have argued that it is wrong for me to hunt deer. Well, you eat hamburger, and that involves the killing of cows. Moreover, it is obvious that there is no moral difference between killing cows and killing deer, so your argument is unsound.

* 28. The poor people in many Third World countries are malnourished and highly susceptible to disease. These people are in need of help for their poverty is so great that many of them can do little to help themselves. But many Americans have discretionary income well beyond what they need personally and these (relatively) wealthy Americans could help the poor in the Third World—at least to some extent. Moreover, from a moral point of view, it is good to help those who really need help. So, from a moral point of view, it would be a good thing for these (relatively) wealthy Americans to help the poor in the Third World.

29. I don't deserve a speeding ticket, officer. Yes, I admit I was doing 60 in a school zone. But I've had a really rough day. I was angry about some stuff that happened at work. Everybody has to let some steam off once in a while, don't they? Give me a break.

30. Your Honor, the witness has just lied to the court three times. This has been verified by the tape recordings and by the reports of all of the other witnesses. Therefore, I submit that the witness's testimony is untrustworthy.

6.2 Fallacies Involving Insufficient Evidence

The first set of fallacies involved premises that are irrelevant to their conclusions. The second set involves premises that are in some degree relevant to their conclusions but nevertheless provide insufficient support for them. We shall call these *fallacies involving insufficient evidence*.

6. Appeal to Ignorance (Ad Ignorantiam Fallacy)

The *appeal to ignorance* (or *ad ignorantiam* fallacy) involves one of the following: either (a) the claim that a statement is true (or may be reasonably believed true) simply because it hasn't been proven false or (b) the claim that a statement is false (or may be reasonably believed false) simply because it hasn't been proven true. Here are two corresponding examples:

21. After centuries of trying, no one has been able to prove that reincarnation occurs. So, at this point, I think we can safely conclude that reincarnation does not occur.

22. After centuries of trying, no one has been able to show that reincarnation does not occur. Therefore, reincarnation occurs.

Put starkly, the claim that a statement is false because it hasn't been proven is manifestly erroneous. By such logic, scientists would have to conclude that their unproven hypotheses are false. And surely it is wiser for scientists to take a "wait-

and-see" attitude. After all, we do not have to believe or disbelieve every statement we consider, for we often have the option of suspending judgment—that is, of not believing the statement is true and (simultaneously) not believing it is false. We can remain neutral. Similarly, the claim that a statement is true (or may reasonably be believed true) simply because it hasn't been disproven is illogical. By this principle, every new scientific hypothesis is true (or at least it can reasonably be believed to be true) unless it has been disproven—*no matter how flimsy the evidence for it is.*

The *ad ignorantiam* fallacy is often committed in organizations during periods of change. Those opposing change may argue along the following lines:

> 23. It has not been proven that the proposed changes will be beneficial. Therefore, they will not be beneficial.

And the counterargument may be this:

> 24. There is no solid evidence showing that the proposed changes will not be beneficial. Therefore, they will be beneficial.

Both arguments are flawed. As for (23), there may be no way of obtaining the evidence apart from organizational experimentation—that is, trying the proposal. So, demanding the evidence may be unrealistic and unreasonable. As for (24), problems with the proposal may become evident once it is tried, so the current lack of evidence against it is obviously no guarantee that it will work.

Although the appeal to ignorance is a fallacy, the failure to discover evidence for (or against) a statement can be relevant in establishing its truth value. To illustrate, suppose an employee is accused of theft by her employer. If the security department conducts a thorough investigation and turns up no evidence of theft, this fact is certainly relevant in establishing the innocence of the employee. However, this type of reasoning makes sense, from a logical point of view, only to the extent that it is reasonable to assume that evidence would probably turn up if an investigation were conducted.

Some confusion regarding the *ad ignorantiam* fallacy may stem from the assumption used in courts of law that a defendant is *innocent until proven guilty.* This important legal principle is *not* a principle of logic. The legal principle is designed primarily to prevent the unjust punishment of the innocent, *not* to increase the chances of correctly identifying *all* those who have committed crimes. Undoubtedly, many defendants have committed the crimes they are accused of even though the evidence is not sufficient to prove them guilty according to accepted legal standards. Our legal system is deliberately designed to prevent one kind of unwanted result (namely, the punishment of the innocent) at the risk of allowing another unwanted result (namely, letting persons who have committed crimes go free). But we can recognize the usefulness and wisdom of the legal principle that "one is innocent until proven guilty" *without* supposing that it is a correct principle of logic.

7. Appeal to Unreliable Authority (Ad Verecundiam Fallacy)

The *appeal to unreliable authority* (or *ad verecundiam* fallacy) is an appeal to an authority *when the reliability of the authority may reasonably be doubted.* (*Ad vere-cundiam* is Latin for "appeal to authority.") A reliable authority is one who can be counted on, for the most part, to provide correct information in a given area. And it is important to keep in mind that an appeal to *reliable* authority is generally appropriate. For example, when we cite encyclopedias, dictionaries, textbooks, or maps, we make an appeal to the authority of experts. This makes perfectly good sense as long as we are appealing to authorities whose reliability is not in doubt. However, when there is legitimate doubt about whether an authority is reliable, then the appeal to authority is weak. Such an appeal may provide *some* evidence for the conclusion, but not enough to establish it.

Ad verecundiam fallacies are common in advertising, when celebrities who lack the relevant expertise endorse products. For example:

> 25. Mike "Monster" Malone, left tackle for the Seattle Sea Lions, says that Chocolate Zonkers are a nutritional breakfast cereal. So, Chocolate Zonkers are a nutritional breakfast cereal.

Malone may be a fine athlete, but we need to know whether he is an expert in nutrition, and the argument leaves us in doubt on that point. Thus, an *ad vere-cundiam* fallacy has occurred.

A more subtle appeal to unreliable authority occurs when a well-known expert in one field is cited as an expert in another field even though he or she lacks expertise in it. This form of the fallacy is especially subtle if the two fields are related (at least in the minds of the audience). For example:

> 26. Professor Bloggs, the well-known astronomer, has done extensive research on distant galaxies. He points out that human bodies are composed of atoms that were once part of distant stars. According to Bloggs, this gives human life a sense of drama and significance equal to that inherent in the world's great mythologies and theologies. Thus, Bloggs corrects the common error of supposing that materialism reduces the drama or significance of human life.

Even if it *is* an error to suppose that materialism reduces the drama or significance of human life, the reasoning in argument (26) is flawed. An astronomer is an expert in the science of the stars and other heavenly bodies. So, as an astronomer, Professor Bloggs is in a position to tell us that the atoms in our bodies once belonged to the stars. But his authority about these matters does not automatically transfer to such philosophical topics as the comparative merits of mythologies, theologies, or worldviews in general. Expertise in one area doesn't necessarily "rub off" on another.

Argument (26) also reminds us of another point to keep in mind when evaluating an appeal to authority—namely, that the appeal to authorities in matters of controversy is often problematic. After all, in such matters, the authorities themselves often disagree. And when this occurs, if we have no good reason to suppose that one authority is more likely to be correct than another, then the appeal to authority is weak.

In conversation and in popular writing, one often encounters arguments of the form "Studies have shown X. So, X." In many cases, such arguments are *ad verecundiam* fallacies. What studies? When were they conducted? By whom? Were the studies conducted in a scientific fashion? Are there equally scientific studies that contradict the ones cited? Thus, the appeal to unreliable authority is a common fallacy, but it sometimes requires research or careful questioning to expose it.

8. False Cause Fallacy

The *false cause* fallacy occurs when one possible cause of a phenomenon is assumed to be a (or the) cause *although reasons are lacking for excluding other possible causes*. This fallacy comes in various forms. Perhaps the most common form is called in Latin, *Post hoc, ergo propter hoc*, which means "after this, therefore because of this." This form of the false cause fallacy occurs whenever an arguer illegitimately assumes that because event X preceded event Y, X caused Y. Here is an example:

> 27. Since I came into office two years ago, the rate of violent crime has decreased significantly. So, it is clear that the longer prison sentences we recommended are working.

The longer prison sentences may be a causal factor, of course, but the mere fact that the longer sentences preceded the decrease in violent crime does not prove this. Many other possible causal factors need to be considered. For example, have economic conditions improved? Are more jobs available? Have the demographics of the area changed, so that the population of young men (statistically the group mostly likely to commit violent crimes) is smaller relative to the population as a whole? Has there been an increase in the number of police officers on patrol?

Consider another example of the false cause fallacy:

> 28. Since sex education has become common, we've had a marked increase in promiscuity. So, sex education causes promiscuity.

Here, the arguer fails in two ways: (a) by ignoring other possible causal factors and (b) by failing to explain the alleged linkage between sex education and promiscuity. Regarding (a), it may be that promiscuity actually results from a third factor, such as the breakdown of the broadly Protestant sexual code that historically typified American attitudes. (This breakdown seems to have occurred gradually during the first half of the 20th century and then to have accelerated rapidly during the 1960s and 1970s.) Regarding (b), the arguer ignores the possibility that the causation may go *from* the phenomenon of promiscuity *to* sex education, rather than vice versa. But surely the reason many people advocate sex education is that they are concerned about the increase in sexual activity among young people and seek to mitigate its negative consequences. So, it may be that promiscuity gives rise to sex education, rather than vice versa. Again, the main point is that we cannot rightly assume that sex education causes promiscuity merely on the grounds that it precedes an increase in promiscuity.

Not all false cause fallacies involve the unwarranted assumption that if X precedes Y, then X causes Y. For instance:

29. The best professional athletes receive big salaries. Therefore, in order to guarantee that Smith will become one of the best professional athletes, we should give him a big salary.

Although a big salary may encourage a fine athlete to try even harder, argument (29) confuses the cause with the effect. It is successful athletic performance (in conjunction with the popular demand for spectator sports) that leads to big salaries for some athletes. Obviously, one cannot turn a mediocre athlete into a star simply by paying him a big salary.

Another version of the false cause fallacy occurs when many causes are (or may well be) operative but one of them is illegitimately claimed to be the sole cause:

30. The scores on standardized tests have been dropping for several decades. What accounts for this? Well, during these same decades, the average time a child spends watching TV (per day) has increased. So, the cause is obvious: Kids are watching too much TV when they need to be reading instead.

The increase in time spent watching TV is a likely contributor to a drop in scores on such standardized tests as the SAT. But insufficient evidence is provided for the conclusion that the time spent watching TV is the *sole* cause. Other factors may be at work, such as a decrease in parental involvement or deficiencies in the public school system.

One special variety of the false cause fallacy is the *slippery slope* fallacy. This fallacy occurs when the arguer claims that a chain reaction will occur but there is insufficient evidence that one (or more) events in the chain will cause the others. The chain of causes is supposedly like a steep slope—if you take one step on the slope, you'll slide all the way down. And since you don't want to slide all the way down, don't take the first step. Here is an example:

31. Never buy a lottery ticket. People who buy lottery tickets soon find that they want to gamble on horses. Next, they develop a strong urge to go to Las Vegas and bet their life savings in the casinos. The addiction to gambling gradually ruins their family life. Eventually, they die, homeless and lonely.

Now, the links in this alleged causal chain clearly are weak. This is not to say that gambling is a risk-free practice. It is only to say that, logically speaking, when causal connections are claimed, there needs to be sufficient evidence that the connections are genuine. And to claim that buying a lottery ticket will cause one to die homeless and lonely is plainly to make a claim that is insufficiently supported by the evidence.

Slippery slope fallacies often play on our deepest fears. During the Vietnam War, it was frequently claimed that if Vietnam fell to communism, a chain reaction would occur, with the result that many countries would come under communist rule. From a historical perspective, it seems apparent that there was never any solid evidence that such a chain reaction would have occurred. Nevertheless, many Americans feared that it would. Thus, the slippery slope fallacy was persuasive because it played on people's fears.

Therapists sometimes call the slippery slope fallacy "catastrophizing." For example, a person's fears may lead him to think that a relatively minor incident will lead to utter catastrophe:

32. I told a joke at the party. It flopped. So, everyone there thought I was a loser. So, I'll never be invited again. In fact, if word gets out, I won't be invited anywhere. And I'm sure they're all talking about my stupid joke. So, I've completely ruined my chances for a decent social life. There's nothing left for me now but years of loneliness and misery. How I wish I'd never told that joke!

Although this example is extreme, it is a common human tendency to make rash assumptions about causal chains. The slippery slope fallacy is alive and well in the human heart.

False Cause Fallacy

Multiple Possible Causes

○
○
○

Assuming that one possible cause is a (or the) cause when reasons are lacking for excluding other possible causes.

The following exercise gives you an opportunity to identify examples of the fallacies discussed in this section. More examples of these types of fallacies can be found in exercise 6.3, part B ("Argument Diagrams and Multiple Fallacies").

Summary of Fallacies Involving Insufficient Evidence

The premises of these arguments are (or at least can be) relevant to their conclusions, but the premises do not provide sufficient evidence to establish the conclusions.

6. The **appeal to ignorance** (or *ad ignorantiam* fallacy): The claim that a statement is true (or may be believed true) simply because it has not been proven false; or the claim that a statement is false (or may be believed false) simply because it has not been proven true.

7. The **appeal to unreliable authority** (or *ad verecundiam* fallacy): An appeal to authority when the reliability of the authority may reasonably be doubted.

8. The **false cause fallacy**: Occurs when one possible cause of a phenomenon is assumed to be a (or the) cause although reasons are lacking for excluding other possible causes.

◆ Exercise 6.2

Fallacies Involving Insufficient Evidence   Most of the following passages exemplify a fallacy discussed in this section. If a fallacy is committed, name the type of fallacy and explain why the passage is an example of that type. If no fallacy is committed, simply write "not a fallacy."

* 1. In a recent speech, the president of General Motors asserted that our country has drifted dangerously away from its religious and ethical moorings. In light of this pronouncement, the cheery optimism of the liberals is no longer reasonable.

2. Although they've certainly tried, scientists have not been able to demonstrate that ESP is a myth. So, ESP is probably real.

3. On Monday, Bill drank scotch and soda and noticed that he got drunk. On Tuesday, Bill drank whiskey and soda, and noticed that he got drunk. On Wednesday, Bill drank bourbon and soda and noticed that he got drunk. Bill concluded that soda causes drunkenness.—Adapted from Wesley Salmon, *Logic*, 3rd ed. (Englewood Cliffs, NJ: Prentice-Hall, 1984), p. 112.

* 4. If smoking is not harmful, then it is not wrong. And the tobacco companies say that smoking is not harmful. Therefore, smoking is not wrong.

5. Of course it is reasonable to believe that we have been visited by extraterrestrial beings. After all, plenty of skeptics have tried, but none has been able to disprove that such visitations have occurred.

6. Left turn signals frequently occur just before an automobile turns left. Right turn signals frequently occur just before an automobile turns right. Consequently, turn signals cause automobiles to turn.

* 7. My psychology professor says that religious experience is generated out of the deep human need for a father-figure, not by an encounter with an actual deity. So, religious experience is not really an experience of God.

8. Leonardo da Vinci's paintings are immoral if they incite rape. And the Reverend Posner states that da Vinci's paintings incite rape. Hence, da Vinci's paintings are immoral.

9. I do not have very much information about Mr. Reed, but there is nothing in his file to disprove that he's a communist. So, he probably is one.

* 10. We never lost a war prior to Vietnam. What had changed? Well, I'll tell you: The generation that went off to fight in the Vietnam War was the first generation in this country to grow up on rock music. It was rock music that brought about our downfall.

11. Keegan is a reliable authority on military history. Keegan says that it was morally wrong for the Americans to fight in World War I. Hence, it was morally wrong for the Americans to fight in World War I.

12. Day always follows night. The two are perfectly correlated. Therefore, night causes day.

* 13. In 1742, Christian Goldbach conjectured that every even number greater than 2 is the sum of two primes. Mathematicians have been trying to prove Goldbach's conjecture ever since, but no one has succeeded in doing so. After two and a half centuries, I think we can safely conclude that Goldbach was wrong.

14. That young man was just fine until he read Kierkegaard's *Fear and Trembling*. It wasn't but a week or so later that he began to walk in his sleep and to emit those awful moans. Therefore, *Fear and Trembling* is a dangerous book.

15. According to the *Encyclopaedia Britannica*, Mary Cassatt, who is often considered American's greatest woman painter, was born in 1844 and died in 1926. So, Cassatt lived from 1844 till 1926.

* 16. After centuries of trying, no one has been able to prove that God exists. The attempt seems to be futile. So, at this point, I think we can safely conclude that there is no God.

17. We could get control of the crime problem in the United States if we would just punish criminals harshly. In Saudi Arabia, for example, thieves get their hands chopped off. Murderers are immediately put to death. And the rate of crime in Saudi Arabia is much lower than the rate of crime in the United States. Therefore, harsh punishments would greatly reduce the rate of crime in the United States.

18. After centuries of trying, no one has been able to disprove the existence of God. And how they've tried! Some philosophers and skeptics have devoted their lives to it. Therefore, God exists.

* 19. Without the discoveries of the great physicist Albert Einstein, the atomic bomb could not have been invented. And Einstein said that it was immoral for America to drop the atomic bomb on Hiroshima. Therefore, it was immoral for America to drop the atomic bomb on Hiroshima.

20. The largest slave revolt in U.S. history was one that occurred near New Orleans in 1811. Four or five hundred slaves were involved, lightly armed with cane knives, axes, and clubs. They wounded a plantation owner and killed his son. The revolt was put down by the U.S. Army, which attacked the slaves, killing 66 of them.

This is all true, for I read about it in Howard Zinn's *A People's History of the United States* (New York: HarperCollins, 1995). And Dr. Zinn is a well-known historian.

21. No one has ever proven that miracles do not happen. Therefore, miracles do happen.

* 22. Folk dancing is bad because it leads to ballroom dancing, which in turn leads to modern dancing. And modern dancing leads to promiscuity, which causes a total breakdown in the moral fabric of a country, and hence a lapse into primitive avagery.

23. Scientists have shown that a person loses a very small but measurable amount of weight at the time of death. This weight loss is probably due to the soul's leaving the body at that time. What else could account for this phenomenon? Here we have unexpected scientific evidence for the existence of an immaterial soul.

24. Violent crime has been on the increase for the past two decades. The quantity of violent movies has also increased during this time. Therefore, in all likelihood, the cause of the increase in violent crime is the increase in the quantity of violent movies.

* 25. I have worn these socks to the last five baseball games. Each time, I've gotten a base hit. So, these are my lucky socks. I play better when I wear them.

26. No one has been able to prove that astrology is nonsense. For this reason I have concluded that astrology is not nonsense—rather, it is an insightful way of viewing our lives and the world around us.

27. I warned those boys not to stand on Prince Valdinsky's grave. He was murdered, you know. And when he was being buried, his mother put a curse on anyone who showed disrespect for his grave. I was there—it was a very eerie thing to watch. Anyway, those boys wouldn't listen, and now look a them, all broken up from that automobile crash. I tell you, that curse worked!

* 28. My sociology professor says that monogamy is an unjust form of social organization. Therefore, monogamy is an unjust form of social organization.

29. According to Lillian Roxon's *Rock Encyclopedia,* it was an English band called the Zombies that came out with the hit record "She's Not There" in 1965. So, while you say "She's Not There" was by the Beatles, it was really by the Zombies.

30. Before television came along, we didn't have much of a problem with illegal drugs. But people learn about drugs on TV, and then they want the drugs. So, TV is ruining this country.

6.3 Fallacies Involving Ambiguity and Fallacies Involving Unwarranted Premises

In this section, we will discuss two rather different types of informal fallacies: (A) fallacies involving ambiguity and (B) fallacies involving unwarranted premises.

A. Fallacies Involving Ambiguity

Arguments are sometimes flawed because they contain ambiguous words (phrases or statements) or because they involve a subtle confusion between two closely related concepts. These we will call *fallacies involving ambiguity*, and we will discuss four kinds of them.

9. Equivocation

We first discussed this fallacy in chapter 4. Recall that *equivocation* occurs when two (or more) meanings of a word (or phrase) are used in a context in which validity requires a single meaning of that word (or phrase). Previously, we considered equivocations involving two meanings for a single *term* (roughly, a word or phrase that can serve as a subject of a statement). Let us here consider a more subtle version of equivocation, in which the double meaning involves a verb:

> 33. I agree with Christians in their claim that God is love. But unlike Christians, I'm not afraid to draw the obvious logical consequence: Love is God.

The gist of the argument is this: "God is love; therefore, love is God." And it might be tempting to suppose that the argument has this form:

> 34. X is identical with Y; therefore Y is identical with X.

Form (34) is valid—for example, "Samuel Clemens is identical with Mark Twain; therefore, Mark Twain is identical with Samuel Clemens." But argument (33) does not really have form (34), for when Christians say, "God is love," they don't mean that God is identical with love. Rather, they mean that God has the attribute of being loving. Thus, in the premise of (33), "is" means "has the attribute of," while in the conclusion, "is" means "is identical with." These two meanings differ, and the difference renders (33) invalid. To see this, compare the following arguments:

> 35. The earth is (i.e., has the attribute of being) round. So, roundness is identical with the earth.
> 36. The moon is (i.e., has the attribute of being) round. So, roundness is identical with the moon.

Arguments (35) and (36) are invalid. The premises are true, but the conclusions are false (for if the earth and the moon are each *identical* to roundness, then the earth and the moon are identical to each other—which is obviously false). Thus, the following form of argument is invalid:

> 37. X has attribute Y. So, Y is identical with X.

But this appears to be the form of argument (33): "God is love (i.e., has the attribute of being loving). So, love is identical with God." Therefore, a careful analysis of the content of argument (33) reveals that it is invalid due to the shift in meaning of the verb "is."

10. Amphiboly

The fallacy of *amphiboly* is similar to equivocation except that the double meaning is due to a syntactic deficiency, such as a grammatical error or a mistake in punctuation (rather than to an ambiguous word or phrase). In other words, an *amphiboly* is an inference that is invalid because of its dependence on an ambiguity *that is due to sentence structure*. Here is an example:

> 38. Author Myron Mobbins warns about the negative effects of subtle lies in his book *Liars Tell Lies*. So, given that Mobbins's book contains subtle lies, perhaps it is best not to read it.

Presumably, Mobbins is not warning people about subtle lies *that occur in his own book*; rather, in his book, he is warning people about the negative effects of subtle lies that originate from other sources. But the conclusion drawn in argument (38) results from a different interpretation of the syntactically flawed premise. Amphiboly often occurs when someone interprets a syntactically deficient statement in a way that was not intended by the original author (or speaker).

Here is another example of amphiboly:

> 39. Professor Warren gave a lecture on homicide in Tiffany Hall, Room 208. I gather that a lot of people have been murdered in that room.

While amphibolies are often easily spotted, they can be rather subtle. In later chapters, we will examine some amphibolies that are easily overlooked.*

11. Composition

The label "fallacy of composition" applies to two similar types of invalid inference. The first type is *an invalid inference from the nature of the parts to the nature of the whole*. For instance:

> 40. Each of the parts of this airplane are very light. Therefore, the airplane itself is very light.

---

*Here is an example that we will discuss in chapter 12: "If God foreknows that I'll sin tomorrow, then necessarily I'll sin tomorrow. God foreknows that I'll sin tomorrow. So, necessarily I'll sin tomorrow." The amphiboly results from the placement of the word "necessarily."

Of course, if enough light parts are conjoined, the airplane itself may be quite heavy, and so the argument is invalid. Here is another example of the parts-to-whole type of fallacy of composition:

> 41. Each player on the football team is outstanding. Hence, the team itself is outstanding.

Even if each of the players on a team is outstanding, the team itself may not be outstanding if there is a lack of teamwork or insufficient opportunity to practice together.

It should be noted that not all inferences from part to whole are invalid. For example:

> 42. Each part of the machine weighs more than one pound, and the machine has five parts. Consequently, the machine itself weighs more than one pound.

Obviously, argument (42) is valid. But (40) and (41) make it clear that the following argument form is *not* in general valid: "Each part of X has attribute Y; therefore, X itself has attribute Y." However, since composition is an *informal* fallacy, it cannot be detected simply by identifying the argument form. One must also examine the content, especially the attribute in question, before passing judgment on the validity of part-to-whole inferences. And there is no simple formula for determining whether a given attribute will lead to fallacies of composition. One must evaluate part-to-whole inferences on a case-by-case basis.

The second type of fallacy of composition is *an invalid inference from attributes of members of a group to attributes of the group itself*. Here is an example:

> 43. Elephants eat more than humans. So, elephants taken as a group eat more than humans taken as a group.

This argument illustrates the traditional distinction between *distributive* and *collective* predication. In the premise, "Elephants eat more than humans," the attribute of "eating more than" is predicated distributively; that is, each *individual* elephant is said to eat more than any *individual* human eats. In the conclusion, however, the attribute of "eating more than" is predicated collectively; that is, elephants *taken as a group* are said to eat more than humans *taken as a group*. Thus, while the premise of (43) is true, its conclusion is false simply because there are so many more humans than elephants.

The two forms of the fallacy of composition are related, because the relationship of parts to a whole is analogous to the relationship of members to a group (or collective). However, these relationships are not identical. A whole must have its parts organized or arranged in a particular way. For instance, if we take an automobile apart and ship the parts to hundreds of different locations, the automobile no longer exists, but the collection of parts still exists.

The fallacy of composition is here classified as a fallacy of ambiguity because it often gains its persuasive force from a confusion of concepts. Consider again this example: "The team members are excellent; so the team is excellent." While on reflection there is a clear distinction between the team members and the team, the two concepts are easily confused, since the team is merely its members *organized in a certain way*. So, a less-than-clear grasp of the concepts involved may obscure the error in reasoning.

It should be noted that in some cases, it is a matter of controversy whether an argument exemplifies the fallacy of composition. For instance, some philosophers think the following argument is an example of the fallacy of composition while others do not:

44. Each part of the universe is a dependent entity (i.e., depends for its existence on some other entity). So, the universe itself is a dependent entity.

The conclusion of argument (44) has been used by some philosophers to argue for the existence of God. But does the premise of (44) support the conclusion? Some philosophers doubt that the concept of dependence is understood well enough to legitimate a conclusion about the universe as a whole (even if each part of the universe *is* a dependent entity). This controversy has yet to be settled in a definitive way.

Fallacy of Composition

Parts or members have this attribute.   therefore   The whole (or group) has this attribute.

12. Division

The fallacy of *division* is the reverse of the fallacy of composition. That is, the fallacy of division involves *an invalid inference from the nature of the whole to the nature of the parts, or from the nature of a group to the nature of its members*. Here is an example of the whole-to-part type of fallacy:

45. The airplane is heavy. So, each of its parts is heavy.

Of course, some of the parts of a heavy airplane may be very light. Thus, the argument is invalid. Here is another example of the whole-to-part variety of the fallacy of division:

46. The soccer team is excellent. Hence, each member of the team is excellent.

A team may be excellent due to teamwork and a few outstanding players and yet have members who are not themselves excellent players.

The fallacy of division does not always involve an inference from a whole to its parts. It may involve an inference from a group (or collective) to its members. For instance:

> 47. Grizzly bears are rapidly disappearing. So, Freddy, the grizzly bear at the zoo, must be rapidly disappearing.

This argument moves invalidly from a statement about grizzly bears (taken as a group) to a statement about a member of that group. The fallacy of division (like the fallacy of composition) is classified as a fallacy of ambiguity because it gains its persuasive force from a confusion of meanings or concepts. For instance, "grizzly bears" may mean "grizzly bears taken as group" or "individual grizzly bears." If one fails to distinguish these two meanings, one is readily taken in by the fallacy.

Fallacy of Division

The whole (or group) has this attribute.	therefore	The parts or members have this attribute.
		☐ ☐ ☐ ☐
		☐ ☐ ☐ ☐

B. Fallacies Involving Unwarranted Premises

All of the fallacies we have considered thus far have involved an invalid (or weak) inference. In other words, all the fallacies we have considered so far are **non sequiturs**. ("Non sequitur" means "it does not follow" in Latin.) But not all fallacies are non sequiturs. Some are valid (or strong) but involve the use of *unwarranted* premises. We will now examine two examples of this type of fallacy.

13. Begging the Question (Petitio Principii)

An argument *begs the question* when it *assumes the point to be proved*. Begging the question is also known as arguing in a circle. (The Latin expression *petitio principii* means roughly "begging the first principle." It is pronounced variously but may be pronounced as "peh-TIT-ee-o prin-KIP-ee-ee.") Here is an example:

> 48. The defendant is not guilty of the crime, for she is innocent of having committed it.

The conclusion of this argument is merely a slightly rephrased version of the premise. So, the conclusion cannot be false given that the premise is true. And hence, argument (48) is valid. Therefore, if the premise is, as a matter of fact, true, then the argument is deductively sound (by definition). Still, even if (48) is deductively sound, one can see that it is defective in that it *assumes the point to be proved.*

The phenomenon of begging the question is interesting from the standpoint of logical theory, for it shows us that ultimately, we want something more than valid (or strong) arguments *with true premises.* But what is that something more? Here, we must keep in mind the two basic purposes for arguing: (a) convincing others and (b) discovering truth. From the standpoint of convincing others, we need premises that are somehow more acceptable to them than the conclusion. Of course, it's one of the facts of life that we cannot always convince others. As the old saying goes, "Convince a man against his will, he's of the same opinion still." But insofar as we wish to use an argument to persuade a person or group on a given issue, we need to employ premises that are more plausible to that person or group than the conclusion. And obviously, what's "more plausible" is, at least to some extent, relative to the person or group. We can sum this up by saying that in many cases, we need not only sound arguments but also convincing or persuasive ones.

But we use arguments not only to convince others but also to discover truth. And arguments that beg the question are flawed from this perspective as well, because obviously one cannot reasonably claim to discover a truth *by inference* when that truth is itself included in the premises of one's argument. To discover a given truth via argument, each premise must be a different statement than the conclusion. Moreover, we usually want premises that we (rightly) take to be more probable than the conclusion prior to considering the argument.*

In sum, when an argument begs the question, it has an *unwarranted* premise. Both from the standpoint of convincing others and from the standpoint of discovering truth, an argument that begs the question has a premise that is ill-suited to (or inappropriate for) the purpose and, in that sense, unwarranted or unjustified. This is not to deny, of course, that question-begging arguments *do* sometimes convince a person or group. But such arguments *should not* be convincing and *would not* convince an ideally rational and alert audience.

Consider another example of begging the question:

49. Boeing makes the best airliners in the world. Why? Because Boeing has the best aeronautical engineers. And why is that? Because Boeing pays the highest salaries. Of course, the Boeing Company can afford this because they make the best airliners in the world.[3]

---

*I say "usually" because sometimes a conclusion is well known on grounds independent of the premises of the argument, and yet the argument may be helpful from the standpoint of discovering the truth, because it shows that the conclusion is supported by *more than one* line of evidence.

Here, the fallacy is slightly disguised because the unwarranted premise (i.e., the one that rephrases the conclusion) is used along with more appropriate supporting material.

It is not always immediately obvious whether an argument involves a fallacy of begging the question. Consider the following case:

> 50. God exists because the Bible says so. But how do I know that what the Bible says is true? Because it is God's Word.

In textbook form, argument (50) would look like this:

> 1. The Bible is God's Word.
> So, 2. What the Bible says is true. [from (1)]
> 3. The Bible says that God exists.
> So, 4. God exists. [from (2) and (3)]

None of the premises here simply *restates* the conclusion that God exists. But the first premise (all by itself) *presupposes* that God exists. Therefore, the argument seems to beg the question.[4]

Sometimes, there is reasonable disagreement about whether an argument assumes the point to be proved. For one thing, there can be borderline cases because the extent to which a premise contains the information in the conclusion is a matter of degree. Furthermore, this entire issue is complicated by the fact that the premises of a *valid* argument, taken together, *must contain* the information in the conclusion. Ultimately, to identify a fallacy of begging the question, we need to determine whether each premise, taken by itself, is better known or more reasonably believed than the conclusion of the argument. If a given premise is similar in content to the conclusion but is *not* better known (or more reasonably believed) than the conclusion, then the argument begs the question. But there will sometimes be reasonable disagreement about whether a given premise is better known (or more reasonably believed) than the conclusion of the argument.

14. False Dilemma

The fallacy of *false dilemma* occurs when one uses a premise that unjustifiably reduces the number of alternatives to be considered. For example:

> 51. I'm tired of all these young people criticizing their own country. What I say is this, "America—love it or leave it!" And since these people obviously don't want to leave the country, they should love it instead of criticizing it.[5]

The argument allows us only two options: We can love America (uncritically) or we can emigrate. But there seem to be other possibilities. For example, surely one can be critical of one's country, insofar as it has fallen short of its own ideals, and yet still be devoted to it. And perhaps it is morally permissible for one to respect one's country (i.e., respect its laws and traditions) without loving it (assuming that loving one's country involves being especially fond of it).

Notice that the fallacy of false dilemma is not a non sequitur. Given that I have just two options ("love it" or "leave it"), and given that one of these ("leave it") is ruled out, I must take the other. Thus, as in the case of begging the question, the fallacy of false dilemma consists in employing an *unwarranted* (or unjustified) premise. In a false dilemma, the disjunctive premise is unwarranted because it omits an alternative that needs to be considered. Here is a second example:

> 52. I do not know whether God's existence can be proven, but I do know that each person must be either a theist or an atheist. And by your own admission, you're no theist. Therefore, you must be an atheist.

This argument ignores or overlooks the possibility of agnosticism. While the theist believes that God exists and the atheist believes that God does not exist, the agnostic suspends judgment or remains neutral as regards the proposition that God exists. That is, the agnostic is not confident that this proposition is true, but he or she is not confident that it is false, either. The agnostic's mental state is a philosophical shrug of the shoulders, generally based on the principle that *one's confidence in a proposition should be proportional to the evidence for it*, and therefore, when the evidence doesn't settle a matter, belief is inappropriate. In any case, since people often suspend judgment on an issue when they feel they have inadequate evidence, the agnostic's attitude is at least a possible one.

We can't identify a false dilemma unless we can specify at least one alternative that has been ignored. This is not always easy. Consider the following example:

> 53. Either your reasoning in any given case is based on an assumption or you have no place to start in your reasoning. If your reasoning is based on an assumption, then your conclusions are no more certain than a mere assumption. And if your conclusions are no more certain than a mere assumption, you do not gain knowledge by reasoning. Of course, if you have no place to start in your reasoning, then you are unable to make any inferences, and hence (once again) you do not gain knowledge by reasoning. Therefore, you do not gain knowledge by reasoning.

A chain of inferences has to start somewhere. And it seems that one cannot always defend one's premises with further arguments. Apparently, then, some of one's premises will be unsupported by further statements. Let us call these "first premises." Do first premises have the status of mere assumptions? If so, it would appear that all our reasoning is based on mere assumptions, in which case our reasoning never yields knowledge.

Many philosophers think there is a class of statements that do not *need* to be supported by further statements in order to be known or well grounded. But

Summary of Fallacies Involving Ambiguity

These fallacies result from double meanings or from a confusion between two closely related concepts.

9. **Equivocation:** An inference that is invalid because of its dependence on an ambiguous word (or phrase).

10. **Amphiboly:** An inference that is invalid because of its dependence on an ambiguity that is due to sentence structure.

11. **Composition:** An invalid inference from the nature of the parts to the nature of the whole, or from the nature of the members to the nature of the group (or collective).

12. **Division:** An invalid inference from the nature of the whole to the nature of the parts, or from the nature of the group (or collective) to the nature of the members.

Summary of Fallacies Involving Unwarranted Premises

These fallacies involve not invalid or weak inferences, but the use of premises that are unwarranted or unjustified given the purpose for the argument or its context.

13. **Begging the question** (*petitio principii*): Assuming the point to be proved.

14. **False dilemma:** Using a premise that unjustifiably reduces the number of alternatives to be considered.

how do such statements differ from mere assumptions? How can a statement be known, warranted, or well grounded without being based on further statements? Here, some philosophers have called attention to allegedly self-evident statements, such as "No circles are squares." These are not *mere assumptions*, they claim, because to understand the statements is to see that they are true. Other philosophers have called attention to observation statements, such as "I see a piece of paper now." These are not mere assumptions, it is claimed, because they are somehow grounded in our sensory experience. But other philosophers have expressed doubts about the attempt to identify a privileged class of first premises. These philosophers are skeptical about the categories of self-evident statements and observation statements. The point here is simply that it takes philosophical creativity to explain how a first premise can be more than a mere assumption. Thus, it sometimes takes both creativity and hard intellectual work to make the case that a false dilemma fallacy has been committed.

The following exercises perform two separate functions. First, exercise 6.3, part A, gives you an opportunity to identify examples of the fallacies introduced in this section. Second, exercise 6.3, part B, tests your ability to identify all the types of fallacies introduced in this chapter.

◆ *Exercise 6.3*

Part A: Fallacies Involving Ambiguity and Fallacies Involving Unwarranted Premises
Most of the following passages exemplify a fallacy discussed in this section. If a fallacy is committed, name the type of fallacy and explain why the passage is an example of that type. If no fallacy is committed, simply write "not a fallacy."

* **1.** The leader of this new religious group preaches the following message: "We shall wear no clothes to distinguish ourselves from our Christian brethren." Therefore, this religious group should be opposed. For it advocates nudity.

  2. Every American is either a Republican or a Democrat. Dr. Porter is an American, but she is not a Republican. So, she must be a Democrat.

  3. Monty is so much fun at a party! He's a real ham! But if he's a ham, then he is high in cholesterol. So, he is high in cholesterol.

* **4.** Every sentence in my book is well written. Accordingly, my book is well written.

  5. Sleeping pills work because they cause people to go to sleep.

  6. A hit man is a person. A 200-pound hit man is a 200-pound person. Therefore, a good hit man is a good person.

* **7** Either men are superior to women or women are superior to men. Men are not superior to women. Hence, women are superior to men.

  8. No member of the crew can lift over 100 pounds. Therefore, the entire crew cannot lift over 100 pounds.

  9. The Acme Corporation is very important. So, since Ms. Griggs works for the Acme Corporation, she must be very important.

* **10.** Obviously, humans have free will, since they have the power to make choices.

 11. Your Honor, the witness said he saw a photograph of the defendant lying on the coffee table. Therefore, the defendant must have lain on the coffee table at some point.

 12. Please don't tell me you think that human vegetables should be kept on respirators! After all, brain-dead humans are already dead. We know this because they are not alive.

* **13** The Germans are mostly Lutheran. Karl Schmidt is a German. Accordingly, Karl is mostly Lutheran.

 14. You either hate parties or you love them. So, since you say you don't hate parties, you must love them.

 15. Each cell in the human body is invisible. Therefore, the human body itself is invisible.

* **16.** I was there, I tell you. I stood within 10 feet of the man. Either I was hallucinating or he levitated. And I wasn't hallucinating. Therefore, he levitated.

 17. Surely Anthony loves me. For he told me he loves me and he wouldn't lie to someone he loves.

 18. Sparrows are plentiful. Pete, my pet bird, is a sparrow. Therefore, Pete is plentiful.

* **19.** Each square inch of the car's surface is red. It follows that the whole car is red.

20. Either nonhuman animals are robots or they have thoughts and feelings just like humans have. Nonhuman animals are not robots. Hence, they have thoughts and feelings just like humans have.

21. Religion is the opiate of the people. Therefore, religion is like a drug that can be used to make people forget or ignore the miserable conditions they live in.

* **22.** If I have a strong desire to believe in God, then I have a motive for believing in God. And if I have a motive for believing in God, then I have a reason for believing in God. However, if I have a reason for believing in God, then I have evidence for my belief in God. Therefore, if I have a strong desire to believe in God, then I have evidence for my belief in God.

23. Nuclear weapons are more destructive than conventional weapons. Therefore, over the course of human history, more destruction has resulted from nuclear weapons than from conventional weapons.

24. People are either good or evil. And Doris is not good. Therefore, she is evil.

* **25.** Immigrants come from every country in the world. Ms. Bashir is an immigrant. Consequently, Ms. Bashir comes from every country in the world.

26. Either you believe that the doctrine of reincarnation is true or you believe that it is false. Clearly, you do not believe that the doctrine of reincarnation is true. Accordingly, you must believe that it is false.

27. When it comes to morality, a person is either a cultural relativist or a dogmatist. Since you won't allow that infanticide is right for the Eskimos if they approve of it, you obviously aren't a cultural relativist. So, you must be a dogmatist.

* **28.** That which can not-be at some time is not. Therefore, if everything can not-be, then at one time there was nothing in existence. —St. Thomas Aquinas, *Summa Theologica* (I, Q. 2. Art. 3), in Anton C. Pegis, ed., *Introduction to St. Thomas Aquinas* (New York: Random House, 1948), p. 26

29. God is love. Love is a character trait. Therefore, God is a character trait.

30. Sixty percent of the students at Seattle Pacific University are female. Pat is a student at Seattle Pacific. So, Pat is 60 percent female.

Part B: Argument Diagrams and Multiple Fallacies   Photocopy the following arguments. Then, on your photocopy, bracket and number the statements in the arguments and construct diagrams (following the principles outlined in chapter 3). Finally, identify any fallacies that occur. Each of the arguments involve *two or more* fallacies discussed in this chapter.

* **1.** Christians teach the doctrine of the Triune God, namely, that "One God plus one God plus one God equals one God." But this doctrine is false, for it is obviously a mathematical impossibility, and only fools believe mathematical impossibilities.

2. Thomas Jefferson said that all men are created equal. Therefore, all men are created equal. On the other hand, humans clearly differ in important respects from birth (e.g., intelligence, athletic ability, physical beauty). And if people differ in important respects from birth, then they are not created equal. It follows that humans aren't created equal. And therefore, at least one contradiction is true.

3. Here's how to win the lottery: Consult an astrologer. How do I know this? Well, I was watching a TV program recently and there was an interview with this very intelligent man who said that astrology is based on scientific principles. So, astrology is based on science. Furthermore, last week I took the advice of an astrologer who gave me a number based on my astrological sign. Using the number, I won the lottery. So, obviously, astrology works on things like the lottery.

* 4. When it comes to criminal punishment, one must favor either rehabilitation or deterrence. The rehabilitationists think criminals are sick and need treatment. The deterrence crowd wants harsh punishments that will put a stop to crime. Since it is just silly to suppose that every shoplifter or car thief is mentally ill, the rehabilitationists are mistaken. Hence, the deterrence view is correct. And by the way, here's another way to see the same point: Rehabilitationists hold that even the most hardened criminals can be cured in a few sessions with a psychotherapist. But hardened criminals cannot be cured so easily! Once again, then, we see that rehabilitationists are mistaken.

5. You should stop reading your horoscope. Why? First, because reading your horoscope is a waste of time. After all, you could be reading great literature instead. Second, people will think you are superstitious if you read your horoscope. Third, you should quit reading your horoscope because horoscopes are for idiots. Fourth, you don't want to turn out like that weird guy at work, Bob Crombie. And Bob reads horoscopes! So, obviously, horoscopes produce weirdness. Hence, you've got to stop reading them.

6. Gauguin's painting *The Spirit of the Dead Watching* is pornographic. How do I know? First, it is a picture of a naked woman lying on a bed. And either you are a pervert yourself or you'll agree that pictures of that type are pornographic. And I know you're not a pervert. Second, a young man looking at *The Spirit of the Dead Watching* might have lustful thoughts. So, once again, we have evidence that the painting is pornographic. Third, there was a criminal case in which a man visited an art museum, looked at *The Spirit of the Dead Watching*, and then went out and committed rape. Seriously, this really happened! My cousin told me about it. So, the painting caused this man to commit rape! And even a birdbrain can see that any painting that causes rape is pornographic. Finally, the painting incites lust because it causes men to have strong sexual urges.

* 7. When you get down to it, philosophers are just logic choppers who sit around trying to put reality into little boxes made of words. So, the philosophical arguments against time travel prove nothing. Hence, time travel is possible. Anyway, I know it's possible because it can happen. And besides, just about everyone *but* philosophers thinks that time travel is possible, so once again, time travel probably is possible.

8. How do I know that mantras work? Consider this: Last week I said a mantra on Tuesday and on Friday. And guess what? Those days really went well for me. Fur-

thermore, mantras work because they are effective. Finally, mantras are recommended by many great movie stars.

9. Ingres' *Odalisque* is not a sexist painting. Of course, I admit that *Odalisque* is sexist if it treats women as sex objects. But you'd have to be the worst sort of uptight prude to think that *Odalisque* treats women as sex objects. In addition, no one has ever proven that *Odalisque* treats women as sex objects. Therefore, Odalisque does not treat women as sex objects, and so it is not sexist.

* 10. Logic varies as languages vary. For logic is based on grammar. My chemistry professor said so. And any intelligent person will agree that different languages have different grammars. But if logic varies as languages vary, then logic is relative to cultures. Consequently, logic is relative to cultures.

11. The will states that the painting of a beautiful woman in the storage bin shall be given to the brother of the deceased. But this is not a painting of a beautiful woman in a storage bin. It is a painting of a beautiful woman walking across a field. Therefore, this painting does not belong to the brother of the deceased. Yes, I realize that the brother *thinks* the painting is his by right, but his mind is clouded by greed, and so his arguments are without force.

12. According to mind–body dualism, human beings have both a body and a nonphysical soul. But if mind–body dualism is true, then new energy is introduced from the soul into the brain. But dualists have never been able to prove that new energy is introduced from the soul into the brain. Thus, we can safely conclude that new energy is not introduced from the soul into the brain. Furthermore, it's just crazy to suppose that a nonphysical thing (i.e., the soul) can have causal interactions with a physical thing (i.e., the brain). This, too, supports the claim that new energy is not introduced from the soul into the brain. I must conclude that mind–body dualism is not true.

13. Last night we went to see *Hamlet*. The play was excellent since each scene was excellent. Plus, everybody who is anybody is raving about the play. I mean, the play was just excellent because it was really superb!

14. Either God created everything (including human beings) in six days or else human life evolved gradually out of lower life forms over a very long period of time apart from any divine activity. But you are not a religious fanatic, so you know about fossils. And hence, you know that human life evolved gradually out of lower life forms over a very long period of time. Thus, God did not create everything in six days. I mean, I hate to break the news, but you are just about the last person on earth who believes that humans were created by God.

15. Suicide is wrong for many reasons. First, because it involves killing. And killing is wrong because it is wrong to take a life. Second, suicide is wrong because it deeply wounds one's family and friends. Third, suicide is the coward's way out. It's for weaklings who collapse the first time they run into a little adversity. Fourth, suicide is wrong because it's not cool—not cool at all.

16. Real men drink El Belcho beer. Wimps drink the inferior brands. I can see you're a real man. So, El Belcho is the beer for you.

17. My dear sir, there are two reasons why you should agree that the money in your wallet is rightfully mine. First, I've had a lot of bad luck in my life, but you obviously enjoy health, wealth, and prosperity. So, if you are a man of compassion, you'll see that I deserve the wallet. Second, since I'm pointing a gun at your head, you owe your very life to my generosity and patience.

18. Time is composed of moments. Moments have no duration. Therefore, time has no duration. This rather surprising thesis is further supported by the following considerations: Time is illusory because time seems real but isn't real. Furthermore, down through the ages, the best and brightest people have always thought time was illusory.

19. You have asked Lolla Lodge to contribute to the Krazykids Preschool fundraiser. I am sorry to inform you that we are unable to honor your request. Lolla Lodge must either give all its discretionary funds to the preschool or else donate them to St. Mary's Hospital. And as we have been giving to St. Mary's for many years now, we have decided to continue that tradition. We realize that you are under the impression that our previous director promised you that we would make a contribution this year. But what the previous director actually said was, "We promise to give $1000 and our best wishes to St. Mary's Hospital and Krazykids Preschool." So, St. Mary's gets the $1000 and Krazykids gets our best wishes.

20. I've heard that St. Andrew's Episcopal Church is very wealthy. You are a member of St. Andrew's, so you must be wealthy. Anyway, I can tell you're wealthy because you have a lot of money.

Notes

1. *The Guide to American Law: Everyone's Legal Encyclopedia*, Vol. 4 (New York: West, 1984), p. 352.
2. Anthony Flew, *A Dictionary of Philosophy*, rev. 2nd ed. (New York: St. Martin's Press, 1979), p. 104. I have slightly altered the punctuation.
3. This example is inspired by one in Patrick Hurley, *A Concise Introduction to Logic*, 4th ed. (Belmont, CA: Wadsworth, 1991), p. 143.
4. Not everyone agrees. See, for example, John Lamont, "Believing That God Exists Because the Bible Says So," *Faith and Philosophy* (Journal of the Society of Christian Philosophers) 13(1) (1966): 121–124.
5. I owe this example to Anthony Weston, *A Rulebook for Arguments* (Indianapolis, IN: Hackett, 1987), p. 88. I have elaborated the example somewhat.

Chapter 7

Statement Logic: Truth Tables

The history of the discipline of logic is not a continuous, upward progression from one discovery to the next. Rather, it is characterized by episodes of discovery followed by lengthy periods in which little creative work was done. The philosopher Aristotle (384–322 B.C.E.) is generally considered the father of logic. His syllogistic logic was the first great systematic development in the field. The Stoic philosopher Chrysippus (279–206 B.C.E.) also made important contributions to logic by developing the rudiments of statement logic. For example, Chrysippus analyzed compound statements such as disjunctions and conditionals and identified the patterns of reasoning that we now refer to as *modus ponens* and *modus tollens*. But for over a thousand years after the death of Chrysippus, there were few significant advances in the field of logic. Most philosophers were content to write commentaries on the works of Aristotle and Chrysippus.

During the medieval period, there was a resurgence of interest in logic. Philosophers such as Peter Abelard (1079–1142) and William of Ockham (c. 1285–1349) made important contributions to the field. Some of the medieval logicians offered subtle insights into *modal logic* (roughly, the logic of possibility and necessity), which we will consider in chapter 12. However, at the end of the medieval period, logic again entered a time of relative neglect, so that there was little creative work in the field from the middle of the 15th century until the time of the German philosopher Gottfried Wilhelm Leibniz (1646–1716). Leibniz stimulated interest in a more symbolic approach to logic.

Since the mid-19th century, the field of logic has developed at a rapid pace. We have already examined the work of John Venn (1834–1923), whose diagram method is perhaps the most intuitive means of evaluating categorical syllogisms. In this chapter, we will focus primarily on the truth table method developed by the American philosopher Charles Sanders Peirce (1839–1914).[1] However, before we can apply the truth table method, we must first learn how to translate English arguments into symbols.

7.1 Symbolizing English Arguments

In chapter 2, we saw that arguments are valid by virtue of having a valid form. Modern logicians have developed very useful ways of symbolizing an argument's form. And as we will see, symbolizing an argument enables us to apply certain powerful techniques in order to determine its validity.

To symbolize statements properly, we must distinguish between atomic and compound statements. An **atomic statement** is one that does not have any other statement as a component. For example:

1. Shakespeare wrote *Hamlet.*

2. China has a large population.

3. Roses are red.

A **compound statement** is one that has at least one atomic statement as a component. For instance:

4. It is not the case that Ben Jonson wrote *Hamlet.*

5. China has a large population and Luxembourg has a small population.

6. Either Palermo is the capital of Sicily or Messina is the capital of Sicily.

7. If Sheboygan is in Wisconsin, then Sheboygan is in the U.S.A.

8. The Democrats win if and only if the Republicans quarrel.

We can symbolize the *atomic* statements in these compounds with capital letters, as follows:

B: Ben Jonson wrote *Hamlet.*
C: China has a large population.
L: Luxembourg has a small population.
P: Palermo is the capital of Sicily.
M: Messina is the capital of Sicily.
S: Sheboygan is in Wisconsin.
U: Sheboygan is in the U.S.A.
D: The Democrats win.
R: The Republicans quarrel.

The compounds themselves can then be written as follows (in order):

9. It is not the case that B.

10. C and L.

11. Either P or M.

12. If S, then U.

13. D if and only if R.

Note that statement (9) counts as a compound even though it has only one statement as a component. It is a compound consisting of an atomic statement and the phrase "it is not the case that."

Throughout this chapter and the next, we will use capital letters to stand for atomic statements. We will also use symbols to stand for the key logical words in our example compounds, namely, "it is not the case that," "and," "or," "if . . . then . . . ," and "if and only if." We will symbolize these English expressions by means of **logical operators**. We can sum up the symbol system as follows:*

Operator	Name	Translates	Type of Compound
~	tilde	not	negation
•	dot	and	conjunction
∨	vee	or	disjunction
→	arrow	if-then	conditional
↔	double-arrow	if and only if	biconditional

Negations

The " ~ " symbol, called the **tilde**, is used to translate the English word "not" and its stylistic variants. Take the following example:

14. Roses are not blue. (R: Roses are blue)

The **scheme of abbreviation** on the right assigns a distinct capital letter to each atomic statement in the English. Using the tilde, we can then symbolize statement (14) as follows:

15. ~R

Of course, the English language provides a number of ways of negating a statement. For example:

a. It is not the case that roses are blue.

b. It is false that roses are blue.

c. It is not true that roses are blue.

d. Roses fail to be blue.

---

*From a historical point of view, symbolic logic is relatively new, and its notation is not yet standardized. Thus, although the symbols provided in this text are in common use, they are not the only ones in common use. Many texts employ one or more of the following alternatives: "¬" to symbolize negations; "&" to symbolize conjunctions; "⊃" to symbolize conditionals, and "≡" to symbolize biconditionals. The lack of standard notation in logic is inconvenient, but it is not difficult to move from one notation to another once the basic principles have been mastered.

Statement (15) translates each of these English expressions into symbols.

> Each of the statements below is a **negation**. The main operator is the *tilde*.
> ~C
> ~(A ∨ B)
> ~(F → G)

Conjunctions

The "•" sign (called the **dot**) is used to translate the English word "and" as well as its stylistic variants. Take the following example:

> 16. Hobbes was born in 1588 *and* Descartes was born in 1596. (H: Hobbes was born in 1588; D: Descartes was born in 1596)

Using the scheme of abbreviation indicated, statement (16) translates into symbols as follows:

> 17. (H • D)

Note that parentheses have been placed around the letters connected by the dot. As we will see, these are often necessary to avoid the fallacy of amphiboly (i.e., ambiguity due to flawed sentence structure).[2] The statements composing a conjunction (*H* and *D* in this case) are called **conjuncts**. A partial list of stylistic variants for "and" is provided by the following set of sentences:

a. Hobbes was born in 1588, *but* Descartes was born in 1596.

b. Hobbes was born in 1588; *however,* Descartes was born in 1596.

c. *While* Hobbes was born in 1588, Descartes was born in 1596.

d. *Although* Hobbes was born in 1588, Descartes was born in 1596.

e. Hobbes was born in 1588, *yet* Descartes was born in 1596.

f. Hobbes was born in 1588; *nevertheless,* Descartes was born in 1596.

g. Hobbes was born in 1588 *even though* Descartes was born in 1596.

h. Hobbes was born in 1588 *though* Descartes was born in 1596.

(17) correctly symbolizes each of these variants. You may be thinking that such words as "but," "while," and "although" do not have quite the same connotation as "and" in ordinary English. Indeed, these words convey a sense of contrast that is lacking in "and." But bear in mind that some distortion often results when one language is translated into another. Moreover, *for the purpose of evaluating arguments for validity*, the expressions in the previous list can usually be translated adequately by means of the dot.

It should be noted, however, that the dot does not correctly translate *every* use of the English word "and." Consider the following statements:

18. Jane became pregnant and got married. (P: Jane became pregnant; M: Jane got married)

19. Jane got married and became pregnant.[3]

In ordinary conversation, these two statements do not mean the same thing. Here, the word "and" has the force of "and then." In other words, it indicates a temporal order. But the dot does not indicate any such temporal order, so the dot cannot adequately translate statements (18) and (19). Can the dot provide an adequate translation of the following statements?

20. Jack and Jill are married. (J: Jack is married; M: Jill is married)

21. Jack and Jill are persons. (J: Jack is a person; P: Jill is a person)

Statement (20) would normally be taken to mean that Jack and Jill are married *to each other*. But if we translate (20) via the dot, we get a statement that could be true even if Jack and Jill are *not* married to each other, namely, $(J \cdot M)$. On the other hand, (21) *can* be adequately translated by means of the dot: $(J \cdot P)$.

The importance of parentheses is evident when we consider negated conjunctions, such as this one:

22. It is not true that both Clinton and Bush won. (C: Clinton won; B: Bush won)

The correct symbolization is as follows:

23. $\sim(C \cdot B)$

If we remove the parentheses, we get this:

24. $\sim C \cdot B$

(24) says, "Clinton did not win, and Bush won," which is not at all the meaning of (22). So, the placement of parentheses is important when translating English into symbols.

In longer statements, we may alternate parentheses and brackets since multiple sets of parentheses can become confusing. For instance:

25. Al is old, but Ben and Cindy are young. (A: Al is old; B: Ben is young; C: Cindy is young)

The comma indicates the main break, and statement (25) may be symbolized as follows:

26. $[A \cdot (B \cdot C)]$

Each of the statements below is a **conjunction**. The main operator is the *dot*.

(E • ~F)
(G ∨ H) • K]
(L → M) • (N ∨ O)]

Disjunctions

The "∨" sign (called the **vee**) is used to symbolize disjunctions. (This symbol is borrowed from the first letter of the Latin word *vel*, meaning "or.") The vee means "either . . . or . . . *or both*," which is commonly referred to as the *inclusive* sense of the word "or." The vee does *not* mean "either . . . or . . . *but not both*," which is commonly referred to as the *exclusive* sense of the word "or."[4] Consider this example:

> 27. Either Carol attends college or she gets a job (or both). (C: Carol attends college; J: Carol gets a job)

Statement (27) can be translated into symbols this way:

> 28. (C ∨ J)

Note that parentheses have been placed around the vee. As with the dot, these are often necessary to prevent structural ambiguities. (28) also translates the stylistic variants of (27), such as the following:

> a. Carol attends college *and/or* she gets a job.
>
> b. Carol attends college *or* she gets a job.
>
> c. *Either* Carol attends college *or* she gets a job.
>
> d. Carol attends college *unless* she gets a job.

As a general rule, when symbolizing arguments containing disjunctions, assume that the word "or" is used in the inclusive sense unless this assumption renders the argument invalid. For example, consider the following argument, which has the form of a *disjunctive syllogism*:

> 29. Lassie is either a cat or a dog. Lassie is not a cat. So, Lassie is a dog. (C: Lassie is a cat; D: Lassie is dog)

This argument is correctly symbolized as follows:

> 30. (C ∨ D), ~C ∴ D

Several things should be noted here. First, a comma is used to punctuate (or separate) the premises. Second, the vee is used in the first premise even though C and D cannot in fact both be true. The argument form is valid even if the "or" is inclusive: "Either C or D (or both) are true. It is not true that C. So, D is true." Third, note the use of the triple-dot symbol to mark the conclusion. This is customary among logicians.

What if we need the exclusive "or" to represent an argument fairly? For example:

31. Either the Sonics won or the Bulls won. The Sonics won. So, the Bulls did not win. (S: The Sonics won; B: The Bulls won)

Intuitively, the argument is valid, but the following symbolized version is invalid:

32. (S ∨ B), S ∴ ~B

Here's a counterexample: "Either trees are plants or flowers are plants (or both are plants). Trees are plants. So, flowers are not plants." To present the argument fairly, we need to interpret the first premise as follows:

33. Either the Sonics won or the Bulls won, but it is not true that both the Sonics won and the Bulls won.

The comma indicates that the main logical connective in (33) is the word "but," which is symbolized by the dot. The left conjunct is a disjunction ("Either the Sonics won or the Bulls won"), and the right conjunct is the negation of a conjunction ("It is not true that both the Sonics won and the Bulls won"). So, in symbols, (33) looks like this:

34. [(S ∨ B) • ~(S • B)]

Here again, we use brackets around the whole statement because adding another set of parentheses would make the symbols rather difficult to read. With (34) as its first premise, argument (31) as a whole is symbolized as follows:

35. [(S ∨ B) • ~(S • B)], S ∴ ~B

This argument is intuitively valid, and we will prove that it is valid later in this chapter.

Before leaving disjunctions, let us note that statements of the form "Neither A nor B" can be symbolized in two ways. For instance:

36. Neither Sue nor Fred is happy. (S: Sue is happy; F: Fred is happy)

We can symbolize statement (36) by means of the vee, as follows:

>   37. ~(S ∨ F)

But we can also symbolize it by means of the dot, like this:

>   38. (~S • ~F)

Each of the statements below is a **disjunction**. The main operator is the *vee*.
(~P ∨ Q)
(R • S) ∨ ~T]
(U → W) ∨ ~(X • Y)]

Conditionals

The "→" sign (called the **arrow**) is used to symbolize conditionals. For example:

>   39. If Fido is a dog, then he is an animal. (D: Fido is a dog; A: Fido is an animal)

(39) can be symbolized as follows:

>   40. (D → A)

Again, we use parentheses (and brackets) to avoid structural ambiguities. As we observed in chapter 2, there are many stylistic variants for if-then statements. We will use the arrow to symbolize all of them. For example, expression (40) symbolizes not only (39) but also each of the following:

  a. *Given that* Fido is a dog, Fido is an animal.
  b. Fido is an animal *given that* he is a dog.
  c. *Assuming that* Fido is a dog, he is an animal.
  d. Fido is an animal *assuming that* he is a dog.
  e. *Provided that* Fido is a dog, he is an animal.
  f. Fido is an animal *provided that* he is a dog.
  g. *On the condition that* Fido is a dog, he is an animal.
  h. Fido is an animal *on the condition that* he is a dog.
  i. Fido is an animal *if* he is a dog.
  j. Fido is a dog *only if* he is an animal.
  k. Fido's being a dog *is a sufficient condition for* Fido's being an animal.
  l. Fido's being an animal *is a necessary condition for* Fido's being a dog.

Items (k) and (l) merit comment. A *sufficient condition* is a condition which guarantees that a statement is true (or that a phenomenon will occur). For instance, *Fido's being a dog* guarantees that he is an animal. By contrast, *Fido's being an animal* does not guarantee that he is a dog, for he might be some other kind of animal. The *antecedent* (if-clause) of a true conditional statement provides a sufficient condition for the truth of the *consequent* (then-clause).

A *necessary condition* is a condition which, if lacking, guarantees that a statement is false (or that a phenomenon will not occur). Thus, *Fido's being an animal* is a necessary condition for *Fido's being a dog*, for if Fido is not an animal, then he is not a dog. The consequent (then-clause) of a true conditional statement provides a necessary condition for the truth of the antecedent (if-clause).

Each of the statements below is a **conditional**. The main operator is the *arrow*.
$(\sim X \rightarrow Y)$
$[Z \rightarrow (A \vee B)]$
$(C \bullet \sim D) \rightarrow (E \vee \sim F)]$

Let us now symbolize an argument involving a conditional statement:

41. If humans have souls, then immaterial things can evolve from matter. Immaterial things cannot evolve from matter. So, humans do not have souls. (H: Humans have souls; M: Immaterial things can evolve from matter)

Using the scheme of abbreviation provided, argument (41) can be symbolized like this:

42. $(H \rightarrow M), \sim M \therefore \sim H$

Again, we use the triple-dot symbol to mark the conclusion. Can you identify the form employed in argument (42)? It is *modus tollens*.

Before leaving our discussion of conditionals, let us note that the word "unless" can be translated by means of the arrow as well as the vee. For example:

43. We will lose unless we do our best. (L: We will lose; B: We will do our best)

As we have already seen, (43) can be symbolized as follows:

44. $(L \vee B)$

But it can also be symbolized by a combination of the arrow and the tilde, like this:

45. $(\sim B \rightarrow L)$

In other words, (43) has the same meaning as "If we do not do our best, then we will lose."

Biconditionals

The "↔" sign (called the **double-arrow**) is used to symbolize biconditionals. For example:

> 46. Mary is a teenager *if and only if* she is from 13 to 19 years of age. (M: Mary is a teenager; Y: Mary is from 13 to 19 years of age)

This statement may be symbolized as follows:

> 47. (M ↔ Y)

As before, we use parentheses (and brackets) to prevent structural ambiguities. And (47) symbolizes not only (46) but also its stylistic variants, such as these:

> a. Mary is a teenager *just in case* she is from 13 to 19 years of age.
>
> b. Mary's being a teenager is *a necessary and sufficient condition for* Mary's being from 13 to 19 years of age.

Each of the following statements is a **biconditional**. The main operator is the *double-arrow*.

(~H ↔ J)

[~K ↔ (P ∨ Q)]

(L • M) ↔ (N → T)]

Let us now consider an example that illustrates some of the finer points of translating arguments into symbols:

> 48. If Dostoyevsky was right, then everything is permissible if God does not exist. But it is not true that if God does not exist, everything is permissible. Therefore, Dostoyevsky was not right. (D: Dostoyevsky was right; E: Everything is permissible; G: God exists)

The first premise may be symbolized as follows:

> 49. [D → (~G → E)]

In this case, we can drop the brackets without altering the meaning, so the following is also an acceptable translation of the first premise:

> 50. D → (~G → E)

Note, however, that we cannot remove the parentheses from (50), for if we did, we would alter the meaning:

> 51. D → ~G → E

Statement (51) is ambiguous because it could be interpreted as (50) or as follows:

52. (D → ~G) → E

And these two statements have different meanings. (52) translates sentences that are difficult to put gracefully into English, such as the following:

53. If Dostoyevsky was right only if God does not exist, then everything is permitted.

54. If God doesn't exist given that Dostoyevsky was right, then everything is permitted.

This should make it clear that (52) is not an accurate translation of the first premise of the argument.

Now, let us symbolize the second premise of argument (48), that is, "It is not true that if God does not exist, everything is permissible":

55. ~(~G → E)

Note that there must be a tilde *outside* the parentheses in this case, because "it is not true that" precedes the word "if" in the English statement. Moreover, we cannot drop the parentheses. If we did, we would get this:

56. ~~G → E

Statement (56) says, "If it is not true that God does not exist, then everything is permissible." In other words, since the two "nots" cancel each other out, it says, "If God exists, everything is permissible," which is not at all the meaning of the English.

Finally, let us symbolize the conclusion of argument (48), that is, "Dostoyevsky was not right":

57. ~D

Note that we use no parentheses in symbolizing the conclusion. For example, do *not* write ~(D). We do not put parentheses around a single statement letter because this only adds clutter. Nor do we write (~D). *Parentheses are used with the dot, the vee, the arrow, and the double-arrow, but not with the tilde itself.*

Now, let's put all the pieces together. Here is the original argument and our symbolization of it:

If Dostoyevsky was right, then everything is permissible if God does not exist. But it is not true that if God does not exist, everything is permissible. Therefore, Dostoyevsky was not right. (D: Dostoyevsky was right; E: Everything is permissible; G: God exists)

In symbols: D → (~G → E), ~(~G → E) ∴ ~D

In closing this section, let us summarize what sorts of symbolic expressions are properly formed or grammatical. A grammatically correct symbolic expression is called a **well-formed formula** (WFF for short). To sum up what counts as a WFF, let us use the italicized, lower case letters *p* and *q* as **statement variables**, which can stand for any statement. For instance, in the following summary, the statement variable *p* could stand for A, for ~B, for (C ∨ ~D), for (E • F), for (G → H), and so on. A symbolic expression is a WFF under the following conditions:

(1) Capital letters (which stand for atomic statements) are WFFs.

(2) If *p* is a WFF, then so is ~*p*.

(3) If *p* and *q* are WFFs, then so is (*p* • *q*).

(4) If *p* and *q* are WFFs, then so is (*p* ∨ *q*).

(5) If *p* and *q* are WFFs, then so is (*p* → *q*).

(6) If *p* and *q* are WFFs, then so is (*p* ↔ *q*).

Nothing counts as a WFF unless it can be demonstrated to be one by applications of the above conditions. Consider a symbolic expression that violates the above conditions:

58. (A ∨ B • C)

We cannot tell whether the main operator in (58) is the vee or the dot. Thus, (58) is ambiguous between the following:

59. ((A ∨ B) • C)
60. (A ∨ (B • C))

Both of these formulas are WFFs. Let us examine (59) in detail. Its main operator is the dot. To apply condition (3) above, replace *p* with (A ∨ B) and *q* with C. Thus, (59) is a WFF given that (A ∨ B) and C are WFFs. Condition (1) assures us that C is a WFF. Condition (4) assures us that (A ∨ B) is a WFF if A is a WFF and B is a WFF; and of course A and B are WFFs according to condition (1). Hence, (59) is itself a WFF.

Note: While nothing is a WFF unless it can be demonstrated to be one via the above six conditions, for the sake of convenience, certain abbreviations are permitted, e.g., we can drop parentheses in some cases *without creating ambiguity*, and we will do so to avoid clutter. Thus, we may write (A ∨ B) • C instead of ((A ∨ B) • C). Also, we may alternate parentheses with brackets to make statements easier to read. So, we may write ~[F • (G ∨ H)] rather than ~(F • (G ∨ H)).

The symbolic language we have developed in this section is extremely useful as a means of representing the forms of arguments. But, as with any language, practice is essential to facility. The following exercises provide you with an opportunity to practice translating English into symbols.

◆ **Exercise 7.1**

Part A: Well-Formed Formulas? Which of the following symbolic expressions are well-formed formulas (WFFs)? Which are not?

* 1. $(A \rightarrow B \rightarrow C)$ 5. $\sim((H \rightarrow J) \rightarrow (K \rightarrow L))$ 8. $((Q \rightarrow S) \rightarrow T)$

  2. $(\sim B)$ 6. $(M \rightarrow \sim\sim N)$ 9. $(\sim U \rightarrow (W))$

  3. $(\sim(C) \rightarrow F)$ * 7. $(O \rightarrow \sim(P \rightarrow R))$ *10. $\sim Z$

* 4. $(E \rightarrow (\sim F \rightarrow G)$

Part B: Symbolizing Translate the following statements into symbols, using the schemes of abbreviation provided.

* 1. The crops will fail unless it rains. (C: The crops will fail; R: It rains)

  2. Humans are animals if they are mammals. (A: Humans are animals; M: Humans are mammals)

  3. The statement "If humans are rational, then they are not animals" is false. (R: Humans are rational; A: Humans are animals)

* 4. Bats are mammals only if they nourish their young with milk. (M: Bats are mammals; N: Bats nourish their young with milk)

  5. Coffee isn't good if it isn't fresh-brewed. (G: Coffee is good; F: Coffee is fresh-brewed)

  6. Assuming that your test scores are high and you get your paper in on time, you will do well. (T: Your test scores are high; P: You get your paper in on time; W: You will do well)

* 7. Roberto lacks wisdom. (R: Roberto has wisdom)

  8. The statement "Humans lack rationality" is false. (H: Humans have rationality)

  9. Polly fails to be a parrot provided that she cannot talk and does not want a cracker. (P: Polly is a parrot; T: Polly can talk; C: Polly wants a cracker)

* 10. Neither birds nor snakes are mammals. (B: Birds are mammals; S: Snakes are mammals)

  11. Given that Linda is both smart and diligent, she will do well; but Linda is not diligent. (S: Linda is smart; D: Linda is diligent; W: Linda will do well)

  12. Al wins only if Ed does not win; and Ed wins only if Al does not win. (A: Al wins; E: Ed wins)

* 13. If Smith fails to win, then either Jones wins or Smith and Jones are tied. (S: Smith wins; J: Jones wins; T: Smith and Jones are tied)

  14. Assuming that Julio is a bachelor, he is a man who is unmarried. (B: Julio is a bachelor; M: Julio is a man; J: Julio is married)

  15. Erin's being penniless is a sufficient condition for her being miserable. (P: Erin is penniless; M: Erin is miserable)

* 16. Kareem's being tall is a necessary condition for his being on the team. (K: Kareem is tall; T: Kareem is on the team)

17. The statement "Santa does not exist" is false. (S: Santa exists)

18. Although reindeer exist, Santa does not exist; but adults are not honest if Santa does not exist. (R: Reindeer exist; S: Santa exists; H: Adults are honest)

* 19. While Joe and Sue are married, both have friends of the opposite sex. (M: Joe and Sue are married; J: Joe has friends of the opposite sex; S: Sue has friends of the opposite sex)

20. Paula will pass the test just in case she studies diligently. (P: Paula will pass the test; S: Paula studies diligently)

Part C: More Symbolizing Translate the following statements into symbols, using the schemes of abbreviation provided.

* 1. The picture frame is square only if it is rectangular. (S: The picture frame is square; R: The picture frame is rectangular)

2. You will not succeed if you lack common sense. (S: You will succeed; C: You have common sense)

3. If Sammy is a penguin, then Sammy is a bird that cannot fly. (P: Sammy is a penguin; B: Sammy is a bird; F: Sammy can fly)

* 4. Either you work hard or you have fun, but not both. (W: You work hard; F: You have fun)

5. Given that Bozo has a bill, Bozo is either a duck or a platypus. (B: Bozo has a bill; D: Bozo is a duck; P: Bozo is a platypus)

6. Neither penguins nor ostriches can fly. (P: Penguins can fly; O: Ostriches can fly)

* 7. If Alvin has a bill, then he is not a platypus if he has feathers. (B: Alvin has a bill, P: Alvin is a platypus; F: Alvin has feathers)

8. Neither Smith nor Jones wins if there is a tie; but Jones does not win given that Smith wins. (S: Smith wins; J: Jones wins; T: There is a tie)

9. While Miriam is both competent and hard-working, she is not interested in the job. (C: Miriam is competent; H: Miriam is hard-working; J: Miriam is interested in the job)

* 10. Given that Murphy is a bat only if he can fly, Murphy is not a bat. (B: Murphy is a bat; F: Murphy can fly)

11. Sally will pass unless her mind goes blank. (P: Sally will pass; M: Sally's mind goes blank)

12. Either Tyson wins or Holyfield wins, but not both. (T: Tyson wins; H: Holyfield wins)

13. Stella's being in Arkansas is a sufficient condition for her being in the U.S.A. (A: Stella is in Arkansas; U: Stella is in the U.S.A.)

14. Humberto's being competent is a necessary and sufficient condition for his being hired. (C: Humberto is competent; H: Humberto is hired)

15. Solomon's growing older is a necessary condition for his becoming wiser, but it is not a sufficient condition for his becoming wiser. (S: Solomon grows older; W: Solomon becomes wiser)

16. Dan's being in Pennsylvania is a necessary condition for his being in Philadelphia. (D: Dan is in Pennsylvania; P: Dan is in Philadelphia)

17. It is always wrong to kill the innocent only if it is wrong to kill an insane person in self-defense. (K: It is always wrong to kill the innocent; S: It is wrong to kill an insane person in self-defense)

18. It is not the case that if the Seahawks win, the Cowboys win. (S: The Seahawks win; C: The Cowboys win)

19. It is not always wrong to kill the innocent just in case it is not wrong to kill an insane person in self-defense. (K: It is always wrong to kill the innocent; S: It is wrong to kill an insane person in self-defense)

20. Plato's being a rational animal is a necessary and sufficient condition for his being human. (R: Plato is rational; A: Plato is an animal; H: Plato is human)

Part D: Schemes of Abbreviation and Symbols   Provide schemes of abbreviation for each of the following statements, and then translate the statements into symbols.

1. Fido is a dog only if Fido is an animal.

2. Josey is a mammal if Josey is a cat.

3. Physical laws cannot be changed given that they are either necessary or eternal.

4. Snakes are mammals only if snakes nourish their young with milk; but snakes do not nourish their young with milk.

5. The statement "If evil exists, then God does not exist" is false.

6. If Smith is guilty only if Smith's blood is on the murder weapon, then Smith is not guilty if Smith's blood is not on the murder weapon.

7. It is not true that if the Eiffel Tower is in Ohio, then it is in Europe.

8. Romeo and Juliet are not married, but they are in love.

9. Jane will fail unless she studies.

10. Assuming Fred is both rational and an animal, Fred is human; but Fred is not rational.

7.2 Truth Tables

Truth tables can be used to determine the validity (or invalidity) of a large class of arguments. In this section, we will examine the truth tables for the five basic types of compounds formed via the operators introduced in the previous section: the tilde, the dot, the vee, the arrow, and the double-arrow.

The main idea behind truth tables is that the truth value of certain compound statements is a function of the truth value of the atomic statements that make them up. A compound statement is said to be **truth-functional** if its truth value is completely determined by the truth value of the atomic statements that compose it. Let us now examine a series of truth-functional compounds.

We will again use the italicized, lowercase letters *p* and *q* as statement variables that can stand for any statement. For instance, the statement variable *q* can stand for A, for ~B, for ~C ∨ D, for E ↔ F, and so on.

Negations

A *negation has the opposite truth value of the statement negated.* For example, the statement "Bertrand Russell was born in 1872" is true; so its negation, "Bertrand Russell was not born in 1872," is false. And "John F. Kennedy was born in 1872" is false; so its negation, "John F. Kennedy was not born in 1872," is true. Thus, negations are *truth-functional* compounds. We can present this in a kind of diagram, called a **truth table**, as follows:

p	~*p*
T	F
F	T

This truth table has two vertical **columns**, one on the left and one on the right. The column on the left gives the possible truth values for any statement *p*, namely, T (true) and F (false). The column on the right gives the corresponding truth values for the negation, ~*p*. The table also has two horizontal **rows**. In the first (or top) row, *p* is true, so its negation is false. In the second (or bottom) row, *p* is false, so its negation is true.

Conjunctions

A *conjunction is true if both its conjuncts are true; otherwise, it is false.* Thus, one false conjunct renders an entire conjunction false. For example, "St. Augustine and Abraham Lincoln were both born in 354" is false, for although St. Augustine was born in 354, Lincoln was not. We can sum up the relationship between the truth value of a conjunction and the truth value of its conjuncts as follows:

p	*q*	(*p* • *q*)
T	T	T
T	F	F
F	T	F
F	F	F

Here, the two columns on the left list all the possible truth value assignments for any two statements. Row 1 represents the situation in which both statements are true. Rows 2 and 3 represent the *two* situations in which the statements *differ* in truth value (*p* true, *q* false; and *p* false, *q* true). Finally, row 4 represents the situation in which both statements are false. The column under the dot indicates that the conjunction as a whole is true *only if* both conjuncts are true (namely, in row 1); otherwise, the conjunction as a whole is false.

Disjunctions

A disjunction (represented by the vee) is false if both its disjuncts are false; otherwise, it is true. Consider the following examples:

61. Either George Washington or John F. Kennedy was born in 1999 (or both were).

62. Either Abraham Lincoln or Andrew Jackson was born in 1809 (or both were).

63. Either Franklin D. Roosevelt or Jimmy Carter was a Democrat (or both were).

Statement (61) is false because both its disjuncts are false. (62) is true since Lincoln was born in 1809. (The statement as a whole is true even though Jackson was born not in 1809, but in 1767.) And (63) is true because both Roosevelt and Carter were Democrats. We can present these possibilities succinctly in a truth table as follows:

p	q	$(p \vee q)$
T	T	T
T	F	T
F	T	T
F	F	F

Again, the columns on the left represent the four possible combinations of truth values for any two statements. The column under the vee indicates that the disjunction is false only when both disjuncts are false (namely, in row 4); otherwise, the disjunction as a whole is true.

Material Conditionals

A material conditional (represented by the arrow) is false if its antecedent is true and its consequent is false; otherwise, it is true. However, English conditionals are rather complicated, and so we need to discuss the relationship between the arrow and the English if-then in some detail. Consider the following examples:

64. If some dogs are collies, then no dogs are collies.

65. If George Washington was born before Jimmy Carter, then Jimmy Carter was born before George Washington.

66. If physical objects exert a gravitational attraction on each other, then a fist-sized chunk of lead released 3 feet from the surface of the earth will always float in midair.

Each of these conditionals has a true antecedent and a false consequent, and each conditional *is itself* false. Indeed, *an English conditional is always false when its antecedent is true and its consequent is false.* As it turns out, this fact is so important as regards the validity of arguments that logicians have defined a special type of conditional, called the **material conditional**, that is false *only* when its antecedent is true and its consequent is false. The truth table for the material conditional, which is represented by the arrow, is as follows:

p	q	$(p \rightarrow q)$
T	T	T
T	F	F
F	T	T
F	F	T

Again, note that the material conditional is false *only* in the situation in which the antecedent is true and the consequent is false (row 2).

Now consider the following four English sentences, which correspond to the four rows in the truth table for the material conditional:

a. If the Eiffel Tower is in France, then the Eiffel Tower is in Europe.

b. If the Eiffel Tower is in France, then the Eiffel Tower is in the U.S.A.

c. If the Eiffel Tower is in Germany, then the Eiffel Tower is in Europe.

d. If the Eiffel Tower is in Ohio, then the Eiffel Tower is in the U.S.A.

With the exception of (b), each of these conditionals is true. In (a), both antecedent and consequent are true. In (c), the antecedent is false while the consequent is true; however, the conditional itself is true, since if the Eiffel Tower *is* in Germany, it is certainly in Europe. It may seem odd that a conditional could be true when both antecedent and consequent are false, but (d) illustrates that this can be so: If the Eiffel Tower *is* in Ohio, then of course it is in the U.S.A.

At this point, it may seem that the English if-then is truth-functional and that the truth table for the material conditional is also a truth table for the English if-then. Unfortunately, things are not that simple. Consider the following conditionals:

a. If $1 + 1 = 2$, then the Eiffel Tower is in France.

b. If the Eiffel Tower is in Ohio, then it is in Europe.

c. If the Eiffel Tower is in Germany, then it is in the U.S.A.

In (a), both antecedent and consequent are true, yet the conditional as a whole seems false. At any rate, most people would hesitate to pronounce it true, since there is no relevance between the antecedent and the consequent. But if (a) is false, then English conditionals are not in general truth-functional. Obviously, if they *are* truth-functional, then any conditional with a true antecedent *and* a true consequent must be true. It appears, then, that there is a significant difference between the material conditional, defined by the preceding truth table, and ordinary English conditionals. This is born out if we examine rows 3 and 4 of the truth table in the light of (b) and (c). (b) corresponds to row 3, since it has a false antecedent and true consequent. If we went by the truth table, we would say that (b) is true, but from the standpoint of common sense, it is false. If the Eiffel Tower *is* in Ohio, then it certainly is not in Europe. Similarly, (c) seems false. If the Eiffel Tower *is* in Germany, then it certainly is not in the U.S.A. Yet, if we go by the truth table for the material conditional, we must pronounce (c) true, since both antecedent and consequent are false.

Why are logicians so interested in the material conditional if it doesn't correspond to English conditionals? What good does it do to have a truth table for conditionals if we can see that the truth table does not give an accurate picture of the relationship between the truth value of English conditionals (in general) and the truth value of their constituent parts? As it turns out, when the truth table method is applied to arguments, it nicely corroborates our belief in the validity of such intuitive inference rules as those introduced in chapter 2— *modus ponens*, *modus tollens*, hypothetical syllogism, disjunctive syllogism, and constructive dilemma. Moreover, it confirms our belief in the *invalidity* of such common, formal fallacies as denying the antecedent and affirming the consequent. In short, the material conditional captures that part of the meaning of the English conditional that is essential for the validity of the basic argument forms of statement logic.

Material Biconditionals

A *material biconditional* (represented by the double-arrow) *is true when its two constituent statements have the same truth value; and it is false if the two statements differ in truth value.* Thus, the truth table for the material biconditional is as follows:

p	q	$(p \leftrightarrow q)$
T	T	T
T	F	F
F	T	F
F	F	T

Notice that the material biconditional is true when its constituent parts are both *false* (row 4), as well as when they are both true (row 1).

The truth table for the biconditional is perhaps more readily understandable if one realizes that a biconditional is in effect a conjunction of two conditionals. Consider an example:

67. Clinton won the election *if and only if* Bush lost the election.

Statement (67) can be broken down into two conditional statements, as follows:

68. Clinton won the election *if* Bush lost the election.

69. Clinton won the election *only if* Bush lost the election.

In standard form, (68) and (69) look like this (respectively):

70. If Bush lost the election, then Clinton won the election.

71. If Clinton won the election, then Bush lost the election.

So, (67) can be rewritten as a conjunction of two conditionals:

72. If Clinton won the election, then Bush lost the election; and if Bush lost the election, then Clinton won the election. (C: Clinton won the election; B: Bush lost the election)

Similar remarks could be made about any biconditional. Let us symbolize (67) and (72) and then check to see if the truth tables for these statements are alike. In symbols, (67) and (72) look like this (respectively):

73. $C \leftrightarrow B$

74. $(C \rightarrow B) \bullet (B \rightarrow C)$

Let us work out the truth table for (74). The first row looks like this:

C	B	$(C \rightarrow B) \bullet (B \rightarrow C)$		
T	T	T	T	T

When C and B are both true, then of course $(C \rightarrow B)$ is true, and so is $(B \rightarrow C)$. Hence, we place a "T" under the main operator, the dot, because both conjuncts are true. (Strictly speaking, we only need the "T" under the dot; the others are merely "scratch work" to ensure accuracy.) Now let us add the second row to the truth table:

C	B	$(C \rightarrow B) \bullet (B \rightarrow C)$		
T	T	T	T	T
T	F	F	F	T

With C true and B false, $(C \rightarrow B)$ is false while $(B \rightarrow C)$ is true. (Remember, the material conditional is false *only when* its antecedent is true and its consequent is false.) So, we have a conjunction with one false conjunct and one true conjunct. We place an "F" under the dot, since one false conjunct makes the entire conjunction false.

Summary of Truth Tables for the Five Compounds												
Negation		**Conjunction**			**Disjunction**			**Conditional**			**Biconditional**	
p	*~p*	*p* *q*		*(p•q)*	*p* *q*		*(p∨q)*	*p* *q*		*(p→q)*	*p* *q*	*(p↔q)*
T	F	T T		T	T T		T	T T		T	T T	T
F	T	T F		F	T F		T	T F		F	T F	F
		F T		F	F T		T	F T		T	F T	F
		F F		F	F F		F	F F		T	F F	T

Next, we fill in truth values for the third row:

C B	(C → B) • (B → C)
T T	T T T
T F	F F T
F T	T F F

With C false and B true, (C → B) is true; however, (B → C) is false. So, we again place an "F" under the dot, since we have one false conjunct. We can now add the fourth and final row to the truth table:

C B	(C → B) • (B → C)
T T	T T T
T F	F F T
F T	T F F
F F	T T T

With C and B both false, (C → B) is true, and so is (B → C). We place a "T" under the dot, since both conjuncts are true.

The column under the dot gives us the truth value of the entire statement, row by row. (As mentioned previously, the columns under the arrows are merely scratch work and, as such, are not essential to the truth table.) And the column under the dot is exactly like the column under the double-arrow in the truth table for the biconditional:

C B	C ↔ B
T T	T
T F	F
F T	F
F F	T

To check your understanding of the truth-functional compounds discussed in this section, complete the following exercises.

◆ **Exercise 7.2**

Part A: True or False?   Determine the truth value of the following compound statements. Make the following assumptions: A is true, B is true, C is false, and D is false.

* 1. A • C
  2. A ∨ C
  3. ~ A
* 4. B → D
  5. D → B
  6. A ↔ B
* 7. C ↔ D
  8. ~(A • B)
  9. C ∨ D
* 10. ~(C ∨ D)
  11. ~C → D
  12. ~(D → A)
* 13. (A • C) → B

14. C → (A → D)
15. (C → A) → D
* 16. ~(A ↔ D)
17. ~C • ~D
18. ~(~A ↔ ~B)
* 19. (A • C) ∨ (B • D)
20. (C ∨ A) • (D ∨ B)
21. ~[A → (C ∨ B)]
* 22. (D ↔ A) ∨ (C → B)
23. (~C → A) ↔ (~A ∨ D)
24. ~B ↔ (A • C)
* 25. ~(D ∨ C) → B

Part B: More True or False.   Determine the truth value of the following compound statements.

* 1. It is not the case that Abraham Lincoln was born in 1997.
  2. If water is H₂O, then water is not wet.
  3. Either New York City is the capital of Montana or Seattle is the capital of Montana.
* 4. Hillary Clinton is a married man if and only if Hillary Clinton is a husband.
  5. If Reno is in Nevada, then Reno is in the U.S.A.
  6. Either Alabama is a southern state (of the U.S.A.) or Maine is a southern state.
* 7. It is not the case that both Charlie Chaplin and George Washington are past presidents of the U.S.A.
  8. If either Mozart or Beethoven was born in Korea, then it is false that both Mozart and Beethoven were born in Australia.
  9. If the Taj Mahal is green, then the Taj Mahal is not invisible.

* **10.** If Paris is the capital of France, then neither Seattle nor Spokane is the capital of France.

 11. Samuel Clemens wrote *Huckleberry Finn* if and only if Samuel Clemens is Mark Twain.

 12. If Reno is in Nevada, then Reno is in Canada.

* **13.** If the Statue of Liberty is in Kentucky, then the Statue of Liberty is in the U.S.A.

 14. Either Bruce Willis or Clint Eastwood is president of the U.S.A.

 15. If Reno is in Nevada, then either Reno is in Canada or Reno is in the U.S.A.

7.3 Using Truth Tables to Evaluate Arguments

We are now in a position to use truth tables to establish the validity and invalidity of arguments. Let's begin by examining an argument having the form *modus tollens*:

> **75.** If Lincoln is 8 feet tall, then Lincoln is over 7 feet tall. But it is not the case that Lincoln is over 7 feet tall. It follows that Lincoln is not 8 feet tall. (L: Lincoln is 8 feet tall; S: Lincoln is over 7 feet tall)

The argument may be symbolized as follows:

> **76.** $L \rightarrow S$, $\sim S$ $\therefore$ $\sim L$

First, we generate all the possible truth value assignments for L and S. Since there are two truth values (truth and falsehood), our truth table must have 2^n rows, where n is the number of statement letters in the symbolic argument. In this case, we have just two statement letters, L and S, so our truth table will have 2^2 rows ($2^2 = 2 \times 2 = 4$). The truth value assignments can be generated in a completely mechanical way; indeed, it is important to generate them mechanically both to avoid error and to facilitate communication. In the column nearest to the vertical line (in this case, the column under S), simply alternate Ts and Fs. In the next column to the left (in this case, the column under L), alternate couples (two Ts, followed by two Fs). Like this:

L	S	
T	T	
T	F	
F	T	
F	F	

We then write the steps of the argument out on the line at the top of the table and fill in the columns under each step of the argument, row by row. Row 1 looks like this:

L	S	L → S,	~S	∴ ~L
T	T	T	F	F

As we have seen, $L \to S$ is true when L and S are both true. Of course, $\sim S$ is false when S is true; and $\sim L$ is false when L is true.

Next, we fill in truth values in row 2:

L	S	L → S,	~S	∴ ~L
T	T	T	F	F
T	F	F	T	F

With its antecedent true and consequent false, $L \to S$ is false in this row of the table. Since S is false, $\sim S$ must be true. And since L is true, $\sim L$ must be false.

Now we add row 3:

L	S	L → S,	~S	∴ ~L
T	T	T	F	F
T	F	F	T	F
F	T	T	F	T

The conditional premise is true when its antecedent is false and its consequent is true. Obviously, $\sim S$ is false when S is true; and $\sim L$ is true when L is false.

To complete the table, we add the fourth and final row.

L	S	L → S,	~S	∴ ~L
T	T	T	F	F
T	F	F	T	F
F	T	T	F	T
F	F	T	T	T

The conditional premise is true in row 4. (The material conditional is false *only* when its antecedent is true and its consequent is false; otherwise, it is true.) Since L and S are both false in this row, $\sim S$ and $\sim L$ are true.

Now, what does the truth table tell us about the argument? Each row in the table describes a possible situation in very abstract terms. For example, row 1 describes a situation in which both *L* and *S* are true. *L* and *S* could be about any topic—science, sorcery, celery, whatever. As long as the statements are both true, row 1 tells us that the first premise is true, the second premise is false, and the conclusion is false. *What we are looking for is a row, and hence a possible situation, in which the premises are all true but the conclusion is false.* If we can find such a row (or situation), then the argument form is invalid. Recall that validity preserves truth—if you start with truth and reason validly, you'll get a true conclusion. So, if a form of argument *can* lead from true premises to a false conclusion, that form of argument is invalid. As we look at the table for the symbolic argument (76), which has the form *modus tollens*, we see that there is no row in which all of the premises are true and the conclusion is false. This means that the argument has a valid form; hence, the argument itself is valid. And because the English argument (75) has the same form, it too is valid.

Now let's see what happens when we apply the truth table method to one of the formal fallacies. Here is an argument having the form of the fallacy of denying the antecedent:

77. If society approves of genetic engineering, then genetic engineering is morally permissible. But society does not approve of genetic engineering. Therefore, genetic engineering is not morally permissible. (S: Society approves of genetic engineering; G: Genetic engineering is morally permissible)

We translate the argument into symbols as follows:

78. S → G, ~S ∴ ~G

The truth table looks like this:

S	G	S → G	~S	∴ ~G
T	T	T	F	F
T	F	F	F	T
F	T	T	T	F
F	F	T	T	T

Is there a row in which the premises are all true and the conclusion is false? Yes, row 3. This shows that the argument form is invalid, for it does not preserve truth. The table gives us the additional bit of information that the invalidity of the form is revealed in situations in which the antecedent of the conditional premise (i.e., S) is false and its consequent (i.e., G) is true. This gives us a strong hint about how to write an English **counterexample** that will connect what we have learned from the truth table with our intuitions as speakers of English. As you will recall from chapter 2, a good counterexample has the following features: (a) It has the same form as the original argument, (b) its premises are *well-known* truths, and (c) its conclusion is a *well-known* falsehood. Here is a counterexample to argument (78):

> 79. If George Washington was 8 feet tall, then he was over 2 feet tall. But Washington was not 8 feet tall. So, he was not over 2 feet tall.

Note that the conditional premise has a false antecedent but a true consequent: Washington wasn't 8 feet tall, but he was certainly over 2 feet tall. Moreover, the conditional premise as a whole is plainly true: Anyone who is 8 feet tall is certainly over 2 feet tall. And, of course, the second premise is true while the conclusion is false. So, this English example illustrates the sort of situation described by the third row of the truth table. The pattern of reasoning is *always* invalid, since it allows for true premises and a false conclusion.

Of course, not all truth tables are as short as those we've examined thus far. Let us see what happens when we apply the truth table method to arguments having three statement letters.

> 80. If the equatorial rain forests produce oxygen used by Americans, then either Americans ought to pay for the oxygen or they ought to stop complaining about the destruction of the rain forests. But either it is false that Americans ought to pay for the oxygen or it is false that Americans ought to stop complaining about the destruction of the rain forests. Therefore, it is false that the equatorial rain forests produce oxygen used by Americans. (E: The equatorial rain forests produce oxygen used by Americans; P: Americans ought to pay for the oxygen; S: Americans ought to stop complaining about the destruction of the rain forests)

Using the scheme of abbreviation provided, the argument translates into symbols as follows:

> 81. $E \rightarrow (P \vee S)$, $\sim P \vee \sim S$ $\therefore$ $\sim E$

Now we are ready to construct a truth table. We list the statement letters *in the order in which they appear* in our symbolization: *E, P, S*. Since a truth table must have 2^n rows, where *n* is the number of statement letters, in this case we need a table with eight rows ($2^3 = 2 \times 2 \times 2 = 8$). To generate every possible combination of truth values for the three statement letters *mechanically*, we alternate Ts and Fs in the column nearest the vertical line, under *S*. Then we alternate couples (two Ts, followed by two Fs, etc.) in the next column to the left, under *P*. Finally, we alternate quadruples (four Ts followed by four Fs) in the column on the far left, under *E*, like this:

E	P	S	
T	T	T	
T	T	F	
T	F	T	
T	F	F	
F	T	T	
F	T	F	
F	F	T	
F	F	F	

It's important to generate the possible truth value combinations *in the manner indicated*, for two reasons. First, doing so will enable you to construct truth tables quickly and accurately. Second, for purposes of communication, a *standard method* of generating truth value combinations is needed. Without a standard method, truth tables cannot readily be compared or checked for accuracy.

Next, we fill in the truth values for the premises and conclusion, row by row. Check out each row of the following table. Only the circled columns are absolutely essential. The other columns are scratch work done to guarantee accuracy. For example, because the first premise is a conditional, only the column under the arrow is essential to the table. But filling in some other columns often helps one to avoid errors.

E	P	S	E → (P ∨ S),		~P ∨ ~S		∴ ~E
T	T	T	T	T	F F	F	F
T	T	F	T	T	F T	T	F
T	F	T	T	T	T T	F	F
T	F	F	F	F	T T	T	F
F	T	T	T	T	F F	F	T
F	T	F	T	T	F T	T	T
F	F	T	T	T	T T	F	T
F	F	F	T	F	T T	T	T

Once the table is complete, we examine it to see if there are any rows in which the premises are all true while the conclusion is false. Rows 2 and 3 meet this condition, so the argument is invalid. (An argument is invalid as long as *at least one* row meets this condition.)

Using the hints provided by row 3 of the truth table, we can construct a counterexample to argument (81):

82. If George Washington was born before Harry Truman, then either Abraham Lincoln was born before George Washington or Abraham Lincoln was born

before Harry Truman. Either it is false that Abraham Lincoln was born before George Washington or it is false that Abraham Lincoln was born before Harry Truman. So, it is false that George Washington was born before Harry Truman. (E: George Washington was born before Harry Truman; P: Abraham Lincoln was born before George Washington; S: Abraham Lincoln was born before Harry Truman)

Note that the counterexample matches the scenario described in row 3 of the truth table perfectly: *E* (i.e., Washington was born before Truman) is true, *P* (i.e., Lincoln was born before Washington) is false, and *S* (i.e., Lincoln was born before Truman) is true.

Truth tables can be used to evaluate for validity even when our English intuitions fail us. For example, is the following argument valid? Most people find it difficult to answer simply on the basis of logical intuition.

83. If Socrates works hard, he gets rich. But if Socrates doesn't work hard, he enjoys life. Moreover, if Socrates does not get rich, then he does not enjoy life. Hence, Socrates gets rich. (H: Socrates works hard; R: Socrates gets rich; L: Socrates enjoys life)

Using the scheme of abbreviation provided, the argument may be symbolized as follows:

84. H → R, ~H → L, ~R → ~L ∴ R

The truth table looks like this:

H	R	L	H → R	~H → L	~R → ~L	∴ R
T	T	T	T	T	T	T
T	T	F	T	T	T	T
T	F	T	F	T	F	F
T	F	F	F	T	T	F
F	T	T	T	T	T	T
F	T	F	T	F	T	T
F	F	T	T	T	F	F
F	F	F	T	F	T	F

There is no row in which the premises are true and the conclusion is false; therefore, the argument form is valid. Since argument (83) is one that most people find difficult to assess through unaided logical intuition, the fact that a truth table enables us to achieve a definitive evaluation illustrates the power of this method.

The truth table method does have an important limitation: It becomes unwieldy as arguments become longer. For instance, suppose we wish to evaluate an argument having the form of a constructive dilemma. In symbols, we have the following:

85. $A \lor B, A \to C, B \to D \therefore C \lor D$

Here, we have four statement letters, so we need 2^4 rows in our truth table ($2^4 = 2 \times 2 \times 2 \times 2 = 16$). The truth table looks like this:

A	B	C	D	$A \lor B,$	$A \to C,$	$B \to D$	$\therefore$ $C \lor D$
T	T	T	T	T	T	T	T
T	T	T	F	T	T	F	T
T	T	F	T	T	F	T	T
T	T	F	F	T	F	F	F
T	F	T	T	T	T	T	T
T	F	T	F	T	T	T	T
T	F	F	T	T	F	T	T
T	F	F	F	T	F	T	F
F	T	T	T	T	T	T	T
F	T	T	F	T	T	F	T
F	T	F	T	T	T	T	T
F	T	F	F	T	T	F	F
F	F	T	T	F	T	T	T
F	F	T	F	F	T	T	T
F	F	F	T	F	T	T	T
F	F	F	F	F	T	T	F

The argument is valid, for there are no rows in which all the premises are true and the conclusion is false. Note that the initial truth value assignments on the left are generated in the mechanical way previously described: alternate Ts and Fs under the letter closest to the vertical line (*D* in the table); alternate couples under the next letter to the left (*C*); alternate quadruples under the next letter (*B*); finally, alternate groups of eight. How many rows would be needed for a truth table involving five statement letters? Thirty-two ($2^5 = 2 \times 2 \times 2 \times 2 \times 2 = 32$). And if six statement letters were involved, we would need a truth table with 64 rows. So, the truth table method is cumbersome when applied to arguments involving many statement letters. Nevertheless, it is a powerful method that is useful in many cases.

Check your understanding by completing the following exercises.

◆ *Exercise 7.3*

Part A: Truth Tables   Construct truth tables to determine whether the following arguments are valid. Make initial truth value assignments in the mechanical fashion described in this section. That is, list statement letters *in the order in which they appear* in the argument; then alternate Ts and Fs in the column under the letter *closest* to the vertical line; alternate couples (two Ts, two Fs, etc.) under the next letter on the left; and so on.

* 1. A ∨ B, ~A ∴ B
  2. F → G, F ∴ G
  3. (A ∨ B) • ~(A • B), ~A ∴ B
* 4. ~P → ~R ∴ ~(P → R)
  5. ~(X → Y) ∴ ~X → ~Y
  6. E ∴ D ∨ E
* 7. A • B ∴ B
  8. ~(N • L) ∴ ~N ∨ ~L
  9. (A ∨ B) • ~(A • B), A ∴ ~B
* 10. ~F • ~G ∴ ~F ↔ ~G
  11. ~(S • ~R), ~R ∴ ~S

  12. A ↔ B ∴ A • B
* 13. D ↔ (E ∨ C), ~D ∴ ~C
  14. (A • B) → C ∴ A → (B → C)
  15. N ↔ (M • L), ~L ∴ ~N
* 16. A → B, B → C ∴ A → C
  17. (Q ∨ U) → Z, ~Z ∴ ~Q
  18. (E ↔ G) → H, ~H ∴ ~E ∨ ~G
* 19. A ∨ B, A → C, B → C ∴ C
  20. A → C, B → D, ~C ∨ ~D
      ∴ ~A ∨ ~B

Part B: More Truth Tables   Construct truth tables to determine whether the following arguments are valid.

* 1. A • ~B ∴ ~(A → B)
  2. F → G ∴ ~F → ~G
  3. ~E → ~G ∴ G → E
* 4. ~(H • K) ∴ ~H • ~K
  5. A → B, B ∴ A
  6. X ∨ Y, Y ∴ ~X
* 7. A ∴ (A ∨ B) • ~(A • B)
  8. ~(T ↔ ~S) ∴ ~T ∨ S
  9. ~F ∨ ~G ∴ ~(F ∨ G)
* 10. ~(H ↔ J) ∴ ~H ↔ ~J
  11. ~(A → B) ∴ A • ~B
  12. ~(N ↔ P) ∴ N → ~P
  13. ~(A ↔ B) ∴ (A • ~B) ∨ (B • ~A)
  14. (H • B) → S ∴ B → S
  15. P → Q, S → Q, ~Q ∴ ~P • ~S
  16. Z → (S ∨ G), Z ∴ S
  17. ~(L ∨ M), ~M ↔ ~N ∴ ~N
  18. P → (~Q ∨ R), P • ~R ∴ ~Q
  19. A → (B → C) ∴ (A • B) → C
  20. ~[~(D • E) ∨ (F ∨ ~D)] ∴ D • (E • ~F)

Part C: English Arguments   Symbolize the following arguments. Then use truth tables to determine whether they are valid.

* **1.** Not having exceeded our natural resources is a necessary condition for its being appropriate to expand our city. Unfortunately, we have exceeded our natural resources. Consequently, it is not appropriate to expand our city. (E: We have exceeded our natural resources; A: It is appropriate to expand our city)

  2. Humans evolved from lower life forms given that either human life evolved from inanimate matter apart from divine causes or God created human life via the long, slow process we call evolution. God created human life via the long, slow process we call evolution. It follows that humans evolved from lower life forms. (H: Humans evolved from lower life forms; M: Human life evolved from inanimate matter apart from divine causes; G: God created human life via the long, slow process we call evolution)

  3. American foreign policy is bankrupt unless it is based on clear moral principles. American foreign policy is not based on clear moral principles just in case it is based primarily on the national interest. Unfortunately, American foreign policy is based primarily on the national interest. We may infer that American foreign policy is bankrupt. (B: American foreign policy is bankrupt; M: American foreign policy is based on clear moral principles; N: American foreign policy is based primarily on the national interest)

* **4.** You won't get an A unless you do well on all the exams. Therefore, if you do well on all the exams, you will get an A. (A: You will get an A; W: You do well on all the exams)

  5. There are necessary truths (i.e., truths that cannot be false under any possible circumstances). For assuming that there are no necessary truths, there are no necessary connections between premises and conclusions. But there are no valid arguments if there are no necessary connections between premises and conclusions; and there are valid arguments. (N: There are necessary truths; C: There are necessary connections between premises and conclusions; V: There are valid arguments)

  6. On the condition that land mines are designed to inflict horrible suffering, they ought to be banned unless inflicting horrible suffering is sometimes justified. It is not true that inflicting horrible suffering is sometimes justified, but it is true that land mines are designed to inflict horrible suffering. Accordingly, land mines ought to be banned. (L: Land mines are designed to inflict horrible suffering; B: Land mines ought to be banned; S: Inflicting horrible suffering is sometimes justified)

* **7.** The reduction of violence is a necessary and sufficient condition for making drugs legal. But more people will use drugs if drugs are made legal. And violence is not reduced if more people will use drugs. Hence, drugs are not made legal. (V: Violence is reduced; L: Drugs are made legal; P: More people will use drugs)

8. Augustine achieves heaven if Augustine is virtuous. But Augustine is happy provided that he is not virtuous. Augustine does not achieve heaven only if he is not happy. Therefore, Augustine achieves heaven. (A: Augustine achieves heaven; V: Augustine is virtuous; H: Augustine is happy)

9. Not all living things are able to feel pain. For all living things are able to feel pain only if all living things have nervous systems. But not all living things have nervous systems given that plants do not have nervous systems. And plants do not have nervous systems. (L: All living things are able to feel pain; N: All living things have nervous systems; P: Plants have nervous systems)

10. It is morally permissible for mentally superior extraterrestrials to eat humans on the condition that it is morally permissible for humans to eat animals. But either it is not morally permissible for mentally superior extraterrestrials to eat humans or human life lacks intrinsic value. However, human life has intrinsic value. We are forced to conclude that it is not morally permissible for humans to eat animals. (E: It is morally permissible for mentally superior extraterrestrials to eat humans; H: It is morally permissible for humans to eat animals; V: Human life has intrinsic value)

7.4 Abbreviated Truth Tables

As we have seen, the truth table method is rather cumbersome when applied to arguments having more than three statement letters. But there are ways to make it less cumbersome, and we will explore one of them in this section, namely, the **abbreviated truth table method**. The essential insight behind abbreviated truth tables is this: If we can construct *one* row of a truth table, *making all the premises true while the conclusion is false*, then we have shown that the argument form in question is invalid. Here's an example:

> 86. If I am thinking, then my neurons are firing. Hence, if my neurons are firing, then I am thinking. (A: I am thinking; N: My neurons are firing)

Using the scheme of abbreviation provided, we may symbolize the argument as follows:

> 87. A → N ∴ N → A

We begin by hypothesizing that all the argument's premises are true while its conclusion is false:

$$
\begin{array}{c|cc}
 & A \to N & \therefore\ N \to A \\
\hline
 & T & F
\end{array}
$$

Now we work backward. If the conclusion is false, then N must be true and A must be false. We fill in these values uniformly throughout the argument:

	$A \rightarrow N$ $\therefore$ $N \rightarrow A$
	F T T T F F

This truth assignment does indeed make the conclusion false and the premise true. We have in effect constructed a row in the truth table that shows the argument to be invalid: It is the row in which A is false and N is true. We add this information at the left to complete our abbreviated truth table:

A N	$A \rightarrow N$ $\therefore$ $N \rightarrow A$
F T	F T T T F F

We have thus shown the argument to be invalid. And as before, our truth-functional assessment of the argument gives a strong hint about how to construct an English counterexample:

88. If Thomas Jefferson was 500 years old when he died, then he lived to be more than a year old. Therefore, if Jefferson lived to be more than a year old, then he was 500 years old when he died.

The premise of argument (88) is plainly true, even though its antecedent is false. And, of course, the conclusion of the argument is false, too.

Let's try a more complicated example. Consider the following symbolic argument:

89. $E \vee S$, $E \rightarrow (B \cdot U)$, $\sim S \vee \sim U$ $\therefore$ B

Again, we hypothesize that all the premises can be true while the conclusion is false:

	$E \vee S$, $E \rightarrow (B \cdot U)$, $\sim S \vee \sim U$ $\therefore$ B
	T T T F

Then we work backward to determine the truth value of each constituent statement letter. Since we have assigned "F" to B in the conclusion, we must assign "F" to B uniformly throughout the argument. (Remember, we are in effect constructing a single row in a truth table.) This means that $(B \cdot U)$ is also false. Hence, we must assign "F" to E; otherwise, the second premise will be false, which contradicts our hypothesis. Now, if E is false, we must make S true;

otherwise, the first premise will be false, which contradicts our hypothesis. And if S is true, then $\sim S$ is false, so we must make $\sim U$ true (and hence U false) to make the third premise true. Thus, we arrive at our abbreviated truth table:

E	S	B	U	$E \vee S$,	$E \rightarrow (B \cdot U)$,	$\sim S \vee \sim U$	$\therefore$ B
F	T	F	F	F T T	F T	F F F	F T T T F	F

In this case, an argument that would require a 16-row truth table can be dealt with quickly by means of an abbreviated truth table.

The abbreviated truth table method can also be used to show that an argument is valid. Let's try it out on an old friend, disjunctive syllogism. Again, we begin by hypothesizing that the conclusion can be false while the premises are true:

	$A \vee B$,	$\sim A$	$\therefore$ B
	T	T	F

If $\sim A$ is true, then A is false. But since B is also false, $A \vee B$ is false, contrary to our hypothesis. Thus, in trying to assign values so that the premises are all true and the conclusion is false, we are forced to contradict ourselves. This means the argument is valid. We indicate that we were forced to assign truth values inconsistently by writing "T/F" under the first premise:

	$A \vee B$,	$\sim A$	$\therefore$ B	
	F (T/F) F	T F	F	Valid

Using an abbreviated truth table is a bit more complicated when the conclusion of the argument is false on *more than one* assignment of truth values—for example, when the conclusion is a conjunction or a biconditional. In such cases, the following principles will suffice:

Principle 1: If there is *any* assignment of values in which the premises are all true and the conclusion is false, then the argument is invalid.

Principle 2: If more than one assignment of truth values will make the conclusion false, then consider each such assignment; if each assignment that makes the conclusion false makes *at least one* premise false, then the argument is valid.

For instance, consider the following symbolic argument:

90. F → G, G → H ∴ ~F • H

There are three ways to make the conclusion false: (a) make both conjuncts false, (b) make the left conjunct false and the right one true, or (c) make the left conjunct true and the right one false. If we neglect this complexity, we can easily fall into error, for not every assignment that makes the conclusion false makes the premises true. For instance:

	F → G, G → H ∴ ~F • H
	T T/F F F T F F T F F

With this assignment, the first premise is false. (We could make the first premise true by assigning "T" to G, but then the second premise would be false.) If we overlook the fact that other truth value assignments render the *conclusion* false, we might suppose that this abbreviated truth table shows that the argument is valid. But it does not, because there is a way of assigning "F" to the conclusion that makes all the premises true, namely:

F G H	F → G, G → H ∴ ~F • H
F F F	F T F F T F T F F F

And this proves that the argument form is invalid.

To show that an argument is valid, we must consider every truth value assignment in which its conclusion is false. Consider the following example:

91. P → Q, Q → P ∴ P ↔ Q

A biconditional is false whenever its two constituent statements *differ* in truth value. So, in this case, we must consider the assignment in which *P* is true and *Q* is false, *and also* the assignment in which *P* is false and *Q* is true.

	P → Q, Q → P ∴ P ↔ Q
	T (T/F) F F T T T F F
	F T T T (T/F) F F F T Valid

Here, each assignment that makes the conclusion false also makes one of the premises false (which contradicts our hypothesis that all the premises can be true while the conclusion is false). Thus, we have shown the argument to be valid.

◆ Exercise 7.4

Part A: Abbreviated Truth Tables   Use abbreviated truth tables to show that the following arguments are invalid.

*   1.   A → (B → C) ∴ B → C

    2.   ~(E ↔ F) ∴ ~E • ~F

    3.   ~(G ↔ H) ∴ ~G → ~H

*   4.   J → ~K ∴ ~(J ↔ K)

    5.   (P • Q) → R, ~R ∴ ~P

    6.   ~(Z • H), ~Z → Y, W → H ∴ ~W → Y
         How many rows would be needed in a complete truth table for argument 6?

*   7.   ~(S • H), (~S • ~H) → ~U ∴ ~U

    8.   (F • G) ↔ H, ~H ∴ ~G

    9.   ~(B → C), (D • C) ∨ E ∴ ~B

* 10.   (P → ~Q) ↔ ~R, R ∴ ~P

  11.   S → (T → V) ∴ (S → T) → V

  12.   A → (B → C) ∴ A → (B • C)

* 13.   (Z • Y) → W ∴ Z → (Y • W)

  14.   ~(C ∨ D), (~C • ~E) ↔ ~D, ~E → (C ∨ F), S ∨ F ∴ S
         How many rows would be needed in a complete truth table for argument 14?

  15.   (F ↔ G) ↔ H, ~H ∴ ~F • ~G

* 16.   P → Q, P → R, Q ↔ R, S, S → R ∴ P • Q

  17.   S → (A • O), ~P ∨ ~R, P → (S ∨ Z), Z → (O → R) ∴ Z ∨ ~P

  18.   A ∨ (B • C), ~A ∴ (A • B) ∨ (A • C)

* 19.   ~(Q ∨ S), ~T ∨ S, (U • W) → Q ∴ (~T • ~U) • W

  20.   ~J • ~K, L → J, M → K, (M → ~L) → ~(N • O) ∴ ~N

Part B: More Abbreviated Truth Tables   Use abbreviated truth tables to show that the following arguments are invalid.

*   1.   ~(A • B), ~A → C, ~B → D ∴ C • D

    2.   L ↔ (M • N), M ∨ N, ~L ∴ ~M

    3.   (O ↔ P) → R, ~R ∴ ~O ∨ P

*   4.   ~(V • X) → ~Y ∴ ~(V • X) → Y]

    5.   ~(Z • H), ~Z → Y, W → H ∴ ~W → Y

    6.   ~X ∨ (C • A), ~Y ∨ ~B, ~Y ∨ (X ∨ T), T → (A → B) ∴ T ∨ ~Y

*   7.   ~(Z → A), Z → B, ~A → C ∴ C • ~B

8. B → (C • D), ~E ∨ ~F, E → (B ∨ G), G → (D → F) ∴ G ∨ ~E
   How many rows would be needed in a complete truth table for item 8?

9. ~(D ↔ E), ~D → F, E → G ∴ F • G

* 10. H ∨ ~S, H → Z, ~S → P ∴ P ↔ Z

11. ~[(J • K) → (M ∨ N)] ∴ K • N

12. A → B, C → ~D, ~B ∨ D ∴ ~A ↔ ~C

13. ~E → (G • A), ~(P ↔ ~L) ∨ E, ~(P • L) ∨ Q, ~N → ~G ∴ Q • A

14. (G → E) ↔ S, ~(S ∨ H), ~(P • ~H) ∴ G • E

15. ~(C ↔ ~D) ∨ E, ~E → (G • H), (C • D) → K, ~N → ~G ∴ K • H
    How many rows would be needed in a complete truth table for item 15?

Part C: Valid or Invalid?   Some of the following arguments are valid, and some are invalid. Use abbreviated truth tables to determine which are valid and which are invalid.

* 1. ~A ∨ B ∴ A → B

2. F → (G ↔ H), ~F • ~H ∴ ~G

3. ~M ∴ ~N ∨ ~M

* 4. A ∨ (B • C) ∴ (A • B) ∨ (A • C)

5. P → ~(Q • R), P • R ∴ ~Q

6. X → Z, Y → Z, ~Z ∴ X ↔ Y

7. ~(S → R), S → J, ~R ↔ W ∴ W → ~J

8. ~M → O, ~N → O, ~O ↔ ~P, ~P ∴ M • N
   How many rows would be needed in a complete truth table for item 8?

9. (A ∨ B) • (A ∨ C) ∴ A • (B ∨ C)

10. R ↔ ~Q, R ∨ Q, R ∨ P ∴ (P • Q) → R

Part D: English Arguments   Translate the following English arguments into symbols, using the schemes of abbreviation provided. Use abbreviated truth tables to determine whether the arguments are valid.

* 1. If you want to mess up your life, you should drink a lot of booze. Therefore, if you don't want to mess up your life, you should not drink a lot of booze. (W: You want to mess up your life; B: You should drink a lot of booze)

2. Being undetermined is a necessary but not a sufficient condition for human behavior's being free. The laws of subatomic physics are statistical only if human behavior is not determined. And the laws of subatomic physics are statistical. It follows that human behavior is free. (D: Human behavior is determined; F: Human behavior is free; L: The laws of subatomic physics are statistical)

3. Given that nuclear energy is needed if and only if solar energy cannot be harnessed, nuclear energy is not needed. For solar energy can be harnessed provided

that funds are available; and funds are available. (N: Nuclear energy is needed; S: Solar energy can be harnessed; F: Funds are available)

* **4.** If the Gulf War was about oil and if human life is more valuable than oil, then the Gulf War was immoral. Human life is more valuable than oil, but the Gulf War was not about oil. Therefore, the Gulf War was not immoral. (G: The Gulf War was about oil; H: Human life is more valuable than oil; I: The Gulf War was immoral)

5. The rate of teenage drunk driving will decrease just in case the taxes on beer increase. The taxes on beer increase only if either the federal government or the state government will resist the liquor lobby. The state government will resist the liquor lobby, but the federal government will not. Accordingly, the rate of teenage drunk driving will not decrease. (R: The rate of teenage drunk driving will decrease; B: The taxes on beer increase; F: The federal government will resist the liquor lobby; S: The state government will resist the liquor lobby)

6. Erik attains Valhalla given that he is valiant. And Erik is depressed assuming that he is not valiant. Furthermore, Erik fails to attain Valhalla only if he is not depressed. Thus, Erik is depressed. (E: Erik attains Valhalla; V: Eric is valiant; D: Eric is depressed)

* **7.** If society is the ultimate source of moral authority, then if society approves of polygamy, polygamy is right. But it is not true that either society is the ultimate source of moral authority or society approves of polygamy. Hence, polygamy is not right. (S: Society is the ultimate source of moral authority; P: Society approves of polygamy; R: Polygamy is right)

8. Either the earth is millions of years old or it is only 6000 years old. If the earth is millions of years old, then the traditional story of creation is a myth and ultimate reality is nothing but atoms in motion. Now, either it is false that the earth is only 6000 years old or it is false that ultimate reality is nothing but atoms in motion. Therefore, the traditional story of creation is a myth. (E: The earth is millions of years old; S: The earth is only 6000 years old; B: The traditional story of creation is a myth; U: Ultimate reality is nothing but atoms in motion)

9. Wittgensteinians are right if logic is embedded in language. But logic is embedded in language if and only if logic varies as language varies. And logic is language-relative if logic varies as language varies. Moreover, given that logic is language-relative, contradictions may be true in some languages. Therefore, Wittgensteinians are right only if contradictions may be true in some languages. (W: Wittgensteinians are right; E: Logic is embedded in language; V: Logic varies as language varies; R: Logic is language-relative; C: Contradictions may be true in some languages)

10. Although most Americans approve of gun control, gun control is neither wise nor moral. For gun control is wise if and only if it prevents criminals from obtaining weapons. And gun control is moral if and only if it preserves our liberty. But it is not the case that gun control both preserves our liberty and prevents criminals from obtaining weapons. (W: Gun control is wise; M: Gun control is moral; P: Gun control prevents criminals from obtaining weapons; L: Gun control preserves our liberty)

7.5 Tautology, Contradiction, Contingency, and Logical Equivalence

Truth tables can be used to sort compound statements into logically significant categories: tautologies, contradictions, and contingent statements. A compound statement is called a **tautology** if *it is true regardless of the truth values assigned to the atomic statements that compose it.* The tautologies of statement logic belong to a class of statements that are true simply by virtue of their form.* Here are some examples:

92. Either it is raining or it is not raining. (R: It is raining)

93. If trees are plants, then trees are plants. (P: Trees are plants)

94. If neither atoms nor molecules exist, then atoms do not exist. (A: Atoms exist; M: Molecules exist)

These statements can be translated into symbols as follows, in order:

95. R ∨ ~R

96. P → P

97. ~(A ∨ M) → ~A

If we construct truth tables for these statements, then every row under the main logical operator will contain a "T":

R	R ∨ ~R
T	T
F	T

P	P → P
T	T
F	T

A	M	~(A ∨ M) → ~A
T	T	T
T	F	T
F	T	T
F	F	T

Tautologies have some interesting and paradoxical properties. For example, every argument whose conclusion is a tautology is valid—regardless of the content of the premises. Consider the following example:

98. The moon is made of green cheese. So, either Santa is real or Santa is not real. (M: The moon is made of green cheese; S: Santa is real)

---

*Not all statements that are true by virtue of their form are tautologies in the sense here defined. For example, the following statement is not a tautology, but it is true by virtue of its form: "If everything is human, then something is human." We will examine statements of this type in chapter 9, "Predicate Logic." According to many philosophers, statements that are true by virtue of their form (including tautologies) belong to a larger class of statements called *necessary truths*. Necessary truths are truths that cannot be false under any possible circumstances. Here is an example of a necessary truth that does not appear to be true simply by virtue of its form: "If Al is older than Bob, then Bob is younger than Al." We will examine the concept of necessary truths more closely in chapter 12, "Modal Logic."

Here is a symbolization and truth table for argument (98):

M	S	M	∴	S ∨ ~S
T	T	T		T
T	F	T		T
F	T	F		T
F	F	F		T

As you can see, there is no row in which the premise is true while the conclusion is false, and so the argument is valid. This may seem puzzling because intuitively the premise is irrelevant to the conclusion. But the argument does satisfy our definition of validity, for since the conclusion is a tautology, it is impossible for the conclusion to be false while the premise is true.

A compound statement is called a **contradiction** if *it is false regardless of the truth values assigned to the atomic statements that compose it*. The contradictions of statement logic belong to a class of statements that are false simply by virtue of their form. Here are two examples:

99. Ants exist and yet they do not exist. (A: Ants exist)

100. If lemons are yellow, then they are not blue; but lemons are both blue and yellow. (Y: Lemons are yellow; B: Lemons are blue)

In symbols, we have this:

101. A • ~A

102. (Y → ~B) • (B • Y)

If we construct a truth table for a contradiction, then every row under the main logical operator will contain an "F":

A	A • ~A
T	F
F	F

Y	B	(Y → ~B) • (B • Y)
T	T	F
T	F	F
F	T	F
F	F	F

Like tautologies, contradictions have some interesting logical properties. For example, any argument that has a contradiction among its premises is a valid argument. For instance:

103. Atoms exist and yet they do not exist. So, God exists. (A: Atoms exist; G: God exists)

Here is the truth table:

A G	A • ~A ∴ G	
T T	F	T
T F	F	F
F T	F	T
F F	F	F

Note that there is no row in which the premise is true and the conclusion is false; hence, the argument is valid. This may seem strange, but the argument does satisfy our definition of validity. It is impossible for the conclusion to be false while the premise is true (because it is impossible for the premise to be true). Notice, however, that all arguments having a contradiction among their premises are *unsound,* since contradictions are always false.

We can go a step further here: Any argument with logically inconsistent premises will be valid yet unsound. If the premises of an argument are inconsistent, then if we form a conjunction of the premises, that conjunction will be a contradiction. Here is an example:

104. P → Q, ~P → Q, ~Q ∴ R

If we form a conjunction of the premises, the argument looks like this:

P Q R	(P → Q) • [(~P → Q) • ~Q] ∴ R			
T T T	T	F	F	T
T T F	T	F	F	F
T F T	F	F	T	T
T F F	F	F	T	F
F T T	T	F	F	T
F T F	T	F	F	F
F F T	T	F	F	T
F F F	T	F	F	F

The truth table reveals that the conjunction is a contradiction. Again, the point is that, paradoxically, every argument with inconsistent premises is valid. (Of course, all such arguments are *unsound* due to having one or more false premises.) How will you know if the premises of an argument are inconsistent?

Here's how: There will be no row in the truth table in which all of the premises are true. For instance:

M	N	L	M ↔ N,	M • ~N	∴ L
T	T	T	T	F	T
T	T	F	T	F	F
T	F	T	F	T	T
T	F	F	F	T	F
F	T	T	F	F	T
F	T	F	F	F	F
F	F	T	T	F	T
F	F	F	T	F	F

Because there is no row in which all the premises are true, the premises are inconsistent, and the argument is valid.

A **contingent statement** is *one that is true in at least one row of the truth table and false in at least one row.* Here is an example:

105. $P • (P \rightarrow R)$

The truth table looks like this:

P	R	$P • (P \rightarrow R)$
T	T	T
T	F	F
F	T	F
F	F	F

Contingent statements have important logical relations to both tautologies and contradictions. For example, any argument that has a tautology as its premise but a contingent statement as its conclusion is invalid. (The premise will be true in every row of the truth table while the conclusion will be false in at least one row.) And suppose that the premises of an argument, when made into a conjunction, form a contingent statement. Then, if the conclusion of the argument is a contradiction, the argument is invalid. (The conclusion will be false in every row while the premise will be true in at least one row.)

Notice that tautologies and contradictions place limitations on the method of abbreviated truth tables which was introduced in the previous section. For instance, if an argument has a tautology as its conclusion, then there is no way to assign truth values so that the conclusion is false. One way to deal with such a case is to use a complete truth table to prove that the conclusion is a tautology (which simultaneously proves that the argument is valid). Similarly, if at least one premise is a contradiction (or if the premises are inconsistent), then there is no way to assign values so that the premises are all true, and a complete truth table may be needed to establish this, as in the case of argument (103). However, a complete truth table is not always needed in such cases, for consider the following (admittedly odd) argument:

106. B • ~B ∴ B

We can deal with this argument by means of an abbreviated truth table:

	B • ~B ∴ B	
	F (T/F) T F	Valid

Since there is only one way to make B false, and it forces an assignment of "F" to the premise, the abbreviated truth table works in this case.

Two statements are said to be **logically equivalent** if they have the following relationship: *Each validly implies the other.* And truth-functional compounds are logically equivalent provided that the columns in the truth table *under their main operators* are exactly alike. For example:

A B	A → B	~A ∨ B
T T	T	T
T F	F	F
F T	T	T
F F	T	T

Note that the columns under the arrow and the vee are exactly the same, row by row.

The concept of logical equivalence has an important relationship to the concept of a tautology—namely, if a biconditional statement is a tautology, then its two constituent statements (joined by the double-arrow) are logically equivalent. For instance, consider the following tautology:

F G	(F → G) ↔ (~G → ~F)		
T T	T	T	T
T F	F	T	F
F T	T	T	T
F F	T	T	T

From the fact that $(F \rightarrow G) \leftrightarrow (\sim G \rightarrow \sim F)$ is a tautology, we may infer that the following two statements are logically equivalent:

107. $F \rightarrow G$

108. $\sim G \rightarrow \sim F$

Note also that the columns in the truth table under $F \rightarrow G$ and $\sim G \rightarrow \sim F$ are exactly alike, row by row.

To sum up, truth tables can be used to sort statements into logically significant categories: tautologies, contradictions, and contingent statements. And, as we have seen, each of these types of statements has important logical properties. In addition, we have noted that if two statements *joined with the double-arrow* form a tautology, then the two statements are logically equivalent.

To check your understanding of these concepts, complete the following exercises.

◆ Exercise 7.5

Part A: Tautologies, Contradictions, and Contingent Statements   Use truth tables to determine whether the following statements are tautologies, contradictions, or contingent statements.

* 1. $\sim A \rightarrow (A \rightarrow B)$
  2. $\sim F \rightarrow G$
  3. $\sim S \leftrightarrow S$
* 4. $B \rightarrow (A \rightarrow B)$
  5. $F \rightarrow [\sim(F \cdot G) \rightarrow \sim G]$
  6. $A \rightarrow [(A \rightarrow B) \rightarrow B]$
* 7. $P \rightarrow (P \rightarrow Q)$
  8. $(A \leftrightarrow B) \rightarrow (\sim A \cdot \sim B)$
  9. $\sim P \cdot \sim(\sim P \vee \sim Q)$
* 10. $(R \cdot \sim R) \rightarrow S$
  11. $B \rightarrow [\sim(A \cdot B) \rightarrow A]$
  12. $\sim(F \rightarrow G) \cdot G$
  13. $\sim(N \leftrightarrow M) \rightarrow (N \cdot \sim M)$
  14. $[A \rightarrow (B \vee C)] \rightarrow [(A \rightarrow B) \vee (A \rightarrow C)]$
  15. $(\sim P \leftrightarrow P) \rightarrow Q$
  16. $\sim(K \rightarrow L) \rightarrow (K \cdot \sim L)$
  17. $[A \rightarrow (B \rightarrow C)] \rightarrow [(A \rightarrow B) \rightarrow (A \rightarrow C)]$

18. $(H \rightarrow J) \rightarrow \sim(H \cdot \sim J)$
19. $(\sim Z \cdot \sim W) \rightarrow (Z \leftrightarrow W)$
20. $[(A \rightarrow B) \rightarrow A] \rightarrow A$

Part B: Logical Equivalence   Use truth tables to prove that the following statements are tautologies. This shows that in each case, the statements joined by the double-arrow are logically equivalent. It will be useful to know these particular equivalences as we move on to the material in the next chapter.

* 1. $\sim(A \cdot B) \leftrightarrow (\sim A \vee \sim B)$
  2. $\sim(F \vee G) \leftrightarrow (\sim F \cdot \sim G)$
  3. $[P \cdot (Q \vee R)] \leftrightarrow [(P \cdot Q) \vee (P \cdot R)]$
  4. $(S \rightarrow U) \leftrightarrow (\sim S \vee U)$
  5. $Q \leftrightarrow \sim\sim Q$
  6. $[P \vee (Q \cdot R)] \leftrightarrow [(P \vee Q) \cdot (P \vee R)]$
  7. $(F \leftrightarrow G) \leftrightarrow [(F \cdot G) \vee (\sim F \cdot \sim G)]$
  8. $(A \vee B) \leftrightarrow (B \vee A)$
  9. $(K \cdot K) \leftrightarrow K$
  10. $(U \leftrightarrow Z) \leftrightarrow [(U \rightarrow Z) \cdot (Z \rightarrow U)]$

Part C: English Arguments   Symbolize the following arguments. Then use truth tables to determine whether they are valid. Most of these arguments illustrate important logical properties of tautologies, contradictions, or contingent statements.

* 1. Grass is green. So, if Clinton wins, then Clinton wins. (G: Grass is green; W: Clinton wins)

  2. Light is both a wave and a particle. But if light is a wave, then it is not a particle. So, physicists are profoundly mistaken. (W: Light is a wave; P: Light is a particle; M: Physicists are profoundly mistaken)

  3. Either unicorns exist or unicorns do not exist. Therefore, trees exist. (U: Unicorns exist; T: Trees exist)

* 4. Pain is an illusion if and only if it is not an illusion. It follows that everything is an illusion. (P: Pain is an illusion; E: Everything is an illusion)

  5. If it is wet, then it is wet if it is raining. Consequently, either Sasquatch exists or Sasquatch fails to exist. (W: It is wet; R: It is raining; S: Sasquatch exists)

  6. Human behavior is determined only if human behavior is not free. Human behavior is determined; nevertheless, it is free. Therefore, life is but a dream. (D: Human behavior is determined; F: Human behavior is free; L: Life is but a dream)

  7. The sky's being colored is a necessary condition for its being blue. It follows that the sky's being blue is a sufficient condition for its being colored. (C: The sky is colored; B: The sky is blue)

8. It is not the case both that electrons exist and electrons do not exist. Hence, electrons exist. (E: Electrons exist)

9. If ultimate reality is divine, then it can be described in human language if and only if it cannot be described in human language. So, ultimate reality is not divine. (U: Ultimate reality is divine; L: Ultimate reality can be described in human language)

10. If you do not accept me as I am, then you do not love me. You accept me as I am if and only if you accept me as a violent criminal. You love me, but you do not accept me as a violent criminal. Consequently, you do not love me. (A: You accept me as I am; L: You love me; C: You accept me as a violent criminal)

Notes

1. C. S. Peirce, "On the Algebra of Logic: A Contribution to the Philosophy of Notation," *American Journal of Mathematics* 7 (1885): 180–202. The credit for the inven-
   tion and development of truth tables should probably be spread around a bit. The
   idea occurs informally in Gottlob Frege's *Begriffsschrift* (Halle, Germany: L. Nebert,
   1879). And the Austrian philosopher Ludwig Wittgenstein developed truth tables
   independently in his famous *Tractatus Logico-philosophicus* (London: Routledge &
   Kegan Paul, 1922).
2. To review the fallacy of amphiboly, see section 6.3.
3. The example is borrowed from Wesley Salmon, *Logic*, 3rd ed. (Englewood Cliffs, NJ:
   Prentice-Hall, 1984), p. 39.
4. Some logicians deny that the word "or" has two meanings. These logicians hold that
   the word "or" always means "either . . . or . . . *or both*," but they would agree that in
   many contexts both disjuncts cannot in fact be true—for instance, "Either all trees
   are plants or some trees are not plants." I do not wish to enter into the dispute about
   whether "or" has two meanings. I will only venture to say that I have found it peda-
   gogically useful to speak of an *inclusive* and *exclusive* sense of the word "or," and so I
   have freely done so in this book.

Chapter 8

Statement Logic: Proofs

In the previous chapter, we used truth tables to evaluate arguments in statement logic (the part of logic in which atomic statements are the basic units). We saw, however, that truth tables are cumbersome when applied to arguments involving numerous statement letters. In this chapter, we will develop a system of natural deduction that has certain advantages over the truth table method. In a system of *natural deduction*, one uses a set of inference rules to prove that the conclusion of an argument follows from its premises. And for the purpose of proving arguments valid, a system of natural deduction has at least two advantages over the truth table method. First, it is less cumbersome. Second, such systems more clearly mirror our intuitive patterns of reasoning (the ways we ordinarily argue) than do truth tables. The German logician and mathematician Gerhard Gentzen (1909–1945) was the first to develop a system of natural deduction.[1]

Our system of natural deduction will be introduced in stages. Section 8.1 gives us eight initial rules of inference that permit us to construct a limited variety of proofs. Sections 8.2 and 8.3 each introduce 5 more rules, bringing the total to 18 rules. In section 8.4, we add a proof procedure called "conditional proof." With the addition of conditional proof, our system of natural deduction can prove as valid any argument that is valid according to the truth table method. And since each of our rules of inference is itself valid, *any argument that can be proved valid in our system of natural deduction is indeed valid*. In section 8.5, we add a proof procedure, called "reductio ad absurdum," that makes many proofs either shorter or more intuitive. Finally, in section 8.6, we discuss proving theorems.

8.1 Implicational Rules of Inference

Let us use the word "proof," in a technical sense, to refer to a series of steps that leads from the premises of a symbolic argument to its conclusion. The fundamental idea is to show that the premises lead, by way of valid rules of inference, to the conclusion. The underlying principle is this: *Whatever follows from a set of statements by means of valid inferences is true if all the statements in the set are true.*

Our first set of inference rules is mostly familiar. The first five were introduced as argument forms in chapter 2. Once again, we use italicized, lowercase letters as variables that stand for any given statement: *p*, *q*, *r*, and *s*.

Rule 1: *Modus ponens* (MP): $p \rightarrow q$
  p
  $\therefore q$

Rule 2: *Modus tollens* (MT): $p \rightarrow q$
  $\sim q$
  $\therefore \sim p$

Rule 3: Hypothetical syllogism (HS): $p \rightarrow q$
  $q \rightarrow r$
  $\therefore p \rightarrow r$

Rule 4: Disjunctive syllogism (DS), in two forms:
  $p \lor q$ $\qquad\qquad$ $p \lor q$
  $\sim p$ $\qquad\qquad\quad$ $\sim q$
  $\therefore q$ $\qquad\qquad\quad$ $\therefore p$

Rule 5: Constructive dilemma (CD): $p \lor q$
  $p \rightarrow r$
  $q \rightarrow s$
  $\therefore r \lor s$

Note that each rule is given an abbreviation designed to cut down on the amount of writing involved in constructing proofs. To these familiar forms, we add three additional patterns of inference, two involving conjunctions and one involving disjunctions.

Rule 6: Simplification (Simp), in two forms:
  $p \cdot q$ $\qquad\quad$ $p \cdot q$
  $\therefore p$ $\qquad\quad$ $\therefore q$

Simplification says, in effect, that if you have a conjunction, then you may infer either conjunct. Here is an English example:

1. Both Pierre Curie and Marie Curie were physicists. Therefore, Marie Curie was a physicist.

This type of inference may seem so obvious as to be trivial, but it is nonetheless valid. And one aspect of the power of logic is its capacity to break complex reasoning down into easy steps.

The next rule tells us that if we have two statements as steps in an argument, we may conjoin them.

Rule 7: Conjunction (Conj):   *p*

q

∴ *p • q*

Again, this rule is obviously valid. Here is an example:

2. Thomas Aquinas died in 1274. William Ockham died in 1349. Consequently, Aquinas died in 1274 *and* Ockham died in 1349.

The rule of addition is perhaps a bit less obvious than the rules we have considered so far.

Rule 8: Addition (Add):   *p*

∴ *p ∨ q*

This schema tells us that from any given statement *p*, one may infer a disjunction that has *p* as one of its disjuncts—and the other disjunct may be anything you please. For instance:

3. Thomas Paine wrote *Common Sense*. Hence, either Thomas Paine wrote *Common Sense* or Patrick Henry wrote *Common Sense* (or both did).

This type of inference may seem odd, but it is valid. Recall that only one disjunct must be true for an inclusive disjunction to be true. Thus, "Either $1 + 1 = 2$ or $2 + 2 = 22$ (or both)" is true, even though "$2 + 2 = 22$" is false. And hence, every instance of addition is valid since it is impossible for the conclusion of an argument of this form to be false *given that its premise is true*.

Is the following argument an example of addition?

4. Adam stole the money. It follows that either Adam stole the money or Betty stole the money, but not both. (A: Adam stole the money; B: Betty stole the money)

No. Argument (4) has the following invalid form:

5. A ∴ (A ∨ B) • ~(A • B)

And it is easy to construct a counterexample to this pattern of reasoning. For instance:

6. Four is an even number. So, either four is even or six is even, *but not both*.

Because the premise is obviously true but the conclusion is obviously false, the counterexample proves that form (5) is invalid. So, it is important not to confuse form (5) with the rule of addition.

The italicized, lowercase letters in the previous argument schemas play a special role. They can be replaced by any symbolic sentence *as long as the replacement is uniform throughout the argument.* For example, both of the following count as instances of *modus ponens*:

$$\sim F \rightarrow G \qquad\qquad L \rightarrow (M \rightarrow N)$$
$$\sim F \qquad\qquad\qquad L$$
$$\therefore\ G \qquad\qquad\qquad \therefore\ M \rightarrow N$$

In the inference on the left, $\sim F$ is substituted for the letter p while G is substituted for the letter q in the original schema: $p \rightarrow q, p \therefore q$. Note that we have replaced p with $\sim F$ throughout the argument schema; substitutions must be uniform in this sense. In the example on the right, L is substituted for p while $(M \rightarrow N)$ is substituted for q in the original schema. In both cases, the pattern of reasoning is *modus ponens* because one premise is a conditional, the other is the antecedent of the conditional, and the conclusion is the consequent of the conditional.

In substituting symbolic formulas for lowercase letters, precision is required. Consider the following argument. Is it an instance of *modus tollens*?

$$C \rightarrow \sim D$$
$$D$$
$$\therefore\ \sim C$$

No, it is not. The schema for *modus tollens* is $p \rightarrow q, \sim q \therefore \sim p$. If we replace the letter q with $\sim D$ in the first premise, we must replace q with $\sim D$ in the second premise as well, in which case we obtain the following argument:

$$C \rightarrow \sim D$$
$$\sim\sim D$$
$$\therefore\ \sim C$$

This *is* an instance of *modus tollens*. To apply *modus tollens*, we need a conditional *and* the negation of its consequent. If the consequent of the conditional is itself a negation, such as $\sim D$, the other premise will be a double-negation, such as $\sim\sim D$ above.

To ensure an understanding of our new inference rules, let us consider a series of examples. Which rules of inference, if any, are exemplified by the following arguments?

$$\sim P \rightarrow (Q \cdot R) \qquad\qquad X \vee (Y \leftrightarrow Z)$$
$$(Q \cdot R) \rightarrow S \qquad\qquad\quad \sim(Y \leftrightarrow Z)$$
$$\therefore\ \sim P \rightarrow S \qquad\qquad\quad \therefore\ X$$

The argument on the left is an example of hypothetical syllogism. Note that $\sim P$ replaces p, $(Q \cdot R)$ replaces q, and S replaces r in the original schema: $p \rightarrow q$,

$q \rightarrow r \therefore p \rightarrow r$. The argument on the right is an example of disjunctive syllogism. Here, X replaces p and $(Y \leftrightarrow Z)$ replaces q in the second form of disjunctive syllogism: $p \vee q, \sim q \therefore p$.

Which rules of inference, if any, are exemplified by the following arguments?

$$\sim M \vee \sim N$$
$$\sim M \rightarrow \sim O$$
$$\sim N \rightarrow \sim P \qquad\qquad \sim(B \bullet \sim C)$$
$$\therefore \sim O \vee \sim P \qquad\qquad \therefore \sim(B \bullet \sim C) \vee \sim D$$

The argument on the left is an example of constructive dilemma. Here, $\sim M$ replaces p, $\sim N$ replaces q, $\sim O$ replaces r, and $\sim P$ replaces s in the schema for constructive dilemma: $p \vee q, p \rightarrow r, q \rightarrow s \therefore r \vee s$. The argument on the right is an example of addition. Note that $\sim(B \bullet \sim C)$ replaces p while $\sim D$ replaces q in the original schema: $p \therefore p \vee q$.

Which rules of inference, if any, are exemplified by the following arguments?

$$A \vee \sim B$$
$$(C \rightarrow D) \bullet (E \vee F) \qquad\qquad B$$
$$\therefore E \vee F \qquad\qquad \therefore A$$

The argument on the left is an example of simplification. Here, $(C \rightarrow D)$ replaces p while $(E \vee F)$ replaces q in the second form of simplification: $p \bullet q \therefore q$. The argument on the right, however, does *not* exemplify any of our inference rules. But if we changed the second premise to $\sim\sim B$, then we would have an instance of the second form of disjunctive syllogism: $p \vee q, \sim q \therefore p$. (Substitute A for p and $\sim B$ for q.)

Let us now use our new inference rules to construct some proofs. We begin with an English argument:

7. If some employees deserve five times the wages of others, then some employees are five times more valuable than others. It is not true that some employees are five times more valuable than others. So, it is not true that some employees deserve five times the wages of others. (D: Some employees deserve five times the wages of others; V: Some employees are five times more valuable than others)

Using the scheme of abbreviation provided, the argument should be symbolized as follows:

1. $D \rightarrow V$
2. $\sim V \qquad\qquad \therefore \sim D$

The first lines of our proof contain the premises of the argument. And we write the conclusion off to the side to remind ourselves of what we are trying to derive from the premises. (Thus, the expression $\therefore$ ~D is not really a part of the proof, but merely a reminder of what we need to prove.) What we want to do is to arrive at the conclusion, ~D, by means of our inference rules. We have a conditional premise, and we also have the negation of its consequent. That is, we have here the makings of a *modus tollens*–type argument. To see this, substitute D for p and substitute V for q in the original diagram for *modus tollens*: $p \rightarrow q$, ~q $\therefore$ ~p. Proper proof procedure requires that *we list the lines to which we are applying the rule of inference, as well as the abbreviation of the inference rule*. Accordingly, our completed proof looks like this:

    1. $D \rightarrow V$
    2. ~V $\therefore$ ~D
    3. ~D 1, 2, MT

Line (3) tells us that ~D follows from lines (1) and (2) by *modus tollens*. We have shown that the premises of the argument lead to the conclusion by way of a valid rule of inference. Notice that the only lines in the proof without annotation (without an explicit indication of how we arrived at them) are the premises. *Let us adopt the convention that any step in an argument without annotation will be understood to be a premise.*

Consider a slightly more complicated example:

8. If the workplace is a meritocracy, then the most qualified person always gets the job. But the most qualified person does not always get the job if networking plays a role in who gets most jobs. Furthermore, networking does play a role in who gets most jobs. Therefore, the workplace is not a meritocracy. (W: The workplace is a meritocracy; M: The most qualified person always gets the job; N: Networking plays a role in who gets most jobs)

Using the scheme of abbreviation provided, the argument should be symbolized as follows:

    1. $W \rightarrow M$
    2. $N \rightarrow$ ~M
    3. N $\therefore$ ~W

As before, the first lines of our proof contain the premises of the argument, with the conclusion written off to one side. The completed proof runs as follows:

    1. $W \rightarrow M$
    2. $N \rightarrow$ ~M
    3. N $\therefore$ ~W
    4. ~M 2, 3, MP
    5. ~W 1, 4, MT

Lines (2) and (3) imply ~M by the rule *modus ponens*. To see this, replace *p* with N and *q* with ~M in the schema for *modus ponens*: $p \rightarrow q, p \therefore q$. Lines (1) and (4) imply ~W by the rule *modus tollens*: $p \rightarrow q, \sim q \therefore \sim p$ (replacing *p* with W and *q* with M).

Let us now consider a proof that employs our inference rules involving conjunctions:

> 9. Women earn only 75¢ for every dollar earned by men. If women earn only 75¢ for every dollar earned by men and 90% of children who live with one parent live with their mothers, then men are better off than women and women are victims of injustice. Ninety percent of children who live with one parent live with their mothers. Feminists are right if women are victims of injustice. So, feminists are right. (W: Women earn only 75¢ for every dollar earned by men; C: 90% of children who live with one parent live with their mothers; M: Men are better off than women; V: Women are victims of injustice; F: Feminists are right)

Using the scheme of abbreviation provided, the translation into symbols looks like this:

> 1. W
> 2. (W • C) → (M • V)
> 3. C
> 4. V → F   ∴ F

The proof may be completed thus:

> 5. W • C   1, 3, Conj
> 6. M • V   2, 5, MP
> 7. V   6, Simp
> 8. F   4, 7, MP

Note that line (5) comes from lines (1) and (3) by substituting W for *p* and C for *q* in the schema for conjunction: $p, q \therefore p \cdot q$. And line (7) comes from line (6) by substituting M for *p* and V for *q* in the second form of simplification: $p \cdot q \therefore q$.

One last example will demonstrate some of the inference rules involving disjunctions.

> 10. If Pierre is an assassin, then either he should be put to death or he should be given a life sentence. He should be put to death only if murderers deserve death. He should be given a life sentence only if murderers forfeit their right to liberty. Pierre is an assassin, but murderers do not deserve death. Therefore, murderers forfeit their right to liberty. (A: Pierre is an assassin; D: Pierre should be put to death; L: Pierre should be given a life sentence; M: Murderers deserve death; F: Murderers forfeit their right to liberty)

Using the scheme of abbreviation provided, the argument may be symbolized like this:

> 1. $A \rightarrow (D \vee L)$
> 2. $D \rightarrow M$
> 3. $L \rightarrow F$
> 4. $A \cdot \sim M$ $\therefore$ F

The proof may be completed as follows:

> 5. A   4, Simp
> 6. $D \vee L$ 1, 5, MP
> 7. $M \vee F$ 6, 2, 3, CD
> 8. $\sim M$ 4, Simp
> 9. F   7, 8, DS

Note that line (7) derives from the steps indicated by substituting D for p, L for q, M for r, and F for s in the original schema for constructive dilemma: $p \vee q$, $p \rightarrow r, q \rightarrow s \therefore r \vee s$. And line (9) derives from lines (7) and (8) by substituting M for p and F for q in the first form of disjunctive syllogism: $p \vee q$, $\sim p \therefore q$.

Our first eight inference rules are called **implicational rules** to set them apart from equivalence rules, which will be introduced in the next section. The basic difference is this: Implicational rules *cannot* be applied to *parts* of a line in a proof, whereas equivalence rules can be applied to parts of a line in a proof. To illustrate, consider the following inference:

> 1. $F \rightarrow (G \rightarrow H)$
> 2. $\sim H$ $\therefore F \rightarrow \sim G$
> 3. $F \rightarrow \sim G$???

Does line (3) follow from lines (1) and (2) by *modus tollens*? No. *Modus tollens* must be applied to entire lines in a proof. So, in order to have an instance of *modus tollens*, we need two things:

- ■ A conditional statement that is an entire line in a proof
- ■ Another line that is *the negation of the consequent of that conditional*

In the preceding example, the first is satisfied, but the second is not. Line (1) *is* a conditional that represents an entire line in the proof. But the negation of its consequent is $\sim(G \rightarrow H)$, not $\sim H$. So, line (3) does not follow from lines (1) and (2) by *modus tollens*.

The following hints or rules of thumb may help you as you construct proofs:

Rule of Thumb 1: It usually helps to work backward. So, start by looking at the conclusion, and then try to find the conclusion (or elements thereof) in the premises.

For example:

1. A → [B → (C ∨ D)]
2. B • A
3. ~D   ∴ C

The conclusion here is C. Does it appear anywhere in the premises? Yes, it is embedded in the consequent of premise (1). And if we could obtain (C ∨ D) from premise (1), we could combine it with ~D—that is, premise (3)—to get C, by disjunctive syllogism. But how can we obtain (C ∨ D)? Consider a second rule of thumb:

Rule of Thumb 2: Apply the inference rules to break the premises down.

We could get A from line (2) by simplification and use it together with line (1) to obtain B → (C ∨ D), by *modus ponens*. Then we could get B from line (2) (by simplification) and apply *modus ponens* again, to obtain (C ∨ D). The whole proof would then look like this:

1. A → [B → (C ∨ D)]
2. B • A
3. ~D   ∴ C
4. A   2, Simp
5. B → (C ∨ D)   1, 4, MP
6. B   2, Simp
7. C ∨ D   5, 6, MP
8. C   3, 7, DS

Let's consider another example:

1. E ∨ F
2. E → G
3. F → H
4. (G ∨ H) → J   ∴ J ∨ K

Using Rule of Thumb 1, we start by examining the conclusion. We look to see if the conclusion (or parts thereof) appear in the premises, noting that J is the consequent of premise (4). Now, is there any way to break premise (4) down, as Rule of Thumb 2 suggests? Yes, we can use the rule of constructive dilemma to obtain G ∨ H from premises (1), (2), and (3), and then use *modus ponens* to get J. But

Summary of Implicational Rules

1. *Modus ponens* (MP):

$$p \rightarrow q$$
$$p$$
$$\therefore q$$

2. *Modus tollens* (MT):

$$p \rightarrow q$$
$$\sim q$$
$$\therefore \sim p$$

3. Hypothetical syllogism (HS):

$$p \rightarrow q$$
$$q \rightarrow r$$
$$\therefore p \rightarrow r$$

4. Disjunctive syllogism (DS), in two forms:

$p \vee q$	$p \vee q$
$\sim p$	$\sim q$
$\therefore q$	$\therefore p$

5. Constructive dilemma (CD):

$$p \vee q$$
$$p \rightarrow r$$
$$q \rightarrow s$$
$$\therefore r \vee s$$

6. Simplification (Simp), in two forms:

$p \bullet q$	$p \bullet q$
$\therefore p$	$\therefore q$

7. Conjunction (Conj):

$$p$$
$$q$$
$$\therefore p \bullet q$$

8. Addition (Add):

$$p$$
$$\therefore p \vee q$$

where do we go from there? In particular, how can we obtain K when it appears nowhere in the premises? At this point, it will be helpful to bear in mind an additional rule of thumb:

> Rule of Thumb 3: If the conclusion contains a statement letter that does not appear in the premises, use the rule of addition.

The whole proof looks like this:

1. $E \vee F$
2. $E \rightarrow G$
3. $F \rightarrow H$
4. $(G \vee H) \rightarrow J$ $\therefore J \vee K$
5. $G \vee H$ 1, 2, 3, CD
6. J 4, 5, MP
7. $J \vee K$ 6, Add

These rules of thumb are helpful in many cases, but a certain amount of ingenuity is required when doing proofs. Furthermore, to gain facility in constructing proofs, one must practice. Hence, the following exercises are provided.

◆ Exercise 8.1

Part A: Annotating   For each of the following proofs, indicate from which steps each inference is drawn and by which rule the inference is made. (See the Answer Key for an illustration.)

* **1.** 1. $F \rightarrow G$
      2. $G \rightarrow H$ ∴ $F \rightarrow H$
      3. $F \rightarrow H$

  2. 1. $\sim S \rightarrow \sim P$
      2. $\sim S$ ∴ $\sim P \vee K$
      3. $\sim P$
      4. $\sim P \vee K$

  3. 1. $E \rightarrow (T \rightarrow S)$
      2. $\sim (T \rightarrow S)$
      3. $\sim R \vee E$ ∴ $\sim R$
      4. $\sim E$
      5. $\sim R$

* **4.** 1. $H \vee \sim C$
      2. $H \rightarrow \sim B$
      3. $\sim C \rightarrow D$
      4. $(\sim B \vee D) \rightarrow (K \cdot J)$ ∴ J
      5. $\sim B \vee D$
      6. $K \cdot J$
      7. J

  5. 1. D
      2. $\sim H$
      3. $(D \cdot \sim H) \rightarrow (E \vee H)$ ∴ E
      4. $D \cdot \sim H$
      5. $E \vee H$
      6. E

  6. 1. $\sim A \rightarrow \sim B$
      2. $\sim\sim B \cdot C$ ∴ $\sim\sim A \cdot C$
      3. $\sim\sim B$
      4. $\sim\sim A$
      5. C
      6. $\sim\sim A \cdot C$

* **7.** 1. $\sim (P \cdot Q) \vee R$
      2. $\sim R$

  3. $E \rightarrow (P \cdot Q)$
  4. $(\sim E \cdot \sim R) \rightarrow (A \cdot B)$
      ∴ $B \vee (F \cdot G)$
  5. $\sim (P \cdot Q)$
  6. $\sim E$
  7. $\sim E \cdot \sim R$
  8. $A \cdot B$
  9. B
  10. $B \vee (F \cdot G)$

  8. 1. $F \vee S$
      2. G
      3. $[G \cdot (F \vee S)] \rightarrow \sim T$
      4. $(\sim B \rightarrow T)$ ∴ $\sim\sim B$
      5. $G \cdot (F \vee S)$
      6. $\sim T$
      7. $\sim\sim B$

  9. 1. $F \rightarrow B$
      2. $\sim D$
      3. $(\sim D \cdot G) \rightarrow (B \rightarrow S)$
      4. G
      5. $\sim S$ ∴ $G \cdot \sim F$
      6. $\sim D \cdot G$
      7. $B \rightarrow S$
      8. $F \rightarrow S$
      9. $\sim F$
      10. $G \cdot \sim F$

* **10.** 1. $W \rightarrow (X \vee \sim Y)$
      2. $\sim\sim Y \cdot W$ ∴ $X \vee \sim Z$
      3. W
      4. $X \vee \sim Y$
      5. $\sim\sim Y$
      6. X
      7. $X \vee \sim Z$

Part B: Correct or Incorrect?   Some of the following inferences are correct applications of the eight rules introduced in this section and some are not. If an inference is a correct application of a rule, name the rule. If an inference is not a correct application of a rule, explain why it is not. (The question is whether the conclusion in each case can be reached *in a single step* from the premise(s) by an application of one of the rules.)

* 1.   K → L
         ~L
         ∴ ~K

  2.   ~E ∨ G
         ~G
         ∴ ~E

  3.   M → N
         ~M
         ∴ ~N

* 4.   ~B ∨ ~Y
         ~B → ~X
         ~Y → Z
         ∴ ~X ∨ Z

  5.   (E • F) ∨ G
         ~(E • F)
         ∴ G

  6.   (N • P) → (O ∨ S)
         O ∨ S
         ∴ N • P

* 7.   ~E ∨ ~F
         ~~F
         ∴ ~E

  8.   A → ~~B
         ~B
         ∴ ~A

  9.   (P → Q) ∨ R
         P
         ∴ Q ∨ R

* 10.   (R • S) → T
         ∴ S → T

  11.   (K ∨ L) → M
         ~M
         ∴ ~(K ∨ L)

  12.   (H ∨ ~S) → ~W
         H ∨ ~S
         ∴ ~W

* 13.   T → ~U
         U
         ∴ ~T

  14.   P • Q
         ∴ (P • Q) ∨ (R → S)

  15.   R → ~S
         ~~S
         ∴ ~R

* 16.   ~C ∨ ~D
         X → C
         Y → D
         ∴ ~X ∨ ~Y

  17.   ~G ∨ ~P
         G
         ∴ ~P

  18.   A → (B → C)
         B
         ∴ A → C

* 19.   (~B ∨ D) → E
         ~~B
         ∴ D → E

  20.   ~T → ~N
         ~~N
         ∴ ~~T

Part C: Proofs   Construct proofs to show the following symbolic arguments valid. Commas mark the breaks between premises. (See the Answer Key for an illustration.)

* 1. H → ~B, D → B, H ∴ ~D
  2. F → (G → H), ~F → J, ~(G → H) ∴ J
  3. (E ∨ F) → ~D, S ∨ D, E ∴ S
* 4. ~A → F, A → D, ~D, F → S ∴ S ∨ X
  5. (A • E) → F, E, F → (D • ~C), A ∴ ~C

6. ~F ∨ ~G, ~F → Z, ~G → ~R, (Z ∨ ~R) → (U → P), ~P ∴ ~U

* 7. ~(S ∨ R), B → (S ∨ R), B ∨ P, ~Q ∨ B ∴ P • ~Q

8. C → (T → L), ~L, ~E → C, L ∨ ~E ∴ ~T

9. ~~A, B → ~A ∴ ~B

* 10. (B • A) → C, ~D → (B • A), ~C ∴ ~~D

11. (~B • ~C) → (D → C), ~B, C → B ∴ ~D

12. (D • H) → R, S → (D • H) ∴ S → R

* 13. (T → C) → ~F, S → C, T → S, F ∨ ~P ∴ ~P

14. (A ∨ ~B) → (F ∨ (R • G)), A, F → L, (R • G) → T, (L ∨ T) → S ∴ S

15. P ∨ Q, (Q • ~R) → S, R → P, ~P ∴ S

* 16. (E ∨ F) → ~G, ~H, H ∨ K, (K ∨ L) → E ∴ ~G

17. (M ∨ N) → ~S, T → (M ∨ N), ~S → ~(M ∨ N) ∴ T → ~(M ∨ N)

18. (E ∨ ~B) → (~S ∨ T), E, ~S → L, T → ~C, (L ∨ ~C) → A ∴ A

* 19. ~~B, ~C → ~B, (~~C ∨ T) → P ∴ P

20. B ∨ ~C, B → E, ~~C ∴ E ∨ ~B

Part D: More Proofs   Construct proofs to show that the following arguments are valid. Commas mark the breaks between premises.

* 1. P → Q, R → ~S, P ∨ R, (Q ∨ ~S) → (~T ∨ ~W), ~~T ∴ ~W

2. (A ∨ G) → K, K → (B → F), A • B ∴ F

3. ~M, (~M • ~N) → (Q → P), ~N, P → R ∴ Q → R

* 4. ~(R ∨ S), ~(T • V) → (R ∨ S), ~~(T • V) → W ∴ W ∨ ~R

5. ~W • ~~Z, (~W • X) → Y, ~Z ∨ X ∴ Y

6. F → A, ~J • ~K, H → (G → F), (~K → (~J → H) ∴ G → A

* 7. ~F → J, ~F ∨ ~G, ~G → ~H, (J ∨ ~H) → ~K, ~L → K ∴ ~~L

8. Y → W, (Z → W) → (V • ~T), Z → Y, Q → T ∴ ~Q

9. (~N • M) → T, ~O → M, ~O • ~N ∴ T ∨ S

* 10. ~A • ~C, ~C → D, (D • ~A) → (E → ~H), E • (~F → H) ∴ ~~F

11. R → D, B → R, (B → D) → (E ∨ F), ~E ∴ F

12. ~F → ~G, P → ~Q, ~F ∨ P, (~G ∨ ~Q) → (L • M) ∴ L

13. (Z • A) ∨ ~Y, (Z • A) → U, W ∨ ~U, ~W ∴ ~Y

14. (D • E) ∨ F, F → C, (D • E) → ~B, (~B ∨ C) → (A → P), ~P ∴ ~A

15. O → N, ~M, S → R, P → O, R → P, (S → N) → (M ∨ L) ∴ L ∨ ~P

Part E: English Arguments   Symbolize the following arguments. If a scheme of abbreviation is provided, use it. If a scheme of abbreviation is not provided, create your own. Then construct proofs to show that the arguments are valid.

* 1. No one can know anything. For every piece of reasoning must start somewhere. And if every piece of reasoning must start somewhere, then every piece of reasoning begins with an unsupported premise. Now, if every piece of reasoning begins with an unsupported premise, then all human thinking is based on mere

assumption. And if all human thinking is based on mere assumption, no one can know anything. (S: Every piece of reasoning must start somewhere; U: Every piece of reasoning begins with an unsupported premise; A: All human thinking is based on mere assumption; K: No one can know anything)

2. Theists say that God created the world. They say that the world must have a cause. But why? The world must have a cause only if everything must have a cause. But if everything must have a cause, then God has a cause. However, God isn't God if God has a cause. And if God isn't God, God doesn't exist. So, if the world must have a cause, there is no God. (W: The world must have a cause; E: Everything must have a cause; H: God has a cause; G: God is God; X: God exists)

3. Either we should stop going places, or we should develop solar-powered cars or we should go on driving gasoline-powered cars. We should go on driving gasoline-powered cars only if we should destroy the ozone layer. We should not stop going places and we should not destroy the ozone layer. Therefore, we should develop solar-powered cars.

* 4. Dinosaurs are extinct. And given that dinosaurs are extinct, they suffered some catastrophe if they died suddenly. The dinosaurs died suddenly assuming that they froze due to a sudden drop in temperature or were attacked by a lethal virus. The dinosaurs froze due to a sudden drop in temperature provided that the sun's rays were blocked. The earth's atmosphere was filled with dust due to the impact of a comet and the sun's rays were blocked. Therefore, the dinosaurs suffered some catastrophe. (E: Dinosaurs are extinct; C: The dinosaurs suffered some catastrophe; D: The dinosaurs died suddenly; F: The dinosaurs froze due to a sudden drop in temperature; V: The dinosaurs were attacked by a lethal virus; S: The sun's rays were blocked; A: The earth's atmosphere was filled with dust due to the impact of a comet)

5. In spite of the fact that advocates of suicide and euthanasia often claim that every right—including the right to life—can be waived, I think it's absurd to suggest that every right can be waived. (To waive a right is to agree, for good moral reasons, not to exercise it.) For if every right can be waived, then if I announce that I am waiving my right to liberty, you are morally permitted to enslave me. But obviously, it is not true that if I announce that I am waiving my right to liberty, then you are morally permitted to enslave me. (E: Every right can be waived; A: I announce that I am waiving my right to liberty; P: You are morally permitted to enslave me)

6. If morality is not subjective, then either morality is relative to cultures or God is the source of all moral values. If morality is subjective, then if I approve of racism, racism is right. Plainly, it's false that if I approve of racism, racism is right. Furthermore, if morality is relative to cultures, then the cannibalism in New Guinea is right and the caste system in India is right. The statement "The cannibalism in New Guinea is right and the caste system in India is right" is false. God exists if God is the source of all moral values. Accordingly, God exists. (S: Morality is subjective; M: Morality is relative to cultures; V: God is the source of all moral val-

ues; A: I approve of racism; R: Racism is right; C: The cannibalism in New Guinea is right; I: The caste system in India is right; G: God exists)

* **7.** Al has precognition. And assuming that Al has precognition, Al experiences events prior to their occurrence. But if Al experiences events prior to their occurrence, then either events exist prior to their occurrence or Al predicts the future on the basis of what he knows about the past and present. It is simply nonsense to say that events exist prior to their occurrence. We may infer that Al predicts the future on the basis of what he knows about the past and present. (P: Al has precognition; A: Al experiences events prior to their occurrence; E: Events exist prior to their occurrence; F: Al predicts the future on the basis of what he knows about the past and present)

8. God's existence is either necessary or impossible, if it is not contingent. God's existence is a matter of metaphysical luck if it is contingent. God's existence is emphatically not a matter of metaphysical luck. God's existence is not impossible if the concept of an omnipotent and perfectly good being is coherent. The concept of an omnipotent and perfectly good being is coherent. Therefore, God's existence is necessary.

9. Either the "eye for an eye" principle is interpreted literally or it is interpreted figuratively. If it is interpreted literally, then the state must do to criminals what they have done to their victims. If the state must do to criminals what they have done to their victims, then the state must torture torturers. On the other hand, if the "eye for an eye" principle is interpreted figuratively, the state need only mete out punishments that are proportional to the crime. If the state need only mete out punishments that are proportional to the crime, then the state is free to give murderers life imprisonment rather than the death penalty. Now, the state must not torture torturers if such acts are immoral. And it is indeed immoral to torture torturers. Hence, the state is free to give murderers life imprisonment rather than the death penalty. (L: The "eye for an eye" principle is interpreted literally; F: The "eye for an eye" principle is interpreted figuratively; C: The state must do to criminals what they have done to their victims; T: The state must torture torturers; P: The state need only mete out punishments that are proportional to the crime; S: The state is free to give murderers life imprisonment rather than the death penalty; I: It is immoral to torture torturers)

10. Either Mary is in much pain or she isn't in much pain. And Mary lacks a capacity to make a rational decision about ending her life if she is in a lot of pain. On the other hand, given that Mary isn't in much pain, she is in no position to know what she will want when she is in much pain. Furthermore, Mary has no right to end her life if either she lacks a capacity to make a rational decision about ending her life or she is in no position to know what she will want when she is in much pain. But Mary has no right to "die with dignity" if she has no right to end her life. Therefore, Mary has no right to "die with dignity." (M: Mary is in much pain; R: Mary lacks a capacity to make a rational decision about ending her life; K: Mary is in no position to know what she will want when she is in much pain; E: Mary has no right to end her life; D: Mary has no right to "die with dignity")

8.2 Five Equivalence Rules

In developing a system of natural deduction, the logician is torn in two directions. On the one hand, it is possible to develop a system with a small number of inference rules. But in systems with only a few rules, the proofs are often quite long and require much ingenuity. Moreover, the proof strategies tend to depart substantially from those employed in ordinary reasoning. On the other hand, it is possible to develop a system with a very large number of rules. Such systems allow for relatively short proofs, but most people find it difficult to remember a large number of rules. The present system is a compromise that includes 18 rules. (In addition to the rules, a special procedure called "conditional proof" is also needed, as we will see in section 8.4.)

Five equivalence rules are introduced in this section, and five more in the next section. We will use the four-dot symbol (: :) to indicate logical equivalence. Recall that two statements are *logically equivalent* if they validly imply each other. And within statement logic, two statements are logically equivalent if they have the same truth value in every row of the truth table.[2]

We can state our first equivalence rule, the rule of **double-negation**, as follows:

> **Rule 9:** Double-negation (DN): p : : $\sim\sim p$

The four-dot symbol tells us that we may move validly from $\sim\sim p$ to p, as well as from p to $\sim\sim p$. All our equivalence rules are two directional in this sense, unlike the implicational rules introduced in the previous section. For example, the rule of addition allows one to move from p to $p \lor q$, but it does not allow one to move from $p \lor q$ to p. Indeed, the latter move is invalid; here is a counterexample: "Either the number 3 is even or the number 2 is even. So, the number 3 is even."

The rule of double-negation formalizes the intuition that any statement implies, and is implied by, the negation of its negation. Here are two English examples:

> 11. It is not true that Booth did not kill Lincoln. So, Booth killed Lincoln.
>
> 12. Booth killed Lincoln. So, it is not true that Booth did not kill Lincoln.

The usefulness of this rule is illustrated in constructing a proof for the following short argument:

> 13. If humans do not have free will, then they are not responsible for their actions. But obviously, humans are responsible for their actions. Thus, humans have free will. (F: Humans have free will; R: Humans are responsible for their actions)

Using the scheme of abbreviation provided, argument (13) translates into symbols as follows:

1. ~F → ~R
2. R   ∴ F

The proof must include two applications of the double-negation rule:

3. ~~R   2, DN
4. ~~F   1, 3, MT
5. F   4, DN

Note that we cannot obtain F from the premises in one step by applying MT. MT tells us that if we have a conditional in one line of a proof and have *the negation of the conditional's consequent* in another line of the proof, then we can infer the negation of the antecedent. But line (2) of the proof does not give us the negation of the consequent of line (1). The negation of ~R is ~~R, and hence we must use the double-negation rule prior to applying MT.

As mentioned in the previous section, there is an important difference between implicational and equivalence rules as regards the construction of proofs. *We can apply equivalence rules to parts of lines in a proof and to entire lines.* We can do this because we never change the truth value of a statement by replacing some part of it with a logically equivalent expression. By contrast, *we can apply implicational rules only to entire lines in a proof.* The need for this restriction is illustrated by the following fallacious argument:

14. If Harry Truman was president in 1950 and Dwight Eisenhower was president in 1950, then America had two presidents in 1950. Therefore, if Truman was president in 1950, then America had two presidents in 1950. (T: Truman was president in 1950; E: Eisenhower was president in 1950; A: America had two presidents in 1950)

Without our restriction on implicational inference rules, we could construct the following proof:

1. (T • E) → A   ∴ T → A
2. T → A   1, *incorrect use of Simp* [not permitted]

Plainly, we do not want to allow this type of move. (An abbreviated truth table quickly reveals that the argument is invalid.) The proper use of both implicational and equivalence rules is illustrated in the following proof:

1. (A → B) → (A → ~~C)
2. A
3. A → D
4. D → B   ∴ C

At this point, if we tried to apply MP to lines (1) and (2) to derive B or ~~C, we would be misapplying MP. An implicational rule such as MP cannot be applied to a *part* of line (1); it must be applied to the whole line. So, we would need A → B to get A → ~~C from line (1) by MP. On the other hand, since double-negation is an equivalence rule, we can, if we wish, apply double-negation to a part of a line. Thus, we can complete our proof as follows:

5. (A → B) → (A → C)	1, DN
6. A → B	3, 4, HS
7. A → C	5, 6, MP
8. C	2, 7, MP

The fact that equivalence rules can be applied to parts of lines makes them very flexible tools to work with. But error will result if one fails to keep the distinction between implicational and equivalence rules firmly in mind. To repeat: The eight rules introduced in the previous section are all implicational rules (*modus ponens, modus tollens,* hypothetical syllogism, disjunctive syllogism, constructive dilemma, simplification, conjunction, and addition, The 10 rules introduced in this section and the next are all equivalence rules. For easy reference, a table of inference rules is provided on the inside front cover of this book.

Our second equivalence rule is **commutation**, which applies to both disjunctions and conjunctions:

Rule 10: Commutation (Com): $(p \lor q) :: (q \lor p)$
$(p \cdot q) :: (q \cdot p)$

Here are two English examples of commutation:

15. Either Sarah loves psychology or Harlan hates history. So, either Harlan hates history or Sarah loves psychology.

16. Frege is a logician and Russell is a logician. So, Russell is a logician and Frege is a logician.

The utility of the rule of commutation is revealed in constructing a proof for the following argument:

17. If pointless suffering occurs, then God is not both benevolent and omnipotent. But God is both omnipotent and benevolent. So, pointless suffering doesn't occur. (P: Pointless suffering occurs; B: God is benevolent; O: God is omnipotent)

1. P → ~(B • O)	
2. O • B	∴ ~P
3. B • O	2, Com
4. ~~(B • O)	3, DN
5. ~P	4, 1, MT

To underscore the difference between implicational and equivalence rules, it may be helpful to note that the following alternative proof is also correct:

    3. P → ~(O • B)   1, Com
    4. ~~(O • B)   2, DN
    5. ~P   3, 4, MT

Here, the rule of commutation is applied to *part* of line (1) to obtain line (3).

The rule of **association** is so obvious that you may not have thought of it as involving an inference. It comes in two forms, one governing disjunctions and one governing conjunctions:

Rule 11: Association (As): $(p \lor (q \lor r)) :: ((p \lor q) \lor r)$
$(p \bullet (q \bullet r)) :: ((p \bullet q) \bullet r)$

In English, this sort of inference would normally be signaled by a shift in punctuation. Here is an example of the first form of association:

> 18. Either the alleged eyewitnesses of UFO landings are telling the truth, or they are lying or they've been duped. So, either the alleged eyewitnesses of UFO landings are telling the truth or they are lying, or they've been duped.

In our symbolic language, the parentheses play the role that the commas play in the English example. The practical value of the rule of association is illustrated in constructing a proof for the following short argument:

> 19. Either cigarette manufacturers are greedy or they are ignorant of cancer research, or they dislike young people. But it is not true that either cigarette manufacturers are ignorant of cancer research or they dislike young people. Therefore, cigarette manufacturers are greedy. (C: Cigarette manufacturers are greedy; R: Cigarette manufacturers are ignorant of cancer research; D: Cigarette manufacturers dislike young people)

    1. (C ∨ R) ∨ D
    2. ~(R ∨ D)   ∴ C
    3. C ∨ (R ∨ D)   1, As
    4. C   2, 3, DS

Our next rule was first made explicit by the English logician Augustus De Morgan (1806–1871) and so is named after him. It comes in two forms. **De Morgan's laws** delineate the logical relations of negated conjunctions and of negated disjunctions.

Rule 12: De Morgan's laws (DeM): $\sim(p \bullet q) :: (\sim p \lor \sim q)$
$\sim(p \lor q) :: (\sim p \bullet \sim q)$

Here is an English example of an inference endorsed by the first of De Morgan's laws:

> **20.** Spot is not both a dog and a cat. So, either Spot is not a dog or Spot is not a cat.

The first law also tells us that we may reverse this reasoning and infer the *premise* of argument (20) from its conclusion. (This should make sense as the premise and conclusion are logically equivalent.) Here is an English example of the second law:

> **21.** It's not true that either hydrogen or oxygen is a metal. So, hydrogen is not a metal and oxygen is not a metal.

The second law also tells us that we may reverse this reasoning and infer the premise from the conclusion. As the following example illustrates, De Morgan's laws are quite useful in constructing proofs.

> **22.** Either people are equal and deserve equal pay for equal work or else people are not equal and do not deserve equal pay for equal work. People are not equal. So, people do not deserve equal pay for equal work. (E: People are equal; D: People deserve equal pay for equal work)
>
> 1. $(E \cdot D) \lor (\sim E \cdot \sim D)$
> 2. $\sim E$ $\therefore \ \sim D$
> 3. $\sim E \lor \sim D$ 2, Add
> 4. $\sim(E \cdot D)$ 3, DeM
> 5. $\sim E \cdot \sim D$ 1, 4, DS
> 6. $\sim D$ 5, Simp

The strategy required in this proof is a bit indirect. The basic insight is that the second premise, $\sim E$, is clearly incompatible with the left disjunct of the first premise, $E \cdot D$. This means that an application of disjunctive syllogism is in the offing. But we have to use addition and one of De Morgan's laws before we can apply disjunctive syllogism.

Our next rule of inference relies on the logical equivalence between a conditional and its contrapositive. To form the contrapositive of a conditional, switch the antecedent and consequent, and negate both. To illustrate, the contrapositive of "If Bob is an uncle, then Bob is male" is "If Bob is not male, then Bob is not an uncle." Let us call the inference rule itself **contraposition**.

> **Rule 13:** Contraposition (Cont): $(p \rightarrow q) :: (\sim q \rightarrow \sim p)$

The utility of this rule becomes apparent in evaluating the following argument:

23. If it is wrong to use drugs only if they impair the user's mental functions, then it is not wrong to use caffeine. And if drugs do not impair the user's mental functions, then it is not wrong to use drugs. Hence, it is not wrong to use caffeine. (W: It is wrong to use drugs; D: Drugs impair the user's mental functions; C: It is wrong to use caffeine)

1. $(W \rightarrow D) \rightarrow \sim C$
2. $\sim D \rightarrow \sim W$ $\therefore \sim C$
3. $W \rightarrow D$ 2, Cont
4. $\sim C$ 1, 3, MP

To emphasize the point that equivalence rules can be applied to *part* of a line, let us note that the proof could also be completed as follows:

3. $(\sim D \rightarrow \sim W) \rightarrow \sim C$ 1, Cont
4. $\sim C$ 2, 3, MP

Here, contraposition is applied to *part* of line (1) to obtain line (3).

    The five rules introduced in this section may seem obvious or even trivial, but some logicians have rejected one or more of them. This results from skepticism about the **law of the excluded middle**, which says that for any given statement, either it or its negation is true. Using statement variables, we can state the law of the excluded middle as follows: $p \lor \sim p$. One group of logicians who reject the law of the excluded middle is the intuitionists. The intuitionists hold that the truth of a statement consists in there being a proof of it. Thus, to prove that any statement of the form $p \lor q$ is true, we must either prove that p is true or prove that q is true. Now, consider Goldbach's conjecture, which states that every even number greater than 2 is equal to the sum of two primes. No one has proved that this conjecture is true, and no one has proved that it is not true. Let us symbolize Goldbach's conjecture with the letter G. According to the intuitionists, then, the statement $G \lor \sim G$ is not true because neither disjunct has been proved, and so the law of the excluded middle is not true.[3]

    However, given the rules introduced in this section, we cannot deny the law of the excluded middle unless we are prepared to deny the **law of noncontradiction**, which states that contradictions are never true. Using statement variables, the law of noncontradiction can be expressed as follows: $\sim(p \cdot \sim p)$. And all logicians endorse the law of noncontradiction. Now, consider the following proof:

1. $\sim(G \cdot \sim G)$ $\therefore G \lor \sim G$
2. $\sim G \lor \sim \sim G$ 1, DeM
3. $\sim G \lor G$ 2, DN
4. $G \lor \sim G$ 3, Com

Summary of the First Set of Equivalence Rules

9. Double-negation (DN):	$p : : \sim\sim p$
10. Commutation (Com):	$(p \lor q) : : (q \lor p)$
	$(p \bullet q) : : (q \bullet p)$
11. Association (As):	$(p \lor (q \lor r)) : : ((p \lor q) \lor r)$
	$(p \bullet (q \bullet r)) : : ((p \bullet q) \bullet r)$
12. De Morgan's laws (DeM):	$\sim(p \bullet q) : : (\sim p \lor \sim q)$
	$\sim(p \lor q) : : (\sim p \bullet \sim q)$
13. Contraposition (Cont):	$(p \to q) : : (\sim q \to \sim p)$

The premise says that Goldbach's conjecture is not both true and false (or that Goldbach's conjecture and its negation are not *both* true). And the conclusion says that Goldbach's conjecture is either true or false (or that either Goldbach's conjecture or its negation is true). It appears, then, that if we wish to reject the law of the excluded middle, we must also reject at least one of the following: De Morgan's laws, double-negation, commutation, or the law of noncontradiction. But each of these is very hard to deny.

As you complete the exercises that follow, keep in mind that the three rules of thumb provided in the previous section still apply: Start with the conclusion and work backward; break premises down into simpler components using MP, MT, Simp, DS, and so on; and if a "new" statement letter appears in the conclusion, use addition. To these three rules of thumb, we now add the following:

> **Rule of Thumb 4:** It is often useful to consider logically equivalent forms of the conclusion.

For example, suppose the conclusion is $\sim(A \bullet B)$. Then it may help to notice that the conclusion is logically equivalent to $\sim A \lor \sim B$, according to De Morgan's laws. Or if the conclusion is $\sim D \to \sim C$, it may be helpful to note that the conclusion is equivalent to $C \to D$, by contraposition.

> **Rule of Thumb 5:** Both conjunction and addition can lead to useful applications of De Morgan's laws.

Consider the following examples:

1. $\sim E$			1. $\sim G$		
2. $\sim F$			2. $\sim G \lor \sim H$	1, Add	
3. $\sim E \bullet \sim F$	1, 2, Conj		3. $\sim(G \bullet H)$	2, DeM	
4. $\sim(E \lor F)$	3, DeM				

As before, rules of thumb are to be taken as helpful hints. They do not automatically provide a solution in every case. A summary of rules of thumb for constructing proofs appears at the end of section 8.5 on page 296.

◆ *Exercise 8.2*

Part A: Annotating   Annotate the following short proofs. (In each case, the argument has only one premise.)

* **1.** 1. ~~A → B ∴ A → B
   2. A → B

 2. 1. ~C → ~D ∴ D → C
   2. D → C

 3. 1. ~(E • ~D) ∴ D ∨ ~E
   2. ~E ∨ ~~D
   3. ~E ∨ D
   4. D ∨ ~E

* **4.** 1. ~(E ∨ D) ∴ ~D
   2. ~E • ~D
   3. ~D

 5. 1. ~A • [(A ∨ B) ∨ C] ∴ B ∨ C
   2. ~A
   3. (A ∨ B) ∨ C
   4. A ∨ (B ∨ C)
   5. B ∨ C

 6. 1. F • (G • R) ∴ G • F
   2. (F • G) • R
   3. F • G
   4. G • F

* **7.** 1. [(P → Q) → R] • (~Q → ~P) ∴ ~~R
   2. ~Q → ~P
   3. P → Q
   4. (P → Q) → R
   5. R
   6. ~~R

 8. 1. [~(S • T) ∨ ~~U] • (T • S) ∴ U
   2. T • S
   3. S • T
   4. ~(S • T) ∨ ~~U
   5. ~~(S • T)
   6. ~~U
   7. U

 9. 1. ~W ∨ (~X ∨ ~Y) ∴ ~Y ∨ ~(W • X)
   2. (~W ∨ ~X) ∨ ~Y
   3. ~(W • X) ∨ ~Y
   4. ~Y ∨ ~(W • X)

* **10.** 1. [~O → (~M → ~N)] • ~(N → M) ∴ O
  2. ~O → (~M → ~N)
  3. ~(N → M)
  4. ~(~M → ~N)
  5. ~~O
  6. O

Part B: Correct or Incorrect? Some of the following inferences are correct applications of our rules and some are not. If an inference is a correct application of our rules, name the rule. If an inference is not a correct application of our rules, explain why it is not. (The question is whether the conclusion in each case can be reached *in a single step* from the premise(s) by an application of one of our rules.)

* **1.**   ~(~E ∨ B)
      ∴ ~~E • ~B

   2.   ~B → ~C
      ∴ C → B

   3.   ~(F ∨ G)
      ∴ ~F ∨ ~G

* **4.**   ~W ∨ ~Z
      ∴ ~(W • Z)

   5.   A • ~B
      ∴ ~B • A

   6.   ~D → ~E
      ∴ ~~E → ~~D

* **7.**   ~S ∨ T
      ∴ ~(S • ~T)

   8.   ~J ∨ ~~K
      ∴ ~(J • ~K)

   9.   P → ~Q
      ∴ Q → ~P

* **10.**   O → R
      ∴ ~R → ~O

   11.   [B ∨ (C ∨ A)] ↔ D
      ∴ [(C ∨ B) ∨ A] ↔ D

   12.   ~(D • C) → E
      ∴ (~D ∨ ~C) → E

* **13.**   ~(L • ~M)
      ∴ ~(~M • L)

   14.   ~(U • ~Z)
      ∴ ~U ∨ ~~Z

   15.   (~~N ∨ ~M) ↔ (L • K)
      ∴ ~(~N • M) ↔ (L • K)

* **16.**   ~[(O • ~P) • W]
      ∴ ~[O • (~P • W)]

   17.   ~(R ∨ ~Q)
      ∴ ~R • ~~Q

   18.   ~~S ↔ T
      ∴ S ↔ T

* **19.**   ~~(U ∨ W)
      ∴ ~(~U • ~W)

   20.   ~(X → Y)
      ∴ ~X → ~Y

Part C: Proofs Construct proofs for each of the following symbolic arguments. Commas are used to mark the breaks between premises. (Each proof can be completed in two to four steps.)

* **1.** ~(C • D), ~C → S, ~D → T ∴ S ∨ T
   2. (W → U) • ~X ∴ ~U → ~W
   3. F → ~G, G ∴ ~F
* **4.** ~(~A ∨ B) ∴ A
   5. (~P → Q) • ~Q ∴ P
   6. ~(N ∨ M), ~L → (M ∨ N) ∴ L
* **7.** (A ∨ B) ∨ C, ~A ∴ C ∨ B
   8. (W • ~X) ∨ (Y • Z), (~X • W) → U, (Y • Z) → T ∴ U ∨ T

    9. ~(S ∨ R), P → R ∴ ~P
* **10.** F → (G • H), (H • G) → J ∴ F → J
  11. K ∨ (L ∨ S), ~(K ∨ L) ∴ S
  12. ~P, ~(P ∨ Q) → ~R, ~Q ∴ ~R
* **13.** ~S → (T • U), (~S → X) → ~Z, (U • T) → X ∴ ~Z
  14. ~(~B → A), C → (~A → B) ∴ ~C
  15. ~E, F → (D ∨ E), ~D ∴ ~F
* **16.** (K ∨ P) ∨ X, K → ~O, (P ∨ X) → ~L ∴ ~(O • L)
  17. (G ∨ H) → (J ∨ K) ∴ ~(J ∨ K) → ~(H ∨ G)
  18. ~A → ~~R, G → ~U, ~A ∨ G ∴ ~(~R • U)
* **19.** ~(L • M) → ~(N ∨ O) ∴ (O ∨ N) → (M • L)
  20. B → E, (B ∨ C) ∨ D, (D ∨ C) → F ∴ E ∨ F

Part D: Longer Proofs   Construct proofs to show that the following arguments are valid. Commas are used to mark the breaks between premises.

* **1.** ~~T ∨ ~R, ~(S ∨ ~R), (T • ~S) → ~Q, W → Q ∴ ~W
  2. ~(J • L), (~J ∨ ~L) → ~M, ~E ∨ (M ∨ ~S) ∴ ~(S • E)
  3. E → [~(H ∨ K) → R], ~~E • (~H • ~K) ∴ ~~R
* **4.** B → E, ~F ∨ G, (B • C) • D, (D • C) → F ∴ E • G
  5. P ∨ (Q ∨ R), (Q ∨ P) → ~S, R → ~T, U → (S • T) ∴ ~U ∨ Z
  6. ~~W • [(X ∨ W) → Y], H → ~Y ∴ ~H
* **7.** ~(B • ~C), ~B → D, C → ~E ∴ ~E ∨ D
  8. (F • G) → (H • J), (J • H) → (K ∨ L), (L ∨ K) → M ∴ (G • F) → M
  9. ~Y ∨ N, (Y • ~N) ∨ (Y • Z), (Z • Y) → ~~U ∴ U ∨ ~V
* **10.** ~A → ~B, D → E, (B → A) → (C ∨ D), C → F ∴ E ∨ F
  11. ~(H ↔ G) ∨ ~J, K → (H ↔ G), ~L → J ∴ ~(K • ~L)
  12. (X • Q) → (Z • ~T), R • (T ∨ ~Z) ∴ (~X ∨ ~Q) • R
  13. ~[(M ∨ N) ∨ O], (P • R) → N, ~P → T, ~R→ S ∴ T ∨ S
  14. Z → (U • X), ~[(U • W) • X], W ∴ ~Z
  15. ~(~A • B) ↔ ~(C ∨ ~D) ∴ (~B ∨ A) ↔ (D • ~C)
  16. ~[(E • F) ∨ G], (H ∨ ~E) → G ∴ ~(F ∨ H)
  17. ~(R → S) → ~(~T → ~U), ~W → T, U → ~W, ~S ∴ ~R
  18. ~[(L ∨ M) • N], (P → ~Q) → N, Q → ~P ∴ ~M
  19. ~(X ∨ Y) → Z, [(A • B) ∨ ~C] → (~X • ~Y), ~C ∴ Z
  20. H ∨ G, ~(~D → E), (F ∨ G) → (~E → D) ∴ H ∨ ~J

8.3 *Five More Equivalence Rules*

To this point, our system of natural deduction includes eight implicational rules and five equivalence rules. With these 13 rules, we can construct proofs for many valid arguments in statement logic. But we need five more equivalence rules (plus a special proof procedure called "conditional proof") if our system of natural deduction is to be able to *prove valid* every argument that is valid according to the truth table method. So, in this section, we add five more equivalence rules to our system.

The rule of **distribution** tells us how certain combinations of the dot and the vee interrelate. It comes in two forms.

Rule 14: Distribution (Dist): $(p \cdot (q \vee r)) :: ((p \cdot q) \vee (p \cdot r))$
$(p \vee (q \cdot r)) :: ((p \vee q) \cdot (p \vee r))$

To grasp these inferences, think about them truth functionally, e.g., consider the first form of distribution: Suppose $(p \cdot (q \vee r))$ is true; then p is true and $(q \vee r)$ is true; so either $(p \cdot q)$ is true or $(p \cdot r)$ is true (or both). Similarly, suppose $((p \cdot q) \vee (p \cdot r))$ is true. If $(p \cdot q)$ is true, then $(p \cdot (q \vee r))$ must be true too; but if $(p \cdot r)$ is true, then, again, $(p \cdot (q \vee r))$ must be true. Here are some English examples of disribution:

24. "Bats are animals, and they are either mammals or birds" implies (and is implied by) "Either bats are animals and mammals, or bats are animals and birds."

25. "Either Bill lost the lottery, or Bill won and he is rich" implies (and is implied by) "Either Bill lost the lottery or he won, and either Bill lost the lottery or he is rich."

The utility of the rule of distribution is brought out when we construct a proof of the following argument:

26. Either Fiona is insane, or she is guilty and a liar. But if Fiona is either insane or a liar, then she is dangerous. It follows that Fiona is dangerous. (F: Fiona is insane; G: Fiona is guilty; L: Fiona is a liar; D: Fiona is dangerous)

    1. $F \vee (G \cdot L)$
    2. $(F \vee L) \rightarrow D$ $\therefore$ D
    3. $(F \vee G) \cdot (F \vee L)$ 1, Dist
    4. $F \vee L$ 3, Simp
    5. D   2, 4, MP

Perhaps because distribution appears a bit complex, there is some tendency to overlook occasions for its use when constructing proofs, but it is often quite useful.

The rule of **exportation** tells us that statements of the form "If p and q, then r" are logically equivalent to statements of the form "If p, then if q, then r." In symbols, we have the following:

Rule 15: Exportation (Ex): $((p \cdot q) \rightarrow r) :: (p \rightarrow (q \rightarrow r))$

Here is an English example:

27. "If Sue is intelligent and she studies hard, then she gets good grades" implies (and is implied by) "If Sue is intelligent, then if she studies hard, she gets good grades."

A proof of the following argument will illustrate a typical usage of exportation.

28. If World War I was not a war in defense of the U.S.A. and only wars of defense are just, then the American participation in World War I was not just. World War I was not a war in defense of the U.S.A. It follows that if only wars of defense are just, then the American participation in World War I was not just. (W: World War I was a war in defense of the U.S.A.; D: Only wars of defense are just; J: American participation in World War I was just)

1. $(\sim W \cdot D) \rightarrow \sim J$
2. $\sim W$ $\therefore D \rightarrow \sim J$
3. $\sim W \rightarrow (D \rightarrow \sim J)$ 1, Ex
4. $D \rightarrow \sim J$ 2, 3, MP

The **redundancy** rule is obviously valid, and as the name suggests, it allows us to eliminate certain types of redundancy.

Rule 16: Redundancy (Re): $p :: (p \cdot p)$
                          $p :: (p \vee p)$

A proof of the following argument reveals a typical use of this rule.

29. Either pain is real or it is an illusion. If pain is real, then pain is bad. And if pain is an illusion, then pain is bad. Accordingly, pain is bad. (R: Pain is real; I: Pain is an illusion; B: Pain is bad)

1. $R \vee I$
2. $R \rightarrow B$
3. $I \rightarrow B$ $\therefore B$
4. $B \vee B$ 1, 2, 3, CD
5. B 4, Re

In this case, the rule allows us to eliminate redundancy in a disjunction. Note that the rule also allows us to eliminate redundancy in a conjunction.

The rule of **material equivalence** gives us a way of handling biconditionals. It comes in two forms. The first form tells us that a biconditional is logically equivalent to a *conjunction* of two conditionals. The second form tells us that a biconditional is logically equivalent to a *disjunction* of two conjunctions. The second form makes sense if you remember the truth table for the biconditional: $(p \leftrightarrow q)$ is true if either p and q are both true or p and q are both false; otherwise, $(p \leftrightarrow q)$ is false.

Rule 17: Material equivalence (ME): $(p \leftrightarrow q) :: ((p \rightarrow q) \cdot (q \rightarrow p))$
                                          $(p \leftrightarrow q) :: ((p \cdot q) \vee (\sim p \cdot \sim q))$

A proof of the following argument will illustrate a typical usage of material equivalence.

30. Withholding medical treatment is wrong if and only if either the patient has a valuable future life or the family insists on medical treatment. But the patient is brain dead. And if the patient is brain dead, then he has not got a valuable future life. Furthermore, it is not the case that the family insists on medical treatment. It follows that withholding medical treatment is not wrong. (W: Withholding medical treatment is wrong; L: The patient has a valuable future life; F: The family insists on medical treatment; B: The patient is brain dead)

   1. W ↔ (L ∨ F)
   2. B
   3. B → ~L
   4. ~F   ∴ ~W
   5. ~L   2, 3, MP
   6. [W → (L ∨ F)] • [(L ∨ F) → W]   1, ME
   7. W → (L ∨ F)   6, Simp
   8. ~L • ~F   5, 4, Conj
   9. ~(L ∨ F)   8, DeM
   10. ~W   7, 9, MT

The last of our equivalence rules is called **material implication**. It is based on the logical equivalence between statements of the form $(p \rightarrow q)$ and a *disjunction* whose disjuncts are the consequent of the conditional and the negation of its antecedent. This equivalence can easily be demonstrated with a truth table.

Rule 18: Material implication (MI): $(p \rightarrow q)$: : $(\sim p \lor q)$

Without material implication, our proof system would lack the capacity to prove valid every argument that is valid according to the truth table method. But it is important to remember that $\sim p \lor q$ and $p \rightarrow q$ are equivalent because of the truth-functional definition we have given the arrow. As we saw in chapter 7, not every English statement of the form "If p, then q" is equivalent to "Either not p or q." For example, "If the Eiffel Tower is in Ohio, then it is in France" is intuitively false; but the disjunction "Either the Eiffel Tower is not in Ohio or the Eiffel Tower is in France" is true, since the Eiffel Tower is in fact in France (and not in Ohio). Accordingly, we include the rule of material implication in our system, but with the realization that if a proof relies on this rule, it may fail to mirror our intuitive logical convictions about English conditionals.

A proof of the following argument demands a strategic use of both material implication and the rule of distribution.

31. If either humans do not need meat or eating meat is unhealthy, then humans should not eat meat. Hence, if humans do not need meat, then humans should not eat meat. (N: Humans need meat; E: Eating meat is unhealthy; S: Humans should eat meat)

1. $(\sim N \vee E) \rightarrow \sim S$ $\therefore \sim N \rightarrow \sim S$
2. $\sim(\sim N \vee E) \vee \sim S$ 1, MI
3. $(\sim\sim N \bullet \sim E) \vee \sim S$ 2, DeM
4. $(N \bullet \sim E) \vee \sim S$ 3, DN
5. $\sim S \vee (N \bullet \sim E)$ 4, Com
6. $(\sim S \vee N) \bullet (\sim S \vee \sim E)$ 5, Dist
7. $\sim S \vee N$ 6, Simp
8. $S \rightarrow N$ 7, MI
9. $\sim N \rightarrow \sim S$ 8, Cont

This proof is rather complex, and it suggests the following rules of thumb (to be added to the five rules of thumb introduced previously):

Rule of Thumb 6: Material implication can lead to useful applications of distribution.

This is illustrated by lines (2) through (6) in the previous proof. But here is a simpler case:

1. $A \rightarrow (B \bullet C)$
2. $\sim A \vee (B \bullet C)$ 1, MI
3. $(\sim A \vee B) \bullet (\sim A \vee C)$ 2, Dist

Rule of Thumb 7: Distribution can lead to useful applications of simplification.

This rule of thumb is illustrated in lines (5) through (7) in the previous proof, but here is another example:

1. $(D \bullet E) \vee (D \bullet F)$
2. $D \bullet (E \vee F)$ 1, Dist
3. D 2, Simp

At least one more rule of thumb (not suggested by the previous proof) may be helpful as you complete the exercises at the end of this section:

Rule of Thumb 8: Addition can lead to useful applications of material implication.

Here are two examples:

1. B 1. $\sim F$
2. $B \vee \sim A$ 1, Add   2. $\sim F \vee G$ 1, Add
3. $\sim A \vee B$ 2, Com   3. $F \rightarrow G$ 2, MI
4. $A \rightarrow B$ 3, MI

Summary of the Second Set of Equivalence Rules	
14. Distribution (Dist):	$(p \cdot (q \lor r)) :: ((p \cdot q) \lor (p \cdot r))$ $(p \lor (q \cdot r)) :: ((p \lor q) \cdot (p \lor r))$
15. Exportation (Ex):	$((p \cdot q) \to r) :: (p \to (q \to r))$
16. Redundancy (Re):	$p :: (p \cdot p)$ $p :: (p \lor p)$
17. Material equivalence (ME):	$(p \leftrightarrow q) :: ((p \to q) \cdot (q \to p))$ $(p \leftrightarrow q) :: ((p \cdot q) \lor (\sim p \cdot \sim q))$
18. Material implication (MI):	$(p \to q) :: (\sim p \lor q)$

A summary of rules of thumb for constructing proofs is provided at the end of section 8.5 on page 296.

In closing this section, let us reflect briefly on the value of proofs. What good are they? First, many valid arguments are sufficiently complex to dazzle one's logical intuitions. In such cases, our proof system comes into its own by enabling us to show how we can get from the premises to the conclusion *using only the rules we have explicitly adopted*. So, unless we have doubts about our 18 rules, a proof should settle all doubts about the validity of even very complicated arguments. Second, suppose you claim that an argument is valid and someone else claims that it isn't. What can you do? Well, if the argument can be shown to be valid by means of a proof, then this should settle the matter (unless the other person rejects one or more of the rules in our system). The power of logic consists partly in the fact that in so many cases, it can settle the question of an argument's validity. And once we determine that an argument is valid, the question of its soundness turns entirely on whether its premises are true.

◆ Exercise 8.3

Part A: Annotating   Annotate the following short proofs. (In each case, the argument has only one premise.)

* 1. 1. $B \leftrightarrow E$ ∴ $E \to B$
      2. $(B \to E) \cdot (E \to B)$
      3. $E \to B$

  2. 1. $(B \cdot C) \lor (\sim B \cdot \sim C)$ ∴ $B \leftrightarrow C$
      2. $B \leftrightarrow C$

  3. 1. $\sim(A \cdot A) \lor (B \lor B)$ ∴ $A \to B$
      2. $\sim(A \cdot A) \lor B)$
      3. $(A \cdot A) \to B$
      4. $A \to B$

* 4. 1. $H \to (J \to \sim H)$ ∴ $H \to \sim J$
      2. $H \to (\sim\sim H \to \sim J)$
      3. $(H \cdot \sim\sim H) \to \sim J$
      4. $(H \cdot H) \to \sim J$
      5. $H \to \sim J$

  5. 1. $P \cdot \sim Q$ ∴ $P \cdot (\sim Q \lor R)$
      2. $(P \cdot \sim Q) \lor (P \cdot R)$
      3. $P \cdot (\sim Q \lor R)$

6. 1. F ∨ (~G • H) ∴ G → F
   2. (F ∨ ~G) • (F ∨ H)
   3. F ∨ ~G
   4. ~G ∨ F
   5. G → F

* 7. 1. M → ~N ∴ N → ~M
   2. ~M ∨ ~N
   3. ~N ∨ ~M
   4. N → ~M

8. 1. ~S ↔ T ∴ (~S • T) ∨ (S • ~T)
   2. (~S • T) ∨ (~~S • ~T)
   3. (~S • T) ∨ (S • ~T)

9. 1. (B • B) ∨ (C • D) ∴ B ∨ D
   2. B ∨ (C • D)
   3. (B ∨ C) • (B ∨ D)
   4. B ∨ D

* 10. 1. (U → U) ∨ (~U → U)
   ∴ ~U ∨ U
   2. (~U ∨ U) ∨ (~U → U)
   3. (~U ∨ U) ∨ (~~U ∨ U)
   4. (~U ∨ U) ∨ (U ∨ U)
   5. (~U ∨ U) ∨ U
   6. ~U ∨ (U ∨ U)
   7. ~U ∨ U
   8. U ∨ ~U

Part B: Correct or Incorrect? Some of the following inferences are correct applications of our rules and some are not. If an inference is a correct application of our rules, name the rule. If an inference is not a correct application of our rules, explain why it is not. (The question is whether the conclusion in each case can be reached *in a single step* from the premise by an application of one of our rules.)

* 1.   (~B ∨ ~B) ↔ A
   ∴ ~B ↔ A

2.   N ∨ M
   ∴ ~N → M

3.   ~~P ∨ Q
   ∴ ~P → Q

* 4.   (C • ~L) ∨ (C • S)
   ∴ C • (~L ∨ S)

5.   (~M • N) → ~L
   ∴ ~M → (N → ~L)

6.   S → (R • R)
   ∴ S → R

* 7.   K ∨ (X • R)
   ∴ (K • X) ∨ (K • R)

8.   ~H → P
   ∴ H ∨ P

9.   X → (Y → Z)
   ∴ (X • Y) → Z

* 10.   (~U ∨ S) → Q
   ~~U
   ∴ S → Q

11.   (~W ∨ ~U) → (~F ∨ ~F)
   ∴ (~W ∨ ~U) → ~F

12.   ~A → ~B
   ∴ ~~A ∨ ~B

* 13.   ~A ∨ (N • Z)
   ∴ (~A ∨ N) • (~A ∨ Z)

14.   F → (G • H)
   ∴ F → (G → H)

15.   (~J • ~K) ∨ (~J • ~L)
   ∴ ~J • (~K ∨ ~L)

* 16.   M • (O ∨ U)
   ∴ (M • O) ∨ (M • U)

17.   (S ∨ T) • (S ∨ ~W)
   ∴ S ∨ (T • ~W)

18.   A • (~B ∨ C)
   ∴ (A ∨ ~B) • (A ∨ C)

* 19.   (E • H) → V
   ∴ E

20.   (B → C) ∨ K
   B
   ∴ C ∨ K

Part C: Proofs   Construct proofs for each of the following symbolic arguments. Each proof can be completed in two or three steps.

* 1. ~M ∨ N ∴ ~N → ~M
  2. ~B ↔ C, ~B ∴ C
  3. ~S ∨ (R • T), ~R ∴ ~S
* 4. ~A ∨ ~A, A ∨ P ∴ P
  5. (D → C) • (C → D), E → ~(D ↔ C) ∴ ~E
  6. F • (G ∨ H), ~F ∨ ~H ∴ F • G
* 7. (~J • K) → L, ~J ∴ ~L → ~K
  8. (~N ∨ M) • (~N ∨ O) ∴ ~(M • O) → ~N
  9. P • P, Q → ~P ∴ ~Q
* 10. ~R, (R → S) → T ∴ T
  11. U → (X → W), Z → ~[(U • X) → W] ∴ ~Z
  12. ~D ∴ C → ~D
* 13. E → H, [(E ∨ F) • (E ∨ G)] • [(F • G) → H] ∴ H
  14. (~J • K) ∨ (~J • L), M → J ∴ ~M
  15. ~N ↔ ~O, (~O → ~N) → P ∴ P
* 16. ~~(R • S), T → (R → ~S) ∴ ~T
  17. ~C, (~A • B) ∨ (~A • C) ∴ B
  18. (~D ∨ E) • (~D ∨ ~F), (E • ~F) → ~G, ~D → ~G ∴ ~G
* 19. H ∨ H, H ↔ ~J ∴ ~J
  20. X ↔ Y, ~~(X ∨ Y) ∴ X • Y

Part D: More Proofs   Construct a proof for each of the following symbolic arguments.

* 1. (Z ∨ ~Y) • (Z ∨ W), Z → ~~U, ~Y → (W → U) ∴ U
  2. ~U → ~B, S → ~B, ~(U • ~S), T ∨ B ∴ T
  3. (Q • R) ∨ (~Q • ~R), N → ~(Q ↔ R), E ∨ N ∴ E
* 4. ~H ∨ (G ∨ F), ~F, S → ~(H → G) ∴ ~S
  5. ~(J • L), (J → ~L) → (~M • ~X), E ∨ (M ∨ X) ∴ E
  6. (L ∨ M) • (L ∨ ~S), A → ~L, A → (~M ∨ S) ∴ ~A
* 7. B ∨ (C • ~D), (D → B) ↔ P ∴ P
  8. (G • S) ∨ (G • ~T), ~R → ~G, (T → S) → Q ∴ R • Q
  9. ~X ↔ ~Y, ~X ∨ ~Y, Z ↔ Y ∴ ~Z

* 10. $(B \cdot C) \rightarrow D, B, Q \rightarrow \sim(\sim C \vee D), \sim Q \leftrightarrow T \therefore T$
  11. $(F \cdot G) \vee (F \cdot \sim H), (H \rightarrow G) \rightarrow L, L \rightarrow (P \rightarrow \sim F) \therefore \sim P$
  12. $\sim X \vee (M \cdot O), (X \rightarrow O) \rightarrow \sim M \therefore \sim X$
  13. $(\sim Z \cdot W) \rightarrow Q, \sim Z, R \leftrightarrow (W \cdot \sim Q) \therefore \sim R$
  14. $A \leftrightarrow B, \sim\sim(A \vee B) \therefore B$
  15. $(A \vee B) \cdot (A \vee G), M \rightarrow \sim A, \sim Q \rightarrow (\sim B \vee \sim G) \therefore M \rightarrow Q$
  16. $Y \cdot (\sim N \vee A), \sim Y \vee N, (A \cdot Y) \rightarrow \sim\sim K \therefore K$
  17. $\sim G \rightarrow \sim F, (\sim F \vee G) \rightarrow (H \vee J), H \rightarrow Z, J \rightarrow \sim P \therefore P \rightarrow Z$
  18. $(D \cdot E) \vee (\sim D \cdot \sim E), (H \cdot J) \rightarrow \sim(D \leftrightarrow E), \sim\sim H \vee J \therefore J \leftrightarrow \sim H$
  19. $(\sim E \vee Z) \cdot (\sim E \vee W), \sim K \rightarrow E, \sim K \rightarrow (\sim Z \vee \sim W), K \leftrightarrow U \therefore R \rightarrow U$
  20. $(R \cdot S) \vee (R \cdot \sim E), (Y \cdot O) \rightarrow (E \cdot \sim S), (O \rightarrow \sim Y) \rightarrow L \therefore L$

Part E: English Arguments Symbolize the following arguments and then construct proofs to show that they are valid.

* 1. If workers should be paid, then either they should be paid according to their needs (as Marx asserted) or they should be paid for services rendered. If workers should be paid according to their needs, then single mothers should be paid more (other things being equal) than their co-workers, and so should workers who have large families. If workers should be paid for services rendered, then workers should receive equal pay for equal work. Workers should be paid, but it is not the case that workers having large families should be paid more (other things being equal) than their co-workers. Hence, workers should receive equal pay for equal work. (P: Workers should be paid; N: Workers should be paid according to their needs; S: Workers should be paid for services rendered; M: Single mothers should be paid more (other things being equal) than their co-workers; F: Workers who have large families should be paid more (other things being equal) than their co-workers; E: Workers should receive equal pay for equal work)

  2. If either the defendant refuses to take the stand or he confesses, then he is guilty. We may infer that the defendant is guilty if he refuses to take the stand. (R: The defendant refuses to take the stand; C: The defendant confesses; G: The defendant is guilty)

  3. If beauty is in the eye of the beholder, then beauty is not objective. But beauty is objective if it is observable. And beauty can be seen, can't it? Furthermore, beauty can be seen if and only if beauty is observable. Therefore, popular opinion to the contrary, beauty is not in the eye of the beholder. (E: Beauty is in the eye of the beholder; B: Beauty is objective; O: Beauty is observable; S: Beauty can be seen)

* **4.** Either sex is for procreation or it is for interpersonal union and pleasure. If sex is for either procreation or interpersonal union, then societal rules are needed to regulate sex. It follows that societal rules are needed to regulate sex. (S: Sex is for procreation; U: Sex is for interpersonal union; P: Sex is for pleasure; R: Societal rules are needed to regulate sex)

5. Young smokers either identify with their future selves or fail to identify with their future selves. If young smokers identify with their future selves, then they are irrational if they know smoking causes cancer. If young smokers fail to identify with their future selves, then they act without due regard for another person (namely, their future self), assuming that they know smoking causes cancer. And given that young smokers act without due regard for another person, they are immoral. But while young smokers do know that smoking causes cancer, they are not immoral. Therefore, young smokers are irrational and they identify with their future selves. (I: Young smokers identify with their future selves; R: Young smokers are irrational; K: Young smokers know that smoking causes cancer; A: Young smokers act without due regard for another person; M: Young smokers are immoral) —This argument makes use of material in Derek Parfit, *Reasons and Persons* (New York: Oxford University Press, 1986), pp. 319–320

6. It is a biological fact that animals in most species will make greater sacrifices for near relatives than for others. (For instance, a calf's mother will defend it to the death but will not defend the calf of another cow.) Given this fact, there is a general law that animals act so as to preserve genes similar to their own. But if there is a general law that animals act so as to preserve genes similar to their own, then sociobiologists are right and it is biologically impossible to treat all people equally. Now, if it is biologically impossible to treat all people equally, then it is futile to preach the ideal of equality and futile to preach the ideal of universal love. Hence, it is futile to preach universal love if sociobiologists are right. [Hint: In symbolizing the argument, ignore the parenthetical remark.] (B: It is a biological fact that animals in most species will make greater sacrifices for near relatives than for others; G: There is a general law that animals act so as to preserve genes similar to their own; S: Sociobiologists are right; E: It is biologically impossible to treat all people equally; P: It is futile to preach the ideal of equality; U: It is futile to preach the ideal of universal love)

7. You can walk to the door only if you can walk to the halfway point between yourself and the door. But unfortunately, you can walk to the halfway point between yourself and the door only if you can walk to a point *halfway* to the halfway point! Now, if you cannot walk halfway to the halfway point only if you cannot walk to the door, then you can walk to the door only if you can perform an infinite number of acts in a finite period of time. Obviously, you cannot perform an infinite number of acts in a finite period of time. So, as Zeno of Elea concluded, in spite of what your senses may tell you, you cannot walk to the door. (D: You can walk to the door; H: You can walk to the halfway point between yourself and the door; P: You can walk halfway to the halfway point; F: You can perform an infinite number of acts in a finite period of time)

8. This is the best of all possible worlds. For God exists; and if God is not both morally perfect and omnipotent, then God does not exist. Now, if God is omnipotent, God can create just any possible world. And if God is morally perfect, God will create the best possible world if He can create it. And God can create the best of all possible worlds if and only if God can create just any possible world. Moreover, this is the best of all possible worlds given that God will create the best of all possible worlds. (G: God exists; M: God is morally perfect; O: God is omnipotent; A: God can create just any possible world; W: God will create the best possible world; C: God can create the best possible world; B: This is the best of all possible worlds)

9. God cannot know the future free acts of his creatures if God is in time. For if God is in time, God's knowledge of the future is a prediction based on the past and present. However, if humans have free will, then their future acts are not infallibly predictable based on the past and the present. If the future acts of humans are not infallibly predictable based on the past and the present, then God cannot know the future free acts of his creatures if God is in time. Finally, if humans do not have free will, then God's knowledge of the future is not a prediction based on the past and the present. (T: God is in time; P: God's knowledge of the future is a prediction based on the past and present; F: Humans have free will; I: The future acts of humans are infallibly predictable based on the past and present; K: God can know the future free acts of his creatures)

10. All inductive arguments presuppose that the unobserved resembles the observed. (For example, "All observed emeralds have been green; therefore, the next emerald to be found will be green.") Given that all inductive arguments presuppose that the unobserved resembles the observed, induction is unjustified unless we have good reason to believe that the unobserved resembles the observed. If we have good reason to believe that the unobserved resembles the observed, then either we have a good deductive argument or a good inductive argument. We have a good inductive argument only if not all inductive arguments presuppose that the unobserved resembles the observed. We have a good deductive argument only if valid reasoning can begin with the observed and end with the unobserved. Sad to say, valid reasoning cannot begin with the observed and end with the unobserved. It thus appears that David Hume's skeptical conclusion is inescapable: induction is unjustified. [*Hint:* In symbolizing the argument, ignore the parenthetical remark.] (P: All inductive arguments presuppose that the unobserved resembles the observed; J: Induction is justified; R: We have good reason to believe that the unobserved resembles the observed; D: We have a good deductive argument; I: We have a good inductive argument; V: Valid reasoning can begin with the observed and end with the unobserved)

8.4 Conditional Proof

Consider the following argument.

> 32. If Hank is a horse, then Hank is not a bird. So, if Hank is a horse, then Hank is a horse and not a bird. (H: Hank is a horse; B: Hank is a bird)

This argument may seem a bit odd, but it is plainly valid. Its form is as follows:

> 33. $H \rightarrow {\sim}B \therefore H \rightarrow (H \cdot {\sim}B)$

Unfortunately, we cannot prove that the argument is valid using only our system of 18 rules.[4] In fact, to make our system of statement logic complete, we need to add one further element, a proof procedure called "conditional proof" (CP for short). Without this proof procedure (or some equivalent addition to our system), we would be unable to construct proofs for many valid arguments. And, as it turns out, CP also greatly simplifies many proofs that could in principle be done without it but would require much ingenuity.

The basic idea behind CP is that *we can prove a conditional true by assuming that its antecedent is true and showing that its consequent can be derived from this assumption* (together with whatever premises are available). For example, take argument (33). We have $H \rightarrow {\sim}B$ as a premise. We need to show that the premise validly implies the conclusion, which is a conditional statement: $H \rightarrow (H \cdot {\sim}B)$. We assume H, the antecedent of the conclusion. Now, from the assumption H and the premise $H \rightarrow {\sim}B$, we can derive ${\sim}B$ by *modus ponens*. And from the assumption H and ${\sim}B$, we can obtain $H \cdot {\sim}B$ by conjunction. This shows that the antecedent, H, of the conditional conclusion leads logically to its consequent, $H \cdot {\sim}B$, given the premise. Therefore, the argument is valid.

Now, we need to formalize this intuitive proof technique. This means we need a way to include assumptions in our proofs, bearing in mind that an assumption is not a premise. In fact, since conditionals are hypothetical, the antecedent of a conditional may be false (and may be admitted to be false by the arguer) even though the conditional itself is true. So, we need a way of using assumptions temporarily—a way that keeps it clear that we are not treating them as premises. As an example, the formal proof of argument (33) would look like this:

1. $H \rightarrow {\sim}B$	$\therefore H \rightarrow (H \cdot {\sim}B)$
2. H	Assume
3. ${\sim}B$	1, 2, MP
4. $H \cdot {\sim}B$	2, 3, Conj
5. $H \rightarrow (H \cdot {\sim}B)$	2–4, CP

The word "Assume" indicates the special status of H. The box indicates the *scope* of the assumption (i.e., the part of the proof in which the assumption is made). The steps from line (2) to line (4) do not prove that $H \cdot {\sim}B$ follows from the argument's premise. (They *would* prove this if H were a premise and not a mere assumption.) Rather, lines (2) through (4) show only that $H \cdot {\sim}B$ is true *on the assumption that H is true*. We box the steps in and enter line (5) to make it clear that only a conditional conclusion has been established. The annotation of line (5) mentions the steps falling within the scope of the assumption, as well as the type of proof used (CP). It is crucial to note that line (5) follows logically from the premise of the argument, namely, $H \rightarrow {\sim}B$. We haven't added a premise to the argument in line (2). We have merely introduced a temporary assumption for the purpose of proving that the *conditional* conclusion follows from the premise.

Using Greek letters as statement variables, we can make a diagram of conditional proof as follows:

Premises

$$\begin{array}{ll} \boxed{\begin{array}{l} p \\ \cdot \\ \cdot \\ \cdot \\ q \end{array}} & \text{Assume} \\[4pt] p \rightarrow q & \text{CP} \end{array}$$

The vertical dots here stand for inferences from the premises and the assumption. In the typical case, $(p \rightarrow q)$ is the conclusion of the argument, though as we will see, this is not necessarily the case.

Let's consider another example:

34. If most Americans favor gun control, then if lobbies block gun control proposals, democracy is hindered. If most Americans favor gun control, then lobbies do block gun control proposals. Therefore, if most Americans favor gun control, democracy is hindered. (M: Most Americans favor gun control; L: Lobbies block gun control proposals; D: Democracy is hindered)

$$\begin{array}{lll} 1. & M \rightarrow (L \rightarrow D) & \\ 2. & M \rightarrow L & \qquad \therefore \ M \rightarrow D \\ 3. & M & \text{Assume} \\ 4. & L \rightarrow D & 1, 3, \text{MP} \\ 5. & L & 2, 3, \text{MP} \\ 6. & D & 4, 5, \text{MP} \\ 7. & M \rightarrow D & 3\text{--}6, \text{CP} \end{array}$$

Notice that it would be a mistake to suppose that the statements within the box have been shown to follow from the premises alone. We box the statements in precisely to remind ourselves of their tentative status, dependent as they are on the assumption in line (3). We stop making our assumption at line (7). And our proof shows that line (7) follows logically from the premises—that is, lines (1) and (2).

When you are making an assumption for the purpose of conditional proof, always select the *antecedent* of the conditional statement that you are trying to obtain. CP is often useful when the conclusion of an argument is a conditional statement. So, we can state the following rule of thumb:

> **Rule of Thumb 9:** If the conclusion of an argument is a conditional statement, use CP.

For instance, consider the following symbolic argument:

35. $\sim S \rightarrow W$, $\sim R \rightarrow U$, $(U \vee W) \rightarrow T$ $\therefore$ $\sim(S \cdot R) \rightarrow (T \vee Z)$

Because the conclusion of this argument is a conditional statement, CP is a good method to try. And we should assume the *antecedent* of the conclusion, $\sim(S \cdot R)$. Accordingly, the proof looks like this:

1. $\sim S \rightarrow W$	
2. $\sim R \rightarrow U$	
3. $(U \vee W) \rightarrow T$	$\therefore$ $\sim(S \cdot R) \rightarrow (T \vee Z)$
4. $\sim(S \cdot R)$	Assume
5. $\sim S \vee \sim R$	4, DeM
6. $W \vee U$	5, 1, 2, CD
7. $U \vee W$	6, Com
8. T	3, 7, MP
9. $T \vee Z$	8, Add
10. $\sim(S \cdot R) \rightarrow (T \vee Z)$	4–9, CP

Again, we box in the lines of the proof that fall within the *scope* of the assumption (the part of the proof in which the assumption is made). These lines tell us that if we have $\sim(S \cdot R)$, then we can obtain $T \vee Z$. The boxed-in steps are *hypothetical* in nature, for they depend on the assumption in line (4). We stop making our assumption at line (10). And our proof shows that line (10) follows validly from the premises—that is, lines (1), (2), and (3).

So far, we have considered cases in which only one assumption is introduced. But sometimes it is helpful to introduce more than one assumption—for example, when you are trying to prove a conditional whose *consequent* is a conditional. Here is an example:

36. If space travelers from another galaxy visit Earth, then aliens will rule us if our technology is inferior. But if our technology is inferior and aliens will rule us, then our liberty will decrease. So, if space travelers from another galaxy visit Earth, then our liberty will decrease if our technology is inferior. (S: Space

travelers from another galaxy visit Earth; A: Aliens will rule us; T: Our technology is inferior; L: Our liberty will decrease)

We symbolize the argument and begin a conditional proof in line (3). But having derived line (4), we "get stuck"—there seems to be no useful move to make.

$$1. \; S \rightarrow (T \rightarrow A)$$
$$2. \; (T \cdot A) \rightarrow L \qquad \therefore \; S \rightarrow (T \rightarrow L)$$
$$3. \; S \qquad \text{Assume}$$
$$4. \; T \rightarrow A \qquad 1, 3, \text{MP}$$

We note, however, that the conditional we are trying to obtain has a conditional as its consequent, namely, $T \rightarrow L$. So, we make a second assumption (again, the antecedent of a conditional), like this:

$$1. \; S \rightarrow (T \rightarrow A)$$
$$2. \; (T \cdot A) \rightarrow L \qquad \therefore \; S \rightarrow (T \rightarrow L)$$
$$3. \; S \qquad \text{Assume}$$
$$4. \; T \rightarrow A \qquad 1, 3, \text{MP}$$
$$5. \; T \qquad \text{Assume}$$
$$6. \; A \qquad 4, 5, \text{MP}$$
$$7. \; T \cdot A \qquad 5, 6, \text{Conj}$$
$$8. \; L \qquad 2, 7, \text{MP}$$
$$9. \; T \rightarrow L \qquad 5–8, \text{CP}$$

Now, at this point, we have shown that if T, then L, for by assuming T, we were able to obtain L. But all of this occurs within the scope of our first assumption (i.e., S), and a proof is always incomplete as long as we are still making an assumption. Furthermore, we have not yet reached the conclusion of the argument, so we need one additional step:

$$1. \; S \rightarrow (T \rightarrow A)$$
$$2. \; (T \cdot A) \rightarrow L \qquad \therefore \; S \rightarrow (T \rightarrow L)$$
$$3. \; S \qquad \text{Assume}$$
$$4. \; T \rightarrow A \qquad 1, 3, \text{MP}$$
$$5. \; T \qquad \text{Assume}$$
$$6. \; A \qquad 4, 5, \text{MP}$$
$$7. \; T \cdot A \qquad 5, 6, \text{Conj}$$
$$8. \; L \qquad 2, 7, \text{MP}$$
$$9. \; T \rightarrow L \qquad 5–8, \text{CP}$$
$$10. \; S \rightarrow (T \rightarrow L) \qquad 3–9, \text{CP}$$

Lines (3) through (9) indicate that if we have S, we can obtain $T \rightarrow L$. In other words, the proof shows that line (10) follows logically from the premises—that is, lines (1) and (2). So, the argument is valid.

Here is the place to issue two important warnings: First, because the statements within the boxes are dependent on assumptions, we cannot make use of boxed-in statements in later parts of a proof. For example, in the previous proof, it may appear that we could write L on line (9) by applying *modus ponens* to lines (7) and (2), but line (7) is available only because of the assumption in line (5). And the box indicates that we *discharged* (i.e., ceased to make) that assumption when we got to line (9). So, we cannot make use of line (7) in subsequent parts of the proof. In general, boxed-in lines cannot be used to justify later steps in a proof, for the boxes indicate that we have ceased to make the assumption in question. Second, no proof involving CP is complete until all assumptions are discharged.

It should be noted that CP is sometimes useful even when the conclusion of the argument is not a conditional. Here is an example:

37. If God stops people from performing acts that cause unnecessary suffering, then *either* God denies creatures a choice between good and evil *or* God can cause the free acts of his creatures. If God can cause the free acts of his creatures, then the concept of free will is empty. The concept of free will is not empty. So, either God does not stop people from performing acts that cause unnecessary suffering or else God denies creatures a real choice between good and evil. (S: God stops people from performing acts that cause unnecessary suffering; G: God denies creatures a choice between good and evil; F: God can cause the free acts of his creatures; W: The concept of free will is empty)

We symbolize the argument and begin a conditional proof in line (4). This makes sense if one realizes that the conclusion, $\sim S \vee G$, is logically equivalent to $S \rightarrow G$.

```
1. S → (G ∨ F)
2. F → W
3. ~W              ∴  ~S ∨ G
 ┌ 4. S            Assume
 │ 5. G ∨ F        1, 4, MP
 │ 6. ~F           2, 3, MT
 └ 7. G            5, 6, DS
   8. S → G        4–7, CP
   9. ~S ∨ G       8, MI
```

Note that *by CP we always obtain a conditional,* and this case is no exception. Lines (4) through (7) establish $S \rightarrow G$. We then apply MI to obtain the conclusion of the argument.

CP can be used when the conclusion of an argument is a biconditional. For example:

38. $(B \vee A) \rightarrow C, A \rightarrow \sim C, \sim A \rightarrow B \therefore B \leftrightarrow C$

The basic strategy is to prove two conditionals, conjoin them, and then use ME:

```
    1. (B ∨ A) → C
    2. A → ~C
    3. ~A → B                        ∴ B ↔ C
   ┌ 4. B                            Assume
   │  5. B ∨ A                       4, Add
   └  6. C                           1, 5, MP
    7. B → C                         4–6, CP
   ┌ 8. C                            Assume
   │  9. ~~C                         8, DN
   │ 10. ~A                          2, 9, MT
   └ 11. B                           3, 10, MP
   12. C → B                         8–11, CP
   13. (B → C) • (C → B)             7, 12, Conj
   14. B ↔ C                         13, ME
```

Note that although two assumptions are made in this proof, neither falls within the scope of the other. So, at line (13), we are free to conjoin lines (7) and (12).

It is possible to construct a direct proof for the previous argument, a **direct proof** being one that makes no use of assumptions. (Try it!) The direct proof is slightly longer than the one just presented, but more importantly, the direct proof is less intuitive, as it involves the use of MI. We have noted more than once that MI is not an intuitive rule when applied to some English conditionals. Accordingly, it is reassuring that we can often construct a conditional proof without MI when a direct proof would require an application of MI.

Conditional proof renders our system of statement logic complete. Whatever can be proved valid through the truth tables can be proved valid using our 18 inference rules and CP. It is interesting to note that some systems achieve completeness in a different way, by adding the rule of *absorption*, which countenances inferences from $p \rightarrow q$ to $p \rightarrow (p \cdot q)$. However, CP tends to make proofs both shorter and more intuitive than absorption does.[5]

Note: As you complete the following exercises, it may be helpful to refer to the summary of rules of thumb for constructing proofs, appearing on page 296.

◆ *Exercise 8.4*

Part A: Conditional Proof Use CP (together with the 18 rules of inference) to show that each of the following symbolic arguments is valid.

* **1.** $Z \rightarrow (\sim Y \rightarrow X), Z \rightarrow \sim Y \therefore Z \rightarrow X$

  2. $P \rightarrow Q \therefore P \rightarrow (Q \vee R)$

  3. $(F \vee \sim G) \rightarrow \sim L \therefore L \rightarrow G$

* **4.** $A \rightarrow B, A \rightarrow C \therefore A \rightarrow (B \cdot C)$

  5. $(H \vee E) \rightarrow K \therefore E \rightarrow K$

  6. $(B \rightarrow \sim C) \rightarrow D \therefore B \rightarrow (\sim C \rightarrow D)$

* 7. P ∴ (P → Q) → Q

   8. S ∴ ~(S • R) → ~R

   9. (G → H) → J ∴ H → J

* 10. C → (~D → E), (D → ~D) → (E → G) ∴ C → (~D → G)

   11. H → (J • K), ~L → (J • M) ∴ (~L ∨ H) → J

   12. ~X ∨ (O • W), (X → O) → (W → X) ∴ W → X

* 13. (A ∨ N) → ~S, M → [N → (S • T)] ∴ ~(~M ∨ ~N) → (S • ~A)

   14. ~P ∨ (Q • ~R) ∴ (R ∨ R) → ~P

   15. (S ∨ T) ↔ ~E, S → (F • ~G), A → W, T → ~W ∴ (~E • A) → ~G

* 16. A → (B → C) ∴ (A → B) → (A → C)

   17. (G • P) → K, E → Z, ~P → ~Z, G → (E ∨ L) ∴ (G • ~L) → K

   18. S → (~T → U), ~T → (U → O) ∴ ~S ∨ [(T → ~T) → O]

* 19. A → (B • C), B → D, C → ~D ∴ A → X

   20. B → [(E • ~G) → M], ~(~E ∨ G) → (M → R) ∴ B → [~(~G → ~E) → R]

Part B: English Arguments   Symbolize the following arguments, using the schemes of abbreviation provided. Then use CP to show that the arguments are valid.

* 1. If Jones doesn't vote, then he shouldn't vote. For after all, if Jones doesn't vote, then either he lacks intelligence or he lacks a proper value system. And Jones shouldn't vote if he lacks intelligence. Furthermore, Jones shouldn't vote if he lacks a proper value system. (V: Jones does vote; I: Jones has intelligence; P: Jones has a proper value system; S: Jones should vote)

   2. Euthanasia is wrong if either the patient prefers to go on living or she still maintains her higher faculties. Therefore, if the patient still maintains her higher faculties, then euthanasia is wrong. (P: The patient prefers to go on living; F: The patient maintains her higher faculties; E: Euthanasia is wrong)

   3. If we should forgive our enemies, then it is wrong to punish criminals. For if we should forgive our enemies, then we should forget the offense and behave as if the offense never occurred. And we should punish criminals if and only if we should not behave as if the offense never occurred. Furthermore, it is wrong to punish criminals if and only if we should not punish criminals. (F: We should forgive our enemies; W: It is wrong to punish criminals; O: We should forget the offense; B: We should behave as if the offense never occurred; S: We should punish criminals)

   4. If God believes on Monday that I'll tell a lie on Tuesday, then either I have the power to make one of God's past beliefs false or I cannot refrain from lying on Tuesday. I do not have the power to make one of God's past beliefs false if either God is infallible or the past is unalterable. The past is unalterable. It follows that if God believes on Monday that I'll tell a lie on Tuesday, then I cannot refrain from lying on Tuesday. (B: God believes on Monday that I'll tell a lie on Tuesday; F: I have the

power to make one of God's past beliefs false; R: I can refrain from lying on Tuesday; I: God is infallible; P: The past is unalterable)

5. If humans lack free will, then there is no moral responsibility. Materialism is true if and only if only matter exists. Assuming that only matter exists, every event is the result of past states of the world plus the operation of natural laws. Now, if every event is the result of past states of the world plus the operation of natural laws, then human acts are under human control only if either humans have control over the past or humans have control over the natural laws. Humans do not have control over the past, and they do not have control over the natural laws. Finally, if human acts are not under human control, then humans do not have free will. We may conclude that if materialism is true, then there is no moral responsibility. (F: Humans have free will; R: There is moral responsibility; M: Materialism is true; O: Only matter exists; E: Every event is the result of past states of the world plus the operation of natural laws; C: Human acts are under human control; P: Humans have control over the past; N: Humans have control over the natural laws)

Part C: Valid or Invalid?   Symbolize the following arguments. If an argument is invalid, prove this by means of an abbreviated truth table. If an argument is valid, construct a proof to demonstrate its validity.

1. If either moral judgments are products of biological causes or moral judgments are not based on empirical evidence, then morality is not objective. But if moral judgments are not products of biological causes, then moral judgments are not based on empirical evidence. Hence, morality is not objective. (M: Moral judgments are products of biological causes; E: Moral judgments are based on empirical evidence; O: Morality is objective)

2. It is false that if we continue to use gasoline, then the air will not be polluted. Either we do not continue to use gasoline or we use solar power. If we continue to use gasoline and air-pollution control devices are perfected, then the air will not be polluted. Therefore, we use solar power if and only if air-pollution control devices are perfected. (G: We continue to use gasoline; A: The air will be polluted; S: We use solar power; P: Air-pollution control devices are perfected)

3. Given that Henri Rousseau's *The Dream* is pornographic if and only if Rousseau painted it with the intention of inciting lust in the viewers, Rousseau's *The Dream* is not pornographic. For Rousseau painted it with the intention of inciting lust in the viewers only if every nude painting is painted with the intention of inciting lust in the viewers. And the latter suggestion is wildly false! (P: Henri Rousseau's *The Dream* is pornographic; L: Rousseau painted *The Dream* with the intention of inciting lust in the viewers; N: Every nude painting is painted with the intention of inciting lust in the viewers)

4. If Boethius is morally virtuous, then he achieves heaven. But if he isn't morally virtuous, then his longings are satisfied. On the other hand, if Boethius doesn't achieve heaven, then his longings are not satisfied. So, Boethius's longings are satisfied. (M: Boethius is morally virtuous; H: Boethius achieves heaven; L: Boethius's longings are satisfied)

5. Either God has a reason for his commands or morality is ultimately arbitrary. If God has a reason for his commands, then reasons that are independent of God's will make actions right. Consequently, reasons that are independent of God's will make actions right provided that morality is not ultimately arbitrary. (R: God has a reason for his commands; M: Morality is ultimately arbitrary; I: Reasons that are independent of God's will make actions right)

8.5 Reductio ad Absurdum

Although our system of statement logic is already complete, we will add one more technique that simplifies proofs in many cases. This is the method of *reductio ad absurdum* (RAA for short). The basic principle behind the RAA method of proof is this: *Whatever implies a contradiction is false*. Using the italicized, lower-case letters *p* and *q* as statement variables (which can stand for any statement), we can see that RAA is closely related to *modus tollens*. Suppose we know that a given statement ~*p* implies a contradiction:

39. $\sim p \rightarrow (q \cdot \sim q)$

Now, we know that contradictions are false. So, we also know this:

40. $\sim (q \cdot \sim q)$

But then, if we apply *modus tollens* to (39) and (40), we get ~~*p*, and hence *p* by DN. This is the essential logic underlying a *reductio ad absurdum* proof. Since ~*p* leads to (or "reduces" to) a logical absurdity (i.e., a contradiction), ~*p* must be false, and hence *p* is true. Now, in practice, the contradiction does not usually follow from a single statement all by itself. Rather, the contradiction usually follows from the premises of the argument (which are taken as true for the purpose of establishing validity) *together with* the temporary assumption, ~*p*, where *p* is the conclusion of the argument.

   Look at it this way. Suppose we have three statements that together imply a contradiction. For instance:

$\sim A \rightarrow (B \cdot \sim C)$
$B \rightarrow C$
$\sim A$

Using MP, Simp, and Conj, one can derive C • ~C from these statements in only a few steps. Because these statements imply a contradiction, we know that at least one of them is false. Now, given that the first two statements are true, we can conclude that ~A is false, and hence that A is true. This reasoning shows the following argument to be valid:

41. $\sim A \rightarrow (B \cdot \sim C), B \rightarrow C \therefore A$

The formal proof runs as follows:

```
  1. ~A → (B • ~C)
  2. B → C              ∴ A
┌ 3. ~A                 Assume
│ 4. B • ~C             1, 3, MP
│ 5. B                  4, Simp
│ 6. C                  2, 5, MP
│ 7. ~C                 4, Simp
└ 8. C • ~C             6, 7, Conj
  9. A                  3–8, RAA
```

For the purpose of establishing the *validity* of an argument, the truth of the premises is a given. So, since the premises, together with ~A, imply a contradiction, we may conclude that ~A is false, and hence that A is true. As with CP, we box in the lines that fall within the scope of the assumption and add line (9) to indicate that A follows, not from our assumption but from the premises of the argument. The annotation for line (9) mentions the lines falling within the scope of the assumption and adds "RAA" for *reductio ad absurdum*.

When the conclusion of an argument is the *negation* of a statement, (e.g., ~B), your assumption line should usually be the statement itself (in this case, B) rather than a double-negation. This procedure will usually save some steps. For example, consider the following proof:

```
  1. B ↔ ~A
  2. ~A → ~C
  3. C ∨ D
  4. ~C → ~D            ∴ ~B
┌ 5. B                  Assume
│ 6. (B → ~A) • (~A → B)  1, ME
│ 7. B → ~A             6, Simp
│ 8. ~A                 5, 7, MP
│ 9. ~C                 8, 2, MP
│ 10. D                 9, 3, DS
│ 11. ~D                9, 4, MP
└ 12. D • ~D            10, 11, Conj
  13. ~B                5–12, RAA
```

Note that in line (5), we assume B rather than ~~B. It wouldn't be a logical error to assume ~~B, but it would add an unnecessary step. (We'd have to apply DN to drop the double-negation prior to performing a *modus ponens* step.)

Thus, an RAA proof may proceed in two ways. When we are trying to prove a negation, we obtain our assumption line simply by dropping the tilde. When we are trying to prove a statement that is not a negation, we obtain our assumption line by *adding* a tilde sign. Using Greek letters as statement variables, we can make a diagram of these two forms of RAA as follows:

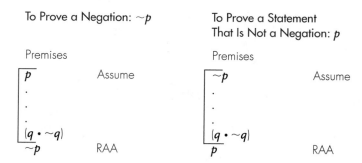

The procedure is essentially the same in both cases: We show that a statement (together with the premises) implies a contradiction and conclude that the statement is false. Note: As with CP, no proof involving RAA is complete until all assumptions have been discharged.

Many proofs are simplified when the RAA method is employed. Consider the following symbolic argument and the proofs provided for it.

42. ~F → G, S ∨ (G • R), ~S ∨ ~F ∴ G

The proof on the top is a direct proof (one that does not involve any assumptions). The proof on the bottom employs the RAA method.

1. ~F → G
2. S ∨ (G • R)
3. ~S ∨ ~F   ∴ G
4. S → ~F   3, MI
5. S → G   1, 4, HS
6. ~~S ∨ (G • R)   2, DN
7. ~S → (G • R)   6, MI
8. ~G → ~S   5, Cont
9. ~G → (G • R)   7, 8, HS
10. ~~G ∨ (G • R)   9, MI
11. G ∨ (G • R)   10, DN
12. (G ∨ G) • (G ∨ R)   11, Dist
13. G ∨ G   12, Simp
14. G   13, Re

1. ~F → G
2. S ∨ (G • R)
3. ~S ∨ ~F   ∴ G
4. ~G   Assume
5. ~~F   4, 1, MT
6. ~S   5, 3, DS
7. G • R   6, 2, DS
8. G   7, Simp
9. G • ~G   4, 8, Conj
10. G   4–9, RAA

A close inspection of these two proofs reveals that the proof on the bottom, which employs RAA, is not only shorter but also more intuitive than the direct proof on the top. This suggests the following rule of thumb:

> Rule of Thumb 10: If the conclusion of an argument is not a conditional, and direct proof is long or difficult, try RAA.

(Of course, if the conclusion of the argument is a conditional statement, CP is usually the best strategy.)

RAA and CP are closely related from a theoretical standpoint. For example, we can always use CP whenever we use RAA. To illustrate, consider the following proofs:

1. $\sim P \to (Q \cdot R)$		
2. $R \to \sim Q$	$\therefore$ P	
3. $\sim P$	Assume	
4. $Q \cdot R$	1, 3, MP	
5. R	4, Simp	
6. $\sim Q$	2, 5, MP	
7. Q	4, Simp	
8. $Q \lor P$	7, Add	
9. P	6, 8, DS	
10. $\sim P \to P$	3–9, CP	
11. $\sim\sim P \lor P$	10, MI	
12. $P \lor P$	11, DN	
13. P	12, Re	

Note: As with CP, because the statements within the boxes of an RAA proof are dependent on assumptions, we cannot make use of boxed-in statements in *later* parts of a proof.

1. $\sim P \to (Q \cdot R)$	
2. $R \to \sim Q$	$\therefore$ P
3. $\sim P$	Assume
4. $Q \cdot R$	1, 3, MP
5. R	4, Simp
6. $\sim Q$	2, 5, MP
7. Q	4, Simp
8. $Q \cdot \sim Q$	6, 7, Conj
9. P	3–8, RAA

Note that the CP on the top is exactly like the RAA proof down to line (7). The remaining steps are characteristic of ones we could employ *whenever we have derived a contradiction from an assumption*. So, there is a close theoretical relationship between CP and RAA. RAA proofs, however, will typically be shorter *except when* the conclusion of the argument is a conditional.

It is also worth noting that in principle, we could dispense with CP and use RAA to complete our system of statement logic, for RAA works whenever CP works. To illustrate, consider the following RAA proof for an argument having a conditional as its conclusion:

Summary of Rules of Thumb for Constructing Proofs

1. It usually helps to work backward. So, start by looking at the conclusion. Try to find the conclusion (or elements thereof) in the premises.
2. Apply the inference rules to break the premises down.
3. If the conclusion contains a statement letter that does not appear in the premises, use the rule of addition.
4. It is often useful to consider logically equivalent forms of the conclusion.
5. Both conjunction and addition can lead to useful applications of De Morgan's laws.
6. Material implication can lead to useful applications of distribution.
7. Distribution can lead to useful applications of simplification.
8. Addition can lead to useful applications of material implication.
9. If the conclusion of an argument is a conditional statement, use CP.
10. If the conclusion of an argument is not a conditional, and direct proof is long or difficult, try RAA.

$$
\begin{array}{lll}
1. & Z \rightarrow (\sim Y \rightarrow X) & \\
2. & Z \rightarrow \sim Y & \therefore\ Z \rightarrow X \\
3. & \sim(Z \rightarrow X) & \text{Assume} \\
4. & \sim(\sim Z \vee X) & 3, \text{MI} \\
5. & \sim\sim Z \cdot \sim X & 4, \text{DeM} \\
6. & \sim\sim Z & 5, \text{Simp} \\
7. & Z & 6, \text{DN} \\
8. & \sim Y & 7, 2, \text{MP} \\
9. & \sim Y \rightarrow X & 7, 1, \text{MP} \\
10. & X & 8, 9, \text{MP} \\
11. & \sim X & 5, \text{Simp} \\
12. & X \cdot \sim X & 10, 11, \text{Conj} \\
13. & Z \rightarrow X & 3\text{--}12, \text{RAA}
\end{array}
$$

While from a purely theoretical standpoint we do not need both CP *and* RAA, both are intuitive methods of proof, and both are quite useful. Thus, it is important to be able to employ both of them. In this regard, we can note that it is easy to construct a *seven*-step CP proof for the previous argument, a fact that underscores Rule of Thumb 9: If the conclusion of an argument is a conditional, use CP.

It is possible to combine RAA and CP, and in some cases the combination is helpful. Consider an example:

$$
\begin{array}{lll}
1. & A \rightarrow (B \vee C) & \\
2. & D \rightarrow \sim C & \therefore\ A \rightarrow \sim(D \cdot \sim B) \\
3. & A & \text{Assume (for CP)} \\
4. & B \vee C & 1, 3, \text{MP}
\end{array}
$$

In line (3), we begin a conditional proof. But we get stuck at line (4): There seems to be no useful move to make. We note, however, that having begun a CP proof, we need to obtain the *consequent* of the conditional in question, namely, $\sim(D \cdot \sim B)$. If we assume $D \cdot \sim B$ and derive a contradiction, we will have shown that $\sim(D \cdot \sim B)$ must be true given that A is true. The entire proof looks like this:

1. $A \rightarrow (B \vee C)$		
2. $D \rightarrow \sim C$	$\therefore\ A \rightarrow \sim(D \cdot \sim B)$	
3. A	Assume (for CP)	
4. $B \vee C$	1, 3, MP	
5. $D \cdot \sim B$	Assume (for RAA)	
6. D	5, Simp	
7. $\sim C$	2, 6, MP	
8. $\sim B$	5, Simp	
9. C	8, 4, DS	
10. $C \cdot \sim C$	9, 7, Conj	
11. $\sim(D \cdot \sim B)$	5–10, RAA	
12. $A \rightarrow \sim(D \cdot \sim B)$	3–11, CP	

Here, our RAA proof falls within the scope of a CP proof.

As you complete the exercises for this section, you may find the summary of rules of thumb helpful.

◆ Exercise 8.5

Part A: Proofs Construct proofs to show that the following symbolic arguments are valid. Use only RAA.

* 1. $A \rightarrow B \therefore \sim(A \cdot \sim B)$
  2. $P \rightarrow Q, \sim P \rightarrow J, \sim Q \rightarrow \sim J \therefore Q$
  3. $F \rightarrow G, F \vee G \therefore G$
* 4. $(H \vee R) \cdot (H \vee \sim R) \therefore H$
  5. $(M \rightarrow L) \rightarrow M \therefore M$
  6. $\sim P \leftrightarrow Q,\ \sim(Q \vee R), (P \cdot \sim R) \rightarrow S \therefore S$
* 7. $Z \rightarrow (X \vee Y), X \rightarrow \sim W, Y \rightarrow \sim W, \sim W \rightarrow \sim Z \therefore \sim Z$
  8. $E \vee T, T \rightarrow (B \cdot H), (B \vee E) \rightarrow K \therefore K$
  9. $(O \vee N) \rightarrow (O \cdot N) \therefore N \leftrightarrow O$
* 10. $\sim A \cdot \sim B \therefore A \leftrightarrow B$
  11. $\sim W \vee (Z \rightarrow Y), \sim X \rightarrow (W \vee Y), W \rightarrow Z \therefore Y \vee X$
  12. $\sim P \rightarrow (R \cdot S), \sim Q \rightarrow (R \cdot T), \sim(S \vee T) \therefore P \cdot Q$
* 13. $D \rightarrow \sim(A \vee B), \sim C \rightarrow D \therefore A \rightarrow C$
  14. $E \therefore (E \cdot H) \vee (E \cdot \sim H)$
  15. $\sim Q \rightarrow (L \rightarrow F), Q \rightarrow \sim A, F \rightarrow B, L \therefore \sim A \vee B$

* 16. $W \rightarrow (X \vee G), G \rightarrow M, \sim M \therefore \sim W \vee X$
  17. $(\sim H \vee K) \cdot (\sim H \vee L), \sim N \rightarrow H, \sim N \rightarrow (\sim L \vee \sim K), P \leftrightarrow N$
     $\therefore S \rightarrow P$
  18. $C \rightarrow (D \rightarrow H), D \cdot \sim H, H \vee T \therefore \sim C \cdot T$
* 19. $\sim S \rightarrow (T \cdot U), \sim R \rightarrow \sim (T \vee U), (T \leftrightarrow U) \rightarrow (\sim \sim S \cdot R) \therefore R \cdot S$
  20. $(A \rightarrow B) \rightarrow (C \rightarrow A) \therefore C \rightarrow A$

Part B: Valid or Invalid?   For each of the following pairs of arguments, one is valid and one is invalid. Use an abbreviated truth table to determine which argument is invalid. Then construct a proof to show that the other member of the pair is valid using either RAA or CP.

* 1. $(F \rightarrow G) \rightarrow H \therefore F \rightarrow (G \rightarrow H)$
* 2. $F \rightarrow (G \rightarrow H) \therefore (F \rightarrow G) \rightarrow H$
  3. $\sim L \rightarrow L, \sim L \leftrightarrow N \therefore \sim N$
  4. $(E \cdot F) \rightarrow G \therefore F \rightarrow G$
  5. $(\sim D \vee H) \cdot (\sim D \vee \sim P), \sim D \rightarrow S, (H \cdot P) \rightarrow \sim U \therefore S \vee \sim U$
  6. $\sim (S \rightarrow R) \therefore S \cdot \sim R$
  7. $(Z \vee Y) \cdot (Z \vee W) \therefore Z \cdot (Y \vee W)$
  8. $P \rightarrow \sim Q \therefore Q \rightarrow \sim P$
  9. $\sim S \rightarrow (F \rightarrow L), F \rightarrow (L \rightarrow P) \therefore \sim S \rightarrow (F \rightarrow P)$
  10. $A \rightarrow (B \vee C) \therefore (A \rightarrow B) \cdot (\sim A \vee C)$

Part C: English Arguments   Symbolize the following arguments using the schemes of abbreviation provided. Then construct proofs to show that the arguments are valid. Use only RAA.

* 1. If the rate of literacy has declined, then either TV or parental neglect is the cause. If TV is the cause, then we can't increase literacy unless we can get rid of TV. If parental neglect is the cause, then we can't increase literacy unless we are willing to support early childhood education with our tax dollars. The rate of literacy has declined, but we can't get rid of TV and we certainly aren't willing to support early childhood education with our tax dollars. So, we can't increase literacy. (R: The rate of literacy has declined; T: TV is the cause of the decline in the rate of literacy; P: Parental neglect is the cause of the decline in the rate of literacy; L: We can increase literacy; C: We can get rid of TV; W: We are willing to support early childhood education with our tax dollars)

  2. Either vegetarians are misguided, or factory farming is cruel and the grain fed to animals could save thousands of starving people. Vegetarians are misguided only if feeding grain to animals is an efficient way to make protein. And if the grain fed to animals could save thousands of starving people, then American consumers are

insensitive if they insist on eating meat at the current rate. American consumers insist on eating meat at the current rate. Therefore, either American consumers are insensitive or feeding grain to animals is an efficient way to make protein. (V: Vegetarians are misguided; F: Factory farming is cruel; G: The grain fed to animals could save thousands of starving people; E: Feeding grain to animals is an efficient way to make protein; A: American consumers are insensitive; M: American consumers insist on eating meat at the current rate)

3. We should maximize the general welfare if and only if utilitarianism is true. If we should maximize the general welfare, we should promote the greatest sum of pleasure. If we should promote the greatest sum of pleasure, then we are morally obligated to increase the size of the population provided that we can increase the size of the population without reducing the standard of living. We can increase the size of the population without reducing the standard of living, but we are not morally obligated to increase the size of the population if either increasing the size of the population will destroy the environment or no individual experiences the sum of pleasure. Obviously, no individual experiences the sum of pleasure. It follows that utilitarianism is not true. (W: We should maximize the general welfare; U: Utilitarianism is true; P: We should promote the greatest sum of pleasure; M: We are morally obligated to increase the size of the population; R: We can increase the size of the population without reducing the standard of living; E: Increasing the size of the population will destroy the environment; N: No individual experiences the sum of pleasure)

4. According to some Hindu traditions, reincarnation is true but reality is undifferentiated being. However, it is not the case that *both* reincarnation is true *and* reality is undifferentiated being. For reincarnation is true if and only if a person's soul transfers to another body at death. But if a person's soul transfers to another body at death, then each individual soul is real and each individual soul differs from all other souls. But if reality is undifferentiated being, then all apparent differences are illusory. And if each individual soul is real, then souls are not illusory. However, if each individual soul differs from all other souls and souls are not illusory, then not all apparent differences are illusory. (R: Reincarnation is true; U: Reality is undifferentiated being; T: A person's soul transfers to another body at death; E: Each individual soul is real; D: Each individual soul differs from all other souls; S: Souls are illusory; A: All apparent differences are illusory)

5. Some hold the view that while contradictions *could* be true, we happen to know that they are always false. This view is mistaken. For if contradictions could be true, then if the evidence for some statements is counterbalanced by equally strong evidence for their negations, some contradictions are true for all we know. Now, if there are areas of controversy among scholars, then the evidence for some statements is counterbalanced by equally strong evidence for their negations. And it almost goes without saying that there are areas of controversy among scholars. Finally, some contradictions are true for all we know if and only if we do not know that contradictions are always false. (C: Contradictions could be true; K: We know that contradictions are always false; E: The evidence for some statements is counterbalanced by equally strong evidence for their negations; S: Some

contradictions are true for all we know; A: There are areas of controversy among scholars)

Part D: Valid or Invalid?   Symbolize the following arguments using the schemes of abbreviation provided. If an argument is invalid, demonstrate this by means of an abbreviated truth table. (Only one of the arguments is invalid.) If an argument is valid, demonstrate this by constructing a proof. You can use either CP, RAA, or direct proof.

1. If Smith works hard, then he gets elected. But if he doesn't work hard, then he is happy. Moreover, if he doesn't get elected, then he isn't happy. We may infer that Smith gets elected. (W: Smith works hard; E: Smith gets elected; H: Smith is happy)

2. If either mathematical laws are due to arbitrary linguistic conventions or mathematical laws are not based on empirical evidence, then math is merely a game played with symbols. If mathematical laws are not based on empirical evidence, then they are not due to arbitrary linguistic conventions. So, math is merely a game played with symbols. (M: Mathematical laws are due to arbitrary linguistic conventions; E: Mathematical laws are based on empirical evidence; G: Math is merely a game played with symbols)

3. God is not outside of time if time is real. For, as St. Thomas Aquinas pointed out, if God is outside of time, then God sees all of time (past, present, and future) at a glance. But if God sees all of time at a glance, then all of time (past, present, and future) already exists. Now, if all of time already exists, then the future already exists. However, if the future already exists, then I have already committed sins that I will commit in the future. But if time is real, I have emphatically *not* already committed sins that I will commit in the future. (O: God is outside of time; S: God sees all of time at a glance; A: All of time already exists; F: The future already exists; I: I have already committed sins that I will commit in the future; T: Time is real)

4. Television has destroyed the moral fiber of our country if it has both stifled creativity and substantially interfered with communication between children and parents. Of course, television has not destroyed the moral fiber of our country assuming that our country still has moral fiber. However, one must admit that television has substantially interfered with communication between children and parents. Furthermore, the statement "Television has stifled creativity if and only if television is a good thing" is false. It follows that television is a good thing given that our country still has moral fiber. (T: Television has destroyed the moral fiber of our country; S: Television has stifled creativity; C: Television has substantially interfered with communication between children and parents; M: Our country still has moral fiber; G: Television is a good thing)

5. There is life after death if and only if there is a God. For either God exists or only matter exists. And if only matter exists, then when we die our bodies simply decay and we cease to exist permanently. Of course, if we cease to exist permanently, then there is no life after death. But God exists if and only if God is both

perfectly good and omnipotent. If God is omnipotent, God is able to raise humans from the dead. If God is perfectly good, then God wants to raise humans from the dead if resurrection is necessary for their fulfillment. Resurrection is necessary for human fulfillment if most people die with their deepest longings unsatisfied; and as a matter of fact most people do die in that condition. If God is able to *and* wants to raise humans from the dead, then there is life after death. (L: There is life after death; G: God exists; M: Only matter exists; D: When we die our bodies simply decay; E: We cease to exist permanently; P: God is perfectly good; O: God is omnipotent; A: God is able to raise humans from the dead; W: God wants to raise humans from the dead; R: Resurrection is necessary for human fulfillment; U: Most people die with their deepest longings unsatisfied)

8.6 Proving Theorems

A **theorem** is a statement that can be proved independently of any premises. The theorems of statement logic are identical with the tautologies of statement logic. (Recall that a *tautology* is a statement that is true in every row of its truth table.) Theorems belong to a class of statements that are true by virtue of their logical form. Many philosophers regard theorems as one type of necessary truth. A **necessary truth** is a truth that cannot be false under any possible circumstances.

Theorems have some rather paradoxical logical properties. For instance, any argument that has a theorem as its conclusion is valid, regardless of the information in the premises. This is so because it is impossible for a theorem to be false, and hence it is impossible for the conclusion of such an argument to be false while the premises are true. Note that this implies that each theorem is validly implied by any other theorem.

To prove a theorem, use either CP or RAA. If the theorem is itself a conditional statement, it is usually best to use CP. Here is an example:

$$\therefore \ \sim A \to [(A \lor B) \to B]$$

1.	$\sim A$	Assume
2.	$A \lor B$	Assume
3.	B	1, 2, DS
4.	$(A \lor B) \to B$	2–3, CP
5.	$\sim A \to [(A \lor B) \to B]$	1, 4, CP

The theorem itself is indicated by the triple-dot symbol. This proof shows that if we have $\sim A$, then if we have $A \lor B$, we can derive B. In other words, the proof shows that the statement beside the triple-dot symbol is indeed a theorem: It can be proved without appealing to any premises.

In some cases, RAA is the best approach. Here is a simple example:

$$\therefore \ P \vee \sim P$$

1. $\sim(P \vee \sim P)$	Assume
2. $\sim P \bullet \sim\sim P$	1, DeM
3. $P \vee \sim P$	1–2, RAA

In other cases, a combination of CP and RAA works best. For instance:

$$\therefore \ [(F \rightarrow G) \rightarrow F] \rightarrow F$$

1. $(F \rightarrow G) \rightarrow F$	Assume (for CP)
2. $\sim F$	Assume (for RAA)
3. $\sim(F \rightarrow G)$	1, 2, MT
4. $\sim(\sim F \vee G)$	3, MI
5. $\sim\sim F \bullet \sim G$	4, DeM
6. $\sim\sim F$	5, Simp
7. $\sim F \bullet \sim\sim F$	2, 6, Conj
8. F	2–7, RAA
9. $[(F \rightarrow G) \rightarrow F] \rightarrow F$	1–8, CP

Sometimes it is necessary to introduce multiple assumptions to prove a theorem. Here is an example:

$$\therefore \ (A \rightarrow (B \rightarrow C)) \rightarrow ((A \rightarrow B) \rightarrow (A \rightarrow C))$$

1. $A \rightarrow (B \rightarrow C)$	Assume
2. $A \rightarrow B$	Assume
3. A	Assume
4. B	2, 3, MP
5. $B \rightarrow C$	1, 3, MP
6. C	4, 5, MP
7. $A \rightarrow C$	3–6, CP
8. $(A \rightarrow B) \rightarrow (A \rightarrow C)$	2–7, CP
9. $(A \rightarrow (B \rightarrow C)) \rightarrow ((A \rightarrow B) \rightarrow (A \rightarrow C))$	1–8, CP

There is an important connection between valid arguments and theorems. To understand this connection, we first need the concept of a **corresponding conditional**. In the case of an argument with a single premise, one forms the corresponding conditional simply by connecting the premise and conclusion with an arrow. Here is an example:

Argument: $\sim(A \vee \sim B) \ \therefore \ B$

Corresponding conditional: $\sim(A \vee \sim B) \rightarrow B$

In the case of an argument with multiple premises, forming the corresponding conditional is a two-step process. First, one conjoins the premises—that is, one forms a conjunction of the premises. Second, one connects this conjunction with the conclusion of the argument by means of an arrow. To illustrate:

Argument: P → Q, ~Q ∴ ~P

Conjunction of premises: (P → Q) • ~Q

Corresponding conditional: [(P → Q) • ~Q] → ~P

Note that in this case, the form of the argument is *modus tollens*. Of course, the argument is valid, and the corresponding conditional is a theorem. This is a relationship that can be counted on for every symbolic argument of statement logic: A symbolic argument is valid if and only if its corresponding conditional is a theorem.

Consider a second example. The argument form is traditionally known as *destructive dilemma:*

Argument: ~A ∨ ~B, C → A, D → B ∴ ~C ∨ ~D

To form the corresponding conditional, we first make a conjunction out of the premises, like this:

(~A ∨ ~B) • [(C → A) • (D → B)]

Next, we connect this conjunction to the conclusion of the argument with an arrow, to obtain the corresponding conditional:

((~A ∨ ~B) • [(C → A) • (D → B)]) → (~C ∨ ~D)

Now, we can prove that the argument is valid by proving that its corresponding conditional is a theorem:

∴ ((~A ∨ ~B) • [(C → A) • (D → B)]) → (~C ∨ ~D)

1. (~A ∨ ~B) • [(C → A) • (D → B)]	Assume
2. ~A ∨ ~B	1, Simp
3. (C → A) • (D → B)	1, Simp
4. C → A	3, Simp
5. D → B	3, Simp
6. ~(~C ∨ ~D)	Assume
7. ~~C • ~~D	6, DeM
8. ~~C	7, Simp
9. C	8, DN
10. A	9, 4, MP
11. ~~A	10, DN
12. ~B	11, 2, DS
13. ~~D	7, Simp
14. D	13, DN
15. B	14, 5, MP
16. B • ~B	15, 12, Conj
17. ~C ∨ ~D	6–16, RAA
18. ((~A ∨ ~B) • [(C → A) • (D → B)]) → (~C ∨ ~D)	1–17, CP

The following exercises will provide you with practice in constructing proofs for theorems.

◆ Exercise 8.6

Part A: Proofs   Prove the following theorems using either CP or RAA.

* 1. ~(P → Q) → (P • ~Q)
  2. ~(A • ~A)
  3. [(S ∨ R) • ~R] → S
* 4. (X → Y) → ~(X • ~Y)
  5. (~F • ~G) → (F ↔ G)
  6. ~(H • [(H → J) • (H → ~J)])
* 7. K → [(K → L) → L]
  8. ~(M ↔ ~M)
  9. (~N → O) ∨ (N → O)
* 10. (P • ~Q) → ~(P ↔ Q)
  11. [(~B → ~A) → A] → A
  12. ~[(X ↔ Y) • ~(X ∨ ~Y)]
  13. ~F → (F → G)
  14. (~H ∨ (~J ∨ K)) → ((~H ∨ J) → (~H ∨ K))
  15. [(~M ∨ M) → M] → M
  16. [(P → Q) • (R → ~Q)] → ~(P • R)
  17. D → (C → D)
  18. ~[(E ∨ F) • ((E → G) • [(F → G) • ~G])]
  19. (~X → Y) ∨ (X → Z)
  20. [(A → B) ∨ (A → C)] → [A → (B ∨ C)]

Part B: Corresponding Conditionals   Form the corresponding conditional for each of the following symbolic arguments. Then construct a proof to show that each of the conditionals is a theorem.

* 1. ~A ∨ ~B, B ∴ ~A
  2. C ↔ D, C ∴ D
  3. ~E ∴ E → F
  4. G → J, ~K → ~H, G ∨ H ∴ J ∨ K
  5. ~M ∨ ~S, ~L ∴ (~L • ~M) ∨ (~L • ~S)
  6. N • O ∴ P → N

7. ~R, Q ∴ ~(Q → R)
8. ~S ∨ T, ~T ∨ U ∴ U ∨ ~S
9. ~(W → X), Z → X ∴ ~Z
10. A ↔ ~A ∴ B

Notes

1. The relevant work is Gerhard Gentzen, "Untersuchungen über das logische Schliessen," *Mathematische Zeitschrift* 39 (1934): 176–210, 405–431.
2. For more on logical equivalence, see section 7.5.
3. The most famous intuitionist is the Dutch mathematician Luitzen Egbertus Jan Brouwer (1881–1966). See Anthony Flew, *A Dictionary of Philosophy* (New York: St. Martin's Press, 1979), p. 178.
4. The form of the argument and the observation that it cannot be proved directly from our 18 rules of inference are borrowed from Howard Kahane, *Logic and Philosophy: A Modern Introduction*, 6th ed. (Belmont, CA: Wadsworth, 1990), p. 88.
5. This observation is borrowed from Kahane, *Logic and Philosophy*, p. 88. A popular text that uses absorption instead of CP is Irving M. Copi and Carl Cohen, *Introduction to Logic*, 8th ed. (New York: Macmillan, 1990), chap. 9.

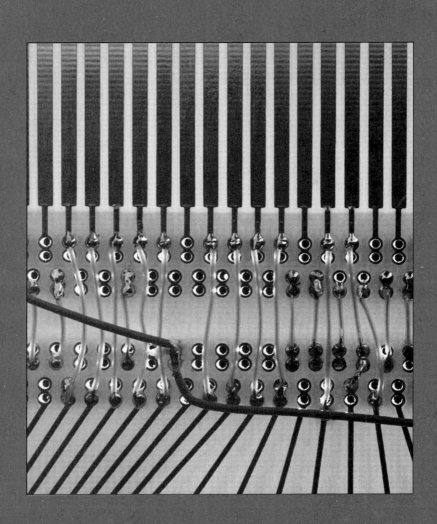

Chapter 9

Predicate Logic

Many arguments cannot be evaluated properly via the tools of statement logic. Take the following example:

> 1. All skeptics are depressed. Some logicians are skeptics. So, some logicians are depressed.

Argument (1) is obviously valid, but suppose we try to symbolize it, using the techniques of statement logic. Our scheme of abbreviation would look something like this:

> S: All skeptics are depressed; L: Some logicians are skeptics; D: Some logicians are depressed.

Using this scheme of abbreviation, (1) translates into symbols as follows:

> 2. S, L ∴ D

But argument (2) is invalid. We can easily show this with an abbreviated truth table. (Simply assign falsehood to D and truth to S and L.) So, the validity of (1) is not revealed through the techniques of statement logic.

As we learned in chapter 5, argument (1) is a categorical syllogism. In this chapter, we will see how categorical logic can be developed by adding elements to our system of statement logic. From a historical point of view, the connections between statement logic and categorical logic were poorly understood until quite recently. In fact, it was Gottlob Frege (1848–1925), a German professor of mathematics, who first demonstrated the conceptual links between them.[1] This chapter on predicate logic, which depends heavily on Frege's pioneering work, covers not only forms of argument that can be evaluated via the methods of Aristotle and Venn (see chapter 5) but also forms that lie well beyond the range of these earlier methods.

9.1 Predicates and Quantifiers

To apply the most powerful methods available to arguments within categorical logic, we must first learn how to symbolize categorical statements. For example, before we can evaluate categorical syllogisms, such as argument (1), we must learn how to symbolize the four types of categorical statements that play a central role in Aristotelian logic. By way of review, here is an example of each of the four main types of categorical statements:

Name	Form	Example
Universal affirmative	All S is P.	All trees are plants.
Universal negative	No S is P.	No trees are animals.
Particular affirmative	Some S is P.	Some dogs are collies.
Particular negative	Some S is not P.	Some dogs are not collies.

This section explains how to symbolize not only these types of statements but also a much wider range of categorical statements.

Consider this atomic sentence:

3. Aristotle is a logician.

We need a way of symbolizing this sentence that reveals its subject-predicate structure. Sentence (3) says that a particular thing or entity, namely, Aristotle, has a certain property or attribute, namely, the property or attribute of being a logician. If we let the lowercase letter *a* name the individual, Aristotle, and let the capital letter *L* stand for the predicate "is a logician," we can symbolize (3) as follows.

4. La

And if we use the lowercase letter *b* to name the Roman philosopher Boethius, the statement "Both Aristotle and Boethius are logicians" translates as follows:

5. La • Lb

In this chapter, we will use capital letters A through Z to designate properties (such as being human, being mortal, being rational, etc.). When so used, we will call these symbols **predicate letters**. (Note that capital letters can still be used to stand for statements, as needed, but we are here expanding their use.) Lowercase letters *a* through *u* will be used to name individuals. We will call these symbols **individual constants**. "Individuals" in this context refers not only to individual persons, such as Boethius and Aristotle, but also more generally to things or objects *as opposed to properties*. For example, in the statement "Seattle is beautiful," the name "Seattle" denotes an individual, a particular city, while the predicate "is beautiful" attributes a property to that city. And in the statement "Mount Rainier is snow-covered," the name "Mount Rainier" denotes an individual, a particular mountain, while the predicate "is snow-covered" attributes a property to that mountain.

The remaining lowercase letters—*v, w, x, y,* and *z*—will serve as **individual variables.** Variables do not name individuals, but rather serve primarily as placeholders. To grasp the idea of a placeholder, consider the following expression:

6. _____ is Greek.

The blank space here can be filled with the name of any individual. If we place a name denoting the ancient Greek philosopher Socrates or Plato in the blank, a true statement results. If we place a name denoting the American president George Washington or Abraham Lincoln in the blank, a false statement results. Now, if we use G to stand for "is Greek," the following expression, which contains a variable, says the same thing as expression (6):

7. Gx

(We could just as well have written Gy or Gz.) The expression "x is Greek" is neither true nor false, just as "_____ is Greek" is neither true nor false. So, Gx is not a statement (i.e., a sentence that is either true or false). Rather, we will call it a **statement function,** for if we replace x with an individual constant, we get a statement. For example:

8. Gs

(8) is true if s denotes the ancient Greek philosopher Socrates. So, it is important to keep in mind the distinction between individual constants and individual variables. Whereas the individual constants (*a* through *u*) are always used to name specific individuals, the individual variables (*v* through *z*) are primarily used as placeholders. (We will consider other uses of individual variables shortly, but for now think of them simply as placeholders.)

When is a capital letter used as a predicate letter? As a statement letter? When a capital letter is coupled with an individual constant or an individual variable, it is a predicate letter, used to designate a property or attribute. For example, in the following expressions, the capital letters are used as predicate letters: *Fa, Gd,* and *Px.* When a capital letter is not coupled with an individual constant or an individual variable, then in our symbol system it is used to stand for a statement—for instance, *F, G,* and *P.*

Suppose we want to symbolize the statement "Everything is human." How do we go about this? Of course, we need a scheme of abbreviation to tell us what capital letter stands for the predicate "is human." We indicate the scheme of abbreviation in parentheses following the statement to be symbolized, like this:

9. Everything is human. (Hx: x is human)

Now, to symbolize this statement, we must employ a **quantifier**. A quantifier is used to indicate how many things have the property (or properties) in question. For example, the words "all" and "some" are quantifiers in English. To get at the concept of a quantifier, let us note that statement (9) bears a close relationship to the following expression:

> 10. _____ is human.

Everything is human if and only if (10) is true regardless of which "fillers" we place in the blank. Therefore, we could express (9) this way:

> 11. For any individual thing x, x is human. (Hx: x is human)

For the sake of brevity, we will use a variable enclosed in parentheses to stand for the phrase "For any individual thing x." Thus, we can symbolize statement (11) as follows:

> 12. (x)Hx

(12) correctly symbolizes both (11) and (9). The symbol (x) is called a **universal quantifier**. It may be read variously as "for any x," "for all x," "for each x," and "for any individual thing x." By the way, we could use a variable other than x to translate statement (9), "Everything is human," for the variables in the scheme of abbreviation are merely placeholders. So, the following is also a correct symbolization of (9):

> 13. (y)Hy

Now, suppose we wish to symbolize a **universal affirmative** statement, such as the following:

> 14. All humans are mortal. (Hx: x is human; Mx: x is mortal)

Let us begin by rephrasing this universal affirmative. Statement (14) says, in effect, that *if anything is human, then it is mortal*. In other words, it says that the following expression is true *for any "filler"* we place in the blank spaces: "If _____ is human, then _____ is mortal." Consequently, we can rewrite "All humans are mortal" in rather technical logical language, as follows:

> 15. For any individual thing x, if x is human, then x is mortal.

The advantage of this technical logical language, which we will call "logicese," is that it is easily translated into symbols. Using the scheme of abbreviation provided, we can translate statement (15), and hence (14), into symbols, as follows:

> 16. (x)(Hx → Mx)

Note that *universal affirmative statements involve the arrow*. This analysis of universal statements partially in terms of *conditionals* provides one of the crucial links between statement logic and categorical logic. Momentarily, we will provide a similar analysis of universal negatives, particular affirmatives, and particular negatives. Each of these analyses essentially involves elements of statement logic. These Frege-style analyses of Aristotelian categorical statements enable us to develop a system of proof for predicate logic that builds on, and is an extension of, the system of proof for statement logic.

Note that it would be quite wrong to symbolize "All humans are mortal" as follows:

    17. $(x)(Hx \cdot Mx)$

This says that everything in the entire universe is both human and mortal! So, obviously, (17) is not equivalent to (16): $(x)(Hx \rightarrow Mx)$. *We need the arrow rather than the dot when symbolizing universal affirmatives*.

Universal affirmatives can be expressed in a variety of ways in English. For example, each of the following is a stylistic variant of "All humans are mortal":

    a. Every human is mortal.

    b. Each human is mortal.

    c. Humans are mortal.

    d. Any human is mortal.

    e. If anything is a human, then it is mortal.

    f. Anything that is a human is a mortal.

    g. A thing is human only if it is mortal.

    h. Only mortals are humans.

Each of (a) through (h) is correctly symbolized by (16): $(x)(Hx \rightarrow Mx)$. Note that in (h), the order of the terms is reversed. The word "only" often causes confusion. For example, "All trees are plants," which is a true statement, is *not* equivalent to "Only trees are plants," which is a false statement. Rather, "All trees are plants" is equivalent to "Only plants are trees," because "Only plants are trees" is equivalent to "If a thing is not a plant, then it is not a tree," which, in turn, is equivalent to "If a thing is a tree, then it is a plant."

In a more technical vein, let us examine the use of parentheses in the statement $(x)(Hx \rightarrow Mx)$. The parentheses indicate the scope of the quantifier, (x). The **scope** of the quantifier is the statement function over which it ranges. In $(x)(Hx \rightarrow Mx)$, the quantifier ranges not just over Hx, but, as the parentheses indicate, over $Hx \rightarrow Mx$. Suppose we had left off the parentheses around $Hx \rightarrow Mx$. Then we would have this:

    18. $(x)Hx \rightarrow Mx$

Now, the scope of the quantifier is merely Hx. But (18) does not say that if anything is human, then it is mortal. Rather, it says that if everything in the entire universe is human, then _____ is mortal. Thus, (18) is not equivalent to $(x)(Hx \rightarrow Mx)$. In fact, (18) expresses neither a truth nor a falsehood, but is merely a statement function.

The expression $(x)Hx \rightarrow Mx$ also illustrates the difference between **free** and **bound** variables. In this expression, the x in Hx is bound because it is quantified. The x in Mx, on the other hand, is free because it is not quantified (due to the lack of parentheses). To further clarify the idea of free and bound variables, consider this formula:

19. $(y)(Hx \rightarrow My)$

Here, the parentheses tell us that the y in My is bound by the quantifier (y). However, the x in Hx is not bound, because a quantifier must contain the same variable it quantifies. Thus, (y) cannot bind any x-variables; it can only bind y-variables.

Let us now consider **universal negative** statements. How will we symbolize them? For example:

20. No trees are animals. (Tx: x is tree; Ax: x is an animal)

This says, in effect, that if anything is a tree, then it is not an animal. In logicese, statement (20) looks like this:

21. For any x, if x is a tree, then x is not an animal.

So, we can symbolize (20) by means of a universal quantifier, the arrow, and the tilde:

22. $(x)(Tx \rightarrow \sim Ax)$

There are various ways of expressing universal negatives in English. For example, (20) has the following stylistic variants:

   a. Nothing that is a tree is an animal.
   b. All trees are nonanimals.
   c. If anything is tree, then it is not an animal.
   d. A thing is a tree only if it is not an animal.
   e. Nothing is a tree unless it is not an animal.

(22) symbolizes each of (a) through (e).

Our examination of universal negative statements raises further questions about the placement of tildes. How would you translate the following statements into symbols?

23. Nothing is human. (Hx: x is human)
24. Not everything is human. (Hx: x is human)
25. Not every human is a hero. (Hx: x is a human; Ox: x is a hero)

In logicese, (23) becomes, "For all x, x is not human." In symbols, we have $(x)\sim Hx$. We can rephrase (24) as "It is not the case that, for every x, x is human." In symbols, we have $\sim(x)Hx$. And (25) translates into "It is not true that for every x, if x is a human, then x is a hero." In symbols, we have $\sim(x)(Hx \rightarrow Ox)$. These examples underscore the fact that the placement of tildes requires careful attention.

A second quantifier, called the **existential quantifier**, is used to assert that at least one thing has a specified property. Our symbol for the existential quantifier looks like this: $(\exists x)$. (The "E" is backwards so it won't be confused with a predicate letter.) This symbol is read, "There is at least one x such that" or "There exists an x such that" or simply "There is an x such that." Consider the following statement:

26. Something is mortal. (Mx: x is mortal)

In logicese, (26) looks like this: "There exists an x such that x is mortal." In symbols, we have this:

27. $(\exists x)Mx$

With the existential quantifier in hand, we can symbolize **particular affirmatives**, such as:

28. Some dogs are collies. (Dx: x is a dog; Cx: x is a collie)

"Some" means "at least one." So, in logicese, statement (28) looks like this: "There is at least one x such that x is both a dog and a collie." In symbols, we have this:

29. $(\exists x)(Dx \cdot Cx)$

Note that (29) is *not* equivalent to either of the following:

30. There is an x such that *if* x is a dog, *then* x is a collie.
31. $(\exists x)(Dx \rightarrow Cx)$.

Both (30) and (31) tell us merely that something is such that *if* it is a dog, *then* it is a collie. Applying the rule MI, we see that (31) is logically equivalent to $(\exists x)(\sim Dx \vee Cx)$. But this statement is true given that something is *either* not a dog *or* a collie. So, the mere existence of one thing that is not a dog—say, a desk or a duck—is sufficient to ensure the truth of (31). Hence, (31) is a far cry from

"Some dogs are collies." Therefore, *when symbolizing particular affirmatives, we need to combine the existential quantifier with the dot rather than the arrow.*

Stylistic variants of "Some dogs are collies" include the following:

a. At least one dog is a collie.

b. There are dogs that are collies.

c. Something is both a dog and a collie.

d. There exists a dog that is a collie.

Each of these is correctly symbolized as follows: $(\exists x)(Dx \cdot Cx)$.

Occasionally, the English word "some" has the force of "some but not all." We will assume, however, that "some" means "at least one" unless the context demands otherwise. For example, the context demands otherwise when the locution "some but not all" is used or when the argument would be invalid unless the qualifier "but not all" was added. We can symbolize the expression "some but not all" using the existential and universal quantifiers in concert. For example:

32. Some but not all humans are rational

33. Some humans are rational, but not all humans are rational. (Hx: x is human; Rx: x is rational)

Statements (32) and (33) are equivalent, so each translates into symbols as follows:

34. $(\exists x)(Hx \cdot Rx) \cdot \sim(x)(Hx \rightarrow Rx)$

Note that (34) is a conjunction. Its left conjunct says, "Some humans are rational," and its right conjunct says, "Not all humans are rational." The parentheses around $Hx \cdot Rx$ indicate the scope of the existential quantifier. They tell us that $(\exists x)$ governs $Hx \cdot Rx$ but nothing more. Thus, the scope of the existential quantifier does not extend to the right conjunct.

The symbolization for **particular negative** statements is now apparent. Consider:

35. Some dogs are not collies. (Dx: x is a dog; Cx: x is collie)

Statement (35) translates into logicese as follows: "There is an x such that x is a dog and x is not a collie." In symbols, we have this:

36. $(\exists x)(Dx \cdot \sim Cx)$

There are numerous ways of expressing particular negatives in English. For example, stylistic variants of "Some dogs are not collies" include the following:

a. At least one dog is not a collie

b. There are dogs that are not collies

c. Something is a dog but not a collie

d. Not all dogs are collies.

e. Not every dog is a collie.

Note that (d) and (e) can be translated using either the existential quantifier or the universal quantifier:

37. $(\exists x)(Dx \cdot \sim Cx)$

38. $\sim(x)(Dx \to Cx)$

Later in the chapter, we will be able to prove that these two statements are logically equivalent.

To avoid mistakes when symbolizing English statements, it often helps to translate them into logicese first. The following list of examples should serve as a helpful guide for this process.

English	Logicese	Symbols
1. All ruffians are dangerous. (Rx: x is a ruffian; Dx: x is dangerous)	For any x, if x is a ruffian, then x is dangerous.	$(x)(Rx \to Dx)$
2. No plants are minerals. (Px: x is a plant; Mx: x is a mineral)	For all x, if x is a plant, then x is not a mineral.	$(x)(Px \to \sim Mx)$
3. Some people are stingy. (Px: x is a person; Sx: x is stingy)	There is an x such that x is a person and x is stingy.	$(\exists x)(Px \cdot Sx)$
4. Some students are not bored. (Sx: x is a student; Bx: x is bored)	There exists an x such that x is a student and x is not bored.	$(\exists x)(Sx \cdot \sim Bx)$
5. Electrons exist. (Ex: x is an electron)	There exists a y such that y is an electron.	$(\exists y)Ey$
6. Everything is an electron. (Ex: x is an electron)	For any z, z is an electron.	$(z)Ez$
7. Vampires do not exist. (Vx: x is a vampire)	For all x, it is not the case that x is a vampire.	$(x)\sim Vx$
8. Something is a logician. (Lx: x is a logician)	There is an x such that x is a logician.	$(\exists x)Lx$
9. Someone is a logician. (Px: x is a person; Lx: x is a logician)	There is a y such that y is a person and y is a logician.	$(\exists y)(Py \cdot Ly)$
10. If Aristotle is a logician, then there is at least one logician. (Lx: x is a logician; a: Aristotle)	If Aristotle is a logician, then there is an x such that x is a logician.	$La \to (\exists x)Lx$

11. Either Abelard is a logician or no one is a logician.(Lx: x is a logician; a: Abelard; Px: x is a person)

Either Abelard is a logician or (for all x, if x is a person, then x is not a logician).

La ∨ (x)(Px → ~Lx)

12. If everything is beautiful, then nothing is ugly. (Bx: x is beautiful; Ux: x is ugly)

If (for all x, x is beautiful), then (for all x, x is not ugly).

(x)Bx → (x)~Ux

13. Only women are mothers. (Wx: x is a woman; Mx: x is a mother)

For any y, if y is a mother, then y is a woman.

(y)(My → Wy)

14. If no one is a father, then Adam is not a father. (Px: x is a person; Fx: x is a father; a: Adam)

If (for all x, if x is a person, then x is not a father), then Adam is not a father.

(x)(Px → ~Fx) → ~Fa

15. If anything is either red or blue, then it has a color. (Rx: x is red; Bx: x is blue; Cx: x has a color)

For any x, if either x is red or x is blue, then x has a color.

(x)[(Rx ∨ Bx) → Cx]

Let us now describe the language of predicate logic more precisely. The vocabulary consists of: statement letters (capital letters A through Z), individual constants (lowercase letters *a* through *u*), individual variables (*v, w, x, y,* and *z*), predicate letters (capital letters A through Z coupled with individual constants or variables, e.g., *Fa, Gx,* and *Hxy*), the logical operators (~, ∨, •, →, and ↔), the quantifier symbols, and parentheses. An *expression* of predicate logic is *any* sequence of symbols in this vocabulary, such as (B → Fy ∨ (∃z)~. An a*tomic formula* of predicate logic is either a statement letter or a predicate letter coupled with individual constants or variables, such as *Bc, Cx,* or *Dyz.*

In what follows we will use the capital, cursive letters $\mathcal{P}$ and $\mathcal{Q}$ to stand for any expressions in the language of predicate logic. And we will use the bold letter **x** to stand for any individual variable (*v, w, x, y,* and *z*). The **well-formed formulas** (WFFs) of predicate logic can be characterized as follows:

Any atomic formula is a WFF. Examples: A, Ba, Cx, and Dxb.

If $\mathcal{P}$ is a WFF, then so is ~$\mathcal{P}$. *Examples:* ~M, ~Ga, and~ Hx.

If $\mathcal{P}$ and $\mathcal{Q}$ are WFFs, then so are ($\mathcal{P}$• $\mathcal{Q}$), ($\mathcal{P}$∨ $\mathcal{Q}$), ($\mathcal{P}$→ $\mathcal{Q}$), and ($\mathcal{P}$↔ $\mathcal{Q}$). *Examples:* (Fa • Gb), (Hx ∨ Kd), (Sy → Ry), and (Lb ↔ Mc).

If $\mathcal{P}$ is a WFF and **x** is any variable, then (**x**)$\mathcal{P}$ and (∃**x**)$\mathcal{P}$ are WFFs. *Examples:* (y)Ny, (∃z)Az, (x)(Sx → Ra), and (x)(y)Fxy.

Nothing counts as a WFF of predicate logic unless it can be demonstrated to be one by application of the above conditions. (The meaning of some of the examples above may be unclear at the moment but it will be explained later in this chapter.)*

Although nothing counts as a WFF unless it can be demonstrated to be one via the above conditions, we continue to allow some informal uses for the sake of convenience, e.g., we permit the omission of parentheses when no ambiguity results. Thus, we may write $Fa \lor (y)Gy$ instead of $(Fa \lor (y)Gy)$. Similarly, brackets may be employed to increase readability; accordingly, we may write $(x)[(Ax \bullet Bx) \to Cx]$ instead of $(x)((Ax \bullet Bx) \to Cx)$.

The following exercises will give you practice in using quantifiers, predicate letters, individual variables, and individual constants.

◆ *Exercise 9.1*

Part A: WFFs? Which of the following are well-formed formulas (WFFs)? Which are not?

* **1.** $(x)Ax$ **8.** Cx **15.** $(y)(My \to \sim Oy)$
  2. $(x)(Ax)$ **9.** $(z)P\sim z$ *16. $\sim b$
  3. $\sim(\exists y)By$ *10. $(\sim y)Sy$ **17.** $(y)(Hy)$
* **4.** $(a)Ca$ **11.** $(\exists u)Gu$ **18.** $((y)Ry \lor (\exists z)\sim Sz)$
  5. $(z)\sim Tz$ **12.** $(w)(\sim Dw)$ *19. $(x)((Fx \lor Gx) \to Hx)$
  6. $(\sim x)Hx$ *13. $(P \bullet (x)Fx)$ **20.** $(Q \bullet (Rg \lor (x)Ex))$
* **7.** $\sim(x)\sim Jx$ **14.** $((x)Gx \to (x)Nx)$

Part B: Symbolizing   Symbolize the following statements using the schemes of abbreviation provided.

* **1.** No Zoroastrians are Moslems. (Zx: x is a Zoroastrian; Mx: x is a Moslem)
  2. All kangaroos are marsupials. (Kx: x is a kangaroo; Mx: x is a marsupial)
  3. Peter Abelard is a logician, but Jacob Boehme is not. (Lx: x is a logician; a: Peter Abelard; b: Jacob Boehme)
* **4.** Not every marsupial is a kangaroo. (Mx: x is a marsupial; Kx: x is a kangaroo)
  5. Nothing is right. (Rx: x is right)
  6. Not everything is right. (Rx: x is right)
* **7.** Something is right. (Rx: x is right)
  8. Something is not right. (Rx: x is right)
  9. Only dogs are animals. (Dx: x is a dog; Ax: x is an animal)
* **10.** At least one mortal is human. (Mx: x is mortal; Hx: x is human)

---

*The notation for predicate logic (like the notation for statement logic) is not yet standardized. Although "(x)" is the most frequently used symbol for the universal quantifier, "($\forall$x)" is not uncommon. And in place of "($\exists$x)" for the existential quantifier, some systems employ "Vx".

11. A thing is a logician only if it is rational. (Lx: x is a logician; Rx: x is rational)

12. All trees are nonanimals. (Tx: x is tree; Ax: x is an animal)

* 13. Some people are good and some people are not good. (Px: x is a person; Gx: x is good)

14. Something is both good and evil. (Gx: x is good; Ex: x is evil)

15. There exists a person who is good. (Px: x is a person; Gx: x is good)

* 16. Only blue things are sky-blue. (Bx: x is blue; Sx: x is sky-blue)

17. If Socrates is not a philosopher, then Aristotle is not a philosopher. (s: Socrates; Px: x is a philosopher; a: Aristotle)

18. Not all animals are rational. (Ax: x is an animal; Rx: x is rational)

* 19. There exists an animal that has a soul. (Ax: x is an animal; Sx: x has a soul)

20. If all bats are mammals, then some mammals have wings. (Bx: x is a bat; Mx: x is a mammal; Wx: x has wings)

Part C: More Symbolizing   Symbolize the following statements using the schemes of abbreviation provided.

* 1. A thing is a cat only if it is an animal. (Cx: x is cat; Ax: x is an animal)

2. Some people are wicked. (Px: x is a person; Wx: x is wicked)

3. Some diseases are not fatal. (Dx: x is a disease; Fx: x is fatal)

* 4. Every logic student is wise. (Lx: x is a logic student; Wx: x is wise)

5. No soldier is a sailor. (Sx: x is a soldier; Ax: x is a sailor)

6. Only animals are wolves. (Ax: x is an animal; Wx: x is wolf)

* 7. Everything is an illusion. (Ix: x is an illusion)

8. Not everything is an illusion. (Ix: x is an illusion)

9. Either something is an illusion or nothing is an illusion. (Ix: x is an illusion)

* 10. Nothing is right unless it is not wrong. (Rx: x is right; Wx: x is wrong)

11. If neither Aristotle nor Boole is a logician, there are no logicians. (Lx: x is a logician; a: Aristotle; b: Boole)

12. Some but not all paintings are forgeries. (Px: x is a painting; Fx: x is a forgery)

* 13. If everything is mental, then nothing is physical. (Mx: x is mental; Px: x is physical)

14. If nothing is mortal, then nothing is human. (Mx: x is mortal; Hx: x is human)

15. If everyone is sad, then no one is happy. (Sx: x is sad; Px: x is a person; Hx: x is happy)

* 16. If anyone is sad, then he or she is not happy. (Sx: x is sad; Px: x is a person; Hx: x is happy)

17. If Cudworth is a logician and all logicians are bores, then he is a bore. (Lx: x is a logician; Bx: x is a bore; c: Cudworth)

18. Something is red all over and something is green all over, but it is not true that something is both red all over and green all over. (Rx: x is red all over; Gx: x is green all over)

* 19. If ghosts do not exist, then no houses are haunted. (Gx: x is ghost; Hx: x is a house; Nx: x is haunted)

20. If any number is odd, then not every number is even. (Nx: x is a number; Ox: x is odd; Ex: x is even)

Part D: Quiz on Symbolizing   Symbolize the following statements using the schemes of abbreviation provided.

1. Every wombat is a marsupial. (Wx: x is a wombat; Mx: x is a marsupial)

2. No wombat is a duck. (Wx: x is a wombat; Dx: x is a duck)

3. Some rectangles are squares. (Rx: x is a rectangle; Sx: x is square)

4. At least one rectangle is not a square. (Rx: x is a rectangle; Sx: x is square)

5. Not every person is a vegetarian. (Px: x is a person; Vx: x is a vegetarian)

6. Something is both green and not green. (Gx: x is green)

7. Only cats are mammals. (Cx: x is a cat; Mx: x is mammal)

8. A thing is a sphere only if it is not a cube. (Sx: x is sphere; Cx: x is a cube)

9. There exists a tree that is an oak. (Tx: x is tree; Ox: x is an oak)

10. If everything is blue, then nothing is red. (Bx: x is blue; Rx: x is red)

Part E: Schemes of Abbreviation   After constructing your own schemes of abbreviation for each of the following statements, symbolize them.

1. If everything is flawed, then nothing is perfect.

2. Some diamonds are gems, but no emeralds are diamonds.

3. Any given number is odd only if it is not even.

4. Unicorns do not exist, but horses do exist.

5. If anyone is a criminal, he or she deserves to be punished. [*Hint:* "anyone" means "any person."]

6. Either everything is perfect or at least one thing is not perfect.

7. Every criminal is either guilty or unlucky.

8. Some but not all politicians are hypocrites.

9. Something is not physical if and only if not everything is physical.

10. If anything is perfect, then it has no flaws.

Part F: Challenging Translations   Translate the following statements into symbols using the schemes of abbreviation provided. (*Note:* Some of these are rather difficult.)

* **1.** No rectangle is a square unless it is equilateral. (Rx: x is a rectangle; Sx: x is a square; Ex: x is equilateral)

2. Not all murderers deserve capital punishment, but Smith is a murderer who deserves capital punishment. (Mx: x is a murderer; Dx: x deserves capital punishment; s: Smith)

3. If Darwin is not a biologist, then no one is a biologist. (d: Darwin; Bx: x is a biologist; Px: x is a person)

* **4.** None but citizens can vote. (Cx: x is citizen; Vx: x is a thing that can vote)

5. Only citizens can vote. (Cx: x is citizen; Vx: x is a thing that can vote)

6. If everything is a human, then Fido is a human. (Hx: x is a human; f: Fido)

* 7. If all humans are mortal but Socrates is not mortal, then Socrates is not human. (Hx: x is human; Mx: x is mortal; s: Socrates)

8. If everyone is wise, then no one is a fool. (Px: x is a person; Wx: x is wise; Fx: x is a fool)

9. If anyone is wise, then he or she is not a fool. (Px: x is person; Wx: x is wise; Fx: x is a fool)

* 10. Fetuses lack a right to life if they are neither humans nor moral agents. (Fx: x is a fetus; Rx: x has a right to life; Hx: x is human; Mx: x is a moral agent)

11. None but men are fathers. (Mx: x is a man; Fx: x is a father)

12. If anyone is either courageous or just, then he is virtuous. (Px: x is a person; Cx: x is courageous; Jx: x is just; Vx: x is virtuous)

* 13. If Bob is a dog and all dogs are animals, then Bob is an animal. (b: Bob; Dx: x is a dog; Ax: x is an animal)

14. Either no one is wise or Solomon is wise. (Px: x is a person; Wx: x is wise; s: Solomon)

15. All and only married men are husbands. (Mx: x is married; Nx: x is a man; Hx: x is a husband)

* 16. If anyone is both happy and sad, then he is confused. (Px: x is a person; Hx: x is happy; Sx: x is sad; Cx: x is confused)

17. At least one nonphysical thing exists given that God exists. (Px: x is physical; G: God exists)

18. Only benevolent deities are worthy of worship. (Bx: x is benevolent; Dx: x is a deity; Wx: x is worthy of worship)

* 19. Nothing is good unless something is evil. (Gx: x is good; Ex: x is evil)

20. No animal is a dog unless it is a mammal. (Ax: x is an animal; Dx: x is a dog; Mx: x is a mammal)

9.2 Demonstrating Invalidity

An **algorithm** is a precisely described and finite procedure for solving a problem. The truth tables we studied in chapter 7 are an algorithm for statement logic. If we follow the correct procedures for constructing a truth table, we can determine the validity of any argument within statement logic. Unfortunately, there is no such algorithm for predicate logic. This was proved in 1936 by the American logician Alonzo Church.[2] Nevertheless, there are methods similar to truth tables that can be used to evaluate many arguments in predicate logic. We will examine one such method in this section, the **finite universe method**.

An argument is invalid if it is *possible* for its conclusion to be false while its premises are true. Thus, if we can describe a possible situation in which the conclusion of an argument is false while its premises are true, then we have shown the argument to be invalid. This is the essential principle underlying the finite universe method. And the finite universe method enables us to describe such situations simply and abstractly by imagining universes with a small number of objects.

To understand the finite universe method, we must first understand the meaning of quantified statements in universes containing a small number of objects. For instance, let us imagine a universe containing only two objects— *a* and *b*. We can picture it like this:

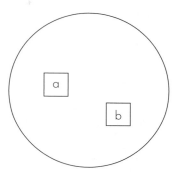

Two-Object Universe

Let us first consider the meaning of universal statements in a two-object universe. A **universal statement** is one of the form $(\mathbf{x})\mathcal{P}\mathbf{x}$, where bold $\mathbf{x}$ stands for any variable and $\mathcal{P}\mathbf{x}$ for any WFF containing at least one free occurrence of $\mathbf{x}$. Example:

39. Everything is red. (Rx: x is red)
   In symbols: (x)Rx

Since *a* and *b* are the only items in this universe, $(x)Rx$ is equivalent *in this universe* to the following conjunction:

Ra • Rb

In general, in a finite universe, a universal statement is equivalent to a certain conjunction.

We also need to consider the meaning of particular statements. A **particular statement** is one of the form $(\exists \mathbf{x})\mathcal{P}\mathbf{x}$, where bold $\mathbf{x}$ stands for any variable and $\mathcal{P}\mathbf{x}$ for any WFF containing at least one free occurrence of $\mathbf{x}$. Example:

40. Something is red. (Rx: x is red)
   In symbols: (∃x)Rx

This statement is equivalent, in our two-object universe, to the following disjunction:

Ra v Rb

In general, in a finite universe, a particular statement is equivalent to a certain disjunction.

To ensure understanding, let us consider a slightly larger universe containing three objects—*a*, *b*, and *c*:

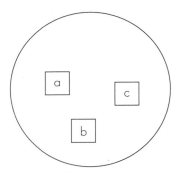

Three-Object Universe

In this universe, $(x)Rx$ is equivalent to the following conjunction:

Ra • (Rb • Rc)

And in this universe, $(\exists x)Rx$ is equivalent to the following disjunction:

Ra v (Rb v Rc)

Obviously, we could continue working out these equivalences for universes of larger (but finite) sizes. However, the general principle should be clear at this point: Universal statements become conjunctions; particular statements become disjunctions.

A special case worth noting is that of a universe with only one object:

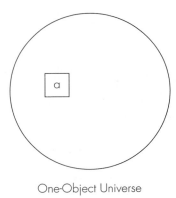

One-Object Universe

In this universe, "Everything is red" is equivalent to "*a* is red" (in symbols, *Ra*). But "Something is red" is also equivalent (in our one-object universe) to "*a* is red" (in symbols, *Ra*). Thus, in a one-object universe, $(x)Rx$ is equivalent to $(\exists x)Rx$. If $(x)Rx$ is true, then $(\exists x)Rx$ must be true; and if $(\exists x)Rx$ is true, then $(x)Rx$ must be true.

Let us now consider the meaning of *universal affirmative* and *particular affirmative* statements in a two-object universe. Here is a universal affirmative statement in both English and symbols:

41. All collies are dogs. (Cx: x is a collie; Dx: x is a dog)

    In symbols: (x)(Cx → Dx)

In a universe containing just two objects, *a* and *b*, this universal affirmative statement is equivalent to the following conjunction:

(Ca → Da) • (Cb → Db)

As before, universal statements become conjunctions, but note that an arrow appears in each conjunct.

Here is a particular affirmative statement in both English and symbols:

42. Some dogs are collies. (Dx: x is a dog; Cx: x is a collie)

    In symbols: (∃x)(Dx • Cx)

In a universe containing only two objects, *a* and *b*, this particular affirmative statement is equivalent to the following disjunction:

(Da • Ca) ∨ (Db • Cb)

Note that the dot appears in each disjunct.

The process of translating universal and particular statements into conjunctions and disjunctions, respectively, should now be clear. To apply the finite universe method, we first translate the premises and conclusion of an argument into conjunctions and disjunctions, as we have been doing. We then apply the method of abbreviated truth tables to determine whether the conclusion can be false while the premises are true. The basic idea is that the validity of an argument does not depend on there being a large number of objects in the universe. For instance, if a pattern of reasoning allows for true premises and a false conclusion in a two-object universe, then that pattern of reasoning is invalid. No further proof is needed.

Let's try the method out on a short argument:

43. Nothing red is blue. Something is not blue. So, something is red. (Rx: x is red; Bx: x is blue)

    In symbols: (x)(Rx → ~Bx), (∃x)~Bx ∴ (∃x)Rx

To keep things as simple as we can, we first translate the premises and conclusion for a one-object universe, like this:

Ra → ~Ba, ~Ba ∴ Ra

Now, we apply the method of abbreviated truth tables. If we can find a truth value assignment in which the premises are true while the conclusion is false, we have shown the argument to be invalid:

Ra Ba	Ra → ~Ba, ~Ba ∴ Ra
F F	F T T F T F F

This assignment does the job. We have shown that it is possible for an argument of the preceding pattern to have true premises and a false conclusion. Hence, the form is invalid. (We could obtain the same result by translating the premises and conclusion for a two-object universe, a three-object universe, and so on, but there is no need to do so.)

A one-object universe will not always be adequate for our purposes. Consider the following argument:

44. Nothing good is evil. Something is good. So, nothing is evil. (Gx: x is good; Ex: x is evil)

    In symbols: (x)(Gx → ~Ex), (∃x)Gx ∴ (x)~Ex

For a one-object universe, the argument translates as follows:

Ga → ~Ea, Ga ∴ ~Ea

Now, we apply the abbreviated truth table method:

Ga Ea	Ga → ~Ea, Ga ∴ ~Ea
T T	T TF F T T F T

Although we hypothesized that the premises could be true (while the conclusion is false), we were forced to contradict the hypothesis, as the symbol "T/F" indicates. So, let's try a two-object universe:

Ga Ea Gb Eb	(Ga → ~Ea) • (Gb → ~Eb), Ga ∨ Gb ∴ ~Ea • ~Eb
T F F T	T T TF T F T F T T T F T F F T

Here, the premises are true and the conclusion is false. This shows that the argument form is invalid, for there are circumstances in which it leads from true premises to a false conclusion.

To show that certain kinds of arguments are invalid, we need to consider a universe containing at least three objects. Here is an example:

45. (∃x)(Ax • ~Bx), (∃x)(Bx • ~Ax) ∴ (x)(Ax ∨ Bx)

Aa Ba Ab Bb Ac Bc	(Aa • ~Ba) ∨ [(Ab • ~Bb) ∨ (Ac • ~Bc)],
F F T F F T	F F T F T T T T F T F F F T

(Ba • ~Aa) ∨ [(Bb • ~Ab) ∨ (Bc • ~Ac)]   ∴ (Aa ∨ Ba) • [(Ab ∨ Bb) • (Ac ∨ Bc)]

F F T F T F F F T T T T T F   F F F F T T F T F T T

Obviously, this method becomes rather unwieldy as we consider universes with more than two members. The good news is that in many cases, a one- or two-object universe will be sufficient to reveal the invalidity of an argument.

The bad news here is multiple. First, there are invalid arguments within predicate logic whose invalidity *cannot* be shown via the finite universe method. These arguments belong to the logic of relations, the more advanced part of predicate logic (see section 9.5).[3] Second, there are cases in which a large (though finite) universe would be needed to apply the finite universe method, making it impractical without a computer. For instance, some invalid arguments can be shown to be invalid only in a universe with at least 2^n objects, where n is the number of predicate letters. So, if such an argument has only three predicate letters, then the finite universe method would require a universe with eight objects.

In spite of these limitations, the finite universe method can deepen our understanding of the meaning of quantified statements by revealing a great many invalid inferences. In practice, it is usually best to consider a one-object universe first and then to try a two- or three-object universe as needed. Of course, if an argument is valid, it cannot be shown to be invalid by means of the finite universe method.

Using the finite universe method, we can now sort out some issues that arose in chapter 5 as we discussed the Aristotelian Square of Opposition. Recall that *corresponding* categorical statements have the same subject and predicate terms. And from an Aristotelian perspective, a universal affirmative statement implies its corresponding particular affirmative—for example, "All unicorns are animals" implies "Some unicorns are animals." Similarly, a universal negative statement implies its corresponding particular negative—for example, "No unicorns are horses" implies "Some unicorns are not horses." Modern logicians, following George Boole, deny that these inferences are valid. Let's examine the inference from a universal affirmative to its corresponding particular affirmative, using the finite universe method.

46. All unicorns are animals. So, some unicorns are animals. (Ux: x is a unicorn; Ax: x is an animal)

   In symbols: (x)(Ux → Ax) ∴ (∃x)(Ux • Ax)

The invalidity is demonstrable in a one-object universe:

Ua Aa	Ua → Aa ∴ Ua • Aa
F T	F T T F F T

In general, the inference from a universal affirmative to its corresponding particular affirmative will move from truth to falsehood when the subject terms denote an empty class. The inference from universal negative statements to their corresponding particular negatives is invalid for the same reason.

Here is a related point. In the Aristotelian scheme, corresponding universal affirmative and universal negative statements are said to be **contraries**. Contraries cannot both be true, but they can both be false. To illustrate, "All unicorns are animals" and "No unicorns are animals," according to Aristotelians, are contraries. But according to modern logicians, these statements are not contraries, because they can both be true. Now, if the Aristotelians are right, the following argument should be valid:

47. All unicorns are animals. So, it is false that no unicorns are animals. (Ux: x is a unicorn; Ax: x is an animal)

That is, if "All unicorns are animals" and "No unicorns are animals" are contraries, then if "All unicorns are animals" is true, "No unicorns are animals" must be false. Here's the argument in symbols:

   (x)(Ux → Ax) ∴ ~(x)(Ux → ~Ax)

We translate for a one-object universe and assign truth values as follows:

Ua Aa	Ua → Aa ∴ ~(Ua → ~Aa)
F T	F T T F F T F T

On this truth value assignment, the premise is true and the conclusion is false, so the inference is invalid. This reason is this: The conditionals *Ua → Aa* and *Ua → ~Aa* are both true when *Ua* is false. And, of course, *Ua* is false assuming the class of unicorns is empty. We can generalize this point as follows: *Whenever the subject term of corresponding universal affirmative and universal negative statements denotes an empty class, both statements are true.* This is why modern logicians deny the Aristotelian thesis that corresponding universal affirmative and universal negative statements are contraries.

Although we have mentioned some limitations of the finite universe method, the following exercises will help you to understand the power of the method. It is indeed useful in a wide range of cases. Incidentally, all of the arguments in these exercises can be shown to be invalid in either a one-object or a two-object universe.

◆ Exercise 9.2

Part A: Demonstrating Invalidity   Use the finite universe method to show that the following symbolic arguments are invalid.

*   1. $(x)(Ax \rightarrow Bx)$ ∴ $(\exists x)(Ax \cdot Bx)$
   2. $(\exists x)Cx$ ∴ $(x)Cx$
   3. $(z)(Fz \rightarrow \sim Gz)$, $(\exists z)(Fz \cdot \sim Hz)$ ∴ $(\exists z)(Gz \cdot Hz)$
*   4. $(\exists y)Ky \rightarrow (\exists y)Ly$ ∴ $(y)(Ky \rightarrow Ly)$
   5. $(\exists x)(Ax \rightarrow Bx)$ ∴ $(x)(Ax \rightarrow Bx)$
   6. $(\exists x)(Rx \rightarrow Sx)$ ∴ $(x)Rx \rightarrow (x)Sx$
*   7. $(x)Hx \rightarrow (x)\sim Jx$ ∴ $(x)(Jx \rightarrow \sim Hx)$
   8. $(\exists z)Mz$, $(\exists z)Nz$ ∴ $(\exists z)(Mz \cdot Nz)$
   9. $(x)(Ax \rightarrow Bx)$, $(\exists x)Bx$ ∴ $(\exists x)Ax$
* 10. $(\exists y)(Ry \rightarrow Sy)$ ∴ $(\exists y)Ry \rightarrow (\exists y)Sy$
  11. $(x)(Cx \rightarrow \sim Dx)$ ∴ $\sim(x)(Cx \rightarrow Dx)$
  12. $(\exists z)(Nz \leftrightarrow Pz)$ ∴ $(z)(Nz \leftrightarrow Pz)$
* 13. $(y)(Ay \rightarrow By)$, Bd ∴ Ad
  14. $(x)Fx \rightarrow (x)Gx$ ∴ $(x)(Fx \rightarrow Gx)$
  15. $(\exists x)Dx$, $(\exists x)Cx$ ∴ $(x)(Dx \cdot Cx)$
* 16. $(x)(Mx \rightarrow Nx)$, $(\exists x)Mx$ ∴ $(x)Nx$
  17. $\sim(\exists y)(Sy \cdot Py)$ ∴ $(\exists y)(Sy \cdot \sim Py)$
  18. $(x)Tx \leftrightarrow (x)Ux$ ∴ $(x)(Tx \leftrightarrow Ux)$
* 19. $(\exists z)(Az \cdot Bz)$, $(\exists z)(Cz \cdot Bz)$ ∴ $(\exists z)(Az \cdot Cz)$
  20. $(x)(Ox \lor Px)$ ∴ $(x)Ox \lor (x)Px$

Part B: English Arguments   Translate the following English arguments into symbols. Then use the finite universe method to show that the arguments are invalid.

*   1. All students who take logic are courageous. Therefore, some students who take logic are courageous. (Sx: x is a student; Lx: x takes logic; Cx: x is courageous)

   2. All human beings are moral agents. Hence, all moral agents are human beings. (Hx: x is a human being; Mx: x is a moral agent)

   3. Every general is arrogant. There are lieutenants who are not generals. It follows that at least one lieutenant is not arrogant. (Gx: x is a general; Ax: x is arrogant; Lx: x is a lieutenant)

* **4.** All saints are good people. Some bankers are good people. Consequently, some bankers are saints. (Sx: x is saint; Gx: x is a good person; Bx: x is a banker)

  5. Nothing is a lover unless it is not a fighter. If anything is a fighter, then it is not a peacemaker. Accordingly, no lovers are peacemakers. (Lx: x is a lover; Fx: x is a fighter; Px: x is a peacemaker)

  6. There is an x such that if x is a tycoon, then x is a rapscallion. Thus, some tycoons are rapscallions. (Tx: x is a tycoon; Rx: x is a rapscallion)

  7. If everything is a circle, then everything is a square. Therefore, if anything is a circle, then it is square. (Cx: x is a circle; Sx: x is a square)

  8. Something is guilty. We may infer that Bob Smith is guilty. (Gx: x is guilty; b: Bob Smith)

  9. Nothing that is a ghost is also a vampire. So, there exists a ghost who is not a vampire. (Gx: x is a ghost; Vx: x is a vampire)

  10. All anarchists are fanatics. All communists are fanatics. We may infer that all communists are anarchists. (Ax: x is an anarchist; Fx: x is a fanatic; Cx: x is a communist)

  11. If anything is a human, then it is a sinner. Dracula is not a human. Hence, Dracula is not a sinner. (Hx: x is a human; Sx: x is a sinner; d: Dracula)

  12. Everything that is fully caused by material antecedents is determined. Some determined events are not free. Consequently, some things that are fully caused by material antecedents are not free. (Cx: x is fully caused by material antecedents; Dx: x is a determined event; Fx: x is free)

  13. Only acts that promote the general happiness are morally obligatory. Not all acts that promote the general happiness are socially acceptable. Therefore, at least one act that is socially acceptable is not morally obligatory. (Ax: x is an act; Px: x promotes the general happiness; Mx: x is morally obligatory; Sx: x is socially acceptable)

  14. All scientists who are engaged in cancer research are vivisectionists. Some vivisectionists are well intentioned but misguided. Therefore, some scientists who are engaged in cancer research are well intentioned but misguided. (Sx: x is a scientist; Cx: x is engaged in cancer research; Vx: x is a vivisectionist; Wx: x is well intentioned; Mx: x is misguided)

  15. Only things approved of by either God or society are morally permissible. Some acts of violence are approved of by either God or society. Hence, some acts of violence are morally permissible. (Gx: x is approved of by God; Sx: x is approved of by society; Mx: x is morally permissible; Vx: x is an act of violence)

9.3 Constructing Proofs

In this section and the next, we will continue and extend our practice of employing proofs to establish validity. Let us begin by observing that all the rules of statement logic still apply within predicate logic. For example, consider the following argument:

48. If Gretchen is not rational, then she is not a moral agent. But Gretchen is a moral agent. So, she is rational. (g: Gretchen; Rx: x is rational; Mx: x is a moral agent)

We can symbolize this argument and prove it valid as follows:

1. ~Rg → ~Mg
2. Mg   ∴ Rg
3. ~~Mg   2, DN
4. ~~Rg   1, 3, MT
5. Rg   4, DN

Because *Rg* and *Mg* are statements, they can be moved about, in accordance with all the rules of statement logic, just as statement letters can. Here's another example:

49. For all x, it is not the case that *either* x is red *or* x is blue. So, for all x, x is not red *and* x is not blue. (Rx: x is red; Bx: x is blue)

1. (x)~(Rx ∨ Bx)   ∴ (x)(~Rx • ~Bx)
2. (x)(~Rx • ~Bx)   1, DeM

This inference is permitted because De Morgan's laws are equivalence rules, and equivalence rules, unlike implicational rules, can be applied to parts of lines in a proof (as well as to entire lines).

Universal Instantiation

We will now add four implicational rules of inference for predicate logic.[4] Our first new rule is called **universal instantiation** (UI for short). The following simple argument illustrates the need for this new rule:

50. All humans are mortal. Socrates is human. Therefore, Socrates is mortal. (Hx: x is human; Mx: x is mortal; s: Socrates)

1. (x)(Hx → Mx)
2. Hs   ∴ Ms

Now, one might be tempted to apply *modus ponens* to lines (1) and (2), but this would be a mistake. The raw materials for a *modus ponens*–type inference are not present. We need a conditional, namely, *Hs* → *Ms*, to apply *modus ponens*. And our first premise is not a conditional (though it contains an arrow), but a universal statement. However, the first premise tells us that for every x, if x is human, then x is mortal. And what's true of every individual thing must also be true of Socrates, right? So, from line (1), we can infer the following:

3. Hs → Ms   1, UI

We call the rule of inference that permits this move "universal instantiation" (UI) because it allows us to derive a specific instance from a universal statement. The remainder of the proof is now merely statement logic:

1. (x)(Hx → Mx)
2. Hs   ∴ Ms
3. Hs → Ms   1, UI
4. Ms   2, 3, MP

While the basic idea behind UI is quite intuitive, the formal statement of the rule is a bit complex. The rule is designed to permit such inferences as the following:

A. 1. (x)Tx
   2. Ta   1, UI
B. 1. (x)Tx
   2. Tx   1, UI
C. 1. (x)Tx
   2. Ty   1, UI
D. 1. (y)(Pa → Fy)
   2. Pa → Fb   1, UI
E. 1. (z)~[(Az • Bz) v Cz]
   2. ~[(Aa • Ba) v Ca]   1, UI
F. 1. (x)(Bx v (z)Cz)
   2. Ba v (z)Cz   1, UI

Take a close look at these inferences. In each case, a universal quantifier is dropped, and the variables to which it is bound are replaced by an individual constant or individual variable. Notice that variables *not bound* by the quantifier must be left alone—see inference (F). Note also that a variable can be replaced by itself—see inference (B).

We must now attempt a more precise and technical statement of the rule of universal instantiation. UI comes in two forms. The first form involves instantiating to an individual constant. Let us combine the cursive letter $\mathcal{P}$ and the bold **x** to symbolize any formula containing a variable, like this: $\mathcal{P}$**x** (the bold **x** stands for *any* variable). And let us use the bold lowercase letter **c** to symbolize any constant (lowercase letters from *a* through *u*).The first form of universal instantiation permits the following pattern of inference:

(**x**)$\mathcal{P}$**x**
∴ $\mathcal{P}$**c**

Here, we get $\mathcal{P}$**c** from $\mathcal{P}$**x** by substituting **c** for each free occurrence of **x** in $\mathcal{P}$**x**. For example:

$$(x)(Hx \rightarrow Mx)$$
$$\therefore Hb \rightarrow Mb$$

Note that we substituted b for each free occurrence of x in $Hx \rightarrow Mx$. Bear in mind that individual constants designate specific individuals. Suppose b stands for an individual named Bob, H for the predicate "is a husband," and M for the predicate "is married." Then we can write the preceding inference in logicese as follows: "For any x, if x is a husband, then x is married. So, if Bob is a husband, then Bob is married."

The second form of universal instantiation involves instantiating to a variable. It permits inferences of the following sort, where the bold letters **x** and **y** stand for any of our variables (v, w, x, y, and z):

$$(\mathbf{x})\mathcal{P}\mathbf{x}$$
$$\therefore \mathcal{P}\mathbf{y}$$

Here, we get $\mathcal{P}\mathbf{y}$ from $\mathcal{P}\mathbf{x}$ by replacing every free occurrence of **x** in $\mathcal{P}\mathbf{x}$ with a free occurrence of **y** in $\mathcal{P}\mathbf{y}$. All three of the following inferences are correct according to this rule:

$(x)Rx$	$(y)(Cy \bullet Dy)$	$(z)(Sz \rightarrow (z)Tz)$
$\therefore Rx$	$\therefore Cx \bullet Dx$	$\therefore Sy \rightarrow (z)Tz$

Note that we can substitute the same variable (e.g., x for x), as illustrated by the inference on the far left. Also note that we cannot replace variables if they are not free, as illustrated by the inference on the far right: There are no free variables in the expression $(z)Tz$. Finally, note that in each of these inferences, we move from a statement to a statement function, whereas in the first form of UI, we move from a statement to another statement. For example, if R stands for the predicate "is red," then we can translate the first inference into logicese as follows: "Everything is red. So, x is red." And, as we have seen, "x is red" is a statement *function*, not a statement.

To ensure understanding, let us consider three moves that are not permitted by UI. First, UI does *not* permit this:

1. $\sim(y)Gy$
2. $\sim Gs$ 1, *incorrect use of UI*

This is like arguing, "Not everything is Greek; therefore, Socrates is not Greek," which is plainly invalid. Our formulation of the rule of UI does not permit this inference, because according to our formulation, UI can be applied only to a line that is a universal statement. A universal statement has the form $(\mathbf{x})\mathcal{P}\mathbf{x}$. Line (1) in the preceding erroneous proof is not a universal statement, but the *negation* of a universal statement.

Universal Instantiation (UI), in Two Forms

$(x)\mathcal{P}x$
$\therefore \mathcal{P}c$

Where the bold **x** stands for any individual variable and the bold **c** stands for any individual constant, and $\mathcal{P}c$ comes from $\mathcal{P}x$ by substituting **c** for each free occurrence of **x** in $\mathcal{P}x$.

$(x)\mathcal{P}x$
$\therefore \mathcal{P}y$

Where the bold **x** and **y** stand for individual variables, and $\mathcal{P}y$ comes from $\mathcal{P}x$ by replacing each free occurrence of **x** in $\mathcal{P}x$ with a free occurrence of **y** in $\mathcal{P}y$.

Correct Applications

1. $(z)Az$	
2. Ab	1, UI

1. $(x)(Bx \rightarrow Cx)$	
2. $Bx \rightarrow Cx$	1, UI

Errors to Avoid

1. $\sim(x)Ax$	
2. $\sim Ax$	1, *incorrect use of UI*

1. $(x)Dx \rightarrow (y)Ey$	
2. $Dx \rightarrow (y)Ey$	1, *incorrect use of UI*

The incorrect applications on the right both involve the same basic error—that is, applying UI to *part* of a line instead of a whole line. UI can be applied only to an entire line that has the form of a universal statement: $(x)\mathcal{P}x$.

Second, UI does *not* permit the following sort of inference:

1. $(x)Ex \rightarrow (y)Dy$
2. $Es \rightarrow (y)Dy$ 1, *incorrect use of UI*

This is like arguing, "If everything is an even number, then everything is divisible by two (without remainder). Hence, if 6 is an even number, then everything is divisible by 2 (without remainder)." The premise of this argument is true but the conclusion is false. (The conclusion is false because it has a true antecedent and false consequent.) So, the argument is invalid. In this erroneous proof, the error consists in applying UI to *part* of a line (in this case, the antecedent of a conditional). As an implicational rule, UI must be applied to an entire line of a proof. Moreover, UI can only be applied to a line that is a universal statement, but line (1) of the preceding "proof" is a conditional, not a universal statement.

Third, UI does *not* permit the following inference:

1. $(x)(Ex \rightarrow Dx)$
2. $Es \rightarrow Dn$ 1, *incorrect use of UI*

This is like arguing, "All even numbers are exactly divisible by 2. So, if 6 is even, then 9 is exactly divisible by 2." Since this argument has a true premise but a false conclusion, it is invalid. The problem is that we failed to replace all free occurrences of x in $Ex \rightarrow Dx$ with *the same* individual constant.

Existential Instantiation

Our second new inference rule is called **existential instantiation** (EI). Just as UI allows us to drop universal quantifiers, EI allows us to drop existential quantifiers. EI is commonly used in mathematics. Here's an example: "Something when added to 13 equals 29. So, $x + 13 = 29$." If this seems less like an inference and more like a decision to call an unknown quantity "x," so be it—the usefulness of EI in proofs will become evident momentarily. Here are some typical inferences permitted by existential instantiation:

A. 1. (∃x)Fx
    2. Fy   1, EI
B. 1. (∃x)Fx
    2. Fx   1, EI
C. 1. (∃y)(Sy • (x)Rx)
    2. Sz • (x)Rx   1, EI
D. 1. (∃z)(Pz → Tz)
    2. Px → Tx   1, EI

To avoid fallacies, however, we need a careful formulation of the EI rule. Again, we use the bold **x** and **y** to stand for any of our variables (v, w, x, y, and z). EI permits inferences of the following form:

$$(\exists \mathbf{x})\mathcal{P}\mathbf{x}$$
$$\therefore \mathcal{P}\mathbf{y}$$

Here, we get $\mathcal{P}\mathbf{y}$ from $\mathcal{P}\mathbf{x}$ by replacing all of the free occurrences of **x** in $\mathcal{P}\mathbf{x}$ with free occurrences of **y** in $\mathcal{P}\mathbf{y}$. Note that **y** stands for variables, not for individual constants. To avoid fallacies, we must also add this condition: The variable we instantiate to (**y** in the preceding formulation) may not occur *free* earlier in our proof. Why are these restrictions needed? To see why, let's examine some incorrect uses of EI.

     Consider the following erroneous proof:

1. (∃x)Sx
2. (∃x)Cx   ∴ Sx • Cx
3. Sx   1, EI (correct)
4. Cx   2, *incorrect use of EI*
5. Sx • Cx   3, 4, Conj

This is like arguing, "Something is a square. Something is a circle. So, x is a square circle." Because no individual thing can be a square circle, there can be no such x. Yet, the premises of the argument are true. So, it is invalid. The error results from our failure to honor the restriction that we cannot existentially

---

Existential Instantiation (EI)

$(\exists \mathbf{x})\mathcal{P}\mathbf{x}$
$\therefore \mathcal{P}\mathbf{y}$

Where the bold **x** and **y** stand for variables, and $\mathcal{P}\mathbf{y}$ comes from $\mathcal{P}\mathbf{x}$ by replacing all the free occurrences of **x** in $\mathcal{P}\mathbf{x}$ with free occurrences of **y** in $\mathcal{P}\mathbf{y}$. *Restriction:* the variable we instantiate to (**y** in the above formulation) may not occur *free* previously in the proof.

Correct Applications		**Errors to Avoid**	
1. $(\exists z)Fz$		1. $(\exists y)Ay$	
2. Fz	1, EI	2. Ab	1, *incorrect use of EI*
1. $(\exists x)(Dx \cdot Ex)$		1. $(x)Gx$	
2. $Dy \cdot Ey$	1, EI	2. $(\exists x)Hx$	
		3. Gx	1, UI
		4. Hx	2, *incorrect use of EI*

The incorrect uses on the right involve two distinct errors: (a) existentially instantiating to an individual constant, and (b) existentially instantiating to a variable that has occurred free earlier in the proof.

---

instantiate to a variable *if that variable occurs free earlier in the proof.* The variable *x* occurs free in line (3), so we may not existentially instantiate to *x* in line (4).

Consider a second abuse of EI:

1. $(\exists y)Ey$
2. En 1, *incorrect use of EI*

This is like arguing, "Something is an even number. So, 9 is an even number." The invalidity is obvious. The problem here is that we have employed an *individual constant rather than a variable* in our application of EI. We have to use variables because they serve, in this case, as names of unknowns. As noted previously, this use of variables is common in math. For example, in "$x - 23 = 49$," x is used as the name of an unknown quantity.

Finally, note that EI is an implicational rule, and *not* an equivalence rule. Consider the following misapplication of EI:

1. $(\exists x)Fx \rightarrow (y)Gy$
2. $Fx \rightarrow (y)Gy$ 1, *incorrect use of EI*

The problem here is that the premise is not a particular statement, but a conditional. A particular statement is one of the form $(\exists \mathbf{x})\mathcal{P}\mathbf{x}$. Thus, to apply EI in this way is to apply EI to the antecedent of a conditional, and hence to a part of a line (instead of to an entire line).

Universal Generalization

UI and EI allow us to drop quantifiers. But when the conclusion of an argument is a quantified statement, we may need to introduce a quantifier into a proof. Our third new inference rule, **universal generalization** (UG), permits us to introduce a universal quantifier under certain conditions. Consider the following argument and the accompanying proof, which illustrates a typical use of UG.

51. All trees are plants. All plants are living things. So, all trees are living things. (Tx: x is a tree; Px: x is a plant; Lx: x is a living thing)

    1. (x)(Tx → Px)
    2. (x)(Px → Lx)   ∴ (x)(Tx → Lx)
    3. Tx → Px   1, UI
    4. Px → Lx   2, UI
    5. Tx → Lx   3, 4, HS
    6. (x)(Tx → Lx)   5, UG

The addition of the universal quantifier in line (6) is legitimate, because the validity of the earlier steps in the proof did not require any specific lowercase letter. We instantiated to x, but we could have instantiated to any lowercase letter: y, z, a, b—you name it. In fact, we could have instantiated to every letter (one at a time) had we so desired.

The inference from line (5) to (6) is similar to certain types of inferences made in mathematics. For example, a geometer may prove that all rectangles have such-and-such a property by arguing that a certain figure, X, about which we assume *only* that it is a rectangle, has that property. If one makes no assumption about X other than that it is a rectangle, the conclusion about X may be generalized to all rectangles.

Using the bold **x** and **y** to stand for any of our variables, UG may be stated formally as follows:

$$\mathcal{P}\mathbf{y}$$
$$\therefore (\mathbf{x})\mathcal{P}\mathbf{x}$$

Here, $\mathcal{P}\mathbf{x}$ comes from $\mathcal{P}\mathbf{y}$ by replacing all free occurrences of **y** in $\mathcal{P}\mathbf{y}$ with free occurrences of **x** in $\mathcal{P}\mathbf{x}$. Note that **y** stands for individual variables, not for individual constants. Otherwise, the rule would endorse such blatantly invalid inferences as the following:

    1. Os
    2. (x)Ox   1, incorrect use of UG

Universal Generalization (UG)

$\mathcal{P}y$
$\therefore (\mathbf{x})\mathcal{P}\mathbf{x}$

Where the bold **x** and **y** stand for individual variables, and $\mathcal{P}\mathbf{x}$ comes from $\mathcal{P}y$ by replacing all free occurrences of **y** in $\mathcal{P}y$ with free occurrences of **x** in $\mathcal{P}\mathbf{x}$. *Restriction:* **y** must not be free in a line arrived at by EI.

Correct Applications

1. (x)Fx	
2. Fx	1, UI
3. (y)Fy	2, UG

1. (x)Sx	
2. (x)Tx	
3. Sx	1, UI
4. Tx	2, UI
5. Sx • Tx	3, 4, Conj
6. (x)(Sx • Tx)	5, UG

Errors to Avoid

1. Ba	
2. (x)Bx	1, *incorrect use of UG*

1. (∃x)Ax	
2. (x)(Ax → Bx)	
3. Ax	1, EI
4. Ax → Bx	2, UI
5. Bx	3, 4, MP
6. (x)Bx	5, *incorrect use of UG*

The incorrect uses on the right involve two distinct errors: (a) universally generalizing on the basis of a statement about a single individual, and (b) universally generalizing on the basis of a *variable* that *is free in a line arrived at by applying EI.*

This is like arguing, "Seven is an odd number. So, everything is an odd number."

A crucial restriction on UG must be emphasized at this time. To avoid fallacies, **y** *must not be free in a line arrived at by EI.* Without this restriction, we could argue as follows:

1. (∃x)Rx	
2. Rx	1, EI
3. (x)Rx	2, *incorrect use of UG*

Clearly, this is invalid—like arguing, "Something is red. So, everything is red." (Another restriction on UG will be mentioned in section 9.4, in our discussion of conditional proof and *reductio ad absurdum*.)

UG and UI can be combined to prove the validity of many categorical syllogisms. Here is a typical example:

52. No scientists are astrologers. All biologists are scientists. So, no biologists are astrologers. (Sx: x is scientist; Ax: x is an astrologer; Bx: x is a biologist)

    1. (x)(Sx → ~Ax)
    2. (x)(Bx → Sx) $\therefore$ (x)(Bx → ~Ax)

3. Sy → ~Ay   1, UI
4. By → Sy   2, UI
5. By → ~Ay   3, 4, HS
6. (x)(Bx → ~Ax)   5, UG

Here, we instantiated to y in lines (3) and (4), but we could have instantiated to any of our variables and then applied UG in line (6).

Existential Generalization

The need for our fourth new inference rule, **existential generalization** (EG), is illustrated by the following argument and proof:

53. All rock stars are musicians. Sheryl Crow is a rock star. So, there is at least one musician. (Rx: x is a rock star; Mx: x is a musician; c: Sheryl Crow)

    1. (x)(Rx → Mx)
    2. Rc   ∴ (∃x)Mx
    3. Rc → Mc   1, UI
    4. Mc   2, 3, MP
    5. (∃x)Mx   4, EG

The move from line (4) to (5) is intuitive: "Sheryl Crow is a musician; therefore, there is at least one musician."

There are two forms of EG. Using bold **c** to stand for any individual constant (*a* through *u*) and bold **x** to stand for any individual variable, we can state the first form of EG as follows:

$$\mathcal{P}\mathbf{c}$$
$$\therefore (\exists \mathbf{x})\mathcal{P}\mathbf{x}$$

Here, $\mathcal{P}\mathbf{x}$ comes from $\mathcal{P}\mathbf{c}$ by replacing one or more occurrences of **c** in $\mathcal{P}\mathbf{c}$ with occurrences of **x** free in $\mathcal{P}\mathbf{x}$. (*Note:* While one *typically* replaces *all* occurrences of **c** with free occurrences of **x**, the rule does not require that one replace them all.) Each of the following are correct applications of this form of EG:

A. 1. Fa
   2. (∃x)Fx   1, EG
B. 1. Ac • Bc
   2. (∃z)(Az • Bz)   1, EG
C. 1. Hd ∨ Pd
   2. (∃y)(Hy ∨ Py)   1, EG
D. 1. Ma • Sa
   2. (∃x)(Mx • Sa)   1, EG

Note especially application (D). Not all occurrences of the individual constant *a* are replaced by the variable *x*. Nevertheless, this use of EG is permitted by our rule. And the inference is valid. For instance, "Al is mad and Al is sad" implies "At least one *x* is such that (*x* is mad and Al is sad)."

Using the bold **x** and **y** to stand for individual variables, the second form of EG may be formulated as follows:

$$\mathcal{P}\mathbf{y}$$
$$\therefore (\exists\mathbf{x})\mathcal{P}\mathbf{x}$$

Here, $\mathcal{P}\mathbf{x}$ comes from $\mathcal{P}\mathbf{y}$ by replacing one or more occurrences of **y** free in $\mathcal{P}\mathbf{y}$ with occurrences of **x** free in $\mathcal{P}\mathbf{x}$. (Note that the rule does not require that one replace *every* occurrence of **y**.) Here are some typical inferences permitted by the second form of EG:

A. 1. Gx
   2. (∃x)Gx   1, EG
B. 1. Az → Bz
   2. (∃x)(Ax → Bx)   1, EG
C. 1. Tz ∨ Rz
   2. (∃y)(Ty ∨ Ry)   1, EG
D. 1. Lx • Kx
   2. (∃y)(Ly • Kx)   1, EG

Note (D): Not all occurrences of *x* are replaced by *y*. Again, this use of EG is permitted by our rules.

It is noteworthy that the following proof is correct, given our rules:

1. (x)Rx   ∴ (∃x)Rx
2. Ry   1, UI
3. (∃x)Rx   2, EG

In other words, given that everything has property *R*, we may conclude that something has *R*. Here, we move from a universal premise to a particular conclusion. The fact that this proof is valid in our system shows that our system contains an assumption that is standard in classical systems of logic—namely, at least one thing exists. Without this assumption, we could not instantiate to *y* in line (2).*

---

*Not all systems of logic involve the assumption that at least one thing exists. Those that do not make this assumption are called "Free Logics." ("Free Logic" means "Logic free of assumptions about existence.") For an excellent discussion of Free Logics, see Stephen Read, *Thinking About Logic: An Introduction to the Philosophy of Logic* (New York: Oxford University Press, 1995), pp. 131–144.

With the addition of EG, we can now handle syllogisms having particular statements as conclusions. For instance:

54. All artists are highly creative. Some photographers are artists. So, some photographers are highly creative. (Ax: x is an artist; Cx: x is highly creative; Px: x is a photographer)

1. $(x)(Ax \rightarrow Cx)$
2. $(\exists x)(Px \cdot Ax)$ $\therefore (\exists x)(Px \cdot Cx)$
3. $Px \cdot Ax$ 2, EI
4. $Ax \rightarrow Cx$ 1, UI
5. Ax 3, Simp
6. Cx 4, 5, MP
7. Px 3, Simp
8. $Px \cdot Cx$ 7, 6, Conj
9. $(\exists x)(Px \cdot Cx)$ 8, EG

Note that we applied EI before UI. What if we had reversed these inferences? Consider:

1. $(x)(Ax \rightarrow Cx)$
2. $(\exists x)(Px \cdot Ax)$ $\therefore (\exists x)(Px \cdot Cx)$
3. $Ax \rightarrow Cx$ 1, UI
4. $Px \cdot Ax$ 2, *incorrect use of EI*

Line (4) violates one of the restrictions on EI. We may not existentially instantiate to a variable that occurs free earlier in a proof. As we noted, without this restriction, our EI rule would permit fallacies. This leads to our first rule of thumb for predicate logic:

Rule of Thumb 1: Apply EI before you apply UI.

Consider the following alternative attempt to prove argument (54). Can we apply MP to lines (6) and (4) to obtain Cx?

1. $(x)(Ax \rightarrow Cx)$
2. $(\exists x)(Px \cdot Ax)$ $\therefore (\exists x)(Px \cdot Cx)$
3. $Py \cdot Ay$ 2, EI
4. $Ax \rightarrow Cx$ 1, UI
5. Py 3, Simp
6. Ay 3, Simp
7. ???

Existential Generalization (EG), in Two Forms

$\mathcal{P}c$
$\therefore (\exists x)\mathcal{P}x$

Where the bold letter **c** stands for any individual constant and **x** is an individual variable and $\mathcal{P}x$ comes from $\mathcal{P}c$ by replacing one or more occurrences of **c** in $\mathcal{P}c$ with occurrences of **x** free in $\mathcal{P}x$.

$\mathcal{P}y$
$\therefore (\exists x)\mathcal{P}x$

Where the bold **x** and **y** stand for individual variables, and $\mathcal{P}x$ comes from $\mathcal{P}y$ by replacing one or more free occurrences of **y** in $\mathcal{P}y$ with occurrences of **x** free in $\mathcal{P}x$.

Correct Applications

1. Ka
2. $(\exists y)$Ky   1, EG

1. Lx • Nx
2. $(\exists x)$(Lx • Nx)   1, EG

1. My ∨ Oy
2. $(\exists x)$(Mx ∨ Oy)   1, EG

Errors to Avoid

1. Az → (y)By
2. $(\exists z)$Az → (y)By   1, *incorrect use of EG*

1. (x)(Dx → Eb)
2. (x)(Dx → $(\exists y)$Ey)   1, *incorrect use of EG*

The incorrect uses on the right involve the same basic error: applying EG to part of a line instead of to an entire line. Like all of the other inference rules introduced in this section, EG is an implicational rule, not an equivalence rule.

No. To apply MP, we need a conditional on one line and the antecedent of that conditional on another line. And the antecedent of line (4) is Ax, not Ay. This suggests a second rule of thumb for predicate logic:

> Rule of Thumb 2: Universally instantiate to free variables or individual constants and apply the rules of statement logic.

Is the following alternative proof for argument (54) correct?

1. (x)(Ax → Cx)
2. $(\exists x)$(Px • Ax) $\therefore (\exists x)$(Px • Cx)
3. Py • Ay   2, EI
4. Ay → Cy   1, UI
5. Ay   3, Simp
6. Py   3, Simp
7. Cy   4, 5, MP
8. Py • Cy   6, 7, Conj
9. $(\exists x)$(Px • Cx)   8, EG

Yes. First, existentially instantiate to the variable y. Next, universally instantiate to y and apply the rules of statement logic. Line (8) tells us that y has attributes P and C; so, we may conclude in line (9) that *something* has attributes P and C.

The following exercises will give you some practice in applying the four rules of inference introduced in this section.

◆ *Exercise 9.3*

Part A: Annotating   Annotate the following proofs.

* **1.** 1. (x)(Rx → Tx)
     2. ~Tc ∴ ~Rc
     3. Rc → Tc
     4. ~Rc

  2. 1. Km
     2. (∃x)Kx → (x)Lx ∴ Lm
     3. (∃x)Kx
     4. (x)Lx
     5. Lm

  3. 1. (z)(Az → Bz)
     2. (∃y)Ay ∴ (∃y)By
     3. Ay
     4. Ay → By
     5. By
     6. (∃y)By

* **4.** 1. Hn ∴ (∃x)Hx
     2. (∃x)Hx

  5. 1. (x)(Rx → ~Ox)
     2. (∃y)(Sy • Ry) ∴ (∃z)(Sz • ~Oz)
     3. Sy • Ry
     4. Ry → ~Oy
     5. Ry
     6. ~Oy
     7. Sy
     8. Sy • ~Oy
     9. (∃z)(Sz • ~Oz)

  6. 1. (z)(Mz • Lz)
     2. (z)Mz → Kd ∴ (∃y)Ky
     3. Mz • Lz
     4. Mz
     5. (z)Mz
     6. Kd
     7. (∃y)Ky

* **7.** 1. (y)(Ry → Ny)
     2. ~Ng ∴ (∃y)~Ry
     3. Rg → Ng
     4. ~Rg
     5. (∃y)~Ry

  8. 1. Ab ∨ (Bb · Cb)
     2. (x)~Cx ∴ (∃x)Ax
     3. (Ab ∨ Bb) • (Ab ∨ Cb)
     4. Ab ∨ Cb
     5. ~Cb
     6. Ab
     7. (∃x)Ax

  9. 1. (x)(Fx → Gx)
     2. (x)(Gx → Fx) ∴ (x)(Fx ↔ Gx)
     3. Fx → Gx
     4. Gx → Fx
     5. (Fx → Gx) • (Gx → Fx)
     6. Fx ↔ Gx
     7. (x)(Fx ↔ Gx)

* **10.** 1. (∃y)Py → (z)(~Nz ∨ Oz)
      2. Pn
      3. ~Om ∴ (∃x)~Nx
      4. (∃y)Py
      5. (z)(~Nz ∨ Oz)
      6. ~Nm ∨ Om
      7. ~Nm
      8. (∃x)~Nx

Part B: Correct or Incorrect   Which of the following inferences are permitted by our inference rules? Which are not permitted?

* **1.** 1. $(x)Ax \rightarrow (x)Bx$
     2. $Ax \rightarrow (x)Bx$ 1, UI

  2. 1. $(\exists x)(Dx \cdot Fx)$
     2. $(\exists x)Gx$
     3. $Dx \cdot Fx$ 1, EI
     4. Dx 3, Simp
     5. $(x)Dx$ 4, UG
     6. Fx 3, Simp
     7. $(\exists x)Fx$ 6, EG
     8. Gx 2, EI

  3. 1. $(\exists y)Hy \rightarrow (\exists y)Jy$
     2. $Hy \rightarrow (\exists y)Jy$ 1, EI

* **4.** 1. $(\exists z)(Kz \cdot Lz)$
     2. $(\exists z)Kz$ 1, Simp

  5. 1. $(\exists y)(Ry \cdot Sy)$
     2. $Rb \cdot Sb$ 1, EI

  6. 1. $(x)(Mx \rightarrow Nx)$
     2. $(x)(Nx \rightarrow Ox)$
     3. $Mx \rightarrow Nx$ 1, UI
     4. $Nx \rightarrow Ox$ 2, UI
     5. $Mx \rightarrow Ox$ 3, 4, HS
     6. $(x)(Mx \rightarrow Ox)$ 5, UG
     7. $Md \rightarrow Od$ 6, UI
     8. $(\exists y)(My \rightarrow Oy)$ 7, EG

* **7.** 1. $(x)(y)(My \leftrightarrow Nx)$
     2. $(y)(My \leftrightarrow Ny)$ 1, UI

  8. 1. $\sim(x)(Tx \vee Ax)$
     2. $\sim(Tx \vee Ax)$ 1, UI

  9. 1. $(x)[(y)Fy \vee Hx]$
     2. $(y)Fy \vee Hx$ 1, UI
     3. $(y)Fy \vee (\exists z)Hz$ 2, EG

* **10.** 1. $(x)(Bx \rightarrow (x)Cx)$
     2. $(x)Bx$
     3. $(x)Cx$ 1, 2, MP

Part C: Proofs   Construct proofs to show that the following symbolic arguments are valid. Use direct proof rather than CP or RAA.

*   **1.** Ja → Hb, (y)~Hy ∴ (∃x)~Jx
    2. (x)(~Tx → ~Hx), Ha ∴ Ta
    3. (x)Mx → (y)Ny, (x)~~Mx ∴ Nd
*   **4.** (z)(Nz → ~Ez), (z)(Sz → Nz) ∴ (z)(Sz → ~Ez)
    5. (∃x)(Ax • Bx) ∴ (∃x)Ax • (∃x)Bx
    6. (y)(Fy → Gy), Fb ∴ (∃y)(Fy • Gy)
*   **7.** (x)(Dx → Lx), (∃x)Dx ∴ (∃x)(Dx • Lx)
    8. (z)(Hz → Jz), (∃z)(Hz • Kz) ∴ (∃z)(Jz • Kz)
    9. (x)[(Ax ∨ Bx) → Cx], (∃x)Bx ∴ (∃x)Cx
* **10.** (y)(~Py → ~Ly), Lc ∨ Ld ∴ Pd ∨ Pc
  11. (∃x)(Dx • ~Rx), (x)(Dx → Wx) ∴ (∃x)(Wx • ~Rx)
  12. (z)[Uz → (Kz ∨ Sz)], (z)Uz, (∃z)~Sz ∴ (∃z)Kz
* **13.** (x)(Ax ↔ ~Ax) ∴ Bc
  14. (x)(Jx → ~Ex), (∃x)(Jx ∨ Jd) ∴ (∃y)(Ey → ~Ed)
  15. (x)(Lx → Mx) → (x)(Nx → Lx), (x)~Lx ∴ (x)~Nx
* **16.** (∃y)Fy → (y)My, Fg ∴ Mg
  17. (x)(Sx → Tx), (∃y)(Ry • ~Ty) ∴ (∃z)(Rz • ~Sz)
  18. (x)(Bx → Cx), (x)(Ax → Bx), (x)(Cx → Dx), (∃x)~Dx ∴ (∃x)~Ax
* **19.** (x)[Px → (∃y)Oy], (∃z)Pz ∴ (∃y)Oy
  20. (x)(Dx → ~Kx), (∃x)(Ex • Hx), (x)(Hx → Dx), (x)(Jx → Kx)
    ∴ (∃x)(Ex • ~Jx)

Part D: English Arguments Symbolize the following arguments using the schemes of abbreviation provided. Then construct proofs to show that the arguments are valid. Use direct proof rather than CP or RAA.

*   **1.** Only humans have inherent value. No chimps are humans. So, no chimps have inherent value. (Hx: x is a human; Ix: x has inherent value; Cx: x is a chimp)

    2. Every fetus has an immortal soul. A thing has an immortal soul only if it has a right to life. Hence, each and every fetus has a right to life. (Fx: x is fetus; Sx: x has an immortal soul; Rx: x has a right to life)

    3. There are rights that cannot be waived. But alienable rights can be waived. It follows that some rights are inalienable. (Rx: x is right; Wx: x can be waived; Ax: x is an alienable right)

*   **4.** God is a perfect being. Nothing perfect is unreal. Therefore, God is real. (g: God; Px: x is a perfect being; Rx: x is real)

5. At least one instance of intentional killing is not wrong. But every murder is wrong. Hence, some instances of intentional killing are not murder. (Kx: x is an instance of intentional killing; Mx: x is murder; Wx: x is wrong)

6. Some wars are just. No war of aggression is just. Accordingly, there are wars that are not wars of aggression. (Wx: x is a war; Jx: x is just; Ax: x is a war of aggression)

* 7. A person deserves the death penalty if and only if he is a serial killer. Bundy is a serial killer, but Oswald is not. Both Bundy and Oswald are persons. Hence, Bundy deserves the death penalty, but Oswald does not. (Px: x is a person; Dx: x deserves the death penalty; Sx: x is a serial killer; b: Bundy; o: Oswald)

8. All contingent beings are causally dependent. No necessary beings are causally dependent. Every physical entity is contingent. All atoms are physical entities. We may conclude that no atom is a necessary being. (Cx: x is a contingent being; Dx: x is causally dependent; Nx: x is a necessary being; Px: x is a physical entity; Ax: x is an atom)

9. At least one instance of killing an innocent human is not wrong. For some instances of killing an innocent human are either accidental or in self-defense. But neither accidental killing nor killing in self-defense is wrong. (Kx: x is an instance of killing an innocent human; Wx: x is wrong; Ax: x is an accidental killing; Sx: x is a case of killing in self-defense)

10. Only things having human bodies are human. No unembodied soul has a human body. Only unembodied souls survive the death of the body. Thus, no humans survive the death of the body. (Bx: x has a human body; Hx: x is human; Ux: x is an unembodied soul; Sx: x survives the death of the body)

9.4 Quantifier Negation, RAA, and CP

In this section, we add two equivalence rules to our system of proof and explain how to use conditional proof and *reductio ad absurdum* within predicate logic.

Consider the following pair of statements:

55. Everything is nonred (or nothing is red).

56. It is not the case that something is red.

It should be obvious that each of these statements validly implies the other. In symbols, these intuitive inferences would look like this (using R to stand for "is red"):

$$(x){\sim}Rx \qquad\qquad {\sim}(\exists x)Rx$$
$$\therefore\ {\sim}(\exists x)Rx \qquad\qquad \therefore\ (x){\sim}Rx$$

In both cases, one begins with a quantifier having a tilde on one side. One then switches the tilde to the opposite side and changes the type of quantifier.

It should also be obvious that the following two statements validly imply each other:

57. Something is not red.

58. Not everything is red.

In symbols, the inferences would look like this:

$$(\exists x)\sim Rx \qquad\qquad \sim(x)Rx$$
$$\therefore \sim(x)Rx \qquad\qquad \therefore (\exists x)\sim Rx$$

Such inferences are permitted by the rule of **quantifier negation** (QN). To state this rule, we will use the cursive letter $\mathcal{P}$ to stand for any WFF and the bold **x** to stand for any variable. QN comes in two forms, as follows:

$$\sim(\exists \mathbf{x})\mathcal{P} :: (\mathbf{x})\sim\mathcal{P}$$
$$\sim(\mathbf{x})\mathcal{P} :: (\exists \mathbf{x})\sim\mathcal{P}$$

The four-dot symbols indicate that both of these rules are equivalence rules. In each case, we can move logically from the formula on the left to the formula on the right, *and vice versa*. In each case, one begins with a quantifier having a tilde on one side. One then switches the tilde to the opposite side and changes the type of quantifier.

Here are some typical examples of inferences permitted by the QN rule:

A. 1. $(x)\sim Fx$
    2. $\sim(\exists x)Fx$ 1, QN
B. 1. $\sim(\exists x)(Sx \vee Rx)$
    2. $(x)\sim(Sx \vee Rx)$ 1, QN
C. 1. $\sim(y)(Ay \rightarrow By)$
    2. $(\exists y)\sim(Ay \rightarrow By)$ 1, QN
D. 1. $(\exists z)\sim(Cz \cdot Dz)$
    2. $\sim(z)(Cz \cdot Dz)$ 1, QN

Because QN is an *equivalence* rule, it can be applied to *parts* of a line. For example:

E. 1. $(x)\sim Hx \rightarrow (y)Ky$
    2. $\sim(\exists x)Hx \rightarrow (y)Ky$ 1, QN
F. 1. $(y)By \rightarrow \sim(x)Ax$
    2. $(y)By \rightarrow (\exists x)\sim Ax$ 1, QN

Note that in example (E), QN is applied to the antecedent of a conditional, while in example (F), it is applied to the consequent of a conditional.

The following argument and proof illustrate the utility of the quantifier negation rule:

59. Not all animals are moral agents. Only moral agents have rights. Hence, some animals do not have rights. (Ax: x is an animal; Mx: x is a moral agent; Rx: x has rights)

1. ~(x)(Ax → Mx)	
2. (x)(Rx → Mx)	∴ (∃x)(Ax • ~Rx)
3. (∃x)~(Ax → Mx)	1, QN
4. ~(Ax → Mx)	3, EI
5. ~(~Ax v Mx)	4, MI
6. ~~Ax • ~Mx	5, DeM
7. ~Mx	6, Simp
8. Rx → Mx	2, UI
9. ~Rx	7, 8, MT
10. ~~Ax	6, Simp
11. Ax	10, DN
12. Ax • ~Rx	11, 9, Conj
13. (∃x)(Ax • ~Rx)	12, EG

When a tilde appears on the left side of a universal or particular statement, it is often useful to apply QN so that one can apply EI or UI. Lines (1), (3), and (4) illustrate this type of sequence, which suggests a third rule of thumb for predicate logic:

Rule of Thumb 3: When a tilde appears on the left side of a universal or particular statement, it is often useful to apply QN and instantiate. (But keep in mind that EI and UI are implicational rules and cannot be applied to parts of a line.)

Using QN, we can prove the equivalence of statements such as these:

60. Not all animals are cats. (Ax: x is an animal; Cx: x is a cat)

61. Some animals are not cats. (Ax: x is an animal; Cx: x is a cat)

The following proofs show that we can move logically from either one of these statements to the other; hence, they are logically equivalent.

1. ~(x)(Ax → Cx)	∴ (∃x)(Ax • ~Cx)
2. (∃x)~(Ax → Cx)	1, QN
3. (∃x)~(~Ax v Cx)	2, MI

4. (∃x)(~~Ax • ~Cx)   3, DeM
5. (∃x)(Ax • ~Cx)   4, DN

1. (∃x)(Ax • ~Cx)   ∴ ~(x)(Ax → Cx)
2. (∃x)(~~Ax • ~Cx)   1, DN
3. (∃x)~(~Ax ∨ Cx)   2, DeM
4. (∃x)~(Ax → Cx)   3, MI
5. ~(x)(Ax → Cx)   4, QN

Sometimes, the QN rule enables us to make use of statement logic rules without instantiating. Here is an example:

1. (x)~Ax → (z)Bz
2. (∃z)~Bz   ∴ (∃x)Ax
3. ~(z)Bz   2, QN
4. ~(x)~Ax   1, 3, MT
5. (∃x)~~Ax   4, QN
6. (∃x)Ax   5, DN

The QN rule is often useful when employing the *reductio ad absurdum* (RAA) method. For example:

1. (x)(Lx → Mx)
2. (∃x)Lx   ∴ (∃x)Mx
3. ~(∃x)Mx   Assume
4. (x)~Mx   3, QN
5. Lx   2, EI
6. Lx → Mx   1, UI
7. Mx   5, 6, MP
8. ~Mx   4, UI
9. Mx • ~Mx   7, 8, Conj
10. (∃x)Mx   3–9, RAA

But while RAA and CP can be used in predicate logic as well as in statement logic, *the use of these methods demands an additional restriction on universal generalization (UG).* We previously stated the UG rule as follows:

$\mathcal{P}$**y**
∴ (**x**)$\mathcal{P}$**x**

Where the bold **x** and **y** stand for individual variables, and $\mathcal{P}$**x** comes from $\mathcal{P}$**y** by replacing all free occurrences of **y** in $\mathcal{P}$**y** with free occurrences of **x** in $\mathcal{P}$**x**. *Restriction:* **y** must not be free in a line arrived at by EI.

Now, we must add the following:

> *Restriction:* UG cannot be used within the scope of an assumption for RAA or CP if **y** occurs *free* in the assumption.

To understand the need for this restriction, consider the following invalid argument and erroneous proof:

62. If everything is red, then everything is blue. So, all red things are blue. (Rx: x is red; Bx: x is blue)

In symbols: (x)Rx → (x)Bx ∴ (x)(Rx → Bx)

1. (x)Rx → (x)Bx	∴ (x)(Rx → Bx)
2. Rx	Assume
3. (x)Rx	2, *incorrect use of UG* [violates the new restriction]
4. (x)Bx	1, 3, MP
5. Bx	4, UI
6. Rx → Bx	2–5, CP
7. (x)(Rx → Bx)	6, UG

To see that the argument is invalid, consider this: The premise is true because its antecedent is false—not everything is red. But the conclusion, "All red things are blue," is obviously false. And, of course, any argument with a true premise and a false conclusion is invalid. The invalidity of the argument is also revealed if we apply the finite universe method:

Ra Rb Ba Bb	(Ra • Rb) → (Ba • Bb) ∴ (Ra → Ba) • (Rb → Bb)
T F F T	T F F T F F T T F F F F T T

Our new restriction on UG prevents us from "proving" that such invalid arguments are valid.

Let us consider some further examples of CP and RAA in predicate logic. Here is a correct use of CP:

1. (x)(Rx → Bx)	∴ (x)Rx → (x)Bx
2. (x)Rx	Assume
3. Rx → Bx	1, UI
4. Rx	2, UI
5. Bx	3, 4, MP
6. (x)Bx	5, UG
7. (x)Rx → (x)Bx	2–6, CP

Here, we have *not* violated the new restriction on UG because the variable x does not occur free in the assumption in line (2). Note that this proof shows that one can move logically from the *conclusion* of argument (62) to its *premise*. The following use of CP is also permissible:

1. $(x)(Fx \rightarrow Gx)$		
2. $(x)(Fx \rightarrow Hx)$	$\therefore (x)[Fx \rightarrow (Gx \cdot Hx)]$	
3. Fx	Assume	
4. $Fx \rightarrow Gx$	1, UI	
5. $Fx \rightarrow Hx$	2, UI	
6. Gx	3, 4, MP	
7. Hx	3, 5, MP	
8. $Gx \cdot Hx$	6, 7, Conj	
9. $Fx \rightarrow (Gx \cdot Hx)$	3–8, CP	
10. $(x)[Fx \rightarrow (Gx \cdot Hx)]$	9, UG	

This proof does *not* violate our new restriction on UG because UG is not used *within the scope of the assumption*. Rather, we apply UG after we have discharged the assumption. Here, we may add a fourth rule of thumb for predicate logic:

> **Rule of Thumb 4:** If the conclusion is a universal statement containing an arrow, use CP to prove the relevant conditional and then apply UG.

When the conclusion of an argument is a particular statement, RAA is often useful. For example:

1. $(x)(Px \rightarrow Sx)$	
2. $Pa \lor Pb$	$\therefore (\exists x)Sx$
3. $\sim(\exists x)Sx$	Assume
4. $(x)\sim Sx$	3, QN
5. $Pa \rightarrow Sa$	1, UI
6. $\sim Sa$	4, UI
7. $\sim Pa$	5, 6, MT
8. Pb	2, 7, DS
9. $Pb \rightarrow Sb$	1, UI
10. Sb	8, 9, MP
11. $\sim Sb$	4, UI
12. $Sb \cdot \sim Sb$	10, 11, Conj
13. $(\exists x)Sx$	3–12, RAA

This argument illustrates our fifth and final rule of thumb for predicate logic:

> **Rule of Thumb 5:** When the conclusion of an argument is a particular statement, RAA is often useful.

Summary of Rules of Thumb for Predicate Logic

1. Apply EI before you apply UI.
2. Universally instantiate to free variables or individual constants and apply the rules of statement logic.
3. When a tilde appears on the left side of a universal or particular statement, it is often useful to apply QN and instantiate. (But keep in mind that EI and UI are implicational rules and cannot be applied to parts of a line.)
4. If the conclusion is a universal statement containing an arrow, use CP to prove the relevant conditional and then apply UG.
5. When the conclusion of an argument is a particular statement, RAA is often useful.

As in statement logic, it is sometimes useful to employ more than one assumption in the same proof. In the following proof, CP and RAA are combined:

1. (x)Ax ∨ (x)Bx	∴ (x)(~Ax → Bx)
2. ~Ax	Assume (for CP)
3. (x)Ax	Assume (for RAA)
4. Ax	3, UI
5. Ax • ~Ax	4, 2, Conj
6. ~(x)Ax	3–5, RAA
7. (x)Bx	1, 6, DS
8. Bx	7, UI
9. ~Ax → Bx	2–8, CP
10. (x)(~Ax → Bx)	9, UG

This proof does not violate our new restriction on UG because UG is not used within the scope of the assumption in line (2). We could also construct a proof for this argument using RAA alone. But we would still need two assumptions, and the proof would be 18 steps long. (Try it!) So, combining CP and RAA is sometimes very efficient.

These exercises provide you with practice in using QN, RAA, and CP.

◆ Exercise 9.4

Part A: Annotating Annotate the following proofs. Some of the proofs involve assumptions.

* **1.** 1. (x)Ax → (x)Bx
   2. ~(x)Bx ∴ (∃x)~Ax
   3. ~(x)Ax
   4. (∃x)~Ax

2. 1. ~(∃y)Cy
 2. (y)~Cy → (z)Dz ∴ Db
 3. (y)~Cy
 4. (z)Dz
 5. Db

3. 1. ~(x)~Fx ∴ (∃x)Fx
 2. ~~(∃x)Fx
 3. (∃x)Fx

* **4.** 1. ~(∃x)~Gx ∴ (x)Gx
 2. (x)~~Gx
 3. (x)Gx

5. 1. (∃y)Hy → (∃y)Jy
 2. (y)~Jy ∴ ~Ha
 3. ~(∃y)Jy
 4. ~(∃y)Hy
 5. (y)~Hy
 6. ~Ha

6. 1. (z)[(Kz ∨ Lz) → Mz] ∴ (z)(Lz → Mz)
 2. Lz
 3. Lz ∨ Kz
 4. Kz ∨ Lz
 5. (Kz ∨ Lz) → Mz
 6. Mz
 7. Lz → Mz
 8. (z)(Lz → Mz)

* **7.** 1. (x)(Nx → Ox) ∴ ~(x)Ox → ~(x)Nx
 2. ~(x)Ox
 3. (∃x)~Ox
 4. ~Ox
 5. Nx → Ox
 6. ~Nx
 7. (∃x)~Nx
 8. ~(x)Nx
 9. ~(x)Ox → ~(x)Nx

8. 1. ~(∃x)~Px
 2. ~(∃y)Sy ∨ ~(x)Px ∴ ~Sd
 3. ~~(x)Px
 4. ~(∃y)Sy
 5. (y)~Sy
 6. ~Sd

9. 1. (x)~Rx → (∃x)~~Tx ∴ (x)~Tx → (∃x)Rx
 2. ~(∃x)Rx → (∃x)~~Tx
 3. ~(∃x)Rx → ~(x)~Tx
 4. (x)~Tx → (∃x)Rx

10. 1. $(x)(Ax \rightarrow \sim Bx)$
    2. $(y)Ay \therefore (z)\sim Bz$
    3. $\sim(z)\sim Bz$
    4. $(\exists z)\sim\sim Bz$
    5. $\sim\sim Bz$
    6. Bz
    7. $Az \rightarrow \sim Bz$
    8. Az
    9. $\sim Bz$
    10. $Bz \cdot \sim Bz$
    11. $(z)\sim Bz$

Part B: Proofs Construct proofs to show that the following symbolic arguments are valid. You may use direct proof, CP, or RAA.

* 1. $(\exists x)Fx \rightarrow (\exists x)(Gx \cdot Hx), (\exists x)Hx \rightarrow (x)Jx \therefore (x)(Fx \rightarrow Jx)$

   2. $(x)(Wx \rightarrow Sx) \therefore (\exists x)Wx \rightarrow (\exists x)Sx$

   3. $(x)\sim Kx \vee (\exists x)Lx, (x)\sim Lx \therefore \sim Kb$

* 4. $\sim(\exists x)Mx \rightarrow (\exists x)(Nx \cdot Px), (x)\sim Px \therefore (\exists x)Mx$

   5. $\sim(\exists x)(Rx \vee Sx) \vee (x)Tx, (\exists x)\sim Tx \therefore \sim(\exists x)Sx$

   6. $(x)(Ax \rightarrow (x)Bx) \therefore (x)Ax \rightarrow (x)Bx$

* 7. $(x)(Cx \rightarrow Dx), \sim(\exists x)Cx \rightarrow (\exists x)Dx \therefore \sim(x)\sim Dx$

   8. $(z)(Ez \rightarrow (\exists z)Fz), (z)Gz \rightarrow (\exists z)Ez \therefore (z)Gz \rightarrow (\exists z)Fz$

   9. $\sim(x)\sim Ax, (\exists x)Ax \rightarrow (x)Bx, (x)[(Bx \vee Cx) \rightarrow Dx] \therefore (x)Dx$

* 10. $(\exists x)\sim Kx \rightarrow \sim(\exists x)Dx, \sim(x)Kx, Db \leftrightarrow Qa \therefore \sim Qa$

 11. $\sim[(x)Fx \vee (\exists x)Gx], (\exists x)\sim Fx \rightarrow (y)Hy, (x)\sim Gx \rightarrow (z)Jz \therefore (x)(Hx \cdot Jx)$

 12. $\sim(x)Kx \rightarrow (\exists x)Lx, (\exists x)\sim Kx \rightarrow (x)(Lx \rightarrow Mx) \therefore \sim(x)Kx \rightarrow (\exists x)Mx$

* 13. $\sim[(x)Ax \rightarrow (\exists x)Bx], (\exists x)\sim Cx \rightarrow (\exists x)Bx, (x)[(Ax \cdot Cx) \rightarrow Da] \therefore Da$

 14. $\sim[(y)Zy \cdot (y)Wy], (\exists y)\sim Zy \rightarrow (y)Uy, (\exists y)Ry \rightarrow (y)Wy \therefore (y)(Uy \vee \sim Ry)$

 15. $Ba \leftrightarrow \sim(\exists x)Cx, (\exists x)Ax \vee (x)Bx, (x)\sim Ax \therefore \sim Ce$

* 16. $\sim(x)Mx \vee (\exists x)\sim Mx, (\exists x)Sx \rightarrow (x)Mx, Sb \vee (x)\sim Px \therefore \sim Pa$

 17. $[(x)Hx \rightarrow (\exists x)Gx] \rightarrow \sim(\exists y)(Fy \vee (\exists z)Tz), \sim(x)Fx \rightarrow (\exists x)Gx,$
     $(x)Hx \rightarrow (\exists x)\sim Fx \therefore (\exists x)\sim Tx$

 18. $(x)Hx \vee [(x)Kx \cdot (\exists x)\sim Lx], (x)Hx \rightarrow \sim(x)Nx, \sim(x)Lx \rightarrow (\exists x)\sim Nx,$
     $(x)Mx \vee (x)Nx \therefore Mc$

* 19. $(\exists x)[Bx \rightarrow (y)\sim Cy], \sim(\exists y)Cy \rightarrow \sim(\exists z)Dz \therefore (x)Bx \rightarrow (z)\sim Dz$

 20. $(x)Ax \vee (x)Bx \therefore (x)(Ax \vee Bx)$ [*Hint:* Use two assumptions.]

Part C: Logical Equivalents Construct proofs to show that the following are valid. By constructing these proofs, you will show that each pair of statements is logically equivalent. *Note:* In the last five pairs, *P* is a statement letter and so plays the role of any formula in which there is no free occurrence of *x*—for example, the role of (x)Bx in (x)[(x)Bx → Ax]. Take special note of the fourth and fifth pairs, as these indicate the somewhat surprising behavior of quantifiers that bind variables in the antecedent of a conditional.

* **1.** (x)(Ax • Bx) ∴ (x)Ax • (x)Bx

   2. (x)Ax • (x)Bx ∴ (x)(Ax • Bx)

   3. (∃x)(Ax ∨ Bx) ∴ (∃x)Ax ∨ (∃x)Bx

* **4.** (∃x)Ax ∨ (∃x)Bx ∴ (∃x)(Ax ∨ Bx)

   5. (x)(P → Ax) ∴ P → (x)Ax

   6. P → (x)Ax ∴ (x)(P → Ax)

* **7.** (x)(Ax → P) ∴ (∃x)Ax → P

   8. (∃x)Ax → P ∴ (x)(Ax → P)

   9. (∃x)(Ax → P) ∴ (x)Ax → P

  10. (x)Ax → P ∴ (∃x)(Ax → P)

  11. (∃x)(P → Ax) ∴ P → (∃x)Ax

  12. P → (∃x)Ax ∴ (∃x)(P → Ax)

  13. (x)Ax ∨ P ∴ (x)(Ax ∨ P)

  14. (x)(Ax ∨ P) ∴ (x)Ax ∨ P

Part D: English Arguments   Symbolize the following arguments using the schemes of abbreviation provided. Then construct proofs to show that the arguments are valid. You may use either direct proof, CP, or RAA.

* **1.** Every act of terrorism is deplorable. If there is an act of terrorism that either promotes the general welfare or corrects an injustice, then some acts of terrorism are not deplorable. So, no act of terrorism corrects an injustice. (Tx: x is an act of terrorism; Dx: x is deplorable; Wx: x promotes the general welfare; Cx: x corrects an injustice)

  2. All brain processes are physical processes. No mental processes are tangible. Therefore, every brain process that is a mental process is also an intangible physical process. (Bx: x is a brain process; Px: x is a physical process; Mx: x is a mental process; Tx: x is tangible)

  3. Either Smith is a criminally insane person or all kleptomaniacs are criminally insane persons. But it is not the case that there are persons who are criminally insane. We may infer that Smith is not a kleptomaniac. (Cx: x is criminally insane; Px: x is a person; Kx: x is a kleptomaniac; s: Smith)

* **4.** An act of killing is wrong if and only if it eliminates the prospect of future valuable life. To kill a potential person is to kill. To kill a fetus is to kill a potential person. To kill a potential person is to eliminate the prospect of future valuable life. It follows that killing a fetus is wrong. (Kx: x is an act of killing; Wx: x is wrong; Ex: x eliminates the prospect of future valuable life; Px: x is an act of killing a potential person; Fx: x is an act of killing a fetus)

  5. If there are any gods, then all free creatures are predestined. If there are any free creatures, then whatever is predestined is morally responsible. Accordingly, if there are any gods, then all free creatures are morally responsible. (Gx: x is a god; Fx: x is a free creature; Px: x is predestined; Mx: x is morally responsible)

  6. No absolute right can be denied. Every right can be denied if one person's right to life can conflict with another person's right to life. Unfortunately, one person's right to life can conflict with another person's right to life. Therefore, no rights are absolute rights. (Ax: x is an absolute right; Rx: x is a right; Dx: x can be denied; P: One person's right to life can conflict with another person's right to life)

* **7.** Some reprobates are boring. Some highly moral individuals are humorous. If there are any reprobates, then highly moral individuals are fascinating if they are humorous. We may conclude that there are highly moral individuals who are fascinating. (Rx: x is a reprobate; Bx: x is boring; Mx: x is highly moral; Hx: x is humorous; Fx: x is fascinating)

8. If some poltergeists are not ghosts, then some haunted houses are dangerous. But it is not the case that there are any ghosts or haunted houses. Therefore, it is not the case that there are any poltergeists. (Px: x is a poltergeist; Gx: x is a ghost; Hx: x is a haunted house; Dx: x is dangerous)

9. Contraception is not right if it violates the purpose of sex or obviates valuable life. Some acts of contraception obviate valuable life. If a thing is not right, then it is wrong. Hence, some acts of contraception are wrong. (Cx: x is an act of contraception; Rx: x is right; Vx: x violates the purpose of sex; Ox: x obviates valuable life; Wx: x is wrong)

10. If some acts of torturing the innocent are not wrong, then all acts of torturing the innocent are right. Some acts of torturing the innocent are approved by society. Consequently, if no acts of torturing the innocent are right, then some things approved by society are wrong. (Tx: x is an act of torturing the innocent; Wx: x is wrong; Rx: x is right; Sx: x is approved by society)

9.5 The Logic of Relations

Thus far, we have considered only **monadic** (one-place) predicate letters, such as Ax, By, and Cz. Monadic predicate letters are adequate for ascribing an attribute (e.g., being human) to an individual. But individuals not only have attributes, they also bear relations to one another. For example, we can say that Smith *is older than* Jones or that Elizabeth *is a sister of* John. Modern predicate logic encompasses the logic of relations, but to symbolize relations, we need predicate letters with more than one place. For instance, we can use Oxy to stand for "x is older than y" or Sxy to stand for "x is a sister of y."

Here is a simple example of an argument that involves a relational predicate:

63. Al is taller than Bob. Bob is taller than Chris. If one thing is taller than a second and the second is taller than a third, then the first is taller than the third. So, Al is taller than Chris.

We need a two-place predicate letter to symbolize the relation "x is taller than y," so here is a scheme of abbreviation for argument (63):

Txy: x is taller than y; a: Al; b: Bob; c: Chris

Using this scheme of abbreviation, "Al is taller than Bob" becomes simply *Tab*, and "Bob is taller than Chris" becomes: *Tbc*. To symbolize the third premise, we first translate it into logicese: "For all x, for all y, for all z, if x is taller than y and y is taller than z, then x is taller than z." The complete symbolization looks like this:

64. Tab, Tbc, $(x)(y)(z)[(Txy \cdot Tyz) \rightarrow Txz]$ ∴ Tac

And the proof runs as follows:

1. Tab
2. Tbc
3. $(x)(y)(z)[(Txy \cdot Tyz) \rightarrow Txz]$ ∴ Tac
4. $(y)(z)[(Tay \cdot Tyz) \rightarrow Taz]$ 3, UI
5. $(z)[(Tab \cdot Tbz) \rightarrow Taz]$ 4, UI
6. $(Tab \cdot Tbc) \rightarrow Tac$ 5, UI
7. Tab $\cdot$ Tbc   1, 2, Conj
8. Tac   6, 7, MP

When instantiating formulas with multiple quantifiers, such as line (3) in this proof, one must carefully note which variables are governed by which quantifier. Thus, in line (4), a is substituted for x in $(y)(z)[(Txy \cdot Tyz) \rightarrow Txz]$ but for no other variable in the formula.

One aspect of the rule UI should be reemphasized at this point. The second form of UI allows us to move from $(x)\mathcal{P}x$ to $\mathcal{P}y$, where $\mathcal{P}y$ is obtained by replacing each occurrence of **x** free in $\mathcal{P}x$ by an occurrence of **y** free in $\mathcal{P}y$. The following inference violates this rule:

1. $(x)(\exists y)Gyx$
2. $(\exists y)Gyy$ 1, *incorrect use of UI*

This is like arguing, "For every natural number x, there is a natural number y such that y is greater than x. So, there is a natural number y such that y is greater than y." Since no number is greater than itself, we have moved from a true premise to a false conclusion, and the inference is invalid. Thus, care must be taken when applying UI in contexts in which the variable one instantiates to is liable to be bound by another quantifier.

The logic of relations enables us to see the subtlety of many rather ordinary-looking English sentences. For example, consider the following argument:

65. Each thing causes at least one thing. So, something causes something.
(Cxy: x causes y)
In symbols: $(x)(\exists y)Cxy$ ∴ $(\exists x)(\exists y)Cxy$

Note that it would be wrong to switch the order of the quantifiers in the premise as follows: $(\exists y)(x)Cxy$. This formula says that *at least one thing is such that everything causes it*, which is quite different from the premise of argument (65). The proof for (65) is short and simple:

    1. (x)(∃y)Cxy   ∴ (∃x)(∃y)Cxy
    2. (∃y)Cxy   1, UI
    3. (∃x)(∃y)Cxy   2, EG

Now, compare argument (65) to the following fallacious argument:

66. Each thing causes at least one thing. So, at least one thing is such that everything causes it. (Cxy: x causes y)

   In symbols: (x)(∃y)Cxy ∴ (∃y)(x)Cxy

Even if each thing causes at least one thing, we cannot infer that something is caused by everything. So, we shouldn't be able to construct a (correct) proof for argument (66). Which of the following steps cannot be justified by our rules?

    1. (x)(∃y)Cxy   ∴ (∃y)(x)Cxy
    2. (∃y)Cxy   ?
    3. Cxy   ?
    4. (x)Cxy   ?
    5. (∃y)(x)Cxy   ?

Line (2) follows from line (1) by UI, and line (3) follows from line (2) by EI. The problem comes at line (4). It may seem that line (4) derives from line (3) by UG, but this is not so. UG allows us to move from $\mathcal{P}$y to (x)$\mathcal{P}$x (where **x** and **y** stand for any of our variables), but there are certain restrictions—for example, **y** must not be free in a line arrived at by EI. But x is free in line (3), and line (3) is arrived at by EI. Therefore, we cannot apply UG in line (4).

    Arguments involving relations can be rather difficult to symbolize. But much of the difficulty can be removed by working through a series of well-chosen examples. Perhaps the most important skill to develop here is that of translating English into logicese. How would you symbolize the following sentence?

67. Someone loves everyone. (Px: x is a person; Lxy: x loves y)

First, let's rewrite it in logicese: "There exists an x such that x is a person, and, for every y, if y is a person, then x loves y." Once we have the logicese, symbolizing is easy:

68. (∃x)[Px • (y)(Py → Lxy)]

    Now, examine the following closely related sentences, along with their symbolic translations. (The scheme of abbreviation remains the same.)

69. Everyone loves someone.

In logicese, we have "For any x, if x is a person, then there exists a y such that y is a person and x loves y." In symbols:

70. $(x)[Px \rightarrow (\exists y)(Py \cdot Lxy)]$

How would you symbolize the following sentence?

71. No one loves everyone.

In logicese, we have "For every x, if x is a person, then it is not true that for every y, if y is a person, x loves y." In symbols:

72. $(x)[Px \rightarrow \sim(y)(Py \rightarrow Lxy)]$

Statement (71) can also be translated into logicese as follows: "It is not the case there is an x such that x is a person and for all y, if y is a person, then x loves y." So, we can also symbolize (71) this way:

73. $\sim(\exists x)[Px \cdot (y)(Py \rightarrow Lxy)]$

We can prove that statements (72) and (73) are logically equivalent. To do this, we must show that (72) implies (73), and vice versa. The following abbreviated proof shows that (73) implies (72). That (72) implies (73) is left as an exercise (Exercise 9.5, part E, item 8).

1. $\sim(\exists x)[Px \cdot (y)(Py \rightarrow Lxy)]$	$\therefore (x)[Px \rightarrow \sim(y)(Py \rightarrow Lxy)]$	
2. Px	Assume (for CP)	
3. $(x)\sim[Px \cdot (y)(Py \rightarrow Lxy)]$	1, QN	
4. $(y)(Py \rightarrow Lxy)$	Assume (for RAA)	
5. $\sim[Px \cdot (y)(Py \rightarrow Lxy)]$	3, UI	
6. $\sim Px \vee \sim(y)(Py \rightarrow Lxy)$	5, DeM	
7. $\sim\sim(y)(Py \rightarrow Lxy)$	4, DN	
8. $\sim Px$	6, 7, DS	
9. $Px \cdot \sim Px$	2, 8, Conj	
10. $\sim(y)(Py \rightarrow Lxy)$	4–9, RAA	
11. $Px \rightarrow \sim(y)(Py \rightarrow Lxy)$	2–10, CP	
12. $(x)[Px \rightarrow \sim(y)(Py \rightarrow Lxy)]$	11, UG	

Now, try to symbolize the following sentence:

74. No one loves anyone.

In logicese, we have "For any x, if x is a person, then for any y, if y is a person, x does not love y." In symbols:

75. $(x)[Px \rightarrow (y)(Py \rightarrow \sim Lxy)]$

Statement (74) can also be translated into logicese as follows: "It is not the case that there is an *x* such that *x* is a person and there is a *y* such that *y* is a person, and *x* loves *y*." In symbols:

76. ~(∃x)[Px • (∃y)(Py • Lxy)].

Exercise 9.5, part E, items 9 and 10, provides you with an opportunity to prove that (75) and (76) are logically equivalent.

Now, let's consider an argument involving a grammatically complex state-ment similar to those we've just been symbolizing.

77. The *Mona Lisa* is beautiful. So, anyone who steals the *Mona Lisa* steals something beautiful. (a: The *Mona Lisa*; Bx: x is beautiful; Px: x is a person; Sxy: x steals y)

The symbolization is as follows:

78. Ba ∴ (x)[(Px • Sxa) → (∃y)(By • Sxy)]

Here is a proof for argument (78). Note the use of two assumptions.

1. Ba		∴ (x)[(Px • Sxa) → (∃y)(By · Sxy)]
2. Px • Sxa		Assume (for CP)
3. ~(∃y)(By • Sxy)		Assume (for RAA)
4. (y)~(By • Sxy)		3, QN
5. ~(Ba • Sxa)		4, UI
6. ~Ba ∨ ~Sxa		5, DeM
7. ~~Ba		1, DN
8. ~Sxa		6, 7, DS
9. Sxa		2, Simp
10. Sxa • ~Sxa		9, 8, Conj
11. (∃y)(By • Sxy)		3–10, RAA
12. (Px • Sxa) → (∃y)(By • Sxy)		2–11, CP
13. (x)[(Px • Sxa) → (∃y)(By • Sxy)]		12, UG

Predicate letters can be of more than two places. For example, the follow-ing sentence involves the three-place relation "*x* steals *y* from *z*":

79. Every thief steals something valuable from someone. (Tx: x is a thief, Sxyz: x steals y from z; Vx: x is valuable; Px: x is a person)

In logicese, we have "For any *x*, if *x* is a thief, then there is a *y* such that *y* is valu-able, and there is a *z* such that *z* is a person, and *x* steals *y* from *z*." The symbol-ization looks like this:

80. (x)(Tx → (∃y)[Vy • (∃z)(Pz • Sxyz)])

Again, our symbolization brings out the logical complexity that can be present in rather ordinary English sentences.

As mentioned previously, the best way to ensure accuracy of translation into symbols within predicate logic is first to translate English into logicese and then to translate logicese into symbols. The following short list of examples should serve as a useful guide for this process.

English	Logicese	Symbols
1. No woman is smarter than Eve. (Wx: x is a woman; Sxy: x is smarter than y; e: Eve)	For all x, if x is woman, then it is not the case that x is smarter than e.	$(x)(Wx \rightarrow \sim Sxe)$
2. If Adam is taller than Eve, then someone is taller than Eve. (a: Adam; e: Eve; Txy: x is taller than y; Px: x is a person)	If a is taller than e, then there is an x such that x is a person and x is taller than e.	$Tae \rightarrow (\exists x)(Px \cdot Txe)$
3. No one is shorter than himself. (Px: x is a person; Sxy: shorter than y)	For all x, if x is a person, then it is not the case that x is shorter than x.	$(x)(Px \rightarrow \sim Sxx)$
4. No one is shorter than everyone. (Px: x is a person; Sxy: x is shorter than y)	For all x, if x is a person, then it is not the case that for all y, if y is a person, then x is shorter than y.	$(x)[Px \rightarrow \sim(y)(Py \rightarrow Sxy)]$
5. Everyone is shorter than someone. (Px: x is a person; Sxy: x is shorter than y)	For any x, if x is a person, then there is a y such that y is a person and x is shorter than y.	$(x)[Px \rightarrow (\exists y)(Py \cdot Sxy)]$
6. Every adult gives a present to some child. (Ax: is an adult; Gxyz: x gives y to z; Px: x is a present; Cx: x is a child)	For all x, if x is an adult, then there is a y such that y is a present and there is a z such that z is a child, and x gives y to z.	$(x)[Ax \rightarrow (\exists y)(Py \cdot (\exists z)(Cz \cdot Gxyz)]]$

In closing this section, let us take note of certain general characteristics of relations. Some relations are **symmetrical**. If a relation R is symmetrical, then if *a* bears R to *b*, *b* bears R to *a*. For example, the relation "being a sibling of" is symmetrical, for if Jeff is a sibling of Jane, then Jane must be a sibling of Jeff. On the other hand, the relation "being a mother of" is **asymmetrical**, for if Thelma is the mother of Sharlene, then Sharlene is not the mother of Thelma. To generalize: If a relation R is asymmetrical, then if *a* bears R to *b*, *b* does not bear R to *a*. Note that some relations are **nonsymmetrical**—that is, they are neither symmetrical nor asymmetrical. The relation "being a sister of" is nonsymmetrical, for if Jane is a sister of Chris, Chris may or may not be a sister of Jane—it all depends on whether Chris is male or female.

A relation R is **reflexive** if things must bear R to themselves. For example, each thing is identical with itself. So, identity is a reflexive relation. An **irreflexive** relation is one an entity cannot bear to itself. For example, since nothing can be larger than itself, "being larger than" is an irreflexive relation. And a **nonreflexive** relation is one that is neither reflexive nor irreflexive. "Being proud of" is nonreflexive because a person may or may not be proud of him- or herself.

If a relation R is **transitive**, then if *a* bears R to *b* and *b* bears R to *c*, *a* bears R to *c*. "Being taller than" is transitive. To illustrate: If Al is taller than Bob, and Bob is taller than Chris, then Al must be taller than Chris. On the other hand, "being father of" is an **intransitive** relation, for if Earl is the father of John and John is the father of Drew, then Earl cannot be the father of Drew. To generalize: If a relation R is intransitive, then if *a* bears R to *b* and *b* bears R to *c*, *a* does not bear R to *c*. Finally, a relation is **nontransitive** if it is neither transitive nor intransitive. The relation "being an acquaintance of" is nontransitive. If Rick is an acquaintance of Dawn and Dawn is an acquaintance of Pete, then Rick may or may not be an acquaintance of Pete.

The following exercises provide you with an opportunity to explore the logic of relations.

◆ Exercise 9.5

Part A: Matching   Match the item on the left with the appropriate characteristic on the right.

_____ 1. If x is older than y and y is older than z, then x is older than z.

_____ 2. Nothing is bigger than itself.

_____ 3. If x is shorter than y, then y is not shorter than x.

_____ 4. Everything is the same size as itself.

_____ 5. If x is married to y, then y is married to x.

_____ 6. If x is greater than y, then y is not greater than x.

_____ 7. If x is equal to y, then y is equal to x.

_____ 8. If x is the mother of y and y is the mother of z, then x is not the mother of z.

_____ 9. If x loves y and y loves z, then x may or may not love z.

A. Symmetrical
B. Asymmetrical
C. Nonsymmetrical
D. Reflexive
E. Irreflexive
F. Nonreflexive
G. Transitive
H. Intransitive
I. Nontransitive

____ **10.** If x admires y, then y may or may not
admire x.

____ **11.** A person may or may not hate himself.

____ **12.** If x is obligated to y and y is obligated to z,
then x may or may not be obligated to z.

Part B: Symbolizing   Symbolize the following statements using the schemes of abbreviation provided.

* **1.** Nothing stands to the left of itself. (Lxy: x stands to the left of y)

2. No human is taller than Goliath. (Hx: x is human; Txy: x is taller than y;
g: Goliath)

3. No human is taller than himself. (Hx: x is human; Txy: x is taller than y)

* **4.** Some financier is richer than everyone. (Fx: x is a financier; Rxy: x is richer than y;
Px: x is a person)

5. Someone gives everyone something. (Px: x is a person; Gxyz: x gives to y [object]
z)

6. Someone gives someone everything. (Px: x is a person; Gxyz: x gives to y [object]
z)

* **7.** No deity is weaker than some human. (Dx: x is a deity; Hx: x is human; Wxy: x is
weaker than y)

8. No one gives anyone anything. (Px: x is a person; Gxyz: x gives to y [object] z)

9. Everyone gives someone something. (Px: x is a person; Gxyz: x gives to y [object] z)

* **10.** No one who is poor is richer than someone who is wealthy. (Ox: x is a person; Px:
x is poor; Rxy: x is richer than y; Wx: x is wealthy)

11. No one is more fun than Chris. (Px: x is person; Fxy: x is more fun than y;
c: Chris)

12. No cat is smarter than some horse. (Cx: x is cat; Sxy: x is smarter than y;
Hx: x is a horse)

* **13.** No mouse is mightier than himself. (Mx: x is a mouse; Mxy: x is mightier than y)

14. Every woman is stronger than some man. (Wx: x is a woman; Sxy: x is stronger
than y; Mx: x is a man)

15. If Apollo is better than Hera and Hera is better than Cronos, then Apollo is better
than Cronos. (Bxy: x is better than y; a: Apollo; h: Hera; c: Cronos)

* **16.** Every moviegoer admires Bogart. (Mx: x is moviegoer; Axy: x admires y;
b: Bogart)

17. Some moviegoers admire themselves as well as Bogart. (Mx: x is a moviegoer; Axy:
x admires y; b: Bogart)

18. Some saints help someone everyday. (Sx: x is a saint; Hxyz: x helps y on z; Px: x is
person; Dx: x is a day)

* **19.** No saint helps everyone everyday. (Sx: x is a saint; Hxyz: x helps y on z; Px: x is person; Dx: x is a day)

  20. Everyone falls in love with someone at some enchanted moment. (Px: x is a person; Lxyz: x falls in love with y at z; Ex: x is enchanted; Mx: x is a moment)

  21. The relation "being older than" is asymmetrical. (Oxy: x is older than y)

* **22.** The relation "being the father of" is intransitive. (Fxy: x is the father of y)

  23. The relation "being larger than" is irreflexive. (Lxy: x is larger than y)

  24. The relation "being south of" is transitive. (Sxy: x is south of y)

* **25.** The relation "being near to" is symmetrical. (Nxy: x is near to y)

Part C: More Matching   Match the item on the left with the appropriate characteristic on the right.

_____   **1.** Nothing is smaller than itself.

_____   **2.** If x hates y, then y may or may not hate x.

_____   **3.** If x is the same size as y, then y is the same size as x.

_____   **4.** Everything is the same weight as itself.

_____   **5.** If x is near y, then y is near x.

_____   **6.** If x is less than y, then y is not less than x.

_____   **7.** If x likes y and y likes z, then x may or may not like z.

_____   **8.** If x is the father of y and y is the father of z, then x is not the father of z.

_____   **9.** If x is taller than y, then y is not taller than x.

_____   **10.** If x is younger than y and y is younger than z, then x is younger than z.

A. Symmetrical
B. Asymmetrical
C. Nonsymmetrical
D. Reflexive
E. Irreflexive
F. Nonreflexive
G. Transitive
H. Intransitive
I. Nontransitive

Part D: More Symbolizing   Symbolize the following arguments using the schemes of abbreviation provided.

* **1.** Someone gets angry at everyone. (Px: x is a person; Axy: x gets angry at y)

  2. Everyone laughs at someone. (Px: x is a person; Lxy: x laughs at y)

  3. Everything is either colorless or the same color as itself. (Cx: x has a color; Sxy: x has the same color as y)

* **4.** Some people like themselves, but some people do not like themselves. (Px: x is a person; Lxy: x likes y)

5. No one laughs at anyone. (Px: x is a person; Lxy: x laughs at y)

6. Some students find Kant boring, but Amy is a student who does not find Kant boring. (Sx: x is a student; Bxy: x finds y boring; k: Kant; a: Amy)

* 7. Everything is caused by something (or other). (Cxy: x is caused by y)

8. Nothing causes everything. (Cxy: x causes y)

9. Something causes everything. (Cxy: x causes y)

* 10. Nothing causes anything. (Cxy: x causes y)

11. Everyone gets angry at someone about something. (Px: x is a person; Axyz: x gets angry at y about z)

12. Everything has a cause; but for all x and y, if x precedes y, then y does not cause x. (Cxy: x causes y; Pxy: x precedes y)

13. Every entity is either necessary or dependent on a necessary entity. (Nx: x is necessary; Dxy: x is dependent on y)

14. No logician argues about every subject with everyone. (Lx: x is a logician; Sx: x is a subject; Px: x is a person; Axyz: x argues about y with z)

15. Either nothing is dependent on anything or everything is dependent on something. (Dxy: x is dependent on y)

16. No one is obligated to everyone. (Px: x is a person; Oxy: x is obligated to y)

17. Everyone is obligated to someone. (Px: x is a person; Oxy: x is obligated to y)

18. The relation "being to the north of" is transitive. (Nxy: x is north of y)

19. The relation "being next to" is symmetrical. (Nxy: x is next to y)

20. The relation "being the same shape as" is reflexive. (Sxy: x is the same shape as y)

21. Some number is greater than itself. (Nx: x is a number; Gxy: x is greater than y)

22. God will punish the wicked. (g: God; Wx: x is wicked; Pxy: x will punish y)

23. Some philosopher studies every book with some teacher. (Px: x is a philosopher; Sxyz: x studies y with z; Bx: x is a book; Tx: x is a teacher)

24. Every philosopher studies some book with every teacher. (Px: x is a philosopher; Sxyz: x studies y with z; Bx: x is a book; Tx: x is a teacher)

25. No philosopher studies any book with any teacher. (Px: x is a philosopher; Sxyz: x studies y with z; Bx: x is a book; Tx: x is a teacher)

Part E: Proofs Construct proofs to show that the following arguments are valid. You may use direct proof, CP, or RAA.

* 1. $(x)(y)(Rxy \rightarrow Ryx)$, Rab $\therefore$ Rba

2. $(\exists x)\sim Rxx$, $\sim(x)Rxx \rightarrow (x)(y)\sim Txy$ $\therefore$ $\sim Tba$

3. $(x)(y)(z)[(Wxy \cdot Wyz) \rightarrow Wxz]$, Wab, Wbc $\therefore$ Wac

* 4. $(y)(Bay \vee Bya)$ $\therefore$ Baa

5. Meb $\rightarrow$ Nbb, $(z)\sim Nzz$ $\therefore$ $\sim$Meb

6. $(x)(Tx \to (y)[Vy \to (\exists z)(Pz \cdot Sxyz)])$, $Tb \cdot Ve$ $\therefore$ $(\exists z)(Pz \cdot Sbez)$

* 7. $(\exists x)[Hx \cdot (y)(Hy \to Lyx)]$ $\therefore$ $(\exists x)(Hx \cdot Lxx)$

8. $(x)[Px \to \sim(y)(Py \to Lxy)]$ $\therefore$ $\sim(\exists x)[Px \cdot (y)(Py \to Lxy)]$

9. $(x)[Px \to (y)(Py \to \sim Lxy)]$ $\therefore$ $\sim(\exists x)[Px \cdot (\exists y)(Py \cdot Lxy)]$

* 10. $\sim(\exists x)[Px \cdot (\exists y)(Py \cdot Lxy)]$ $\therefore$ $(x)[Px \to (y)(Py \to \sim Lxy)]$

11. $(\exists y)(z)\sim Kzy$ $\therefore$ $(y)(\exists z)\sim Kyz$

12. $(x)(y)(Sxy \to \sim Syx)$ $\therefore$ $(x)\sim Sxx$

13. $(x)[Px \to \sim(\exists y)Mxy]$ $\therefore$ $\sim(\exists x)(Px \cdot Mxb)$

14. $(\exists x)(y)(Jx \cdot Ny)$, $(\exists x)(Jx \cdot Nx) \to \sim(\exists x)Ux$ $\therefore$ $\sim Ud$

15. $(x)(Kbx \to Gxc)$, $(\exists x)Gxc \to (\exists y)Gcy$ $\therefore$ $(\exists x)Kbx \to (\exists y)Gcy$

16. $(\exists y)(x)(Lxy \to Mxy)$ $\therefore$ $(\exists x)(y)Lxy \to (\exists y)(\exists x)Mxy$

17. $(x)(Gx \to Fx)$, $(\exists x)Fx \to \sim(\exists y)(\exists z)Hyz$ $\therefore$ $(\exists x)Gx \to \sim Hbc$

18. $(x)[Fx \to (y)(Sy \to Rxy)]$, $(x)[Px \to (y)(Rxy \to Ty)]$,
    $\therefore$ $(\exists x)(Fx \cdot Px) \to (y)(Sy \to Ty)$

19. $(x)(\sim Rx \lor Nx)$, $\sim(\exists x)Nx \lor (\exists y)(z)Szy$ $\therefore$ $\sim(\exists x)Rx \lor (z)(\exists y)Szy$

20. $(x)(y)[\sim Cxy \lor (Dx \leftrightarrow Dy)]$, $(x)(\sim Dx \to \sim Ax)$, $(x)[Ax \to (\exists y)(By \cdot Cxy)]$,
    $(\exists x)Ax$ $\therefore$ $(\exists x)(Bx \cdot Dx)$

Part F: English Arguments   Symbolize and construct proofs to show that the following arguments are valid.

* 1. Ormazd is morally superior to Ahriman. For all x, for all y, if x is morally superior to y, then y is not morally superior to x. Hence, Ahriman is not morally superior to Ormazd. (o: Ormazd; a: Ahriman; Sxy: x is morally superior to y)

2. Whatever is not observable by both Einstein and Feynman is outside the realm of science. If an electron is observable by Feynman, then it is observable by Einstein. Accordingly, if any electron is not observable by Einstein, then it is outside the realm of science. (Oxy: x is observable by y; e: Einstein; f: Feynman; Sx: x is outside the realm of science; Ex: x is an electron)

3. There is at least one person. For all x, for all y, x loves y if and only if x loves x. Mad Dog MacKenzie loves no one. It follows that Mad Dog does not love himself. (Px: x is a person; Lxy: x loves y; m: Mad Dog MacKenzie)

* 4. Any rational animal is of greater intrinsic value than any nonrational animal. Karen is a rational animal, but she is not of greater intrinsic value than George. So, if George is an animal, then he is rational. (Rx: x is rational; Ax: x is an animal; Gxy: x is of greater intrinsic value than y; k: Karen; g: George)

5. Carl is not on the team. For Carl is a sprinter, and Carl is faster than any sprinter on the team. But no sprinter is faster than himself. (c: Carl; Sx: x is a sprinter; Fxy: x is faster than y; Tx: x is on the team)

6. Something is such that everything was created by it. We may infer that everything was created by something. (Cxy: x was created by y)

* **7.** All horses are animals. Therefore, every tail of a horse is a tail of an animal. (Hx: x is a horse; Ax: x is animal; Txy: x is a tail of y)

8. Every act is caused by a desire. Every desire is caused by a brain process. For all x, y, and z, if x is caused by y and y is caused by z, then x is caused by z. Thus, every act is caused by a brain process. (Ax: x is an act; Dx: x is a desire; Cxy: x is caused by y; Bx: x is brain process)

9. Either every being is causally dependent on some being (or other), or some being is not causally dependent on any being. If every being is causally dependent on some being (or other), then either there is an infinite chain of dependent beings or some being is causally dependent on itself. It is false that there is an infinite chain of dependent beings. No being is causally dependent on itself. So, some being is not causally dependent on any being. (Dxy: x is causally dependent on y; I: There is an infinite chain of dependent beings)

* **10.** There are sets. Hence, it is not the case that there is a set that contains all and only those sets that do not contain themselves. (Sx: x is a set; Cxy: x contains y)

9.6 Identity

Among the many different types of relations, one is particularly important for logic, namely, identity. For instance, consider the following argument:

> **81.** George Orwell wrote *1984*. George Orwell is identical with Eric Blair. Therefore, Eric Blair wrote *1984*. (o: George Orwell; Wxy: x wrote y; n: *1984*; Ixy: x is identical with y; b: Eric Blair)

This argument is obviously valid, but we cannot prove it valid given the inference rules introduced thus far. Using the scheme of abbreviation provided, the symbolization looks like this:

> 1. Won
> 2. Iob ∴ Wbn

Now what do we do? We have no useful moves to make because as yet we have no inference rules concerning the identity relation.

To introduce identity into our system of logic, we will borrow a symbol from arithmetic—namely, the equality sign—but we will refer to it as the **identity sign**. Except for the addition of the identity sign, the language for predicate logic with identity is exactly like the language for predicate logic. So, we can symbolize the statement "George Orwell is identical with Eric Blair" as follows:

> 82. $o = b$

Here are some additional examples of identity claims, together with their symbolizations:

83. Thomas Edward Lawrence was Lawrence of Arabia. (t: T. E. Lawrence; a: Lawrence of Arabia)

    In symbols: $t = a$

84. Kareem Abdul-Jabbar is Lew Alcindor. (k: Kareem Abdul-Jabbar; a: Lew Alcindor)

    In symbols: $k = a$

85. Muhammed Ali is the same individual as Cassius Clay. (m: Muhammed Ali; c: Cassius Clay)

    In symbols: $m = c$

And we can symbolize negations of identity statements by means of the negation sign, as follows:

86. Sarah Jessica Parker is not identical with Clint Eastwood. (s: Sarah Jessica Parker; c: Clint Eastwood)

    In symbols: $\sim s = c$

87. John Milton is distinct from William Shakespeare. (m: John Milton; s: William Shakespeare)

    In symbols: $\sim m = s$

To construct proofs involving the identity relation, we will add three new rules of inference.[5] The first of these is called **Leibniz' law** (LL) after the philosopher who first made it explicit, Gottfried Wilhelm Leibniz (1646–1716). Leibniz' law is the principle that if x and y are identical, then every property of x is a property of y, and vice versa. Here are some typical inferences permitted by Leibniz' law:

A. 1. $a = b$
   2. Fa
   3. Fb 1, 2, LL

B. 1. $x = y$
   2. $Fx \cdot Gx$
   3. $Fy \cdot Gy$ 1, 2, LL

C. 1. $x = d$
   2. Wxn
   3. Wdn 1, 2, LL

D. 1. $y = e$
   2. $\sim Lxy$
   3. $\sim Lxe$ 1, 2, LL

In each case, we substitute an individual variable or individual constant for another that denotes the same entity. To state our inference rules in a general fashion, we will use the bold letters **m** and **n** to stand for any individual constant *or* individual variable. And we will use $\mathcal{P}$**m** and $\mathcal{P}$**n** to stand for WFFs containing **m** and **n**, respectively. Leibniz' law comes in two forms, as follows:

$$\mathbf{m} = \mathbf{n} \qquad\qquad \mathbf{n} = \mathbf{m}$$
$$\mathcal{P}\mathbf{m} \qquad\qquad\quad \mathcal{P}\mathbf{m}$$
$$\therefore\ \mathcal{P}\mathbf{n} \qquad\qquad \therefore\ \mathcal{P}\mathbf{n}$$

Here, we obtain $\mathcal{P}$**n** by replacing *one or more* free occurrences of **m** in $\mathcal{P}$**m** with free occurrences of **n** in $\mathcal{P}$**n**. *Note:* To grasp this rule, it is important to understand that individual constants (unlike individual variables) are always free because they cannot be bound by quantifiers. Which of the following are correct applications of LL? Which are incorrect?

A. 1. b = c
   2. (x)(Ax → Bx)
   3. Ab → Bb   2, UI
   4. Ac → Bc   1, 3, (?)

B. 1. Cx • Dx
   2. y = x
   3. Cy • Dy   1, 2, (?)

C. 1. (y)(My ∨ Ny)
   2. x = d
   3. Mx ∨ Nx   1, UI
   4. Md ∨ Nx   2, 3, (?)

D. 1. (y)Gyo
   2. o = y
   3. (y)Gyy   1, 2, (?)

All are correct except for application (D). Regarding (D), the problem is that *o* is free in line (1) but is replaced by *y*, which is bound in line (3). The inference in (D) is like arguing, "Every positive number is greater than zero and zero is equal to *y*; therefore, every positive number is greater than itself." The invalidity is obvious. Note that in (C) only one occurrence of *x* in line (3) is replaced by *d* in line (4). This is permitted by Leibniz' law.

    Armed with Leibniz' law, we can easily prove the validity of the argument that appears at the beginning of this section: "George Orwell wrote *1984*. George Orwell is identical with Eric Blair. Therefore, Eric Blair wrote *1984*." The symbolization and proof are as follows:

1. Won
2. o = b   ∴ Wbn
3. Wbn   1, 2, LL

The following argument and proof illustrate another application of LL:

88. William Ockham died of the black plague. Billy the Kid did not die of the black plague. So, William Ockham is not Billy the Kid. (o: William Ockham; Dx: x died of the black plague; b: Billy the Kid)

> 1. Do
> 2. ~Db   ∴ ~o = b
> | 3. o = b   Assume
> | 4. Db   1, 3, LL
> | 5. Db • ~Db   4, 2, Conj
> 6. ~o = b   3–5, RAA

This proof illustrates the general principle that if *x* has a certain property and *y* lacks that property, then *x* is not identical to *y*.

Our next inference rule is called **symmetry** (Sm). Where the bold **m** and **n** stand for either individual constants or individual variables, the rule may be stated as follows. It comes in two forms:

$$\mathbf{m = n} \qquad \sim\mathbf{m = n}$$
$$\therefore \mathbf{n = m} \qquad \therefore \sim\mathbf{n = m}$$

Symmetry justifies such intuitive inferences as these:

89. Lewis Carroll was Charles Lutwidge Dodgson. Therefore, Charles Lutwidge Dodgson was Lewis Carroll. (c: Lewis Carroll; d: Charles Lutwidge Dodgson)

90. Woody Allen is not Gottfried Wilhelm Leibniz. So, Gottfried Wilhelm Leibniz is not Woody Allen. (a: Woody Allen; g: Gottfried Wilhelm Leibniz)

The proofs are short and simple:

> 1. c = d   ∴ d = c   1. ~a = g   ∴ ~g = a
> 2. d = c   1, Sm   2. ~g = a   1, Sm

Our third and final rule of inference governing the logic of identity is the principle that *each thing is identical with itself*. We will call this simply the **identity** (Id) rule. It differs from all our previous rules in that it does not involve a premise. We may represent it as follows:

$$\therefore \mathbf{n = n}$$

Here, the bold **n** stands for any individual constant or individual variable. The Id rule allows us to enter statements of self-identity, such as $b = b$, as lines in a proof. This rule isn't used very often in constructing proofs, but our system of logic would not be complete without it. Here is an argument, symbolization, and proof that illustrate an application of Id.

> 91. Everything that is identical with Bill Cosby is a comedian. So, Bill Cosby is a comedian. (b: Bill Cosby; Cx: x is a comedian)
>
> *In symbols:* $(x)(x = b \rightarrow Cx) \therefore Cb$
>
> 1. $(x)(x = b \rightarrow Cx)$ $\therefore Cb$
> 2. $b = b \rightarrow Cb$ 1, UI
> 3. $b = b$ Id
> 4. Cb 2, 3, MP

Note: the parentheses in premise (1) indicate that the *scope* of the quantifier is $x = b \rightarrow Cx$. Without the parentheses we would have $(x)x = b \rightarrow Cx$, in which case the scope of the quantifier would be $x = b$, and we could not apply UI at step 2.

By means of the identity sign we can symbolize many complicated types of statements. The following list provides you with a guide for moving from English to logicese to symbols. Since these translations often involve lengthy conjunctions or disjunctions, we will allow some informal abbreviations to reduce the number of parentheses, e.g., a long conjuction such as $(Fa \cdot (Gb \cdot Hc))$ can be abbreviated like this: $Fa \cdot Gb \cdot Hc$. After all, the rule of association tells us that, however we group these conjuncts, the resulting statement will be logically equivalent to the original.

Only

English: Only Edison invented the phonograph. (e: Edison; Px: x invented the phonograph)

Logicese: e invented the phonograph, and for all x, if x invented the phonograph, then x is identical with e.

Symbols: $Pe \cdot (x)(Px \rightarrow x = e)$

The Only

English: The only person who is guilty is David. (Px: x is person; Gx: x is guilty; d: David)

Logicese: d is a person and d is guilty, and for all x, if x is a person and x is guilty, then x is identical with d.

Symbols: $Pd \cdot Gd \cdot (x)[(Px \cdot Gx) \rightarrow x = d]$

No . . . Except

English: No one except Bell invented the telephone. (Px: x is a person; b: Bell; Tx: x invented the telephone)

Logicese: b is a person and b invented the telephone, and for all x, if x is a person and x invented the telephone, then x is identical with b.

Symbols: $Pb \cdot Tb \cdot (x)[(Px \cdot Tx) \rightarrow x = b]$

All . . . Except

English: All European countries except Switzerland declared war. (Ex: x is a European country; s: Switzerland; Dx: x declared war)

Logicese: s is a European country and s did not declare war, and for all x, if x is a European country and x is not identical with s, then x declared war.

Symbols: Es • ~Ds • (x)[(Ex • ~x = s) → Dx]

Superlatives

English: The tallest mountain is Mount Everest. (Mx: x is a mountain; Txy: x is taller than y; e: Mount Everest)

Logicese: e is a mountain, and for all x, if x is a mountain and x is not identical with e, then e is taller than x.

Symbols: Me • (x)[(Mx • ~x = e) → Tex]

Note: The strategy regarding superlatives is to say, first, that a certain individual *x* falls into a class and, second, that *x* has a certain property in greater degree than anything else that falls into that class.

At Most

English: There is at most one god. (Gx: x is a god)

Logicese: For all x, for all y, if x is a god and y is a god, then x is identical with y.

Symbols: (x)(y)[(Gx • Gy) → x = y]

English: There are at most two gods. (Gx: x is a god)

Logicese: For all x, for all y, for all z, if x is a god and y is a god and z is a god, then either x is identical with y or x is identical with z or y is identical with z.

Symbols: (x)(y)(z)[(Gx • Gy • Gz) → (x = y ∨ x = z ∨ y = z)]

Note: These "at most" statements do not assert that there are any gods. The first merely states that if there are any gods, then the maximum number is one. And the second states that if there are any gods, then the maximum number is two.

At Least

English: There is at least one god. (Gx: x is a god)

Logicese: There exists an x such that x is a god.

Symbols: (∃x)Gx

English: There are at least two gods. (Gx: x is a god)

Logicese: There exists an x and there exists a y such that x is a god and y is a god and x is distinct from y.

Symbols: (∃x)(∃y)(Gx • Gy • ~x = y)

Note: If we had omitted ~$x = y$ from our symbolization of "There are at least two gods," we would have left open the possibility that x and y are one and the same thing.

Exactly One

English: There is exactly one God. (Gx: x is a god)

Logicese: There is an x such that x is a god, and for all x, for all y, if x is a god and y is a god, then x is identical with y.

Symbols: $(\exists x)Gx \cdot (x)(y)[(Gx \cdot Gy) \rightarrow x = y]$

Note: "Exactly one" is a conjunction of "at least one" and "at most one." We could symbolize "There are exactly two gods" by conjoining our symbolizations of "There are at least two gods" and "There are at most two gods."

Definite Descriptions

English: The discoverer of polonium is Polish. (Dx: x discovered polonium; Px: x is Polish)

Logicese: There is an x such that x discovered polonium, and for all y, if y discovered polonium, y is identical with x, and x is Polish.

Symbols: $(\exists x)[Dx \cdot (y)(Dy \rightarrow y = x) \cdot Px]$

Note: A *definite description* is an expression of the form "The so-and-so" that denotes an individual person or thing.

According to an influential analysis provided by the English logician Bertrand Russell, statements involving definite descriptions, such as "The discoverer of polonium is Polish," make three claims: (a) A thing of a certain type exists (in this case, a discoverer of polonium), (b) that thing is unique, and (c) it has a certain property (in this case, it is Polish). Because Russell's analysis of statements involving definite descriptions has been very influential, we will adopt it here on a provisional basis. How would you symbolize the following statement?

92. The author of *War and Peace* is Tolstoy. (Wxy: x wrote y; p: *War and Peace*; t: Tolstoy)

Using Russell's approach, we get: $(\exists x)[Wxp \cdot (y)(Wyp \rightarrow y = x) \cdot x = t]$.

In closing, let us take note of a subtle ambiguity that can arise in statements involving definite descriptions:

93. The king of Kentucky is not bald. (Kx: x is a king of Kentucky; Bx: x is bald)

(93) can be taken to mean that there is exactly one king of Kentucky and he is not bald. In symbols: $(\exists x)[Kx \cdot (y)(Ky \rightarrow y = x) \cdot \sim Bx]$. This is a false statement since Kentucky has no king. But (93) can also be taken to mean that it is false that there is exactly one king of Kentucky (whether bald or not). In

symbols: $\sim(\exists x)[Kx \cdot (y)(Ky \rightarrow y = x) \cdot Bx]$. This is a true statement by virtue of the fact that Kentucky has no king.

The following exercises provide you with an opportunity to explore the logic of identity.

◇ Exercise 9.6

Part A: Symbolizing   Symbolize the following sentences using the schemes of abbreviation provided.

* **1.** Cameron Diaz is not identical with Linda Fiorentino. (d: Cameron Diaz; f: Linda Fiorentino)

  2. Samuel Clemens is identical with Mark Twain. (s: Samuel Clemens; m: Mark Twain)

  3. Everything is identical with something.

* **4.** Nothing is distinct from itself.

  5. Everything differs from something.

  6. Nothing differs from everything.

* **7.** Each thing is identical with itself.

  8. If two things are identical to a third thing, then they are identical to each other.

  9. Only Faraday discovered electromagnetic induction. (f: Faraday; Dx: x discovered electromagnetic induction)

* **10.** At least two people invented the airplane. (Px: x is a person; Ax: x invented the airplane)

  11. No one except Dostoyevsky wrote *Crime and Punishment*. (Px: x is a person; d: Dostoyevsky; Wxy: x wrote y; c: *Crime and Punishment*)

  12. Goliath is the tallest human. (g: Goliath; Hx: x is human; Txy: x is taller than y)

  13. At most two persons invented the airplane. (Px: x is a person; Ax: x invented the airplane)

  14. There is exactly one dollar in my wallet. (Dx: x is a dollar in my wallet)

  15. At least two physicists discovered polonium. (Px: x is a physicist; Dx: x discovered polonium)

  16. Eddie Murphy is the funniest comedian. (m: Eddie Murphy; Cx: x is a comedian; Fxy: x is funnier than y)

  17. Every star except the sun is outside our solar system. (Sx: x is a star; s: The sun; Ox: x is outside our solar system)

  18. The most brilliant physicist is Einstein. (Px: x is a physicist; Bxy: x is more brilliant than y; e: Einstein)

  19. There is at most one mountain in Ohio. (Mx: x is a mountain; Ox: x is in Ohio)

  20. There are at most two wizards. (Wx: x is a wizard)

21. There are at least two honest politicians. (Hx: x is honest; Px: x is a politician)

22. Everything but God is created. (g: God; Cx: x is created)

23. Exactly one person shot Abraham Lincoln. (Px: x is a person; Sxy: x shot y; a: Abraham Lincoln)

24. The author of *The Brothers Karamazov* is Russian. (Wxy: x wrote y; Rx: x is Russian; b: *The Brothers Karamazov*)

25. The star of the movie *Patton* is George C. Scott. (Sxy: x is a star of y; p: *Patton*; g: George C. Scott)

Part B: Proofs Construct proofs to show that the following arguments are valid.

* 1. Na • ~Nb ∴ ~a = b

  2. ~a = b ∴ (∃x)(∃y)~x = y

  3. Rab • (∃x)~Rxb ∴ (∃x)~x = a

* 4. c = d → e = g, d = c, Fg ∴ Fe

  5. (x)x = a → ~b = b ∴ ~a = x

  6. (x)(~Gx → ~x = d) ∴ Gd

* 7. (y)(Ay → By), Ab, b = c ∴ Bc

  8. (z)(Cz → Dz), ~Dg • Ca ∴ ~g = a

  9. (x)(~Fx → ~Ex), (x)(Fx → Gx), ~Gb • Ea ∴ ~a = b

* 10. (x)(Hx → Jx), (x)(Kx → Lx), Hd • Kc, c = d ∴ Jc • Ld

  11. (x)(Gx → x = d), (∃x)(Fx • Gx) ∴ Fd

  12. (x)(y)[Cyx → ~(z)Dz], (x)n = x, (∃x)[Ax • (y)(Ay → Cxy)] ∴ ~Dn

* 13. (∃x)Hx, (x)(y)[(Hx • Hy) → x = y] ∴ (∃x)[Hx • (y)(Hy → x = y)]

  14. (x)(y)y = x, (x)Mxx ∴ Mab

  15. (x)[(∃y)Kxy → (∃z)Kzx], (x)(Kxg • x = b) ∴ (∃z)Kzb

Part C: English Arguments Symbolize the following arguments using the schemes of abbreviation provided. Then construct proofs to show that the arguments are valid.

* 1. No one antedates himself. Augustine antedates Boethius. Augustine and Boethius are both persons. Therefore, Augustine is not identical with Boethius. (Px: x is a person; Axy: x antedates y; a: Augustine; b: Boethius)

  2. I am not my body. The clump of cells in the corner of the room is my body. It follows that I am not identical with the clump of cells in the corner of the room. (i: I; b: my body; c: the clump of cells in the corner of the room)

  3. Every mental state is identical with some brain state or other. All mental states are introspectible. There is at least one mental state. Hence, some brain state is introspectible. (Mx: x is a mental state; Bx: x is a brain state; Nx: x is introspectible)

* 4. There are exactly two omniscient beings. Apollo is omniscient. We may infer that there is an omniscient being distinct from Apollo. (Ox: x is omniscient; a: Apollo)

5. The only suspect who confessed is Benjamin Bondurant. The only suspect with a motive is Charles Ashworth. At least one suspect who confessed also has a motive. Consequently, Benjamin Bondurant is one and the same individual as Charles Ashworth. (Sx: x is suspect; Cx: x confessed; b: Benjamin Bondurant; c: Charles Ashworth; Mx: x has a motive)

6. The perfect triangle is not a material object. Hence, there is a perfect triangle. (Px: x is perfect; Tx: x is a triangle; Mx: x is a material object)

7. There are at least two physical objects. Jupiter is a physical object. Accordingly, there is at least one physical object other than Jupiter. (Px: x is a physical object; j: Jupiter)

8. The perfect being is divine. All divine beings are benevolent. We may conclude that the perfect being is benevolent. (Px: x is a perfect being; Dx: x is a divine being; Bx: x is benevolent)

9. The greatest painter is Rembrandt. Michelangelo is greater than Rembrandt. Michelangelo is not the same individual as Rembrandt. If one thing is greater than another, then the latter is not greater than the former. Therefore, Michelangelo is not a painter. (Px: x is a painter; Gxy: x is greater than y; r: Rembrandt; m: Michelangelo)

10. The most powerful person is God. The most powerful person is not morally weak. If one thing is more powerful than another, then the latter is not more powerful than the former. If God is not morally weak, then God is morally good. It follows that God is morally good. (Mxy: x is more powerful than y; Px: x is a person; g: God; Wx: x is morally weak; Gx: x is morally good)

Notes

1. See A. N. Prior, "History of Logic," in Paul Edwards, ed., *The Encyclopedia of Philosophy*, Vol. 4 (New York: Macmillan Free Press, 1967), p. 520; and Anthony Flew, "Logic," *A Dictionary of Philosophy*, 2nd ed. (New York: St. Martin's Press, 1979), pp. 208–212. Flew remarks, "The advance in Frege's system . . . is the introduction of quantifiers. . . . This enabled him to unify the logic of propositions [i.e. statement logic] . . . with the study of those logical relationships which had previously been treated in the theory of the syllogism" (p. 211). Gottlob Frege's *Begriffsschrift* was first published in 1879; an English translation is available in J. van Heijnoort, ed., *From Frege to Godel: A Source Book in Mathematical Logic, 1879–1931* (Cambridge, MA: Harvard University Press, 1967).

2. See Flew, *Dictionary of Philosophy*, p. 63. The relevant work is Alonzo Church, "A Note on the *Entscheidungsproblem*," *Journal of Symbolic Logic* I (1936): pp. 40–41.

3. See Donald Kalish, Richard Montague, and Gary Mar, *Logic: Techniques of Formal Reasoning*, 2nd ed. (New York: Harcourt Brace Jovanovich, 1980), p. 238. These authors give the following example: $(x)(y)(z)[(Fxy \cdot Fyz) \rightarrow Fxz]$, $(x)(\exists y)Fxy \therefore (\exists x)Fxx$.

4. The system of rules here employed for predicate logic is based on a system developed by Howard Kahane, *Logic and Philosophy: A Modern Introduction*, 6th ed. (Belmont, CA: Wadsworth, 1990), chap. 6 and 7.

5. The system of rules here employed for the logic of identity is based on a system developed by Kalish, Montague, and Mar, *Logic*, chap. 5.

Chapter 10

Induction

So far, we have focused primarily on deductive logic, and hence on tests for the validity and invalidity of arguments. But as we saw in chapter 1, the premises of some *invalid* arguments provide a significant degree of support for their conclusions. We will now look into some of these types of arguments in greater detail. In short, we will take up the subject of inductive logic. **Inductive logic** is the part of logic that is concerned with tests for the strength and weakness of arguments. To date, logicians have made far more headway in deductive logic than in inductive logic, so that inductive logic is relatively less developed. For example, effective tests for strength and weakness have so far proven more elusive than tests for validity and invalidity. Our approach will be to examine common forms of argument that can be strong and to describe some of the main evaluative techniques available.

10.1 Inductive and Deductive Logic: Contrasts and Clarifications

Recall that a **strong argument** has the following essential feature: It is unlikely (though possible) that its conclusion is false while its premises are true. For example:

> 1. Ninety percent of 40-year-old American women live to be at least 50. Helen is a 40-year-old American woman. So, Helen will live to be at least 50.

Argument (1) is not valid, but its premises do provide some support for its conclusion. Just consider this: If you have to place a bet, and the premises of (1) sum up the relevant information you have in hand, then you should bet on the conclusion of (1) rather than on its negation.

A **weak argument** has the following essential feature: It is not likely that if its premises are true, then its conclusion is true. For example:

> 2. Fifty percent of 30-year-old American women live to be 80. Alice is a 30-year-old American woman. So, Alice will live to be 80.

Is it likely that if the premises of this argument were true, then its conclusion would be true? Let us assume for the moment that the premises are true. If 50 percent of 30-year-old American women will live to be 80, then 50 percent of 30-year-old American women will *not* live to be 80. So, given only the information provided in the premises, we could just as well conclude that *Alice will not live to be 80*. In short, the premises give us no reason to prefer the conclusion of the argument to its negation. Thus, it is *not* likely that if the premises were true, then the conclusion would be true. Hence, the argument is weak.

An **inductively sound argument** is one that has two essential features: (a) It is strong, and (b) all its premises are true. An **inductively unsound argument** is one that is either (a) weak or (b) strong with at least one false premise. Note that "inductively unsound argument" is *not* defined as follows: an argument that either is weak or has a false premise. This latter definition is too broad because it would classify *valid arguments with false premises* as inductively unsound. It is unhelpful to classify valid arguments as inductively unsound since they meet a higher logical standard than strength.

Inductively Sound Arguments Can Have False Conclusions

Let us now contrast deduction and induction. First, note that a deductively sound argument cannot have a false conclusion, but an inductively sound argument can have a false conclusion. A deductively sound argument cannot have a false conclusion, because if an argument is valid and has only true premises, then it must have a true conclusion. But if an argument is strong and has only true premises, it is still possible (though unlikely) that its conclusion is false. To illustrate, suppose the premises of the following argument are true:

> 3. Ninety percent of the cars in the parking lot were vandalized last night. My car was in the parking lot. So, my car was vandalized last night.

But suppose I go to the parking lot and discover that my car was not vandalized. Does that mean the argument is weak? No, it simply means that my car was among the 10 percent not vandalized. Again, the main point is that the conclusion of an inductively *sound* argument can be false.

Form Does Not Ensure Strength

Second, while every argument with a valid form is valid, the strength of an argument is not ensured by its form. To grasp this point, let us consider a form of argument that can be strong under certain conditions, **statistical syllogism**. Here is an example:

> 4. Ninety-five percent of women over 30 years of age cannot run the mile in under 5 minutes. Rebekah is a woman over 30 years of age. Hence, Rebekah cannot run the mile in under 5 minutes.

The form of a statistical syllogism can be represented as follows:

> 1. _____ percent of A is B.
> 2. c is an A.
> So, 3. c is a B.

In our example, A stands for the set of women over 30, while B stands for the set of things that cannot run the mile in under 5 minutes. The lowercase letter c stands for a particular person, Rebekah. (In another case, c might stand for a particular thing, event, or situation.) The blank space is to be filled with numbers greater than 50 and less than 100. If we place the number 50 in the blank, we get a weak argument. If we place the number 100 in the blank, we get a valid argument—it is as if we had said, "All A is B." So, we will stipulate that the numbers filling the blank in a statistical syllogism must lie between 50 and 100 *exclusive*. By the way, in ordinary English, a statistical syllogism may be formulated without the use of specific percentages. For instance, the following counts as a statistical syllogism: "The vast majority of violent criminals are unhappy. Jones is a violent criminal. So, Jones is unhappy."

Now, consider argument (4) in light of the following statistical syllogism:

> 5. Eighty percent of women over 30 who are world-class marathoners can run the mile in under 5 minutes. Rebekah is a woman over 30 who is a world-class marathoner. Therefore, Rebekah can run the mile in under 5 minutes.

The premises of arguments (4) and (5) could all be true. But their conclusions contradict each other (assuming "Rebekah" names the same person in both arguments). This situation cannot arise in the case of valid arguments. If the premises of two *valid* arguments can be combined to form a consistent set of statements, then the conclusions of those arguments must be consistent as well.

What is going on? Assuming one is fully aware of the information contained in the premises of argument (5), one cannot rightly pronounce argument (4) strong. Yet, (4), like (5), has the form of a statistical syllogism. So, while it is obvious that arguments having the form of a statistical syllogism *can* be strong, it is also clear that having that form is not a guarantee of strength.

Logicians are not agreed on how to characterize what is wrong with argument (4) *given that* the premises of both arguments are true. Perhaps the best we can say is this: If someone were to advance (4) *while aware* of the information contained in the premises of (5), that person would be leaving out relevant evidence, evidence that has a bearing on the truth of the conclusion of (4). We might call such a culpable omission the **fallacy of incomplete evidence**.[1] And, in general, when one seeks to meet the standard of strength but *knowingly omits relevant evidence*, one is apt to fall short of the standard. The main point for the moment, however, is simply that form does not ensure strength. This fact greatly complicates the process of testing arguments for strength and weakness. Let us amplify this point briefly.

We have already seen that a knowledge of valid argument forms is a powerful tool in evaluating arguments for validity. But when evaluating arguments for strength, the identification of form only serves to rule out certain types of errors. For example, consider the following argument:

6. Five percent of adults can do 50 push-ups. John Barton is an adult. So, John Barton can do 50 push-ups.

This argument may appear to be a statistical syllogism, but it is not really of that form, because the percentage is too low. The percentage must lie between 50 and 100 (exclusive) to meet the requirements for a statistical syllogism. And given only the information provided in the premises of (6), we have more reason to deny the conclusion than to affirm it. ("Ninety-five percent of adults cannot do 50 push-ups. John is an adult. So, John cannot do 50 push-ups.") Accordingly, the form of argument (6) is flawed.

As we have just seen, however, *given only the information provided in the premises*, arguments having a certain form will appear strong, and yet they may be weak, if relevant information has been omitted. This is so, for example, whenever the argument has the form of a statistical syllogism. And this leaves us with the question, When does the omission of relevant evidence count as a logical error? It is clearly an error to omit evidence (or information) when one knows full well that it reduces the strength of one's argument. But consider the following cases:

■ The relevant evidence is readily available and most people are aware of it. The arguer is not aware of it, but his ignorance is excusable for some reason (e.g., due to illness or other circumstances beyond his control, he has been isolated from the ordinary sources of information).

■ The relevant evidence is readily available and most people are aware of it. The arguer is not aware of it but her ignorance is culpable (i.e., she should be aware of it).

■ The relevant evidence is available but only through some investigation (e.g., a trip to the library), and the arguer is not aware of the evidence.

Do we want to say that a fallacy of incomplete evidence has been committed in some or all of these kinds of cases? This issue is under dispute among logicians, and we cannot attempt to resolve it here. But the very nature of the issue underscores the fact that induction is far less tidy than deduction.

Strength Comes in Degrees

Here is a third important contrast between deduction and induction. Validity is an all-or-nothing affair; it does not come in degrees. For instance, if two arguments are valid, it makes no sense to say that one of them is more valid than the other. But strength does come in degrees. Statistical syllogisms nicely illustrate this fact. An argument of the form "___ percent of A are B; c is an A; so, c is a B" will be stronger as the number in the blank nears 100, and it will be less strong as the number nears 50 (assuming that no fallacy of incomplete evidence has been committed). Accordingly, if two arguments are strong, one of them may well be stronger than the other.

Myths About Inductive Logic

We close this section by challenging two commonly held beliefs about induction.

A Flawed Definition of "Inductive Argument"

Consider the following definitions of "deductive argument" and "inductive argument," which are similar to those provided in many textbooks:

> A **deductive argument** is an argument in which the premises are claimed to support the conclusion in such a way that it is *impossible* for the premises to be true and the conclusion false. [. . .] On the other hand, an **inductive argument** is an argument in which the premises are claimed to support the conclusion in such a way that it is *improbable* that the premises be true and the conclusion false.[2]

In essence, these definitions tell us that a deductive argument is one *claimed to be valid* while an inductive argument is one *claimed to be strong*. There are many problems lurking here in the word "claimed." First, arguments themselves do not make claims; people do. And, in many cases, we have no way of knowing whether the arguer claims (or claimed) that the premises support the conclusion in a certain way. For example, a written argument may be unclear, and the arguer herself may be unavailable (e.g., anonymous or deceased). Second, the same argument may be advanced by more than one person, with some claiming it to be valid and others claiming it to be strong. Is the argument then both deductive and inductive? Third, people may be very vague or confused about what they are claiming. Suppose an arguer has *never thought of* the distinction between validity and strength and merely claims that his premises support a given conclusion. Is his argument deductive or inductive? It seems to be neither, given the definitions just cited. Fourth, suppose the arguer gives a valid argument but explicitly claims that it is strong. Do we count the argument as inductive? Apparently so, given the definitions just cited, but that answer seems wrong. Finally, suppose the arguer gives a strong argument but explicitly claims that it is valid. Do we classify the argument as deductive? Again, apparently so, but the answer seems wrong.

We are free, of course, to define "inductive argument" in some other way. For example, we can make a list of forms of argument that are strong when properly constructed and call all arguments having these forms "inductive arguments." (This approach classifies the arguments without regard for whether the premises are *claimed* to support the conclusion in a certain way.) The point here is simply that the typical definitions of "inductive argument" and "deductive argument" are flawed because they rest on the shaky notion that arguments can be neatly sorted on the basis of whether they are *claimed* to be strong or valid.

To sum up, attempts to define "inductive argument" often are deficient. For the most part, we are better off asking not whether an argument is deductive or inductive, but whether it is valid or strong. Nevertheless, we can, if we wish, use the phrase "inductive argument" to refer to a class of arguments that, when well constructed, are strong.

Do Strong Arguments Always Move from Particular Statements to General Statements?

One often hears it said that "deductive arguments proceed from the general to the specific while inductive arguments proceed from the specific to the general." To avoid the possibility of mingling this myth with the previous one, we can restate it as follows: "Valid arguments proceed from the general to the specific, while strong arguments proceed from the specific to the general." To see the problems with this thesis, consider the following examples.[3]

Some valid arguments move from general premises to a general conclusion:

> 7. All Shiites are Moslems. All Moslems are monotheists. Hence, all Shiites are monotheists.

Some valid arguments go from particular premises to a particular conclusion:

> 8. William of Ockham died in 1349. Bertrand Russell did not die in 1349. Therefore, William of Ockham is not identical with Bertrand Russell.

Perhaps surprisingly, some valid arguments even go from particular to general:

> 9. Bill Clinton is a Democrat. So, anyone who votes for Clinton votes for a Democrat.

Furthermore, some strong arguments have a general premise but a particular conclusion:

> 10. All lemons previously tasted have been sour. Therefore, the next lemon to be tasted will be sour.

Note that the premise here concerns only *previously* tasted lemons while the conclusion concerns a lemon as yet untasted. So, the argument is not valid, but it is nevertheless strong. And certain types of strong arguments move from particular premises to particular conclusions:

> 11. Jeff Lyle is similar to Jim Gossett in that each weighs 150 pounds. My CD player broke when Jeff sat on it. So, my CD player will break if Jim sits on it.

By some fluke, or perhaps because the CD player is on a softer surface, the conclusion of this argument could be false even if the premises are true. So, the argument is not valid, but it does appear to be strong. Finally, some strong arguments have general premises and a general conclusion:

> 12. All five starters on the basketball team performed well throughout the season. All five starters have shown a willingness to sacrifice personal glory for the sake of the team throughout the season. All five starters are experienced competitors. All five starters are rested and in good health. All five starters are highly motivated to do their best. So, all five starters on the basketball team will perform well in the competition tomorrow.

Note that the conclusion of argument (12) could be false even if the premises are true. For instance, one of the players may perform poorly due to receiving some dismaying news just prior to the game. So, the argument is not valid, but it seems to be strong.

To sum up, it is a mistake to suppose that strong arguments always move from particular statements to general statements. And it is equally erroneous to suppose that valid arguments always move from general statements to particular ones. These characterizations are at best gross oversimplifications.

The following exercises will test your understanding of the material in this section.

◆ *Exercise 10.1*

Part A: True or False? Which of the following statements are true? Which are false?

* 1. If an argument is inductively sound, then it has true premises.

2. If an argument is inductively sound, then it is strong.

3. If an argument is inductively sound, then it is invalid.

* 4. If an argument is strong and has only true premises, then it is inductively sound.

5. If an argument is weak, then it is probable that if its premises are true, its conclusion is false.

6. If an argument is strong, then it is possible that its conclusion is false even if its premises are true.

* 7. If an argument is weak, then it is inductively unsound.

8. If an argument has a false premise, then it must be inductively unsound.

9. If an argument has true premises and a false conclusion, then it is weak.

* 10. If an argument is valid, then it is strong.

11. If an argument is strong, then it is valid.

12. If an argument is inductively unsound, then it is weak.

* 13. If an argument is weak, then it must be invalid.

14. If the conclusion of an argument is *exactly as probable* as its negation, given the premises of the argument, then the argument is weak.

15. If an argument is inductively unsound, then it is strong but has at least one false premise.

* 16. Strong arguments always proceed from the specific to the general.

17. Valid arguments always proceed from the general to the specific.

18. Some valid arguments proceed from the general to the general.

* 19. If an argument is valid and has at least one false premise, then it is inductively unsound.

20. If an argument is weak, then it is not likely that if its premises are true, then its conclusion is true.

Part B: Identifying and Evaluating Statistical Syllogisms   Which of the following arguments have the form of a statistical syllogism? Which do not? Some of the arguments contain information that suggests a possible fallacy of incomplete evidence. Explain why.

* 1. Fifty percent of the marbles in container 3 are green. The next marble to be drawn is a marble from container 3. Hence, the next marble to be drawn is green.

2. Two-thirds of the students at Seattle Pacific University are women. Chris is a student at Seattle Pacific. Consequently, Chris is a woman.

3. The vast majority of Americans approve of the Gulf War. John Montgomery is an American. So, John Montgomery approves of the Gulf War even though he belongs to a religious group most of whose members are pacifists.

* 4. More than half of all voters in the state of Washington favor campaign reform. Gordon Johnark, a U.S. senator, is a voter in the state of Washington. Accordingly, Gordon Johnark favors campaign reform.

5. Philosophy 301 is similar to Philosophy 101 in that both are philosophy courses. Philosophy 101 is a course Diana dislikes. So, Philosophy 301 is a course Diana dislikes.

6. Most college students do not work full-time. Jane is a college student. Therefore, Jane does not work full-time.

* 7. Seventy percent of the citizens of Salt Lake City do not drink coffee. Phil Goggans is a citizen of Salt Lake City. So, even though Phil owns and operates the Caffeine Club Coffee House, he probably does not drink coffee.

8. One hundred percent of Texans love Texas. Marla Miller is a Texan. Therefore, Marla loves Texas.

9. Eighty-two percent of those in a randomly chosen sample of 4000 Americans eat meat. Therefore, about 82 percent of Americans eat meat.

* 10. Nearly all Mennonites are (were, and will be) pacifists. John Howard Yoder was a Mennonite. Accordingly, John Howard Yoder was a pacifist.

11. According to the *National Enquirer*, last week a woman gave birth to a baby whose father came from Mars. Therefore, last week a woman gave birth to a baby whose father came from Mars.

12. Fifty-one percent of Marines are under 19 years old. Captain Lawrence is a Marine. So, Captain Lawrence is under 19 years old.

* 13. Jack is 65 years old. So, Jack is not currently making a living as a professional boxer.

14. Ninety percent of abortions in the 1980s were performed in the first 12 weeks of pregnancy. Ms. Brown's abortion occurred in the 1980s. Thus, Ms. Brown's abortion was performed in the first 12 weeks of her pregnancy.

15. Ninety-nine percent of lemons are sour. The fruit I am about to eat is a lemon. Therefore, the fruit I am about to eat is sour.

10.2 Arguments from Authority and Induction by Enumeration

In this section, we will examine two common types of arguments that are strong when properly constructed. In this context, a "properly constructed" argument is not merely one that conforms to a certain pattern or form, but also one that avoids any fallacy of incomplete evidence.

Arguments from Authority

Let us begin with **arguments from authority**, which have the following form:

> 1. *R* is a reliable authority regarding *S*.
> 2. *R* sincerely asserts that *S*.
> So, 3. *S*.

Here, *R* stands for any reliable source of information (e.g., an acknowledged expert, a group of experts, or a reference work), while *S* stands for any statement. We use arguments from authority when we appeal to dictionaries, encyclopedias, or maps, or to experts in any field. For instance:

> 13. In his *Dictionary of Philosophy,* Anthony Flew defines "logicism" as the view that "mathematics, in particular arithmetic, is part of logic." So, that is what logicism is.[4]

Arguments from authority are strong given that the authority in question is reliable, and the more reliable the authority, the stronger the argument. An authority is reliable to the extent that he or she can be counted on to provide true statements on the subject at issue. However, even reliable authorities can make mistakes, and for this reason, arguments from authority are not valid. (Incidentally, an appeal to an *infallible* authority would be a special type of valid argument, for an infallible cognitive authority is one that cannot make mistakes. Thus, "R is an infallible authority regarding S, and R sincerely asserts S; therefore, S" is a valid form. Of course, it is one thing to observe that this form of argument is valid, and another thing altogether to claim to know that there is an infallible authority who has sincerely asserted such-and-such statements.)

Note that the word "authority" is ambiguous. In this context, "authority" means "cognitive authority." A *cognitive* authority is a person or group possessing a special fund of knowledge. In other contexts, however, "authority" means "organizational authority." An *organizational* authority is a person or group whose particular office or role involves the responsibility of making certain decisions that affect others in the organization (e.g., school, corporation, or nation). It is vital that these two meanings of "authority" not be confused, for the following form of argument is weak: "An organizational authority asserts that S is true; therefore, S is true." Except when organizational authorities happen also to be cognitive authorities regarding S, the fact that they assert S does not provide good evidence that S is true. While this is obvious on reflection, the trust placed in organizational authorities often leads to a confusion between the two types of authority in ordinary life.

The *ad verecundiam* fallacy (or appeal to unreliable authority) masquerades as an argument from authority, but as presented in chapter 6, this fallacy really has a slightly different form, namely: "An authority *whose reliability can be reasonably doubted* asserts S. Therefore, S."

As regards arguments from authority, the *fallacy of incomplete evidence* typically arises when the arguer fails to note that an equally reliable authority (or a more reliable authority) denies the conclusion (either explicitly or implicitly). For example, suppose you look up a historical personage, such as Thomas Aquinas, in a reliable source, and reason as follows:

14. In Cahn's *Classics of Western Philosophy*, we read that Thomas Aquinas was born in 1225. So, Aquinas was born in 1225.[5]

However, you later find another reliable source stating that Aquinas was born in 1224.[6] The difference may simply be due to honest error (e.g., a printer's error or a mistake on the part of the author). Alternatively, it may be due to a difference of opinion among historians. Assuming the authorities *are* both *generally reliable* on the subject in question, the premises of the original argument remain true (i.e., Cahn is a reliable authority on the subject in question, and he does assert that Aquinas was born in 1225), but the strength of the inference is called into doubt by the conflict between reliable authorities. In such a case, one can often avoid a fallacy of incomplete evidence simply by drawing on a wider range of reliable authorities. If nearly all of the most reliable authorities agree on a point, then the appeal to authority can still render a conclusion probable. Or one may appeal to an authority with a specialized expertise in the issue in question.[7] However, it may happen that the more one looks into the matter, the more it appears that the authorities are not basing their assertions on solid evidence. In such a case, the appeal to authority is weak.

Arguments from authority often fail in another way. The authority may be misquoted or misinterpreted. When this occurs, the second premise of the argument, "R sincerely asserts that S," is false. The reliable authority didn't really assert S; rather, the reliable authority asserted some other statement P, which may (or may not) be easily confused with S. In this case, the argument is inductively unsound because it has a false premise.

To sum up, arguments from authority can be inductively sound, but several errors must be avoided. For example, fallacies of incomplete evidence can occur if the relevant authorities disagree. Moreover, arguments from authority often fail to be inductively sound because the arguer misquotes (or misinterprets) the relevant authorities. In this case, the argument has a false premise of the form. "R sincerely asserts that S." Finally, if there is reasonable doubt about the reliability of the alleged authority, an *ad verecundiam* fallacy is committed.

Induction by Enumeration

Let us now consider another type of argument that is strong when properly constructed. This type of argument is called **induction by enumeration**, and the form is as follows:

> 1. _____ percent of a sample of A is B.
> So, 2. Approximately _____ percent of A is B.

The **sample** consists of the members of set A that have been observed. Thus, the sample is a subset of set A. Set A itself is called the **population**. The blanks may be filled by numbers from zero to 100, inclusive. For instance:

> 15. Twenty-five percent of a sample of the students at St. Ambrose College are members of the Republican Party. So, approximately 25 percent of the students at St. Ambrose College are members of the Republican Party.

Here, "twenty-five" fills the blanks, the set of students at St. Ambrose College replaces A, and the set of persons belonging to the Republican Party replaces B. Argument (15) is correct in form, but it may still be weak. The *fallacy of incomplete evidence* arises if our sample is too small or if it is biased. For instance, if our sample consists of only 4 students and St. Ambrose has 3000 students enrolled, then our sample is just too small to warrant the inference. Or suppose our sample is large but biased—it was taken at a meeting of the Young Democrats Club.

Then, again, the argument will be weak. Our sample must be *representative* of set A or else the premise will not support the conclusion.

How large does a sample need to be? How can one avoid biased samples? These are important questions that we cannot explore in great detail. But even a small amount of information about sampling errors can help one avoid them. Let us here consider three features of a good sample. A good sample is *random*, of *appropriate size*, and not distorted by *psychological factors*.[8]

Random Samples

A good sample is *random* as opposed to *biased*. "Random" here has a technical meaning. A sample is **random** if (and only if) each member of the population has an equal chance of being selected for observation. A famous case of a biased sample illustrates the need for random samples. In 1936, *Literary Digest* magazine conducted a poll to determine who would win the presidential election—Republican Alf Landon or Democrat Franklin D. Roosevelt. The *Digest* sent out 10 million questionnaires, of which roughly 2 million were returned. A sample of 2 million is a very large sample compared to those used in a Gallup poll, so there was no problem with the size of the sample. And based on the sample, the *Digest* predicted that Landon would win the election, but in fact Roosevelt won by a landslide. What went wrong? At least in part, this: The names of those to be polled had been taken mainly from lists of telephone subscribers and lists of automobile registrations. However, the election occurred during the Great Depression, when many people could not afford a telephone or an automobile. And a very large percentage of those on government relief voted for Roosevelt.

How can a random sample be obtained? In some cases, the randomness of a sample is fairly easy to obtain. This is especially so when the members of a population are known to have a high degree of uniformity. To take an extreme case, suppose our argument concerns hydrogen atoms. Hydrogen atoms are exceedingly similar to one another, each having one proton and one electron. So, although the total number of hydrogen atoms is very large (according to physicists, there are about 10^{80} hydrogen atoms!), a relatively small sample would support an inference about the total population. Similarly, police detectives can learn much from a few strands of hair or a few drops of blood at the scene of a crime. A person's hairs tend to be very similar to one another, and one drop of a victim's (or suspect's) blood will be very similar to another.

However, if we are concerned with human opinions about, say, which foods taste best, our population will have a very low degree of uniformity, for humans have widely varying views about which foods taste best. And thus, we will need to take elaborate precautions to ensure a random sample. Bias can creep into a sample in many ways, some of them rather subtle. To cite just one common problem, when a sample consists of questionnaires that must be voluntarily returned, people on one side of an issue may have much stronger feelings than those on the other side, and those with stronger feelings may be more likely to return the questionnaire, which skews the result.

To avoid such biased samples, researchers use elaborate methods to obtain a genuinely random sample. In essence, a city, state, or country is divided into geographical areas (taking population density into account), and then, within each area, those to be interviewed are selected on a chance basis:

> The most common procedure is to divide the overall population into separate categories (or "strata") according to the size of the locality the people live in. Specific geographical areas are then determined on a systematic (or on a random) basis in which a specified number of interviews are to be conducted. The people actually interviewed fall into the sample on a chance basis. They are not interviewed because they are representative of any particular population characteristic. Rather, they are interviewed solely because the area in which they live has fallen into the sample.[9]

Here is a rough, oversimplified illustration: The total U.S. population is about 250 million. Suppose we divide the United States into 250 geographical areas with 1 million people in each area. If six persons are then chosen randomly from each area, we have a sample of 1500.[10]

Appropriate Sample Size

A good sample is of the appropriate size. It would be nice if a simple mathematical formula could be applied to determine the appropriate sample size in any given case. Unfortunately, no such formula is available. As we have just seen, the appropriate size of the sample depends on such factors as the degree of uniformity within the population. It also depends on (a) the size of the population and (b) the acceptable degree of error.

Size of the Population   To some extent, the size of the sample depends on the size of the population. This is especially true when the population is relatively small. For instance, if we are taking an opinion poll at a small college with only a few hundred students enrolled, our sample can be smaller than it would need to be if we were polling students at a university with 20,000 enrolled. However, one common misconception about samples is that the larger the population, the larger the sample should be. The fact is that problems with samples depend

> only slightly upon the size of the population under study if it is a large population. To achieve a sampling error of plus or minus three percentage points requires a sample of 1500 interviews—regardless of whether one is surveying a city, a state, or the nation.[11]

We can perhaps best understand this point by means of an illustration. Suppose we are drawing a sample of 500 marbles from a barrel containing 10,000 marbles, half of them red and half blue. And let us stipulate that our sample is chosen randomly, so that each marble in the barrel has an equal chance of being selected. Our sample likely will contain approximately 250 red marbles (give or take a few), and approximately 250 blue ones (give or take a few). Now, suppose the barrel contains 1 million marbles instead of 10,000. If we select 500 marbles at random, we should still get approximately 250 red and 250 blue. Thus, a larger population does not necessarily require a larger sample.[12]

Acceptable Degree of Error   The **sampling error** is the difference between the percentage of the sample that has the attribute in question and the percentage of the population that has it. For instance, suppose we take a random sample of 10 marbles from a population of 100: 6 marbles in our sample are red, 4 are blue. We conclude that 60 percent of the marbles in the population are red. In fact, let us suppose, exactly 50 percent of the marbles in the population are red. The sampling error in this case is 10 percent.

   Based on experience with the Gallup polls, the relationship between sample size and sampling error can be stated with remarkable precision for studies of large populations. Consider the following data:[13]

Number of Interviews	Margin of Error (in percentage points)
4000	± 2
1500	± 3
1000	± 4
750	± 4
600	± 5
400	± 6
200	± 8
100	±11

Let us suppose that we are conducting a poll, and our (randomly selected) sample contains 1000 registered voters, of whom 700 say they currently favor Smith for president. We conclude that 70 percent of the registered voters currently favor Smith for president, with a sampling error of ±4 percent. In other words, given our evidence, it is probable that between 66 and 74 percent of the registered voters currently favor Smith for president. And, as the data indicate, we can reduce the margin of error by increasing the size of our sample. Of course, it takes more time and effort to obtain larger samples (and hence, more money), so we may rest content with a smaller sample if we do not have a strong need for greater accuracy.

Psychological Factors

One last potential problem with samples should be noted: distortion due to psychological factors. Even if a sample is randomly chosen and of the appropriate size, an induction by enumeration can still be weak if psychological factors enter the picture in certain ways. For instance, the nature of the questions asked in a survey may be such as to produce inaccuracies. If people are asked, "How often have you driven your car while intoxicated?" or "Have you stolen anything in the past year?", they may not wish to answer truthfully. Furthermore, the answers may be influenced by the interviewer. For instance, a frown or a shocked tone of voice may cause the interviewee to modify his or her answers.

To sum up, arguments having the form of an induction by enumeration can be strong, but several errors must be avoided. Most importantly, the sample must be sufficiently large and random. Furthermore, care must be taken to ensure that psychological factors do not produce an inaccurate sample.

The following exercise gives you practice in evaluating both arguments from authority and inductions by enumeration.

◆ *Exercise 10.2*

Identifying Inductive Arguments   Which of the following arguments are examples of the types of inductive argument introduced in this section? Which are not? (a) If an argument is not an example of any of the types of arguments introduced in this section, simply write "incorrect form." (b) If an argument is an example of a type of argument introduced in this section, identify the type. (c) Specify the sampling error wherever possible. (d) Identify any fallacies of incomplete evidence and briefly indicate why a fallacy has been committed.

* **1.** One hundred percent of the dogs that have been dissected have had kidneys. Hence, 100 percent of the members of the class of dogs have kidneys.

  2. In a recent study, a randomly chosen sample of 1500 American husbands were asked how many times they had had extramarital affairs. Eighty-four percent of those in the sample stated that they had never had an extramarital affair. Hence, approximately 84 percent of American husbands have never had an extramarital affair.

  3. The word *obviate* means "to do away with or prevent" because that is what *Webster's Dictionary* says it means.

* **4.** According to a recent poll, 50 percent of a random sample of 1500 voters in Ohio favor Quigley for governor. Thus, roughly 50 percent of voters in Ohio favor Quigley for governor.

  5. Bertrand Russell, a noted logician, states that the social mores concerning sex outside of marriage are harmful and oppressive. So, the social mores concerning sex outside of marriage are harmful and oppressive.

  6. According to a recent poll, 65 percent of a randomly chosen sample of 1000 voters in San Francisco are Democrats. Thus, 65 percent of American voters are Democrats.

* **7.** The *Bantam Medical Dictionary* says that an *ectopic pregnancy* is "the development of a fetus at a site other than the womb" (e.g., the fallopian tube). So, an ectopic pregnancy is the development of a fetus at a site outside the womb.

8. According to a recent poll, zero percent of a randomly chosen sample of five U.S. voters favor Mack Smith for president. So, zero percent of U.S. voters favor Mack Smith for president.

9. According to a recent poll, only 15 percent of a randomly chosen sample of 750 Oregon voters favor McKay for senator. Thus, approximately 15 percent of Oregon voters favor McKay for Senator.

* 10. The noted astrologer Vashti Zinia states that the stars determine the course of human history. So, our fate is in the hands of the stars.

11. The following information is gleaned from Howard Zinn, *A People's History of the United States* (New York: HarperCollins, 1995), p. 585: In February 1991, U.S. aircraft dropped bombs on an air raid shelter in Baghdad. Between 400 and 500 people were killed. The Pentagon claimed the shelter was a military target. But reporters who were allowed to inspect the site asserted that there was no evidence of any military presence. Now, given this information from Zinn, we may conclude that the Pentagon was right: The shelter was a military target.

12. In a recent study involving 600 male prison inmates in Georgia, 80 percent of those in the sample indicated disapproval of the death penalty. Hence, 80 percent of men in Georgia disapprove of the death penalty.

* 13. Sixty-seven percent of those in a randomly chosen sample of 4000 Americans are overweight. Therefore, about 67 percent of Americans are overweight.

14. In a recent study, a randomly chosen sample of 400 clergymen were asked whether they have had sexual fantasies involving same-sex partners. Only four of the clergymen answered in the affirmative. Thus, only about 1 percent of clergymen have had sexual fantasies involving same-sex partners.

15. Eighty-two percent of a randomly chosen sample of 600 American college students are sleep-deprived. Therefore, approximately 82 percent of American college students are sleep-deprived.

* 16. According to a recent poll, 80 percent of a randomly chosen sample of 10 Americans prefer football to soccer. Hence, about 80 percent of Americans prefer football to soccer.

17. Of a randomly selected sample of 1000 Americans, only 140 had red hair. So, about 14 percent of Americans have red hair.

18. In a recent study involving a randomly chosen sample of 200 college sophomores, none of those polled planned to take a course in symbolic logic. Hence, no college sophomores plan to take a course in symbolic logic.

* 19. According to Dee Brown, *Bury My Heart at Wounded Knee* (New York: Washington Square Press, 1981), 153 Native Americans are known to have been killed in the massacre at Wounded Knee, although the actual number may well be as high as 300. Only 25 U.S. soldiers were killed, most of them by "friendly fire" from other soldiers. According to Brown, the soldiers ordered the Native Americans to give up their rifles, but a young Minneconjou named Black Coyote did not give up his

rifle. Some eyewitnesses say that Black Coyote opened fire on the soldiers; others say he was deaf and did not understand the soldiers. Therefore, based on this information, we may conclude that Black Coyote started the incident at Wounded Knee by firing on the soldiers.

20. According to a recent poll, 90 percent of a randomly chosen sample of 4000 women in Mississippi reported that they believe that God exists. Hence, approximately 90 percent of American women believe that God exists.

10.3 Mill's Methods and Scientific Reasoning

Mill's methods provide us with patterns of reasoning to use in reaching conclusions of the form "A causes B." These patterns of reasoning are not valid, but the premises can provide significant support for their conclusions. Mill's methods are useful in many kinds of situations, from mundane cause-and-effect issues to the rarefied and technical areas of modern science. Because Mill's methods are used routinely by scientists, a discussion of Mill's methods leads naturally to a consideration of scientific reasoning.

Mill's Methods

We often want to know what has caused some event or phenomenon. For example, when one is ill, one may visit a physician to discover the cause. When one's automobile will not run, one tries to find a competent mechanic to identify the cause. And when a friendship ceases to be enjoyable, one may speculate on the cause(s).

Unfortunately, the word "cause" is ambiguous. Sometimes, it is used to refer to a **sufficient condition** for some event or phenomenon: If X is a sufficient condition for Y, then if X occurs, Y occurs. In other cases, the word "cause" may be used to refer to a **necessary condition** for some event or phenomenon: If X is a necessary condition for Y, then Y occurs *only if* X occurs. Consider some examples:

16. For humans, being beheaded is a sufficient condition for death.

17. For flowers, water is a necessary condition for growth.

If a person is beheaded, he or she dies. So, being beheaded is a sufficient condition for death. But other conditions are also sufficient for death—for example, having one's air supply cut off for a day. By contrast, water is a necessary condition for the growth of flowers, but it is not a sufficient condition—light is also necessary, as are the proper nutrients in the soil. When an event or phenomenon occurs, all the necessary conditions must be present. (They wouldn't be necessary conditions if the event could occur without them.) And "cause" is often ambiguous—it may denote either a necessary or a sufficient condition. Furthermore, "cause" is sometimes used to refer to a condition that is neither sufficient nor necessary. For example, a forest ranger may tell us that lightning caused a forest fire. The lightning immediately preceded the fire, but it wouldn't have caused the fire if the weather had been wet and cold. So, the lightning is not by itself a sufficient condition. Nor is it a necessary condition, for a carelessly discarded cigarette might also have ignited the forest fire (in the absence of any lightning). So, in this case, the lightning is simply the most obvious or salient condition in a group of conditions that, *taken together, form a sufficient condition*—for example, (a) lightning strikes timber, (b) the timber is dry, and (c) oxygen is present.

In his book *A System of Logic,* the English philosopher John Stuart Mill (1806–1873) developed five methods for establishing conclusions of the form "A causes B." We will examine four of Mill's methods.

First, Mill proposed the **method of agreement**. To apply this method, one attempts to identify a common factor in a range of cases. For example, suppose five students at Vernon Elementary School become nauseous shortly after lunch. The school nurse forms a list of what each student ate for lunch:

Student 1: Milk, tuna salad, candy bar
Student 2: Tuna salad, coke, potato chips
Student 3: Milk, tuna salad, chocolate cake
Student 4: Apple, orange juice, tuna salad
Student 5: Tuna salad, milk, carrots, cupcake

The nurse observes that all of these students ate the tuna salad in the school cafeteria. Thus, eating the tuna salad is a factor common to all five cases. Of course, this is not enough, by itself, to prove that the tuna salad caused the nausea, but the search for a common factor gives us a good place to start in identifying the cause.

Second, Mill proposed the **method of difference**. To apply this method, we compare two cases, one in which the effect is present and one in which the effect is absent. To continue with our school lunch example, the "effect" is the nausea. To apply this method, the school nurse would find out what one or more students *who didn't become nauseous* ate for lunch. For example, suppose students (6) and (7) didn't become nauseous:

Student 6: Pizza, coke, tossed salad
Student 7: Hot dog, milk, potato chips

Since the effect (nausea) is absent, the cause is absent as well. And since students (6) and (7) did not eat the tuna salad, the nurse gains an additional line of evidence in favor of the tuna salad as the cause of the nausea. (Of course, it could be that those who became ill just happen to have an intolerance for tuna.

Then the common factor is more subtle and complex—a combination of the material ingested and the conditions specific to the students who became ill, such as food allergies.)

Mill's third method, his so-called **joint method**, is simply a combination of the method of agreement and the method of difference. And, as we have just seen, it is entirely natural to combine the two.

Mill's fourth method is called the **method of concomitant variation**. To employ this method, we show that as one factor varies, another varies in a corresponding way. A simple example would be the speed of a car and the extent to which the accelerator is pressed down. The more you press down on the accelerator, the faster the car goes. In the case of the nauseous schoolchildren, the nurse may find that some students are sicker than others and that the more tuna salad a student ate, the sicker he or she is. This would give the nurse yet further evidence that eating the tuna salad caused the nausea.

It should be obvious that arguments employing Mill's methods are not valid, for even if the premises are true, it is possible that the conclusion is false. The following example (which we first encountered in chapter 6) illustrates this point:

> 18. On Monday, Bill drank scotch and soda, and noticed that he got drunk. On Tuesday, Bill drank whiskey and soda, and noticed that he got drunk. On Wednesday, Bill drank bourbon and soda, and noticed that he got drunk. Bill concluded that soda causes drunkenness.[14]

Here, Bill applies the method of agreement. Soda is indeed a common factor in the three cases. And yet Bill has arrived at a false conclusion. The problem is that Bill failed to recognize another, very important common factor, namely, alcohol. In this case, Bill's oversight is outlandish. But in the history of science, there are many cases in which the most important common factor was something that most people did not even regard as a possible cause. For example, prior to Louis Pasteur's famous experiments in 1881, virtually no one thought that vaccination could produce immunity to anthrax. And until 1900, when Walter Reed proved that mosquitoes can transmit yellow fever, most people had never even regarded mosquito bites as a possible cause of the disease.

The soda and alcohol example illustrates something very important about Mill's methods: To make effective use of the methods, we have to make intelligent guesses about which conditions are causally relevant in a given case. For example, just prior to Bill's getting intoxicated, he may have been wearing a white shirt, breathing regularly, thinking about summer vacation, and eating a sandwich. Why do we ignore these prior conditions as we consider possible causes of Bill's inebriated state? Well, our background knowledge gives us some ideas about the kinds of conditions that might produce the effect in question. Accordingly, out of the myriad conditions present in any given case, we hypothesize that only some of them are causally relevant. Thus, our discussion of Mill's methods leads naturally to a discussion of the formation and testing of hypotheses. In other words, our discussion of Mill's methods leads naturally to a discussion of scientific reasoning.*

Scientific Reasoning

Boiled down to its essentials, scientific reasoning involves (a) describing the problem, (b) formulating hypotheses, and (c) testing the hypotheses. To illustrate this process, let us consider the work of one scientist, Ignaz Semmelweis, a physician who worked in the Vienna General Hospital. In the 1840s, he made an important discovery concerning the cause of childbed (puerperal) fever. At that time, childbed fever was a frequent cause of death among pregnant women in Europe.[15]

Describing the Problem

The Vienna General Hospital had two maternity divisions. In one of these divisions, the First Maternity Division, 8.2 percent of the mothers died of childbed fever in 1844; 6.8 percent died in 1845; and 11.4 percent died in 1846. In the Second Maternity Division, however, the death rate was much lower: 2.3, 2.0, and 2.7 during the same years.

Formulating and Testing Hypotheses

Semmelweis formulated a number of hypotheses. Because some people thought that the crowded conditions in the First Maternity Division might be the cause of the problem, Semmelweis formulated the following hypothesis:

> H_1: Childbed fever is caused by the crowded conditions in the First Maternity Division.

Semmelweis tested this hypothesis by considering its implications. He observed that the Second Division was actually more crowded than the First. (Due to the notorious reputation of the First Division, women understandably went to great lengths to avoid being assigned to it.) Thus, he reasoned that if H_1 were true, then the rate of childbed fever should be at least as high in the Second Division as in the First. But, as noted previously, the rate was in fact lower in the Second Division. So, Semmelweis concluded that H_1 is false. (*Note:* In rejecting H_1, Semmelweis made use of Mill's method of difference. Since the *effect*—that is,

---

*For the curious, here is a brief description of Mill's fifth method, called the *method of residues*. The method of residues is applied when some of the causes of a phenomenon have already been identified; we then conclude that a remaining factor completes the causal account. For example, a room in your house is unusually cold in the winter. You identify three possible causes: (a) a broken windowpane, (b) a hole in the ceiling, or (c) a clogged furnace duct. You replace the windowpane and unclog the furnace duct; the room is not as cold as it was, but still a bit cool. You conclude that the hole in the ceiling accounts for the residual coldness.

the higher rate of mortality due to childbed fever—was lacking in the Second Division, the cause should also have been absent. But the crowded conditions were present; therefore, they must not have been the cause.)

Semmelweis observed that the women in the two divisions delivered their babies in different positions; those in First Division delivered lying on their backs, while those in the Second Division delivered lying on their sides. Accordingly, Semmelweis formulated the following hypothesis:

> H_2: Childbed fever is caused by the position of delivery (specifically, by the mother lying on her back rather than on her side).

To test this hypothesis, Semmelweis instructed the First Division to use the same method of delivery as that used in the Second Division. But this change did not affect the rates of mortality, so Semmelweis concluded that H_2 is false.

Desperate for answers, Semmelweis tried a psychological hypothesis. He noted that the priest who administered the sacraments to the dying women was readily visible to the women in the First Division, so he formulated this hypothesis:

> H_3: The appearance of the priest terrifies the patients, making them more susceptible to childbed fever.

To test this hypothesis, Semmelweis instructed the priest to come by a different route, so that he would not be seen or heard except by those who were already gravely ill. But this made no difference in the rate of childbed fever or the rate of death; accordingly, Semmelweis inferred that H_3 is false.

At length, a tragic accident led Semmelweis to an insightful hypothesis. A colleague of Semmelweis's named Kolletschka was accidentally cut by an assistant's scalpel while performing an autopsy. Shortly thereafter, Kolletschka died of an illness whose symptoms were the same as those of childbed fever. Semmelweis intuited that Kolletschka's death had been caused by the "cadaveric matter" introduced into his bloodstream during the autopsy. Furthermore, Semmelweis knew that the doctors and medical students often examined the women in the First Division immediately after performing dissections in the autopsy room, and although the medical personnel washed their hands, an unmistakable odor indicated that some of the cadaveric matter was still present. This led Semmelweis to the following hypothesis:

> H_4: Childbed fever is caused by cadaveric matter on the hands of medical examiners.

Again, Semmelweis tested the hypothesis by considering its implications. If H_4 was correct, then childbed fever could be prevented by removing the infectious material from the hands of those examining the pregnant women. Accordingly, he required all those who participated in such examinations to wash their hands in a solution containing chlorinated lime. As a result of this measure, the rate of childbed fever dropped dramatically in the First Division: indeed, it became lower than the rate in the Second Division.

Semmelweis also noted that H_4 explained why the rates of disease and mortality had differed between the two divisions, for the patients in the Second Division had been cared for by midwives rather than by those whose training involved the dissection of cadavers. (Note the use of Mill's method of difference here: The effect is absent in the Second Division, and so is the cause.) Semmelweis concluded that H_4 is true.

Let us now consider the general principles involved in testing hypotheses. Let us use H to stand for a hypothesis and I to stand for an implication of the hypothesis. You may have noticed that Semmelweis employed the following pattern of reasoning in rejecting hypotheses:

1. If H, then I.
2. It is not the case that I.
So, it is not the case that H.

This is the general pattern for rejecting an empirical hypothesis as a result of an unfavorable test outcome (i.e., one that conflicts with the predictions made on the basis of the hypothesis). Note that the form is *modus tollens,* which meets the standard of deductive logic, namely, validity. For this reason, and also because valid forms may be employed in deriving test implications from a hypothesis, this picture of scientific hypothesis testing is often called the "hypothetico-deductive method."

It would, however, be a gross oversimplification to suggest that rejecting a scientific hypothesis is simply a matter of applying *modus tollens.* In a typical case, one must make many background assumptions to obtain the premises. For example, suppose an astronomical hypothesis implies that a planet will be in a certain location at a certain time. An astronomer uses her telescope to observe whether the planet is present at the location and time implied by the hypothesis, but she does not see the planet. Has the hypothesis been disproved? Not necessarily. The astronomer may have made an error in aiming the telescope. The telescope may have malfunctioned. And note that using the telescope presupposes that the various hypotheses concerning optics, which are employed in the design and construction of the telescope, are true. So, in testing one hypothesis, we may need to assume that another hypothesis or theory is true. The point is that while *modus tollens* may be employed in testing hypotheses, applying it in scientific situations involves making many background assumptions that may be open to question in a given case (e.g., the telescope did not malfunction, the astronomer used the telescope properly, and so on).

How is a hypothesis confirmed? It may seem that Semmelweis used the following pattern of reasoning (where H stands for the hypothesis and I stands for an implication of the hypothesis):

1. If *H*, then *I*.
2. *I*.
So, *H*.

("If cadaveric matter causes childbed fever, then the patients currently being treated in the First Division do not get childbed fever when the cadaveric matter is absent. The patients currently being treated in the First Division do not get childbed fever when the cadaveric matter is absent. So, cadaveric matter causes childbed fever.") But the form of argument here is the fallacy of affirming the consequent. Are we saying, then, that scientific reasoning rests on a fallacy? No. It would indeed be a fallacy to argue that if one specific implication of a hypothesis holds true, then the hypothesis holds true. But if we can identify many specific implications of a hypothesis, and observation (or experiment) indicates that all the implications are true, we can accumulate a significant amount of support for the hypothesis. Each instance in which an implication of a hypothesis is observed to be true is called a **confirming instance**. And, at some point, as the number (and/or kind) of confirming instances for a hypothesis increases, scientists find it unreasonable to attribute this to chance or mere coincidence. However, it is extremely difficult to specify clear and general logical principles for determining when a hypothesis is strongly supported by the evidence, and we cannot enter into a discussion of these complicated issues here.[16]

What do scientists look for in a hypothesis?[17] At least four things. First, generally speaking, a hypothesis should be logically consistent with hypotheses or theories that are already well established. There are exceptions to this general rule, however. For example, Einstein's theories were not consistent with Newton's, and yet they came to be accepted because they explained things Newton's theories could not explain.

Second, a hypothesis should have explanatory power. A hypothesis has explanatory power to the extent that known facts can be inferred from it. And, of course, the "known facts" mentioned here must include those we are seeking to explain; otherwise, the hypothesis is irrelevant. To illustrate, Semmelweis's hypothesis that cadaveric material (when introduced into the bloodstream) causes childbed fever has explanatory power. From it, we can infer that persons who have had cadaveric material introduced into their bloodsteams are apt to contract childbed fever, which explains the high rate of childbed fever in the First Maternity Division.

Third, a good scientific hypothesis should be liable to empirical tests. Suppose Semmelweis had hypothesized that the higher rate of childbed fever in the First Division was caused by ghosts who haunt the First Division (but not the Second Division). Is there any way to test this hypothesis? There might be. Perhaps the ghosts can be seen or heard at certain times, or perhaps their influences can be thwarted by the work of an exorcist. But suppose no tests are allowed. The alleged ghosts, it is asserted, cannot be seen or heard. No traces of them can be found, not even in principle. Nor are they the type of ghosts who will respond to the work of exorcists. And so on. Such an untestable hypothesis is not acceptable within any scientific discipline.

But at least two cautionary remarks are warranted here. First, scientists routinely form hypotheses concerning entities that are not directly observable, such as electrons and protons. Nevertheless, many observable events can be explained in terms of these unobserved entities. For instance, if a hypothesis states that electrons behave in such-and-such a way, implications concerning observable events can be derived from the hypothesis. Scientists can then check to see if these events occur. Second, it is one thing to say that an untestable hypothesis is unscientific, and another to say that it is untrue. There may well be things that cannot be explained scientifically—for example, the very existence of physical reality—and such things may have to be explained via untestable hypotheses or else not explained at all.

Finally, other things being equal, scientists generally prefer a simpler hypothesis to one that is more complicated. But consider an example outside of science for a moment. When investigating a murder, police do not typically begin with a complicated hypothesis to the effect that the victim was assassinated as part of an international conspiracy. Rather, it seems best to start with a relatively simple hypothesis and to complicate it only as necessary to explain the phenomenon.

To take a scientific case, suppose we are testing a steel spring that hangs from the ceiling.[18] We place a 1-pound weight on the spring and it extends 1 inch; we place a 2-pound weight on the spring and it extends 2 inches; we place a 3-pound weight on the spring and it extends 3 inches; and so on. We hypothesize that the behavior of the spring conforms to the formula $x = y$ (where x is the force in pounds and y is the extension in inches).

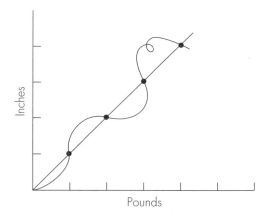

In the accompanying graph, our hypothesis is represented by the straight, diagonal line. The dots stand for specific observations we have made—for example, "A 2-pound weight extends the spring 2 inches." The curvy line represents an

---

Summary of Mill's Methods

The **method of agreement** involves identifying a "common factor," that is, one that is present whenever the effect is present.

The **method of difference** involves comparing two cases, one in which the effect is present and one in which it is absent. If when the effect is absent the possible cause C is also absent, the test lends support to C as the cause.

The **joint method** involves combining the first two methods.

The **method of concomitant variation** involves showing that as one factor varies, another varies in a corresponding way.

---

alternative hypothesis that is far more complicated but that still accounts for each of the observations. The point, once again, is that a good scientific hypothesis avoids unnecessary complications. If a relatively simple hypothesis works, one should not complicate it.

To sum up, Mill's methods provide us with some helpful strategies for reaching conclusions of the form "A causes B." But in order to use Mill's methods effectively, we have to make intelligent guesses about which conditions are apt to cause the phenomenon in question. That is, we have to formulate hypotheses. Scientific reasoning involves describing a problem, formulating hypotheses, and testing them. Hypotheses are tested by drawing out their implications and checking to see if the implications are true. A good scientific hypothesis is consistent with well-established hypotheses, has explanatory power, can be tested, and is relatively simple.

The following exercises give you some practice in applying the concepts introduced in this section.

◆ Exercise 10.3

Part A: Mill's Methods   Which of Mill's methods is illustrated in each of the following examples? If, in your opinion, the conclusion reached indicates that an inadequate hypothesis was employed, formulate a better hypothesis.

* **1.** By his third shot of whiskey, Robert noticed that he was feeling intoxicated. He drank another shot of whiskey and found that the feeling increased. Curious, he drank yet another shot, and his head really began to spin. Robert concluded that the whiskey was making him drunk.

2. Dick and Jane took a history exam. Both did poorly although both studied for many hours. Both had pulled an "all-nighter." They concluded that the cause of their poor performance on the exam was a lack of sleep.

3. Tom, Tanya, and Teri ate dinner at a Japanese restaurant. Tom had rice, squid, and salad. Tanya had rice, octopus, and salmon. Teri had rice, squid, and cucumber rolls. After the meal, Tom and Teri had upset stomachs, but Tanya did not. They concluded that the squid caused their upset stomachs.

* 4. Alonzo has done well on his last three math exams. In each case, he studied very intensely for 3 hours the night before the exam. Also, in each case, he departed from his usual informal style of dress and wore a tie to the exam. Alonzo concluded that wearing a tie increases the quality of his performance on examinations.

5. Marla ate some cookies that she obtained from a vending machine. Shortly after she ate the cookies, her lips began to tingle, and then they swelled up. Because the swelling didn't last very long, she quickly forgot about the incident. But a few weeks later, she again ate some cookies from a vending machine, and once again, her lips swelled up immediately. She concluded that something in the cookies was causing her lips to swell up.

6. An economist noted a correlation between the length of women's skirts and the price of stocks. As fashion trends moved in the direction of shorter skirts, stock prices increased. But as fashion trends moved in the direction of longer skirts, stock prices fell. The economist concluded that fashion trends regarding the length of women's skirts cause stock prices to rise and fall.

* 7. A certain physics professor got into his car to drive home from work. As he backed out of the parking place, he noticed a large oil spot. The next day he parked in a different parking place, one that had no oil spot. But as he backed out of the parking place at the end of the day, he once again noticed a large oil spot. He concluded that an oil leak from his car had caused the oil spots.

8. Pasteur gave 25 farm animals a vaccination for anthrax. These animals, as well as 25 who had not been vaccinated, were subsequently given a large dose of anthrax germs. None of the vaccinated animals came down with the disease, but all of the others died of anthrax. Pasteur concluded that his vaccine produced immunity to anthrax.

9. Colette took one benedryl capsule and felt a bit drowsy. She took a second Benedryl capsule and began to feel very sleepy. She took a third benedryl capsule and could scarcely keep her eyes open. She concluded that benedryl causes sleepiness.

* 10. A doctor had 10 patients suffering from a rare form of cancer. By investigating the life histories of his patients, he found that each of them had worked for several years at a nuclear power plant and each had been exposed to significantly high amounts of radiation on at least one occasion. The doctor concluded that the radiation was the cause of cancer in each of the 10 cases.

11. Bobby pulled the lever on the little black box. His electric train began to move forward. He pulled the lever a bit further. The train went faster. He pulled the lever further, and the train went so fast it flew off the track. Bobby concluded that pulling the lever caused the train to go faster.

12. A psychiatrist treated five soldiers who wished to stop stuttering. He discovered that each of the soldiers had begun to stutter shortly after undergoing a frightening experience in combat. The psychiatrist concluded that the stuttering was caused by extreme fear.

* 13. Galvani was dissecting a dead frog. By chance, he touched the nerves of the frog's leg with an instrument that conveyed an electrical impulse. The frog's leg muscles contracted suddenly. Galvani touched the frog's nerves many times with the instrument, and each time the frog's leg muscles contracted sharply. Galvani then touched the frog's nerves with a metal instrument that did not convey an electrical impulse. The frog's leg did not contract. Galvani concluded that an electrical impulse had caused the dead frog's muscles to contract.

14. A Martian visited a large city in North America. While walking the streets incognito, he observed the traffic closely. He noted that when lights blinked on the left side of a vehicle, it nearly always turned left; and when lights blinked on the right side of a vehicle, it nearly always turned right. The Martian concluded that the blinking lights caused the vehicles to turn.

15. A sociologist closely observed correlations between demographics and the rate of violent crime. He noted that the rate of violent crime rose as the percentage of young men (15 to 25 years of age) *relative to the rest of the population* increased. For example, he noted that about 15 years after each baby boom, there is an increase in the rate of violent crime, and the rate remains high for approximately 10 years. After about 10 years, the rate of violent crime falls off. The sociologist concluded that increases in the rate of violent crime are largely caused by an increase in the number of young men (as a percentage of the population).

* 16. On Wednesday night, Fran had shrimp, fries, and a salad with blue cheese dressing. She broke out in hives. The following Sunday, she ate the same meal, and again she broke out in hives. She suspected that the blue cheese dressing was the problem. So, a few days later, she ate shrimp, fries, and a salad with Italian dressing. She did not break out in hives. Fran concluded that the blue cheese dressing had indeed caused the hives.

17. Sharon drank one cup of coffee with cream on an empty stomach. She began to feel more alert. So, she had a second cup of coffee, again with cream. She noticed that she felt a bit jittery, but the coffee was delicious, so she had a third cup, adding a generous portion of cream. Suddenly, Sharon began to feel very nervous and to talk excitedly. She concluded that the cream was making her feel nervous.

18. A psychiatrist treated six men who wanted to be married but always wound up in profoundly unsatisfying relationships with women. He found that all of the men had been neglected by their parents as children. He concluded that parental neglect had left the men without resources for maintaining satisfying relationships with women.

* 19. At one point in his research on the causes of yellow fever, Walter Reed confined some volunteers to a carefully sealed room. The room contained a number of mosquitoes who were known to have bitten persons having yellow fever. All the volunteers were bitten by the mosquitoes and all contracted yellow fever. In another room, mosquitoes were carefully sealed out, and the people staying in that room did not contract yellow fever. Reed concluded that the mosquitoes were spreading yellow fever.

20. On one occasion, . . . [Semmelweis] and his associates, having carefully disinfected their hands, examined first a woman in labor who was suffering from a festering cervical cancer; then they proceeded to examine twelve other women in the same room, after only routine washing without renewed disinfection. Eleven of the twelve patients died of puerperal fever. Semmelweis concluded that childbed fever can be caused not only by cadaveric material, but also by "putrid matter derived from living organisms" —Carl G. Hempel, *Philosophy of Science* (Englewood Cliffs, NJ: Prentice-Hall, 1966), p. 6

Part B: Hypotheses   In the following arguments, identify any hypotheses that fail to meet the four criteria for good scientific hypotheses. State which criterion is violated, and explain your answer.

* 1. Frederick has been having trouble with his watch. It keeps losing time. He had the battery replaced, but that didn't help. So, Frederick hypothesized that an invisible demon had possessed his watch, slowing down the mechanism. He took the watch to a priest for an exorcism, but that didn't help either. Frederick concluded that the demon must be the type of demon that cannot be exorcised.

2. Robert was behind in his lab work in Chemistry 101. He heated some chemicals in a test tube. A gas was generated, and Robert filled a balloon with the gas. The balloon floated upward when released. Robert concluded that boiling the chemicals had somehow produced a situation in which the law of gravity was temporarily suspended. He excitedly wrote up his lab reports, expecting an A for his remarkable discovery.

3. Jennifer has been having trouble with her computer. For example, occasionally a few letters in a document get misplaced (without any action on her part). In an effort to account for these glitches, Jennifer hypothesizes that the computer has developed free will and is now occasionally making its own choices.

* 4. A certain biology professor noted a correlation between increased activity among bees and the beginning of spring. He hypothesized that as bees flap their wings, their body heat increases, which warms the air around them, thus bringing about the changes in seasons from winter to spring.

5. A mechanic is trying to discover why your car won't start. He hypothesizes that the trouble is due to poltergeistic activity. When you state your intention of obtaining a second opinion, he indicates that this will do you no good, since he is the only mechanic who can intuit the presence of poltergeists in cars and no observational checks are possible.

6. A certain professor got into his car to drive home from work. As he backed out of the parking place, he noticed a large oil spot. The next day he parked in a different parking place, one that had no oil spot. But as he backed out of the parking place at the end of the day, he once again noticed a large oil spot. He concluded that a group of pranksters had lifted his car up via blimp and poured oil under it on both days.

* **7.** A detective is trying to explain two murders that are remarkably similar in detail, yet happened at the same time in very different locations—one in Florida and one in Alaska. The detective hypothesizes that the murderer has somehow learned to travel faster than the speed of light.

8. A biologist is trying to account for the extinction of the dinosaurs. He hypothesizes that the dinosaurs simply decided to stop having sex.

9. A detective is assigned to a murder case. The victim has been shot six times with a large-caliber handgun. Forensic tests indicate that the bullets all came from the same gun. With virtually no other facts to go on, the detective hypothesizes that there were six murderers who took turns shooting the victim, each of them firing one shot.

10. Martha has received her logic exam back from the instructor. She did well but lost a few points on one item. Specifically, on the exam, an inference of the form "If A, then B; not A; so not B" is identified as *modus tollens*. The answer is in Martha's handwriting. But since Martha knows that the inference form is in fact the fallacy of denying the antecedent, she hypothesizes that the CIA stole her exam from the instructor, erased her original answer, and wrote in an incorrect answer in her handwriting.

10.4 Arguments from Analogy

Another type of argument which can be strong, when properly constructed, is the argument from analogy. **Arguments from analogy** have the following form:

> 1. A is similar to B in relevant respects.
> 2. B has property P.
> So, 3. A has property P.

Here, A and B can stand for many different things. They may stand for a specific object or person (e.g., my car or Socrates). They may stand for a type or kind of object (e.g., cars in general or human beings). They may stand for specific events or situations (e.g., the situation in which your car has broken down). P stands for any sort of property (e.g., the property of being fast, the property of being intelligent, or the property of being dangerous). Let's consider an example:

> **19.** *The Tempest* and *A Midsummer Night's Dream* are both plays written by William Shakespeare. These two plays are very similar in length. I was able to read *A Midsummer Night's Dream* in the space of an evening. So, I am able to read *The Tempest* in the space of an evening.

Here, "*The Tempest*" replaces A and "*A Midsummer Night's Dream*" replaces B in the original schema. P is the property of being readable (by me) in the space of an evening.

How, in general, do we go about evaluating the strength of an argument from analogy? Basically, we have to evaluate to what degree (if any) A's similarity to B provides support for the statement that A has property P. Unfortunately, there is no formula or mechanical method for evaluating arguments from analogy. But in assessing the logical connection between the premises and the conclusion, it usually helps to ask the following three questions:

> **Question 1**: What are the relevant respects in which A and B are similar? Ideally, the one who offers the argument supplies this information, but often the information is provided only in part. Similarities are relevant if they increase the likelihood of A's having property P. And, generally speaking, the more relevant respects A and B share, the stronger the argument.
>
> **Question 2**: Are A and B dissimilar in any relevant respects? That is, does the analogy between A and B break down at any relevant points? Dissimilarities are relevant if they decrease the likelihood of A's having property P. Relevant differences between A and B tend to weaken the argument.
>
> **Question 3**: Are there things (other than A) that are similar to B in the relevant respects? If so, do these things have property P? To the extent that there are things relevantly similar to B that lack P, the analogy breaks down. To the extent that there are things relevantly similar to B that have P, the analogy holds up.

Let us evaluate argument (19) in terms of these three questions.

Question 1: In what relevant respects are A (*The Tempest*) and B (*A Midsummer Night's Dream*) similar? They are similar in length, and both are written in Elizabethan English. The style of writing is also similar.

Question 2: Are A (*The Tempest*) and B (*A Midsummer Night's Dream*) dissimilar in any relevant respects? *The Tempest* is a more serious play than *A Midsummer Night's Dream*, and in places *The Tempest*, unlike *A Midsummer Night's Dream*, is rather pessimistic in tone. So, it might take a little longer to read *The Tempest*.

Questions 3: Are there things other than A (*The Tempest*) that are similar to B (*A Midsummer Night's Dream*) in the relevant respects and that have property P (i.e., can be read by me in an evening)? Yes, I once read another of Shakespeare's plays, *As You Like It*, in an evening. And it is similar in length, type of English, and style to *A Midsummer Night's Dream*.

To sum up, the answer to Question 1 indicates that there are several relevant respects in which *The Tempest* and *A Midsummer Night's Dream* are similar. The answer to Question 2 notes a relevant dissimilarity, but the dissimilarity does not seem to weaken the analogy much. The answer to Question 3 indicates that as we consider related examples, the analogy holds up. Accordingly, the argument appears to be strong.

Let's consider a second argument from analogy:

20. Parrots and humans can both talk. Humans can think rationally. Therefore, parrots can think rationally.

Here, "parrots" replaces A and "humans" replaces B in the original schema. P is the property of being able to think rationally.

Question 1: What are the relevant similarities between parrots and humans? The chief relevant similarity is the ability to talk. Of course, it is true that both parrots and humans can talk. And there is *some* sort of linkage between the ability to talk and the ability to think rationally, since it is primarily in the linguistic behavior of humans that their capacity for rational thought is exhibited.

Question 2: Are parrots dissimilar to humans in any relevant respects? Yes, in at least two relevant respects. First, as far as we can tell, parrots merely *mimic* what they hear. They do not produce their own sentences in a spontaneous, creative fashion. And, of course, mimicking is not a reliable indication of rational thought. Second, the brain of a parrot is much smaller than that of a human. And this raises a legitimate doubt as to whether parrots are capable of the kind of thinking humans are capable of.

Incidentally, it must be understood that not all dissimilarities are relevant ones. For example, parrots have feathers and humans do not. But this dissimilarity has no apparent bearing on the issue at hand (i.e., can parrots think rationally?), and so it is irrelevant for present purposes. Relevant dissimilarities are those that affect the likelihood of A's having property P.

Question 3: Are there any examples of things (other than parrots) that can talk but cannot think rationally? Apparently so, for some deranged persons are able to talk but only in a highly disconnected and illogical fashion. So, apparently, there are things that talk but do not think rationally. This observation again draws attention to a weakness in the analogy between parrots and humans (in general).

To sum up, our answer to Question 1 indicates that there are *some* relevant similarities between parrots and humans, but not many. Our answers to Questions 2 and 3 indicate that these similarities are *not* sufficient to make it likely that if the premises of argument (20) are true, then its conclusion is true. Therefore, argument (20) is weak.

Arguments from analogy are often used in moral and legal reasoning. Let us consider an argument from analogy on a very controversial issue, not with a view to settling the issue, but simply to illustrate the process of evaluating such arguments.

21. The prohibition of so-called hard drugs such as cocaine and heroin is similar to the prohibition of alcohol. The prohibition of alcohol was well intentioned and based on legitimate concerns about the dangers of alcohol consumption. The

> prohibition of alcohol also led to a highly profitable black market ruled by organized crime and marked by violence. Now, we can all agree that the prohibition of alcohol was, in the last analysis, a mistake. Therefore, the prohibition of hard drugs is also a mistake—hard drugs should be legalized.

Here, A is the prohibition of hard drugs, and B is the prohibition of alcohol. Property P is that of being a mistake. Again, we use our three questions as tools for analyzing the argument.

Question 1: In what ways are A and B relevantly similar? The premises spell out a number of relevant similarities between the prohibition of hard drugs and the prohibition of alcohol—certainly enough relevant similarities to give the argument some initial plausibility.

Question 2: Are A and B dissimilar in any relevant respects? Critics of argument (21) might claim that prohibiting hard drugs is relevantly different from prohibiting alcohol in at least two ways. For instance:

a. Drugs such as cocaine and heroin are more addictive than alcohol, and hence are, in some respects, potentially more harmful to individuals and society than alcohol.

b. The current social context is different than that in which alcohol was legalized. When alcohol was legalized, drug abuse was not a serious social problem in America. But now it is. Therefore, legalizing hard drugs will probably add to currently severe problems such as death and injury resulting from traffic accidents, babies born with health problems because their mothers abuse chemical substances, and a workplace that is less efficient because of the number of people who use drugs while working.

Surely, these alleged dissimilarities, if accurate, are relevant and weaken the analogy at least to some degree.

Question 3: Are there things other than A (the prohibition of hard drugs) that are similar to B (the prohibition of alcohol) in the relevant respects but that lack P (the property of being a mistake)? Critics of argument (21) may point out that there are many drugs that cannot be used legally without a doctor's prescription. Surely, then, it is not in general a mistake to prohibit the use of a drug (except under doctor's orders). Proponents of argument (21) might reply, however, that prescription drugs are not in general relevantly similar to cocaine and heroin, for prescription drugs are not being sold in large quantities through black markets, and they are not under the control of organized criminals.

Our purpose at present is the limited one of illustrating the appropriate method of evaluating an argument from analogy. So, we will make no effort to render a final judgment on the strength of argument (21). But in a case such as this, where highly controversial claims are at issue, we may learn valuable truths and become aware of important questions by exploring an analogy to the best of our ability, even if it is difficult or impossible to reach a clear verdict on the

---

Summary of Arguments from Analogy

Form

      1. *A* is similar to *B* in relevant respects.
      2. *B* has property *P.*
So, 3. *A* has property *P.*

Questions to Ask

1. What are the relevant respects in which *A* and *B* are similar? In general, the more relevant respects *A* and *B* share, the stronger the argument.

2. Are *A* and *B* dissimilar in any relevant respects?

3. Are there things (other than *A*) that are similar to *B* in the relevant respects? If so, do these things have property *P?* To the extent that there are things relevantly similar to *B* that lack *P,* the analogy breaks down. To the extent that there are things relevantly similar to *B* that have *P,* the analogy holds up.

---

strength of the argument. Thus, an argument from analogy can be useful even when its strength is in dispute.

The following exercise provides you with an opportunity to evaluate a series of arguments from analogy.

◆ *Exercise 10.4*

Analyzing and Evaluating Analogies   Analyze the following arguments in terms of the schema for arguments from analogy, identifying *A* and *B* (the things being compared) and property *P.* Below each argument is a suggested criticism or reply. Does the reply point to an important weakness in the analogy? Why or why not? Wherever possible, briefly state at least one additional criticism that calls the strength of the argument into question.

* **1.** Mars is similar to the earth in that both are planets that orbit the sun. The earth is inhabited by living things. Therefore, Mars is inhabited by living things.
    Reply: The moon also orbits the sun, but we know that the moon is not inhabited by living things.

  2. Having an abortion is like using contraception. In both cases, the intent is the same: to avoid having a baby. And plainly, contraception is morally permissible. Thus, abortion is morally permissible also.
    Reply: Abortion involves taking life while contraception prevents life from occurring.

  3. Marijuana is as much a gift from God as lettuce. Therefore, since it not wrong to enjoy lettuce, it is not wrong to enjoy marijuana.
    Reply: Marijuana is usually smoked while lettuce is eaten.

* **4.** Logic, like whiskey, loses its beneficial effects when taken in very large quantities. Therefore, very large quantities of logic should be avoided. —Lord Dunsany, *My Ireland*, as quoted in H. L. Mencken (ed.), *A New Dictionary of Quotations* (New York: Knopf, 1978), p. 705 (*Note:* This quotation is slightly altered—I've made the conclusion explicit, and the original has "too" where I've used "very.")
Reply: Whereas whiskey has alcohol in it, logic does not.

5. Suppose Buddhists became politically powerful in America and succeeded in having Buddhism taught in the public schools. Would that be morally acceptable? Of course not. Therefore, it is not morally acceptable to have Christianity taught in the public schools.
Reply: Until recently, Buddhism has not been very influential in America, while Christianity has been influential in America from the beginning.

6. Can nonhuman animals feel pain? Well, the higher mammals have nervous systems that are similar to human nervous systems. Furthermore, higher mammals behave in ways similar to humans when damage is inflicted. (For example, just as a human is apt to cry out and withdraw his finger if it is stabbed with a pin, so a dog is apt to yelp and withdraw its paw if it is stabbed with a pin.) Therefore, higher mammals can feel pain.
Reply: Animals cannot talk to us and explain how they feel, but humans can.

7. Taxation of earnings from labor is on a par with forced labor . . . it is like forcing the person to work *n* hours for another's purpose. Therefore, since it is wrong to force one person to work for another's purpose, it is wrong for the government to tax our earnings.—(Robert Nozick, *Anarchy, State, and Utopia* (New York: Basic Books, 1974), p. 169 (*Note:* I have made the conclusion explicit.)
Reply: All governments tax their citizens, but only corrupt or tyrannical governments have programs of forced labor.

8. If at times force can be used to counter force, why should lies never be used to counter lies? . . . just as someone forfeits his rights to noninterference by others, when he threatens them forcibly, so a liar has forfeited the ordinary right to be dealt with honestly. —(Sissela Bok, *Lying: Moral Choice in Public and Private Life* (New York: Random House, 1979), p. 133 (*Note:* Bok states the argument in order to discuss it, not to endorse it.)
Reply: Lying involves the use of language whereas force need not involve the use of language.

9. For the first six to eight weeks of pregnancy, the fetus has no brain waves. So, during this period, the fetus is similar to a brain-dead adult. Therefore, if a brain-dead adult is not living, neither is a fetus during the first six to eight weeks of pregnancy. —Adapted from Baruch Brody, "Fetal Humanity and the Theory of Essentialism," in Robert Baker and Frederick Elliston, eds., *Philosophy and Sex* (Buffalo: Prometheus Books, 1975), pp. 348–352
Reply: A brain-dead adult is not growing and gaining new powers, but a fetus is growing and gaining new powers.

10. Belief in God is like belief in electrons. For example, no one has ever seen an electron, just as no one has ever seen God. Similarly, the concept of an electron plays an important role in physical theory, just as the concept of God plays an important role in theology. Furthermore, one can reasonably believe that electrons exist even if one cannot summarize the evidence for their existence, for one can reasonably believe in electrons on the basis of authority (e.g., a physics textbook). Thus, one can reasonably believe in God even if one cannot summarize the evidence for God's existence.

Reply: Whereas electrons are physical objects, God (if God exists) is not physical.

10.5 Metaphors and Arguments from Analogy

Metaphors are often used in stating an argument from analogy. For example:

> 22. Philosophy is a game of chess. Therefore, in philosophy, a slight oversight or slip in reasoning can have disastrous ramifications.

Here, the premise is metaphorical—philosophy isn't literally a game of chess. And, often, when a metaphor is used in formulating an argument from analogy, the metaphor is left unexplained. This complicates the attempt to evaluate for strength. Thus, a deeper understanding of the nature of metaphors is an aid in evaluating those arguments from analogy that employ metaphorical language.

Identifying Metaphors

A **metaphor** is a similarity statement; that is, a metaphorical statement draws attention to a similarity between two objects, persons, events, or situations. However, not all similarity statements are metaphorical. For example, the similarity statements "Your car and mine are similar in that both have four wheels" and "These two cats are similar in that both are gray in color" are entirely literal.

In practice, we often find ourselves forced to take a statement as metaphorical when taking it literally would require us to suppose that the speaker (or author) is expressing a blatantly false proposition. For example, Sylvester Prierias, a member of the Order of St. Dominic and a hostile critic of Martin Luther, once said that Luther had "a brain of brass and a nose of iron."[19] Obviously, Prierias's comment was intended not as a literal statement about the composition of Luther's body parts (in which case it would be wildly false), but as a metaphorical one concerning Luther's intellectual qualities and/or character traits.

However, metaphors are not always false if taken literally. Consider John Donne's famous line: "No man is an island." In this case, the statement, taken literally, is true but utterly trivial; hence, we rightly understand that a deeper, metaphorical usage is intended. This phenomenon is common in the case of *negations* of metaphors—for instance, "Mrs. Billings is no *spring chicken*" and "I am your employee, not your *doormat*."[20]

Thus, we test for metaphorical usage primarily by asking these two questions:

> Is the statement *clearly false if taken literally,* and the context such that the speaker (author) seems not to intend to assert a falsehood?
>
> Is the statement *trivially true if taken literally,* and the context such that the speaker (author) seems to intend to assert something nontrivial?

A "yes" answer to either question is generally a good indication of a metaphorical usage.

Here, it may be well to note the distinction between a metaphor and a simile. A *simile* is a figure of speech that involves an explicit comparison, usually indicated by the words "like" or "as"—for instance, "The man cried like a baby." In the typical case, a simile is designed to draw attention to one respect in which two quite different things are alike (e.g., the man cried in an uninhibited way). The test for identifying metaphors does not work for similes. To illustrate: It may be literally true that the man cried *like* a baby. Nevertheless, much of what follows can be applied to similes as well as to metaphors.

We now have some idea about how to spot a metaphorical usage, but let us examine the nature of metaphors more closely.[21] When we use a predicate term metaphorically, we do not simply discard the literal meaning of the term. We do two things. First, we call to mind something the word applies to literally. Let us call the thing the word applies to literally "the model."[22] Second, we invite the audience to compare the model with a certain person, place, or thing. Let us call that person, place, or thing the "subject" of the metaphor. Here is an example:

> 23. Jake Jones (a human being) is a bull in a china shop.

The *model* here is a certain large farm animal, specifically, a male bovine, who happens to be in a room full of fine porcelain dishware. Jake Jones is the *subject.* The predicate "being a bull in a china shop" is metaphorical. It does not apply literally to Jake, but rather calls our attention to some significant way in which Jake is similar to the model (e.g., Jake is apt to destroy things nearby).

When one uses a metaphor, however, one is not (normally) saying only that there is *some sort* of useful comparison to be made between the model and the subject:

> More typically the speaker is concerned to exploit the model in a particular way; he will "have in mind" one or more particular points of resemblance (between model and subject) that he intends to be attributing to the subject. Thus, when Churchill said "Russia has dropped an iron curtain across Europe," he wasn't just throwing the image of an iron curtain up for grabs, leaving it to his auditors to make of it what they would. He meant to be exploiting the model in a certain way—to assert that Russia has made it almost impossible to exchange information, goods, and persons between her sphere of influence and western Europe.[23]

But how does a metaphor succeed in drawing attention to some points of comparison between two objects and not others? First, since some metaphors are frequently used, they have a more or less "standard" interpretation. For example, one would be violating a convention if one were to interpret "The boxer has a glass jaw" as meaning that his jaw is transparent or translucent. Rather, the conventional interpretation is along these lines: "The boxer can easily be defeated by a punch to the jaw." Speakers and authors often count on such conventions to ensure that their intentions aren't misunderstood. So, in many cases, linguistic conventions help to specify a range of relevant features in the model.

Second, in many cases, we must rely on the context. The context will generally include parts of the text in question (or even the whole text), but it may also include relevant background information regarding the situation in which the statement was written or uttered. For example, take Prierias's statement that Luther had "a brain of brass." The context would include the letters, speeches, or conversations in which Prierias made the remark, but it might also include historical information, such as statements from contemporaries of Prierias to the effect that he was a hostile critic of Luther. If we took Prierias's remark out of context, we might possibly suppose that Prierias intended to compliment Luther on his tough-mindedness, though in fact Prierias's statement was a deliberate insult. He may have meant to imply that Luther had a "thick skull" (to resort to a contemporary metaphor). Or perhaps he meant that Luther's brain was of inferior quality, being brass rather than gold or silver.

Incidentally, Prierias's metaphor underscores the important fact that we cannot always be sure precisely which features of the model the speaker (author) intends us to focus on. Is it the hardness of the brass or its inferior quality relative to more precious metals (or both) that Prierias had in mind? We may not be certain. Thus, metaphors can be open-ended or ambiguous. Frequently, we must be content to specify a *range* of possible interpretations. On the other hand, we cannot (reasonably) interpret metaphors any way we wish. Certainly, Prierias did not mean that Luther's brain was of a color similar to the color of brass, nor did he mean that Luther's brain was heavy like brass. More to the point, given the historical context, we can be sure beyond a reasonable doubt that Prierias' statement was derogatory.

Third, we must often rely on explicit clarification by the speaker (author). Thus, we are aided in understanding Donne's "No man is an island" metaphor by the fact that he immediately adds, "entire of itself; every man is a piece of the continent, a part of the main."[24] Given Donne's elaboration, his point seems to be this: "No human being is so constituted as to live well (or flourish) in isolation." Obviously, explicit interpretation by the speaker (or author) is often an aid in identifying those aspects of the model that he or she wishes us to focus upon.

Of course, in some cases, we just don't have many interpretive clues to go on. There may be no conventions. The context may be unclear. The author or speaker may not be available for further comment. In such cases, we are obviously in the dark as to which points of comparison the metaphor highlights.

To bring our discussion of the nature of metaphor to a close, let us consider two points about literal language. First, the word "literal" has misleading associations in the minds of many. And since "metaphorical" and "literal" are contrasting terms, confusion about one is likely to create confusion about the other. For example, some people tend to equate "literal" with "precise." But, as a matter of fact, literal usages also can be vague. The statement "We fly at dawn" is vague (do we fly at 4:00 A.M.? 4:30? 5:00?) but literal. Furthermore, some people tend to equate "literal" with "unambiguous." But literal usages also can be ambiguous. The statement "I shall wear no clothes to distinguish me from my fellow Christians" is ambiguous, but it is not metaphorical.[25] Finally, some people equate "literal" with "physical." But the statement "Humans have nonphysical souls" can certainly be used in a literal fashion, and indeed, it has often been so used by philosophers and theologians. A literal use is nonfigurative, but it need not be precise or unambiguous, and it need not concern physical or observable realities.

Second, metaphors can normally be translated *at least partially* into literal terms. For example, "The Lord is my shepherd" can be partially translated as follows: "God will take care of me." And when Shakespeare has Romeo say, "What light through yonder window breaks? It is the East, and Juliet is the sun," the word "sun" is a metaphor that can be partially translated into literal terms along the following lines: "Juliet's presence has an effect on me [Romeo] similar to the effect of the rising sun, that is, her presence brings me hope and joy."[26]

Metaphors in Arguments from Analogy

Let us now illustrate the process of evaluating an argument from analogy that involves a metaphor. We return to argument (22), which appears at the beginning of this section: "Philosophy is a game of chess. Therefore, in philosophy, a slight oversight or slip in reasoning can have disastrous ramifications." Here, "philosophy" replaces A and "a game of chess" replaces B in the original schema. P is the property of being such that a slight oversight or slip in reasoning can have disastrous ramifications.

Since "Philosophy is a game of chess" is false, if taken literally, the first premise is metaphorical. We must therefore explore the metaphor by asking, "In what relevant respects are chess and philosophy similar?" Well, both philosophy and chess are activities involving a series of moves that must be thought out logically. And, in both philosophy and chess, the reasoning is extremely complicated. Furthermore, just as in chess one plays against an opponent, in philosophy one encounters opposing points of view. Moreover, these points of view are generally defended by philosophers who are skilled in argument and eager to point out the errors of those with whom they disagree. Thus, philosophy does resemble a game of chess in many important ways. Now, as everyone knows, a slight oversight or slip in reasoning can have *disastrous* ramifications in chess, namely, checkmate. Therefore, it seems likely that a slight oversight or slip in reasoning can have disastrous ramifications in philosophy too—for example, self-contradiction. Thus, the analogy between philosophy and chess is strong, and so is the argument.

Let us consider a second example, an analogical version of the so-called design or teleologial argument for God's existence. The argument is a simplified version of one offered by the famous English theologian William Paley (1743–1805). Arguments of this sort were very influential in Britain and America during the 19th century.

> **24.** The physical universe is a clock. Clocks are produced by intelligent designers. Therefore, the physical universe was produced by an Intelligent Designer.

Here, "physical universe" replaces A and "clock" replaces B in the original schema. P is the property of being produced by an intelligent designer(s).

Let us now consider argument (24) in light of our three questions for evaluating arguments from analogy. Because the issues involved in argument (24) are major philosophical ones, however, we cannot hope to reach a definitive evaluation here. Our goal is the more limited one of illustrating how our three questions can serve as a useful guide even when the issues involved are quite complex.

Question 1: How is the universe relevantly similar to a clock? Obviously, this premise is a metaphorical statement. No one would suppose that the universe is, *literally speaking,* a clock. But how is the universe like a clock? Perhaps the suggestion is that both the universe and a clock display intricate orderliness. This orderliness is visible to the eye when a clock is disassembled, while the orderliness of the universe is perhaps best revealed by the discovery of those regularities called scientific laws. But is this shared orderliness enough to indicate that the argument is strong? We must ask further questions.

Question 2: Are there relevant dissimilarities between the physical universe and a clock? Many philosophers would claim that there are. For instance, the various parts of the clock work together to serve a purpose, that of telling time. Because we can see that the various parts of the clock work together to serve an identifiable purpose, we are confident that it was produced by an intelligent designer. But can we see that the various parts of the physical universe work together to serve an identifiable purpose? According to many philosophers, we cannot. To do so, we would have to both know the purpose of the universe and verify that the various parts of the universe fulfill that purpose. And if we are to avoid begging the question, we must specify the purpose of the universe without assuming that some sort of God or Intelligent Designer has created the universe for its own purposes.

Some philosophers would reply that we do not need to be able to identify the purpose of a clock in order to infer that it is designed. The high degree of intricate orderliness a clock displays is sufficient to indicate that it is produced by some sort of intelligent being. Similarly, the physical universe displays a striking degree of order as indicated by the fact that scientists have discovered (and continue to discover) natural laws that can be formulated with great precision. And, according to these philosophers, the orderliness of the physical universe, as codified in scientific laws, is sufficient to indicate that it occurred not by chance, but by design.

Question 3: Are there things that exhibit a high degree of orderliness and yet are not produced by an intelligent designer? We might be tempted to say that animals or animal parts (such as eyes) exhibit orderliness and are produced through the natural processes of evolution rather than by an Intelligent Designer. But these examples beg the question, for animals (and animal organs) are parts of the physical universe that the arguer claims is produced by an Intelligent Designer. Indeed, since evolution is itself a process subject to scientific laws, the arguer will presumably view the processes of evolution as a further illustration of the remarkable orderliness of the physical universe.

Now, our answer to Question 1 indicates that there are some relevant similarities between the universe and a clock. But our attempt to answer Questions 2 and 3 indicates that it is not easy to determine whether the relevant similarities are sufficient to render the argument strong. As expected, our brief discussion of the argument does not yield a definitive verdict on its strength. But by pressing our three questions, we are apt to come to a better understanding both of the argument and of related issues. (Incidentally, it should be kept in mind that there are many other arguments for the existence of God. Thus, one might reject argument (24) while thinking that some other argument for God's existence is sound. Alternatively, one might hold that belief in God need not be supported by any argument at all.)

The following exercises provide you with an opportunity to evaluate a series of arguments from analogy, many of which employ metaphorical statements.

◆ Exercise 10.5

Part A: Identifying and Analyzing Metaphors   Which of the following statements are metaphorical? Which are literal? If a statement involves a metaphor, paraphrase it in literal terms, making use of relevant conventions or contextual clues. (Your paraphrase should be only a sentence or two in length.)

* 1. A marriage is a molecule, not an atom.

  2. Thomas Edison was similar to Benjamin Franklin in that both were inventors.

  3. Religion is the opiate of the people. —Karl Marx, "Toward a Critique of Hegel's *Philosophy of Right,*" in David McLellan, ed., *Karl Marx: Selected Writings* (London: Oxford University Press, 1978), p. 64

* 4. The single life is the flight of a butterfly.

  5. An undisciplined man is a rogue elephant.

  6. My hat is like yours in that both are made of wool.

* **7.** A college education is a ticket to the middle class.

 8. The fog comes on little cat feet. —Carl Sandburg, "Fog," in Laurence Perrine, ed., *Sound and Sense: An Introduction to Poetry* (New York: Harcourt, Brace & World, 1956), p. 84

 9. A virtuous person "is like a tree planted by streams of water, that yields its fruit in season, and its leaf does not wither." —Psalms 1:3

* **10.** I won't take any more of your criticism, Bill. In case you haven't noticed, I'm not a dart board. So, just shut up!

 11. Morality is a cage for little birds.

 12. In this building, the walls have ears.

* **13.** A baseball and a basketball are similar in that both are spherical in shape.

 14. Admittedly, Doug is not a rocket scientist, but he is honest and he's a hard worker. Moreover, he has experience in this type of janitorial work. You should hire him.

 15. A rich tradition is a channel for the stream of life.

Part B: Analogies   Using the form "A is similar to B in relevant respects; B has property P," identify A, B, and P in the following arguments. Also identify any metaphors that occur, and analyze them to discover the "relevant respects" in which A and B are supposed to be similar.

* **1.** Anyone who deliberately murders another human is sick. And we ought not blame people for displaying the symptoms of their sicknesses. For example, if a person has the flu, it doesn't make sense to blame her for having a fever. Hence, we ought not to blame those who commit murder.

 2. The Lord is my shepherd. Hence, the Lord will one day sell me at the meat market or else kill me and eat me himself.

 3. A college is a family. And since you do not *and obviously should not* have to pay tuition to belong to a family, you shouldn't have to pay tuition to attend a college.

* **4.** A corporation is an aircraft carrier, not a patrol boat. Therefore, it is impossible to change the direction of a corporation quickly.

 5. Culture is the life-blood of civilization. Therefore, as cultural illiteracy increases, civilization grows weaker.

 6. Logic is intellectual karate. So, while it takes a long time and a lot of discipline to make the methods of logic second nature, the effort is well worth it.

* **7.** Luther was right: Reason is a harlot that serves any master. Therefore, philosophical argument is futile.

 8. Social Security is automobile insurance. What I mean is this: When you pay auto insurance premiums, you get the money back *only if* you need it (e.g., when you are involved in an accident). Therefore, when you pay into Social Security, you should get your money back only if you need it. And hence, rich retirees should not receive payments from Social Security.

9. Influence is capital. Capital must be economized if it is to last. Thus, influence must be economized if it is to last.

* 10. A university is an ivory tower. And since people need to be in contact with the real world, they shouldn't attend universities.

Part C: More Analogies   Analyze the following arguments in terms of the schema for arguments from analogy, identifying A and B (the things being compared) and property P. Also, identify any metaphors. Below each argument is a suggested criticism or reply. Does the reply point to an important defect in the analogy? Why or why not?

* 1. People often mistreat dogs. But dogs are just mentally deficient people. And a mentally deficient person is still a person. Now, obviously, it is wrong to kill a mentally deficient person *merely on the grounds* that caring for him is inconvenient. Accordingly, it is wrong to kill a dog *merely on the grounds* that caring for it is inconvenient.
  Reply: Dogs do not look very much like people.

  2. Surrogate motherhood is slave owning, for both slave owning and surrogate motherhood involve the buying and selling of human beings. (The only difference is that in the case of surrogate motherhood, the humans who are bought and sold are always babies.) And yet, everyone will agree that slave owning is immoral. We may therefore conclude that surrogate motherhood is immoral also.
  Reply: Surrogate mothers do not sell their babies; rather, surrogate mothers "rent" the use of their own reproductive capacities.

  3. The United States of America is a gentleman's club. The various states freely agree to join the United States, just as gentlemen freely join a club. And take note: In the case of a club, one is free to withdraw at one's own discretion. Thus, any state in the United States is free to withdraw (secede) at its own discretion.
  Reply: The analogy is weak since only men join gentlemen's clubs, but both men and women are citizens of states.

* 4. A computer, like the human brain, is capable of responding to stimuli in astonishingly complex ways. Computers can play chess, enter into dialogues, and solve extremely difficult mathematical problems. Now, humans are aware of their own thoughts and feelings. Therefore, computers are aware of their own thoughts and feelings also.
  Reply: Computers are made mostly of metal and plastic, but humans are not.

  5. Suppose a wicked tyrant threatens to kill 10 innocent people unless you give him all your discretionary income. If you refuse to give the money, you will not be harmed, but the 10 innocent people will be put to death. If you give the money, both you and the 10 innocent people will go unharmed. (Assume that you have no other options such as overthrowing the tyrant or helping the 10 people escape.) Clearly, in such circumstances, you are morally obligated to give up your discretionary income to save the 10 people. Now, you are in fact in a situation quite like this. World hunger is the wicked tyrant. The 10 innocent people are the starving

poor of the Third World. Therefore, you are morally obligated to give up your discretionary income to save the starving poor. —Adapted from Louis Pascal, "Judgement Day," in Peter Singer, ed., *Applied Ethics* (New York: Oxford University Press, 1986), pp. 105–111
Reply: In the wicked tyrant case, you can identify exactly who will die, but in the case of world hunger, you cannot identify the individuals who will die.

6. Suppose you have been kidnapped by the Society of Music Lovers and your kidneys have been connected to the circulatory system of a famous violinist who lies unconscious beside you. You know that if you detach yourself from his circulatory system, the violinist will die. You also know that if you stay attached to the violinist for nine months, he'll regain his health (and your health will not suffer). In such circumstances, would you be morally obligated to remain connected to the violinist? Surely not. It would be very nice of you to remain connected, but it is not your moral duty to do so. Therefore, it is not wrong for a woman to have an abortion in the case of pregnancy through rape. —Adapted from Judith Jarvis Thomson, "A Defense of Abortion," in Peter Singer, ed., *Applied Ethics* (New York: Oxford University Press, 1986), pp. 37–56
Reply: Detaching yourself from the famous violinist is not killing—it is not like shooting him in the head with a gun. In other words, detaching yourself from the violinist is merely letting him die. By contrast, abortion involves killing the fetus.

7. How do I know that other people have inner mental lives of their own? Well, I know that I have such an inner life—I feel pain, I worry, I think thoughts, and I dream dreams. And I know that other people have a central nervous system very similar to mine. Therefore, other people have inner mental lives of their own.
Reply: Chimps also have a central nervous system similar to yours.

8. Rich nations are tiny lifeboats surrounded by masses of drowning people. Thus, it is impossible for rich nations to save many of those living in the poorest nations.—Adapted from Garrett Hardin, "Lifeboat Ethics: The Case Against Helping the Poor," in Stephen Satris, ed., *Taking Sides: Clashing Views on Controversial Moral Issues*, 4th ed. (Guilford, CT: Dushkin, 1994), pp. 350–357
Reply: Rich nations such as the United States own vast amounts of land. So, obviously, they can hold a lot more people than a lifeboat can.

9. When the technique of *in vitro* fertilization is employed, eggs are withdrawn from the woman by laparoscopy and fertilized in a petri dish (usually by the husband's sperm but sometimes by a donor's sperm). A number of eggs are removed at one time and fertilized, for various reasons. For one thing, women who seek *in vitro* fertilization typically have a history of difficulties in achieving pregnancy. Thus, multiple attempts at inserting embryos (i.e., fertilized eggs) into the womb are often required. Also, the pain and expense of multiple surgeries are saved by removing more than one egg per laparoscopy. Now, after the eggs are fertilized they must be frozen, and if the woman becomes pregnant, there may be unneeded or superfluous frozen embryos. These embryos are simply thawed and discarded if the pregnancy results in the birth of a baby. And obviously, there is nothing immoral about discarding such superfluous frozen embryos. But note that this has

implications for the abortion debate. Since discarding a frozen embryo is not and cannot reasonably be equated with murder, early abortions cannot reasonably be equated with murder either.

Reply: Frozen embryos cannot grow; but under normal circumstances, a zygote can.

10. The experiences of a clairvoyant person are similar to the experiences of a sighted person. Both types of experience involve vivid images. And both types of experience *seem* to tell us about events in the real world. Now, admittedly, not everyone is clairvoyant, but not everyone is sighted, either. Furthermore, while the experiences of clairvoyant persons sometimes prove illusory, the experiences of sighted persons sometimes prove to be illusory too. After all, optical illusions are common enough. Nevertheless, it is reasonable to believe that the experience of seeing is a source of truth about the world. Hence, it is reasonable to believe that the experiences of clairvoyant persons are a source of truth about the world.

Reply: Most people are sighted, but at best only a small minority is clairvoyant.

Notes

1. I have borrowed this label from Wesley Salmon, *Logic,* 3rd ed. (Englewood Cliffs, NJ: Prentice-Hall, 1984), p. 97.
2. Patrick Hurley, *A Concise Introduction to Logic,* 6th ed. (Belmont, CA: Wadsworth, 1997), p. 31.
3. My discussion of this common myth about induction is heavily indebted to Brian Skyrms, *Choice and Chance,* 3rd ed. (Belmont, CA: Wadsworth, 1986), pp. 13–15.
4. Anthony Flew, *Dictionary of Philosophy,* rev. ed. (New York: St. Martin's Press, 1979), p. 215.
5. Steven M. Cahn, ed., *Classics of Western Philosophy,* 2nd ed. (Indianapolis, IN: Hackett, 1977), p. 279.
6. For example, James F. Ross, *Introduction to the Philosophy of Religion* (London: Macmillan, 1969), p. 29. Yet another authority states that Aquinas was born in 1225 *or* 1226; see Bertrand Russell, *A History of Western Philosophy* (New York: Simon & Schuster, 1945), p. 452.
7. For example, Frederick Copleston, a well-known authority on Aquinas, states that Aquinas was born *either* at the end of 1224 *or* the beginning of 1225. See Copleston, *A History of Philosophy,* Vol. 2, *Mediaeval Philosophy,* Part II, *Albert the Great to Duns Scotus* (New York: Image Books, 1962), p. 20.
8. My discussion of the features of a good sample is heavily influenced by the discussion in Hurley, *A Concise Introduction to Logic,* pp. 548–552.
9. Charles W. Roll, Jr., and Albert H. Cantril, *Polls: Their Use and Misuse in Politics* (New York: Basic Books, 1972), p. 67.
10. See Roll and Cantril, *Polls,* pp. 82–89 for a detailed discussion of the elaborate methods used to obtain a random sample.
11. Roll and Cantril, *Polls,* p. 74.
12. The illustration is borrowed from Roll and Cantril, *Polls,* p. 75.
13. Roll and Cantril, *Polls,* p. 72.
14. This example is borrowed from Salmon, *Logic,* p. 112. I have paraphrased freely.
15. My account of Semmelweis's work borrows heavily from Carl G. Hempel, *Philosophy of Natural Science* (Englewood Cliffs, NJ: Prentice-Hall, 1966), pp. 3–6.

16. For an accessible discussion of the complexities involved in the confirmation of scientific hypotheses, see Del Ratzsch, *Philosophy of Science* (Downers Grove, IL: InterVarsity Press, 1986), pp. 41–96.

17. My brief summary of criteria for good scientific hypotheses is indebted to the discussion in Irving M. Copi and Carl Cohen, *Introduction to Logic,* 9th ed. (Englewood Cliffs, NJ: Prentice-Hall, 1994), pp. 534–539.

18. This example is borrowed from Salmon, *Logic,* p. 134.

19. See Roland H. Bainton, *Here I Stand: A Life of Martin Luther* (Nashville: Abingdon Press, 1950), p. 68.

20. This point is borrowed from Ted Cohen, "Figurative Speech and Figurative Acts," *The Journal of Philosophy* 72 (1975): 671.

21. My analysis of the nature of metaphors is largely borrowed from William P. Alston, *Divine Nature and Human Language* (Ithaca, NY: Cornell University Press, 1989), p. 22.

22. The term "model" is borrowed from Alston, *Divine Nature,* p. 22.

23. Alston, *Divine Nature,* pp. 22–23.

24. John Donne, "Meditation XVII," *Devotions upon Emergent Occasions.* See M. H. Abrams, ed., *The Norton Anthology of English Literature,* 3rd ed., Vol. 1 (New York: Norton, 1974), p. 1215.

25. The example is borrowed from Wilfrid Hodges, *Logic* (New York: Penguin Books, 1984), p. 26.

26. William Shakespeare, *The Tragedy of Romeo and Juliet,* J. A. Bryant, Jr., ed. (New York: New American Library, 1964), p. 74.

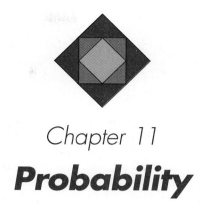

Chapter 11

Probability

In chapter 10, we examined a series of types of arguments that are strong when properly constructed. We defined a strong argument as one having this feature: It is unlikely (but possible) that its conclusion is false while its premises are true. We might also define a strong argument as one having this feature: It is *probable* that if its premises are true, then its conclusion is true. (The word "probable" should here be understood to imply that it is *possible* that the conclusion is false even if the premises are true.) In this chapter, we will take a closer look at the concept of probability, which is a main ingredient in our concept of strength. First, we examine three theories regarding the nature of probability. Second, we consider the elementary rules of probability. Finally, we focus on Bayes' theorem as a tool for determining the probability of a hypothesis given the evidence.

11.1 Three Theories of Probability

Consider the following statements:

1. The probability that *you will select a king from an ordinary deck of playing cards on the next draw* is 4 out of 52.

2. The probability that *a 20-year-old woman will live to be 30* is .913.

3. The probability that *Tom and Sue will like each other* is high.

These three statements correspond to three different understandings of the nature of probability: the classical theory, the relative frequency theory, and the subjectivist theory.[1]

The Classical Theory

This theory stems from the work of two French mathematicians, Blaise Pascal (1623–1662) and Pierre de Fermat (1601–1665). According to the **classical theory**, the probability of an event (or of a statement's being true) is determined by the following formula:

$$P(s) = f/n$$

Here, P is read as "the probability of," s stands for any event or for any statement's being true, f stands for the number of favorable outcomes, and n stands for the number of possible outcomes. For instance, what is the probability that *you will select a king from an ordinary deck of playing cards on the next draw?* The number of favorable outcomes is 4, because there are 4 kings, but the number of possible outcomes is 52, because there are 52 cards in the deck. So, the probability that you will select a king on the next draw is 4/52 or 1/13.

The classical theory involves two noteworthy assumptions:

Assumption 1: All possible outcomes are equally probable.

Assumption 2: All possible outcomes are taken into account.

Assumption 1 is also known as the **principle of indifference**. In our playing card example, this assumption could be false under certain circumstances. For instance, suppose the person drawing the card wants to draw a king and knows the location of one or more of the kings (e.g., on top of the deck). Or suppose the cards have been marked by someone who intends to cheat. The classical theory assumes that one card is just as likely to be drawn as another. Assumption 2 could also be false under certain circumstances—for example, if a card has been removed from the deck or if some cards have been added.

Take another example. What is the probability that *you will get "heads" on the next toss of a fair coin?* There are two possible outcomes: heads or tails. The favorable outcome is heads. So, the probability that you will get heads on the next toss is one out of two, or 1/2 (or .5). Now, you might question whether the two assumptions hold true in this type of case. Is it not possible—however unlikely—that a coin will remain balanced on its edge, in which case we have more than two possible outcomes? The answer, strictly speaking, is yes, but for practical purposes, we may reasonably ignore such remote possibilities. Similarly, any given coin is likely to have imperfections that may affect the outcomes (e.g., it may be slightly out of balance). In this case, the *principle of indifference* is violated, strictly speaking, but again, for practical purposes, it may be reasonable to ignore this.

In some cases, however, the two assumptions of the classical theory clearly do not hold even as rough approximations. How probable is it, for instance, that a 50-year-old man will die of lung cancer within 10 years? What are the possible outcomes here? The outcomes include all the possible ways to die—automobile accident, heart attack, murder, shark attack, nuclear war, and so on—as well as the possibility of not dying within 10 years. There seems to be no way to take all the possible outcomes into account in this sort of case. Furthermore, it does not seem reasonable to suppose that the possible outcomes are equally likely. Surely, for example, most people are more likely to die of a heart attack than of a shark attack.

The Relative Frequency Theory

This theory was developed from the study of mortality records used by life insurance companies. (Life insurance companies obviously have a stake in knowing the probability that persons of any given age will live for a specified period of time, e.g., 10, 20, or 30 years.) According to the **relative frequency theory**, the probability of an event (or of a statement's being true) is given by the following formula:

$$P(s) = f_o/n_o$$

Here, f_o is the number of observed favorable outcomes and n_o is the total number of observed outcomes. For example, suppose we wish to discover the probability that a 20-year-old woman will live 10 more years. We observe a sample of 20-year-old women over a 10-year period. If our sample contains 1000 women and 913 are alive 10 years later, we conclude that the probability that a 20-year-old woman will live 10 more years equals 913/1000, or .913.

The relative frequency theory can also be applied to coin tossing. Suppose you toss a coin 100 times and record that it came up tails 48 times. What is the probability that you will get "tails" on the next toss? By our formula, the probability is 48/100, or 12/25 (or .48). Note that this approach enables us to determine that a coin is loaded or off balance. For example, if, after 100 tosses, you get tails only 13 times, then you would presumably be justified in concluding that the coin is loaded or off balance.

The relative frequency theory can be applied only if an appropriate sample can be identified. And, sometimes, this appears to be impossible. For instance, what sample would one use to calculate the probability that Tom and Sue—two people who have never met—will like each other? So many subtle factors contribute to the phenomenon of mutual liking that there is no clear way to

identify a sample in this case, and hence no clear way to apply the relative frequency theory.

Can we apply the classical theory in this sort of case? Well, we can identify
the possible outcomes: (a) Tom likes Sue and Sue likes Tom, (b) Tom likes
Sue but Sue does not like Tom, (c) Tom does not like Sue but Sue likes Tom,
and (d) Tom does not like Sue and Sue does not like Tom. But is there good reason to assume that these four possible outcomes are equally probable? Certainly,
we cannot in general make such an assumption when two people meet for the
first time. Temperament and personal bias often render liking more (or less)
probable. So, the principle of indifference is apt to be violated in such cases.

Since, in some cases, the classical and relative frequency theories appear
inapplicable, let us consider an additional theory.

The Subjectivist Theory

According to the **subjectivist theory**, probability is interpreted as an individual's
confidence that an event will occur (or that a statement is true). That confidence
(or degree of belief) can be stated in terms of the odds that the individual would
accept on a bet. The odds are the probability that an event will happen *divided by*
the probability that it will not happen (or the probability of a statement's being
true *divided by* the probability of its not being true). For example, you might be
willing to give 3-to-1 odds that *Speedsteed will win the derby,* in which case you
have assigned a probability of $3/(3 + 1) = 3/4$ to that statement. Or you might be
willing to give 2-to-1 odds that *Tom and Sue will like each other,* in which case you
have assigned a probability of $2/(2 + 1) = 2/3$ to that statement.

In general, if you give x-to-y odds for a statement s, then you assign the
following probability to it: $x/(x + y)$. Thus, a subjectivist approach to probability
can be given a quantitative interpretation as follows:

$$P(s) = x/(x + y)$$

Here, x-to-y odds are given for s's occurring or being true. For instance, if you
give 3-to-5 odds that Speedsteed will win, you assign a probability of $3/(3 + 5) =$
$3/8$. If you give 7-to-3 odds that Speedsteed will win, you assign a probability
of $7/(7 + 3) = 7/10$. And if you give *even* odds that Speedsteed will win (such as
1-to-1 odds), you assign a probability of $1/(1 + 1) = 1/2$.

In assigning odds, it is necessary for an individual to be consistent. For
instance, if I lay 3-to-2 odds that Speedsteed will win, then I am assigning that
statement a probability of $3/(3 + 2) = 3/5$. I cannot then consistently give the
same odds that Speedsteed will not win. In fact, for reasons that will be discussed

in the next section, if I lay 3-to-2 odds that Speedsteed will win, I must lay 2-to-3 odds that Speedsteed will not win if I am to be consistent.

One problem with the subjectivist theory is suggested by its name: Different people may assign different probabilities to the same statement. This problem can be mitigated, to some extent, by taking the average of the various probabilities individuals ascribe to a statement, or by applying the theory only when individuals agree about the odds.

The classical, relative frequency, and subjectivist theories give us alternative methods for assigning probability to a statement. In a given case, one of these theories may be easier to apply than another, and in some cases, we may find it difficult to apply any of the theories. However, given that we can assign probabilities to statements F and G, the probability calculus, which we will examine in the next section, tells us how to determine the probabilities of *compounds* involving F and G (e.g., disjunctions and conjunctions). In this way, the probability calculus is similar to truth tables. A truth table does not tell us the truth value of noncompound statements such as F, G, and H, but a truth table does tell us the value of $(F \lor G)$, for example, given truth value assignments for F and for G. Similarly, the probability calculus does not tell us the probability of noncompound statements, but it does enable us to determine the probability of compound statements whenever we can assign probabilities to the noncompound statements involved.

◆ Exercise 11.1

Part A: Classical Theory   Use the classical theory to determine the probability of each of the following statements. Assume you are drawing from an ordinary deck of playing cards and that each card drawn is replaced, so that there are always 52 cards in the deck. (If you are not a cardplayer, the following information may be of use: Each deck of 52 playing cards comes in four suits: hearts, diamonds, clubs, and spades. Each suit contains 13 cards: an ace, a two, a three, a four, a five, a six, a seven, an eight, a nine, a ten, a jack, a queen, and a king. Hearts and diamonds are red; clubs and spades are black.)

* **1.** You select the jack of diamonds on the next draw.
  2. You select a queen on the next draw.
  3. You select a red card on the next draw.
* **4.** You select a heart on the next draw.
  5. You select a black card on the next draw.
  6. You select the ace of spades on the next draw.
* **7.** You select the three of diamonds on the next draw.
  8. You select an ace on the next draw.
  9. You select the five of hearts on the next draw.
 10. You select a club on the next draw.

Part B: Relative Frequency Theory   Use the relative frequency theory to answer each of the following questions. If the classical theory provides a different answer or is inapplicable, explain why.

* **1.** You toss a coin 1000 times, and it turns up heads 503 times. What is the probability that the coin will turn up heads on the next toss?

  2. You toss a coin 100 times, and it turns up tails 51 times. What is the probability that the coin will turn up tails on the next toss?

  3. You roll a die 60 times, getting a five 10 times. What is the probability of getting a five on the next roll?

  4. You roll a die 600 times, getting a three 400 times. What is the probability of getting a three on the next roll? Is the die loaded or off balance?

  5. An urn contains 50 red marbles and 50 blue marbles. You draw marbles one at a time, *replacing each one* after recording the outcome. Between each draw, you shake the urn in an effort to ensure that each marble has an equal chance of being selected. Out of 100 selections, you draw 46 blue marbles. What is the probability of drawing a blue marble on the next draw?

Part C: Subjectivist Theory   Use the subjectivist theory to answer each of the following questions.

* **1.** If you give odds of 4 to 1 that *Andretti will win the Indianapolis 500*, what probability have you assigned to this statement?

  2. If you give odds of 7 to 4 that *Jack and Jill will marry*, what probability have you assigned this statement?

  3. If you give odds of 2 to 3 that *you will sink your next free throw*, what probability have you assigned this statement?

* **4.** If you lay odds of 17 to 2 that *it will rain today*, what probability have you assigned this statement?

  5. If you lay odds of 11 to 14 that *Ken Griffey will hit a homer his next time at bat*, what probability have you assigned this statement?

  6. If you lay odds of 1 to 6 that *Earth has been visited by extraterrestrials*, what probability have you assigned this statement?

* **7.** If you give odds of 2 to 5 that *Smith will win the election*, what probability have you assigned this statement?

  8. If you give odds of 8 to 3 that *Jones will win the election*, what probability have you assigned this statement?

  9. If you lay odds of 2 to 1 that *you will pass your next logic exam*, what probability have you assigned this statement?

  10. If you give even odds that a fair coin will turn up heads on the next toss, does your assignment of probability differ from that of the classical theory?

Part D: For Discussion   Which theory of probability would you use to determine the probability of each of the following statements given the information available? Why? If more than one theory is applicable in a given case, explain why one theory is more applicable than the others (if possible). If two or more theories are equally applicable, explain why.

* **1.** You roll a die 100 times, and get a six 40 times. What is the probability that you will get a six on the next roll?

2. You give 100-to-1 odds that you will drive across town tonight without getting into an accident. What is the probability that you will drive across town tonight without getting into an accident?

3. The Sonics have played the Bulls 10 times this season. The Sonics have won four games and lost six. What is the probability that the Sonics will win tonight's game against the Bulls?

4. You roll a die 120 times, and get a three 20 times. What is the probability that you will get a three on the next roll?

5. Smith and Jones have raced against each other in the 100-yard dash 10 times this season. Smith has won five of these races, and Jones has won five. Smith, however, slightly injured her right ankle in practice yesterday, leading you to give 6-to-4 odds that Jones will win tonight's race between Smith and Jones. What is the probability that Jones will win tonight's race against Smith?

11.2 The Rules of Probability

Pascal and Fermat discovered the basic rules of probability. Oddly, their work was a response to a question about gambling asked by Chevalier de Mere, a friend of Pascal's.[2]

In this section and the next, our discussion of probability presupposes the truth-functional logic introduced in chapter 7. Accordingly, we will employ the symbols for statement logic first introduced in that chapter—specifically, "$\sim$" for negation, "$\vee$" for disjunctions, "$\cdot$" for conjunctions, "$\rightarrow$" for the material conditional, and "$\leftrightarrow$" for the material biconditional.

Probability values are expressed as numbers from zero to one. Zero is the lowest degree of probability; one is the highest. It is customary to assign the tautologies of statement logic (which are true in every row of the truth table) the highest probability, namely, one. So, for example, $P(A \vee \sim A) = 1$. Hence, we may state our first rule of probability theory as follows:

> Rule 1: If a statement *p* is a tautology, then $P(p) = 1$.

Here the italicized, lowercase *p* stands for any statement whatever, including compound statements such as $[B \rightarrow (B \vee C)]$. And since a truth table reveals that $[B \rightarrow (B \vee C)]$ is a tautology, Rule 1 tells us that $P[B \rightarrow (B \vee C)] = 1$.

By contrast, contradictions, which are false in every row of the truth table, receive the lowest probability, namely, zero. This gives us our second rule of probability theory:

Rule 2: If a statement p is a contradiction, then $P(p) = 0$.

For example, Rule 2 tells us that $P(H \cdot \sim H) = 0$, and that $P(B \leftrightarrow \sim B) = 0$.

Two statements are **mutually exclusive** if they cannot both be true. For example:

4. Julian Lennon is exactly 25 years old today.

5. Julian Lennon is exactly 55 years old today.

A set of statements is **exhaustive** if one of the statements must be true. For example:

6. Jody Foster is 35.

7. Jody Foster is 40.

8. It is not the case that either Jody Foster is 35 or Jody Foster is 40.

Note that any statement and its negation are mutually exclusive as well as jointly exhaustive.

Now, suppose two statements, p and q, are mutually exclusive. For example, perhaps we are rolling a single six-sided die of the type used in ordinary board games. Let T stand for "The die will turn up three" and let S stand for "The die will turn up six." Now, assuming the die is not loaded, there is one chance in six that it will turn up on any given side. So, $P(T) = 1/6$ and $P(S) = 1/6$. And our chances of rolling *either three or six* on the next roll are two out of six. In other words, we add the probabilities: $P(T \vee S) = 1/6 + 1/6 = 2/6 = 1/3$. Examples such as this give us an intuitive grasp of the **restricted disjunction rule**:

Rule 3: If p and q are mutually exclusive, then $P(p \vee q) = P(p) + P(q)$.

(This is called the "*restricted* disjunction rule" because it governs only the case in which two statements are mutually exclusive.) The following two examples are designed to enable you to see the intuitive plausibility of the restricted disjunction rule for yourself.

Suppose we are about to draw one card from an ordinary, well-shuffled deck of 52 playing cards. What is the probability that we will select either the ace of clubs or the ace of diamonds? Assuming each of the 52 cards has an equal chance of being drawn, $P(\text{draw ace of clubs}) = 1/52$, and $P(\text{draw ace of diamonds}) = 1/52$. So, intuitively, we have 2 chances out of 52 of selecting either the ace of clubs or the ace of diamonds (on the next draw), and this is just what the restricted disjunction rule tells us:

P(draw ace of clubs ∨ ace of diamonds) = P(draw ace of clubs) + P(draw ace of diamonds) = 1/52 + 1/52 = 2/52 = 1/26

What is the probability of drawing a queen from a well-shuffled deck (on the next draw)? Since there is one queen per suit, and four suits, the intuitively correct answer is 4 out of 52, and again this is just what the restricted disjunction rule tells us:

P(draw queen of clubs ∨ draw queen of hearts ∨ draw queen of diamonds ∨ draw queen of spades) = P(draw queen of clubs) + P(draw queen of hearts) + P(draw queen of diamonds) + P(draw queen of spades) = 1/52 + 1/52 + 1/52 + 1/52 = 4/52 = 1/13

The restricted disjunction rule tells us something important about the probability of negations. Namely, it enables us to calculate the probability of a negation from the probability of the statement negated. Take the statement S. By the restricted disjunction rule, we can conclude:

$$P(S \vee \sim S) = P(S) + P(\sim S)$$

(A statement and its negation are mutually exclusive.) And since S ∨ ~S is a tautology, by Rule 1 we may write:

$$P(S \vee \sim S) = 1$$

Now, it is a general principle of mathematics that two quantities equal to a third quantity are equal to each other. (If x = z and y = z, then x = y.) So, from the two prior equations, we may draw the following conclusion:

$$P(S) + P(\sim S) = 1$$

At this point, we subtract the $P(S)$ from both sides of the equation:

$$P(\sim S) = 1 - P(S)$$

Using the lowercase letter *p* to stand for any statement whatever, we can now generalize this reasoning, and state the **negation rule**:

Rule 4: $P(\sim p) = 1 - P(p)$

The negation rule is very useful. For example, if we know that the probability of rolling a four on the next throw of the die is 1/6, then the negation rule allows us to immediately calculate the probability that a four will not turn up on the next throw:

P(not roll 4) = 1 − P(roll 4) = 1 − 1/6 = 5/6

Since there are 13 cards in each suit, the probability that I will select a spade on the next draw from a well-shuffled deck is 13/52. What is the probability that I will *not* select a spade on the next draw? As follows:

P(not select spade) = 1 − P(select spade) = 52/52 − 13/52 = 39/52 = 3/4

Obviously, not every pair of statements is mutually exclusive. So, we need a more general disjunction rule to take care of cases in which the disjuncts can both be true. For example, suppose we want to know the probability of getting either a king or a club on the next draw. Since there is a king of clubs, these two possibilities are not mutually exclusive. How shall we proceed? We have to subtract the probability of drawing a king that is also a club:

P(draw king ∨ club) = P(draw king) + P(draw club) − P(draw king • club)

If we do not subtract this quantity, in effect, we count the king of clubs twice—once as a king and once as a club, which skews the result. Now, since there is one king per suit, the probability that we will draw a king (on the next draw) is 4/52. The probability that we will draw a club is 13/52, since there are 13 cards in each suit. But what is the probability that we will draw both a king *and* a club? Because there is only one king that is also a club, the probability that we will draw a king and a club is simply the probability that we will draw the king of clubs, that is, 1/52. Plugging these values into our formula, we get:

P(draw king ∨ club) = 4/52 + 13/52 − 1/52 = 16/52 = 4/13

This sort of example gives us an intuitive grasp of the **general disjunction rule**:

Rule 5: $P(p \lor q) = P(p) + P(q) - P(p \cdot q)$

We can apply the general disjunction rule even when *p* and *q* are mutually exclusive, for in such a case, P(*p* • *q*) will always be zero. For example, what is the probability that the next card to be drawn will be either a club or a diamond? Applying Rule 5 we get:

P(club ∨ diamond) = P(club) + P(diamond) − P(club • diamond)

And since a card cannot be both a club and a diamond, we may write:

P(club ∨ diamond) = 13/52 + 13/52 − 0 = 26/52 = 1/2

The following examples should enable you to see the intuitive plausibility of the general disjunction rule for yourself. What is the probability of selecting either the jack of hearts or a red card (on the next draw)? There is one jack of hearts and 26 red cards. So, one might be tempted to say P(jack of hearts ∨ red) = 27/52, but this answer ignores the fact that the jack of hearts is itself red (and hence has been counted twice). The general disjunction rule gives the correct formula to employ:

P(jack of hearts ∨ red) = P(jack of hearts) + P(red) − P(jack of hearts • red)

And since the only card that is both the jack of hearts and red is the jack of hearts, we plug in values as follows:

P(jack of hearts ∨ red) = 1/52 + 26/52 − 1/52 = 26/52 = 1/2

What is the probability of drawing either a red card or an eight (on the next draw)? Because half the cards (i.e., 26) are red, and there are four eights (one in each suit), one might be tempted to answer 30/52. But this would be a mistake, because two of the eights are red, and they've been counted twice. The general disjunction rule gives the correct answer:

P(red ∨ eight) = 26/52 + 4/52 − 2/52 = 28/52 = 7/13

Before leaving our discussion of the general disjunction rule, let us note that it enables us to handle the material conditional, for *p* → *q* is logically equivalent to ~*p* ∨ *q*, and hence P(*p* → *q*) is equal to P (~*p* ∨ *q*). However, as we noted in chapter 7, the material conditional does not adequately capture the meaning of the English "if-then" in every context. For this reason, logicians have developed a rule of probability that is designed to capture the meaning of English conditionals as they are used in contexts involving judgments about probability. Accordingly, we turn now to a rule of probability designed to capture a different sense of "if-then" than the material conditional.

Suppose we want to know the probability that *q* is true *given that p* is true. Following standard notation in probability theory, we will write "The probability of *q* given that *p*" as: P(*q/p*). This notation is read variously as "The probability of *q* on the condition that *p*," "The probability of *q* on *p*," or "The probability of *q* given *p*." The **conditional rule** is as follows:

$$\text{Rule 6: } P(q/p) = \frac{P(p \cdot q)}{P(p)}$$

Stated in the abstract, this rule may not seem at all obvious to you. Why suppose that the probability of a conditional equals the probability of the conjunction of its antecedent and consequent *divided by* the probability of its antecedent? The correctness of this rule is best seen through the lens of specific examples. Suppose I am about to draw exactly one card from a well-shuffled deck. Consider the probability that I will draw a club *given that* I will draw the ace of clubs. Intuitively, the probability is one, since if the card drawn is the ace of clubs, it must be a club. And this is exactly what Rule 6 tells us:

$$P(\text{club/ace of clubs}) = \frac{P(\text{ace of clubs} \cdot \text{club})}{P(\text{ace of clubs})}$$

The probability of drawing the ace of clubs is 1/52. The probability of drawing a club *that is also the ace of clubs* is simply the probability of drawing the ace of clubs. So, we write:

$$P(\text{club/ace of clubs}) = \frac{1/52}{1/52} = 1$$

Consider a second example. What is the probability that I will draw a spade *given that* I will draw a heart? (Remember, I am drawing just one card from a well-shuffled deck.) Intuitively, the probability is zero, since if I draw just one card and it is a heart, I certainly do not draw a spade. Let's see if the conditional rule bears this out:

$$P(\text{spade/heart}) = \frac{P(\text{heart} \cdot \text{spade})}{P(\text{heart})}$$

The probability of drawing a heart on a given draw is 13/52. Because a card cannot be both a heart and a spade, the probability of drawing a heart *and* a spade (on a given draw) is zero. Plugging in these values, we get:

$$P(\text{spade/heart}) = \frac{0}{13/52} = 0$$

Thus, the conditional rule once again gives us the intuitively correct answer.
    A third example: What is the probability that I will draw the king of hearts from a well-shuffled deck *given that* I will draw a king? Since there are four kings

altogether, but only one king of hearts, this probability is intuitively 1/4. Applying the conditional rule, we get:

$$P(\text{king of hearts}/\text{king}) = \frac{P(\text{king} \cdot \text{king of hearts})}{P(\text{king})}$$

The probability of drawing a king on a single draw from a well-shuffled deck is 4/52. The probability of drawing a king that is also the king of hearts is, of course, simply the probability of drawing the king of hearts, that is, 1/52. Therefore:

$$P(\text{king of hearts}/\text{king}) = \frac{1/52}{4/52} = 1/52 \times 52/4 = 52/208 = 1/4$$

Once again, the conditional rule accords with our intuitions.*

One last example: What is the probability that I will draw a club *given that* I will draw a black card? Since half the black cards are clubs and half are spades, the answer is intuitively 1/2. The conditional rule tells us:

$$P(\text{club}/\text{black}) = \frac{P(\text{black} \cdot \text{club})}{P(\text{black})}$$

Now, half the cards in a deck are black and half are red. So, P(black) = 1/2. And the probability of drawing a card that is both black *and* a club is simply the probability of drawing a club, namely, 13/52, or 1/4. Once again, the conditional rule gives us the intuitively correct answer:

$$P(\text{club}/\text{black}) = \frac{1/4}{1/2} = 1/4 \times 2/1 = 2/4 = 1/2$$

Now, the conditional rule is important, not only for what it tells us about the probability of conditionals, but also because from it we can immediately deduce the **general conjunction rule**:

Rule 7: $P(p \cdot q) = P(p) \times P(q/p)$

To prove this, we begin with the conditional rule:

$$P(q/p) = \frac{P(p \cdot q)}{P(p)}$$

---

*Since math skills can become "rusty" with disuse, this note explains how to divide complex fractions, that is, fractions in which the numerator and/or denominator involve fractions. To get right to the point: a/b divided by c/d = a/b times d/c. For example, 1/3 divided by 4/5 = 1/3 times 5/4 = 5/12. Thus, the division of a fraction may be interpreted as multiplication by the reciprocal of its *divisor*. (In the above formula, the divisor is c/d.)

Next, we multiply both sides of the equation by P(*p*):

$$P(p) \times P(q/p) = P(p) \times \frac{P(p \cdot q)}{P(p)}$$

Now, since $a \times \dfrac{b}{a} = \dfrac{a \times b}{a} = \dfrac{a}{a} \times b = 1 \times b = b$, we can transform the right-hand side of the equation as follows:

$$P(p) \times P(q/p) = P(p \cdot q)$$

And this is just what the general conjunction rule says. For example, consider the situation in which one draws a card from a well-shuffled deck and, *without* replacing it, draws a second card. What is the probability of drawing the ace of spades on the first draw *and* the ace of spades on the second draw? The answer is zero, since there is only one ace of spades and it was removed on the first draw. This is exactly the answer given by the general conjunction rule:

P(ace of spades on 1 • ace of spades on 2) = P(ace of spades on 1) × P(ace of spades on 2 *given* ace of spades on 1) = 1/52 × 0 = 0

What is the probability of drawing a red card on the first draw and a red card on the second draw? Of course, P(red on 1) = 1/2. But if we do select a red card on the first draw, only 51 cards will be left, 25 of them red. So, our chances of getting a red card the second time will be 25/51. How do we ascertain P(red on 1 • red on 2)? The general conjunction rule gives the answer:

P(red on 1 • red on 2) = P(red on 1) × P(red on 2 *given* red on 1) = 1/2 × 25/51 = 25/102.

In other words, the probability is just a bit shy of one-fourth. Of course, the numerically precise answer is something virtually no one can directly intuit. But since the general conjunction rule follows from the conditional rule, and we have seen that the conditional rule accords with our intuitions about probability, we can trust the answer given by the general conjunction rule.

What is the probability of drawing an ace on the first draw *and* (without replacing the first card drawn) another ace on the second draw?

P(ace on 1 • ace on 2) = P(ace on 1) × P(ace on 2 *given* ace on 1)

Now, the probability of getting an ace on the first draw is only 4/52. But if we do draw an ace and lay it aside, 51 cards remain in the deck, three of them aces. So, the probability of selecting an ace on the second draw, given that we drew an ace on the first draw, is 3/51. Therefore:

$$P(\text{ace on } 1 \cdot \text{ace on } 2) = 4/52 \times 3/51 = 12/2652 = 1/221$$

In other words, the probability of drawing two consecutive aces is quite low. Here again, although virtually no one can directly intuit the precise numerical probability, the answer is reliable assuming the conditional rule (from which we derived the general conjunction rule) is reliable.

If two statements, *p* and *q*, are such that neither one affects the probability of the other, they are said to be **independent**. In such a case, $P(q/p) = P(q)$ and $P(p/q) = P(p)$. For example, "The German philosopher Gottfried Wilhelm Leibniz died in 1716" and "The next card to be drawn will be a jack" are independent. Thus, the probability that "The next card to be drawn will be a jack *given that* Leibniz died in 1716" is simply the probability that the next card to be drawn will be a jack, namely, 4/52. In such cases, we can apply the **restricted conjunction rule**:

Rule 8: If *p* and *q* are independent, $P(p \cdot q) = P(p) \times P(q)$

For example, consider the probability of selecting an ace twice by drawing from a well-shuffled deck, replacing the card, reshuffling, and drawing a second time. Because, in this sort of case, what one gets on the first draw has no effect on what one gets on the second draw, it is convenient to apply the restricted conjunction rule:

$$P(\text{ace on } 1 \cdot \text{ace on } 2) = P(\text{ace on } 1) \times P(\text{ace on } 2)$$

Plugging in numerical values, we get:

$$P(\text{ace on } 1 \cdot \text{ace on } 2) = 4/52 \times 4/52 = 1/13 \times 1/13 = 1/169$$

It is instructive to compare this with the probability calculated previously of drawing two aces consecutively *without* replacing the card selected on the first draw.

The restricted conjunction rule provides us with an important logical insight. Suppose we have a conjunction of independent statements, each of which has a probability of less than one but greater than one-half. For example, suppose $P(A) = 7/10$, $P(B) = 7/10$, and $P(C) = 7/10$. What is the probability of the whole conjunction?

$$P[A \cdot (B \cdot C)] = 7/10 \times 7/10 \times 7/10 = 343/1000$$

Note that although each conjunct is more probable than not, the entire conjunction has a probability of less than one-half. So, the negation of this conjunction is more probable than the conjunction itself. Therefore, when we

---

Summary of the Rules of Probability

1. If a statement p is a tautology, then $P(p) = 1$.
2. If a statement p is a contradiction, then $P(p) = 0$.
3. Restricted disjunction rule: If p and q are mutually exclusive, then $P(p \vee q)$ $= P(p) + P(q)$.
4. Negation rule: $P(\sim p) = 1 - P(p)$
5. General disjunction rule: $P(p \vee q) = P(p) + P(q) - P(p \cdot q)$
6. Conditional rule: $P(q/p) = \dfrac{P(p \cdot q)}{P(p)}$
7. General conjunction rule: $P(p \cdot q) = P(p) \times P(q/p)$
8. Restricted conjunction rule: If p and q are independent, $P(p \cdot q) = P(p) \times P(q)$.

---

conjoin *probably true but independent* statements—think, for example, of a creed in which some of the statements may be independent—the probability of the compound may sink below 1/2, even though each conjunct is more probable than not. (Of course, it may still be true that the entire creedal statement is more probable than any interesting alternative creed.)

To check your understanding of the basic rules of probability theory, complete the following exercises.

◆ *Exercise 11.2*

Part A: Disjunctions   Suppose you have an ordinary deck of playing cards. Assuming that you are as likely to draw one card as another, what is the probability that on your next draw you will select each of the following?

* 1. A spade or a diamond?
  2. A jack or a queen?
  3. A king or a nonking?
* 4. The queen of diamonds or a heart?
  5. A king or a spade?
  6. A club or a red card?
* 7. A red card or an ace?
  8. A black card or the 10 of hearts?
  9. A black card or the 10 of spades?
  10. A black card or a 10?

Part B: Conjunctions and Conditionals   You have an ordinary deck of cards. You draw one card, do *not* replace it, and then draw a second card. Assuming you are as likely to draw one card as another, find the following probabilities.

* 1. P(jack on first draw • queen on second draw)

  2. P(ace on first draw • ace on second draw)

  3. P(ace of hearts on first • red on second)

* 4. P(club on first • club on second)

  5. P(club on first • diamond on second)

  6. P(black on first • black on second)

* 7. P(queen of hearts on first • queen of hearts on second)

  8. P(spade on first • black on second)

  9. P(king on second draw *given* ace on first draw)

 10. P(red on second *given* jack of spades on first)

Part C: Various Compound Statements   Let G be "God exists," M be "Miracles occur," *T* be "A → A," and *D* be "Ducks exist." Assume that $P(G) = 3/5$, $P(M) = 3/10$, $P(D) = 9/10$, and $P(G/M) = 9/10$. Also assume that D and M are independent. Determine the following probabilities.

* 1. P(~G)   9. P(D/M)

  2. P(~M)   * 10. P[D → (G → D)]

  3. P(G • ~G)   11. P(M/D)

* 4. P(M ∨ ~M)   12. P(~D)

  5. P(T)   13. P(D • M)

  6. P(~T)   14. P(D ∨ M)

* 7. P(M • G)   15. P[G → (M ∨ G)]

  8. P(M ∨ G)

Part D: The Strength of Arguments   Use the rules of probability to determine the strength of the following arguments. In other words, given that the premises are true, how likely is the conclusion?

* 1. The odds are 5 to 1 that Team A will beat Team B in the quarter-finals. The odds are 4 to 1 that Team C will beat Team D in the quarter-finals. Therefore, Team A will play Team C in the semi-finals.

  2. The odds are 6 to 1 that Chris is lying. Therefore, it is not the case that Chris is lying.

3. The odds are 1 to 3 that Mad Dog Mike killed Jones. The odds are 2 to 1 that Bad Dog Bob killed Jones. There is a probability of zero that Mad Dog Mike and Bad Dog Bob *both* killed Jones. Therefore, either Mad Dog Mike or Bad Dog Bob killed Jones.

* 4. The die is fair (not loaded or off balance), and I roll it twice. Therefore, I roll a five twice.

5. The odds are 1 to 4 that Bill stole the TV. The odds are 1 to 3 that Jack stole the TV. The odds are 1 to 9 that Jack and Bill both stole the TV. Therefore, either Jack or Bill stole the TV.

6. Jack and Jill are married, and they are both 30 years of age. The probability that a 30-year-old man will live to age 80 is .63, while the probability that a 30-year-old woman will live to age 80 is .71. Therefore, Jack and Jill will both live to age 80.

* 7. The odds are 15 to 1 that Ted was at the party. Moreover, it is very likely that if Ted was at the party, Sue was also; in fact, the odds are 20 to 1. So, Ted and Sue were both at the party.

8. The odds are 2 to 1 that Radical Jack Jones will defeat Buster Bonzo in the semi-final bout. The odds are even that Crocker Crunch will defeat The Blue Basher in the semifinal bout. Therefore, Radical Jack Jones will meet Crocker Crunch in the championship bout.

9. The odds are 2 to 1 that Zeus exists. And the odds are 2 to 1 that wisdom is a virtue. "Zeus exists" is logically independent of "Wisdom is a virtue." Hence, Zeus exists and wisdom is a virtue.

10. The odds are 9 to 1 that trees are real. And the odds are 0 to 1 that life is but a dream *given that* trees are real. So, trees are real and life is nothing but a dream.

11.3 Bayes' Theorem

Thomas Bayes (1702–1761) was an English theologian and mathematician who made an important contribution to the theory of probability. According to many philosophers, Bayes' theorem gives us an important insight into the relationship between the evidence for a hypothesis and the hypothesis itself. Assuming this is so, Bayes' theorem provides us with important information relative to assessing inductive arguments. Let us see how we can derive Bayes' theorem from the basic rules of probability theory.

Let us use the italicized, lowercase letter *h* to stand for any hypothesis and *e* to stand for a statement that summarizes the observational evidence for that hypothesis. We begin with the conditional rule:[3]

$$P(h/e) = \frac{P(e \cdot h)}{P(e)}$$

This tells us that the probability of a hypothesis *given* the evidence is equal to the probability of the conjunction of the evidence and the hypothesis *divided by* the probability of the evidence.

A proof or truth table will reveal that *e* is logically equivalent to $(e \cdot h) \vee (e \cdot \sim h)$. Therefore, we may replace *e* with $(e \cdot h) \vee (e \cdot \sim h)$ wherever we wish, and it is useful to do so in the denominator:

$$P(h/e) = \frac{P(e \cdot h)}{P[(e \cdot h) \vee (e \cdot \sim h)]}$$

Now, by the restricted disjunction rule, $P[(e \cdot h) \vee (e \cdot \sim h)]$ is equal to $P(e \cdot h) + P(e \cdot \sim h)$. Therefore, we may write:

$$P(h/e) = \frac{P(e \cdot h)}{P(e \cdot h) + P(e \cdot \sim h)}$$

Next, we apply the rule of commutation to the three conjunctions on the right side of the equation, as follows:*

$$P(h/e) = \frac{P(h \cdot e)}{P(h \cdot e) + P(\sim h \cdot e)}$$

Finally, we apply the general conjunction rule three times, to arrive at **Bayes' theorem**:

$$P(h/e) = \frac{P(h) \times P(e/h)}{[P(h) \times P(e/h)] + [P(\sim h) \times P(e/\sim h)]}$$

Now, in order to use Bayes' theorem to discover the degree to which a given hypothesis is supported by the evidence, we need just three pieces of information: $P(h)$, $P(e/h)$, and $P(e/\sim h)$. (Remember, if we have $P(h)$, we can

---

*According to the rule of commutation, statements of the form $(p \cdot q)$ and $(q \cdot p)$ are logically equivalent, and hence may be exchanged whenever it is convenient to do so. In other words, from a logical point of view, it is always permissible to interchange the conjuncts in a conjunction. The rule of commutation also applies to disjunctions, since $(p \vee q)$ is logically equivalent to $(q \vee p)$.

calculate P($\sim h$) using the negation rule.) P(h) stands for the **prior** or **antecedent probability** of the hypothesis—that is, the likelihood of the hypothesis independent of the evidence e. Normally, e is a statement summarizing the latest observational evidence, so that we have some background evidence to appeal to in estimating P(h).* P(e/h) is the likelihood that the evidence (or phenomenon in question) would be present, assuming the hypothesis is true. P($e/\sim h$) is the likelihood that the evidence (or phenomenon in question) would be present, assuming the hypothesis is false. An example will help to make these abstractions concrete.

Suppose a doctor has diagnosed a patient as having *either* some minor stomach troubles *or* stomach cancer. And let us assume that the doctor knows that the patient does not have *both* minor stomach troubles *and* stomach cancer. The doctor also knows that, given the symptoms, 30 percent of patients have stomach cancer; the rest have minor stomach troubles. Accordingly, the doctor initially suspects that the patient has only minor stomach troubles. But the doctor proceeds to conduct a test. Experience indicates that 90 percent of cases of stomach cancer yield a positive result when this test is applied, but only 10 percent of cases of minor stomach troubles yield a positive result. What is the probability that the patient has stomach cancer *given that the test turns out positive?* Using Bayes' theorem, we can readily answer this question.

Our hypothesis and evidence are as follows:

H: The patient has stomach cancer

E: The test is positive.

We want to find P(H/E), that is, the probability that the hypothesis is true given the evidence. To do this, we need three bits of information. First, we need P(H), that is, the prior or antecedent probability of the hypothesis. Second, we need P(E/H), that is, the probability of a positive test result *assuming that* the hypothesis is true. Finally, we need to know P(E/$\sim$H), that is, the probability of a positive test result *assuming that* the hypothesis is not true. It is built into the case that if the patient does not have cancer, then he or she has minor stomach troubles. So, given the parameters of the case, information about $\sim$H is given by way of information about "minor stomach troubles."

The doctor's background knowledge provides the prior or antecedent probability that the patient has stomach cancer, for given the symptoms, 30 percent of patients have stomach cancer. In other words, P(H) = 30/100 = 3/10. We can obtain P($\sim$H) by the negation rule: 1 − 3/10 = 7/10. And since 90 percent of cases of stomach cancer yield a positive result when the test is applied, P(E/H)

---

*If we wish to distinguish background evidence b from e (the "new" evidence or phenomenon to be explained), Bayes' theorem takes on a slightly more complicated appearance:

$$P[h/(e \cdot b)] = \frac{P(h/b) \times P[e/(h \cdot b)]}{\{P(h/b) \times P[e/(h \cdot b)]\} + \{P(\sim h/b) \times P[e/(\sim h \cdot b)]\}}$$

= 90/100 = 9/10. Furthermore, since we are assuming that the patient has minor stomach troubles if he or she does not have stomach cancer, and since 10 percent of cases of minor stomach troubles yield a positive result when the test is applied, then $P(E/{\sim}H) = 10/100 = 1/10$. Plugging these values into Bayes' theorem, we get:

$$P(H/E) = \frac{3/10 \times 9/10}{[3/10 \times 9/10] + [7/10 \times 1/10]} = \frac{27/100}{27/100 + 7/100} = \frac{27}{34}$$

So, the probability of the hypothesis given the evidence is 27/34 or approximately .79.

In many cases, we do not have adequate grounds for assigning precise numerical values to $P(H)$, $P(E/H)$, and/or $P(E/{\sim}H)$. Does it follow that Bayes' theorem is inapplicable in such cases? Not necessarily. Even if we cannot assign precise numerical values, we may be able to assign relative values. For example, in a given case, we may have good reason to suppose that $P(H) \geq P({\sim}H)$. And we may be able to settle, by argument, that $P(E/H) > P(E/{\sim}H)$. In such a case, we can conclude that the evidence under consideration favors H over ${\sim}H$. This is so because whenever $P(H) \geq P({\sim}H)$, evidence E favors H provided that $P(E/H) > P(E/{\sim}H)$. After all, as we saw in section 11.2, $P(H) + P({\sim}H) = 1$. Hence, if $P(H) \geq P({\sim}H)$, then $P(H) \geq 1/2$ and $P({\sim}H) \leq 1/2$. And in this situation, if $P(E/H) > P(E/{\sim}H)$, then $P(H/E) > P({\sim}H/E)$. To illustrate this concretely, suppose $P(H) = P({\sim}H) = 1/2$, $P(E/H) = 3/5$, and $P(E/{\sim}H) = 2/5$. Then, applying Bayes' theorem, we get:

$$P(H/E) = \frac{1/2 \times 3/5}{[1/2 \times 3/5] + [1/2 \times 2/5]} = \frac{3/10}{3/10 + 2/10} = 3/5$$

$$P({\sim}H/E) = \frac{1/2 \times 2/5}{[1/2 \times 2/5] + [1/2 \times 3/5]} = \frac{2/10}{2/10 + 3/10} = 2/5$$

To generalize, if $P(H) \geq P({\sim}H)$ and $P(E/H) > P(E/{\sim}H)$, then $P(H/E) > P({\sim}H/E)$. The important point is that we can sometimes apply Bayes' theorem even when we cannot set precise numerical values. Typically, this occurs when we can provide reasonable arguments to the effect that $P(H) \geq P({\sim}H)$ and $P(E/H) > P(E/{\sim}H)$.

Some philosophers have tried to apply Bayes' theorem to major philosophical issues such as the existence of God.[4] While we cannot here enter into a detailed discussion of such matters, it is important to understand how Bayes' theorem can be used to organize a rational dialogue and develop strategies for argument. To this end, let us briefly consider a version of the cosmological argument for God's existence. Let H be "God exists" and let E be "There is a physical universe." A theist may argue that $P(E/H) > P(E/{\sim}H)$ on the following grounds: first, that God would have a good reason to create the physical universe as an appropriate environment for intelligent creatures; and second, that if there is no God, then there is no explanation for the existence of physical reality—it can only be regarded as a coincidence. Using Bayes' theorem to structure the discussion, the nontheist might respond in three ways:

- Refute the theist's arguments for the thesis that $P(E/H) > P(E/\sim H)$.

- Argue that the prior probability of "God exists" is lower than the prior probability of "God does not exist." If a good case can be made that $P(H) < P(\sim H)$, then this could destroy the force of the cosmological argument, *even if* $P(E/H) > P(E/\sim H)$. (To illustrate, some have argued that $P(H) < P(\sim H)$ because the divine attributes lead to conceptual puzzles—for example, if God is all-powerful, can God create a stone too big for God to lift?)

- Argue that the probability that God exists is low given some evidence *other than* the existence of the physical universe, such as the suffering or evil in the world.

Obviously, these strategies can be combined. The point here is not to recommend either the cosmological argument or any of these strategies for replying to it, but merely to illustrate how the Bayesian perspective can help us to structure a rational dialogue.

Can a Bayesian approach accommodate a situation in which multiple hypotheses are being compared? Yes. To illustrate, if H_1, H_2, and H_3 are *three mutually exclusive hypotheses that exhaust the possibilities*, then:

$$P(H_1/E) = \frac{P(H_1) \times P(E/H_1)}{[P(H_1) \times P(E/H_1)] + [P(H_2) \times P(E/H_2)] + [P(H_3) \times P(E/H_3)]}$$

In other words, we can accommodate as many hypotheses as we like (provided they are mutually exclusive and exhaust the possibilities), simply by adding relevant clauses to the denominator. To apply Bayes' theorem, we must assign values for $P(E/H_1)$, $P(E/H_2)$, and $P(E/H_3)$, as well as for the prior probabilities of at least two of the three hypotheses. Since we are assuming that the three hypotheses are mutually exclusive and exhaust the possibilities, we can assume that the sum of their prior probabilities is one, just as $P(H) + P(\sim H) = 1$. And given that $P(H_1) + P(H_2) + P(H_3) = 1$, then $P(H_1) = 1 - P(H_2) - P(H_3)$. Similarly, $P(H_2) = 1 - P(H_1) - P(H_3)$, and $P(H_3) = 1 - P(H_1) - P(H_2)$.

The following exercises will increase your understanding of Bayes' theorem and of its application to a wide range of issues.

◆ *Exercise 11.3*

Part A: Patterns   Explore Bayes' theorem by answering the following questions.

1. Suppose you are applying Bayes' theorem, and $P(H) = P(E/H) = P(E/\sim H)$. For example, what is $P(H/E)$ in the following cases?

* a. P(H) = 1/2; P(E/H) = 1/2; P(E/~H) = 1/2
   b. P(H) = 2/3; P(E/H) = 2/3; P(E/~H) = 2/3
   c. P(H) = 1/4; P(E/H) = 1/4; P(E/~H) = 1/4

2. Suppose you are applying Bayes' theorem and the prior probability of the hypothesis is low, but P(E/H) and P(E/~H) are high and equal. For instance, what is P(H/E) in the following cases?
* a. P(H) = 1/5; P(E/H) = 9/10; P(E/~H) = 9/10
   b. P(H) = 1/3; P(E/H) = 7/8; P(E/~H) = 7/8
   c. P(H) = 3/8; P(E/H) = 3/4; P(E/~H) = 3/4

3. Suppose you are applying Bayes' theorem and the prior probability of the hypothesis is high, but P(E/H) is low and equal to P(E/~H). For example, what is P(H/E) in the following cases?
* a. P(H) = 9/10; P(E/H) = 2/5; P(E/~H) = 2/5
   b. P(H) = 8/9; P(E/H) = 1/3; P(E/~H) = 1/3
   c. P(H) = 7/10; P(E/H) = 4/9; P(E/~H) = 4/9

4. Suppose you are applying Bayes' theorem and the prior probability of the hypothesis is one-half, but P(E/H) is greater than P(E/~H). For instance, what is P(H/E) in the following cases? What is P(~H/E) in these cases? Is P(~H/E) = 1 − P(H/E)?
* a. P(H) = 1/2; P(E/H) = 9/10; P(E/~H) = 3/5
   b. P(H) = 1/2; P(E/H) = 7/8; P(E/~H) = 3/4

5. Suppose you are applying Bayes' theorem and one of the probability values is zero. Specifically:
   a. Suppose the prior probability of the hypothesis is zero. Can P(E/H) be determined? [Hint: applying the conditional rule, P(E/H) = P(H • E) divided by P(H).]
* b. Suppose P(H) is high, P(E/H) is zero, and P(E/~H) is not zero. For example, suppose P(H) = 9/10, P(E/H) = 0, and P(E/~H) = 1/10. What is P(H/E)? What is P(~H/E)?
   c. Suppose P(H) and P(E/H) are low, but P(E/~H) is zero. For example, suppose P(H) = 1/10, P(E/H) = 3/10, and P(E/~H) = 0. What is P(H/E)? What is P(~H/E)?

6. Suppose you are applying Bayes' theorem, and suppose P(H) and P(E/H) are both moderately high, and P(E/~H) is a bit lower than P(E/H). For example, what is P(H/E) in the following cases? What is P(~H/E)? Is P(~H/E) = 1 − P(H/E)?
   a. P(H) = 7/10; P(E/H) = 7/10; P(E/~H) = 6/10
* b. P(H) = 5/7; P(E/H) = 5/7; P(E/~H) = 4/7

7. Suppose you are applying Bayes' theorem and the prior probability of the hypothesis H is slightly higher than that of its negation, but P(E/H) is slightly lower than P(E/~H). For example, what is P(H/E) in the following cases? What is P(~H/E)?
   a. P(H) = 9/16; P(E/H) = 8/10; P(E/~H) = 9/10
   b. P(H) = 51/100; P(E/H) = 5/10; P(E/~H) = 6/10

Part B: Applying Bayes' Theorem   Bayes' theorem has many interesting applications. Some philosophers even think it can be used to set up certain traditional philosophical problems in a revealing fashion. Of course, like other logical principles, the rules of probability seldom solve philosophical problems—that is not their purpose. But the rules of probability, like other principles of logic, can help us formulate questions in interesting ways that help us to focus our thinking, ask new questions, and identify difficulties. The following exercises ask you to apply Bayes' theorem to a wide range of questions and issues. In a number of cases, the assignment of numerical values is deliberately contrived, for the sake of making a definite answer possible, but keep in mind that Bayes' theorem can sometimes be applied even when precise numerical values cannot be assigned.

* 1. Bloggs is an impoverished college student working 40 hours a week. Due to the shortage of time, Bloggs prepares for only 40 percent of his exams. Bloggs passes 70 percent of the exams he prepares for. But he only passes 30 percent of the exams he does not prepare for. Furthermore, Bloggs passed his most recent exam. How probable is it that Bloggs prepared for his most recent exam?

2. Sally claims to have telekinetic powers. She claims that she can cause a die to turn up any number she chooses. A *fair* die is produced, and Sally predicts that she will role a six three times in a row. She proceeds to do just that. Our evidence and hypothesis are:

    E: Sally rolls a six three times in a row (without cheating).
    H: Sally has telekinetic powers.

    Given that Sally has telekinetic powers, E is just the sort of thing we should expect. So, assume that $P(E/H) = 1$. But *prior* to considering E, we are understandably skeptical, giving odds of 1 to 9 that Sally has telekinetic powers. Assuming chance is the only alternative to Sally's alleged telekinetic powers, what is $P(E/{\sim}H)$? (*Hint:* You will need to use the restricted conjunction rule.) What is $P(H/E)$?

3. Police detectives have determined that Smith and Jones are the only two possible murderers of McCann, and it is known that the murderer acted all by himself. (Thus, Smith and Jones are not both guilty of the murder.) Because Smith has a prior criminal record, Detective Wills initially gives odds of 5 to 3 that Smith is the murderer. However, while at the scene of the crime, Detective Wills finds the murder weapon, which has Jones' fingerprints on it *and not Smith's*. Detective Wills gives 9-to-1 odds that Jones' fingerprints are on the weapon *given that* Jones is the murderer; whereas Wills gives only 3-to-7 odds that Jones' fingerprints are on the weapon *given that* Smith is the murderer. (It is possible, but unlikely, that Smith somehow set Jones up.) Given Detective Wills' assessment of the odds, how likely is it that Jones is the murderer *given that* Jones' fingerprints are on the murder weapon? How likely is it that Smith is the murderer *given that* Jones' fingerprints are on the murder weapon?

* 4. Valerie is trying to assess the evidence for the existence of a God who is all-powerful and perfectly good. Given her background evidence (e.g., she is aware of the cosmological and design arguments for God's existence), Valerie gives even odds that God exists. However, Valerie has recently heard of the so-called problem of evil. She finds it plausible to suppose that some of the suffering in the world, such as the suffering of animals, is not a necessary means to a greater good. Fur-

thermore, Valerie is convinced that if God were all-powerful and perfectly good, then God would not permit any suffering unless it were a necessary means to a greater good. On reflection, Valerie gives only 1-to-3 odds that some unnecessary suffering occurs *given that* an all-powerful and perfectly good God exists. But she gives 2-to-1 odds that some unnecessary suffering occurs *given that* an all-powerful and perfectly good God does *not* exist. Given Valerie's assignments of probability, what is the probability that God exists *given that* some unnecessary suffering occurs?

5. Nate is a sprinter at a college that hosts relatively few track meets. In fact, only 30 percent of Nate's races are at his own college. Nate wins 90 percent of the races held at his own college. But he only wins 40 percent of the races at other colleges. Nate won his last race. How likely is it that the race was at Nate's own college?

6. A veterinarian has diagnosed a dog as having either leukemia or severe anemia (but not both). Given the symptoms, 90 percent of dogs have severe anemia and 10 percent of dogs have leukemia. So, the vet initially surmises that the dog has severe anemia. Later, however, the vet conducts a test on the dog that turns out positive. Seventy percent of cases of leukemia yield a positive result when this test is applied, and 20 percent of cases of anemia yield a positive result. What is the probability that the dog has leukemia given the results of the test?

7. Zachary is evaluating the evidence for two worldviews, theism and naturalism. Theism is the view that a perfectly loving and all-powerful God exists and that God created the physical universe. Naturalism is the view that only matter exists and that matter is entirely governed by natural laws (such as the law of gravity). In Zachary's estimation, the probability that either theism or naturalism is true is very high. In fact, Zachary regards other worldviews as too implausible to be worth serious consideration. Zachary is aware of the standard arguments for God's existence as well as the problem of evil, which is usually considered the strongest argument against the existence of God. On this basis, Zachary initially gives 1-to-2 odds that God exists and 2-to-1 odds that naturalism is true. However, Zachary goes on to consider his firm belief that people are morally responsible. He takes it as obvious that people cannot be morally responsible unless they have free will. Yet, it appears to Zachary that free will is most unlikely given naturalism. For, given naturalism, every event is the result of past states of the physical world plus the operation of natural laws. And since we have no control over the past and no control over which (or whether) natural laws hold, it seems that we humans lack free will *given* naturalism. Accordingly, Zachary gives only 1-to-5 odds that humans have free will given naturalism, while he gives 5-to-1 odds that humans have free will *given* theism. (Zachary reasons that a God of love would likely provide some of his creatures with free will, in order that they might love freely and not of necessity.) Given Zachary's estimates, what is the probability of theism *given that* humans have free will? What is the probability of naturalism *given that* humans have free will?

8. Suppose the police know that either Jones, Smith, or Dobbs stole the jewels. Furthermore, the police know that the thief acted all by himself. H_1 is "Jones stole the jewels," H_2 is "Smith stole the jewels," and H_3 is "Dobbs stole the jewels." The

hypotheses are equally likely on the background evidence (e.g., the criminal records of the three suspects). Also, suppose the evidence at the crime scene allows us to assign these probabilities: $P(E/H_1) = 1/4$, $P(E/H_2) = 1/2$, and $P(E/H_3) = 3/4$. What is $P(H_1/E)$? $P(H_2/E)$? $P(H_3/E)$?

9. Chris thinks the prior probability that reincarnation occurs is low for two reasons. First, it is unclear what links any given soul with any given body (e.g., why does Jones' soul wind up in Smith's body?). Second, there seems to be no good answer to the question, "How long has reincarnation been going on?" The usual answer is that the process is beginningless (infinite). However, this seems unlikely since, according to recent work in physics, the physical universe itself has only been in existence for 15–20 billion years—a finite period of time. (And, obviously, there were no physical bodies for souls to transmigrate to prior to the existence of matter.) For these reasons, Chris initially gives odds of only 1 to 3 that reincarnation occurs. But then Chris encounters new evidence in the form of a book about apparent past-life recall. (In the more interesting cases, a young child claims to be someone else, someone who lived and died in the surrounding area in the recent past. And in some of these cases, the child claims to remember the sort of thing that can be checked—for example, the location of some object—and his or her apparent memory turns out to be correct.) Chris becomes convinced that apparent past-life recall sometimes occurs and that in some cases the apparent memories turn out to be correct. Chris realizes that the probability of accurate (apparent) past-life recall *given reincarnation* is very high. In fact, Chris offers 9-to-1 odds that accurate (apparent) past-life recall occurs *given reincarnation*. Chris finds it rather difficult to assess the probability of accurate, apparent past-life recall *given that reincarnation does not occur*. Chris judges that this depends on the probability of obtaining information about someone else's past life through some paranormal experience or through spiritism (mediumship). Chris is rather skeptical of these possibilities, and hence gives only 2-to-3 odds that accurate (apparent) past-life recall occurs *if reincarnation doesn't occur*. Given Chris's probability estimates, what is the probability that reincarnation occurs given the evidence of accurate (apparent) past-life recall?

10. Suppose there is a fair lottery for which 1000 tickets have been sold. There will be only one winning ticket, and each ticket has a 1 in 1000 chance of being selected. Suppose Smith purchased exactly one ticket. What is the prior probability that Smith will win? Now, let our evidence and hypothesis be:

    E: A reputable local newspaper, which makes a point of reporting lottery winners, carries a story reporting that Smith won the lottery.
    H: Smith won the lottery.

$P(E/H)$ is surely very high. That is, if Smith won, we would expect a reputable local newspaper (that makes a practice of reporting lottery winners) to report that Smith won. Thus, we give 9-to-1 odds that (E/H). However, $P(E/\sim H)$ is surely quite low. How often does a newspaper report that someone won the lottery if he did not in fact win? Very seldom indeed. Accordingly, we give odds of 1 to 99 that (E/~H). What is $P(H/E)$?

11. Let H be "God exists" and let E be "the universe is orderly and its order can be expressed in terms of scientific laws." Suppose $P(H) = P(\sim H)$. Now, some theists have argued that $P(E/H)$ is greater than $P(E/\sim H)$ on the grounds that (a) a good God would have a reason to create intelligent life, and there can be no intelligent life without order, and (b) there can be no scientific explanation of the orderliness because the fact that the universe operates in accordance with scientific laws is part of the phenomenon to be explained. Suppose these theists are right. Can we conclude that $P(H/E)$ is greater than $P(\sim H/E)$?

12. Suppose that there are just three possible hypotheses that can account for E, the fact that I seem to see physical objects:

> H_1: Physical objects exist and my sensory experiences are produced by them.
> H_2: There are no physical objects; I am simply experiencing a vivid dream.
> H_3: There are no physical objects, and I am not dreaming, but a powerful demon is causing me to have hallucinations of physical objects.

Suppose I can somehow prove that $P(E/H_3)$ is less than $P(E/H_2)$, and that $P(E/H_2)$ is less than $P(E/H_1)$. Based on this information, can I rightly conclude that $P(H_1/E)$ is greater than $P(H_3/E)$? Why or why not?

Notes

1. My summary of these three theories of probability borrows heavily from Patrick Hurley, *A Concise Introduction to Logic*, 6th ed. (Belmont, CA: Wadsworth, 1997), pp. 530–533.
2. For more details, see Alban Krailsheimer, *Pascal* (New York: Hill & Wang, 1980), pp. 14–16.
3. My proof of Bayes' theorem follows that of Brian Skyrms, *Choice and Chance* (Belmont, CA: Wadsworth, 1986), p. 153.
4. Perhaps the best-known example is Richard Swinburne, *The Existence of God* (New York: Oxford University Press, 1979).

Chapter 12

Modal Logic

Modal logic is the logic of necessity and possibility. The name "modal logic" stems from the fact that necessity and possibility have traditionally been regarded as *modes* of truth (or *ways* of being true). For example, some propositions, such as "All triangles have three sides," are traditionally regarded as *necessarily* true. Others, such as "Socrates was married to Xanthippe," are traditionally regarded as true *but not necessarily* true. We will explore these modes of truth in section 12.1.

Modal logic has many interesting applications, especially in regard to philosophical issues. For example, here is a modal version of Saint Anselm's famous ontological argument for the existence of God:

> If God exists, then God is a Supremely Perfect Being. If God is a Supremely Perfect Being, then it is impossible that God not exist. It is logically possible that God exists. So, God exists.

Is this argument valid? We will examine it closely in section 12.5. Modal logic has been developed in order to determine the validity of arguments such as this, whose forms make essential use of modal concepts.

Aristotle was the first philosopher to discuss the logical relationships between necessity and possibility. For example, in his *De Interpretatione*, Aristotle identified the following equivalences:[1]

> "It is impossible that ***p***" is logically equivalent to "It is necessary that not ***p***." (For example, "It is impossible that circular squares exist" is logically equivalent to "It is necessary that circular squares do not exist.")

> "It is not possible that not ***p***" is logically equivalent to "It is necessary that ***p***." (For example, "It is not possible that not every square is a rectangle" is equivalent to "Necessarily, every square is a rectangle.")

However, modal logic did not become highly developed until the 20th century. An American logician, C. I. Lewis (1883–1964), was dissatisfied with the so-called paradoxes of material implication. In symbols, they look like this:

$$p \rightarrow (q \rightarrow p)$$
$$\sim p \rightarrow (p \rightarrow q)$$

Both of these formulas are tautologies of statement logic. The first formula says (in effect) that a conditional is true if its consequent is true. The second formula says (in effect) that a conditional is true if its antecedent is false. These tautologies indicate that the material conditional is not very close to the ordinary English "if-then." Lewis wanted to capture the idea of a necessary connection between antecedent and consequent that frequently occurs in philosophical discourse—for example, "Necessarily, if I think, then I exist." In working his ideas out, Lewis made dramatic advances in modal logic. In this chapter, we will see how to develop a system of modal logic by adding to the system of statement logic developed in chapters 7 and 8.

12.1 Modal Concepts

Let us begin our exploration of the basic concepts of modal logic with an examination of the concept of a necessary truth. A **necessary truth** is one that cannot be false under any possible circumstances. Here are some standard examples:

1. Either trees exist or it is not the case that trees exist.
2. One plus one equals two.
3. All cats are cats.
4. All husbands are married.
5. If Sue is older than Tom, then Tom is not older than Sue.
6. Nothing is red all over and blue all over at the same time.
7. No prime minister is a prime number.[2]

These examples fall into certain significant categories. Item (1) is a tautology of statement logic. Recall that a tautology is a statement that is true in every row of its truth table.[3]

Item (2) is a mathematical truth. Since it does not seem possible for mathematical truths to be false, many philosophers regard all mathematical truths as necessary ones.

Items (3) and (4) are examples of what philosophers call analytic statements. Definitions of the term "analytic" vary, but it will be adequate for present purposes to say that an **analytic statement** is one that is either (a) true by virtue of its logical form or (b) transformable into a statement that is true by virtue of its logical form by replacing synonyms with synonyms.[4] Item (3) has the form "All A are A," and since it is not possible for statements of this form to be false, (3) is a necessary truth. As for (4), since the word "husbands" means "married men," we can transform (4) into "All married men are married." Thus, upon analyzing (4), we can see that it has the form "All AB are A." And because statements having this form cannot be false, (4) is necessary.

Items (5) through (7) are not so easily categorized. They do not seem to be analytic. A statement that is not analytic is said to be **synthetic**. But while (5), (6), and (7) are apparently synthetic, many philosophers believe that it is impossible for such statements to be false. In this view, (5), (6), and (7) are synthetic yet necessary. It must be admitted, however, that many philosophers are skeptical about the thesis that there are synthetic necessary truths. However, because this issue is very complicated, we cannot explore it here.

We noted previously that a necessary truth is one that cannot be false in any possible circumstances. What exactly is meant by a "possible circumstance"? We have been making use of this concept throughout this book, for we noted early on that if we can describe a *situation or circumstance* in which the conclusion of an argument is false while its premises are true, then we have demonstrated that the argument is invalid. For instance:

8. Someone is rich. So, Bill Gates (of Microsoft) is rich.

This argument is invalid, though both its premise and its conclusion are true. We can demonstrate the invalidity by describing a possible circumstance in which the premise is true while the conclusion is false. For example, here is a possible circumstance: "Bill Gates donates his entire fortune, every last penny, to charitable causes, freely choosing to live in poverty, but at least one other person who is currently rich remains so." In such a circumstance, the premise of (8) is true, but the conclusion is false.

A possible circumstance is *a way things could (or might) have been*. In ordinary life, we often make use of a distinction between *how things are* and *how they could (or might) have been*. For example, consider what happens when one makes a decision with far-reaching consequences. One may look back on the decision and realize that one's present circumstances could have been different because one's decision could have been different. Philosophers have attempted to analyze talk about "the way things could have been" in terms of the technical concept of possible worlds. So, before going further, we need to clarify the concept of a possible world.

A **possible world** is a *total way* things could have been. To get at this concept, let us begin with the actual world. As philosophers use this expression, the "actual world" is not merely the planet Earth, but the *complete situation* we find ourselves in—the entire universe (including all the stars and galaxies, subatomic particles, and their movements), every person, every object, and all events (past, present, and future). Moreover, as philosophers use the phrase, the "actual world" is one of many possible worlds. We can clarify the idea of possible worlds by considering some ways in which the actual world could have been different from what it is.

Let's start with a trivial case. Yesterday, January 29, 1998, I wore a blue tie all day. I might have chosen a different tie, say, a red one, but I didn't. So, the actual world includes the following circumstance or state of affairs: my wearing a blue tie all day on January 29, 1998. And we can say that there is a possible world that is exactly like the actual world except that on January 29, 1998, I wear a red tie instead of a blue one. Of course, that possible world is not the actual world, but it is a (total) way things could have been, a comprehensive situation.

Once you grasp the idea of a possible world, you can see that there are *lots* of them, for the actual world might have gone differently in all sorts of ways. For instance, it seems possible that some or even all of the persons who do exist might not have. Suppose my parents had never met, but instead had died of a childhood disease. Then, presumably, I would not exist. So, there is a possible world in which I do not exist. Consider another example: In the actual world, Bill Clinton was president of the United States in January 1998, but we can describe a possible world in which this is not so—for example, one in which Clinton resigned from office in December 1997. Likewise, we can conceive of a possible world in which airplanes were never invented or in which the Allies lost World War II. Perhaps we can even conceive of a possible world in which a large asteroid struck the earth in 1850, destroying the entire human race.

There are, in fact, infinitely many possible worlds. To see this, consider the case of Harvey, the sentimental mathematician. There is a possible world in which Harvey's favorite number is the number 1. In that world, Harvey is very fond of the number 1, thinks of it often, and frequently extols it to others. But, there is also a possible world in which Harvey's favorite number is the number 2, a possible world in which Harvey's favorite number is the number 3, and so on. Clearly, there are infinitely many possible worlds.

Because possible worlds are *total* ways things could have been, only one possible world can be actual. Think of it this way. A complete description of a possible world would be a list of statements that express all of what is true (and only what is true) in that world.[5] Now, take any two possible worlds (call them W_1 and W_2). Since these are different possible worlds, and a possible world is a comprehensive situation, there must be something true in one of these worlds that is not true in the other. For instance, suppose W_1 and W_2 are exactly alike, except that in W_1 you are presently wearing a purple hat while in W_2 you are not presently wearing a purple hat. Thus, if W_1 and W_2 are both actual, you are presently wearing a purple hat and yet not wearing a purple hat, which is a contradiction. Obviously, then, at most one of these worlds is actual.

Now that we have the concept of a possible world, we have an alternative way of defining "necessary truth." A **necessary truth** is one that is true in every possible world. And as we will see, this way of characterizing necessary truths has a number of advantages. But before proceeding further, we need to clarify the concept of a necessary truth by distinguishing it from some other concepts with which it is often confused.

First, a "necessary truth," as we have defined the term, is often said to be *logically* necessary as opposed to **physically necessary**. We can get at the concept of a physically necessary truth as follows. Many possible worlds have the same laws of nature (e.g., the law of gravity) as the actual world. Certain truths are true in all of these worlds. For example:

> 9. Each physical object is attracted to every other with a force varying as the product of the masses of the objects and inversely as the square of the distance between them. (Newton's law of gravitation)

> 10. Nothing travels faster than the speed of light.

Statements (9) and (10) are physically necessary truths. But because the laws of nature could have been different than they in fact are, physically necessary truths are not necessary in our sense. Remember, a logically necessary truth is one that is true in *every* possible world. And there are logically possible worlds in which physical objects behave in accordance with a slightly different law of gravity than they do in the actual world. There are also logically possible worlds in which something travels just a bit faster than the speed of light. Our interest is in *logically* necessary truths, which are true in every possible world, not in physically necessary truths, which are false in some possible worlds.

Second, a necessary truth is not the same thing as an **unalterable truth**. To illustrate:

> 11. John Wilkes Booth killed Abraham Lincoln.

Statement (11) seems to be unalterably true at this time. It cannot become false at this late date assuming that the past cannot be changed. But (11) is not a necessary truth, for there is surely a logically possible world in which Booth refrains from killing Lincoln. Booth did not act under logical necessity.

Third, the concept of a necessary truth is not identical to the concept of a **self-evident statement**. A statement is *self-evident* if one can know that it is true simply by grasping the concepts involved. Now, typical examples of self-evident statements do seem to be necessary. For instance:

> 12. No circles are squares.

But some necessary truths seem to be too complicated to be known in this way. Consider, for example, Goldbach's conjecture:

> 13. Every even number greater than 2 is equal to the sum of two prime numbers.

Since Goldbach's conjecture is a mathematical proposition, *either* it *or* its negation is presumably necessary. But neither Goldbach's conjecture nor its negation is obviously true. Moreover, neither Goldbach's conjecture nor its negation has been proved by mathematicians. So, neither Goldbach's conjecture nor its negation appears to be self-evident. Thus, we cannot equate necessary truths with self-evident truths.

Fourth, a necessary truth is not the same thing as an **"un-give-up-able"** **statement**, that is, a statement that *cannot be given up*. The American philosopher and logician Willard van Orman Quine (1908–) has decried the distinction between the necessary and the contingent. According to Quine, the truth is simply that there are some statements we would be very reluctant to give up (i.e., to stop believing) and others we would more readily give up. In other words, there are merely degrees of "un-give-up-ability," and there are no necessary truths at all. But consider the following argument:

> Clearly we cannot equate relative "ungiveupability" with necessity. . . . For a belief may be ungiveupable for reasons that have nothing to do with its truth, and are unrelated to the necessity of its truth. A belief may be a guiding belief for a person's life to such an extent that the person may be psychologically incapable of giving it up. Or I may find the belief that I exist ungiveupable, but its "ungiveupability" has nothing to do with the necessity of its truth.[6]

Thus, to say that a statement is un-give-up-able is to make a psychological claim, namely, that the person who believes it is psychologically incapable of ceasing to believe it. And this psychological concept is very different from the concept of a necessary truth, that is, the concept of a proposition that is true in every possible world.*

In thinking about necessary truths, we are led back to the distinction between statements and propositions, which we discussed briefly in section 4.1. We have said that a necessary truth cannot be false under any possible circumstances. But you may be thinking that linguistic meaning is changeable, and hence that there are possible worlds in which people speak the truth when they say, for example, "Some circles are squares." After all, there are possible worlds in which the word "circles" is synonymous with "rectangle" (as that word is currently used by English speakers). But this line of thinking is deeply flawed, because it confuses sentences with the propositions (truths or falsehoods) those sentences express. In ordinary usage, the English sentence "No circles are squares" expresses a necessary truth. But if the words composing the sentence

---

*Would it be better to interpret Quine as claiming that "Statement S is un-give-up-able" means "One cannot give S up *without doing something irrational*"? On this reading of Quine, "un-give-up-able" becomes an epistemological concept, that is, a concept regarding what is known or rationally believed. But even in this interpretation "un-give-up-able" still cannot be equated with "necessary," for it would surely be irrational for me to give up the statement "I am thinking" and yet "I am thinking" is not a necessary truth. For a closer look at these issues, see Kenneth Konyndyk, *Introductory Modal Logic* (Notre Dame, IN: University of Notre Dame Press, 1964), pp. 14–15.

were to change meaning, we would need to use a different sentence to express that same truth. So, to avoid confusion, we will make free use of the word "proposition" for the remainder of this chapter. A **proposition** is simply a truth or a falsehood. A given proposition may or may not be expressed in a sentence. And whereas a sentence (and hence a statement) belongs to a particular language, such as English or German, a proposition does not.

It may be helpful to depict possible worlds as circles for the sake of illustration. Let us label the actual world A and label two other possible worlds B and C. And, just for the sake of illustration, let us pretend that these three worlds are all of the possible worlds. (Of course, as we have already seen, there are in fact many more possible worlds.) The symbol *P(T)*, when placed in a circle, means that P is true in that world. For example:

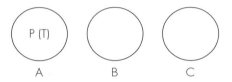

This diagram says that P is true in A (the actual world). Similarly, the symbol *P(F)*, when placed in a circle, means that P is false in that world. Where the symbol *P(?)* appears, the question mark may be replaced with either a "T" or an "F" (as needed). Now, we can make a kind of picture of a necessary truth P as follows:

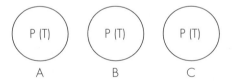

The diagram tells us that P is true in every possible world.

With the concept of a necessary truth in hand, we can readily characterize the other important modal concepts. For instance, a proposition is **impossible** *if and only if* it is necessarily false. Here is an example:

14. Some squares are triangles.

An impossible proposition is false in every possible world. We can depict an impossible proposition P as follows.

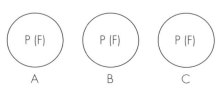

The diagram says that P is false in every possible world.

A proposition is **possible**, or **possibly true**, *if and only if* it is not necessarily false. By this definition, whatever is true is possibly true. Necessary truths also count as possibly true, since they are not necessarily false. In addition, many falsehoods are possibly true, such as this one:

15. Johannesburg, South Africa, is the most highly populated city in the world.

Possibly true propositions are true in *at least one* possible world. We can depict a generic possibly true proposition P as follows:

The diagram indicates that P is true in at least one possible world. Here, we made P true in world B, but of course, P is possibly true as long as P is true in *at least one* possible world, and that world need not be world B. So, our diagram is perhaps slightly misleading. The question marks may be replaced with either a "T" or an "F," depending on the proposition under consideration. For instance, if P is true in the actual world, then we replace the question mark with a "T" in world A.

A further clarification about possibly true propositions is needed. In saying that a proposition is *possibly* true, we are not saying that *for all we know* it is true. Philosophers say that a proposition is **epistemically possible** if it is not known to be false given the information currently available. (Epistemology is the branch of philosophy that concerns the theory of knowledge.) Consider again proposition (15). It is not epistemically possible, for we know it is false. Nevertheless, (15) is *logically* possible, for the following proposition is not a *necessary* falsehood: During the 20th century, Johannesburg grew steadily until it had a larger population than any other city in the world.

A proposition is **possibly false** *if and only if* it is not necessarily true. Possibly false propositions are false in *at least one* possible world. All false propositions (including necessarily false ones) are possibly false. But many true propositions are possibly false as well. For instance:

16. Pierre and Marie Curie discovered radium.

Although the Curies did discover radium, they might not have. For example, because their research was difficult and took a long time, they might easily have given up. We can depict a generic possibly false proposition P as follows:

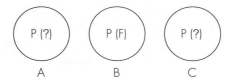

The diagram indicates that P is false in at least one world. Again, the question marks can be replaced by a "T" or an "F," depending on the proposition under consideration.

A proposition is **contingent** *if and only if* it is both possibly true and possibly false. For example, the following proposition is contingent:

17. I exist.

Since proposition (17) is actually true, it is possibly true. But it is also possibly false, for if a certain egg–sperm pair had never united, I presumably would not exist. And many things could have prevented that egg–sperm pair from uniting. If a proposition is contingent, then it is true in at least one possible world and false in at least one possible world. We can depict a generic contingent proposition P as follows:

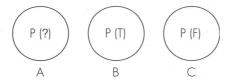

Note that a contingent proposition may or may not be true in the actual world.

A proposition is a **contingent truth** *if and only if* it is true but possibly false. In other words, a contingent truth is true in the actual world but false in at least one possible world. For instance:

18. Socrates died as a result of drinking hemlock.

Socrates did die as a result of drinking hemlock, but he might not have. For example, he might have escaped from prison, or he might simply have refused to drink the hemlock (in which case the Athenians would probably have executed him in some other way). We can depict a generic contingent truth P as follows:

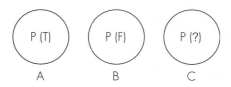

Note that a contingent truth is true in world A, the actual world.

Finally, a proposition is a **contingent falsehood** *if and only if* it is false but possibly true. For example:

19. Socrates died of smallpox.

A contingent falsehood is false in the actual world but true in at least one possible world. We can picture a generic contingent falsehood P as follows:

Note that a contingent falsehood is false in world A, the actual world.

Complete the following exercises to check your understanding of the basic modal concepts.

◆ *Exercise 12.1*

Part A: True or False?   Which of the following statements are true? Which are false?

* 1. A *contingent truth* is defined as a proposition that is true in some possible worlds but false in others.

2. A proposition is *possibly true* if and only if it is true in at least one possible world.

3. The planet Saturn is an example of a *possible world*.

* 4. The actual world is not a possible world.

5. A *necessary truth* is one that cannot be false under any possible circumstances.

6. Every necessary truth is possibly true.

* 7. Every possibly true proposition is either a necessary truth or a contingent truth.

8. A proposition is *possibly true* if and only if it is true in the actual world.

9. A *contingent proposition* is true in at least one possible world and false in at least one possible world.

* 10. A *necessary truth* is one that is true in every possible world.

11. If a proposition is *possibly true*, then it is not known to be false given the information currently available.

12. A proposition is *contingently false* if it is false in the actual world but true in at least one possible world.

* 13. Every contingent proposition is false.

14. If P is a contingent truth, then there is a possible world in which its negation is true.

15. An *impossible proposition* is one that is necessarily false.

* **16.** A *necessarily false* proposition is one that is false in every possible world.

  17. If a proposition is true in some possible worlds but false in others, then it must be a contingent truth.

  18. If an argument is valid, then its conclusion is true in every possible world in which its premises are true.

* **19.** If an argument is invalid, then there is at least one possible world in which its premises are true while its conclusion is false.

  20. An *analytic statement* is one that is true by virtue of its form.

Part B: Identifying Modalities Which of the following propositions are necessary? Contingent? Impossible? If a statement is contingent, also indicate its actual truth value if you can.

*   **1.** Chairs exist.

    2. All uncles are male.

    3. Five plus five equals fifty-five.

*   **4.** One plus one equals two *and* the Eiffel Tower is in France.

    5. $\sim A \rightarrow (A \rightarrow B)$

    6. Benjamin Franklin was the third president of the United States.

*   **7.** The French artist Rodin once made a bronze sculpture that was a spherical cube.

    8. Either grass is green or it is not the case that grass is green.

    9. $A \rightarrow (A \rightarrow B)$

* **10.** Abraham Lincoln was never president of the United States.

  11. $\sim(P \leftrightarrow P)$

  12. John F. Kennedy was assassinated by Lee Harvey Oswald, but Kennedy did not die.

* **13.** Either two plus two equals four or two plus two equals five.

  14. Two plus two equals twenty-two *and* there are some trees.

  15. Either two equals three or two equals four.

* **16.** No human has ever set foot on Neptune.

  17. Two plus three equals five *and* seven plus five equals twelve.

  18. Some people enjoy rock music.

* **19.** There is at least one aunt who has neither a niece nor a nephew.

  20. Alaska was the 49th state to join the United States.

12.2 The Modal Symbols

As noted previously, we can develop a system of modal logic by adding to the system of statement logic developed in chapters 7 and 8. We will use the symbol

"□" (called the "box" or "necessity operator") to stand for "necessarily." Thus, "□*p*" means "necessarily, *p*." To illustrate:

> 20. Necessarily, all sisters are siblings. (S: All sisters are siblings)
>
> *In symbols:* □S

The box can be combined with the tilde. We can say that *p* is *not* a necessary truth in this way: ~□*p*. For instance:

> 21. It is not necessarily true that dogs exist. (D: Dogs exist)
>
> *In symbols:* ~□D

Notice that care must be taken with the placement of the tilde, for we symbolize "*p* is a necessary falsehood" as □~*p*. For example:

> 22. It is necessarily false that two plus two equals five. (T: Two plus two equals five)
>
> *In symbols:* □~T

We will use the symbol "◇" (called the "diamond" or "possibility operator") to stand for "possibly." To illustrate:

> 23. Possibly, Sue is lying. (S: Sue is lying)
>
> *In symbols:* ◇S

We can say that *p* is logically *impossible* using the diamond and a tilde: ~◇*p*. For instance:

> 24. It is logically impossible that zero equals one. (Z: Zero equals one)
>
> *In symbols:* ~◇Z

Again, care must be taken regarding the placement of the tilde. Consider the following:

> 25. It is logically possible that Oswald did not kill Kennedy. (K: Oswald killed Kennedy)
>
> *In symbols:* ◇~K

Using our symbols we can write "*p* is contingent" as ◇*p* • ◇~*p*. In other words, to say that a proposition is contingent is to say that it is logically possible that it is true and logically possible that it is false. For example:

> 26. "Augusta is the capital of Maine" is a contingent statement. (A: Augusta is the capital of Maine)
>
> *In symbols:* ◇A • ◇~A

We can symbolize "*p* is a contingent truth" as *p* • ◇~*p* or as *p* • ~□*p*. For instance:

> 27. It is a contingent truth that Columbus is the capital of Ohio. (C: Columbus is the capital of Ohio)
>
> *In symbols:* C • ◇~C

We could also symbolize (27) as C • ~□C.

We can symbolize "*p* is a contingent falsehood" as ~*p* • ◇*p*. To illustrate:

28. It is contingently false that Dayton is the capital of Ohio. (D: Dayton is the capital of Ohio)

In symbols: ~D • ◇D

We use parentheses to indicate the scope of the modal operators, just as we use parentheses to indicate the scope of the tilde (or the quantifiers in predicate logic). To see the need for this, compare the following statements:

29. Necessarily, both nine is an odd number and there are nine planets in our solar system. (N: Nine is a odd number; P: There are nine planets in our solar system)

In symbols: □(N • P)

30. Necessarily, nine is an odd number, and furthermore there are nine planets in our solar system.

In symbols: □N • P

Statements (29) and (30) are not logically equivalent. (29) says that the conjunction N • P is necessarily true. But a conjunction is necessary *if and only if* both its conjuncts are necessary. (If even one conjunct is not necessary, then there are worlds in which it is false, and in those worlds the conjunction itself is also false.) Moreover, it is not a necessary truth that there are nine planets in our solar system—there might have been more planets or fewer. So, (29) is false. (30), on the other hand, says that N ("Nine is an odd number") is necessary, but that P ("There are nine planets in our solar system") is true. Thus, (30) is a more cautious statement, and indeed a true one.

The main point here is that parentheses are needed to indicate the scope of the modal operators, and a shift in the placement of parentheses can change the meaning substantially. For example, just as ~(A ∨ B) differs in meaning from ~A ∨ B or from ~A ∨ ~B, so □(A ∨ B) differs in meaning from □A ∨ B or from □A ∨ □B. The general rule is that logical operators, such as the box and diamond, apply to the smallest immediately-following component that the punctuation permits. Thus, in the formula ◇(P → Q) • R, the diamond applies only to P → Q; its scope does not extend to R.

It is important to understand that the modal operators are not truth-functional operators; that is, the meaning of the modal operators cannot be specified via truth tables. If the box and the diamond were truth-functional, then we could simply develop truth tables for them and set about evaluating arguments. Let's see what happens when we try to develop truth tables for the box and diamond.

p	□*p*
T	?
F	F

If *p* is false, then of course □*p* is false. A proposition cannot be both false and necessarily true. But if we assume that *p* is true, we do not have enough information to determine that *p* is necessary. If *p* is merely a contingent truth, then □*p* is false; but if *p* is a necessary truth, then □*p* is true. So, the box is not truth-functional.

Now, let's consider the diamond. Is it truth-functional?

p	◇*p*
T	T
F	?

If *p* is true, then of course *p* is possibly true. But suppose *p* is false. What is the truth value of ◇*p*? It may be either true or false, depending on the proposition in question. If *p* is impossible, then ◇*p* is false; if *p* is contingently false, then ◇*p* is true. So, the diamond is not truth-functional.

Truth tables give us the meaning of the tilde, dot, vee, arrow, and double-arrow. But as we have just seen, truth tables cannot give us the meaning for the box and the diamond. Following the work of Saul Kripke, who developed a theory of meaning (or semantics) for modal logic in the late 1950s, we will assign meaning to the box and diamond in terms of possible worlds. □*p* is true in a given possible world *if and only if p* is true in every possible world. And ◇*p* is true in a given possible world *if and only if p* is true in at least one possible world.

The following exercises will give you practice using the new symbols introduced in this section.

◆ Exercise 12.2

Part A: Symbolizing   Express the following statements in symbols, using G to abbreviate "God exists."

* 1. It is logically possible that God exists.

  2. Necessarily, God does not exist.

  3. God exists, but "God exists" is not a necessary truth.

* 4. It is impossible that God does not exist.

  5. It is logically possible that God exists, but in fact God does not exist.

  6. "God exists" is a contingent truth.

* 7. "God exists" is a contingent proposition.

  8. "God exists" is contingently false.

  9. "God exists" is necessarily false.

* 10. "God exists" is either necessary or impossible.

11. There is at least one possible world in which God exists.

12. God exists in every possible world.

* 13. There is no possible world in which God exists.

14. God exists in at least one possible world, but not in every possible world.

15. Either God exists in every possible world or God does not exist in the actual world.

Part B: More Symbolizing Express the following statements in symbols, using the schemes of abbreviation provided.

* 1. It is a contingent truth that Lincoln was the 16th president of the United States. (L: Lincoln was the 16th president of the U.S.)

2. "I exist" is a contingent proposition. (X: I exist)

3. It is necessarily false that Susan is a wife who is not married. (W: Susan is a wife; M: Susan is married)

* 4. George Washington was the first president of the United States, but it is logically possible that Benjamin Franklin was the first president of the United States. (G: George Washington was the first president of the United States; B: Benjamin Franklin was the first president of the United States)

5. It is impossible that if demons are invisible, then my wristwatch is inhabited by blue demons. (I: Demons are invisible; B: My wristwatch is inhabited by blue demons.)

6. It is a necessary truth that either it is raining or it is not raining. (R: It is raining)

* 7. Santa Claus does not exist, but it is logically possible that he does. (S: Santa Claus exists)

8. Either Goldbach's conjecture is necessarily true or its negation is necessarily true. (G: Goldbach's conjecture, that is, every even number greater than 2 is equal to the sum of two prime numbers)

9. Necessarily, if Jane is married, then Jane has a spouse. (M: Jane is married; S: Jane has a spouse)

* 10. It is a contingent truth that Rudolph is both red-nosed and a reindeer. (R: Rudolph is red-nosed; D: Rudolph is a reindeer)

11. Necessarily, both six and eight are divisible by two. (S: Six is divisible by two; E: Eight is divisible by two)

12. Possibly, Seattle is the capital of Washington, but as a matter of fact, Seattle is not the capital of Washington. (S: Seattle is the capital of Washington)

* 13. It is logically possible that if Kyle surfs on a tidal wave, then he surfs from California to Hawaii. (T: Kyle surfs on a tidal wave; C: Kyle surfs from California to Hawaii)

14. It is possible that Joan wins, but it is impossible that both Joan and Marsha win. (J: Joan wins; M: Marsha wins)

15. If it is necessary that five is odd, then it is necessary that six is even. (F: Five is odd; S: Six is even)

* **16.** There is a possible world in which humans have ESP, but in the actual world, humans do not have ESP. (H: Humans have ESP)

17. One plus one equals two in every possible world, and one plus one equals eleven in no possible world. (O: One plus one equals two; E: One plus one equals eleven)

18. There is at least one possible world in which you win an Olympic gold medal and at least one possible world in which you do not win an Olympic gold medal. (Y: You win an Olympic gold medal)

* **19.** There is a possible world in which every trapezoid is blue, but there is no possible world in which some trapezoid is a triangle. (B: Every trapezoid is blue; T: Some trapezoid is a triangle)

20. Although poverty exists in the actual world, it does not exist in every possible world. (P: Poverty exists)

12.3 Constructing Proofs

In this section, we introduce our first set of inference rules for modal logic.[7] Because we are building on the system of statement logic developed in chapter 8, all the rules of statement logic from chapter 8 may be used in proofs throughout this chapter. For reasons mentioned previously, however, we now assume that these rules apply to propositions (truths and falsehoods), as well as to statements (sentences having truth value).

If a proposition is necessarily true, then it is true. In other words, if a proposition is true in *every* possible world, then it is true in the actual world. This obvious principle gives us our first rule of modal logic, **necesse ad esse** (NE). Using the lowercase, italicized *p* to stand for any proposition, the rule may be stated as follows:

$$\Box p$$
$$\therefore\ p$$

Literally translated, *necesse ad esse* means "from being necessary to being." Here is an English example:

31. Necessarily, no immaterial soul weighs 40 pounds. So, no immaterial soul weighs 40 pounds. (S: No immaterial soul weighs 40 pounds)

In symbols, the proof looks like this:

1. $\Box$S $\therefore$ S
2. S   1, NE

Note that NE is an *implicational* rule, not an equivalence rule. Accordingly, it may not be applied to part of a line in a proof; rather, it must be applied to an entire line. For example, the following inference is *not* permitted:

    1. ~□P
    2. ~P   1, *incorrect use of NE*

This is like arguing, "It is not necessarily true that I exist. Therefore, I do not exist." Since the premise is true but the conclusion is false, this argument is invalid. (The premise says that I do not exist in *every* possible world or, in other words, that there is at least one possible world in which I do not exist. But the conclusion says that I do not exist in the actual world.)

    If a proposition is actually true, then it is possibly true. In other words, if a proposition is true in the actual world, then it is true in at least one possible world. (Remember, the actual world is a possible world.) This obvious principle gives us our second rule of modal logic, ***esse ad posse*** (EP):

$$p$$
$$\therefore \ \Diamond p$$

Literally translated, *esse ad posse* means "from being to being possible." Here is an English example:

    32. Some bachelors are party animals. So, it is logically possible that some bachelors are party animals. (B: Some bachelors are party animals)

The proof runs as follows:

    1. B   ∴ ◇B
    2. ◇B   1, EP

Note that EP is an implicational rule. As such, it must be applied to whole lines in a proof, and not to parts of lines. For example, the following inference is not permitted:

    1. C → M
    2. ◇C → M   1, *incorrect use of EP*

This is like arguing, "If Demi Moore is a wife, then she is married. So, if it is *possible* that Demi Moore is a wife, then she is married." Again, the invalidity is obvious. The premise is true in every possible world. But the conclusion is false in those worlds in which Demi Moore is not married (although she could be a wife).

    Our next inference rule is based on the principle that *every theorem of (nonmodal) statement logic is necessarily true*. A *theorem* is a statement that can be proved without any premises. Furthermore, every theorem of (nonmodal) statement logic is a tautology, and every such tautology is a theorem. (A *tautology* is a statement that is true in every row of its truth table.) Since it is impossible to assign truth values in such a way as to make tautologies or theorems false, they are true in every possible world. Our third inference rule, **theorem necessitation** (TN), may be formulated as follows:

> *p* (derived without using any premises)
>
> ∴ □*p*

Here is a proof that involves TN:

$$\therefore \ \Box[A \rightarrow (\sim B \vee A)]$$

1. A	Assume
2. A ∨ ~B	1, Add
3. ~B ∨ A	2, Com
4. A → (~B ∨ A)	1–3, CP
5. □[A → (~B ∨ A)]	4, TN

Note that we arrive at line (4) without using any premises. Here is another example of the use of TN:

1. □(P ∨ ~P) → □Q	∴ □Q
2. ~(P ∨ ~P)	Assume
3. ~P • ~~P	2, DeM
4. P ∨ ~P	2–3, RAA
5. □(P ∨ ~P)	4, TN
6. □Q	5, 1, MP

Here, we first prove the theorem, *P* ∨ ~*P*, without using any premises. Then we apply TN. Finally, we use line (5) together with the premise to obtain line (6), by MP.

Our fourth rule, **modal operator negation** (MN), is an equivalence rule. To understand this rule, consider the following pair of propositions:

33. Possibly, my shirt is green. (G: My shirt is green)
    In symbols: ◇G

34. It is not necessarily true that my shirt is not green.
    In symbols: ~□~G

Proposition (33) says that there is a possible world in which my shirt is green. That being so, the proposition "My shirt is not green" is not true in every possible world. In other words, if (33) is true, then (34) must be true. Similarly, if (34) is true, then (33) must be true, for if "My shirt is not green" is not true in every possible world, then "My shirt is green" is true in at least one possible world. Reflections of this sort should render the following equivalence rule intuitive:

$$\Diamond p :: \sim\Box\sim p$$

The four-dot symbol tells us that $\Diamond p$ implies $\sim\Box\sim p$ and also that $\sim\Box\sim p$ implies $\Diamond p$. This is the first form of modal operator negation (MN). MN comes in four forms. To understand the second form, consider the following pair of propositions:

35. Necessarily, red is a color. (R: Red is a color)
    In symbols: $\Box$R

36. It is not possible that red is not a color.
    In symbols: $\sim\Diamond\sim$R

Proposition (35) tells us that "Red is a color" is true in every possible world. (36) tells us that there is no possible world in which "Red is not a color" is true. It should be clear that each of these propositions implies the other. Our second form of MN is as follows:

$$\Box p :: \sim\Diamond\sim p$$

We can grasp the third form of MN by reflecting on the following pair of propositions:

37. It is not necessarily true that I exist. (X: I exist)
    In symbols: $\sim\Box$X

38. It is logically possible that I do not exist.
    In symbols: $\Diamond\sim$X

Proposition (37) tells us that "I exist" is not true in every possible world. And (38) tells us that there is at least one possible world in which "I do not exist" is true. Again, it should be obvious that each of these propositions implies the other. Stated formally, the third form of MN looks like this:

$$\sim\Box p :: \Diamond\sim p$$

It may be helpful to note that there is an analogy here between the behavior of the box and diamond and the behavior of universal and existential quantifiers. Recall that the QN rule lets us move from $\sim(x)Fx$ to $(\exists x)\sim Fx$, and vice versa. Similarly, MN lets us move from $\sim\Box$A to $\Diamond\sim$A, and vice versa.

The fourth form of MN can readily be understood by reflecting on the following pair of propositions.

39. Necessarily, it is not the case that circular squares exist (C: Circular squares exist)
    In symbols: $\Box\sim$C

40. It is not possible that circular squares exist.

In symbols: $\sim\Diamond C$

Proposition (39) tells us that "Circular squares do not exist" is true in every possible world. (40) tells us that "Circular squares exist" is not true in any possible world. Obviously, these propositions imply each other. And our last form of MN looks like this:

$$\Box\sim p\;::\;\sim\Diamond p$$

Again, the box and diamond behave in a way analogous to universal and existential quantifiers. QN lets us move from $(x)\sim Fx$ to $\sim(\exists x)Fx$, and vice versa. Similarly, MN lets us move from $\Box\sim A$ to $\sim\Diamond A$, and vice versa.

To sum up, the four forms of modal operator negation (MN) are as follows:

$$\Diamond p\;::\;\sim\Box\sim p$$
$$\Box p\;::\;\sim\Diamond\sim p$$
$$\sim\Box p\;::\;\Diamond\sim p$$
$$\Box\sim p\;::\;\sim\Diamond p$$

When we employ any of these four rules in a proof, our annotation is simply MN. Since each form of MN is an equivalence rule, MN may be applied to parts of lines in a proof as well as to entire lines. Let's examine a proof that involves MN:

1. $\sim(\Diamond E \vee \Box F)$		
2. $\Box\sim E \rightarrow \sim\Diamond\sim G$		
3. $\Diamond\sim F \rightarrow \sim\Box\sim H$	$\therefore G \bullet \Diamond H$	
4. $\sim\Diamond E \bullet \sim\Box F$	1, DeM	
5. $\sim\Diamond E$	4, Simp	
6. $\sim\Diamond E \rightarrow \sim\Diamond\sim G$	2, MN	
7. $\sim\Diamond\sim G$	5, 6, MP	
8. $\Box G$	7, MN	
9. G	8, NE	
10. $\sim\Box F$	4, Simp	
11. $\Diamond\sim F$	10, MN	
12. $\sim\Box\sim H$	3, 11, MP	
13. $\Diamond H$	12, MN	
14. $G \bullet \Diamond H$	9, 13, Conj	

Note that MN is applied to part of a line (the antecedent of a conditional) in line (6).

Some of the rules of thumb we have used previously apply in modal logic. For example, it often helps to look at the conclusion first and then work back-

Summary of the First Set of Inference Rules

Necesse ad Esse (NE)   **Esse ad Posse (EP)**

$\Box p$ p

$\therefore p$ $\therefore \Diamond p$

Theorem Necessitation (TN)

p (derived without using any premises)

$\therefore \Box p$

Modal Operator Negation (MN)

$\Diamond p :: \sim\Box\sim p$

$\Box p :: \sim\Diamond\sim p$

$\sim\Box p :: \Diamond\sim p$

$\Box\sim p :: \sim\Diamond p$

ward. Also, if it is possible to apply one of the rules of statement logic, it usually helps to do so. But the following rule of thumb is specific to modal logic:

> **Rule of Thumb 1:** When the tilde is combined with the box or diamond, it often helps to apply MN. Then use statement logic or other rules of modal logic.

Complete the following exercises to ensure your grasp of our first set of inference rules for modal logic.

◆ Exercise 12.3

Part A: Annotating   Annotate the following proofs.

* 1. 1. $\Box$P $\therefore \Diamond$P
      2. P
      3. $\Diamond$P

   2. 1. $\Box\sim$B • T $\therefore \sim\Diamond$B
      2. $\Box\sim$B
      3. $\sim\Diamond$B

   3. 1. $\Box$(A • B) $\therefore \Diamond$B
      2. A • B
      3. B
      4. $\Diamond$B

* **4.** 1. ~◇~G   ∴ G
　　2. □G
　　3. G

　5. 1. □~(B ↔ ~B) → A   ∴ ◇A
　　2. B ↔ ~B
　　3. (B → ~B) • (~B → B)
　　4. B → ~B
　　5. ~B → B
　　6. ~B ∨ ~B
　　7. ~B
　　8. ~~B ∨ B
　　9. B ∨ B
　　10. B
　　11. B • ~B
　　12. ~(B ↔ ~B)
　　13. □~(B ↔ ~B)
　　14. A
　　15. ◇A

　6. 1. ◇H ∨ ~□S
　　2. □~H   ∴ ◇~S
　　3. ~◇H
　　4. ~□S
　　5. ◇~S

* **7.** 1. ◇~W   ∴ ~□W
　　2. ~□W

　8. 1. □S ∨ □P
　　2. ◇~S   ∴ ~◇~P
　　3. ~□S
　　4. □P
　　5. ~◇~P

　9. 1. ~◇E   ∴ ~E
　　2. □~E
　　3. ~E

* **10.**　　∴ □[(A • B) → B]
　　1. A • B
　　2. B
　　3. (A • B) → B
　　4. □[(A • B) → B]

Part B: Correct or Incorrect? Which of the following inferences are permitted by one of our rules, and which are not? If an inference is permitted, indicate the rule that permits it. If it is not permitted, simply write "incorrect." (The question is whether one can move from the first statement to the second, in each instance, by a single application of one of our rules.)

* **1.** 1. $\Box N \rightarrow \Box E$
     2. $N \rightarrow \Box E$

  2. 1. $\Diamond L$
     2. L

  3. 1. $\sim\Diamond\sim K \rightarrow J$
     2. $\Box K \rightarrow J$

* **4.** 1. $A \rightarrow B$
     2. $\Diamond(A \rightarrow B)$

  5. 1. C
     2. $\Box C$

  6. 1. $\Box(\Diamond D \rightarrow E)$
     2. $\Diamond D \rightarrow E$

* **7.** 1. $F \rightarrow G$
     2. $F \rightarrow \Diamond G$

  8. 1. $P \rightarrow \Box Q$
     2. $P \rightarrow Q$

  9. 1. $\Box(H \cdot L)$
     2. $\Box(H \cdot \Diamond L)$

* **10.** 1. $\sim\Box\sim R \leftrightarrow S$
      2. $\Diamond R \leftrightarrow S$

  11. 1. $T \vee \Diamond U$
      2. $T \vee U$

  12. 1. $W \vee X$
      2. $W \vee \Diamond X$

* **13.** 1. $(\Diamond\sim Y \leftrightarrow \sim\Box\sim Z) \rightarrow \sim\Diamond V$
      2. $(\Diamond\sim Y \leftrightarrow \Diamond Z) \rightarrow \sim\Diamond V$

  14. 1. $\Box A \vee \Box B$
      2. $A \vee B$

  15. 1. $(\Diamond C \cdot \sim\Diamond\sim D) \rightarrow \Box E$
      2. $(\Diamond C \cdot \Box D) \rightarrow \Box E$

Part C: Proofs   Construct proofs to show that the following arguments are valid.

* **1.** $\Box C \cdot D, (\Diamond C \cdot D) \rightarrow S \therefore \Diamond S$

  2. $\Box(P \rightarrow P) \rightarrow \Box Q \therefore Q$

  3. $\Diamond J \vee \sim\Box K, \Diamond\sim L \rightarrow \sim\Diamond\sim K, \Box\sim J \therefore L$

* **4.** $\sim\Diamond M \cdot \Box N, \Box\sim M \rightarrow \sim\Diamond Q, \Diamond\sim N \rightarrow \sim\Box P,$
     $(\Box\sim Q \vee \Diamond\sim P) \rightarrow \sim\Diamond R \therefore \sim R$

  5. $\sim(\Box R \rightarrow \Box\sim S), \Diamond S \rightarrow T, \Diamond R \rightarrow U \therefore \Diamond(T \cdot U)$

  6. $(\Box T \cdot \Diamond P) \vee (\Box T \cdot \Diamond\sim W), \Diamond S \rightarrow \sim\Box T, \Box W \therefore \Diamond\sim S \cdot \Diamond P$

* **7.** $\Diamond Z \vee (A \cdot \Box B), \Diamond Z \rightarrow \sim R, \Diamond\sim B \therefore \sim\Box R$

  8. $\sim\Box(K \vee K), \sim\Box L \rightarrow \sim\Diamond\sim K, \Diamond P \rightarrow \Diamond\sim L \therefore \Diamond\sim P$

  9. $\Box(A \rightarrow B), \Diamond\sim(\sim B \rightarrow \sim A) \vee \Box E, \Diamond E \rightarrow D \therefore \Diamond D$

* **10.** $(\Box M \vee \Box F) \cdot (\Box M \vee \sim\Box G), \Box M \rightarrow \sim\Diamond H, (\Box F \cdot \sim\Box G) \rightarrow \sim\Box J$
      $\therefore \Diamond H \rightarrow \Diamond\sim J$

  11. $\Box K \cdot (L \vee M), (\Box K \cdot L) \rightarrow \Box\sim N, (\Box K \cdot M) \rightarrow \Box\sim N,$
      $\Diamond O \rightarrow \Diamond N \therefore \Diamond\sim O$

  12. $\Diamond(P \cdot P), \Diamond\sim\sim P \rightarrow Q, \sim R \rightarrow \sim\Diamond Q \therefore \Diamond R$

* **13.** $\Box(A \vee B), \sim\Diamond\sim(B \vee A) \rightarrow \sim\Diamond C, \sim\Box\sim C \vee R \therefore \Diamond(R \vee S)$

14. ~(□F → ~◇G), ~◇G ∨ □H, ◇~F ∨ □J ∴ ◇H • □J

15. ◇C → ~□[~A → (A → B)] ∴ ~C

* 16. ◇Z • (□Y ∨ ~◇W), □~Z ∨ ◇~Y, □~W → ~◇U,
      ~□~U ∨ □~T ∴ ◇~T

17. ◇~(S → B), ~□C → □(~B → ~S), D → ◇~C ∴ ◇~D

18. □~B → (□~C ∨ ~◇O), H → ~◇B, (~◇C ∨ □~O) → ~◇D,
    □H ∴ D → □E

* 19. P ∨ G, P → □Z, G → ~◇~Z, ◇~S → ◇~Z ∴ □S

20. (□J ∨ ◇K) • (□J ∨ ◇~L), □J → ◇~M, (◇K • ~□L) → ~□M,
    ~◇N ∨ □M ∴ ◇~N

Part D: English Arguments   Symbolize the following arguments and then prove them valid.

* 1. Necessarily, it is false that free acts are coerced. Accordingly, it is impossible that free acts are coerced. (F: Free acts are coerced)

  2. It is not logically possible that God does not exist. Therefore, God exists. (G: God exists)

  3. Necessarily, invisible paintings do not exist. But either it is possible that invisible paintings exist, or it is necessary that all paintings are colored. Hence, all paintings are colored. (P: Invisible paintings exist; C: All paintings are colored)

* 4. It's logically impossible that all paintings are forgeries. Consequently, not all paintings are forgeries. (F: All paintings are forgeries)

  5. It is contingently false that vampires exist. So, it is possible that vampires exist. (V: Vampires exist)

  6. Either it's impossible that humans have souls or it's necessary that moral agents have free will. But humans do have souls. It follows that moral agents have free will. (S: Humans have souls; M: Moral agents have free will)

* 7. It is not possible that time travel occurs but it is necessary that time goes on. If it is possible that time is real and it is impossible that time travel occurs, then it is possible that time does not go on. So, time is not real. (O: Time travel occurs; G: Time goes on; R: Time is real)

  8. It is contingently true that electrons exist. So, it is not necessarily true that electrons exist. (E: Electrons exist)

  9. Either the soul is immortal or it is not necessarily true that if the good is real, then the soul is immortal only if the good is real. We may conclude that the soul is immortal. (S: The soul is immortal; G: the good is real)

  10. If life is meaningless, then possibly happiness is both real and not real. It follows that life is not meaningless. (L: Life is meaningless; H: Happiness is real)

12.4 *Modal Distribution and Strict Implication*

We must now take a close look at inferences involving modal operators, the dot, the vee, and the arrow. We will first consider the behavior of the box and diamond as they relate to the dot and vee.

The **modal operator distribution equivalence** (MODE) rule comes in two forms. The first form governs the box and the dot. Using the lowercase, italicized letters *p* and *q* to stand for any proposition, the first form of MODE may be formulated as follows:

$\square(p \cdot q) :: (\square p \cdot \square q)$

This makes explicit the principle that a conjunction is a necessary truth *if and only if* each of its conjuncts are necessary truths. For example, we can interchange the following statements because they are logically equivalent:

41. Necessarily, both two is even and three is odd.

42. Necessarily, two is even, and necessarily, three is odd.

Since MODE is an equivalence rule, it can be applied to parts of a line.

The second form of MODE governs the diamond and the vee:

$\lozenge(p \vee q) :: (\lozenge p \vee \lozenge q)$

This rule tells us that the diamond distributes over the vee. It makes explicit the logical equivalence between such statements as these:

43. It is logically possible that either Smith wins the election or Jones wins the election (or both).

44. Either it is logically possible that Smith wins the election or it is logically possible that Jones wins the election (or both).

The second form of MODE is also an equivalence rule.

Here is a short proof that involves the MODE rule:

1. $\square(D \cdot E)$
2. $\sim\lozenge\sim E \rightarrow \lozenge(K \vee L)$ $\therefore \lozenge K \vee \lozenge L$
3. $\square D \cdot \square E$ 1, MODE
4. $\square E$ 3, Simp
5. $\sim\lozenge\sim E$ 4, MN
6. $\lozenge(K \vee L)$ 2, 5, MP
7. $\lozenge K \vee \lozenge L$ 6, MODE

The **modal operator distribution implicational** (MODI) rule is, as the name suggests, an implicational rule. As such, MODI may be applied only to entire lines in a proof, and not to parts of lines. The first form of MODI concerns the box and the vee:

$$\Box p \lor \Box q$$
$$\therefore\ \Box(p \lor q)$$

This inference rule is based on the principle that a disjunction is a necessary truth if *at least one* of its disjuncts is a necessary truth. Here is an English example:

> 45. Either "Two plus two equals four" is necessary or "I am wearing a red shirt" is necessary. So, it is a necessary truth that either two plus two equals four or I am wearing a red shirt.

Warning: The first form of MODI does *not* let us move from $\Box(p \lor q)$ to $\Box p \lor \Box q$. The simplest way to see why is to consider the case in which q stands for $\sim p$, for instance, $\Box(A \lor \sim A)$, hence $\Box A \lor \Box \sim A$. It is easy to provide a counterexample to this argument form:

> 46. Necessarily, either Socrates died in 399 B.C.E. or Socrates did not die in 399 B.C.E. Therefore, either "Socrates died in 399 B.C.E." is a necessary truth or "Socrates did not die in 399 B.C.E." is a necessary truth.

Here, the premise is true. All propositions of the form "Either A or not A" are necessary truths. But the conclusion is false. Socrates might have died earlier or later than 399 B.C.E. So, "Socrates died in 399 B.C.E." is not a necessary truth. And since Socrates did in fact die in 399 B.C.E., it is clear that "Socrates did not die in 399 B.C.E." is not a *necessary* truth.

The second form of MODI governs the diamond and the dot:

$$\Diamond(p \cdot q)$$
$$\therefore\ \Diamond p \cdot \Diamond q$$

This rule is based on the principle that if a conjunction is possible, then each of its conjuncts is possible. Here is an English example:

> 47. It is logically possible that both Tom and Fred are lying. So, it is logically possible that Tom is lying and it is logically possible that Fred is lying.

Warning: The second form of MODI does not permit us to move from $\Diamond p \cdot \Diamond q$ to $\Diamond(p \cdot q)$. To see why, consider the following argument:

> 48. It is logically possible that Smith wins the race and logically possible that Jones wins the race. So, it is logically possible that Smith and Jones both win the race.

A tie is logically possible, but it is not logically possible that Smith and Jones both win the same race. Thus, arguments of this form can have a true premise and a false conclusion, and so the form is invalid.

Here is a proof involving the MODI rules:

1. ◇(S • R)
2. ◇R → (~◇W ∨ □Z)   ∴ □(~W ∨ Z)
3. ◇S • ◇R   1, MODI
4. ◇R   3, Simp
5. ~◇W ∨ □Z   2, 4, MP
6. □~W ∨ □Z   5, MN
7. □(~W ∨ Z)   6, MODI

Note that MN is applied in line (6) to set up an application of MODI.

Because confusion between the MODE and MODI rules readily leads to fallacies, it is important to grasp them clearly. So, let us pause here and summarize. Each form of MODE is an equivalence rule. The first form governs the box and the dot, and the second form governs the diamond and the vee:

$$\Box(p \cdot q) :: (\Box p \cdot \Box q) \qquad \text{MODE}$$
$$\Diamond(p \lor q) :: (\Diamond p \lor \Diamond q)$$

The first form tells us that the box can be moved from a conjunction to its conjuncts, and vice versa. The second form tells us that the diamond can be moved from a disjunction to its disjuncts, and vice versa.

Both forms of MODI, on the other hand, are implicational in nature. They govern the box and the vee, and the diamond and the dot.

$$\Box p \lor \Box q \qquad \Diamond(p \cdot q) \qquad \text{MODI}$$
$$\therefore \Box(p \lor q) \qquad \therefore \Diamond p \cdot \Diamond q$$

The form on the left tells us how the box and vee interrelate: The box can be moved from the disjuncts to the whole disjunction, *but not vice versa*. The form on the right tells us how the diamond and dot interrelate: The diamond can be moved from a conjunction to its conjuncts, *but not vice versa*.

Now that we have the MODE and MODI rules, we can add the following rules of thumb for modal logic:

Rule of Thumb 2: When the box is combined with the dot or the diamond is combined with the vee, it often helps to apply MODE.

Rule of Thumb 3: When the box is combined with the vee or the diamond is combined with the dot, it often helps to apply MODI.

As mentioned previously, C. I. Lewis wanted to construct a system of logic with a stronger conditional than the arrow. In particular, he sought a system in which "Necessarily, if P, then Q" was represented. We can construct this sort of conditional out of the arrow and the box, like this:

$$\Box(P \rightarrow Q)$$

It will also be convenient to have a special symbol for this stronger type of conditional, which we will call "strict implication" or "entailment." We will use the symbol "$\Rightarrow$" to indicate that P *strictly implies* Q. (Let us call this symbol "the modal arrow.") The expression $(P \Rightarrow Q)$ may be read variously as "P strictly implies Q" or "P necessarily implies Q" or simply "P entails Q."*

Our first rule governing the modal arrow is called the law of **strict implication** (SI):

$$\Box(p \rightarrow q) :: (p \Rightarrow q)$$

This rule is based on the definition of the modal arrow: "If *p*, then *q*" is necessary *if and only if p* entails *q*. The utility of this equivalence rule will become apparent when we construct proofs involving necessarily true conditionals.

Now that we have two ways of symbolizing "if-then" statements (namely, the arrow and the modal arrow), the question naturally arises as to how we know when to translate the English "if-then" with an arrow and when to use the modal arrow. Of course, technical locutions such as "strictly implies," "necessarily implies," and "entails" call for the modal arrow. For example:

49. "Jill is an aunt" entails "Jill is a woman." (A: Jill is a aunt; W: Jill is woman)

    In symbols: A $\Rightarrow$ W

And if we need to specify the arrow, we can use the locution "materially implies." To illustrate:

50. "Bob studies" materially implies "Bob passes." (S: Bob studies; P: Bob passes)

    In symbols: S $\rightarrow$ P

Expressions of the form "Necessarily, if *p*, then *q*" can be translated in two ways. For example:

51. Necessarily, if Chris is a nephew, then Chris is male. (N: Chris is a nephew: M: Chris is male)

---

*Among logicians, different notations are used to symbolize entailment. In systems in which material implication (our arrow) is symbolized with the horseshoe ($\supset$), the arrow is sometimes used to stand for entailment. The fishhook ($-\!\!3$) is also used to symbolize entailment. I have chosen "$\Rightarrow$" as a natural addition to a system that uses the arrow for material implication.

In symbols: N $\Rightarrow$ M. *Alternatively:* $\Box$(N $\rightarrow$ M).

Of course, in many actual cases, the explicit phrases mentioned here are not used, and so we are forced to rely on the context. In such cases, two general rules apply. First, give the author the benefit of the doubt. Thus, if using the arrow would render the argument invalid but using the modal arrow would render it valid, use the modal arrow. Always try to put the argument in its best possible light when translating into symbols. (This is an application of Principle 4 from chapter 3: Be fair and charitable in interpreting an argument.) Second, since using the modal arrow complicates the argument, do not use it if it is not needed to ensure validity. In general, if a relatively simple symbolization of an argument indicates that it has a valid form, then the original argument is valid *even if it contains complexities of form not represented in the symbolization.* For example, as we have seen previously, truth tables can be used to show many arguments valid even when the arguments contain statements, such as certain types of conditionals, whose meaning cannot be *fully* expressed via truth functional connectives.

Our next rule, modal **operator transfer** (OT), applies to strict implication but not to material implication. OT comes in two forms:

$$p \Rightarrow q \qquad\qquad p \Rightarrow q$$
$$\therefore\ \Box p \Rightarrow \Box q \qquad \therefore\ \Diamond p \Rightarrow \Diamond q$$

Note that both forms of OT are implicational rules, and so they must *not* be applied to parts of a line in a proof—only to entire lines. Here is an English example of each form of OT (assume that "if-then" expresses entailment in each case):

52. If eight is even, then eight is divisible by two (without remainder). So, if it is necessary that eight is even, then it is necessary that eight is divisible by two.

53. If Smith wins the race, then Jones does not win it. So, if it is possible that Smith wins the race, then it is possible that Jones does not win it.

The OT rule enables us to answer the following question: Suppose A entails B, and suppose A is a necessary truth. Does it follow that B is a necessary truth? The following proof reveals that the answer is yes.

1. A $\Rightarrow$ B
2. $\Box$A $\qquad\qquad$ $\therefore\ \Box$B
3. $\Box$A $\Rightarrow$ $\Box$B $\qquad$ 1, OT
4. $\Box$($\Box$A $\rightarrow$ $\Box$B) $\qquad$ 3, SI
5. $\Box$A $\rightarrow$ $\Box$B $\qquad$ 4, NE
6. $\Box$B $\qquad\qquad$ 2, 5, MP

A similar proof reveals that we can move from "A entails B and A is possible" to "B is possible":

1. $A \Rightarrow B$
2. $\Diamond A$ $\therefore \ \Diamond B$
3. $\Diamond A \Rightarrow \Diamond B$ 1, OT
4. $\Box(\Diamond A \to \Diamond B)$ 3, SI
5. $\Diamond A \to \Diamond B$ 4, NE
6. $\Diamond B$ 2, 5, MP

Warning: Neither form of OT is valid for material implication. Consider the following argument form:

$$p \to q \ \therefore \ \Box p \to \Box q$$

This argument form will have a true premise and a false conclusion whenever p is a necessary truth and q is a contingent truth. In these circumstances, $p \to q$ is true, because both the antecedent and the consequent are true. However, $\Box p \to \Box q$ will be false because we have stipulated that p is a necessary truth, but since q is a contingent truth, it is not a necessary truth. In thinking about the following English example, bear in mind that we are assuming (for the sake of illustration) that "if-then" is here to be interpreted as *material* implication:

> 54. If all husbands were (are, and will be) married, then Socrates was married. So, if "All husbands were (are, and will be) married" is a necessary truth, then "Socrates was married" is a necessary truth.

The premise is equivalent to "Either not all husbands were (are, and will be) married or Socrates was married," which is true, since Socrates was married to Xanthippe. But the conclusion is false, since "Socrates was married" is not a necessary truth. (*Note*: If the premise of argument (54) is taken to express *strict* implication, then it is false. Although "All husbands are married" is true in every possible world, there are possible worlds in which Socrates remains a bachelor. So, it is not *necessarily* true that if all husbands are married, then Socrates is married.)

Similarly, the following argument form involving the material conditional is *invalid*:

$$p \to q \ \therefore \ \Diamond p \to \Diamond q$$

Suppose q is necessarily false and $\sim p$ is a contingent truth. Then the premise will be true, since it is equivalent to $\sim p \lor q$. But the conclusion will be false, since it is equivalent to $\sim \Diamond p \lor \Diamond q$. After all, $\sim \Diamond p$ is false, since $\sim p$ is by hypothesis a *contingent* truth (which implies $\Diamond p$); and $\Diamond q$ is false, since q is by hypothesis necessarily false, and hence impossible.

A number of inference rules for modal logic are highly analogous to inference rules in statement logic. For example, the following proof illustrates that an inference rule similar to *modus ponens* holds for strict implication:

1. A ⇒ B
2. A   ∴ B
3. □(A → B)   1, SI
4. A → B   3, NE
5. B   2, 4, MP

Accordingly, let us add the following inference rule to our system, and call it **modal *modus ponens*** (MMP):

$$p \Rightarrow q$$
$$p$$
$$\therefore q$$

MMP will shorten many of our proofs.

A similar proof illustrates that an inference rule analogous to *modus tollens* holds for strict implication:

1. A ⇒ B
2. ~B   ∴ ~A
3. □(A → B)   1, SI
4. A → B   3, NE
5. ~A   2, 4, MT

So, let us also add **modal *modus tollens*** (MMT) to our system of rules:

$$p \Rightarrow q$$
$$\sim q$$
$$\therefore \sim p$$

Note that MMP and MMT are implicational rules. The following proof exemplifies the use of these rules:

1. H ⇒ F
2. ~◇F
3. ~H ⇒ G   ∴ G
4. □~F   2, MN
5. ~F   4, NE
6. ~H   1, 5, MMT
7. G   3, 6, MMP

At this time, let us also add **modal hypothetical syllogism** (MHS) to our system of rules:

$$p \Rightarrow q$$
$$q \Rightarrow r$$
$$\therefore p \Rightarrow r$$

Note that MHS is an implicational rule.

Finally, let us add a rule of strict **logical equivalence** (LE), which governs mutual entailment (or strict biconditionals):

$$p \Leftrightarrow q :: \Box(p \leftrightarrow q)$$

Note that this is an equivalence rule, not an implicational rule. Here is a short proof involving typical applications of LE and MHS:

1. A ⇔ B	
2. B ⇒ ~C	∴ A ⇒ ~C
3. □(A ↔ B)	1, LE
4. □[(A → B) • (B → A)]	3, ME
5. □(A → B) • □(B → A)	4, MODE
6. □(A → B)	5, Simp
7. A ⇒ B	6, SI
8. A ⇒ ~C	7, 2, MHS

There is an important *amphiboly* (i.e., a double meaning due to a structural flaw) in some English conditionals. Our new symbols enable us to identify this amphiboly with precision. For example, consider this sentence:

55. If I think, then necessarily I exist. (T: I think; E: I exist)

It is not entirely clear which of the following symbolic statements translates (55):

56. □(T → E)
57. T → □E

Statement (56) says, "It is a necessary truth that *if* I think, *then* I exist." In other words, the whole conditional is a necessary truth. Medieval logicians called this *necessity of the consequence*, but using contemporary terminology, we might more naturally call it **necessity of the conditional**. Statement (57), on the other hand, says, "If I think, then 'I exist' is a necessary truth." Medieval logicians called this (for obvious reasons) **necessity of the consequent.** There is an important logical difference between (56) and (57), for (56) is obviously true, but (57) is false. (57) is false because its antecedent is true but its consequent is false. I do

---

Summary of the Second Set of Inference Rules

Modal Operator Distribution Equivalence Rule (MODE)

$\Box(p \cdot q) :: (\Box p \cdot \Box q)$

$\Diamond(p \lor q) :: (\Diamond p \lor \Diamond q)$

Modal Operator Distribution Implicational Rule (MODI)

$\Box p \lor \Box q \qquad\qquad \Diamond(p \cdot q)$

$\therefore \Box(p \lor q) \qquad\quad \therefore \Diamond p \cdot \Diamond q$

Strict Implication (SI)

$\Box(p \to q) :: (p \Rightarrow q)$

Operator Transfer (OT)

$p \Rightarrow q \qquad\qquad p \Rightarrow q$

$\therefore \Box p \Rightarrow \Box q \qquad \therefore \Diamond p \Rightarrow \Diamond q$

Modal *Modus Ponens* (MMP)

$p \Rightarrow q$

p

$\therefore q$

Modal *Modus Tollens* (MMT)

$p \Rightarrow q$

$\sim q$

$\therefore \sim p$

Modal Hypothetical Syllogism (MHS)

$p \Rightarrow q$

$q \Rightarrow r$

$\therefore p \Rightarrow r$

Logical Equivalence (LE)

$(p \Leftrightarrow q) :: \Box(p \leftrightarrow q)$

---

in fact think (at least occasionally!), but since, as previously observed, I might not have existed at all, "I exist" is not a necessary truth.

Normally, it is best to translate an English conditional such as (55) as expressing necessity of the conditional. Thus, (56) is probably a better translation than (57). But sometimes it is hard to be sure what the original author intended. In *On Free Choice of the Will*, Saint Augustine considers an argument that could be paraphrased as follows:[8]

> 58. If God foreknows that I'll sin tomorrow, then necessarily I'll sin tomorrow. God foreknows that I'll sin tomorrow. So, necessarily I'll sin tomorrow. (G: God foreknows that I'll sin tomorrow; S: I'll sin tomorrow)

Superficially, this looks like a case of *modus ponens*. But is it really? That depends on how we translate the first premise:

> 59. $G \rightarrow \Box S$, G $\therefore$ $\Box S$
> 60. $\Box(G \rightarrow S)$, G $\therefore$ $\Box S$

Argument (59) is an example of *modus ponens*, so it is valid. However, its first premise is false, or at least highly debatable, for it is natural to think that "I'll sin tomorrow" is a contingent proposition. (There is nothing *logically* impossible about resisting temptation for a day, however difficult it may be in fact.) And presumably, if God exists, then God knows lots of contingent propositions.

Argument (60), on the other hand, is invalid. Consider the following counterexample:

> 61. It is a necessary truth that if Socrates was a husband, then Socrates was married. Socrates was a husband. So, it is a necessary truth that Socrates was married.

The conclusion of this argument is false, for although Socrates was in fact married to Xanthippe, he might have chosen to remain a bachelor. But the premises of the argument are true. So, the argument is invalid. Thus, to analyze argument (58) fully and fairly, we have to consider two possible interpretations of the conditional premise. When we do, a subtle fallacy of amphiboly becomes apparent. In one way of reading the first premise, the argument is valid but the first premise is false (or at least very dubious). In the other way, the premises are true but the argument is invalid. Our symbolic tools give us a very clear way of identifying the problem.

The following exercises will test your understanding of the rules introduced in this section.

◆ *Exercise 12.4*

Part A: Symbolizing   Symbolize the following sentences using the schemes of abbreviation provided.

* 1. "Joe is a man and Joe is not married" strictly implies "Joe is a bachelor." (J: Joe is a man; M: Joe is married; B: Joe is a bachelor)

  2. Necessarily, if Linda is a niece, then she is female. (L: Linda is a niece; F: Linda is female)

3. "Chris is Bob's daughter" entails "Chris is not male." (D: Chris is Bob's daughter; M: Chris is male)

* 4. "Doug does not try" materially implies "Doug fails." (T: Doug tries; F: Doug fails)

5. "Erica is married" does not entail "Erica is happy." (M: Erica is married; H: Erica is happy)

6. "The Eiffel Tower is in Ohio" materially implies, but does not necessarily imply, "The Eiffel Tower is in France." (O: The Eiffel Tower is in Ohio; F: The Eiffel Tower is in France)

* 7. It is a necessary truth that if abortion is murder, then it is wrong. (M: Abortion is murder; W: Abortion is wrong)

8. "Killing innocent humans is always wrong" entails "Euthanasia is wrong." (K: Killing innocent humans is always wrong; E: Euthanasia is wrong)

9. It is necessarily false that some circles are triangles; however, some circles are purple. (T: Some circles are triangles; P: Some circles are purple)

10. Necessarily, if it is necessary that all humans are mortal and necessary that Socrates is human, then it is necessary that Socrates is mortal. (H: All humans are mortal; S: Socrates is human; M: Socrates is mortal)

Part B: Symbolizing and Evaluating Symbolize the following arguments. Which have valid forms? Which have invalid forms? *Note:* Two of the arguments have an amphibolous conditional premise, and hence these arguments can be interpreted as having two different forms. In these cases, identify both forms and indicate which of them is valid and which isn't.

* 1. Possibly Smith is guilty and possibly Jones is guilty. So, it is possible that both Smith and Jones are guilty. (S: Smith is guilty; J: Jones is guilty)

2. The proposition "Betty is an aunt" entails the proposition "Betty is female." Accordingly, the proposition "It is logically possible that Betty is an aunt" strictly implies the proposition "It is logically possible that Betty is female." (A: Betty is an aunt; F: Betty is female)

3. Necessarily, either Santa exists or he doesn't. Hence, either it is necessary that Santa exists or it is necessary that he doesn't exist. (S: Santa exists)

* 4. Either not all husbands are handsome or all wives are beautiful. Therefore, either it is not necessary that all husbands are handsome or it is necessary that all wives are beautiful. (H: All husbands are handsome; W: All wives are beautiful) [*Hint:* Apply MI.]

5. Either it is necessary that all bachelors own Fords or it is necessary that all bachelors own Porsches. Thus, it is necessary that either all bachelors own Fords or all bachelors own Porsches. (F: All bachelors own Fords; P: All bachelors own Porsches)

6. If I see that Al is stealing a TV, then necessarily Al is stealing a TV. I see that Al is stealing a TV. Therefore, it is necessarily true that Al is stealing a TV. (S: I see that Al is stealing a TV; A: Al is stealing a TV)

* **7.** It is logically possible that Fred and Sue are both arrogant. Hence, it is logically possible that Fred is arrogant and logically possible that Sue is arrogant. (F: Fred is arrogant; S: Sue is arrogant)

8. It is necessarily true that either Pat is a man or Pat is a woman. It follows that either it is necessary that Pat is a man or it is necessary that Pat is a woman. (M: Pat is a man; W: Pat is a woman)

9. "The Eiffel Tower is in Ohio" materially implies "The Eiffel Tower is in France." Thus, "It is possible that the Eiffel Tower is in Ohio" materially implies "It is possible that the Eiffel Tower is in France." (O: The Eiffel Tower is in Ohio; F: The Eiffel Tower is in France)

* **10.** If Socrates is sitting, then it must be the case that Socrates is sitting. Socrates is sitting. Therefore, it is necessarily true that Socrates is sitting. (S: Socrates is sitting)

11. Necessarily, either nothing is caused or every event has a cause. Therefore, either it is necessarily true that nothing is caused or it is necessarily true that every event has a cause. (N: Nothing is caused; E: Every event is caused)

12. Monism (i.e., the view that there is only one thing) is possibly true, and so is reincarnation (i.e., the view that when a person dies, his or her soul enters another body). Consequently, it is logically possible both that monism is true and that reincarnation is true. (M: Monism is true; R: Reincarnation is true)

13. Necessarily, if radical skeptics are right, then there is no external world. Radical skeptics are right. So, it is a necessary truth that there is no external world. (R: Radical skeptics are right; E: There is no external world)

14. Either it is necessary that God exists or it is necessary that the physical universe exists. Accordingly, it is necessarily true that either God exists or the physical universe exists. (G: God exists; P: The physical universe exists)

15. Possibly, both Hinduism and Zoroastrianism are true. Therefore, possibly Hinduism is true and possibly Zoroastrianism is true. (H: Hinduism is true; Z: Zoroastrianism is true)

Part C: Annotating   Annotate the following proofs.

* **1.** 1. $\Box(A \cdot \sim B)$ $\therefore \sim \Diamond B$
   2. $\Box A \cdot \Box \sim B$
   3. $\Box \sim B$
   4. $\sim \Diamond B$

2. 1. $\Box C \lor \Box D$ $\therefore C \lor D$
   2. $\Box(C \lor D)$
   3. $C \lor D$

3. 1. $\Diamond E \lor \Diamond F$
   2. $\Diamond(E \lor F) \rightarrow G$ $\therefore \Diamond G$
   3. $\Diamond(E \lor F)$
   4. G
   5. $\Diamond G$

* **4.** 1. $\Diamond(H \cdot J)$
   2. $\Diamond K \Rightarrow \sim \Diamond J$ $\therefore \Box \sim K$
   3. $\Diamond H \cdot \Diamond J$
   4. $\Diamond J$
   5. $\sim \sim \Diamond J$
   6. $\sim \Diamond K$
   7. $\Box \sim K$

5. 1. $L \Rightarrow M$
   2. $\Box \sim M$ $\therefore \Box \sim L$
   3. $\sim \Diamond M$
   4. $\Diamond L \Rightarrow \Diamond M$
   5. $\sim \Diamond L$
   6. $\Box \sim L$

6. 1. $\Diamond A \Rightarrow B \;\therefore\; \Box \sim A \vee B$
    2. $\Box(\Diamond A \rightarrow B)$
    3. $\Box(\sim \Diamond A \vee B)$
    4. $\sim \Diamond A \vee B$
    5. $\Box \sim A \vee B$

* **7.** 1. $N \Leftrightarrow O$
    2. $\Box(N \rightarrow P) \;\therefore\; O \Rightarrow P$
    3. $N \Rightarrow P$
    4. $\Box(N \leftrightarrow O)$
    5. $\Box[(N \rightarrow O) \cdot (O \rightarrow N)]$
    6. $\Box(N \rightarrow O) \cdot \Box(O \rightarrow N)$
    7. $\Box(O \rightarrow N)$
    8. $O \Rightarrow N$
    9. $O \Rightarrow P$

8. 1. $Q \Rightarrow R$
    2. $\Diamond Q \;\therefore\; \Diamond R$
    3. $\Diamond Q \Rightarrow \Diamond R$
    4. $\Diamond R$

9. 1. $S \Rightarrow (T \cdot U)$
    2. $\Box S \;\therefore\; \Box U$
    3. $\Box S \Rightarrow \Box(T \cdot U)$
    4. $\Box(T \cdot U)$
    5. $\Box T \cdot \Box U$
    6. $\Box U$

* **10.** 1. $\Diamond(W \vee X)$
    2. $\Diamond W \Rightarrow \Diamond Z$
    3. $\Diamond X \Rightarrow \Diamond V \quad \therefore \Diamond(Z \vee V)$
    4. $\Diamond W \vee \Diamond X$
    5. $\Box(\Diamond W \rightarrow \Diamond Z)$
    6. $\Box(\Diamond X \rightarrow \Diamond V)$
    7. $\Diamond W \rightarrow \Diamond Z$
    8. $\Diamond X \rightarrow \Diamond V$
    9. $\Diamond Z \vee \Diamond V$
    10. $\Diamond(Z \vee V)$

Part D: Correct or Incorrect?   Which of the following inferences are permitted by one of our rules, and which are not? If an inference is permitted, indicate the rule that permits it. If it is not permitted, simply write "incorrect." (The question is whether one can move from the first statement to the second, in each instance, by a single application of one of our rules.)

* **1.** 1. $\sim A \rightarrow \sim B$
    2. $\Diamond \sim A \rightarrow \Diamond \sim B$

2. 1. $\Box C \Rightarrow \Box D$
    2. $\Box(\Box C \rightarrow \Box D)$

3. 1. $\Diamond(\sim E \cdot F)$
    2. $\Diamond \sim E \cdot \Diamond F$

* **4.** 1. $\Box(G \vee H)$
    2. $\Box G \vee \Box H$

5. 1. $\Diamond J \cdot \Diamond K$
    2. $\Diamond(J \cdot K)$

6. 1. $\sim L \Rightarrow \sim M$
    2. $\Box \sim L \Rightarrow \Box \sim M$

* **7.** 1. $\Diamond(\sim N \vee P)$
    2. $\Diamond \sim N \vee \Diamond P$

8. 1. $Q \Rightarrow R$
    2. $\Diamond Q \Rightarrow R$

9. 1. $\Box S \vee \Box \sim T$
    2. $\Box(S \vee \sim T)$

* **10.** 1. $\Diamond U \vee \Diamond W$
    2. $\Diamond(U \vee W)$

11. 1. $\sim Y \Rightarrow \sim Z$
    2. $\Diamond \sim Y \Rightarrow \Diamond \sim Z$

12. 1. $\sim(A \Rightarrow B)$
    2. $\sim \Box(A \rightarrow B)$

* **13.** 1. $\Box(\sim C \cdot D)$
    2. $\Box \sim C \cdot \Box D$

14. 1. $E \Leftrightarrow F$
    2. $(E \Rightarrow F) \cdot (F \Rightarrow E)$

15. 1. $\sim \Box(G \rightarrow H)$
    2. $\sim(G \Rightarrow H)$

Part E: Proofs   Construct proofs to show that the following symbolic arguments are valid.

* **1.** $A \Rightarrow B \;\therefore\; \sim B \Rightarrow \sim A$

 2. C ⇔ D, D ∴ C

 3. □F ∴ □(F ∨ G)

* 4. □(E → H), ~□~E ∴ ◊H

 5. S ⇒ T ∴ ~◊(S • ~T)

 6. O ⇔ N, ◊O ∴ ◊N

* 7. ◊(L ∨ M), □~L, M ⇒ ~N ∴ ~□N

 8. ◊(~D • ~E), ◊A ⇒ □D ∴ ~A

 9. P ⇔ Q, Q ⇒ ~S ∴ P ⇒ ~S

*10. A ⇒ E, □~E ∴ □~A

 11. □(R ∨ D), □~R ∴ □D

 12. □B • (E ∨ ~G), (□K ∨ ◊H) → ~□B, ◊G ∴ ◊E • ~H

*13. □[~R ∨ (S • T)], ◊R ∴ ◊S • ◊T

 14. ◊[S ∨ (P • R)], ◊Q → ~◊S, ◊Q → ~◊(P • R) ∴ ~Q

 15. □[H → (J → K)], ◊J ∴ ◊(H → K)

*16. ◊[(L ∨ M) • (L ∨ Q)], ◊P ⇒ ~◊Q, □~L ∴ ~P

 17. ~□(P • R), ◊~P ⇒ □Q, ◊~R ⇒ □Q ∴ Q

 18. ~◊(S ∨ T), (U ⇒ W) → ◊S ∴ ◊~W

*19. □[(E • F) → G], □E ∴ ~G ⇒ ~F

 20. □(A • B) ∨ □(~A • ~B), (A ⇔ B) → ~◊C ∴ ◊~C

Part F: English Arguments Symbolize the following arguments, using the schemes of abbreviation provided. Then construct proofs to show that the arguments are valid.

* 1. Necessarily, if a first cause exists, then God exists. But it is not possible that a first cause does not exist. And hence, it is necessary that God exists. (F: A first cause exists; G: God exists)

 2. "Contradictions are false" entails "Circular squares do not exist." And it is necessarily true that contradictions are false. Moreover, "Circular squares do not exist" entails "Some statements about what exists can be known independently of sensory experience." Therefore, necessarily, some statements about what exists can be known independently of sensory experience. (C: Contradictions are false; S: Circular squares exist; E: Some statements about what exists can be known independently of sensory experience)

 3. Either two objects can have all properties in common or two physical objects cannot be in the same place at once. But necessarily, it is not the case that two objects can have all properties in common. Accordingly, two physical objects cannot be in the same place at once. (O: Two objects can have all properties in common; P: Two physical objects can be in the same place at once)

4. Either it is possible that every object has a cause of its existence or it is possible that at least one object exists uncaused. "It is possible that either every object has a cause of its existence or at least one object exists uncaused" strictly implies "Necessarily, it is not the case that some objects bring themselves into existence." Thus, it is impossible that some objects bring themselves into existence. (E: Every object has a cause of its existence; U: At least one object exists uncaused; B: Some objects bring themselves into existence)

5. Necessarily, if God is all-powerful and knowledge is power, then God is all-knowing. It is necessarily true that God is all-powerful. Therefore, the proposition "God is not all-knowing" entails the proposition "It is not the case that knowledge is power." (P: God is all-powerful; K: Knowledge is power; G: God is all-knowing)

12.5 Systems S4 and S5

C. I. Lewis described systems of modal logic in five stages. Each stage corresponds to one of the following principles:

1. If p is a theorem of statement logic, then $\Box p$.
2. If $\Box p$, then p.
3. If $\Box p$ and $p \Rightarrow q$, then $\Box q$.
4. If $\Box p$, then $\Box\Box p$.
5. If $\Diamond\Box p$, then $\Box p$.

The rules we have introduced so far reflect Principles 1, 2, and 3. Some philosophers accept *only* the first three principles. The modal system based on Principles 1–3 (and *not* including 4 and 5) is called system T. Accordingly, the system of modal logic developed in sections 12.3 and 12.4 is a variant of system T. The system of modal logic based on Principles 1–4 is called S4. And the system of modal logic based on all five principles is called S5. In this section, we will explore modal systems S4 and S5.

These various systems of modal logic are progressively stronger. For example, there are arguments that can be proved valid in system S4 that cannot be proved valid in system T. And there are arguments that can be proved valid in system S5 that cannot be proved valid in system S4. On the other hand, if an argument can be proved valid using the rules of system T, then it can be proved valid using the rules of system S4. And if an argument can be proved valid using the rules of system S4, then it can be proved valid using the rules of system S5.

System S4 gives us the following rules that govern repeated (or iterated) modal operators:

$\Box p :: \Box\Box p$
$\Diamond p :: \Diamond\Diamond p$

We will simply call these rules the **S4 rules**. (The annotation in a proof is "S4.") Note that these rules are equivalence rules, so they can be applied to parts of lines in a proof.

The S4 rules may seem initially puzzling. What do the iterated operators mean? For example, what does it mean to say that a proposition is *necessarily necessary*? And what does it mean to say that a proposition is *possibly possible*? Let us take a closer look at both rules.

First, consider $\Box p :: \Box\Box p$. Let's break this down into two separate inferences. The move from $\Box\Box p$ to $\Box p$ is actually redundant within our system. We can already make this move by NE. So, let's focus on the move from $\Box p$ to $\Box\Box p$. It helps to think about this in terms of possible worlds. Suppose $\Box p$ is true. Then p is true in every possible world. Could $\Box\Box p$ be false? Well, if $\Box\Box p$ is false, then $\Box p$ is false in at least one possible world. But if $\Box p$ is false in some possible world, then $\sim p$ is true in some possible world. So, it is not the case that p is true in every possible world, which contradicts our initial supposition that p is necessary. Therefore, when we think about the first S4 rule in terms of possible worlds, it seems clear that $\Box p$ implies $\Box\Box p$.*

Second, consider $\Diamond p :: \Diamond\Diamond p$. Again, break the inference rule down into two parts. The move from $\Diamond p$ to $\Diamond\Diamond p$ is redundant within our system, for we can already make this move by EP. So, let's focus on the move from $\Diamond\Diamond p$ to $\Diamond p$. Again, it helps to think in terms of possible worlds. Suppose $\Diamond\Diamond p$. Could $\Diamond p$ be false? If $\Diamond\Diamond p$, then there is at least one possible world (call it "W") in which p is possibly true. But if p is possibly true in W, then p is true in some possible world. But if $\Diamond p$ is false, then p is impossible, and hence p is false in every world. So, if we assume $\Diamond\Diamond p$, we are forced, on pain of contradiction, to accept $\Diamond p$. Thus, $\Diamond\Diamond p$ implies $\Diamond p$.

Now, consider the following English argument.

62. The proposition "Possibly, morality is relative to culture" entails the proposition "It is not necessarily necessary that torturing people for fun is wrong." But it is a necessary truth that torturing people for fun is wrong. Therefore, morality is not relative to culture. (M: Morality is relative to culture; T: Torturing people for fun is wrong)

Here is the symbolization and proof:

---

*Here is one way of highlighting the philosophical issues that are at stake when the necessity operator is iterated. Some theologians claim that God created logic. This apparently implies that the correct logical rules could have been very different than they are—for example, that contradictions could have been true had God so ordained it. To reduce the philosophical alarm this view often produces, its proponents sometimes suggest that God made the law of noncontradiction a necessary truth in our world (the actual world), but God might have done otherwise. In other words, $\Box\sim(p \cdot \sim p)$, but $\sim\Box\Box\sim(p \cdot \sim p)$, which violates the S4 rules. This scenario is unacceptable if necessary truths are true in every possible world, for if p is necessary but God could have created a world in which p is not necessary, then $\Diamond\sim\Box p$. This means there is a possible world in which p is not necessary. But this could be so only if there is at least one world in which p is false. But then p isn't a necessary truth after all, contrary to our supposition.

1. ◇M ⇒ ~□□T
2. □T   ∴ ~M
3. ◇M ⇒ ~□T   1, S4
4. ~~□T   2, DN
5. ~◇M   3, 4, MMT
6. □~M   5, MN
7. ~M   6, NE

Our final set of rules belongs to Lewis's fifth system of modal logic, S5. We will simply call these rules the **S5 rules** (annotation: S5):

◇□*p* : : □*p*
◇*p* : : □◇*p*

Once again, we have two rules, each of which is an equivalence rule. And once again, these rules are partly redundant within our system. For example, we can move from □*p* to ◇□*p* by EP; and we can move from □◇*p* to ◇*p* by NE. But the move from ◇□*p* to □*p* is new and striking. If a proposition is *possibly* necessary, does it follow that it is necessary? The move from ◇*p* to □◇*p* is new as well. If *p* is possible, does it follow that *p* is *necessarily* possible? A possible-worlds approach helps to explain why many logicians think the S5 rules are valid.

Consider the move from ◇□*p* to □*p*. If ◇□*p*, then there is a possible world in which □*p*. For example, there is a possible world in which "No circles are squares" is necessary. But this means that there is a possible world (call it "W") in which "No circles are squares" is true *in every possible world*. But if in W "No circles are squares" is true in every possible word, then "No circles are squares" is necessary. In other words, if a proposition is necessary in one world, it is necessary in all.

Consider the move from ◇*p* to □◇*p*. This says that if a statement is logically possible, that is, true in at least one possible world, then it can't be impossible in some other world. Suppose ◇*p* but ~□◇*p* (for the sake of the argument). Now, ~□◇*p* implies ◇~◇*p*, by MN. But how could *p* be true in some possible world but impossible, that is, necessarily false, in some other possible world? If a statement is necessarily false in one possible world, then it is false in every possible world. It is reflections such as these that lead many philosophers to accept the S5 rules as valid.

Let us now use our new modal rules to consider a version of the famous ontological argument for the existence of God. The argument was first formulated by Saint Anselm (1033–1109), but we will consider a version that depends heavily on modal terms:

> **63.** If God exists, then God is a Supremely Perfect Being. If God is a Supremely Perfect Being, then it is impossible that God not exist. It is logically possible

Summary of Rules for Systems S4 and S5	
S4 Rules	**S5 Rules**
$\Box p :: \Box\Box p$	$\Diamond\Box p :: \Box p$
$\Diamond p :: \Diamond\Diamond p$	$\Diamond p :: \Box\Diamond p$

that God exists. So, God exists. (G: God exists; S: God is a Supremely Perfect Being)

1. $G \Rightarrow S$	
2. $S \Rightarrow \sim\Diamond\sim G$	
3. $\Diamond G$	$\therefore$ G
4. $\Diamond G \Rightarrow \Diamond S$	1, OT
5. $S \Rightarrow \Box G$	2, MN
6. $\Diamond S \Rightarrow \Diamond\Box G$	5, OT
7. $\Diamond G \Rightarrow \Diamond\Box G$	4, 6, MHS
8. $\Diamond\Box G$	3, 7, MMP
9. $\Box G$	8, S5
10. G	9, NE

This argument is interesting because it reaches a philosophically dramatic conclusion on the basis of rather modest-looking premises. It seems reasonable to suppose that it is logically possible that God exists. (After all, we could say the same about unicorns or Santa Claus, couldn't we?) And if God does exist, then God must be a Supremely Perfect Being. After all, if there is no Supremely Perfect Being, then surely there is no entity that we would regard as God. So, if the argument is unsound, then surely either the second premise is false or at least one of the steps in the proof is invalid.

Philosophers who reject modal system S5 will point out that we made a crucial use of an S5 rule in line (9) of our proof. Others might reject the second premise. Why should we suppose that if God is a Supremely Perfect Being, then "God exists" is necessary? The defense might be that any being that could fail to exist would not be *supremely* perfect, because we could conceive of a more perfect being, namely, one that could not fail to exist.

On the other hand, if "A Supremely Perfect Being exists" is a necessary truth, then "A Supremely Perfect Being does not exist" is impossible. And many philosophers find this implausible. They claim that we must distinguish between *having* a concept (e.g., having the concept of a unicorn or of a Supremely Perfect Being) and *knowing* whether that concept applies to any real object. Furthermore, they claim we cannot tell *merely by examining a concept* whether it applies to anything in reality.

We cannot enter more deeply into these important metaphysical issues here. But our comments on the ontological argument illustrate how modal logic can be used to set philosophical issues up in a revealing fashion. The following exercises indicate how our modal tools can be used to frame several traditional philosophical problems with increased precision.

◆ **Exercise 12.5**

Part A: Symbolizing   Symbolize the following statements using the schemes of abbreviation provided.

* 1. It is necessarily possible that Bozo is president. (B: Bozo is president)

2. "Possibly it is necessary that unicorns exist" strictly implies "necessarily unicorns exist." (U: Unicorns exist)

3. "Possibly, it is necessary that water is wet" materially implies, but does not strictly imply, "It is necessarily necessary that water is clear." (W: Water is wet; C: Water is clear)

* 4. "The Great Pumpkin does not exist" is a contingent truth, and it is necessarily possible that the Great Pumpkin does exist. (G: The Great Pumpkin exists)

5. It is possibly possible that astrologers are wise, but it is not necessarily necessary that astrologers are wise. (A: Astrologers are wise)

6. Necessarily, either it is logically possible that miracles *can* occur or it is necessarily impossible that miracles occur. (M: Miracles occur)

* 7. There is a possible world in which I am rich, but it is not possible that I am rich in every possible world. (R: I am rich)

8. Necessarily, if there is a possible world in which it is necessary that torturing innocent people is wrong, then there is no possible world in which torturing innocent people is not wrong. (T: Torturing innocent people is wrong)

9. "Ants are animals in every possible world" entails "In every possible world 'Ants are animals' is a necessary truth." (A: Ants are animals)

10. It is possibly necessary that if there is no possible world in which it is possible that green things are invisible, then it is necessarily necessary that green things are visible. (G: Green things are visible)

Part B: Annotating   Annotate the following proofs.

* 1. 1. $\Box\Box A \Rightarrow B$
   2. $\Box A$ ∴ B
   3. $\Box\Box A$
   4. B

2. 1. $(\Diamond C \lor \Diamond\Diamond C) \Rightarrow D$ ∴ $\Box(\Diamond C \to D)$
   2. $(\Diamond C \lor \Diamond C) \Rightarrow D$
   3. $\Diamond C \Rightarrow D$
   4. $\Box(\Diamond C \to D)$

3. 1. $\Box\Box E \Rightarrow \Box\Box F$
   2. $\Diamond \sim F$ ∴ $\sim\Box E$
   3. $\sim\Box F$
   4. $\Box\Box E \Rightarrow \Box F$
   5. $\sim\Box\Box E$
   6. $\sim\Box E$

* **4.** 1. ◇G
   2. □◇G ⇒ ◇□H ∴ H
   3. □◇G
   4. ◇□H
   5. □H
   6. H

  5. 1. □~Q ⇒ □□~R
   2. ◇R ∴ ◇Q
   3. □~Q ⇒ □~◇R
   4. □~Q ⇒ ~◇◇R
   5. □~Q ⇒ ~◇R
   6. ~~◇R
   7. ~□~Q
   8. ◇Q

  6. 1. □□◇◇S ∴ ◇S
   2. □◇◇S
   3. □◇S
   4. ◇S

* **7.** 1. ◇□J
   2. ◇◇K ⇒ ~□J ∴ ~◇K
   3. ◇◇K ⇒ ~◇□J
   4. ~~◇□J
   5. ~◇◇K
   6. ~◇K

  8. 1. L ⇒ M
   2. M ⇒ □L
   3. ◇L ∴ L
   4. L ⇒ □L
   5. ◇L ⇒ ◇□L
   6. ◇□L
   7. □L
   8. L

  9. 1. ◇□N ⇒ ◇◇P
   2. ~◇P ∴ ~□N
   3. ◇□N ⇒ ◇P
   4. ~◇□N
   5. ~□N

* **10.** 1. ◇□◇□T ∴ T
   2. □◇□T
   3. □□T
   4. □T
   5. T

Part C: Proofs   Construct proofs to show that the following arguments are valid.

* **1.** □A, A ⇒ B ∴ □□B

  2. ◇◇R ∴ □◇R

  3. ◇□~H, ◇C ⇒ ◇H ∴ ~C

* **4.** □□(A • B) ∴ □A • □□B

  5. ◇◇(P ∨ Q) ∴ ◇P ∨ ◇Q

  6. □◇□◇F ∴ ◇F

* **7.** ◇□◇□~Q ∴ ~Q

  8. ◇◇T ⇒ □◇P ∴ ~◇(◇T • ~◇P)

  9. ~◇(A • ~B) ∴ ◇□A ⇒ ◇□B

* **10.** □□F ⇒ ◇□G ∴ ◇◇(~F ∨ □G)

  11. □R, □□R ⇒ ◇~S ∴ ~□S

  12. ◇□C ∴ ◇D ⇒ □□C

  13. □□(H • ◇□E) ∴ □◇H • ◇E

  14. □M ∨ ◇S ∴ □(M ∨ ◇S)

  15. N ⇒ □N, ◇N ∴ N

16. $\Diamond J, \Box \Diamond J \Rightarrow \Diamond \Box K \therefore K$

17. $\Box \Diamond \Diamond (\sim F \vee \Diamond \sim G) \therefore \Diamond (\sim \Box F \vee \Box \Diamond \sim G)$

18. $\Diamond \Diamond (\sim L \vee \sim M) \therefore \sim (\Box L \cdot \Box M)$

19. $\Diamond E \Rightarrow \sim \Box \Box H, \Box H \therefore \sim E$

20. $\Diamond \sim S \Rightarrow \sim S, \Diamond S \therefore S$

Part D: English Arguments Symbolize the following arguments using the schemes of abbreviation provided. Then construct proofs to show that the arguments are valid.

* 1. Necessarily, if a supremely perfect island exists, then it is necessarily true that a supremely perfect island exists. Possibly, a supremely perfect island exists. Therefore, a supremely perfect island exists. (P: A supremely perfect island exists)

2. Necessarily, if God exists, God is nonphysical but omnipresent. Necessarily, if God is nonphysical, then it is impossible for God to be located anywhere. Necessarily, if God is omnipresent, God is located everywhere. Necessarily, if God is not located anywhere, then God is not located everywhere. Therefore, it is necessarily true that God does not exist. (G: God exists; N: God is nonphysical; O: God is omnipresent; L: God is located somewhere; E: God is located everywhere)

3. The proposition "It is possible that my soul can inhabit another body" strictly implies the proposition "It is not a necessary truth that I am my body." It is not necessary that my soul does not inhabit another body. The proposition "It is possible that I am not my body" entails the proposition "I am not my body." It follows that I am not my body. (B: I am identical with my body; S: My soul inhabits another body)

* 4. Necessarily, both Zeus and Yahweh are omnipotent. Necessarily, if it is necessary that Zeus is omnipotent, then Zeus can thwart Yahweh. Necessarily, if it is necessary that Yahweh is omnipotent, then Yahweh can thwart Zeus. However, "Zeus can thwart Yahweh" entails "It is not necessarily true that Yahweh thwarts Zeus." And necessarily, if it is possible that Yahweh does not thwart Zeus, then it is possible that Yahweh is not omnipotent. We must therefore conclude that Yahweh is not omnipotent. (Z: Zeus is omnipotent; Y: Yahweh is omnipotent; T: Zeus thwarts Yahweh; A: Yahweh thwarts Zeus)

5. Necessarily, it is possible that the word "bachelor" will change meaning over time. Necessarily, if it is possible that the word "bachelor" will change meaning over time, then it is not necessarily true that all bachelors are unmarried. Hence, it is possible that not all bachelors are unmarried. (W: The word "bachelor" will change meaning over time; A: All bachelors are unmarried)

6. The following conditional is logically possible: the proposition "There is a physical universe" entails the proposition "God exists." Therefore, "There is a physical universe" entails "God exists." (P: There is a physical universe; G: God exists)

7. If it is possibly possible that a powerful demon exists, then it is necessarily possible that I am deceived about the existence of an external world. Necessarily, it is possible that a powerful demon exists. If it is possible that I am deceived about the existence of an external world, then it is necessarily possible that I know nothing.

But the proposition "Possibly I know nothing" entails the proposition "I know nothing." Accordingly, I know nothing. (D: A powerful demon exists; E: I am deceived about the existence of an external world; K: I know nothing)

8. If a supremely perfect being created something, then a supremely perfect being created the best of all possible worlds. Possibly, it is necessary that a supremely perfect being created something. If a supremely perfect being created the best of all possible worlds, then the actual world is the best of all possible worlds. Therefore, it is not possible that the actual world is not the best of all possible worlds. (S: A supremely perfect being created something; B: A supremely perfect being created the best of all possible worlds; A: The actual world is the best of all possible worlds)

9. Possibly, it is necessary that if pointless suffering occurs, then God is not both omnipotent and perfectly good. Possibly, pointless suffering occurs. Therefore, necessarily either possibly God is not omnipotent or possibly God is not perfectly good. (S: Pointless suffering occurs; O: God is omnipotent; G: God is perfectly good)

10. Necessarily, using nuclear weapons involves indiscriminate killing if and only if it is wrong to use nuclear weapons. The proposition "It is possible that indiscriminate killing occurred at Hiroshima" strictly implies the proposition "It is possibly necessary that using nuclear weapons involves indiscriminate killing." Indiscriminate killing occurred at Hiroshima assuming that it is possible that any war *can* be won without killing a great many noncombatants. Possibly, any war *is* won without killing a great many noncombatants. Therefore, it is wrong to use nuclear weapons. (N: Using nuclear weapons involves indiscriminate killing; W: It is wrong to use nuclear weapons; H: Indiscriminate killing occurred at Hiroshima; K: Any war is won without killing a great many noncombatants)

Part E: Paradoxes of Strict Implication   As noted previously, C. I. Lewis developed modal logic partly because he was troubled by the so-called paradoxes of material implication. However, the concept of strict implication has results that seem just as paradoxical to many. To understand these paradoxes, construct proofs to show that the following arguments are valid:

1. $\Box B \therefore A \Rightarrow B$

2. $\sim \Diamond A \therefore A \Rightarrow B$

Argument (1) tells us that *a necessary truth is strictly implied by any statement whatsoever.* It follows, for example, that:

3. "Trees exist" strictly implies "No circles are squares."

This is puzzling as the antecedent of (3) seems irrelevant to its consequent. Does it help to note that (3) is equivalent to (4), applying SI and MI?

4. Necessarily, either trees do not exist or no circles are squares.

Argument (2) tells us that *an impossible proposition entails any proposition whatsoever.* It follows, for example, that:

5. "There are circular squares" strictly implies "Santa exists."

Again the antecedent does not seem relevant to the consequent. Does it help to note that (5) is equivalent to (6), applying SI and MI?

6. Necessarily, either there are no circular squares or Santa exists.

Notes

1. The historical observations here regarding Aristotle and the one that follows regarding C. I. Lewis are gleaned from Kenneth Konyndyk, *Introductory Modal Logic* (Notre Dame, IN: University of Notre Dame Press, 1986), pp. 18–19, 26.
2. Example (7) is borrowed from Alvin Plantinga, *The Nature of Necessity* (Oxford: Clarendon Press, 1974), p. 2.
3. For a review of the concept of a tautology, see section 7.5.
4. My definition is adapted from Laurence BonJour, *In Defense of Pure Reason* (New York: Cambridge University Press, 1998), p. 32.
5. This is a note for the metaphysically alert reader. I realize that I am speaking somewhat loosely about statements here. We will take up the issue of statements and propositions momentarily.
6. Konyndyk, *Introductory Modal Logic,* p. 15.
7. The system of rules in this chapter is largely based on a system developed by Richard L. Purtill, *A Logical Introduction to Philosophy* (Englewood Cliffs, NJ: Prentice-Hall, 1989), pp. 171–176.
8. Saint Augustine, *On Free Choice of the Will,* trans. Anna S. Benjamin and L. H. Hackstaff (Indianapolis, IN: Bobbs-Merrill, 1964), pp. 90–93.

Answer Key

◆ Chapter 1

Exercise 1.1
Part A: Recognizing Statements

1. A sentence and a statement
4. A sentence and a statement
7. A sentence and a statement
10. A sentence but not a statement

Part B: True or False?

1. F	10. F	19. T
4. T	13. T	22. F
7. F	16. F	25. F

Part C: Valid or Invalid?

1. Valid	7. Invalid
4. Valid	10. Invalid

Part D: Deductive Soundness

1. Deductively sound.
4. Deductively unsound. The argument is invalid.
7. Deductively sound.
10. Deductively unsound. Valid, but the first premise is false.

Exercise 1.2
Part A: Matching   These are left as exercises.

Part B: True or False?

1. F	10. F
4. F	13. F
7. F	

Part C: Valid or Invalid? Strong or Weak?

1. Invalid and weak	13. Invalid but strong
4. Invalid but strong	16. Invalid and weak
7. Invalid and weak	19. Invalid and weak
10. Valid	

Part D: Inductive Soundness

1. Inductively sound.
4. Inductively unsound. The premise is false (for example, penguins and ostriches cannot fly).
7. Valid, and hence neither inductively sound nor inductively unsound.
10. Inductively unsound. The argument is weak.

◆ Chapter 2

Exercise 2.1: Counterexamples

1. *Form:* No A are B. Some C are not B. So, some C are A.
   Counterexample: No fish are cats. Some collies are not cats. So, some collies are fish.
4. *Form:* No A are B. Some C are B. So, no C are A.
   Counterexample: No collies are cocker spaniels. Some dogs are cocker spaniels. So, no dogs are collies.
7. *Form:* Some A are B. Some B are C. So, some C are not A.
   Counterexample: Some animals are collies. All collies are dogs. So, some dogs are not animals.
10. *Form:* All A are B. Some A are not C. So, some C are not B.
    Counterexample: All dogs are animals. Some dogs are not collies. So, some collies are not animals.
13. *Form:* All A are B. All C are B. So, all A are C.
    Counterexample: All dogs are animals. All cats are animals. So, all dogs are cats.
16. *Form:* Every A is B. No C is A. So, no C is B.
    Counterexample: Every cat is an animal. No dog is a cat. So, no dog is an animal.
19. *Form:* All A are B. No C is A. So, no C is B.
    Counterexample: All fish are animals. No dog is a fish. So, no dog is an animal.

Exercise 2.2
Part A: Stylistic Variants

1. If the Sun is shining, then the room is hot.
4. If Maria is a physicist, then Maria is a scientist.
7. If Joe is late, then Wendy is angry.
10. If Valerie is from Seattle, then she is not from Oregon.
13. If Ted is guilty, then he should go to prison.
16. If Simone is a mathematician, then she is smart.
19. If Van Gogh's *Starry Night* is beautiful, then it is worth big bucks.

Part B: Matching

1. I, AC, 7	10. V, DS, 4
4. V, MP, 1	13. V, CD, 5
7. V, HS, 3	

Part C: Identifying Forms

1. *Modus tollens* (valid)	13. Affirming the consequent (invalid)
4. Denying the antecedent (invalid)	16. Disjunctive syllogism (valid)
7. *Modus ponens* (valid)	19. Unnamed form
10. *Modus ponens* (valid)	

Part D: Constructing Arguments   These are left as exercises.

Part E: Argument Forms   These are left as exercises.

◈ *Chapter 3*
Exercise 3.1: Arguments and Nonarguments

1. Nonargument (explanation).
4. Argument. *Conclusion:* Waging war is always wrong.
7. Argument. *Conclusion:* Without us, light does not exist.
10. Nonargument (explanation).
13. Nonargument (report).
16. Nonargument (illustration).
19. Nonargument (conditional).

Exercise 3.2
Part A: Identifying Arguments

1. 1. The defendant is insane.
    So, 2. The defendant is not guilty.

4. Not an argument.

7. 1. Affirmative action involves giving a less qualified person the job.
    2. The most qualified person deserves the job.
    So, 3. Affirmative action is unjust.

10. Not an argument.

13. 1. The statement "God cannot be proved" may mean that God's existence cannot be proved beyond the shadow of a doubt, but it may also mean, and often does mean, that there is no valid evidence for the existence of God.
    2. These two meanings differ.
    So, 3. The statement "God cannot be proved" is fundamentally ambiguous.

16. 1. Empirical data are scientific.
    2. Only what can in principle be shown false is scientific.
    So, 3. Empirical data can in principle be shown false.

19. Not an argument.

Part B: Identifying Arguments

1. Not an argument.

4. 1. A man in a state of profound hypnosis can be made to remember events that have long vanished from his normal mind and that he is quite unable to recover by ordinary voluntary effort.
    So, 2. Our minds contain elements that are normally inaccessible to us.

7. 1. If each culture should be judged only by its own moral standards, then no culture's moral standards should be criticized.
    2. Some cultures permit slavery, cannibalism, and/or the oppression of women.
    So, 3. The moral standards of some cultures should be criticized. [from 2]
    So, 4. It is not the case that each culture should be judged only by its own moral standards.

10. Not an argument.

13. 1. Deductive reasoning cannot have certainty about its premises.
    2. Inductive reasoning cannot have certainty about its conclusions.
    So, 3. Absolute proof is something that the human being does not and cannot have.

16. 1. The civil disobedient withholds taxes or violates state laws knowing he is legally wrong, but believing he is morally right.
    2. M. L. King led his followers in violation of state laws he believed were contrary to the Federal Constitution.
    3. Supreme Court decisions generally upheld King's many actions.
    So, 4. M. L. King should not be considered a true civil disobedient.

19. Not an argument.

Part C: Argument Forms and Textbook Forms

1.　　1. H.
　　　So, 2. If M, then L.
　　　　3. M.
　　　So, 4. L.　　　　　　　2, 3, *modus ponens*

4.　　1. If P, then C.
　　　　2. If C, then F.
　　　So, 3. If P, then F.　　　1, 2, hypothetical syllogism
　　　　4. Not F.
　　　So, 5. Not P.　　　　　3, 4, *modus tollens*

7.　　1. If L, then C.
　　　　2. Not C.
　　　So, 3. Not L.　　　　　1, 2, *modus tollens*
　　　　5. Either L or U.
　　　So, 6. U.　　　　　　　3, 5, disjunctive syllogism

10.　　1. If S, then C.
　　　　2. If C, then A.
　　　So, 3. If S, then A.　　　1, 2, hypothetical syllogism
　　　　4. If A, then U.
　　　So, 5. If S, then U.　　　3, 4, hypothetical syllogism
　　　　6. If U, then W.
　　　So, 7. If S, then W.　　　5, 6, hypothetical syllogism

Exercise 3.3
Part A: Argument Diagrams

1. [1][Photography makes representational art obsolete] because [2][no one, not even the best artist, can be more accurate than a camera.]

4. While [1][there is much wickedness in the world,] [2][there is also much good.] For [3][if there is evil, then there must be good,] since [4][good and evil are relative, like big and small.] And no one will deny that [5][evil exists.]

7. [1][There is no better way to arouse the American citizen than to order him around or to tell him what to think.] Although [2][there are many people in this country who would like to organize us more thoroughly and tidy up the freedom we have by a little more control,] [3][we still reserve the personal right to plunge our own way into our own mistakes and discoveries, in art, philosophy, education, or politics. . . .]

10. Despite the fact that ¹[contraception is regarded as a blessing by most Americans,] ²[using contraceptives is immoral.] For ³[whatever is unnatural is immoral] since ⁴[God created and controls nature.] And ⁵[contraception is unnatural] because ⁶[it interferes with nature.]

13. ¹[There is no life after death.] For ²[what's real is what you can see, hear, or touch.] And ³[you cannot see, hear, or touch life after death.] Furthermore, ⁴[life after death is possible only if humans have souls.] But ⁵[the notion of a soul belongs to a prescientific and outmoded view of the world.] And hence, ⁶[the belief in souls belongs to the realm of superstition.]

16. ¹[For beginners, portrait painting is perhaps the most difficult branch of art to understand and enjoy *as painting*.] ²[If we happen to know, either from personal acquaintance or from photographs, what the subject of a portrait is actually like in physical appearance, we are inclined to think more about whether it is a good likeness than whether it is a good painting.] And ³[if it is a portrait of someone who lived long ago but is not in the history books, we may think that because the subject is of no interest to us the painting must also be without interest.]

19. ¹[Violence as a way of achieving racial justice is both impractical and immoral.] ²[It is impractical] because ³[it is a descending spiral ending in destruction for all.] ⁴[The old law of an eye for an eye leaves everybody blind.] ⁵[It is immoral] because ⁶[it seeks to humiliate the opponent rather than win his understanding;] ⁷[it seeks to annihilate rather than to convert.] ⁸[Violence is immoral] because ⁹[it thrives on hatred rather than love.] ¹⁰[It destroys community and makes brotherhood impossible.]

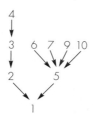

Part B: More Argument Diagrams

1. ¹[John and Robert Kennedy and Martin Luther King were, like them or not, this country's last true national leaders.] ²[None of John Kennedy's successor's in the White House has enjoyed the consensus he built,] and ³[every one of them ran into trouble, of his own making, while in office.] In the same way, [4][none of this country's national spokespeople since Robert Kennedy and Dr. King has had the attention and respect they enjoyed.]

4. For a variety of reasons, [1][private colleges are in trouble.] First, [2][private colleges have repeatedly increased tuition well beyond the rate of inflation.] And [3][any business that increases prices in such a fashion is likely to run into trouble.] Second, [4][many people are beginning to question the value of higher education] since [5][a college degree no longer guarantees an attractive salary.] Third, rightly or wrongly, [6][the American public believes that colleges have not practiced good financial management,] and hence [7][the public thinks that tuition dollars often subsidize inefficiency.]

7. [1][The Peloponnesian War deeply altered the future course of Greek history.] [2][By changing the movement of men, the geographical distribution of genes, values, and ideas, it affected later events in Rome, and through Rome, all Europe.] [. . .] [3][In turn, in the tightly wired world of today, . . . Europeans influence Mexicans and Japanese alike.] [4][Whatever trace of impact the Peloponnesian War left on the genetic structure, the ideas, and the values of today's Europeans is now exported by them to all parts of the world.] Thus [5][today's Mexicans and Japanese feel the distant, twice-removed impact of that war even though their ancestors, alive during its occurrence, did not.] In this way, [6][the events of the past, skipping as it were over generations and centuries, rise up to haunt and change us today.]

10. Not an argument. (*Note:* The passage is an explanation—it explains why the Belgae are the bravest of the Gauls.)

13. While [1][colleges and universities have come under heavy criticism in the last decade,] [2][they will undoubtedly remain a vital force in American social life for generations to come.] For one thing, although [3][both the public and the media seem to have a thirst for stories about people who've gotten rich or famous with only a high school degree,] the fact remains that [4][a college or university degree is the surest way to increase one's social and occupational status.] For another, [5][college grads as a group indicate higher levels of satisfaction with their lives than do those with lesser educational attainments.] Finally, [6][you show me a nation with a weak system of higher education and I'll show you a nation with little power.] And [7][Americans will never willingly accept a position of relative powerlessness among the nations of the world.]

16. Not an argument.

19. [1][The only proof capable of being given that an object is visible, is that people actually see it.] [2][The only proof that a sound is audible, is that people hear it;] and [3][so of the other sources of our experience.] In like manner, I apprehend, [4][the sole evidence it is possible to produce that anything is desirable, is that people do actually desire it.] Thus, [5][no reason can be given why the general happiness is desirable, except that each person . . . desires his own happiness.]

Part C: Diagrams and Argument Forms

1. [1][America must reform its sagging educational system assuming that Americans are unwilling to become a second-rate force in the world economy.] But I hope and trust that [2][Americans are unwilling to accept second-rate status in the international economic scene.] Accordingly, [3][America must reform its sagging educational system.]

4. [1][Either humans evolved from matter or humans have souls.] [2][Humans evolved from matter.] Hence, [3][humans do not have souls.] But [4][there is life after death only if humans have souls.] Therefore, [5][there is no life after death.]

7. [1][Either Boris drowned in the lake or he drowned in the ocean.] [2][But Boris has saltwater in his lungs.] And [3][if Boris has saltwater in his lungs, then he did not drown in the lake.] So, [4][Boris did not drown in the lake.] It follows that [5][Boris drowned in the ocean.]

10. [1][If affirmative action (AA) has better overall consequences than the alternatives, then AA is right.] And [2][if AA promotes social equality by countering unconscious bias among those who interview job candidates, then AA has better overall consequences than the alternatives.] It follows that [3][if AA promotes social equality by countering unconscious bias among those who interview job candidates, then AA is right.] Furthermore, [4][AA does promote social equality by countering unconscious bias among interviewers.] Therefore, [5][AA is right.] Moreover, [6][either we should endorse untrammeled networking or we should endorse AA.] But [7][we should not endorse untrammeled networking if it has the effect (whether intended or not) of excluding minorities.]

And [8][untrammeled networking does have this effect.] So, [9][we should not endorse untrammeled networking.] Hence, [10][we should endorse AA.] Once again, then, we arrive at the conclusion that [11][AA is right.]

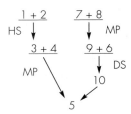

Exercise 3.4: Elaborated Textbook Forms

1.   1. If C, then W.
      [2. Not W.]
      So, 3. Not C.   *modus tollens*

4.   1. If P, then K.
      2. If K, then S.
      So, [3. If P, then S.]   1, 2, hypothetical syllogism
      [4. Not S.]
      So, 5. Not P.   3, 4, *modus tollens*

7.   1. If L, then M.
      [2. L.]
      So, 3. M.   *modus ponens*

10.   1. If J, then W.
      2. V.
      [3. If V, then not W.]
      So, [4. Not W.]   2, 3, *modus ponens*
      So, 5. Not J.   1, 4, *modus tollens*

13.   1. Either P or N.
      [2. Not P.]
      So, 3. N.   disjunctive syllogism

16.   [1. S.]
      2. If S, then T.
      3. If T, then P.
      So, [4. If S, then P.]   2, 3, hypothetical syllogism
      So, 5. P.   1, 4, *modus ponens*

19.   1. If K, then E.
      2. If E, then W.
      So, [3. If K, then W.]   1, 2, hypothetical syllogism
      [4. K.]
      So, 5. W.   3, 4, *modus ponens*

◆ Chapter 4

Exercise 4.1: Cognitive Meaning and Emotive Force

1.   1. Terrorism in the Middle East is one of the greatest threats to world peace today.
      So, 2. We should kill the leaders of each of the main terrorist groups.

4.   1. Playing the lottery involves paying a sum of money with a very low probability of receiving a larger sum in return.
      So, 2. There is nothing wrong with playing the lottery.

7.   1. The work of a garbage collector is of great importance.
2. The pay is good and the hours are reasonable.
So, 3. Your reluctance to take this job is beyond comprehension.

10.   1. If you're against genetic engineering, you're against something recently made possible by science.
So, 2. You should accept the fact that genetic engineering is here to stay.

13.   1. There is a conflict between criminals and those who keep the law.
2. Politicians who promote gun control are aiding criminals.
3. Gun control will not take guns away from criminals.
So, 4. Gun control is misguided.

16.   1. The world is full of cruelty, poverty, starvation, and debilitating illness.
2. Some people believe that a loving God controls the world.
So, 3. People believe what they want to believe regardless of the facts.

19.   1. She is selfish and superficial.
So, 2. You should not marry her.

Exercise 4.2
Part A: Types of Definitions
1. D
4. E
7. C
10. E or F
13. F

Part B: Lexical Definitions
1. Unnecessarily negative.
4. Unsuitable attribute. The conventional meaning is eight-sided figure.
7. Too narrow: leaves out triangles having sides that are unequal in length.
10. Figurative.
13. Too narrow: leaves out lesbians.
16. Unsuitable attribute. The conventional meaning is: having far more material possessions than most people.
19. Figurative.

Part C: More Lexical Definitions
1. Circular.
4. Figurative.
7. OK.
10. Unsuitable attribute. The conventional meaning is: having a round shape.
13. Too narrow: leaves out lizards, turtles, crocodiles, and so on.

Part D: Precising Definitions
1. Too narrow: leaves out inductively sound arguments with false conclusions.
4. Ambiguous: The premises of valid arguments also "support" their conclusions.
7. Ambiguous: The premises of strong arguments also "lead to" their conclusions.
10. Too narrow: leaves out weak arguments in which the premises make the negation of the conclusion *just as likely* as the conclusion.

Part E: Theoretical Definitions   These are left as exercises.

Exercise 4.3
Part A: Equivocation
1. The equivocation is on "nothing." In the first premise, "nothing" means "no job at all," while in the second premise it means something like "no end humans seek."

4. The equivocation is on "faith." Initially, it means "trust in God," but then later it means something like "a willingness to act on the basis of what is probable but not certain."
7. The equivocation is on "miracles." Initially, it means "wonders of science" and then later it means "divine interventions in the natural order."
10. The equivocation is on "nothing." Boiled down, the argument looks like this: When you choose not to exist, you choose nothing. But it makes no sense to prefer nothing to something. So, it makes no sense to prefer not to exist over being unhappy. In premise (1), "nothing" means an end to existence. In premise (2), "nothing" means nothing *whatsoever,* that is, no entity, state of mind, situation, and so on.

Part B: Merely Verbal Disputes and Persuasive Definitions

1. Merely verbal dispute. For Mr. X, "homework" means "any assigned work for class." But for Ms. Y, "homework" means something like "assigned work for class that one doesn't enjoy doing."
4. Persuasive definition. Unsuitable attribute: A more neutral (or less biased) description of the goals or values of the Republican party is needed for a rational evaluation of the party as a whole.
7. Persuasive definition. Unsuitable attribute: For the purpose of a rational discussion of the existence of God, the definition of "wrong" is clearly slanted in favor of theists.
10. Merely verbal dispute. The scare quotes are the key. Ms. Y is saying that polygamy is *considered* right (i.e., regarded as morally permissible) by the members of some societies. Mr. X is making the entirely different claim that polygamy is not right, that is, not morally permissible.
13. Merely verbal dispute. For Ms. Y, "artist" means a person who creates objects having beautiful form. For Mr. X, the forms must *depict* something.

Part C: Argument Diagrams, Equivocation, and Persuasive Definitions

1. [superscript 1][Every free action is prompted by a motive that belongs to the agent (i.e., the person who performs the action).] So, [superscript 2][every free act is pursued in an attempt to satisfy one of the agent's own motives.] But, [superscript 3][by definition, a "self-serving act" is one pursued in an attempt to satisfy one's own motives.] Hence, [superscript 4][every free act is self-serving.]

The definition of "self-serving act" is persuasive. A self-serving act is not merely one that accords with one's own motives; a self-serving act aims at selfish ends.

4. [superscript 1][There ought to be a law against psychiatry,] for [superscript 2]["psychiatrist" means person who makes a living by charging money for talking with deeply troubled people.] And [superscript 3][it is wrong to exploit deeply troubled people.]

The definition of "psychiatrist" is persuasive. Psychiatrists do not merely talk with their patients; psychiatrists treat their patients.

7. [superscript 1][Any fetus of human parents is itself human.] And [superscript 2][if any fetus of human parents is itself human, then abortion is wrong if human life is sacred.] Furthermore, since [superscript 3][being human consists in having faculties higher than those of other animals (such as the capacity to choose between good and evil),] [superscript 4][human life is sacred.] It follows that [superscript 5][abortion is wrong.]

Equivocation on "human": In premise (1) "human" means biologically human, that is, an organism with genes of the type associated with homo sapiens. But in step (4), "human" means animal with higher faculties. (Fetuses presumably do not have such higher faculties.)

◆ Chapter 5

Exercise 5.1: Categorical Statements

Note: The answers are given in the following order:

    (a) standard form (included if the original statement is not in standard form)
    (b) statement form
    (c) subject term
    (d) predicate term.

1. Universal negative, diamonds, emeralds

4. Some persons are nerds. Particular affirmative, persons, nerds

7. No criminals are saints. Universal negative, criminals, saints

10. Particular affirmative, morally virtuous human beings, atheists

13. Some animals that can fly are not birds. Particular negative, animals that can fly, birds

16. All adult male humans who are married are husbands. Universal affirmative, adult male humans who are married, husbands

19. No people who are unlucky are happy people. Universal negative, people who are unlucky, happy people

22. All lizards are reptiles. Universal affirmative, lizards, reptiles

25. All birds are feathered things. Universal affirmative, birds, feathered things

28. Some paintings are not masterpieces. Particular negative, paintings, masterpieces

31. Some mountains are beautiful things. Particular affirmative, mountains, beautiful things

34. Some trees are ugly things. Particular affirmative, trees, ugly things

37. Some animals are vicious things. Particular affirmative, animals, vicious things

40. All female siblings are sisters. Universal affirmative, female siblings, sisters

Exercise 5.2: Venn Diagrams

1. All Athenians are Greeks.
    Some humans are not Athenians.
    So, some humans are not Greeks.

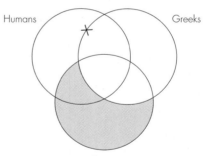

INVALID

4. All liars are self-deceived persons.
    All liars are wicked persons.
    So, all wicked persons are
      self-deceived persons.

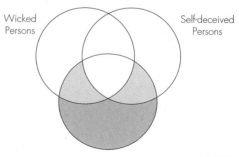

INVALID

7. No human beings are omniscient beings.
   Some divine beings are human beings.
   So, some divine beings are not
      omniscient beings.

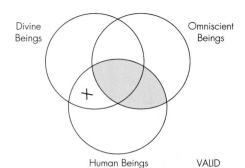

10. All brain events are physical events.
    No mental events are physical events.
    So, no mental events are brain events.

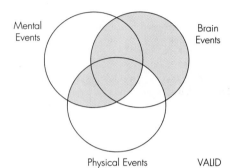

13. All similarity statements are metaphorical
       statements.
    All statements are similarity statements.
    So, all statements are metaphorical
       statements.

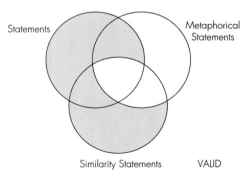

16. No acts foreknown by God are free acts.
    Some acts are acts foreknown by God.
    So, some acts are not free acts.

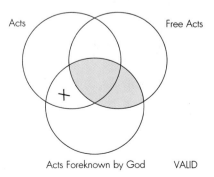

19. All unhappy persons are persons who have inner conflicts.
    Some successful comedians are unhappy persons.
    So, some successful comedians are persons who have inner conflicts.

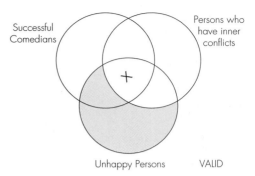

Successful Comedians

Persons who have inner conflicts

Unhappy Persons   VALID

Exercise 5.3
Part A: Matching   These are left as exercises.

Part B: Contraditories, Contraries, and Subcontraries

1. Contradictories	**7.** Subcontraries
4. Contraries	**10.** Contraries

Part C: Valid or Invalid?

1. Valid according to Aristotelians; not valid according to modern logicians.
4. Valid according to Aristotelians; not valid according to modern logicians.
7. Valid according to Aristotelians; not valid according to modern logicians.
10. Valid according to Aristotelians and modern logicians.
13. Not valid according to Aristotelians; not valid according to modern logicians.
16. Valid according to Aristotelians and modern logicians.
19. Valid according to Aristotelians; not valid according to modern logicians.

Part D: Converse, Obverse, and Contrapositive

1. *Converse:* No reprobates are saints. Conversion is valid for **E** statements.
   Obverse: All saints are nonreprobates. Obversion is valid for **E** statements.
   Contrapositive: No nonreprobates are nonsaints. Contraposition is not in general valid for **E** statements.

4. *Converse:* Some grenades are not bombs. Conversion is not in general valid for **O** statements.
   Obverse: Some bombs are nongrenades. Obversion is valid for **O** statements.
   Contrapositive: Some nongrenades are not nonbombs. Contraposition is in general valid for **O** statements.

7. *Converse:* All copies are forgeries. Conversion is not in general valid for **A** statements.
   Obverse: No forgeries are noncopies. Obversion is valid for **A** statements.
   Contrapositive: All noncopies are nonforgeries. Contraposition is valid for **A** statements.

10. *Converse:* Some nonbelievers are theologians. Conversion is valid for **I** statements.
   Obverse: Some theologians are not believers. Obversion is valid for **I** statements.
   Contrapositive: Some believers are nontheologians. Contraposition is not in general valid for **I** statements.

13. *Converse:* All nonmagicians are scientists. Conversion is not in general valid for **A** statements.
   Obverse: No scientists are magicians. Obversion is valid for **A** statements.
   Contrapositive: All magicians are nonscientists. Contraposition is valid for **A** statements.

Exercise 5.4
Part A: Constructing Valid Syllogisms   These are left as exercises.

Part B: Forms
1. **EEE**. Fourth figure. Violates Rule 4: invalid.
4. **AAA**. Second figure. Violates Rule 2: invalid.
7. **AOO**. Second figure. Satisfies all five rules: valid.
10. **OOO**. Second figure. Violates Rule 4: invalid.
13. **OAO**. First figure. Violates Rule 2: invalid
16. **AAI**. First figure. Violates Rule 5: invalid.
19. **III**. Third figure. Violates Rule 2: invalid.

Part C: Valid or Invalid?
1. Some M are P. No S are M. So, some S are not P. *Mood:* **IEO**. First figure. The syllogism violates Rule 3: invalid.
4. All P are M. No S are M. So, no S are P. *Mood:* **AEE**. Second figure. There is an equivocation on the word "animals." In the first premise, "animals" means "nonhuman animals." In the second premise, "animals" means (roughly) "living organism capable of moving about." The syllogism thus violates Rule 1: invalid.
7. All M are P. All S are M. So, some S are P. *Mood:* **AAI**. First figure. Violates Rule 5: invalid.
10. Some M are not P. All S are M. So, some S are not P. *Mood:* **OAO**. First figure. The syllogism violates Rule 2: invalid.

◈ Chapter 6

Exercise 6.1: Fallacies Involving Irrelevant Premises
1. Argument against the person (or *ad hominem* fallacy). "Bonehead" is an abusive term.
4. Appeal to the people (or *ad populum* fallacy). "Hot new thinkers" and "new wave" indicate an appeal to one's desire to be accepted or valued by others.
7. Straw man fallacy. It is a misrepresentation to say that proponents of legalized euthanasia seek the power to kill anyone who has a serious illness. For example, many serious illnesses are not terminal, and some are not especially painful.
10. Appeal to pity (or *ad misericordiam* fallacy). The length of time spent on the paper and the potential probation may arouse pity, but they are not relevant to the conclusion.
13. Appeal to force (or *ad baculum* fallacy). A threat is issued.
16. Argument against the person (or *ad hominem* fallacy). Dr. Herzheimer is attacked as immature and cold-hearted.
19. Argument against the person (or *ad hominem* fallacy). The claim is that Mr. Johnson's argument is worthless because he stands to gain if we accept his conclusion.
22. Appeal to pity (or *ad misericordiam* fallacy). The needs of the children and spouse may arouse the judge's pity, but they are irrelevant to the conclusion.
25. Appeal to force (or *ad baculum* fallacy). Joe is threatened with the loss of a promotion.
28. Not a fallacy.

Exercise 6.2: Fallacies Involving Insufficient Evidence
1. Appeal to unreliable authority (or *ad verecundiam* fallacy). Why suppose that the president of GM is an authority on the religious and ethical state of the country?
4. Appeal to unreliable authority (or *ad verecundiam* fallacy). One may reasonably doubt whether the tobacco companies are reliable authorities on the effects of smoking.
7. Appeal to unreliable authority (or *ad verecundiam* fallacy). Psychologists study human behavior. Their expertise as psychologists does not extend to theological matters.
10. False cause fallacy. The assumption is that since the rock music phenomenon preceded the failure in Vietnam, the rock music phenomenon caused the failure.
13. Appeal to ignorance (or *ad ignorantiam* fallacy). The failure to prove Goldbach's Conjecture does not prove it false.

16. Appeal to ignorance (or *ad ignorantiam* fallacy). The failure to prove that God exists does not show that there is no God.

19. Appeal to unreliable authority (or *ad verecundiam* fallacy). Einstein was an authority in physics, but this does not guarantee that he was an authority about moral issues.

22. False cause fallacy. A chain of causes is described, but there is insufficient evidence that one event in the chain will lead to the next. This variety of false cause fallacy is sometimes called the slippery slope fallacy.

25. False cause fallacy. Mere coincidence is taken as an indication of causation.

28. Appeal to unreliable authority (or *ad verecundiam* fallacy). A sociology professor may be an authority on marital arrangements across cultures, but such expertise does not necessarily translate into expertise about the moral qualities (e.g., just or unjust?) of such arrangements.

Exercise 6.3
Part A: Fallacies Involving Ambiguity and Fallacies Involving Unwarranted Premises

1. Amphiboly. Presumably, the leader was not advocating nudity, but forbidding the wearing of distinctive clothing (e.g., a clerical collar).

4. Composition. Even if every sentence is well written, the book as a whole may not be. For example, perhaps it is poorly organized.

7. False dilemma. Overlooks the possibility that men and women are equal.

10. Begging the question (or *petitio principii*). The premise is just another way of stating the conclusion.

13. Division. From the fact that Germans *as a group* are mostly Lutheran, we cannot rightly conclude that any individual German is mostly Lutheran.

16. False dilemma. The premise, "Either I was hallucinating or he levitated," ignores the possibility that the observer was tricked.

19. Not a fallacy.

22. Equivocation. "Reason to believe" means "something to gain by believing" in premise 2; but in premise 3, "reason to believe" means "evidence in favor of the belief."

25. Division. From the fact that immigrants as a group come from every country in the world, we cannot rightly conclude that any individual immigrant comes from every country in the world.

28. Amphiboly. "That which can not-be at some time is not." Does this mean that those things that can fail to exist will all fail to exist at the same time (call it time "T")? Or does it mean that each thing that can fail to exist will fail to exist at some time or other? The inference drawn assumes the former interpretation, but the latter interpretation makes the first premise much more plausible.

Part B: Argument Diagrams and Multiple Fallacies

1. [1][Christians teach the doctrine of the Triune God, namely, that "One God plus one God plus one God equals one God."] But [2][this doctrine is false,] for [3][it is obviously a mathematical impossibility] and [4][only fools believe mathematical impossibilities.]

The move from 3 and 4 to 2 involves two fallacies. First, to use 3 to support 2 is to commit a straw man fallacy, for "it" refers to the misrepresentation of the doctrine of the Trinity given in statement 1. (The doctrine of the Trinity is the view that there is one God but three divine persons, Father, Son, and Holy Spirit. While this doctrine may be somewhat obscure, it is not represented fairly above.) Second, to use 4 to support 2 is to commit an *ad hominem* fallacy since "fools" is a term of abuse.

4. [1][When it comes to criminal punishment, one must favor either rehabilitation or deterrence.] [2][The rehabilitationists think criminals are sick and need treatment.] [3][The deterrence crowd wants harsh punishments that will put a stop to crime.] Since [4][it is just silly to suppose that every shoplifter or car thief is mentally ill,] [5][the rehabilitationists are mistaken.] Hence, [6][the deterrence view is correct.] And by the way, here's another way to see the same point: [7][rehabilitationists hold that even the most hardened criminals can be cured in a few sessions with a psychotherapist.] But [8][hardened criminals cannot be cured so easily!] Once again, then, we see that [9][rehabilitationists are mistaken.]

The move from 2 and 4 to 5 involves an *ad hominem* fallacy ("it is just silly"). The move from 7 and 8 to 5 in involves a straw man fallacy. (Rehabilitationists do not hold that the most hardened criminals can be cured quickly and easily.) The move from 5 and 1 to 6 involves a false dilemma. For example, retributivists think that the main purpose of criminal punishment is neither rehabilitation nor deterrence—the main purpose is simply to give criminals the punishment they deserve.

7. [1][When you get down to it, philosophers are just logic choppers who sit around trying to put reality into little boxes made of words.] So, [2][the philosophical arguments against time travel prove nothing.] Hence, [3][time travel is possible.] Anyway, I know [4][it's possible] because [5][it can happen.] And besides, [6][just about everyone *but* philosophers thinks that time travel is possible,] so once again, [7][time travel probably is possible.]

The move from 1 to 2 is an *ad hominem* fallacy ("logic choppers" is derogatory). The move from 2 to 3 is an *ad ignorantiam* fallacy. The move from 5 to 3 begs the question. And the move from 6 to 3 is an *ad populum* fallacy (appealing to our desire to be accepted by the majority).

10. [1][Logic varies as languages vary.] For [2][logic is based on grammar.] [3][My chemistry professor said so.] And [4][any intelligent person will agree that different languages have different grammars.] But [5][if logic varies as languages vary, then logic is relative to cultures.] Consequently, [6][logic is relative to cultures.]

The move from 3 to 2 involves an *ad verecundiam* fallacy. (Why should we suppose that a chemistry prof is an authority on the relation between logic and grammar?) The move from 2 and 4 to 1 is an *ad populum* fallacy, appealing to one's desire to be regarded as intelligent.

◆ *Chapter 7*

Exercise 7.1
Part A: Well-Formed Formulas

1. Not a WFF.   7. WFF.
4. Not a WFF.   10. WFF.

Part B: Symbolizing

1. C ∨ R   13. ∼S → (J ∨ T)
4. M → N   16. T → K
7. ∼R   19. M • (J • S)
10. ∼(B ∨ S)

Part C: More Symbolizing

1. S → R   7. B → (F → ∼P)
4. (W ∨ F) • ∼(W • F)   10. (B → F) → ∼B

Part D: Schemes of Abbreviation   These are left as exercises.

Exercise 7.2
Part A: Determining Truth Value

1. F   16. T
4. F   19. F
7. T   22. T
10. T   25. T
13. T

Part B: More Determining Truth Value

1. T   10. T
4. T   13. T
7. T

Exercise 7.3
Part A: Truth Tables

1.

A	B	A ∨ B,	∼A	∴ B	
T	T	T	F	T	
T	F	T	F	F	
F	T	T	T	T	
F	F	F	T	F	valid

4.

P	R	∼P → ∼R	∴ ∼(P → R)	
T	T	T	F	
T	F	T	T	
F	T	F	F	
F	F	T	F	invalid

7.

A B	A • B ∴ B
T T	T T
T F	F F
F T	F T
F F	F F valid

10.

F G	~F • ~G ∴ ~F ↔ ~G
T T	F T
T F	F F
F T	F F
F F	T T valid

13.

D E C	D ↔ (E ∨ C),	~D	∴ ~C
T T T	T	F	F
T T F	T	F	T
T F T	T	F	F
T F F	F	F	T
F T T	F	T	F
F T F	F	T	T
F F T	F	T	F
F F F	T	T	T valid

16.

A B C	A → B,	B → C	∴ A → C
T T T	T	T	T
T T F	T	F	F
T F T	F	T	T
T F F	F	T	F
F T T	T	T	T
F T F	T	F	T
F F T	T	T	T
F F F	T	T	T valid

19.

A B C	A ∨ B,	A → C,	B → C	∴ C
T T T	T	T	T	T
T T F	T	F	F	F
T F T	T	T	T	T
T F F	T	F	T	F
F T T	T	T	T	T
F T F	T	T	F	F
F F T	F	T	T	T
F F F	F	T	T	F valid

Part B: More Truth Tables

1.

A B	A • ~B ∴ ~(A → B)
T T	F F
T F	T T
F T	F F
F F	F F valid

4.

H	K	~(H · K)	∴ ~H · ~K	
T	T	F	F	
T	F	T	F	
F	T	T	F	
F	F	T	T	invalid

7.

A	B	A	∴ (A ∨ B) · ~(A · B)	
T	T	T	F	
T	F	T	T	
F	T	F	T	
F	F	F	F	invalid

10.

H	J	~(H ↔ J)	∴ ~H ↔ ~J	
T	T	F	T	
T	F	T	F	
F	T	T	F	
F	F	F	T	invalid

Part C: English Arguments

1.

A	E	A → ~E,	E	∴ ~A	
T	T	F	T	F	
T	F	T	F	F	
F	T	T	T	T	
F	F	T	F	T	valid

4.

A	W	~A ∨ W	∴ W → A	
T	T	T	T	
T	F	F	T	
F	T	T	F	
F	F	T	T	invalid

7.

V	L	P	V ↔ L,	L → P,	P → ~V	∴ ~L	
T	T	T	T	T	F	F	
T	T	F	T	F	T	F	
T	F	T	F	T	F	T	
T	F	F	F	T	T	T	
F	T	T	F	T	T	F	
F	T	F	F	F	T	F	
F	F	T	T	T	T	T	
F	F	F	T	T	T	T	valid

Exercise 7.4
Part A: Abbreviated Truth Tables

1. $\underline{\text{A} \quad \text{B} \quad \text{C} \mid \text{A} \rightarrow (\text{B} \rightarrow \text{C}) \;\therefore\; \text{B} \rightarrow \text{C}}$
   F T F T F

4. $\underline{\text{J} \quad \text{K} \mid \text{J} \rightarrow \sim\text{K} \;\therefore\; \sim(\text{J} \leftrightarrow \text{K})}$
   F F T F

7. $\underline{\text{S} \quad \text{H} \quad \text{U} \mid \sim(\text{S} \cdot \text{H}), (\sim\text{S} \cdot \sim\text{H}) \rightarrow \sim\text{U} \;\therefore\; \sim\text{U}}$
   F T T T T F

10. $\underline{\text{P} \quad \text{Q} \quad \text{R} \mid (\text{P} \rightarrow \sim\text{Q}) \leftrightarrow \sim\text{R}, \text{R} \;\therefore\; \sim\text{P}}$
    T T T T T F

13. $\underline{\text{Z} \quad \text{Y} \quad \text{W} \mid (\text{Z} \cdot \text{Y}) \rightarrow \text{W} \;\therefore\; \text{Z} \rightarrow (\text{Y} \cdot \text{W})}$
    T F T T F

16. $\underline{\text{P} \quad \text{Q} \quad \text{R} \quad \text{S} \mid \text{P} \rightarrow \text{Q}, \text{P} \rightarrow \text{R}, \text{Q} \leftrightarrow \text{R}, \text{S}, \text{S} \rightarrow \text{R} \;\therefore\; \text{P} \cdot \text{Q}}$
    F T T T T T T T T F

19. $\underline{\text{Q} \quad \text{S} \quad \text{T} \quad \text{U} \quad \text{W} \mid \sim(\text{Q} \vee \text{S}), \sim\text{T} \vee \text{S}, (\text{U} \cdot \text{W}) \rightarrow \text{Q} \;\therefore\; (\sim\text{T} \cdot \sim\text{U}) \cdot \text{W}}$
    F F F F F T T T F

Part B: More Abbreviated Truth Tables

1. $\underline{\text{A} \quad \text{B} \quad \text{C} \quad \text{D} \mid \sim(\text{A} \cdot \text{B}), \sim\text{A} \rightarrow \text{C}, \sim\text{B} \rightarrow \text{D} \;\therefore\; \text{C} \cdot \text{D}}$
   F T T F T T T F

4. $\underline{\text{V} \quad \text{X} \quad \text{Y} \mid \sim(\text{V} \cdot \text{X}) \rightarrow \sim\text{Y} \;\therefore\; \sim[(\text{V} \cdot \text{X}) \rightarrow \text{Y}]}$
   T F F T F

7. $\underline{\text{Z} \quad \text{A} \quad \text{B} \quad \text{C} \mid \sim(\text{Z} \rightarrow \text{A}), \text{Z} \rightarrow \text{B}, \sim\text{A} \rightarrow \text{C} \;\therefore\; \text{C} \cdot \sim\text{B}}$
   T F T T T T T F

10. $\underline{\text{H} \quad \text{S} \quad \text{Z} \quad \text{P} \mid \text{H} \vee \sim\text{S}, \text{H} \rightarrow \text{Z}, \sim\text{S} \rightarrow \text{P} \;\therefore\; \text{P} \leftrightarrow \text{Z}}$
    F F F T T T T F

Part C: Valid or Invalid?

1. $\underline{\text{A} \quad \text{B} \mid \sim\text{A} \vee \text{B} \;\therefore\; \text{A} \rightarrow \text{B}}$
   T F (T/F) F valid

4. $\underline{\text{A} \quad \text{B} \quad \text{C} \mid \text{A} \vee (\text{B} \cdot \text{C}) \;\therefore\; (\text{A} \cdot \text{B}) \vee (\text{A} \cdot \text{C})}$
   F T T T F invalid

Part D: English Arguments

1. $\begin{array}{cc|ccc} \text{W} & \text{B} & \text{W} \rightarrow \text{B} & \therefore & \sim\text{W} \rightarrow \sim\text{B} \\ \hline \text{F} & \text{T} & \text{T} & & \text{F} \end{array}$ invalid

4. $\begin{array}{ccc|ccc} \text{G} & \text{H} & \text{I} & (\text{G} \cdot \text{H}) \rightarrow \text{I}, & \text{H} \cdot \sim\text{G} & \therefore & \sim\text{I} \\ \hline \text{F} & \text{T} & \text{T} & \text{T} & \text{T} & & \text{F} \end{array}$ invalid

7. $\begin{array}{ccc|ccc} \text{S} & \text{P} & \text{R} & \text{S} \rightarrow (\text{P} \rightarrow \text{R}), & \sim(\text{S} \vee \text{P}) & \therefore & \sim\text{R} \\ \hline \text{F} & \text{F} & \text{T} & \text{T} & \text{T} & & \text{F} \end{array}$ invalid

Exercise 7.5

Part A: Tautologies, Contradictions, and Contingent Statements

1. | A | B | $\sim\text{A} \rightarrow (\text{A} \rightarrow \text{B})$ |
    |---|---|---|
    | T | T | T |
    | T | F | T |
    | F | T | T |
    | F | F | T |

    tautology

4. | B | A | $\text{B} \rightarrow (\text{A} \rightarrow \text{B})$ |
    |---|---|---|
    | T | T | T |
    | T | F | T |
    | F | T | T |
    | F | F | T |

    tautology

7. | P | Q | $\text{P} \rightarrow (\text{P} \rightarrow \text{Q})$ |
    |---|---|---|
    | T | T | T |
    | T | F | F |
    | F | T | T |
    | F | F | T |

    contingent statement

10. | R | S | $(\text{R} \cdot \sim\text{R}) \rightarrow \text{S}$ |
    |---|---|---|
    | T | T | T |
    | T | F | T |
    | F | T | T |
    | F | F | T |

    tautology

Part B: Logical Equivalence

1. | A | B | $\sim(\text{A} \cdot \text{B}) \leftrightarrow (\sim\text{A} \vee \sim\text{B})$ |
    |---|---|---|
    | T | T | T |
    | T | F | T |
    | F | T | T |
    | F | F | T |

    equivalent

Part C: English Arguments

1.

G	W	G ∴ W → W	
T	T	T	T
T	F	T	T
F	T	F	T
F	F	F	T

valid

4.

P	E	P ↔ ~P ∴ E	
T	T	F	T
T	F	F	F
F	T	F	T
F	F	F	F

valid

◆ Chapter 8

Exercise 8.1
Part A: Annotating

1.
   1. F → G
   2. G → H   ∴ F → H
   3. F → H   1, 2, HS

4.
   1. H ∨ ~C
   2. H → ~B
   3. ~C → D
   4. (~B ∨ D) → (K • J)   ∴ J
   5. ~B ∨ D   1, 2, 3, CD
   6. K • J   4, 5, MP
   7. J   6, Simp

7.
   1. ~(P • Q) ∨ R
   2. ~R
   3. E → (P • Q)
   4. (~E • ~R) → (A • B)   ∴ B ∨ (F • G)
   5. ~(P • Q)   1, 2, DS
   6. ~E   3, 5, MT
   7. ~E • ~R   2, 6, Conj
   8. A • B   4, 7, MP
   9. B   8, Simp
   10. B ∨ (F • G)   9, Add

10.
   1. W → (X ∨ ~Y)
   2. ~~Y • W   ∴ X ∨ ~Z
   3. W   2, Simp
   4. X ∨ ~Y   1, 3, MP
   5. ~~Y   2, Simp
   6. X   4, 5, DS
   7. X ∨ ~Z   6, Add

Part B: Correct or Incorrect?

1. MT
4. CD
7. DS

10. Incorrect. The main connective of the premise is the arrow rather than the dot, and so simplification cannot be applied.

13. Incorrect. To apply MT, we need both a conditional and the negation of its consequent as premises. And the negation of ~U is ~~U rather than U.

16. Incorrect. This is not CD. To have CD, the disjuncts of the disjunctive premise must be antecedents of the conditional premises.

19. Incorrect. To apply DS, we need a disjunctive premise and the negation of one its disjuncts, but the first premise here is a conditional rather than a disjunction.

Part C: Proofs

1.
1. $H \rightarrow \sim B$
2. $D \rightarrow B$
3. H $\therefore \sim D$
4. $\sim B$ 1, 3, MP
5. $\sim D$ 2, 4, MT

4.
1. $\sim A \rightarrow F$
2. $A \rightarrow D$
3. $\sim D$
4. $F \rightarrow S$ $\therefore S \vee X$
5. $\sim A$ 2, 3, MT
6. F 1, 5, MP
7. S 4, 6, MP
8. $S \vee X$ 7, Add

7.
1. $\sim(S \vee R)$
2. $B \rightarrow (S \vee R)$
3. $B \vee P$
4. $\sim Q \vee B$ $\therefore P \cdot \sim Q$
5. $\sim B$ 1, 2, MT
6. P 3, 5, DS
7. $\sim Q$ 4, 5, DS
8. $P \cdot \sim Q$ 6, 7, Conj

10.
1. $(B \cdot A) \rightarrow C$
2. $\sim D \rightarrow (B \cdot A)$
3. $\sim C$ $\therefore \sim\sim D$
4. $\sim(B \cdot A)$ 1, 3, MT
5. $\sim\sim D$ 2, 4, MT

13.
1. $(T \rightarrow C) \rightarrow \sim F$
2. $S \rightarrow C$
3. $T \rightarrow S$
4. $F \vee \sim P$ $\therefore \sim P$
5. $T \rightarrow C$ 2, 3, HS
6. $\sim F$ 1, 5, MP
7. $\sim P$ 4, 6, DS

16.
1. $(E \vee F) \rightarrow \sim G$
2. $\sim H$
3. $H \vee K$
4. $(K \vee L) \rightarrow E$ $\therefore \sim G$
5. K 2, 3, DS
6. $K \vee L$ 5, Add
7. E 4, 6, MP
8. $E \vee F$ 7, Add
9. $\sim G$ 1, 8, MP

19. 1. ~~B
    2. ~C → ~B
    3. (~~C ∨ T) → P   ∴ P
    4. ~~C   1, 2, MT
    5. ~~C ∨ T   4, Add
    6. P   3, 5, MP

Part D: More Proofs

1. 1. P → Q
   2. R → ~S
   3. P ∨ R
   4. (Q ∨ ~S) → (~T ∨ ~W)
   5. ~~T   ∴ ~W
   6. Q ∨ ~S   1, 2, 3, CD
   7. ~T ∨ ~W   4, 6, MP
   8. ~W   5, 7, DS

4. 1. ~(R ∨ S)
   2. ~(T • V) → (R ∨ S)
   3. ~~(T • V) → W   ∴ W ∨ ~R
   4. ~~(T • V)   1, 2, MT
   5. W   3, 4, MP
   6. W ∨ ~R   5, Add

7. 1. ~F → J
   2. ~F ∨ ~G
   3. ~G → ~H
   4. (J ∨ ~H) → ~K
   5. ~L → K   ∴ ~~L
   6. J ∨ ~H   1, 2, 3, CD
   7. ~K   4, 6, MP
   8. ~~L   5, 7, MT

10. 1. ~A • ~C
    2. ~C → D
    3. (D • ~A) → (E → ~H)
    4. E • (~F → H)   ∴ ~~F
    5. ~C   1, Simp
    6. D   2, 5, MP
    7. ~A   1, Simp
    8. D • ~A   6, 7, Conj
    9. E → ~H   3, 8, MP
    10. E   4, Simp
    11. ~H   9, 10, MP
    12. ~F → H   4, Simp
    13. ~~F   11, 12 MT

Part E: English Arguments

1. 1. S
   2. S → U
   3. U → A
   4. A → K   ∴ K
   5. S → A   2, 3, HS
   6. S → K   5, 4, HS
   7. K   1, 6, MP

4. 1. E
   2. E → (D → C)

3. $(F \lor V) \to D$
4. $S \to F$
5. $A \cdot S$ $\therefore C$
6. S 5, Simp
7. F 4, 6, MP
8. $F \lor V$ 7, Add
9. D 3, 8, MP
10. $D \to C$ 1, 2, MP
11. C 9, 10, MP

7. 1. P
2. $P \to A$
3. $A \to (E \lor F)$
4. $\sim E$ $\therefore F$
5. $P \to (E \lor F)$ 2, 3, HS
6. $E \lor F$ 1, 5, MP
7. F 4, 6, DS

Exercise 8.2
Part A: Annotating

1. 1. $\sim\sim A \to B$ $\therefore A \to B$
2. $A \to B$ 1, DN

4. 1. $\sim(E \lor D)$ $\therefore \sim D$
2. $\sim E \cdot \sim D$ 1, DeM
3. $\sim D$ 2, Simp

7. 1. $[(P \to Q) \to R] \cdot (\sim Q \to \sim P)$ $\therefore \sim\sim R$
2. $\sim Q \to \sim P$ 1, Simp
3. $P \to Q$ 2, Cont
4. $(P \to Q) \to R$ 1, Simp
5. R 3, 4, MP
6. $\sim\sim R$ 5, DN

10. 1. $[\sim O \to (\sim M \to \sim N)] \cdot \sim(N \to M)$ $\therefore O$
2. $\sim O \to (\sim M \to \sim N)$ 1, Simp
3. $\sim(N \to M)$ 1, Simp
4. $\sim(\sim M \to \sim N)$ 3, Cont
5. $\sim\sim O$ 2, 4, MT
6. O 5, DN

Part B: Correct or Incorrect?

1. Correct (DeM)
4. Correct (DeM)
7. Incorrect use of DeM. Correct sequence: from $\sim S \lor T$ to $\sim S \lor \sim\sim T$ by DN; from $\sim S \lor \sim\sim T$ to $\sim(S \cdot \sim T)$ by DeM.
10. Correct (Cont)
13. Correct (Com)
16. Correct (As)
19. Correct (DeM)

Part C: Proofs

1. 1. $\sim(C \cdot D)$
2. $\sim C \to S$
3. $\sim D \to T$ $\therefore S \lor T$
4. $\sim C \lor \sim D$ 1, DeM
5. $S \lor T$ 2, 3, 4, CD

4. 1. ~(~A ∨ B) ∴ A
2. ~~A • ~B 1, DeM
3. ~~A 2, Simp
4. A 3, DN

7. 1. (A ∨ B) ∨ C
2. ~A ∴ C ∨ B
3. A ∨ (B ∨ C) 1, As
4. B ∨ C 2, 3, DS
5. C ∨ B 4, Com

10. 1. F → (G • H)
2. (H • G) → J ∴ F → J
3. (G • H) → J 2, Com
4. F → J 1, 3, HS

13. 1. ~S → (T • U)
2. (~S → X) → ~Z
3. (U • T) → X ∴ ~Z
4. (T • U) → X 3, Com
5. ~S → X 1, 4, HS
6. ~Z 2, 5, MP

16. 1. (K ∨ P) ∨ X
2. K → ~O
3. (P ∨ X) → ~L ∴ ~(O • L)
4. K ∨ (P ∨ X) 1, As
5. ~O ∨ ~L 2, 3, 4, CD
6. ~(O • L) 5, DeM

19. 1. ~(L • M) → ~(N ∨ O) ∴ (O ∨ N) → (M • L)
2. ~(M • L) → ~(N ∨ O) 1, Com
3. ~(M • L) → ~(O ∨ N) 2, Com
4. (O ∨ N) → (M • L) 3, Cont

Part D: Longer Proofs

1. 1. ~~T ∨ ~R
2. ~(S ∨ ~R)
3. (T • ~S) → ~Q
4. W → Q ∴ ~W
5. ~S • ~~R 2, DeM
6. ~~R 5, Simp
7. ~~T 1, 6, DS
8. T 7, DN
9. ~S 5, Simp
10. T • ~S 8, 9, Conj
11. ~Q 3, 10, MP
12. ~W 4, 11, MT

4. 1. B → E
2. ~F ∨ G
3. (B • C) • D
4. (D • C) → F ∴ E • G
5. B • (C • D) 3, As
6. B 5, Simp
7. E 1, 6, MP
8. C • D 5, Simp
9. D • C 8, Com
10. F 4, 9, MP
11. ~~F 10, DN

12. G   2, 11, DS
13. E • G   7, 12 Conj

7. 1. ~(B • ~C
        2. ~B → D
        3. C → ~E   ∴ ~E ∨ D
        4. ~B ∨ ~~C   1, DeM
        5. ~B ∨ C   4, DN
        6. D ∨ ~E   2, 3, 5, CD
        7. ~E ∨ D   6, Com

10. 1. ~A → ~B
        2. D → E
        3. (B → A) → (C ∨ D)
        4. C → F   ∴ E ∨ F
        5. B → A   1, Cont
        6. C ∨ D   3, 5, MP
        7. F ∨ E   2, 4, 6, CD
        8. E ∨ F   7, Com

Exercise 8.3
Part A: Annotating

1. 1. B ↔ E   ∴ E → B
        2. (B → E) • (E → B)   1, ME
        3. E → B   2, Simp

4. 1. H → (J → ~H)   ∴ H → ~J
        2. H → (~~H → ~J)   1, Cont
        3. (H • ~~H) → ~J   2, Ex
        4. (H • H) → ~J   3, DN
        5. H → ~J   4, Re

7. 1. M → ~N   ∴ N → ~M
        2. ~M ∨ ~N   1, MI
        3. ~N ∨ ~M   2, Com
        4. N → ~M   3, MI

10. 1. (U → U) ∨ (~U → U)   ∴ ~U ∨ U
        2. (~U ∨ U) ∨ (~U → U)   1, MI
        3. (~U ∨ U) ∨ (~~U ∨ U)   2, MI
        4. (~U ∨ U) ∨ (U ∨ U)   3, DN
        5. (~U ∨ U) ∨ U   4, Re
        6. ~U ∨ (U ∨ U)   5, As
        7. ~U ∨ U   6, Re

Part B: Correct or Incorrect?

1. Correct (Re).

4. Correct (Dist).

7. Incorrect. From the premise, by Dist, we get (K ∨ X) • (K ∨ R).

10. Incorrect. DS is an implicational rule and cannot be applied to part of line.

13. Correct (Dist).

16. Correct (Dist).

19. Incorrect. Simplification is an implicational rule and may not be applied to part of a line.

Part C: Proofs

1. 1. ~M ∨ N   ∴ ~N → ~M
        2. M → N   1, MI
        3. ~N → ~M   2, Cont

4. 1. ~A ∨ ~A
2. A ∨ P   ∴ P
3. ~A   1, Re
4. P   2, 3, DS

7. 1. (~J • K) → L
2. ~J   ∴ ~L → ~K
3. ~J → (K → L)   1, Ex
4. K → L   2, 3, MP
5. ~L → ~K   4, Cont

10. 1. ~R
2. (R → S) → T   ∴ T
3. (~R ∨ S) → T   2, MI
4. ~R ∨ S   1, Add
5. T   3, 4, MP

13. 1. E → H
2. (E ∨ F) • (E ∨ G)
3. (F • G) → H   ∴ H
4. E ∨ (F • G)   2, Dist
5. H ∨ H   1, 3, 4, CD
6. H   5, Re

16. 1. ~~(R • S)
2. T → (R →~S)   ∴ ~T
3. ~T ∨ (R → ~S)   2, MI
4. ~(~R ∨ ~S)   1, DeM
5. ~(R → ~S)   4, MI
6. ~T   3, 5, DS

19. 1. H ∨ H
2. H ↔ ~J   ∴ ~J
3. (H → ~J) • (~J → H) 2, ME
4. H → ~J   3, Simp
5. H   1, Re
6. ~J   4, 5, MP

Part D: More Proofs

1. 1. (Z ∨ ~Y) • (Z ∨ W)
2. Z → ~~U
3. ~Y → (W → U)   ∴ U
4. Z ∨ (~Y • W)   1, Dist
5. Z → U   2, DN
6. (~Y • W) → U   3, Ex
7. U ∨ U   4, 5, 6, CD
8. U   7, Re

4. 1. ~H ∨ (G ∨ F)
2. ~F
3. S → ~(H → G)   ∴ ~S
4. (~H ∨ G) ∨ F   1, As
5. ~H ∨ G   2, 4, DS
6. H → G   5, MI
7. ~~(H → G)   6, DN
8. ~S   3, 7, MT

7. 1. B ∨ (C • ~D)
2. (D → B) ↔ P   ∴ P
3. (B ∨ C) • (B ∨ ~D)   1, Dist
4. [(D → B) → P] • [P → (D → B)]   2, ME

5. (D → B) → P	4, Simp
6. B ∨ ~D	3, Simp
7. ~D ∨ B	6, Com
8. D → B	7, MI
9. P	5, 8, MP

10.

1. (B • C) → D	
2. B	
3. Q → ~(~C ∨ D)	
4. ~Q ↔ T	∴ T
5. B → (C → D)	1, Ex
6. C → D	2, 5, MP
7. ~C ∨ D	6, MI
8. ~~(~C ∨ D)	7, DN
9. ~Q	3, 8, MT
10. (~Q → T) • (T → ~Q)	4, ME
11. ~Q → T	10, Simp
12. T	9, 11, MP

Part E: English Arguments

1.

1. P → (N ∨ S)	
2. N → (M • F)	
3. S → E	
4. P • ~F	∴ E
5. P	4, S
6. N ∨ S	1, 5, MP
7. (M • F) ∨ E	6, 2, 3, CD
8. ~F	4, Simp
9. ~F ∨ ~M	8, Add
10. ~(F • M)	9, DeM
11. ~(M • F)	10, Com
12. E	7, 11, DS

4.

1. S ∨ (U • P)	
2. (S ∨ U) → R	∴ R
3. (S ∨ U) • (S ∨ P)	1, Dist
4. S ∨ U	3, Simp
5. R	2, 4, MP

Exercise 8.4
Part A: Proofs (using CP)

1.

1. Z → (~Y → X)	
2. Z → ~Y	∴ Z → X
3. Z	Assume
4. ~Y	2, 3, MP
5. ~Y → X	1, 3, MP
6. X	4, 5, MP
7. Z → X	3–6, CP

4.

1. A → B	
2. A → C	∴ A → (B · C)
3. A	Assume
4. B	1, 3, MP
5. C	2, 3, MP
6. B • C	4, 5, Conj
7. A → (B • C)	3–6, CP

7. 1. P   ∴ (P → Q) → Q
    ⌐ 2. P → Q   Assume
    | 3. Q   1, 2, MP
    └ 4. (P → Q) → Q   2–3, CP

10.   1. C → (~D → E)
        2. (D → ~D) → (E → G)   ∴ C → (~D → G)
    ⌐ 3. C   Assume
    | 4. ~D → E   1, 3, MP
    | 5. (~D ∨ ~D) → (E → G)   2, MI
    | 6. ~D → (E → G)   5, Re
    | ⌐ 7. ~D   Assume
    | | 8. E → G   6, 7, MP
    | | 9. E   4, 7, MP
    | |10. G   8, 9, MP
    | └11. ~D → G   7–10, CP
    └ 12. C → (~D → G)   3–11, CP

13.   1. (A ∨ N) → ~S
        2. M → [N → (S · T)]   ∴ ~(~M ∨ ~N) → (S · ~A)
    ⌐ 3. ~(~M ∨ ~N)   Assume
    | 4. ~~M · ~~N   3, DeM
    | 5. ~~M   4, Simp
    | 6. M   5, DN
    | 7. N → (S · T)   2, 6, MP
    | 8. ~~N   4, Simp
    | 9. N   8, DN
    | 10. S · T   7, 9, MP
    | 11. S   10, Simp
    | 12. ~~S   11, DN
    | 13. ~(A ∨ N)   1, 12, MT
    | 14. ~A · ~N   13, DeM
    | 15. ~A   14, Simp
    └16. S · ~A   11, 15, Conj
     17. ~(~M ∨ ~N) → (S · ~A)   3–16, CP

16.   1. A → (B → C)   ∴ (A → B) → (A → C)
    ⌐ 2. A → B   Assume
    | 3. (A · B) → C   1, Ex
    | ⌐ 4. A   Assume
    | | 5. B   2, 4, MP
    | | 6. A · B   4, 5, Conj
    | | 7. C   3, 6, MP
    | └ 8. A → C   4–7, CP
    └ 9. (A → B) → (A → C)   2–8, CP

19.   1. A → (B · C)
        2. B → D
        3. C → ~D   ∴ A → X
    ⌐ 4. A   Assume
    | 5. B · C   1, 4, MP
    | 6. B   5, Simp
    | 7. C   5, Simp
    | 8. D   2, 6, MP
    | 9. ~D   3, 7, MP

```
| 10. D ∨ X          8, Add
| 11. X              9, 10, DS
  12. A → X          4–11, CP
```

Part B: English Arguments

1.   1. ~V → (~I ∨ ~P)
      2. ~I → ~S
      3. ~P → ~S   ∴ ~V → ~S
   ┌──4. ~V   Assume
   │ 5. ~I ∨ ~P   1, 4, MP
   │ 6. ~S ∨ ~S   5, 2, 3, CD
   └──7. ~S   6, Re
      8. ~V → ~S   4–7, CP

Part C: Valid or Invalid?   These are left as exercises.

Exercise 8.5
Part A: Proofs

1.   1. A → B   ∴ ~(A • ~B)
   ┌──2. A • ~B   Assume
   │ 3. A   2, Simp
   │ 4. B   1, 3, MP
   │ 5. ~B   2, Simp
   └──6. B • ~B   4, 5, Conj
      7. ~(A • ~B)   2–6, RAA

4.   1. (H ∨ R) • (H ∨ ~R)   ∴ H
   ┌──2. ~H   Assume
   │ 3. H ∨ (R • ~R)   1, Dist
   │ 4. R • ~R   2, 3, DS
   └──5. H   2–4, RAA

7.   1. Z → (X ∨ Y)
      2. X → ~W
      3. Y → ~W
      4. ~W → ~Z   ∴ ~Z
   ┌──5. Z   Assume
   │ 6. X ∨ Y   1, 5, MP
   │ 7. ~W ∨ ~W   6, 2, 3, CD
   │ 8. ~W   7, Re
   │ 9. ~Z   4, 8, MP
   └──10. Z • ~Z   5, 9, Conj
      11. ~Z   5–10, RAA

10.   1. ~A • ~B   ∴ A ↔ B
   ┌──2. ~(A ↔ B)   Assume
   │ 3. ~[(A • B) ∨ (~A • ~B)]   2, ME
   │ 4. ~(A • B) • ~(~A • ~B)   3, DeM
   │ 5. ~(~A • ~B)   4, Simp
   └──6. (~A • ~B) • ~(~A • ~B)   1, 5, Conj
      7. A ↔ B   2–6, RAA
```
```

13.   1. D → ~(A ∨ B)
       2. ~C → D   ∴ A → C
       3. ~(A → C)   Assume
       4. ~(~A ∨ C)   3, MI
       5. ~~A • ~C   4, DeM
       6. ~C   5, Simp
       7. D   2, 6, MP
       8. ~(A ∨ B)   1, 7, MP
       9. ~A • ~B   8, DeM
      10. ~A   9, Simp
      11. ~~A   5, Simp
      12. ~A • ~~A   10, 11, Conj
      13. A → C   3–12, RAA

16.   1. W → (X ∨ G)
       2. G → M
       3. ~M   ∴ ~W ∨ X
       4. ~(~W ∨ X)   Assume
       5. ~~W • ~X   4, DeM
       6. ~G   2, 3, MT
       7. ~~W   5, Simp
       8. W   7, DN
       9. X ∨ G   8, 1, MP
      10. ~X   5, Simp
      11. G   9, 10, DS
      12. G • ~G   11, 6, Conj
      13. ~W ∨ X   4–12, RAA

19.   1. ~S → (T • U)
       2. ~R → ~(T ∨ U)
       3. (T ↔ U) → (~~S • R)   ∴ R • S
       4. ~(R • S)   Assume
       5. (T ↔ U) → (S • R)   3, DN
       6. (T ↔ U) → (R • S)   5, Com
       7. ~(T ↔ U)   4, 6, MT
       8. ~R ∨ ~S   4, DeM
       9. ~(T ∨ U) ∨ (T • U)   8, 2, 1, CD
      10. (T • U) ∨ ~(T ∨ U)   9, Com
      11. (T • U) ∨ (~T • ~U)   10, DeM
      12. T ↔ U   11, ME
      13. (T ↔ U) • ~(T ↔ U)   12, 7, Conj
      14. R • S   4–13, RAA

Part B: Valid or Invalid?

1.   1. (F → G) → H   ∴ F → (G → H)
       2. F   Assume
       3. G   Assume
       4. ~H   Assume
       5. ~(F → G)   1, 4, MT
       6. ~(~F ∨ G)   5, MI
       7. ~~F • ~G   6, DeM
       8. ~G   7, Simp
       9. G • ~G   3, 8, Conj
      10. H   4–9, RAA
      11. G → H   3–10, CP
      12. F → (G → H)   2–11, CP

2.

F	G	H	F → (G → H)	∴ (F → G) → H
F	F	F	T	F

Part C: English Arguments

1.
1. R → (T ∨ P)
2. T → (~L ∨ C)
3. P → (~L ∨ W)
4. R • (~C • ~W)   ∴ ~L

> 5. L   Assume
> 6. ~C • ~W   4, Simp
> 7. ~C   6, Simp
> 8. ~~L   5, DN
> 9. ~~L • ~C   8, 7, Conj
> 10. ~(~L ∨ C)   9, DeM
> 11. ~T   10, 2, MT
> 12. ~W   6, Simp
> 13. ~~L • ~W   8, 12, Conj
> 14. ~(~L ∨ W)   13, DeM
> 15. ~P   14, 3, MT
> 16. ~T • ~P   11, 15, Conj
> 17. ~(T ∨ P)   16, DeM
> 18. ~R   17, 1, MT
> 19. R   4, Simp
> 20. R • ~R   18, 19, Conj
21. ~L   5–20, RAA

Part D: Valid or Invalid?   These are left as exercises.

Exercise 8.6
Part A: Proofs

1.   ∴ ~(P → Q) → (P • ~Q)

> 1. ~(P → Q)   Assume
> 2. ~(~P ∨ Q)   1, MI
> 3. ~~P • ~Q   2, DeM
> 4. P • ~Q   3, DN
5. ~(P → Q) → (P • ~Q)   1–4, CP

4.   ∴ (X → Y) → ~(X • ~Y)

> 1. X → Y   Assume
> 2. ~X ∨ Y   1, MI
> 3. ~X ∨ ~~Y   2, DN
> 4. ~(X • ~Y)   3, DeM
5. (X → Y) → ~(X • ~Y)   1–4, CP

7.   ∴ K → [(K → L) → L]

> 1. K   Assume
>> 2. K → L   Assume
>> 3. L   1, 2, MP
> 4. (K → L) → L   2–3, CP
5. K → [(K → L) → L]   1–4, CP

10.

	∴ (P • ~Q) → ~(P ↔ Q)
1. P • ~Q	Assume
2. P ↔ Q	Assume
3. (P → Q) • (Q → P)	2, ME
4. P	1, Simp
5. P → Q	3, Simp
6. Q	4, 5, MP
7. ~Q	1, Simp
8. Q • ~Q	6, 7, Conj
9. ~(P ↔ Q)	2–8, RAA
10. (P • ~Q) → ~(P ↔ Q)	1–9, CP

Part B: Corresponding Conditionals

1.

	∴ [(~A ∨ ~B) • B] → ~A
1. (~A ∨ ~B) • B	Assume
2. ~A ∨ ~B	1, Simp
3. B	1, Simp
4. ~~B	3, DN
5. ~A	2, 4, DS
6. [(~A ∨ ~B) • B] → ~A	1–5, CP

◆ Chapter 9

Exercise 9.1
Part A: Well-Formed Formulas?

1. WFF
4. Not a WFF. The problem is that *a* is an individual constant rather than a variable. Quantifiers must contain variables. Note that (*a*)C*a* is nonsense, like saying, "For all Adam, Adam is cold."
7. WFF
10. Not a WFF. Tildes may not be placed inside the parentheses of a quantifier.
13. WFF
16. Not a WFF. The problem is that *b* is an individual constant rather than a formula. Note that ~*b* is nonsense, like saying, "It is not the case that Bob."
19. WFF

Part B: Symbolizing

1. (x)(Zx → ~Mx)
4. ~(x)(Mx → Kx)
7. (∃x)Rx
10. (∃x)(Mx • Hx)
13. (∃x)(Px • Gx) • (∃x)(Px • ~Gx)
16. (x)(Sx → Bx)
19. (∃x)(Ax • Sx)

Part C: More Symbolizing

1. (x)(Cx → Ax)
4. (x)(Lx → Wx)
7. (x)Ix
10. (x)(Rx → ~Wx)
13. (x)Mx → (x)~Px
16. (x)[(Px • Sx) → ~Hx]
19. (x)~Gx → (x)(Hx → ~Nx)

Part D: Quiz on Symbolizing   These are left as exercises.

Part E: Schemes of Abbreviation   These are left as exercises.

Part F: Challenging Translations

    1. *In logicese:* For any x, if x is not equilateral, then it is not the case that x is both a rectangle and a square: $(x)[\sim Ex \rightarrow \sim(Rx \cdot Sx)]$. In other words, for all x, if x is both a rectangle and a square, then x is equilateral: $(x)[(Rx \cdot Sx) \rightarrow Ex]$.

    4. $(x)(Vx \rightarrow Cx)$

    7. $[(x)(Hx \rightarrow Mx) \cdot \sim Ms] \rightarrow \sim Hs$

  10. $(x)[(Fx \cdot \sim(Hx \vee Mx)) \rightarrow \sim Rx]$

  13. $[Db \cdot (x)(Dx \rightarrow Ax)] \rightarrow Ab$

  16. $(x)[(Px \cdot (Hx \cdot Sx)) \rightarrow Cx]$

  19. $(x)\sim Gx \vee (\exists x)Ex$

Exercise 9.2

Part A: Demonstrating Invalidity

    1.   Aa Ba | Aa → Ba ∴ Aa • Ba

          F T | T   F

    4.   Ka Kb La Lb | (Ka ∨ Kb) → (La ∨ Lb) ∴ (Ka → La) • (Kb → Lb)

          T F F T | T   F

    7.   Ha Hb Ja Jb | (Ha • Hb) → (~Ja • ~Jb) ∴ (Ja → ~Ha) • (Jb → ~Hb)

          T F T T | T   F

  10.   Ra Rb Sa Sb | (Ra → Sa) ∨ (Rb → Sb) ∴ (Ra ∨ Rb) → (Sa ∨ Sb)

          F T F F | T   F

  13.   Ad Bd | Ad → Bd, Bd ∴ Ad

          F T | T   T   F

  16.   Ma Mb Na Nb | (Ma → Na) • (Mb → Nb), Ma ∨ Mb ∴ Na • Nb

           F T F T | T   T   F

  19.   Aa Ab Ba Bb Ca Cb | (Aa • Ba) ∨ (Ab • Bb), (Ca • Ba) ∨ (Cb • Bb)

           F T T T T F | T   T

      ∴ (Aa • Ca) ∨ (Ab • Cb)

               F

Part B: English Arguments

    1. *Symbolization:* $(x)[(Sx \cdot Lx) \rightarrow Cx]$ ∴ $(\exists x)[(Sx \cdot Lx) \cdot Cx]$

        Sa La Ca | (Sa • La) → Ca ∴ (Sa • La) • Ca

         F T T | T   F

    4. *Symbolization:* $(x)(Sx \rightarrow Gx)$, $(\exists x)(Bx \cdot Gx)$ ∴ $(\exists x)(Bx \cdot Sx)$

        Sa Ga Ba | Sa → Ga, Ba • Ga ∴ Ba • Sa

         F T T | T   T   F

Exercise 9.3
Part A: Annotating

1.
   1. $(x)(Rx \rightarrow Tx)$
   2. $\sim Tc$ $\therefore \sim Rc$
   3. $Rc \rightarrow Tc$ 1, UI
   4. $\sim Rc$ 2, 3, MT

4.
   1. Hn $\therefore (\exists x)Hx$
   2. $(\exists x)Hx$ 1, EG

7.
   1. $(y)(Ry \rightarrow Ny)$
   2. $\sim Ng$ $\therefore (\exists y)\sim Ry$
   3. $Rg \rightarrow Ng$ 1, UI
   4. $\sim Rg$ 2, 3, MT
   5. $(\exists y)\sim Ry$ 4, EG

10.
    1. $(\exists y)Py \rightarrow (z)(\sim Nz \vee Oz)$
    2. Pn
    3. $\sim Om$ $\therefore (\exists x)\sim Nx$
    4. $(\exists y)Py$ 2, EG
    5. $(z)(\sim Nz \vee Oz)$ 1, 4, MP
    6. $\sim Nm \vee Om$ 5, UI
    7. $\sim Nm$ 6, 3, DS
    8. $(\exists x)\sim Nx$ 7, EG

Part B: Correct or Incorrect?

1.
   1. $(x)Ax \rightarrow (x)Bx$
   2. $Ax \rightarrow (x)Bx$ 1, UI   Incorrect. UI may *not* be applied to part of a line.

4.
   1. $(\exists z)(Kz \cdot Lz)$
   2. $(\exists z)Kz$ 1, Simp   Incorrect. Simp may *not* be applied to part of a line.

7.
   1. $(x)(y)(My \leftrightarrow Nx)$
   2. $(y)(My \leftrightarrow Ny)$ 1, UI   Incorrect. x is free in $(y)(My \leftrightarrow Nx)$, but each occurrence of y is bound in $(y)(My \leftrightarrow Ny)$.

10.
    1. $(x)(Bx \rightarrow (x)Cx)$
    2. $(x)Bx$
    3. $(x)Cx$ 1, 2, MP   Incorrect. To apply MP, we need a conditional on one line and its antecedent on another. Line (1) is not a conditional, but a universal statement.

Part C: Proofs

1.
   1. $Ja \rightarrow Hb$
   2. $(y)\sim Hy$ $\therefore (\exists x)\sim Jx$
   3. $\sim Hb$ 2, UI
   4. $\sim Ja$ 1, 3, MT
   5. $(\exists x)\sim Jx$ 4, EG

4.
   1. $(z)(Nz \rightarrow \sim Ez)$
   2. $(z)(Sz \rightarrow Nz)$ $\therefore (z)(Sz \rightarrow \sim Ez)$
   3. $Sz \rightarrow Nz$ 2, UI
   4. $Nz \rightarrow \sim Ez$ 1, UI
   5. $Sz \rightarrow \sim Ez$ 3, 4, HS
   6. $(z)(Sz \rightarrow \sim Ez)$ 5, UG

7.
   1. $(x)(Dx \rightarrow Lx)$
   2. $(\exists x)Dx$ $\therefore (\exists x)(Dx \cdot Lx)$
   3. Dx 2, EI
   4. $Dx \rightarrow Lx$ 1, UI
   5. Lx 3, 4, MP
   6. $Dx \cdot Lx$ 3, 5, Conj
   7. $(\exists x)(Dx \cdot Lx)$ 6, EG

10. 1. (y)(~Py → ~Ly)
    2. Lc ∨ Ld   ∴ Pd ∨ Pc
    3. ~Pc → ~Lc   1, UI
    4. ~Pd → ~Ld   1, UI
    5. Lc → Pc   3, Cont
    6. Ld → Pd   4, Cont
    7. Pc ∨ Pd   2, 5, 6, CD
    8. Pd ∨ Pc   7, Com

13. 1. (x)(Ax ↔ ~Ax)   ∴ Bc
    2. Ax ↔ ~Ax   1, UI
    3. (Ax → ~Ax) • (~Ax → Ax)   2, ME
    4. Ax → ~Ax   3, Simp
    5. ~Ax ∨ ~Ax   4, MI
    6. ~Ax   5, Re
    7. ~Ax → Ax   3, Simp
    8. ~~Ax ∨ Ax   7, MI
    9. Ax ∨ Ax   8, DN
    10. Ax   9, Re
    11. Ax ∨ Bc   10, Add
    12. Bc   6, 11, DS

16. 1. (∃y)Fy → (y)My
    2. Fg   ∴ Mg
    3. (∃y)Fy   2, EG
    4. (y)My   1, 3, MP
    5. Mg   4, UI

19. 1. (x)[Px → (∃y)Oy]
    2. (∃z)Pz   ∴ (∃y)Oy
    3. Pz   2, EI
    4. Pz → (∃y)Oy   1, UI
    5. (∃y)Oy   3, 4, MP

Part D: English Arguments

1. 1. (x)(Ix → Hx)
    2. (x)(Cx → ~Hx)   ∴ (x)(Cx → ~Ix)
    3. Ix → Hx   1, UI
    4. Cx → ~Hx   2, UI
    5. ~Hx → ~Ix   3, Cont
    6. Cx → ~Ix   4, 5, HS
    7. (x)(Cx → ~Ix)   6, UG

4. 1. Pg
    2. (x)(Px → ~~Rx)   ∴ Rg
    3. (x)(Px → Rx)   2, DN
    4. Pg → Rg   3, UI
    5. Rg   1, 4, MP

7. 1. (x)[Px → (Dx ↔ Sx)]
    2. Sb • ~So
    3. Pb • Po   ∴ Db • ~Do
    4. Pb → (Db ↔ Sb)   1, UI
    5. Pb   3, Simp
    6. Db ↔ Sb   4, 5, MP
    7. (Db → Sb) • (Sb → Db)   6, ME
    8. Sb   2, Simp
    9. Sb → Db   7, Simp
    10. Db   8, 9, MP
    11. Po → (Do ↔ So)   1, UI

12. Po	3, Simp
13. Do ↔ So	11, 12, MP
14. (Do → So) • (So → Do)	13, ME
15. ~So	2, Simp
16. Do → So	14, Simp
17. ~Do	15, 16, MT
18. Db • ~Do	10, 17, Conj

Exercise 9.4
Part A: Annotating

1. 1. (x)Ax → (x)Bx
    2. ~(x)Bx   ∴ (∃x)~Ax
    3. ~(x)Ax   1, 2, MT
    4. (∃x)~Ax   3, QN

4. 1. ~(∃x)~Gx   ∴ (x)Gx
    2. (x)~~Gx   1, QN
    3. (x)Gx   2, DN

7. 1. (x)(Nx → Ox)   ∴ ~(x)Ox → ~(x)Nx
    2. ~(x)Ox   Assume
    3. (∃x) ~Ox   2, QN
    4. ~Ox   3, EI
    5. Nx → Ox   1, UI
    6. ~Nx   4, 5, MT
    7. (∃x) ~Nx   6, EG
    8. ~(x)Nx   7, QN
    9. ~(x)Ox → ~(x)Nx   2–8, CP

Part B: Proofs

1. 1. (∃x)Fx → (∃x)(Gx • Hx)
    2. (∃x)Hx → (x)Jx   ∴ (x)(Fx → Jx)
    3. Fx   Assume
    4. (∃x)Fx   3, EG
    5. (∃x)(Gx • Hx)   4, 1, MP
    6. Gy • Hy   5, EI
    7. Hy   6, Simp
    8. (∃x)Hx   7, EG
    9. (x)Jx   2, 8, MP
    10. Jx   9, UI
    11. Fx → Jx   3–10, CP
    12. (x)(Fx → Jx)   11, UG

4. 1. ~(∃x)Mx → (∃x)(Nx • Px)
    2. (x)~Px   ∴ (∃x)Mx
    3. ~(∃x)Mx   Assume
    4. (∃x)(Nx • Px)   1, 3, MP
    5. Nx • Px   4, EI
    6. ~Px   2, UI
    7. Px   5, Simp
    8. Px • ~Px   7, 6, Conj
    9. (∃x)Mx   3–8, RAA

7. 1. (x)(Cx → Dx)
    2. ~(∃x)Cx → (∃x)Dx   ∴ ~(x)~Dx
    3. (x)~Dx   Assume
    4. ~(∃x)Dx   3, QN
    5. ~~(∃x)Cx   2, 4, MT

6. (∃x)Cx	5, DN
7. Cx	6, EI
8. Cx → Dx	1, UI
9. Dx	7, 8, MP
10. ~Dx	3, UI
11. Dx • ~Dx	9, 10, Conj
12. ~(x)~Dx	3–11, RAA

10.
1. (∃x)~Kx → ~(∃x)Dx	
2. ~(x)Kx	
3. Db ↔ Qa	∴ ~Qa
4. (∃x)~Kx	2, QN
5. ~(∃x)Dx	4, 1, MP
6. (x)~Dx	5, QN
7. ~Db	6, UI
8. (Db → Qa) • (Qa → Db)	3, ME
9. Qa → Db	8, Simp
10. ~Qa	7, 9, MT

13.
1. ~[(x)Ax → (∃x)Bx]	
2. (∃x)~Cx → (∃x)Bx	
3. (x)[(Ax • Cx) → Da]	∴ Da
4. ~[~(x)Ax ∨ (∃x)Bx]	1, MI
5. ~~(x)Ax • ~(∃x)Bx	4, DeM
6. ~(∃x)Bx	5, Simp
7. ~(∃x)~Cx	6, 2, MT
8. ~~(x)Ax	5, Simp
9. ~~(x)Cx	7, QN
10. (x)Ax	8, DN
11. (x)Cx	9, DN
12. (Ax • Cx) → Da	3, UI
13. Ax	10, UI
14. Cx	11, UI
15. Ax • Cx	13, 14, Conj
16. Da	15, 12, MP

16.
1. ~(x)Mx ∨ (∃x)~Mx	
2. (∃x)Sx → (x)Mx	
3. Sb ∨ (x)~Px	∴ ~Pa
4. ~(x)Mx ∨ ~(x)Mx	1, QN
5. ~(x)Mx	4, Re
6. ~(∃x)Sx	5, 2, MT
7. (x)~Sx	6, QN
8. ~Sb	7, UI
9. (x)~Px	8, 3, DS
10. ~Pa	9, UI

19.
1. (∃x)[Bx → (y)~Cy]	
2. ~(∃y)Cy → ~(∃z)Dz	∴ (x)Bx → (z)~Dz
3. (x)Bx	Assume
4. Bx → (y)~Cy	1, EI
5. Bx	3, UI
6. (y)~Cy	4, 5, MP
7. ~(∃y)Cy	6, QN
8. ~(∃z)Dz	7, 2, MP
9. (z)~Dz	8, QN
10. (x)Bx → (z)~Dz	3–9, CP

Part C: Logical Equivalents

1. 1. (x)(Ax • Bx)   ∴ (x)Ax • (x)Bx
   2. Ax • Bx   1, UI
   3. Ax   2, Simp
   4. (x)Ax   3, UG
   5. Bx   2, Simp
   6. (x)Bx   5, UG
   7. (x)Ax • (x)Bx   4, 6, Conj

4.   1. (∃x)Ax ∨ (∃x)Bx   ∴ (∃x)(Ax ∨ Bx)
   2. ~(∃x)(Ax ∨ Bx)   Assume
   3. (x)~(Ax ∨ Bx)   2, QN
   4. (x)(~Ax • ~Bx)   3, DeM
   5. (∃x)Ax   Assume
   6. Ax   5, EI
   7. ~Ax • ~Bx   4, UI
   8. ~Ax   7, Simp
   9. Ax • ~Ax   6, 8, Conj
  10. ~(∃x)Ax   5–9, RAA
  11. (∃x)Bx   10, 1, DS
  12. By   11, EI
  13. ~Ay • ~By   4, UI
  14. ~By   13, Simp
  15. By • ~By   12, 14, Conj
  16. (∃x)(Ax ∨ Bx)   2–15, RAA

7.   1. (x)(Ax → P)   ∴ (∃x)Ax → P
   2. (∃x)Ax   Assume
   3. Ax   2, EI
   4. Ax → P   1, UI
   5. P   3, 4, MP
   6. (∃x)Ax → P   2–5, CP

Part D: English Arguments

1.   1. (x)(Tx → Dx)
   2. (∃x)(Tx • (Wx ∨ Cx)) → (∃x)(Tx • ~Dx)   ∴ (x)(Tx → ~Cx)
   3. Tx   Assume
   4. (x)(Tx → ~~Dx)   1, DN
   5. (x)(~Tx ∨ ~~Dx)   4, MI
   6. (x)~(Tx • ~Dx)   5, DeM
   7. ~(∃x)(Tx • ~Dx)   6, QN
   8. ~(∃x)(Tx • (Wx ∨ Cx))   2, 7, MT
   9. (x)~(Tx • (Wx ∨ Cx))   8, QN
  10. (x)(~Tx ∨ ~(Wx ∨ Cx))   9, DeM
  11. (x)(Tx → ~(Wx ∨ Cx))   10, MI
  12. (x)(Tx → (~Wx • ~Cx))   11, DeM
  13. Tx → (~Wx • ~Cx)   12, UI
  14. ~Wx • ~Cx   3, 13, MP
  15. ~Cx   14, Simp
  16. Tx → ~Cx   3–15, CP
  17. (x)(Tx → ~Cx)   16, UG

4.   1. (x)(Kx → (Wx ↔ Ex))
   2. (x)(Px → Kx)
   3. (x)(Fx → Px)

```
       4. (x)(Px → Ex)                    ∴ (x)(Fx → Wx)
     ┌── 5. Fx                            Assume
     │   6. Fx → Px                       3, UI
     │   7. Px → Ex                       4, UI
     │   8. Px                            5, 6, MP
     │   9. Ex                            7, 8, MP
     │  10. Px → Kx                       2, UI
     │  11. Kx                            8, 10, MP
     │  12. Kx → (Wx ↔ Ex)               1, UI
     │  13. Wx ↔ Ex                       11, 12, MP
     │  14. (Wx → Ex) • (Ex → Wx)        13, ME
     │  15. Ex → Wx                       14, Simp
     └─ 16. Wx                            9, 15, MP
        17. Fx → Wx                       5–16, CP
        18. (x)(Fx → Wx)                  17, UG
```

7. 1. (∃x)(Rx • Bx)
    2. (∃x)(Mx • Hx)
    3. (∃x)Rx → (x)[Hx → (Mx → Fx)]   ∴ (∃x)(Mx • Fx)
    4. Rx • Bx   1, EI
    5. Rx   4, Simp
    6. (∃x)Rx   5, EG
    7. (x)[Hx → (Mx → Fx)]   3, 6, MP
    8. My • Hy   2, EI
    9. Hy → (My → Fy)   7, UI
    10. Hy   8, Simp
    11. My → Fy   9, 10, MP
    12. My   8, Simp
    13. Fy   11, 12, MP
    14. My • Fy   12, 13, Conj
    15. (∃x)(Mx • Fx)   14, EG

Exercise 9.5

Part A: Matching   These are left as exercises.

Part B: Symbolizing

  1. (x)~Lxx
  4. (∃x)[Fx • (y)(Py → Rxy)]
  7. (x)[Dx → ~(∃y)(Hy • Wxy)]
  10. (x)[(Ox • Px) → ~(∃y)((Oy • Wy) • Rxy)]
  13. (x)(Mx → ~Mxx)
  16. (x)(Mx → Axb)
  19. (x)[Sx → ~(y)(Py → (z)(Dz → Hxyz))]
  22. (x)(y)(z)[(Fxy • Fyz) → ~Fxz]
  25. (x)(y)(Nxy → Nyx)

Part C: More Matching   These are left as exercises.

Part D: More Symbolizing

  1. (∃x)[Px • (y)(Py → Axy)]
  4. (∃x)(Px • Lxx) • (∃x)(Px • ~Lxx)
  7. (x)(∃y)Cxy
  10. (x)~(∃y)Cxy

Part E: Proofs

1. 1. (x)(y)(Rxy → Ryx)
2. Rab   ∴ Rba
3. (y)(Ray → Rya)   1, UI
4. Rab → Rba   3, UI
5. Rba   2, 4, MP

4. 1. (y)(Bay ∨ Bya)   ∴ Baa
2. Baa ∨ Baa   1, UI
3. Baa   2, Re

7. 1. (∃x)[Hx • (y)(Hy → Lyx)]   ∴ (∃x)(Hx • Lxx)
2. Hx • (y)(Hy → Lyx)   1, EI
3. Hx   2, Simp
4. (y)(Hy → Lyx)   2, Simp
5. Hx → Lxx   4, UI
6. Lxx   3, 5, MP
7. Hx • Lxx   3, 6, Conj
8. (∃x)(Hx • Lxx)   7, EG

10. 1. ~(∃x)[Px • (∃y)(Py • Lxy)]   ∴ (x)[Px → (y)(Py → ~Lxy)]
2. (x)~[Px • (∃y)(Py • Lxy)]   1, QN
3. ~[Px • (∃y)(Py • Lxy)]   2, UI
4. ~Px ∨ ~(∃y)(Py • Lxy)   3, DeM
5. ~Px ∨ (y)~(Py • Lxy)   4, QN
6. ~Px ∨ (y)(~Py ∨ ~Lxy)   5, DeM
7. Px → (y)(~Py ∨ ~Lxy)   6, MI
8. Px → (y)(Py → ~Lxy)   7, MI
9. (x)[Px → (y)(Py → ~Lxy)]   8, UG

Part F: English Arguments

1. 1. Soa
2. (x)(y)(Sxy → ~Syx)   ∴ ~Sao
3. (y)(Soy → ~Syo)   2, UI
4. Soa → ~Sao   3, UI
5. ~Sao   1, 4, MP

4. 1. (x)[(Rx • Ax) → (y)((~Ry • Ay) → Gxy)]
2. (Rk • Ak) • ~Gkg   ∴ Ag → Rg
3. (Rk • Ak) → (y)((~Ry • Ay) → Gky)   1, UI
4. Rk • Ak   2, Simp
5. (y)((~Ry • Ay) → Gky)   3, 4, MP
6. (~Rg • Ag) → Gkg   5, UI
7. ~Gkg   2, Simp
8. ~(~Rg • Ag)   6, 7, MT
9. ~~Rg ∨ ~Ag   8, DeM
10. ~Ag ∨ ~~Rg   9, Com
11. ~Ag ∨ Rg   10, DN
12. Ag → Rg   11, MI

7. 1. (x)(Hx → Ax)   ∴ (x)[(∃y)(Hy • Txy) → (∃z)(Az • Txz)]
2. (∃y)(Hy • Txy)   Assume
3. Hy • Txy   2, EI
4. Hy → Ay   1, UI
5. Hy   3, Simp
6. Ay   4, 5, MP
7. Txy   3, Simp
8. Ay • Txy   6, 7, Conj
9. (∃z)(Az • Txz)   8, EG
10. (∃y)(Hy • Txy) → (∃z)(Az • Txz)   2–9, CP
11. (x)[(∃y)(Hy • Txy) → (∃z)(Az • Txz)]   10, UG

10.
1. (∃x)Sx   ∴ ~(∃x)[Sx • (y)(Sy → (Cxy ↔ ~Cyy))]
2. (∃x)[Sx • (y)(Sy → (Cxy ↔ ~Cyy))]   Assume
3. Sx • (y)(Sy → (Cxy ↔ ~Cyy))   2, EI
4. Sx   3, Simp
5. (y)(Sy → (Cxy ↔ ~Cyy))   3, Simp
6. Sx → (Cxx ↔ ~Cxx)   5, UI
7. Cxx ↔ ~Cxx   4, 6, MP
8. (Cxx → ~Cxx) • (~Cxx → Cxx)   7, ME
9. Cxx → ~Cxx   8, Simp
10. ~Cxx ∨ ~Cxx   9, MI
11. ~Cxx   10, Re
12. ~Cxx → Cxx   8, Simp
13. Cxx   11, 12, MP
14. Cxx • ~Cxx   13, 11, Conj
15. ~(∃x)[Sx • (y)(Sy → (Cxy ↔ ~Cyy))]   2–14, RAA

Exercise 9.6
Part A: Symbolizing
1. ~d = f
4. ~(∃x) ~x = x
7. (x)x = x
10. (∃x)(∃y)[(Px • Py • Ax • Ay) • ~x = y]

Part B: Proofs

1.
1. Na • ~Nb   ∴ ~a = b
2. a = b   Assume
3. Na • ~Na   1, 2, LL
4. ~a = b   2–3, RAA

4.
1. c = d → e = g
2. d = c
3. Fg   ∴ Fe
4. c = d   2, Sm
5. e = g   1, 4, MP
6. Fe   3, 5, LL

7.
1. (y)(Ay → By)
2. Ab
3. b = c   ∴ Bc
4. Ab → Bb   1, UI
5. Bb   2, 4, MP
6. Bc   3, 5, LL

10.
1. (x)(Hx → Jx)
2. (x)(Kx → Lx)
3. Hd • Kc
4. c = d   ∴ Jc • Ld
5. Hd → Jd   1, UI
6. Kc → Lc   2, UI
7. Hd   3, Simp
8. Jd   5, 7, MP
9. Jc   8, 4, LL
10. Kc   3, Simp
11. Lc   10, 6, MP
12. Ld   4, 11, LL
13. Jc • Ld   9, 12, Conj

13. 1. $(\exists x)Hx$
     2. $(x)(y)[(Hx \cdot Hy) \to x = y]$ ∴ $(\exists x)[Hx \cdot (y)(Hy \to x = y)]$
     3. Hx 1, EI
     ┌ 4. $\sim(\exists x)[Hx \cdot (y)(Hy \to x = y)]$ Assume
     │ 5. $(x)\sim[Hx \cdot (y)(Hy \to x = y)]$ 4, QN
     │ 6. $(x)[\sim Hx \lor \sim(y)(Hy \to x = y)]$ 5, DeM
     │ 7. $\sim Hx \lor \sim(y)(Hy \to x = y)$ 6, UI
     │ 8. $\sim\sim Hx$ 3, DN
     │ 9. $\sim(y)(Hy \to x = y)$ 7, 8, DS
     │ 10. $(\exists y)\sim(Hy \to x = y)$ 9, QN
     │ 11. $(\exists y)\sim(\sim Hy \lor x = y)$ 10, MI
     │ 12. $(\exists y)(\sim\sim Hy \cdot \sim x = y)$ 11, DeM
     │ 13. $(\exists y)(Hy \cdot \sim x = y)$ 12, DN
     │ 14. $Hy \cdot \sim x = y$ 13, EI
     │ 15. $(y)[(Hx \cdot Hy) \to x = y]$ 2, UI
     │ 16. $(Hx \cdot Hy) \to x = y$ 15, UI
     │ 17. Hy 14, Simp
     │ 18. $Hx \cdot Hy$ 3, 17, Conj
     │ 19. $x = y$ 18, 16, MP
     │ 20. $\sim x = y$ 14, Simp
     └ 21. $x = y \cdot \sim x = y$ 19, 20, Conj
        22. $(\exists x)[Hx \cdot (y)(Hy \to x = y)]$ 4–21, RAA

Part C: English Arguments

1. 1. $(x)(Px \to \sim Axx)$
    2. Aab
    3. $Pa \cdot Pb$ ∴ $\sim a = b$
    ┌ 4. $a = b$ Assume
    │ 5. $Pa \to \sim Aaa$ 1, UI
    │ 6. Pa 3, Simp
    │ 7. $\sim Aaa$ 5, 6, MP
    │ 8. $\sim Aab$ 4, 7, LL
    └ 9. $Aab \cdot \sim Aab$ 2, 8, Conj
       10. $\sim a = b$ 4–9, RAA

4. 1. $(\exists x)(\exists y)[(Ox \cdot Oy) \cdot \sim x = y] \cdot (x)(y)(z)([Ox \cdot Oy \cdot Oz]$
       $\to [x = y \lor x = z \lor y = z])$
    2. Oa ∴ $(\exists x)[Ox \cdot \sim x = a]$
    ┌ 3. $\sim(\exists x)[Ox \cdot \sim x = a]$ Assume
    │ 4. $(x)\sim[Ox \cdot \sim x = a]$ 3, QN
    │ 5. $(\exists x)(\exists y)[(Ox \cdot Oy) \cdot \sim x = y]$ 1, Simp
    │ 6. $(\exists y)[(Ox \cdot Oy) \cdot \sim x = y]$ 5, EI
    │ 7. $[(Ox \cdot Oy) \cdot \sim x = y]$ 6, EI
    │ 8. $(x)[\sim Ox \lor \sim\sim x = a]$ 4, DeM
    │ 9. $(x)[\sim Ox \lor x = a]$ 8, DN
    │ 10. $[\sim Ox \lor x = a]$ 9, UI
    │ 11. $Ox \cdot Oy$ 7, Simp
    │ 12. Ox 11, Simp
    │ 13. $\sim\sim Ox$ 12, DN
    │ 14. $x = a$ 10, 13, DS
    │ 15. $\sim x = y$ 7, Simp
    │ 16. $\sim a = y$ 14, 15, LL
    │ 17. $\sim Oy \lor y = a$ 9, UI
    │ 18. Oy 11, Simp
    └ 19. $\sim\sim Oy$ 18, DN

20. y = a	17, 19, DS
21. ~x = a	20, 15, LL
22. x = a • ~x = a	14, 21, Conj
23. (∃x)(Ox • ~x = a)	3–22, RAA

◆ Chapter 10

Exercise 10.1
Part A: True or False?

1. T	**13.** T
4. T	**16.** F
7. T	**19.** F
10. F	

Part B: Identifying and Evaluating Statistical Syllogisms

1. Not a statistical syllogism. (In a statistical syllogism, the percentage is greater than 50 and less than 100.)

4. A statistical syllogism. Since Johnark is a U.S. senator, and many senators oppose campaign reform, there is a possible fallacy of incomplete evidence here.

7. A statistical syllogism. Since Goggans owns a coffee house, however, it seems likely that he drinks coffee; so there is a possible fallacy of incomplete evidence here.

10. A statistical syllogism.

13. Not a statistical syllogism.

Exercise 10.2: Identifying Inductive Arguments

1. Induction by enumeration.

4. Induction by enumeration. Sampling error: ±3.

7. Argument from authority.

10. Incorrect form. (In fact, this is an *ad verecundiam* fallacy.)

13. Induction by enumeration. Sampling error: ±2.

16. Induction by enumeration. The sample is too small.

19. Argument from authority. There is a fallacy of incomplete evidence here, since the authorities (i.e., eyewitnesses) disagree about Black Coyote's role.

Exercise 10.3
Part A: Mill's Methods

1. Method of concomitant variation.

4. Method of agreement. A better hypothesis: Studying intensely for three hours increases the quality of Alonzo's performance on exams.

7. The joint method.

10. Method of agreement.

13. The joint method.

16. The joint method.

19. The joint method.

Part B: Hypotheses

1. There seems to be no way to test the hypothesis.

4. The hypothesis appears to be low in explanatory power. Bees surely do not generate enough body heat to warm the atmosphere.

7. This hypothesis is inconsistent with well-established theories. Nothing can travel faster than the speed of light.

Exercise 10.4: Analyzing and Evaluating Analogies

1. A is Mars; B is the Earth; P is the property of being inhabited by living things. The reply indicates that being a heavenly body that orbits the sun is no guarantee of being inhabited by living things. We might add that Mars and the earth are dissimilar in relevant ways—for example, Mars is much colder than the earth, and its atmosphere contains relatively little oxygen.

4. A is logic; B is whiskey; P is the property of being such that very large quantities should be avoided. The stated reply does not indicate a weakness in the argument, for even if logic does not contain alcohol, one may still be well-advised to avoid taking logic in very large quantities. (The same can be said about aspirin or vitamins.) The vagueness of the phrase "very large quantities" makes it difficult to evaluate the argument. What is a very large quantity of whiskey? Enough to cause drunkenness? Enough to impair one's judgment? Enough so that one is unable to walk? What is a very large quantity of logic? So much that one becomes mentally imbalanced (e.g., unable to appreciate nonlogical aspects of life properly, such as the emotions)? If so, then perhaps the argument is strong. But lovers of logic may rightly observe that very few people take logic in quantities of that magnitude, so the argument is seldom applicable.

Exercise 10.5
Part A: Identifying and Analyzing Metaphors

1. Since a marriage is not literally a molecule, "molecule" is apparently a metaphor here. Also, it is trivially true that a marriage is not an atom, so "atom" also appears to be a metaphor. The atoms in a molecule are closely linked. Similarly, individuals in a good marriage are intimately linked with each other.

4. Since the single life is not literally the flight of a butterfly, the statement is metaphorical. The flight of a butterfly seems relatively aimless. So, the point seems to be this: The lives of single persons are relatively aimless (as compared to the lives of married persons).

7. A college education is not literally a ticket (i.e., a certificate showing that a fee has been paid), so "ticket" is here used metaphorically. The point seems to be this: A college education is a means to higher social status for persons of low socioeconomic status.

10. Since it is trivially true that a person is not a dart board, "dart board" is here used metaphorically. It is appropriate to use a dart board simply as an object to throw darts at. But the point seems to be this: It is not appropriate to use a person simply as an object to be criticized.

13. This statement is entirely literal.

Part B: Analogies

1. A is anyone who deliberately murders another human. B is a sick person. P is the property of being such that one should not be blamed. Sick people have a physical disorder, and they cannot prevent its symptoms from showing. Similarly, according to this argument, murderers have a mental disorder, and they cannot prevent its symptoms from showing.

4. A is a corporation; B is an aircraft carrier. P is the property of being able to change direction quickly. One cannot change the direction of a very large ship, such as an aircraft carrier, quickly. Similarly, one cannot change the direction (i.e., goals, policies, and practices) of a corporation quickly either.

7. A is reason. B is a harlot. P is the property of serving any master. Since reason is not literally a harlot, the word "harlot" is used metaphorically. A harlot will serve anyone who can pay. Similarly, according to Luther, reason can be used to defend any point of view.

10. A is a university; B is an ivory tower. Since a university is not literally an ivory tower, "ivory tower" is used metaphorically. An ivory tower is something removed from practical concerns. Similarly, according to this argument, a university is removed from practical concerns.

Part C: More Analogies

1. A is dogs; B is mentally deficient people. Dogs are not literally mentally deficient people, so "people" is here used metaphorically. P is a complicated moral property: being such that one should not be killed merely on the grounds that caring for one is inconvenient. The main point can be

summed up as follows: If it is wrong to kill a human being who is mentally on the level of a dog (simply on the grounds that caring for the human is inconvenient), then it is wrong to kill a dog (simply on the grounds that caring for it is inconvenient).

The stated reply is certainly open to question. It seems doubtful that the wrongness of killing is grounded in the shape or looks of the thing killed. To illustrate, if something looked like a dog but had the feelings and mental capacities of a normal human adult, wouldn't such a thing have rights similar to a normal human adult?

4. A is a computer; B is a human brain. P is the property of being aware of one's own thoughts and feelings. The words "computer" and "brain" are used literally here.

The stated reply does not seem to point to an important defect in the analogy. Metal, plastic, and brain tissue are all physical in nature. And metal and plastic can be structured so as to simulate SOME functions of the brain. Of course, it remains an open question whether computers have self-awareness.

◆ *Chapter 11*

Exercise 11.1
Part A: Classical Theory
1. 1/52
4. 13/52 = 1/4
7. 1/52

Part B: Relative Frequency Theory
1. Relative frequency theory: .503. Classical theory: 1/2 or 0.5. (The classical theory has no way of accounting for slight imbalances in the coin.)

Part C: Subjectivist Theory
1. 4/(4 + 1) = 4/5
4. 17/(17 + 2) = 17/19
7. 2/(2 + 5) = 2/7

Part D: For Discussion
1. Relative frequency theory. The probability of getting a six on the next roll: 40/100 = 4/10 = 2/5. If we applied the classical theory here the answer would be 1/6. But the classical theory has no way of accounting for irregularities in the die, and the die appears to be off balance or loaded.

Exercise 11.2
Part A: Disjunctions
1. 13/52 + 13/52 = 26/52 = 1/2
4. 1/52 + 13/52 = 14/52 = 7/26
7. 26/52 + 4/52 − 2/52 = 28/52 = 7/13

Part B: Conjunctions and Conditionals
1. 4/52 × 4/51 = 16/2652 = 4/663
4. 13/52 × 12/51 = 156/2652 = 3/51
7. 1/52 × 0 = 0

Part C: Various Compound Statements
1. $P(\sim G) = 1 - P(G) = 5/5 - 3/5 = 2/5$
4. $P(M \vee \sim M) = 1$ (tautology)
7. $P(M \cdot G) = P(M) \times P(G/M) = 3/10 \times 9/10 = 27/100$
10. $P[D \rightarrow (G \rightarrow D)] = 1$ (tautology)

Part D: The Strength of Arguments

1. $5/(5 + 1) = 5/6$ and $4/(4 + 1) = 4/5$. Using the restricted conjunction rule, the probability that Team A will play Team C in the semifinals is $5/6 \times 4/5 = 20/30 = 2/3$.

4. $1/6 \times 1/6 = 1/36$.

7. $15/(15 + 1) = 15/16$. And $20/(20 + 1) = 20/21$. Using the general conjunction rule, the probability that Ted and Sue were both at the party is $15/16 \times 20/21 = 300/336 = 25/28$

Exercise 11.3
Part A: Patterns

1. a. $P(H/E) = \dfrac{1/2 \times 1/2}{[1/2 \times 1/2] + [1/2 \times 1/2]} = \dfrac{1/4}{1/4 + 1/4} = \dfrac{1/4}{2/4} = 1/4 \times 4/2 = 4/8 = 1/2$

2. a. $P(H/E) = \dfrac{1/5 \times 9/10}{[1/5 \times 9/10] + [4/5 \times 9/10]} = \dfrac{9/50}{9/50 + 36/50} = 9/45 = 1/5$

3. a. $P(H/E) = \dfrac{9/10 \times 2/5}{[9/10 \times 2/5] + [1/10 \times 2/5]} = \dfrac{18/50}{18/50 + 2/50} = 18/20 = 9/10$

4. a. $P(H/E) = \dfrac{1/2 \times 9/10}{[1/2 \times 9/10] + [1/2 \times 3/5]} = \dfrac{9/20}{9/20 + 3/10} = 9/15 = 3/5$

   $P(\sim H/E) = \dfrac{1/2 \times 3/5}{[1/2 \times 3/5] + [1/2 \times 9/10]} = \dfrac{3/10}{3/10 + 9/20} = \dfrac{6/20}{6/20 + 9/20} = 6/15 = 2/5$

   Is $P(\sim H/E) = 1 - P(H/E)$? Yes.

5. b. $P(H/E) = \dfrac{9/10 \times 0}{[9/10 \times 0] + [1/10 \times 1/10]} = 0$

   $P(\sim H/E) = \dfrac{1/10 \times 1/10}{[1/10 \times 1/10] + [9/10 \times 0]} = 1$

6. b. $P(H/E) = \dfrac{5/7 \times 5/7}{[5/7 \times 5/7] + [2/7 \times 4/7]} = \dfrac{25/49}{25/49 + 8/49} = 25/33$

   $P(\sim H/E) = \dfrac{2/7 \times 4/7}{[2/7 \times 4/7] + [5/7 \times 5/7]} = \dfrac{8/49}{8/49 + 25/49} = 8/33$

   Is $P(\sim H/E) = 1 - P(H/E)$? Yes.

Part B: Applying Bayes' Theorem

1. $P(\text{Bloggs prepared}) = .40$ or $4/10$
   $P(\text{Bloggs passed } \textit{given } \text{Bloggs prepared}) = .70$ or $7/10$
   $P(\text{Bloggs passed } \textit{given } \text{Bloggs did not prepare}) = .30$ or $3/10$
   $$\dfrac{4/10 \times 7/10}{[4/10 \times 7/10] + [6/10 \times 3/10]} = \dfrac{28/100}{28/100 + 18/100} = \dfrac{28}{46} = \dfrac{14}{23}$$

4. P(God exists) = 1/2

P(some unnecessary suffering occurs *given that* an all-powerful and perfectly good God exists) = 1/(1 + 3) = 1/4

P(some unnecessary suffering occurs *given that* it is not the case that an all-powerful and perfectly good God exists) = 2/(2 + 1) = 2/3

P(God exists *given* some unnecessary suffering) =

$$\frac{1/2 \times 1/4}{[1/2 \times 1/4] + [1/2 \times 2/3]} = \frac{1/8}{1/8 + 2/6} = \frac{3/24}{3/24 + 8/24} = 3/11$$

◆ Chapter 12
Exercise 12.1
Part A: True or False?

1. F	**13.** F
4. F	**16.** T
7. F	**19.** T
10. T	

Part B: Identifying Modalities

1. Contingent and true	**13.** Necessary
4. Contingent and true	**16.** Contingent and true
7. Impossible	**19.** Impossible
10. Contingent and false	

Exercise 12.2
Part A: Symbolizing

1. ◇G	**10.** □G ∨ ~◇G
4. ~◇~G	**13.** ~◇G
7. ◇G • ◇~G	

Part B: More Symbolizing

1. L • ◇~L OR: L • ~□L	**13.** ◇(T → C)
4. G • ◇B	**16.** ◇H • ~H
7. ~S • ◇S	**19.** ◇B • ~◇T
10. (R • D) • ~□(R • D)	

Exercise 12.3
Part A: Annotating

1. 1. □P   ∴ ◇P
      2. P   1, NE
      3. ◇P   2, EP

4. 1. ~◇~G   ∴ G
      2. □G   1, MN
      3. G   2, NE

7. 1. ◇~W   ∴ ~□W
      2. ~□W   1, MN

10.   ∴ □[(A · B) → B]
      ⌐ 1. A • B   Assume
      └ 2. B   1, Simp
        3. (A • B) → B   1–2, CP
        4. □[(A • B) → B] 3, TN

Part B: Correct or Incorrect?

1. 1. □N → □E
   2. N → □E   incorrect (NE is an implicational rule)

4. 1. A → B
   2. ◊(A → B)   1, EP

7. 1. F → G
   2. F → ◊G   incorrect (EP is an implicational rule)

10. 1. ~□~R ↔ S
    2. ◊R ↔ S   1, MN

13. 1. (◊~Y ↔ ~□~Z) → ~◊V
    2. (◊~Y ↔ ◊Z) → ~◊V   1, MN

Part C: Proofs

1. 1. □C • D
   2. (◊C • D) → S   ∴ ◊S
   3. D   1, Simp
   4. □C   1, Simp
   5. C   4, NE
   6. ◊C   5, EP
   7. ◊C • D   3, 6, Conj
   8. S   7, 2, MP
   9. ◊S   8, EP

4. 1. ~(◊M • □N)
   2. □~M → ~◊Q
   3. ◊~N → ~□P
   4. (□~Q ∨ ◊~P) → ~◊R   ∴ ~R
   5. ~◊M ∨ ~□N   1, DeM
   6. ~◊M → ~◊Q   2, MN
   7. ~□N → ~□P   3, MN
   8. ~◊Q ∨ ~□P   5, 6, 7, CD
   9. □~Q ∨ ~□P   8, MN
   10. □~Q ∨ ◊~P   9, MN
   11. ~◊R   10, 4, MP
   12. □~R   11, MN
   13. ~R   12, NE

7. 1. ◊Z ∨ (A • □B)
   2. ◊Z → ~R
   3. ◊~B   ∴ ~□R
   4. (◊Z ∨ A) • (◊Z ∨ □B)   1, Dist
   5. ◊Z ∨ □B   4, Simp
   6. ~□B   3, MN
   7. ◊Z   5, 6, DS
   8. ~R   2, 7, MP
   9. ◊~R   8, EP
   10. ~□R   9, MN

10. 1. (□M ∨ □F) • (□M ∨ ~□G)
    2. □M → ~◊H
    3. (□F • ~□G) → ~□J   ∴ (◊H → ◊~J)
    4. □M ∨ (□F • ~□G)   1, Dist
    5. ~◊H ∨ ~□J   4, 2, 3, CD
    6. ◊H → ~□J   5, MI
    7. ◊H → ◊~J   6, MN

13. 1. □(A ∨ B)
    2. ~◇~(B ∨ A) → ~◇C
    3. ~□~C ∨ R   ∴ ◇(R ∨ S)
    4. ~◇~(A ∨ B)   1, MN
    5. ~◇~(B ∨ A)   4, Com
    6. ~◇C   2, 5, MP
    7. ◇C ∨ R   3, MN
    8. R   6, 7, DS
    9. R ∨ S   8, Add
    10. ◇(R ∨ S)   9, EP

16. 1. ◇Z • (□Y ∨ ~◇W)
    2. □~Z ∨ ◇~Y
    3. □~W → ~◇U
    4. ~□~U ∨ □~T   ∴ ◇~T
    5. (◇Z • □Y) ∨ (◇Z • ~◇W)   1, Dist
    6. ~◇Z ∨ ◇~Y   2, MN
    7. ~◇Z ∨ ~□Y   6, MN
    8. ~(◇Z • □Y)   7, DeM
    9. ◇Z • ~◇W   8, 5, DS
    10. ~◇W   9, Simp
    11. □~W   10, MN
    12. ~◇U   11, 3, MP
    13. ◇U ∨ □~T   4, MN
    14. □~T   12, 13, DS
    15. ~T   14, NE
    16. ◇~T   15, EP

19. 1. P ∨ G
    2. P → □Z
    3. G → ~◇~Z
    4. ◇~S → ◇~Z   ∴ □S
    5. □Z ∨ ~◇~Z   1, 2, 3, CD
    6. ~◇~Z ∨ ~◇~Z   5, MN
    7. ~◇~Z   6, Re
    8. ~◇~S   4, 7, MT
    9. □S   8, MN

Part D: English Arguments

1. 1. □~F   ∴ ~◇F
    2. ~◇F   1, MN

4. 1. ~◇F   ∴ ~F
    2. □~F   1, MN
    3. ~F   2, NE

7. 1. ~◇O • □G
    2. (◇R • ~◇O) → ◇~G   ∴ ~R
    3. (~◇O • ◇R) → ◇~G   2, Com
    4. ~◇O → (◇R → ◇~G)   3, Ex
    5. ~◇O   1, Simp
    6. ◇R → ◇~G   4, 5, MP
    7. □G   1, Simp
    8. ~◇~G   7, MN
    9. ~◇R   6, 8, MT
    10. □~R   9, MN
    11. ~R   10, NE

Exercise 12.4
Part A: Symbolizing
1. $(J \cdot \sim M) \Rightarrow B$
4. $\sim T \rightarrow F$
7. $\square (M \rightarrow W)$

Part B: Symbolizing and Evaluating
1. $\Diamond S \cdot \Diamond J \therefore \Diamond (S \cdot J)$ invalid form
4. $\sim H \vee W \therefore \sim \square H \vee \square W$ invalid form. (*Note:* Applying MI we get: $H \rightarrow W \therefore \square H \rightarrow \square W$, but OT does not apply to the material conditional.)
7. $\Diamond (F \cdot S) \therefore \Diamond F \cdot \Diamond S$ valid form
10. The conditional premise is amphibolous:
    $S \rightarrow \square S, S \therefore \square S$ valid form (*modus ponens*)
    $\square (S \rightarrow S), S \therefore \square S$ invalid form

Part C: Annotating
1.
   1. $\square (A \cdot \sim B)$ $\therefore \sim \Diamond B$
   2. $\square A \cdot \square \sim B$ 1, MODE
   3. $\square \sim B$ 2, Simp
   4. $\sim \Diamond B$ 3, MN

4.
   1. $\Diamond (H \cdot J)$
   2. $\Diamond K \Rightarrow \sim \Diamond J$ $\therefore \square \sim K$
   3. $\Diamond H \cdot \Diamond J$ 1, MODI
   4. $\Diamond J$ 3, Simp
   5. $\sim \sim \Diamond J$ 4, DN
   6. $\sim \Diamond K$ 2, 5, MMT
   7. $\square \sim K$ 6, MN

7.
   1. $N \Leftrightarrow O$
   2. $\square (N \rightarrow P)$ $\therefore (O \Rightarrow P)$
   3. $N \Rightarrow P$ 2, SI
   4. $\square (N \leftrightarrow O)$ 1, LE
   5. $\square [(N \rightarrow O) \cdot (O \rightarrow N)]$ 4, ME
   6. $\square (N \rightarrow O) \cdot \square (O \rightarrow N)$ 5, MODE
   7. $\square (O \rightarrow N)$ 6, Simp
   8. $O \Rightarrow N$ 7, SI
   9. $O \Rightarrow P$ 8, 3, MHS

10.
    1. $\Diamond W \vee X$
    2. $\Diamond W \Rightarrow \Diamond Z$
    3. $\Diamond X \Rightarrow \Diamond V$ $\therefore \Diamond (Z \vee V)$
    4. $\Diamond W \vee \Diamond X$ 1, MODE
    5. $\square (\Diamond W \rightarrow \Diamond Z)$ 2, SI
    6. $\square (\Diamond X \rightarrow \Diamond V)$ 3, SI
    7. $\Diamond W \rightarrow \Diamond Z$ 5, NE
    8. $\Diamond X \rightarrow \Diamond V$ 6, NE
    9. $\Diamond Z \vee \Diamond V$ 4, 7, 8, CD
    10. $\Diamond (Z \vee V)$ 9, MODE

Part D: Correct or Incorrect?
1.
   1. $\sim A \rightarrow \sim B$
   2. $\Diamond \sim A \rightarrow \Diamond \sim B$ incorrect
4.
   1. $\square (G \vee H)$
   2. $\square G \vee \square H$ incorrect

7. 1. ◇(~N ∨ P)
   2. ◇~N ∨ ◇P   MODE
10. 1. ◇U ∨ ◇W
    2. ◇(U ∨ W)   MODE
13. 1. □(~C • D)
    2. □~C • □D   MODE

Part E: Proofs

1. 1. A ⇒ B   ∴ ~B ⇒ ~A
   2. □(A → B)   1, SI
   3. □(~B → ~A)   2, cont
   4. ~B ⇒ ~A   3, SI

4. 1. □(E → H)
   2. ~□~E   ∴ ◇H
   3. ◇E   2, MN
   4. E ⇒ H   1, SI
   5. ◇E ⇒ ◇H   4, OT
   6. ◇H   3, 5, MMP

7. 1. ◇(L ∨ M)
   2. □~L
   3. M ⇒ ~N   ∴ ~□N
   4. ~◇L   2, MN
   5. ◇L ∨ ◇M   1, MODE
   6. ◇M   4, 5, DS
   7. ◇M ⇒ ◇~N 3, OT
   8. ◇~N   6, 7, MMP
   9. ~□N   8, MN

10. 1. A ⇒ E
    2. □~E   ∴ □~A
    3. ◇A ⇒ ◇E   1, OT
    4. ~◇E   2, MN
    5. ~◇A   3, 4, MMT
    6. □~A   5, MN

13. 1. □[~R ∨ (S • T)]
    2. ◇R   ∴ ◇S • ◇T
    3. □[R → (S • T)] 1, MI
    4. R ⇒ (S • T)   3, SI
    5. ◇R ⇒ ◇(S • T) 4, OT
    6. ◇(S • T)   2, 5, MMP
    7. ◇S • ◇T   6, MODI

16. 1. ◇[(L ∨ M) • (L ∨ Q)]
     2. ◇P ⇒ ~◇Q
     3. □~L   ∴ ~P
     4. ◇[L ∨ (M • Q)] 1, Dist
     5. ~◇L   3, MN
     6. ◇L ∨ ◇(M • Q) 4, MODE
     7. ◇(M • Q)   5, 6, DS
     8. ◇M • ◇Q   7, MODI
     9. ◇Q   8, Simp
     10. ~~◇Q   9, DN
     11. ~◇P   10, 2, MMT
     12. □~P   11, MN
     13. ~P   12, NE

19. 1. □[(E • F) → G]
   2. □E   ∴ ~G ⇒ ~F
   3. □[E → (F → G)]   1, Ex
   4. E ⇒ (F → G)   3, SI
   5. □E ⇒ □(F → G)   4, OT
   6. □(F → G)   2, 5, MMP
   7. □(~G → ~F)   6, Cont
   8. ~G ⇒ ~F   7, SI

Part F: English Arguments

1. 1. □(F → G)
   2. ~◊ ~F   ∴ □G
   3. F ⇒ G   1, SI
   4. □F   2, MN
   5. □F ⇒ □G   3, OT
   6. □G   4, 5, MMP

Exercise 12.5
Part A: Symbolizing

1. □◊ B

4. (~G • ◊G) • □◊ G

7. ◊R • ~◊□R

Part B: Annotating

1. 1. □□A ⇒ B
   2. □A   ∴ B
   3. □□A   2, S4
   4. B   1, 3, MMP

4. 1. ◊G
   2. □◊G ⇒ ◊□H   ∴ H
   3. □◊G   1, S5
   4. ◊□H   2, 3, MMP
   5. □H   4, S5
   6. H   5, NE

7. 1. ◊□J
   2. ◊◊K ⇒ ~□J   ∴ ~◊K
   3. ◊◊K ⇒ ~◊□J   2, S5
   4. ~~◊□J   1, DN
   5. ~◊◊K   3, 4, MMT
   6. ~◊K   5, S4

10. 1. ◊□◊□T   ∴ T
   2. □◊□T   1, S5
   3. □□T   2, S5
   4. □T   3, S4 (or NE)
   5. T   4, NE

Part C: Proofs

1. 1. □A
   2. A ⇒ B   ∴ □□B
   3. □A ⇒ □B   2, OT
   4. □A ⇒ □□B   3, S4
   5. □□B   1, 4, MMP

4. 1. $\Box\Box(A \cdot B)$ $\therefore \Box A \cdot \Box\Box B$
     2. $\Box(\Box A \cdot \Box B)$ 1, MODE
     3. $\Box\Box A \cdot \Box\Box B$ 2, MODE
     4. $\Box A \cdot \Box\Box B$ 3, S4

7. 1. $\Diamond\Box\Diamond\Box\sim Q$ $\therefore \sim Q$
     2. $\Box\Diamond\Box\sim Q$ 1, S5
     3. $\Diamond\Box\sim Q$ 2, NE
     4. $\Box\sim Q$ 3, S5
     5. $\sim Q$ 4, NE

10. 1. $\Box\Box F \Rightarrow \Diamond\Box G$ $\therefore \Diamond\Diamond(\sim F \vee \Box G)$
     2. $\Box(\Box\Box F \rightarrow \Diamond\Box G)$ 1, SI
     3. $\Box\Box F \rightarrow \Diamond\Box G$ 2, NE
     4. $\Box F \rightarrow \Diamond\Box G$ 3, S4
     5. $\sim\Box F \vee \Diamond\Box G$ 4, MI
     6. $\Diamond\sim F \vee \Diamond\Box G$ 5, MN
     7. $\Diamond(\sim F \vee \Box G)$ 6, MODE
     8. $\Diamond\Diamond(\sim F \vee \Box G)$ 7, S4

Part D: English Arguments

1. 1. $\Box(P \rightarrow \Box P)$
     2. $\Diamond P$ $\therefore P$
     3. $P \Rightarrow \Box P$ 1, SI
     4. $\Diamond P \Rightarrow \Diamond\Box P$ 3, OT
     5. $\Diamond\Box P$ 2, 4, MMP
     6. $\Box P$ 5, S5
     7. P 6, NE

4. 1. $\Box(Z \cdot Y)$
     2. $\Box(\Box Z \rightarrow \Diamond T)$
     3. $\Box(\Box Y \rightarrow \Diamond A)$
     4. $\Diamond T \Rightarrow \sim\Box A$
     5. $\Box(\Diamond\sim A \rightarrow \Diamond\sim Y)$ $\therefore \sim Y$
     6. $\Box Z \cdot \Box Y$ 1, MODE
     7. $\Box Z \rightarrow \Diamond T$ 2, NE
     8. $\Box Z$ 6, Simp
     9. $\Diamond T$ 7, 8, MP
     10. $\sim\Box A$ 9, 4, MMP
     11. $\Diamond\sim A$ 10, MN
     12. $\Diamond\sim A \Rightarrow \Diamond\sim Y$ 5, SI
     13. $\Diamond\sim Y$ 11, 12, MMP
     14. $\Box Y$ 6, Simp
     15. $\sim\Diamond\sim Y$ 14, MN
     16. $\Diamond\sim Y \vee \sim Y$ 13, Add
     17. $\sim Y$ 15, 16, DS

Part E: Paradoxes of Strict Implication   This is for class discussion.

Glossary/Index

invalidity and, 23–27, 33–35
strength not ensured by, 378–380
validity and, 21–23, 26, 27, 30–33, 35–38
See also specific forms
arguments from analogy: an argument that depends fundamentally on a similarity between two objects, events, or persons, 11–12, **405–409**, 411–416
argument against the person (*ad hominem* fallacy): instead of providing a rational critique of an argument (or statement), one attacks the person who advances the argument (or asserts the statement), 167, **173**
arguments from authority: an argument that depends fundamentally on an appeal to an expert, **11, 385–387**
Aristotelian logic
categorical syllogisms, 154–160
immediate inferences, 143–152
modern logicians' objections to, 145–148, 156, 325–327
Aristotle, 143, 201, 451
arrow: a symbol for the material conditional, 203, **208**
association (As), inference rule, 267
assumptions
in conditional proofs, 284–289, 348
in logic of relations, 358
in probability theory, 424–425, 442
in *reductio ad absurdum*, 292–297, 348
in theorems, proving, 302
universal generalization (UG) and, 348, 349
assurance: an expression indicating that the arguer is confident of a premise or inference, **58,** 59
A statements. *See* universal affirmative statements
asymmetrical relations: if *a* bears relation R to *b*, then *b* does not bear R to *a*, **359**
atomic statement: a statement that does not have any other statement as a component, **202,** 203
authority
appeal to unreliable, 178–179, **182,** 386
arguments from, **11, 385–387**
cognitive *vs.* organizational, 386
infallible, 386

Bayes' theorem, 440–444
Bayes, Thomas, 440
begging the question (*petitio principii*): assuming the point to be proved, 189–191, **193**
biased samples, 388–389
biconditionals: statements of the form, "A if and only if B," **210**

material, 219–221
strict, 482
symbolization of, 203, 210–211, 482
Boole, George, 145, 325
bound variable: a variable that is bound by a quantifier, **312**

categorical statement: a statement that relates two classes, sets, or categories, **127–131**
contrapositive of (*see* contrapositive), **151,** 152
converse of (*see* converse), 149–**150,** 152
obverse of (*see* obverse), 150, 152
particular. *See* particular statements
standard forms of, **128–131**
stylistic variants of, 129–131, 135, 311, 312, 314–315
symbolization of, 308–317, 359
universal. *See* universal statements
Venn diagrams of, 133–141
categorical syllogisms
Aristotelian logic and, 154–160
defined, 132–133
figure of (*see* figure), **155–156**
mood of (*see* mood), **155–156**
standard form of, **154**
terms of, 132–133, 136–137
Venn diagrams of, 133–141
See also syllogisms
causation, reasoning for
Mill's methods, 393–396
scientific reasoning, 396–401
CD. *See* constructive dilemma (CD)
charity, 60, 61–62
Chrysippus, 201
Church, Alonzo, 320
circular definitions, 109
classical theory of probability: P(S) = f/n, where *f* stands for the number of favorable outcomes and *n* stands for the number of possible outcomes, **424–425**
cognitive authority, 386
cognitive meaning, *vs.* **emotive force:** the cognitive meaning is the informational content of a statement while its emotive force is the degree to which it elicits or expresses emotion in a given context, **97–99**
commutation (Com), inference rule, 266–267, 270
complement: the complement of a class X is the class containing all things that are not members of X, **150**
composition, fallacy of: an invalid inference from the nature of the parts (or members) to the nature of the whole (or group), 186–188, **193**

INFERENCE RULES FOR THE LOGIC OF IDENTITY

Leibniz' Law (LL), in two forms

$$m = n$$
$$\mathcal{P}m$$
$$\therefore \mathcal{P}n$$

$$n = m$$
$$\mathcal{P}m$$
$$\therefore \mathcal{P}n$$

Where $\mathcal{P}n$ is obtained by replacing *one or more* free occurrences of **m** in $\mathcal{P}m$ with free occurrences of **n** in $\mathcal{P}n$. (Note: the bold letters **m** and **n** stand for any individual constant *or* individual variable.)

Symmetry (Sm), in two forms

$$m = n$$
$$\therefore n = m$$

$$\sim m = n$$
$$\therefore \sim n = m$$

Where the bold **m** and **n** stand for either individual constants *or* individual variables.

Identity (Id)

$$\therefore n = n$$

Where the bold **n** stands for any individual constant *or* individual variable.

THE RULES OF PROBABILITY

1. If a statement p is a tautology, then $P(p) = 1$.

2. If a statement p is a contradiction, then $P(p) = 0$.

3. **Restricted Disjunction Rule.** If p and q are mutually exclusive, then $P(p \vee q) = P(p) + P(q)$.

4. **Negation Rule.** $P(\sim p) = 1 - P(p)$

5. **General Disjunction Rule.** $P(p \vee q) = P(p) + P(q) - P(p \bullet q)$

6. **Conditional Rule.** $P(q/p) = \dfrac{P(p \bullet q)}{P(p)}$

7. **General Conjunction Rule.** $P(p \bullet q) = P(p) \times P(q/p)$

8. **Restricted Conjunction Rule.** If p and q are independent, $P(p \bullet q) = P(p) \times P(q)$.